A Journey
through
the Cold War

A Journey
through
the Cold War

*A Memoir of Containment
and Coexistence*

Raymond L. Garthoff

Brookings Institution Press
Washington, D.C.

ABOUT BROOKINGS

The Brookings Institution is a private nonprofit organization devoted to research, education, and publication on important issues of domestic and foreign policy. Its principal purpose is to bring knowledge to bear on current and emerging policy problems. The Institution maintains a position of neutrality on issues of public policy. Interpretations or conclusions in Brookings publications should be understood to be solely those of the authors.

Copyright © 2001
THE BROOKINGS INSTITUTION
1775 Massachusetts Avenue, N.W., Washington, D.C. 20036
www.brookings.edu

Library of Congress Cataloging-in-Publication data

Garthoff, Raymond L.
  A journey through the Cold War : a memoir of containment and coexistence / Raymond L. Garthoff.
      p.   cm.
Includes bibliographical references and index.
  ISBN 0-8157-0102-0 (cloth : alk. paper)—
  ISBN 0-8157-0101-2 (pbk. : alk. paper)
    1. Garthoff, Raymond L. 2. Ambassadors—United States—Biography.
3. Intelligence officers—United States—Biography. 4. Ambassadors—
Bulgaria—Biography. 5. Cold War. 6. United States—Foreign relations—
Soviet Union. 7. Soviet Union—Foreign relations—United States.
8. United States—Foreign relations—1945–1989. 9. National security—
United States—History—20th century. 10. World politics—1945– I. Title.
  E748 .G27 2001   2001002502
  327.73′0092—dc21   CIP

9 8 7 6 5 4 3 2 1

The paper used in this publication meets minimum requirements of the
American National Standard for Information Sciences—Permanence of Paper for
Printed Library Materials: ANSI Z39.48-1992.

Typeset in Minion

Composition by Cynthia Stock
Silver Spring, Maryland

Printed by R. R. Donnelley and Sons
Harrisonburg, Virginia

To
My Beloved Wife, Vera,
and Our Son, Alexander,
Companions on the Journey

Contents

Acknowledgments   ix

Preface: Why This Memoir?   xi

1 The Cold War Begins: The Formative Years, 1945–50   1

2 The View from a Think Tank: Soviet Affairs Expert at RAND   9

3 The Thaw: Observing the Soviet Union After Stalin   24

4 CIA and Intelligence Analysis and Estimates   39

5 "Foreign Affairs Adviser" at the Pentagon   61

6 Intelligence Excursions in the Soviet Union   72

7 The Espionage Game   100

8 Department of State: The Kennedy Years (I)   120

9 Department of State: The Kennedy Years (II)   143

10 The Cuban Missile Crisis: Turning Point of the Cold War   168

11 Department of State: The Johnson Years   188

12 The Diplomacy of East-West Relations   220

13 Negotiating on Strategic Arms: SALT and the ABM Treaty   243

14 Developing Détente in U.S.-Soviet Relations   277

15 Inspecting the American Conduct of Foreign Relations   292

16 Ambassador to Bulgaria   302

17 The Decline and Collapse of the Détente of the 1970s   325

18 Witness to the Cold War Endgame: 1980–90   337

19 Reflections on the Cold War   374

Epilogue: A Personal Reminiscence   396

Index   401

Acknowledgments

In a general way, I should like to express thanks to my family, and to my colleagues in varied endeavors, for the support and forbearance they have shown over the many years covered by this memoir (I was sixteen when World War II ended and sixty-one when the Cold War came to a close).

As I wrote the memoir, I had two readers ever ready to offer helpful advice, such as asking whether I really wanted to tell *that*—my wife, Vera, and my brother, Douglas.

For support in writing this memoir, I wish to thank John Steinbruner, director of Foreign Policy Studies at the Brookings Institution, and his successor Richard Haass, for allowing me to maintain an office at Brookings and to draw upon secretarial assistance even though I had already retired. For typing from my handwritten draft through several revisions, I was patiently and efficiently assisted by Louise Skillings, who had put up with me for some years, and then by Stacey Knobler, Megan deLong, Rebecca Over, Catherine Thie, and Mica Kreutz. For assistance in editing the manuscript, I am indebted to Chris Kelaher and Charles Dibble. And in the final stages of production, thanks go to Inge Lockwood for proofreading the pages. To them all, I am most grateful.

I should also like to express my appreciation to the Publications Review Board of the Central Intelligence Agency and the office of the Department of State responsible for classification review for their prompt and professional review of the manuscript to ensure that it would not contain currently classified information. With some deletions as requested, both CIA and the Department of State have posed no objection to publication on grounds of security; such review does not of course constitute confirmation of accuracy or official endorsement of my interpretations or views.

Preface:
Why This Memoir?

My career, as indeed most of my adult life, coincided closely with the Cold War. Moreover, as briefly summarized below, my experiences ranged over a variety of analytical, staff, and diplomatic assignments and work in many aspects of the security field, including intelligence collection and analysis, political-military relations, arms control negotiations with the Soviet Union, and broader East-West diplomacy and alliance relationships. This range of experience provided a variety of vantage points useful for observing different aspects of the history of the Cold War.

Although any memoir account is necessarily based on a slice of the political and historical process, presence inside the policy process at particular places and times can provide the basis for a fuller explication of specific events or developments than a review of public and archival state documents alone can provide, central as documentary sources remain for writing history. The reflections of an observant insider with a range of experience can yield interesting new sidelights on history, and perhaps also insights into broader issues that may differ from and supplement the observations of those who have served in the top levels. In addition to my particular combination of direct experience and observation, I have for some years been studying the historical development of American-Soviet relations, and I have written a number of books on various aspects of the Cold War. This memoir will, however, approach the story of the Cold War from an inside vantage point, or rather a series of such vantage points. While less comprehensive than a conventional historical analysis, it will approach the subjects of American policy and the

history of the period from a different direction: from experience and observation at close hand of some events while they were taking place.

In this brief introduction, to indicate its general scope I shall briefly sketch
the outline of my career experience, of course without raising the many specific events and developments that will form the substance of the account.
This sketch serves only as a bare outline of the vantage points, not a summary
of what was seen from them.

From 1945 to 1950 I was a student at Princeton and Yale universities, keenly
absorbing academic understanding of the field of international relations (with
specialization in Russian area studies). My intellectually formative years in
this field thus coincided with the formative years of the Cold War.

From mid-1950 to mid-1957 I worked as a research analyst on Soviet
affairs at the RAND Corporation, the then novel archetypical "think tank" for
security studies, conducting both classified and open research. I developed
particular expertise in pathfinding research on Soviet military doctrine, leading to a number of books and essays on that general subject, lectures at the
war colleges, and the like, over many years. In mid-1957 I took advantage of a
newly opened opportunity to spend two months in the Soviet Union, before
entering government service.

From late 1957 until the fall of 1961 I worked in the Office of National
Estimates of the Central Intelligence Agency. My responsibility was drafting
national intelligence estimates in the field of Soviet foreign and security pol-
icy. While at CIA, I worked under "cover" as "Foreign Affairs Adviser" in the
Defense Department—which facilitated continuation of my open writing on
Soviet military and political affairs, and on American military policy. In a very
different way, my cover also permitted assignment for two unusually interesting excursions to the Soviet Union in 1959, one accompanying Vice President
Richard Nixon, the other serving as interpreter for an Atomic Energy
Commission delegation headed by John McCone. These trips provided direct
experience both in "overt" intelligence collection and in bridging the relation-
ships between intelligence collection, analysis, and policy application. So did
a "coup" in successful debriefing of important information obtained by a
Swedish military delegation that had visited the Soviet Union. CIA Director
Allen Dulles also brought me into the evaluation of the most important
American agent in Soviet service, Colonel Oleg Penkovsky. My principal work
at CIA, however, remained intelligence analysis and estimates in the field of
Soviet foreign and security policy.

While I greatly enjoyed my four years at CIA, when the Kennedy administration came into office I was eager to get more directly into the policymaking process. I was offered positions as policy planner in the International
Security Affairs office in the Defense Department, and in the Department of
State in a newly created politico-military affairs staff. I chose to go to State, as

special assistant for Soviet Bloc Politico-Military Affairs. I remained in that position for over six years, with a range of responsibilities including direct staff support to Secretary Dean Rusk on arms control and disarmament, serving as executive secretary of an interagency committee on political and security aspects of space reconnaissance (then ultra-secret), a limited role in the Berlin crisis in 1961, and direct involvement in the Cuban missile crisis of 1962. I was closely involved from the start in efforts to engage the Soviet leaders in strategic arms limitation talks (SALT) and served throughout the SALT I negotiations as executive officer and senior State Department adviser on the U.S. delegation.

Meanwhile, from the beginning of 1968 nominally until the fall of 1970, though borrowed for SALT for most of 1969 and 1970, I served as counselor for political-military affairs in the U.S. mission to NATO. This experience added to other occasions for participation in allied consultations and alliance diplomacy. It also was a good vantage point for observing the evolving diplomacy of East-West relations.

In addition to my role on the SALT delegation from November 1969 to January 1973, I served as deputy director of the Bureau of Politico-Military Affairs in the State Department from mid-1970 to mid-1973. From 1973 to 1974 I was president of the State Department's advanced study senior seminar and prepared a comparative study of policy planning in several countries (Germany, France, Italy, Britain, and the Soviet Union) based on interviews in those countries. From 1974 into 1977 I served as a senior Foreign Service inspector, leading teams inspecting our embassies and conduct of relations with various countries (including France, Italy, Spain, and Portugal in Europe; Israel, Iraq, Syria, and Jordan in the Near East; Thailand and the Philippines in Asia; several countries in central Africa; in South America; and Canada). Such "conduct of relations" inspections of our missions abroad (lasting up to three months in the case of our largest embassies) and the associated offices in the department provide a uniquely close and detailed view into the operations of individual missions with varying tasks, of the Foreign Service as a whole, and to some extent the workings of American foreign relations more generally, including the operations of other agencies. I also conducted a sensitive study of internal high-level workings of the Department of State. (Suffice it here to note that as a result of the findings and recommendations of one of my inspections, Secretary of State Henry Kissinger's initial reaction was to call for the abolition of the entire Office of the Inspector General!)

From 1977 through 1979 I served as ambassador to Bulgaria, a relatively quiet assignment that did, however, permit observation of the workings of a communist state, Soviet–East European relations (as well as U.S.–East European relations), and Balkan diplomacy. At the end of 1979, eligible by age and length of service for an early retirement option, I decided to leave government service in order to devote full time to scholarly research and study.

From 1980 through 1994 I was a senior fellow at the Brookings Institution, primarily researching and writing two major studies of American-Soviet relations over the final half of the Cold War. During my years at Brookings, I made nearly a dozen trips to the Soviet Union (and visited China and Cuba). I also participated in a number of international conferences, maintained contacts with Soviet and American diplomats and other officials, in the early 1990s benefited from access to former Soviet Communist Party archives in Moscow, and in other ways engaged in unofficial pursuit of research and related intellectual interests. In the final decade of the Cold War, I was thus following developments actively, although no longer in government service.

This, in bare outline, is the career experience around which this memoir is constructed. Of course, there are many important areas of the recent history of American foreign relations, and of the history of the Cold War, in which I was not involved and on which I have little or no direct experience (including economic relations, the war in Vietnam, and relations with China and in the Third World, to note but a few). On some of these I will have some observations. It is not, however, the purpose of this memoir to be comprehensive, but rather to add to what is known and understood about those specific aspects and episodes in which I had direct experience and knowledge.

Another important role that a memoir can play is to draw attention to conceptions and perceptions prevalent at the time, in an effort to recreate (by anecdote, and reflection, as well as analytical discussion) the context for views, positions, and actions taken in the past which from today's perspective may be difficult to fully comprehend. Indeed, this may be the most important contribution that a memoir can make, to evoke the past empathetically. The aim is neither to criticize nor to justify, but to understand—although criticism and self-criticism, and justification, in reflection may be appropriate.

One advantage of the memoir approach, indeed, is the opportunity to make subjective judgments, based on my personal experience and observations while in government service. The process of reevaluating American security policy from the vantage point of the end of the Cold War is a broad new task, and opportunity, we all face. A memoir provides an additional avenue of approach to this task, supplementing more conventional historical and analytical reexaminations. It adds new grist to the mill for our common efforts at rethinking security policy not only in study of the past but with application to the future. In addition, it permits a participant in the past process to reflect on that experience and draw conclusions from it that can have continuing value.

Most of my account will be focused on American policymaking, with particular attention to American perceptions and assessments of the Soviet adversary and to American-Soviet interactions. Attention to such perceptions and interactions has been a feature of my historical studies of American-Soviet relations, and from a different perspective also underlies this memoir review of the American-Soviet relationship throughout the Cold War experience. Both as a policy and intelligence analyst, and later in negotiation and other contemporary contacts (also continuing today in shared retrospective analysis with a number of former senior Soviet officials), I have had many opportunities to observe and experience this interaction. In reflecting on the broader process of American policymaking and interaction with the Soviet Union, one major conclusion that finds repeated confirmation is the difficulty in visualizing the impact of American actions on the perceptions and hence the decisions and actions of the Soviet adversary. (The reverse, of course, was also true.) The significance of empathy has been greatly underappreciated and even when recognized has been difficult to gear into the process of policymaking. It has too easily been misconstrued or misrepresented as softness, a lack of stalwart pursuit of American interests, even though a really objective and successful advance of one's interest often hinges on correctly understanding the interests and perspective of others—especially an adversary, where there is a divergence or conflict of interests. This kind of conclusion can, of course, be reached on an analytical basis, but it carries particular weight when it is grounded in observation based on experience.

This memoir, in sum, represents one man's journey through the Cold War. The reason for writing it is the belief that it will be of interest and value to readers, most of whom will not have shared the same passage of life and none of whom will have had the same set of experiences inside the American security system. Last, but not least, I hope that I will be able to evoke this important recent chapter of our history by seeing it as I saw it, as "live" history, in a more interesting way than is usually possible with conventional historical writing.

1

The Cold War Begins:
The Formative Years, 1945–50

There is no commonly accepted precise date for the beginning of the Cold War; it emerged during the years 1945 through 1947. Perhaps as good a date as any was the occasion of former British prime minister Sir Winston Churchill's speech in Fulton, Missouri, on March 5, 1946, when he declared that an "Iron Curtain" had descended across the continent of Europe. Less than a month earlier Marshal Josef Stalin, the Soviet leader, had blamed capitalism and the West for both world wars and implied a protracted conflict between the Soviet Union and the West. And two weeks after that the American chargé d'affaires in Moscow, George Kennan, had dispatched his later famous "long telegram" analyzing the sources of Soviet policy in terms that established the basis for the American strategy of containment of communist expansion. Some revisionist historians have contended that the Cold War was prefigured by the American use of the atomic bomb in August 1945, arguing that it had not been militarily necessary to defeat Japan but had been intended to bolster the American postwar position vis-à-vis the Soviet Union. With greater validity, historians have observed that the very success of the allied coalition against the Axis powers had spawned inevitable rivalry among the victors. In any case, over the few years after the end of World War II the Cold War emerged, pitting the "East," the Soviet Union and its satellites, against the "West" led by the United States.

These were the formative years of the Cold War. They were also the formative years of my career. The day the Cold War began, whenever that was, I was in college. I was a student at Princeton University from June 1945 to June 1948, and then in the graduate school of Yale University to June 1950. At

Princeton (where I was six years after George Shultz, and four years ahead of James Baker), I studied in the Woodrow Wilson School of Public and International Affairs, and at Yale in the international relations program with a concentration in Russian studies. From early youth on I had been attracted to contemporary history and world politics, and I naturally applied that interest to the central challenge emerging after the war: American relations with the Soviet Union. At both universities I had multidisciplinary programs, concentrating on modern, diplomatic, and Russian history and international relations, less on political science, and least on economics.

This memoir is not an autobiography, and overall it will have very few references to my personal life. The one exception that seems appropriate, however, is a brief background to my early interest in world affairs, set out in the paragraphs following.

I was born in Cairo, Egypt, on March 26, 1929; my parents were from Iowa, but for five years in the latter 1920s my father was bursar of the American University of Cairo. From early childhood through high school I grew up in Alexandria, Virginia, while my father worked in Washington at the U.S. Department of Agriculture (later serving for several years as the U.S. representative, and then as the chairman, of the International Wheat Council). Although I did not live abroad, I grew up in family surroundings well aware of the world. Growing up in the environs of Washington also contributed a somewhat closer feel for national and international politics.

Some forty years after graduation from George Washington High School in 1945, on the occasion of the school's fiftieth anniversary, I was one of four graduates over that half century honored by awards, in my case for service in international affairs, along with an astronaut, a PulitzerPrize–winning writer, and by far the best-known alumnus, television personality Willard Scott.

I entered Princeton, then on a wartime schedule of three semesters per year, in June 1945 on a scholarship. So, as a sixteen-year-old freshman, I celebrated V-J Day and the end of World War II—and then experienced the events of the next three years as the Cold War descended. As a student of world politics, I was more keenly attuned to what was happening than most of my fellow students, but none of us then quite realized what the Cold War would mean—nor, I believe, did our elders. On the one hand, it was not yet that close to our daily lives; on the other, the few sharpest moments of confrontation (beginning with the Berlin blockade and airlift in 1948) were a reminder that the Cold War could turn hot. But it was not until later, after the outbreak of the Korean War in 1950, that the danger of a "hot war" really seemed to loom.

I had been at Princeton only a short time when the first atomic bombs were dropped on Hiroshima and Nagasaki. Although the terrible power of this new weapon portended a dangerous future, it seemed at the time (and, I remain convinced, was) one of the key factors leading to the early surrender of Japan.

Later, it was a key element in the balance of power as the rivalry of the Cold War grew. But it was not a primary factor in creating that rivalry. Princeton had contributed substantially to the physics research leading to the atomic bomb, several professors and recent graduates worked in the Manhattan Project, and Princeton continued to play an important role in the field. I had chance opportunities in 1945–46 to glimpse two titans of the new atomic age: Niels Bohr and Albert Einstein.

My political inclination was moderate liberal. I wrote my first "published" article in May 1948 titled "The Challenge to Individual Rights," objecting to incipient McCarthyism (before his time), for the campus liberal *New Century* magazine. I joined the newly founded internationalist United World Federalists, one of the national leaders of which was the war veteran Cord Meyer—whom I got to know personally some years later when he headed the international organizations division, and later all covert operations, in the CIA's clandestine services.

Until 1946 I had not had any particular interest in Russia or the Soviet Union or in communism. I recall only two earlier impressions of the Soviet role in the world. The first was a sharp negative reaction to the "Winter War" when the Soviet Union invaded Finland in 1939–40. The second was a positive attitude toward Russia's resistance to the German attack and our wartime alliance against Nazi Germany. One of the first postwar shocks about Soviet behavior for me (as for many others) was the defection of a Soviet military intelligence officer in Ottawa, Igor Guzenko, in September 1945, disclosing that the Soviet Union had been spying on us. I also read and was influenced by the accounts of a series of other defectors, such as Victor Kravchenko, author of *I Chose Freedom*. Intellectually, the most intriguing was Arthur Koestler's *Darkness at Noon*.

The most mobilizing event of the early Cold War years in my own experience was the debate in 1947 surrounding the Marshall Plan. It was the only issue that I recall to have brought many of us out for demonstrations (in my case, and for most but far from all of my fellow students, as advocate). It was an important step in gearing up for the Cold War, but above all it meant American engagement in the world and repudiation of isolationism. The Truman Doctrine, although in effect establishing the general policy of containment as well as specifically aid to Greece and Turkey, was as I recall it curiously less controversial at the time.

For my senior thesis I explored the dual nature of Soviet policy, in the clandestine Soviet-German military collaboration of the 1920s and early 1930s, blending influences of communist ideology and Russian national interest. My formal courses on recent diplomatic history, international organization, international law, foundations of national power, and the like were mostly still focused mainly on the interwar period, but of course also drew on contemporary events such as the establishment of the United Nations, the foreign ministers' meetings addressing peace treaties in Europe, and the like. My courses were mainly oriented on the "realist" school of politics, emphasizing the role of power in international relations, based on such classic texts as E. H. Carr's *The Twenty Years Crisis* (1919–39) and a then new text by Hans J. Morgenthau, still in use today in frequently updated editions, *Politics Among the Nations.*

I was eager to become engaged in the real world of international political affairs. I never even thought of going into any aspect of business, even international business. My main expectation was to join the U.S. Foreign Service, and I obtained and studied the sample examinations as guides on what to expect. My first small direct exposure was accompanying my parents to a meeting at the Waldorf-Astoria of the Arab League in November 1946 to which they were invited by some friends from their Cairo days. In 1947 I also visited my parents' old friend Colonel William Eddy, then heading the intelligence analysis shop transferred to the Department of State from the wartime Office of Strategic Services (OSS). That visit to his imposing office in the old State-War-Navy Building next to the White House (later the Executive Office Building, after the State Department moved to its present location) gave me for the first time a new slant on a possible alternative career—intelligence analysis. Eddy, a much-decorated Marine officer in World War I, had been an important OSS operative in North Africa and the Middle East during the war, and subsequently the American envoy to Saudi Arabia. He was also a Princetonian. Although he did not "recruit" me, our talks did give me a new perspective on opportunities to work in the field of international affairs.

I soon narrowed my choice of graduate school to two, Columbia University, where a special program had just begun in a new Russian Institute, and Yale University, then host to the premier graduate school in the field, the Institute of International Studies. I decided on Yale.[1]

During the summer of 1948, after graduating with honors from Princeton and before beginning at Yale, I took a trip around Western Europe. In Europe, I saw my first live communists, campaigning for election in France and Italy and fully accepted as part of the political scene. I did not doubt they were financially supported by Moscow, as indeed they were, although I did not then know that their rivals in Italy were being financed by the CIA. The trip was broadening, contributed to my general education, and was exciting.

---

1. As a writer on this subject later rightly noted, "In the 1940s, there was no more exciting and stimulating place in the academic world for an international relations scholar to reside than at the Institute for International Studies at Yale." Fred Kaplan, *The Wizards of Armageddon* (Simon & Schuster, 1983), p. 19. In 1951, under a new president of Yale, the institute was closed, and most of its staff moved to a new Center of International Studies at Princeton.

I greatly enjoyed my graduate studies at Yale. By June 1950 I had completed my course requirements and Ph.D. examinations and lacked only a doctoral dissertation, which I could write away from Yale. Although I had begun concentrating on Russian studies at Princeton, under the tutelage of Cyril Black, I had not learned the language. Yale had been one of the few universities during the war pioneering in a new style of language instruction featuring extensive sessions with native language instructors. I could only take Russian alongside my graduate courses, but I took the intensive first-year course my first academic year, a concentrated second-year course during the summer, and skipped to the fourth-year course my second academic year. By 1950 I was reading and using Russian in my research and speaking it fairly freely.

While studying the Russian language and further steeping myself in Russian culture, I came to know a number of émigrés from the "White" emigration that followed the Red victory in the Russian civil war, some of whom had come directly to the United States, others later after years in Europe or China. Among these was the distinguished Russian philosopher Nikolai Lossky, then advanced in years but as sharp and multifaceted as a diamond. Another remarkable man whom I came to know was the noted aircraft and helicopter designer Igor Sikorsky, a technological genius and a religious mystic. I also met some of the new postwar "DPs" (displaced persons) who had left the Soviet Union during the war and later found their way to this country.

Most important, I met my future wife, Vera Alexandrovna Vasilieva, born in Latvia in the White Russian emigration, whose family came to the United States in December 1939 as the war was beginning and the Soviet Union was taking control of Latvia. Her father, of the Russian nobility and an officer in the prerevolutionary Imperial Army and the anti-communist White Army during the Russian civil war, was foremost among my Russian-language instructors at Yale.

At Princeton, as president of the Rifle and Pistol Club, I had become acquainted with Colonel Fox, the head of the Army ROTC program there. Through him in 1947 I learned of a military intelligence reserve program, which I entered at Yale in 1949 (as well as recruiting one of my professors into it!). My strategic intelligence reserve unit (the 469th Strategic Intelligence Research and Analysis Team) engaged in library research on aspects of Soviet war potential—presumably mainly for our own edification, although adding to a massive effort to build up a database on all aspects of the Soviet Union. It was headed by a young Army Reserve captain of Russian-Georgian royal lineage, David Chavchavadze, who had served during the war in liaison for U.S. Air Force supply operations to Russia. We were both also members of an informal Yale Russian Chorus (in later years better known and professionally more accomplished) and often had parties drinking and singing Russian songs as he played a guitar. He later had a long career as an intelligence case officer in the clandestine service of the CIA. On one occasion our intelligence reserve unit attended a lecture given by a recently returned prewar Yale professor who had served in the OSS—and would within a year leave again to join the new CIA. I certainly did not then imagine that within a few years I would be working for him in the CIA. He was Sherman Kent, and in his brief sojourn at Yale between wartime and Cold War intelligence service in Washington he wrote the standard study on strategic intelligence.

I had in 1948 contacted the newly established CIA. I was interviewed by an official whose function was not made entirely clear; I later learned he was a senior official in the clandestine service. He virtually offered me a position on the spot, but when I mentioned that I was considering further graduate work first, he agreed that might be a good idea and remarked that "they" (and presumably a place for me) would always be there.

I also talked with people in the State Department, in particular with several Foreign Service officers in the Soviet affairs field who would later be colleagues and ambassadors to Eastern European countries: Bill Crawford, Dick Davis, and Jack McSweeney. They encouraged me to complete my graduate studies and apply for the Foreign Service and drew my attention to an article in *Foreign Affairs* just published by a colleague (George Morgan) under the pseudonym "Historicus." This article, although far less influential than George Kennan's pseudonymous "X" article two years earlier (which presented the essence of his "long telegram" of 1946), was a careful, scholarly dissection of ideological influences in Soviet foreign policy, along lines of analysis that I was also then pursuing. I was impressed that it was the sort of analysis that would be undertaken by a Foreign Service officer (in fact, it was highly unusual, as was his academic training with a Ph.D in philosophy).

I was very pleased with my courses at Yale, in particular diplomatic history (with Hajo Holborn and George Vernadsky), political science (with Cecil Driver), international relations (with Arnold Wolfers, Frederick Dunn, and William Fox), security studies (with Bernard Brodie and Klaus Knorr), and Soviet studies (with Frederick Barghoorn and Nathan Leites). Perhaps most influential in my thinking was Arnold Wolfers's exposition of Realpolitik. At Princeton I had also studied under another leading exponent of geopolitics, Harold Sprout. Several of these Yale professors had published in 1946 the seminal study of the impact of nuclear weapons (*The Absolute Weapon*, edited by Brodie).

The Cold War had settled into a continuing confrontation during the two years I was at Yale, from fall 1948 to mid-1950. The most dramatic episode was the blockade of Berlin and American airlift in 1948–49, but its resolution suggested that although the confrontations would continue, the conflict would not get out of hand. The signing of the North Atlantic Treaty in 1949, creating NATO, while destined to be important, was not seen at that time as committing the United States to a major military presence on the continent. It was seen mainly as a step in consolidating the political situation in Western Europe.

The Cold War was seen as particularly ominous not only because of a long-standing antipathy and fear of communism, but also owing to the image of Stalin as an inscrutable and diabolical tyrant. The Soviet Union and International Communism under Stalin seemed to present an unprecedented threat, even greater than that posed by Hitler.

The Cold War was not only the dominant aspect of world politics, but also reflected the greatest threat to our nation and our values. It seemed, in essence, to be a conflict between a Free World and a totalitarian Communist World. The Cold War was not only the central threatening fact of the world: it represented the greatest challenge for the United States and the Western (Free) World, and in a special way for those of us entering the field of international relations it seemed clear that we would devote our careers and our lives to waging the Cold War. And, indeed, many of us did. The challenge of the Cold War later changed as the world and the Cold War itself changed, but that was all ahead. In the late 1940s and early 1950s we focused on how to wage the Cold War most effectively.

Although the Soviet consolidation of control in Eastern Europe was of greatest importance to the emergence of the Cold War, the most dramatic development at that time was the communist rise to power in mainland China. It also led to the most divisive debates in domestic American politics. Moreover, it now appeared that the West faced an ominous monolithic "Sino-Soviet bloc." This development overshadowed the earlier indication of a splinter in the world communist movement created by the split in 1948 between Josip Tito's Yugoslavia and the Soviet Union and its satellites.

Another development of paramount significance was the successful Soviet test of an atomic bomb in August 1949. Although eventual Soviet attainment of such a weapon was accepted, and an initial test was only a step toward acquiring a real nuclear weapons capability, a Soviet test had not been expected so soon. The sudden public awareness that the nuclear monopoly of the United States was broken had a powerful psychological impact.

The event that brought these developments together and greatly raised fears was the invasion of South Korea in June 1950. Now the Asian shift toward communism, and image of Stalin's tyranny and of growing Soviet military power, heightened concerns in the United States and opened a new chapter in the Cold War. It also happened to coincide with my move from Yale to Washington, and from the university to a national security "think tank."

Through my mentor in "Kremlinology" at Yale, Nathan Leites, I learned about the recently established RAND Corporation, and in turn I was brought to its attention. Leites was a part-time professor at Yale, but a full-time senior staff member of the social science (political affairs) division of RAND in its Washington office. RAND was then working exclusively for the United States Air Force. In 1949 I was offered a position at RAND as a Soviet affairs analyst, at a salary at least competitive with what I could get in government service and far above an academic salary. I was also offered a position as a research assistant and instructor in the institute at Yale. And when I renewed contact in late 1949, I was offered a position at CIA in political analysis in the area of Soviet affairs. As I considered the three possibilities, it seemed to me that RAND offered the best combination: to engage in scholarly research, and with opportunity for open publication, yet on a security-classified basis on work directed to meeting government policy needs. It combined advantages of both academic and governmental service, and I could later move in either of those two directions. Moreover, I found that I could combine writing my doctoral dissertation with my major project at RAND, a comprehensive analysis of Soviet military doctrine. Washington was also my home town, as well as the center of action for governmental and other work in this field. I decided to go to RAND, and we set my starting date at July 7, 1950.

2

The View from a Think Tank: Soviet Affairs Expert at RAND

The RAND Corporation was established in 1948, although it had originated as a U.S. Army Air Force program, called Project RAND, in 1946. It was envisioned by General "Hap" Arnold, his science adviser Theodore von Karman, and a few other far-seeing Air Force generals as a locus for new broad thinking about military technology and strategy in the budding atomic and air age. RAND's research staff was drawn from many disciplines—physics, mathematics, aeronautics, engineering, economics, and to a lesser degree political and social science and even philosophy. The headquarters, and almost all of the staff, were located in Santa Monica, California. Pay and working conditions were very attractive, especially the opportunity to think and develop ideas in a freewheeling way. The staff was young (averaging in their thirties) but had a high proportion of advanced degrees. Imagination was welcomed.

RAND was the prototype of what eventually became a large number of "think tanks."[1] Although the initial impetus for creating RAND came from recognition of the advances in military technology during the war, what gave momentum to RAND's growth and influence, and spawned the many later imitators and competitors, was the advent of the Cold War in the late 1940s.

---

1. For accounts of the RAND Corporation and the postwar and Cold War environment in which it and other thank tanks developed, see Bruce L. R. Smith, *The RAND Corporation: Case Study of a Nonprofit Advisory Corporation* (Harvard University Press, 1966); Paul Dickson, *Think Tanks* (Ballantine Books, 1971); James A. Smith, *The Idea Brokers: Think Tanks and the Rise of the New Policy Elite* (Free Press/Macmillan, 1991); and most evocative, Fred Kaplan, *The Wizards of Armageddon* (Simon & Schuster, 1983).

In the words of one observer of the origin and development of think tanks, "RAND was the pioneering American institution in the kind of Cold War scholarship that calls for intensive study of a potential enemy from afar."[2] That was what drew me to it.

RAND's very first report, in May 1946, was titled *Preliminary Design of an Experimental World-Circling Spaceship,* and over the years following the institution contributed much to the development of reconnaissance satellites, as well as to development of the intercontinental ballistic missile (ICBM), to redesigning the structure and operations of the bomber force of the Strategic Air Command, and to building the early warning system and other elements of the Air Defense Command. RAND also contributed greatly to the application to strategic problems of "game theory," and to the conception of "systems analysis" (a term coined at RAND), and operations research. Systems analysis and management by program budgeting, together with a bevy of senior RAND members including Charles J. Hitch and Alain Enthoven, moved into a central role in the Department of Defense under Secretary Robert S. McNamara in 1961.

Even more important was the contribution of RAND (with such leading figures as Bernard Brodie, Hans Speier, Herman Kahn, Albert Wohlstetter, Fred Iklé, and Henry Rowen) to military strategic thinking, and above all to deterrence theory and related American policy. Probably the single most influential contribution to the debate among experts was an article by Albert Wohlstetter in *Foreign Affairs* in January 1959 titled "The Delicate Balance of Terror." Deterrence, he held, was fragile and its assurance required continuous intensive military preparations. Herman Kahn's work in the late 1950s and early 1960s at RAND (and later at his own Hudson Institute), devising a typology of deterrents, elaboration of forty-four rungs of a ladder of "escalation" up to a full-fledged thermonuclear "wargasm" (as he called it elsewhere), and finally his idea of a "doomsday machine," guaranteed automatically in retaliation for an attack to kill *everyone,* took the public debate to its utmost extreme.

The views of the "social (political) scientists" tended in my view to be much more keyed to realistic strategic decisions, in particular those of the "Yale school" at RAND (Bernard Brodie, who went to RAND in 1951, and William Kaufmann, who had gone from Yale to Princeton but consulted with RAND and in 1956 joined the staff). Despite RAND's objective of integrating all relevant areas of expertise, the work of the small group of Soviet affairs experts in the social science division located in Washington (until 1957) was not

2. Dickson, *Think Tanks,* p. 69. Dickson also notes that my book on *Soviet Military Doctrine* at RAND was the "first of its kind" anywhere.

geared into the deterrence theorizing, and our findings in fact tended to diverge from it.

When I began working at RAND, in its Washington office in July 1950, the deterrence and strategic debates had not yet been raised. My own work was slated, by mutual decision, to be a study of Soviet military doctrine—surprisingly, a subject not yet analyzed anywhere. In fact, I had begun my research at Yale, and my first published article on the subject, titled "On Soviet Military Strategy and Capabilities," appeared in *World Politics* in October 1950.

No sooner had I been launched on my research in Washington than my U.S. Army strategic intelligence reserve unit was called up for active duty in the Korean War. I had mixed feelings, but RAND took matters in hand and successfully appealed my call-up on the grounds that what I was doing in classified research for the U.S. government at RAND outweighed what I would do in the Army. My military intelligence career was thus aborted. I was caught up in the hectic atmosphere of Washington in the Korean War, although I focused rather exclusively on my study of Soviet military doctrine.

In September, Vera and I were married at St. Nicholas Orthodox Church in Stratford, Connecticut. We were each 21. We settled initially in an apartment in Alexandria, Virginia, but soon moved into Washington. In March 1956 our son Alexander was born.

By the spring of 1951, in less than a year, I had completed a draft of my study. Through the cooperation of Yale and the Air Force, I was able to submit this draft as my dissertation even though it had not yet been cleared as unclassified. It was defended and accepted, and in June 1951 I received my Ph.D. in Russian studies from the international relations department of Yale University. I continued to work on the study, and the completed and declassified version, *Soviet Military Doctrine,* was issued as a RAND report and published as a book by the Free Press in March 1953.

I had been able to use some previously classified sources, mainly wartime German records, but even more important some Soviet military sources not classified but available only in classified collections, including the CIA library and the holdings of Army Intelligence (G-2). In fact, the only problem I had in clearance was objection from one important colonel in Air Force Intelligence who objected to my inescapable conclusion that in the *Soviet* military the predominant role was played by Army generals and Army doctrine! Eventually, he let others who were more reasonable be responsible for clearing my work. I see no need to mention his name, but I will note that some years later he became chief of U.S. Air Force Intelligence.

I recall that while doing research in 1950 in the CIA's Foreign Documents Division, located in a distant temporary building, a large shipment of books in Russian suddenly arrived. They had been picked up in the Soviet embassy in Pyongyang, North Korea, when our troops overran the city. No one knew what they were, except that they were in Russian. I plunged into them and soon discovered they were all classical pre-revolutionary or Soviet literature— Turgenev, Tolstoy, Sholokhov, and others. The lot was of no intelligence interest whatsoever, except for one item that had somehow gotten mixed in: the January 1950 issue of the restricted-circulation General Staff journal *Military Thought!* That was well worth sending back, but the rest of the shipment was not.

During the course of my research on Soviet military doctrine and related matters I developed a good working relationship with analysts in the U.S. government, in particular Army and Air Force Intelligence, and to a lesser extent at what was then called OIR: the Office of Intelligence and Research in the Department of State. Of course, in work on this as well as other subjects in the Soviet affairs field, I and others at RAND had extensive contact with our colleagues in academia, especially at the Russian studies programs at Columbia and Harvard. There were, however, no other specialists in Soviet military doctrine at that time. We drew on the government-sponsored research programs (some secretly funded by CIA, as at Harvard and MIT), including a large-scale interview program run by Harvard to tap the knowledge and experience of former Soviet displaced persons in order to improve our understanding of the operation of the Soviet system. (Also available of course were results of the classified government intelligence émigré and defector "debriefing" programs to sift out intelligence, especially on military and industrial-economic targets, the largest of which was the aptly named U.S. Air Force project "Wringer.") U.S. Army Intelligence had taken a different tack, its interest being more in learning operational doctrine of the Soviet Army. It had brought over a small number of former Soviet field-grade officers soon after the war, who were given access to limited information such as more current Soviet military manuals and other publications to keep up their expertise and assist in interpreting new developments. A few of these were former officers of the "Vlasov army," the wartime German-sponsored "Russian Liberation Army" headed by former Soviet lieutenant general Andrei Vlasov, who had been captured in 1942 and later agreed to cooperate.

One of the officers later added to this group (after initially serving a stint as a Russian-language instructor at the Army language school at Monterey, where I first had met him in 1951) was a former senior Soviet Air Force colonel. He was in fact the most senior former Soviet Air Force officer available, with prewar experience as deputy chief of staff for the air force in Soviet border military districts in the Far East and Central Asia, and he had been selected for promotion to major general when his bomber was shot down and he was captured late in 1941. I learned a lot from him and arranged for him to do some work on contract for RAND and later recommended him to Army

G-2. Aware of this relationship, the FBI asked me to let them know if anything occurred in his behavior that might indicate he was under pressure or had been contacted by Soviet agents. (The only time I had anything to report was when I advised the FBI of his death.) Most, if not all, Vlasov army veterans and later Soviet military defectors had faced difficult choices and were subject to changes of heart. But he stood firm. The only occasion that I had seen him under pressure from an external event that could have led him to some rash change was his angry reaction to a provocative interview by a U.S. Air Force colonel who showed an unseemly avid interest in knowing where the gold fields in Siberia were located. Although anti-Soviet, my friend had not ceased to be a Russian.

My research also led me to interview a number of interesting former Soviet officials, diplomats, military and intelligence officers. (In checking out with the FBI one former NKGB lieutenant I intended to interview, I found that he too had checked on *me*—and RAND—with the FBI.) Some I met were well known, such as former diplomat and general Alexander Barmine. Others were entirely unknown to the public; one was the former senior Soviet diplomat in Italy who had defected in 1940 and was later picked up by Allen Dulles's OSS unit during the war. By 1952, when I met him, under a new identity he had become a very successful American businessman in New York, still a friend of Allen Dulles.

Among the areas of greatest interest to the U.S. government that influenced the subjects studied by the small group of Soviet affairs experts at RAND—and, through research contracts on an unclassified basis, also the academic researchers at Harvard, Columbia, and MIT—were the Soviet system of control, and its obverse: vulnerabilities in the Soviet system. More concretely, this interest embraced psychological, sociological, political, ideological, economic, and institutional aspects of Soviet society and the Soviet polity. Nationality differences, bureaucratic competition, political rivalries within the Communist Party, institutional rivalries within the military or the intelligence services—all these were subjects of great interest and little knowledge during the Cold War 1950s in Washington. Studies at RAND, and elsewhere, addressed many of these subjects. One focus of interest, especially strong in the Air Force, was on targeting for war. Another focus was peacetime psychological warfare. A third, weakly developed in the 1950s but given greater emphasis later, was contributing to a database to support the conduct of U.S.-Soviet relations.

RAND contributed to psychological warfare studies in several ways. One was in theoretical studies based on extrapolation from analysis of wartime experience. For example, a major study by Paul Kecskemeti *(Strategic Surrender: The Politics of Victory and Defeat)* examined insightfully the factors involved in inducing surrender. That particular study, published in 1958, provoked a wholly unjustified protest from some quarters ever suspicious that "Washington" was plotting, and paying researchers, to study how *we* could surrender!

The Truman administration in 1951 had created an interagency body called the Psychological Strategy Board (PSB) to coordinate government planning and activities in waging the Cold War. I came to know several of its members and staff, prominent among whom was the philosopher–Foreign Service officer George Morgan, "Historicus," whom I have mentioned earlier. Under President Eisenhower, the PSB was recast as the Operations Coordinating Board (OCB), to perform essentially the same function, but within a more structured institutional framework under the National Security Council (NSC) along with the NSC Planning Board. In March 1953, when Soviet dictator Josef Stalin died, the new Eisenhower administration quickly turned to see what contingency plans had been developed for that occasion. The PSB had, in fact, been working on that very matter for more than a year, but apart from a file of memorandums there were no concrete "plans." President Eisenhower learned of this with some annoyance, being the product (and a skilled exemplar) of a military staff planning system that sought to plan for all contingencies. The PSB planners, and the intelligence assessors in a special estimate prepared five days after Stalin's death, could say only that the situation might be better, or worse, with Stalin's passing from the scene. We didn't really know. Under the circumstances, no single "contingency plan" *should* have been prepared. RAND had not been directly involved in studies of what Stalin's death would mean, but the Air Force had some ideas of its own. The Psychological Warfare Division (PWD) of the Air Force staff had, on its own, prepared propaganda leaflets to drop in the Soviet Union, in effect calling for a revolution. I vividly recall being told at the time by Colonel Grover, in charge of PWD, that they were even ready to load them on bombers for delivery when higher authority (within the U.S. Air Force, I believe) had stopped them.

The most bizarre example of Cold War political and psychological warfare was a plan called "Project Control," devised by Colonel Raymond Sleeper, a SAC officer serving on the faculty of the Air War College in the early 1950s. In essence, Project Control would have substituted compellence for deterrence and used superior American strategic nuclear air power to compel the Soviet Union virtually to surrender. It postulated unilateral U.S. actions to place nuclear-armed air power over the Soviet Union and dictate terms, including Soviet withdrawal from Eastern Europe. The surprising thing is that the proposal received considerable support from U.S. Air Force leaders and the chairman of the Joint Chiefs of Staff, Admiral Arthur Radford, and less than immediate rejection from some other military and political leaders. I was present at a briefing on the project given at RAND by Colonel Sleeper on July 14, 1954, and can state with confidence that it was received with disbelief, dismay, and alarm at RAND. (Sleeper's own later account was that he had the "impression" of support at RAND, although the audience was "somewhat amazed at the scope of the project and the proposed operations.") At the State Department, policy planning chief Robert Bowie flatly rejected it as "simply another version of preventive war." The project was, of course, never approved.[3]

The idea of U.S. initiation of "preventive war," that is, deliberate U.S. decision to launch a nuclear attack on the Soviet Union at a time of our choice before the Soviet Union could become powerful enough to threaten or attack the West, today seems utterly bizarre and irresponsible. But that was not so self-evident during the early Cold War years, from 1949 (when the Soviet Union tested its first atomic weapon) until 1954 (after Stalin had departed the scene and war seemed less inevitable). In 1952 President Harry S Truman repudiated his secretary of the Navy, Francis Matthews, and the Air Force retired Major General Orvil Anderson, when those officials publicly called for preventive war. But within the government, although the idea was never adopted, it was not flatly excluded as an option until President Eisenhower authoritatively ruled out any concept of preventive war in NSC 5440 in late 1954.[4]

RAND was not immune to thinking about preventive war between 1950 and 1954, and was in fact deeply (if unevenly) divided along a significant fault line. The few advocates of preventive war were among the leading mathematical theoreticians who contributed most to the development of game theory and its application to strategic thought. John Williams was the preeminent advocate of preventive war. Williams was a friend and disciple of John von Neumann, a Manhattan Project veteran and father of game theory, and had brought him aboard as an early RAND consultant. He had also brought in Ed Paxson, author of the "systems analysis" approach to military planning, and another supporter of preventive war. But virtually everyone else, including all of us trained or experienced in politics, history, political or social science, and military strategy, was opposed to preventive war.

RAND never endorsed preventive war. It did, however, by its vigorous lead in applying game theory and systems analysis to military planning, do much

---

3. The twenty-two volumes of documents concerning Project Control have now been declassified. The best account is Tami Davis Biddle, "Handling the Soviet Threat: 'Project Control' and the Debate on American Strategy in the Early Cold War Years," *Journal of Strategic Studies,* vol. 12, no. 3 (September 1989), pp. 273–302, quotations cited from pp. 291 and 301.

4. See NSC 5440, in *Foreign Relations of the United States, 1952–1954,* vol. 2 (U.S. Department of State, 1984), p. 815. For the best review of the subject, see Russell D. Buhite and William Christopher Hamel, "War for Peace: The Question of an American Preventive War Against the Soviet Union, 1945–1955," *Diplomatic History,* vol. 14, no. 3 (Summer 1990), pp. 367–84.

to place military planning at the center of attention. With military theorists such as Albert Wohlstetter (another mathematician by training) and Herman Kahn (a nuclear physicist), RAND contributed importantly—for better or worse, probably both—to conceptualizing and preparing for deterrence of war, and for designing forces and concepts for waging nuclear war if it should come. RAND also worked on both theoretical analyses and case studies of psychological warfare. In addition, RAND in a number of other ways supported a vigorous waging of the Cold War.

RAND was not directly engaged in the U.S. government's burgeoning propaganda and political warfare programs directed at the Soviet Union and its satellites in Eastern Europe in the early 1950s, but we did keep in touch with those developments and in some cases play a supporting role. In 1949 a nongovernmental National Committee for a Free Europe, and a parallel National Committee for the Liberation of the Peoples of the USSR, had been established, with encouragement from George Kennan. Dwight D. Eisenhower, then president of Columbia University (and Allen Dulles, not yet returned to government intelligence service), served on the board of directors. The Voice of America had begun Russian-language broadcasts in early 1947, but it represented official U.S. government views. In mid-1950 (on July 4, to underline the point) the National Committee for a Free Europe launched Radio Free Europe (RFE) broadcasts to eight countries of Eastern Europe under communist domination. Three years later, Radio Liberation (RL, later renamed Radio Liberty, to be less proactive and provocative) began broadcasting in Russian and to fourteen other peoples of the Soviet Union.

CIA through its international organizations division (under Cord Meyer from 1954 until 1962) oversaw and controlled these activities, but although the agency's role was fairly widely known in Washington, it was not publicly revealed or acknowledged until the early 1970s. Several American professors served as advisers to RFE, including William Griffith of MIT. Policy oversight was provided by the PSB (later OCB). RFE/RL, with headquarters in Munich, were funded at $10 million annually in 1950, and by the end of the 1950s this had risen to over $50 million.

The most difficult time for RFE came during the Hungarian uprising of October-November 1956, when excessive expectations for American assistance were held both within RFE itself and in turn by the millions of RFE listeners. Although the American "guidance" precluded direct appeals for revolt, the distinction was lost on many listeners when RFE rebroadcast programs of local rebel Hungarian radios calling for an uprising.

CIA, through the National Committee for the Liberation of the Peoples of the USSR, also organized the Munich-based Institute for the Study of the USSR. Staffed by former Soviet citizens, mostly intellectuals and professionals, it provided them gainful employment, added to the overall

Western public knowledge of the Soviet system, and served to disseminate propaganda against the Soviet system. Professor William Ballis of the University of Washington served as an adviser to the institute for a year, and upon his return urged me to take his place. I considered it, and RAND would probably have given me a leave of absence, but I decided not to do so. At RAND, a few of us kept in touch with developments in the émigré community, but we played no direct role. We did learn, through a consultant who had survived defection from prewar Soviet intelligence, about some current Soviet penetrations of the Organization of Ukrainian Nationalists (OUN) in the mid-1950s and reported this information to CIA. But this was peripheral to our research work.

The Joint Chiefs of Staff, through the U.S. Air Force, in 1948 had asked RAND to study the economic and military capabilities of the Soviet Union. That potentially covered a lot of ground, and so did RAND's efforts. Much of the work in later academic and CIA studies of the Soviet economy was built on the foundation of early RAND work (especially by Abram Bergson) on national income in the Soviet Union, with no gross national product index existing for the USSR, and Soviet statistics both incomplete and suspect.

In our analyses of Soviet political and military developments, I and my colleagues at RAND (and in the Russian studies programs at Harvard and Columbia universities, and in the analytical arm of CIA) were practitioners of the new field of what later came to be called "Sovietology," and its component dealing with the leadership, "Kremlinology." Among the originators and more successful practitioners of Kremlinology were a number of former political rivals of the Bolsheviks, especially some of the émigré Mensheviks (notably Boris Nicolaevsky), and turncoat former communists (such as Franz Borkenau). At RAND, the State Department, CIA (especially the Foreign Broadcast Information Service, FBIS), and the universities, somewhat less attention was given to personal associations and somewhat more to nuances and concealed "Aesopian language" in communications, but both were important elements of Kremlinology. These techniques led some of us at RAND (in the first instance my colleague Robert C. Tucker, who had spent nine years at the embassy in Moscow) to scoop the intelligence community and predict the fall of Georgy Malenkov in February 1955. Sovietology, and Kremlinology, were not "dark arts." They were useful tools for analysis, although with substantial limitations. Personal friendships with other budding Sovietologists of the early postwar generation, as well as a few more senior government experts on the Soviet Union, brought me into contact with colleagues in the Department of State and some other agencies. Incidentally, all of these early centers of Sovietology, including RAND, were heavily salted with veterans of the USSR Division of the Research and Analysis Branch of the wartime Office of Strategic Services (OSS).

In noting earlier the broad policy objectives that attracted RAND and others working on Soviet affairs in the 1950s, I did not mention as one of them the improvement of understanding of Soviet interests and objectives. RAND contributed a number of studies, notably Nathan Leites's *Operational Code of the Politburo*, published in 1951. I wrote several articles in the early to mid-1950s taking a somewhat different approach but also spelling out Soviet foreign policy objectives in terms of application of their ideologically inspired aims, with emphasis on their caution to advance their interests within constraints of opportunity. While such analyses were a useful antidote to those who prophesied rash and unlimited Soviet expansionist offensives, they also contributed to the already prevailing policy assumption that containment of Soviet expansion was a constant, and its corollary: that common interests were absent or at most the product of a temporary balance of contending capabilities. This view was perhaps warranted at the time, but it did not provide a complete picture of Soviet policy based on perceived national interests, even if viewed through ideological lenses, and over time provided a less and less adequate basis for American policy consideration.

While I was still at RAND, the first stirrings of revolt occurred in Eastern Europe, in East Berlin in 1953, and then in Poland and Hungary in 1956. I followed the latter two crises closely and wrote an article titled "The Tragedy of Hungary" soon after the events. Among other things, I concluded that the Soviet leaders had not decided to intervene and suppress the revolt until about October 31, a view that was not then accorded general acceptance. Today we know, from notes in the former Soviet archives regarding the crucial Politburo meetings of October 30 and 31, that indeed the Soviet leaders on October 30 had decided not to intervene, and on the next day reversed themselves and decided to do so.[5] This was my first excursion into dealing with Eastern European affairs, although it was primarily an analysis of Soviet policymaking.

One way in which RAND sought to expand the role that sophisticated political analysis could contribute to policy was by developing the technique of political war-gaming or political gaming. Such "political exercises," as they were sometimes called, went beyond traditional scenarios for analysis and introduced the dynamic of two-sided interplay. At about the same time, in the mid-1950s, and still more later, MIT joined in pioneering this effort. Typically, a crisis situation would be postulated and then two (or more) teams of players, representing the United States and the Soviet Union (and in more complex cases also local parties to a conflict, and perhaps NATO allies), would

5. My 1956 analysis was published as a RAND paper in November 1956 and as an article in *Problems of Communism* in January–February 1957. The Soviet Presidium (Politburo) notes were published in *Istoricheskii arkhiv* (Historical Archives), Moscow, March–April 1996, pp. 73–104, and May–June 1996, p. 87.

simulate the leaderships of those countries and "play" their roles in waging and resolving—or not resolving—their crisis. It was an innovative adaptation of simulated "war games" long played at war colleges.

The most ambitious of these early political games was played in the spring of 1956 in Santa Monica, with RAND and State Department officers on teams representing the United States and the Soviet Union in interactions to simulate developments over the entire next year, 1957. This game was played over a full month of real time. "Control" introduced some elements, but both superpower teams had much more leeway for initiatives of all kinds, rather than reciprocal reactions to events in a time-compressed crisis situation. The teams did not "foresee" all that would in fact occur in 1957 (or indeed in the interim during the remainder of 1956 before the game time was to begin), but that was not the purpose of the exercise. It was, I thought, a very useful experience, and so did most other participants (and it is always the participants themselves who gain most from such games).

Political "war-gaming" developed many variants, but the essential division was between those based on application of some kind of game theory and those simulating real negotiating, crisis management, or other political interplay. The archetype of game theory is, like chess or poker, a zero-sum competition in which one's moves are choices dictated by theoretical logic and a "model" of interaction. A political simulation may employ game theory, but the second variant approach attempts to come closer to reality by introducing other political, doctrinal, and psychological factors through attempts to simulate real-life entities, such as the U.S. and Soviet governments, rather than abstract models ultimately resting on mathematical logic. RAND developed both, but its key analyses (and not only games) tended to be based on game theory applied to deterrence and hence to U.S.-Soviet simulated, or projected, moves. I believe this had a pernicious effect on strategic thinking and, to some extent, on policymaking.[6]

One initiative that I, as a member of the Soviet team, had introduced in the RAND political exercise in the spring of 1956 had been a military-technological demonstration positing Soviet launching in mid-1957 of an artificial satellite of the earth and also of an intercontinental ballistic missile (ICBM). The game umpire (Hans Speier) disallowed the launching of a satellite and downgraded

6. For a good overall review, see Thomas B. Allen, *War Games: The Secret World of the Creators, Players, and Policy Makers Rehearsing World War III Today* (McGraw-Hill, 1987), in particular chapter 7, pp. 141–60; see also Lincoln P. Bloomfield, "Reflections on Gaming," *Orbis*, vol. 27, no. 4 (Winter 1984), pp. 783–90; Bloomfield and Cornelius J. Gearin, "Games Foreign Policy Experts Play: The Political Exercise Comes of Age," *Orbis*, vol. 16, no. 4 (Winter 1973), pp. 1008–31; and Robert Mandel, "Political Gaming and Foreign Policy Making during Crises," *World Politics*, vol. 29, no. 4 (July 1977), pp. 610–25.

the ICBM to an intermediate-range missile (IRBM), despite my insistence that both were quite feasible and indeed likely to occur in 1957. I was right (my date for launching of a Soviet satellite into space was July 4—in reality it came on October 4). But I was not clairvoyant; it was clear to those following the intelligence that the Soviet Union would be putting up a satellite in the international geophysical year (mid-1957 through 1958) and probably testing an intercontinental missile. Yet the Soviet *Sputnik* in October 1957, and ICBM test in August, came as a great surprise and shock to almost all Americans.

RAND, incidentally (notwithstanding Speier's objection), was following Soviet missile, future space, and nuclear weapons developments closely, and a few of us had special access beyond our usual top secret and Q (atomic energy) clearances. The Soviet launch of a satellite in 1957 could have been predicted (and had been in CIA since 1954). During the years I was at RAND, from 1950 until mid-1957, intelligence on Soviet military developments was growing but still insufficient. RAND could not contribute directly to improving intelligence acquisition, but in our research we did seek to broaden intelligence analysis. For example, in 1955 I prepared the first study analyzing Soviet practice and policy on disclosure (and nondisclosure) of new weapons developments.

RAND, especially in Santa Monica, continued to apply its efforts mainly to devising new requirements, techniques, and technologies for enhancing American military power. As earlier noted, from early beginnings in the late 1940s RAND contributed greatly to stimulating Air Force interest in space satellites and later missiles. Titanium was first produced in wrought form suitable for aircraft and missile applications on the basis of RAND research. The 1954 presidential decision to proceed with the *Atlas* ICBM owed much to RAND studies that in 1953 first demonstrated the feasibility of arming an intercontinental missile with a nuclear warhead. RAND was in the forefront in developing computer applications to decisionmaking. (One of the most bizarre examples was a volume published in 1955 to provide truly random numbers—a more complex task than it seems to a layman; the book consisted entirely of a few hundred pages of numbers and had the marvelous title *One Million Random Digits with 100,000 Normal Deviates.*) When we were not ahead of the curve on new weaponry, we caught up fast; for example, Brodie's *Strategy in the Missile Age,* which was published in 1959, had been titled in drafts until sometime in 1958 "Strategy in the Age of Airpower."

RAND and its role gradually came to public attention in the early and mid-1950s, and also to Soviet attention. In late 1951 a Soviet article on RAND appeared titled "Academy of Death and Destruction." Looked upon more objectively, if not without a critical edge, was the title of a later book in the United States devoted largely to the staff of RAND called *Wizards of Armageddon* (by Fred Kaplan). It is true that RAND, and later other think tanks as well, were focused on the "worst-case" threats. Yet that was the cutting edge, the greatest challenge, in the early years of the Cold War. RAND did not demonize the Soviet adversary, nor call for war. At worst, RAND helped to keep a focus on the military competition, and on meeting the most dire possibilities, at great cost and at the expense of efforts at political amelioration; at best, RAND helped to ensure a strong deterrent and to keep dire possibilities from being realized, and at the same time to rein in wilder cold warriors here. In short, in the final analysis RAND may have helped to prolong the Cold War, or it may have helped to win it. Or both. A great deal was yet to occur, in which RAND continued to play a role albeit not a central one, over the last three decades of the Cold War.

I found the environment and my colleagues at RAND stimulating. I was then, and remain today, very happy to have had the opportunity to work at RAND in the early 1950s. We had a privileged position, both "in" on government affairs, and yet "out" of the government bureaucracy. RAND was affected, but only to a small extent, by the wave of McCarthyism in the mid-1950s. I recall sitting with my colleagues in the conference room of the Washington office of RAND transfixed by the televised McCarthy hearings, before returning to our work in combating the *real* enemy in the Soviet Union, not a conjured internal foe.

RAND had also given me the opportunity to gain the reputation of being the leading expert on Soviet military affairs (indeed, at first almost the only one, apart from anonymous officers in G-2). I began to be asked to lecture at the war colleges, my first at the Army War College in 1953, and at the National War College beginning in 1955. I also began to lecture on Soviet military thinking and strategy at various universities and conferences. *Soviet Military Doctrine* was widely cited by authors on American strategic issues looking for the Soviet side of the equation (for example, by Henry Kissinger in his first book, *Nuclear Weapons and Foreign Policy* in 1957). *Soviet Military Doctrine* was also published in England, as *How Russia Makes War,* and was translated into editions in German, French, Spanish, Portuguese (in Brazil), Chinese (in Taiwan), and Turkish. Although without authorization, it was also printed in Russia by the Military Publishing House in Moscow and circulated on a restricted basis. It was also favorably commented on not only in numerous book reviews here and abroad, but also in letters from a number of former German generals. It led to a correspondence of some years with the British military writer Captain Basil H. Liddell Hart, and to my contributions in books edited by him on the Soviet Army and by Wing Commander Asher Lee on the Soviet Air Force. Finally, it also led to my being invited into the circle of military attachés in Washington, where (at receptions hosted by neutral Swedish and Swiss attachés) I first met several Soviet military attachés in the mid-1950s, of course fully reporting such contacts.

After several years, however, I felt that I was getting into something of a rut, essentially updating and continuing my study of Soviet military doctrine. Neither I nor my colleagues in the Soviet field in Washington were really integrated into the central work at RAND, and although I had enjoyed and found interesting and broadening some of my associations on visits to Santa Monica, I did not really want to be integrated into a fundamentally technical, even if broad-gauged, approach to the central problem of the Cold War, which I saw as political or political-military rather than military or military-technical. Coincidentally, in 1957 RAND's management made the decision to move the social science division (including its Soviet experts) from Washington to Santa Monica in order to integrate their work. But by that time I had decided that I wanted to move on, into direct government service.

Two friends in CIA, one a classmate from Princeton and one from Yale, urged me to come to the agency. Both were serving in the clandestine services, but my candidacy was raised with Ray Cline, William Bundy, and several other senior officials in the Directorate of Intelligence, and it was finally proposed that I should at least enter the agency in the intelligence analysis side of its activities, rather than into the intelligence collection or covert action arms, the clandestine services. A particularly interesting position, from my standpoint, was happily available—not merely as an analyst, but as the estimates officer in the Office of National Estimates (ONE) responsible for Soviet foreign policy and strategy. I met several times with Bill Bundy, deputy to the CIA's assistant director for national estimates, Sherman Kent, and John Huizenga, then head of the small Soviet and Eastern European staff of ONE. Kent was forthright, and he put the only reservation he had on the table: Was I just interested in getting a year or two of experience in CIA and then returning to RAND? I assured him that was not my intention, and that disposed of the matter. Bundy told me some time would be required to get full clearance.

I had briefly considered a position in the Pentagon, which a friend in G-2 had urged I consider, working with Lieutenant General James Gavin. I admired Gavin, whom I knew slightly, and he was then believed to be on a fast track to become chief of staff of the U.S. Army (although instead he retired in late 1957). I rejected that possibility because I regarded it as even more "military-technical" than RAND. I did consider the State Department, but if I was to enter the Foreign Service it would have to be at a starting level and with no assurance as to career path. I had also been sounded out by my former professor Cyril Black at Princeton about joining the faculty there. But nothing else appealed to me nearly as much as the position at ONE.

I understood that some time would be required for my CIA clearance, although I already held high clearances at RAND. But rather than stay on at RAND and wait for that clearance, I had another idea. Just the previous year, the Soviet Union had opened to tourist travel. A number of my colleagues in the universities were planning to visit the Soviet Union that summer—for them (and for me) this would be the first chance to actually *see* and experience the Soviet Union. Our studies until then had necessarily been at a distance. I could not travel there as a tourist while at RAND with my security clearances. But if I left RAND, I could visit the Soviet Union as a private tourist before actually joining CIA. Bill Bundy warmly endorsed my plans: it would be an asset to me, and to the agency, for me to have had direct exposure to the Soviet Union before entering on duty. My friends in the clandestine services also welcomed the idea. They informally briefed me on some things that I might find helpful, but of course did not ask or want me to do anything beyond what a tourist and observant scholar would do. (Nor, for that matter, were they even supposed to have talked with me about my trip. And, for that reason, they did not offer to pay any of my expenses, as they then did for some academic tourists—as I learned much later.)

Thus I left RAND after seven years, satisfied with the experience but glad to be moving on. First would be my initial visit to the Soviet Union, then would come the opportunity to participate directly not only in evaluating Soviet intentions and capabilities for U.S. policymakers, but in formulating policy.

3

The Thaw: Observing
the Soviet Union after Stalin

Only gradually—for many only very slowly if at all—did it become clear to those of us in Washington watching Soviet affairs that the Soviet Union after Stalin's death was not the same. Not everything had changed, to be sure, nor were the changes all favorable to the Western world, inasmuch as Nikita Khrushchev and his successors engaged more effectively in a global rivalry. Still, the great internal and external tensions that had been created by Stalin's paranoid totalitarian rule were reduced substantially.

One important difference was the opportunity for much greater, if still constrained, contact between the Soviet and external worlds. Within a few years, by 1956–57, Western unofficial visitors, tourists and scholars as well, could travel to the Soviet Union. And in a much more limited and constrained way, some Soviet citizens could also visit the West in official delegations of various kinds.

The wartime summit meetings of erstwhile allies had ended with Harry Truman's only meeting with Josef Stalin, along with first Winston Churchill and then Clement Atlee representing Great Britain, at Potsdam in July 1945. The first postwar summit did not come until almost exactly ten years later, with new leaders of all three countries (plus France), at Geneva in July 1955. Not much was achieved at the meeting except that it had occurred. President Dwight D. Eisenhower had proposed "Open Skies," but without really expecting it to be accepted by the Soviet leaders (as it was not). It was intended to highlight the closed nature of Soviet society. Nonetheless, there was general satisfaction with an improved international climate, which was sloganized as the "Spirit of Geneva." Khrushchev in his memoirs termed it "an important breakthrough for us [the Soviet leaders] on the diplomatic front. We had established ourselves as able to hold our own in the international arena."[1] The Soviet Union also made its peace with Josip Tito's "National Communist" Yugoslavia, which Stalin had failed either to topple or to hold within the Soviet-led bloc in Eastern Europe.

Partly bolstered by this new mood of confidence, Khrushchev embarked on a risky course of internal change marked by his secret speech to the Twentieth Congress of the Communist Party in February 1956 denouncing the crimes of Stalin. Among the reverberations of that action was the partial loosening of controls in the satellite countries of Eastern Europe, leading in turn to a locally generated change of leadership in Poland and to a short-lived Hungarian Revolution in October–November 1956. Paradoxically, the absence of American or NATO intervention to prevent Moscow's restoration of its control in Hungary confirmed the rhetorical nature of earlier Republican calls for "liberation" and reconfirmed for both sides the geographical line of containment along the Iron Curtain. Although the bloom was off the "Spirit of Geneva," normalization of East-West relations within a divided Europe continued to proceed.

Shortly before the Polish and Hungarian events of late 1956, one of the early Soviet visits to the United States gave me my first opportunity to get to know some Soviet representatives. Somehow my name had been given to the national headquarters of the American Red Cross as a potential interpreter for the exchange visit of a Red Cross delegation from the Soviet Union. RAND was not involved but had no objection to my taking leave for the purpose. Accordingly, my wife Vera and I were engaged by the American Red Cross to serve as the interpreters for a seventeen-day visit to the United States by a delegation of the Union of Red Cross and Red Crescent Societies of the USSR led by its chairman, Professor Georgy Miterev.

Some incidental aspects of the visit cast light on the large gap in early Soviet (and American) efforts at mutual understanding. The only remotely sensitive aspect of respective Red Cross activities was the relationship to civil defense activities. After meeting Ellsworth Bunker, president of the American Red Cross, and other officials, when asked if they had any questions Miterev quickly consulted with his colleague Nikolai Chikalenko (obviously the watchdog of the group) on whether to raise the question of civil defense and decided not to. Accordingly, I did not interpret their remarks—although I had heard the entire conversation. Later Chikalenko did gingerly raise the question and was told that the American Red Cross was concerned only with first aid training and assistance in any kind of disaster situation. When asked, Miterev and Chikalenko denied any interest in civil defense, which we let pass,

1. Nikita Khrushchev, *Khrushchev Remembers* (Little, Brown & Co., 1970), p. 400.

although Soviet civil defense manuals credited the Red Cross of the USSR with civil defense training, and Miterev's own journal had carried articles on medical measures for nuclear war.

There were some interesting sidelights. For example, we visited the New York Stock Exchange. Keith Funston, then president of the exchange, explained the system as our bewildered visitors peered at the active trading floor below, as if looking for the bears and bulls I was quickly translating and explaining. In the directors' conference room, Funston proudly pointed to a huge ornate vase which he noted was a gift from the tsar. "*Our* tsar, the Russian tsar?" asked former People's commissar (of health) Miterev. Chikalenko suspiciously asked where the *other* gifts were. Despite Funston's explanation that it happened to be a gift from Tsar Nicolas II received (in 1904) just as the conference room was dedicated, Chikalenko seemed sure he had uncovered evidence of some clandestine tie between American high-finance capitalism and the Russian monarchy. But Miterev seemed proud of the honor of the Russian vase on display. The visit to Wall Street awed the visitors. By contrast, the Russians were not impressed with the White House or Mount Vernon, much less grand indeed than Russian palaces.

We visited Ames, Iowa, and coincidentally arrived at Des Moines Airport just in time to see President and Mrs. Eisenhower, campaigning for the upcoming election, board their airplane to leave. A reporter asked Miterev his views on President Eisenhower, and he noted that Eisenhower was well known as a great wartime general and patriot. As he was about to go on, an American Red Cross official suggested I remind Miterev that President Eisenhower was one of two competing candidates. Chikalenko later complained to me that obviously that American Red Cross official must be a Democrat who didn't want Miterev to be speaking up for President Eisenhower. I sought to reassure him, without noting that the support of a visiting Soviet official would be unlikely to boost the president's prospects.

More revealing was an incident the next morning. The *Ames Daily Tribune* on September 22 featured a front-page photograph captioned "Russian Red Cross Officials Breakfast"—but depicting the President and Mrs. Eisenhower and others before their departure. Further down the page was the picture of our group eating breakfast the previous day, captioned "Ike and Mamie Introduced to the Crowd . . . ." We Americans in the group found the mixup amusing, but the Russians did not. Miterev took me aside and solemnly asked, "What will happen to the editor?" I assured him that nothing would happen, but he persisted. "But it is a political matter, the President is involved." I attempted to reassure him, but he no doubt had in mind such cases as one where an accidental juxtaposition of Stalin's visage with negative remarks had reportedly cost one Soviet editor his life.

The delegation had been scheduled to meet the governors of Tennessee and Iowa, but both meetings were canceled, probably because of the election campaigns. This was not, however, noticed by the delegation, who seemed unaware and had presumably not expected to meet any government officials. There was, however, a dinner in their honor given by Soviet Ambassador Georgy Zarubin and the Soviet UN representative, Ambassador Arkady Sobolev.

The Soviet representatives were clearly impressed by what they saw, especially the general prosperity of people everywhere. They were particularly taken aback by the evident well-being and occasional affluence of American blacks, who they had been told were harshly repressed. But myths die slowly. In Chicago, when a stylish African American couple strolled by, the Russians agreed among themselves that the couple were, obviously, Ethiopian diplomats! They seemed to remain unshaken in this belief through our efforts to enlighten them, but it may be that they were embarrassed at a slip of their preconceptions and realized they had been wrong. In Ames, when we saw a modern but unpretentious fifty-cow dairy farm (run by three people), I overheard Miterev comment in an aside to Chikalenko, "We would have *fifty* men to run such a farm."

If American political life was enigmatic for the visitors because it was so unfamiliar, their own political system remained in our discussions an enigma because it was *too* familiar to them. I read to Professor Miterev a *New York Times* article in late September reporting a changed Soviet attitude toward Tito, with speculations on shifts in the balance of power among the Soviet leaders. His only comment, in all seriousness, was "I haven't read *Pravda* yet." End of political discussion. We mentioned Khrushchev's famous secret speech denouncing Stalin, but except for confirmation of its general line we could get no real discussion. In more lengthy private talks, one of the group conceded that Stalin's regime (but not Vladimir Lenin's) had been bad, and that the Eastern European regimes might not have been popularly installed.

It is difficult to know what impressions of America the Russians took back with them. Each, of course, reacted as an individual somewhat differently. Needless to say, none was "converted" to capitalism, but all could not fail to see that the United States was not populated with oppressed proletarians and torn asunder by class strife. One of the group, after showing great interest in new things the first few days, retreated to a position of lesser inner turmoil by greeting everything new with remarks like "We have that too" or "Ours is better." In all fairness, there was provocation for some such remarks. It was unintentionally insulting when naive and ignorant Americans would ask the Soviet delegates whether they knew what ice cream was, had they ever seen television, and even did they have theater (!). In one instance a debutante inquired whether all the houses in Russia had onion-shaped domes.

We saw a modern supermarket in St. Louis, but they undoubtedly assumed it was less typical than in fact it was. Similarly, when we visited Ames, Chikalenko discovered that a Soviet agricultural delegation had been there on a visit earlier in the year, and promptly concluded that Ames was a model rural town, an American Potemkin village, to impress foreign visitors. (No doubt Khrushchev was similarly advised when he, too, visited Ames three years later.) This "model farm" idea was so much a part of their own system that it was difficult for them not to expect it here too. Chikalenko, ever on guard and suspicious, also pointed out S-Shelter civil defense signs as evidence of American preparation for war.

One thing the Soviet visitors never did bring themselves to understand was the freedom of the press. In Washington, near the beginning of the trip, a newspaper account of a press conference they had held provoked real consternation. The article was titled "Russian Doctor Says Smoking Causes Lung Cancer." The objection was not that this was untrue, for the story was accurate. But, as Professor Miterev put it, this was only an incidental and unimportant observation he had made in answer to a reporter's query; the main thing, on which he had delivered a short speech, was the common humanitarian and peace-loving aims of the respective Red Cross societies. The article distorted the importance of things: peace was the theme, not cancer. We explained the American conception of freedom for the press to decide what was important and of most interest, but without convincing him.

Seeing America with the *Red* Red Cross was an interesting experience. It was, however, no substitute for visiting the Soviet Union. As earlier noted, an opportunity arose to make such a trip as a tourist in the summer of 1957 in the interim between leaving RAND and starting at CIA.

At that time, the Soviet Union was granting thirty-day visas, rather than keying the length of a visa to a set tour, as they later did. I signed up with a tour group leaving from New York in early July for three weeks. I also reinsured by signing up with a second tour group leaving from Stockholm in early August to use the last of my thirty days. As it turned out, my visa was delayed and I had to fly alone to Moscow, and thence to Kiev and Odessa, to catch up with my tour group traveling through the Ukraine, by ship to the Crimea and Sochi, then on to Georgia, and back to Moscow.

On the cruise ship from Odessa to Sochi, there were not enough cabins for all of our group, so as a Russian-speaker I was assigned instead to share a cabin with some Russians—as it turned out, an Air Force major and his wife and daughter. I didn't learn any military secrets, but I did learn a lot about military life mainly from conversations with the major's wife. Later, on the beach at Sochi, a large crowd gathered around me to ask about America, and a colonel suggested we meet later to talk about more interesting matters. When I saw him the next day at the time he had suggested, however, he acted as though we had never met and walked past me—for good reason. I had noticed someone (not in bathing attire) surreptitiously photographing our conspicuous if spontaneous assembly on the beach the day before, and that person had then come up to me and asked for information about myself, explaining that he was a reporter for the local newspaper. When I asked, he was so flustered that he didn't even know the name of the newspaper he was supposedly representing. By that time the crowd had rapidly dispersed.

In Tbilisi, I rescued a Canadian member of our tour group from arrest, when he was detained for taking notes and photographs on Lenin Square (until four years earlier, Beria Square), unaware that he was facing the headquarters of the Transcaucasian Military District. Also in Tbilisi one evening several members of the group, including two young ladies with very blonde hair, had gone up to a restaurant on a mountain overlooking the city. Suddenly an unrequested bottle of champagne arrived at our table, compliments of some Georgians attracted by the blondes. They had assumed we were Germans and proposed a toast to "Georgian-German friendship." I was interpreting from Russian. When some of my compatriots insisted I explain that we were Americans, I did so, but they persisted in thinking that I was German, and some of the others Americans. Accordingly, they proposed a toast also to Georgian-American friendship, but then told me in an aside that they really *meant* it when they toasted Georgian-*German* friendship! After that, I had to remain a German for the evening. There were none of the usual *Soviet* toasts to peace and friendship. Our hosts were, in fact, part of the local Georgian establishment, members of the Communist Party, but without even a pretense of Soviet veneer on their Georgian nationalism. I visited later the museum built around (and over) Stalin's birthplace in the town of Gori, still a shrine irrespective of Khrushchev's secret speech.

In Moscow, when we returned there, final preparations were under way for the Sixth World Youth Festival in August. Before then, however, my original tour group completed its stay in Moscow and left. Armed with the thirty-day visa, I stayed on, living in the quarters of my good friend the U.S. air attaché, Colonel Tom Wolfe, who was away on a trip but graciously let me stay in his apartment. Later, I went up to Leningrad, joined the second tourist group from Sweden as it entered the Soviet Union, and stayed with them long enough to get my visa extended for another thirty days (under threat of demanding repayment, in dollars, for the prepaid tour if I had to leave). From then on, I stayed in Leningrad and Moscow until my visa expired.

I tried a direct approach for an interview with Marshal Georgy Zhukov, minister of defense and newly named in June as a member of the ruling Party Presidium (as the Politburo was then called). Zhukov's support had been important, possibly decisive, in Khrushchev's successful defeat in June of an alliance of factions of the Party leadership (led by Georgy Malenkov and

Vyacheslav Molotov and later called the "Anti-Party Group") who had gained a majority in the Presidium but not in the larger parent Central Committee. Zhukov was riding high and had publicly pledged support "on behalf of the armed forces" to the Party leadership under Khrushchev. But if Zhukov could pledge the support of the armed forces for one leader, he could conceivably do so for another. In October he was suddenly removed, while on an official visit out of the country. When I sought to see him in August, of course, he was at the peak of his authority. The colonel in the Ministry of Defense external relations office to whom I had addressed my request later conveyed Zhukov's response—regrets. I was told that he had read my book (*Soviet Military Doctrine*) and would very much have liked to talk with me, but "regrettably could not do so in view of the press of his duties, military and political." That way of describing Zhukov's role was quite interesting. I was not surprised that I did not get an interview, although I was a little disappointed.

I did get into the Fundamental Library of the Social Sciences, a Party research organization, where I succeeded in seeing at least the titles of some unpublished dissertations. And I met the editor of *Questions of History*, the main historical journal. I even managed to obtain several classified military histories produced by the Voroshilov General Staff Academy and Frunze (Command and Staff) Academy. But these were chance acquisitions. My main purpose, in any case, was to see and better understand Soviet society.

I had no contacts in Soviet officialdom, with the marginal exception of Professor Miterev of the Red Cross. Miterev greeted me like a long-lost friend and took me to lunch. He opened up much more than he had while in America. He was concerned about the disarray in the Soviet leadership. Moreover, despite his having been removed from office by Stalin in 1947, he referred to him in a respectful and almost nostalgic way. He noted that during the war he had been in charge of all medical affairs except at the front, and there was no question about getting things done. When Stalin had approved something, it would be done. I asked what happened if Stalin had not approved something that needed doing, and he replied that it was then necessary to go about matters in a different way, but officials always knew where they stood. That, by strong implication, was no longer the case. He spoke of Stalin in affectionate terms as "the Old Man" (not, as some others did, as "the Boss").

My most extensive, and by far most interesting, discussions were with students and other Soviet young people. Some I met in Moscow during and after the World Youth Festival. Most dramatic was a meeting with about 150 students at an agricultural college at Pushkin, outside Leningrad. I and a friend and colleague, Alex Dallin (who had just arrived with the Stockholm tour group), took a local train out from Leningrad and arrived at the agricultural school. We were quickly surrounded and two large circles crowded around each of us as soon as it became known that we were Russian-speaking

Americans. Most questions were about life in the United States. But they (as Russian students elsewhere) also asked for "the truth about the Hungarian events." I told them, in a straightforward way, without editorializing on the Soviet actions. When I had finished, one of them apologized for the action of the Soviet government! Only one student objected and tried to defend the Soviet position, but he was quickly talked down and shunted away by the others. When we had to leave to get the last evening train back to Leningrad, the students insisted on escorting us en masse and one almost had the feeling they would raise us on their shoulders in a triumphal march to the station.

In Moscow, I met many other Soviet young people. After the Hungarian uprising, some of them had participated in unpublicized student demonstrations, which they said had taken place in many cities. Even the press confirmed that there had been "demonstrations" (sometimes mis-described as "hooliganism"). Several confirmed that public lecturers were repeatedly asked for the truth about Hungary. In one case, I was told, the whole audience rose and left when the speaker evaded the question; in another case, the lecturer himself fled. I learned of a previously unreported student hunger strike in Moscow and confirmed reports of mass expulsions of students, including about 140 from Moscow State University.

It evidently occurred to the authorities, and I know from some of the students themselves that it occurred to them, that some of the spontaneous discussion groups that sprang up in Moscow in 1956–57 were not unlike the Petofi Circle in Budapest that had sparked the Hungarian Revolution. Some of the students even asked me eagerly for details about the cooperation of students and workers in Budapest. I met young workers who had become informal "liaison" between students and workers in Moscow. Incidentally, an example of the ideological bankruptcy of the regime (and one not lost on the youth) had been an angry extemporaneous remark by Khrushchev in November 1956 to a Moscow youth meeting threatening to send disruptive students to factory work if they didn't behave. In a theoretically proletarian society, that was an insult to the ideology, to the workers, and to the students. An example of the contradictions in Soviet policy was a then new (and short-lived) requirement that all students engage in productive work for two years after finishing the equivalent of high school before they could continue to higher education. This policy was intended to ease the pressure on the Soviet colleges and to introduce the youth to factory service. But it also had the effect of bringing workers and students closer together and "contaminated" the former with the spreading dissatisfaction of the intellectuals. The students became more acutely aware of the unsatisfied needs of the average working-man, and of the contradiction with proclaimed propaganda. Several students insisted on taking me to see the sorry quarters of average workers—indeed a frightful contrast to the model housing to which I had been taken a few weeks earlier as a foreign tourist. Finally, the students knew (and time and again asked me for further details) of the tremendous gap between the living standards of Soviet workers and those in America.

The youths I met and talked with, in various cities and under various circumstances, fell into several categories. First were the naive, especially those recently graduated from secondary school, the seventeen- and eighteen-year-olds. They were usually quite curious and eager to learn, but they had not been around long enough to *experience* the contradictions between what they were told and reality. Here was the greatest reservoir of those who believed the Soviet line. But it was an ever draining reservoir, for those very youngsters usually soon passed on into one of the other three groups. Among them also were the politically precocious younger cynics. A second group were the "believers," those who believed the official myths, either from patriotic desire to believe, or, often, from considerations of career. These Party-liners were but a small minority, even in the Komsomol, the Party youth organization. In contrast, there were the escapists. The "elite" of the escapists were the "golden youth," spoiled sons and daughters of the upper castes of Party, government, Army and official intelligentsia. Others less fortunately endowed by Soviet society became black marketeers, drifters, and hooligans. Still others were the *stilyagy* or zoot-suiters, seeking to escape the constraints and dullness of the officially favored life for youth by the pursuit of pleasure and by adoption of disapproved (and usually grotesquely exaggerated) Westernisms of dress and manner. Finally, there were the alert and increasingly disaffected young intelligentsia, particularly among the college-level students.

These young people displayed an avid hunger for knowledge, which reflected their skepticism, distrust, and disbelief of much of what they were taught and read in *Pravda*. They asked numerous questions about life in the United Sates, about problems of world politics, and about goings-on in the *Soviet* government. But their skepticism of the official line was not matched by knowledge of the falsities underlying it. For example, with real perplexity they asked: "Why does the United States spend half of its budget on military preparations?" I explained that the national budget in the United States did not include the nongovernmental industrial, transportation, and agricultural sectors of our economy, as does the Soviet budget. If the equivalent, the gross national product, were taken, our defense budget was less than ten percent of the total. Invariably, in the many conversations and informal "seminars" where the question was asked, they immediately understood this. Of course! In a capitalist society the entire economy would be in the hands of private enterprise, and the official figure on defense expenditure was quite misleading until this important distinction, deliberately omitted by their own newspapers (as they were quick to realize), was understood. On disarmament, they would ask: "Why doesn't the United States agree to prohibit nuclear weapons?" My explanation involved two points. First, a one-sided approach to disarmament involving reduction or prohibition of one category of weapons, the one in which American military strength lay, would result in a serious imbalance of military power, with the Soviet Union having large non-nuclear military forces unmatched by American and allied NATO strength. Under the circumstances of our lack of confidence in the Soviet leadership, this would be an imprudent and irresponsible act. The second point was a discourse, which always fascinated the young Russians, on the reasons why we did not have confidence in the Soviet regime. I acknowledged that the American people understood that the Russian people also wanted peace (and of this no one who had been there could have had any doubt), but that we had reason to fear that a government not freely representing and responsible to the people would not always reflect in its actions and policies the true interests and desires of the people. I reviewed the growth of the Cold War, from Eastern Europe of 1945–47 to Eastern Europe of October–November 1956; the 1948 Czech coup; the 1948–49 Berlin Blockade; above all, the Korean War. And the Russian students generally agreed, though often ascribing all this to Stalin. But of course Hungary entered and they would fall silent. Only occasionally did they suggest *joint* U.S. and Soviet responsibility for the growth of tensions. This general acceptance of the truth, and even the "conservative" acceptance of half the blame for the Soviets, was a remarkable thing in view of the fact that these Russian youth had had nothing but the official line and their own doubts and skepticism. Again, they had usually not themselves learned the truth, but they were searching and receptive to it.

"Why," they would ask, "can't Russian tourists come to America?" You *can*, I assured them, except that the Soviet government had answered for its citizens in objecting to the "shameful" procedure of fingerprinting, then required by U.S. law. In fact, this was a practice reserved in the USSR for criminals. But, I would note, travelers must always obey the laws and customs of other countries. For example, in the United States we have no internal passports ("Ohs," and "How can that be?"). Anyone in the United States can go from one city or state to another, change jobs, and so on, without any passport or work-book, without registering with the police. I, as a visitor in the Soviet Union, had to surrender my passport for registration with the Ministry of Internal Affairs (MVD) at every hotel, in every city I entered. In the United States, only criminals on parole must register with the police. The parallel was immediately grasped, and the "problem" of fingerprinting understood for what it essentially was: a propaganda ploy of the Soviet regime. (Nonetheless, an effective one; the dropping of that requirement soon after was a welcome shift of the onus for lack of free travel from our government back to theirs, where it belonged.)

Such, then, were the kind of questions they would ask about the United States. One cannot fail to mention also the universal questions on "What does the average worker earn?" "What can he buy with that?" "It isn't true that there is widespread unemployment, is it?" and also "What about discrimination against Negroes and lynchings?" I tried honestly to answer all such queries. That I didn't claim everything in the United States was perfect added credibility. But the truth itself was to them sometimes almost incredible. Some youth, incidentally, had extraordinary fantasies about the United States, assuming that everyone had everything. Their image was America as a land where everyone had servants, but no one was a servant.

The World Youth Festival in August 1957, a major propaganda production, brought some thirty-four thousand young people (ages fifteen to thirty-five) from 131 countries to the Soviet capital. My interest, as an outside observer not officially associated with the event, was in Russian reactions. In passing, however, I might note that a number of Western Europeans who went to the festival as ardent communist and Soviet sympathizers left disillusioned, but most of the much-feted Africans and South Asians seemed tremendously and favorably impressed by Moscow, the Russians, and what they were told was communism.

The Soviets spared little in preparing for the festival. When I was in Moscow about two weeks before its opening, I was amazed at the amount of repair work and painting being done—all on the fronts of buildings on the main streets. This "face-lifting" was eminently required by the normal incredibly sad state of perpetual disrepair cloaking a picturesque city in ragged drabness. (What other country would proudly announce that in 1957 they would repair in Moscow alone 1,600,000 square meters of building *façades?*) The "clean-up" went further. Known undesirables—black marketeers, prostitutes, and the like—were rounded up and taken out of circulation. And goods were withheld from the stores for a number of weeks and then released immediately prior to the festival, so that the shelves would be stocked and people would be spending freely the money they hadn't been able to spend when few goods were there.

I succeeded in obtaining a copy of the *Agitator's Handbook for the Festival* (not for publication) issued by the Propaganda and Agitation Sections of the Moscow and Moscow Regional Committees of the Communist Party. It contained data on the organizing of the festival, on customs of different lands, and on descriptions of the alleged wretched conditions of the workers and students in Great Britain, France, Germany, and other countries (that one really boomeranged when the visiting youth from those countries began to be told how terrible it was that they had to live on the verge of starvation and laughed the propaganda into thin air). But also it announced, along with the official slogan ("Peace and Friendship"), on the very first page, the line toward the West: "The war-mongers continue their dangerous activity, attempting to liquidate the first successes in the reduction of international tensions, increasing war hysteria, the arms race, and suppressing the national-liberation movement of various peoples." Peace was the theme, but it was a very one-sided peace, with Moscow touted as *the* peace capital of the world (the chanting delegations as they passed in the opening parade shouted "peace," "friendship," sometimes with the communist clenched fist—and crying "Moscow-Hanoi," "Moscow-Algiers," "Moscow-London," and so on).

The sham in the festival was by no means apparent to most who were there. But the Russians knew. Several Russians pointed out to me a stand near the housing of the unofficial American delegation where a stack of the U.S. government's Russian-language magazine *Amerika* was plainly displayed. But no one bought them. The Russians had been given to understand that it was not permitted to buy those copies. Ordinarily, I was repeatedly told, those issues actually distributed sold out at once, and indeed would later resell at up to ten times the original price on the black market. Why, then, did these copies not sell? The Soviet authorities wanted the young Americans there to return and say that they had seen piles of *Amerika* freely available to be sold, but not in demand. (Each month the Soviet government returned a big batch to the U.S. Embassy "unsold for lack of interest," keeping the distribution down to the same level as the sales of the Soviet equivalent in the United States, which *was* limited by lack of interest.) *Amerika* had only been allowed again since 1956, having been banned by Stalin in 1952, after an uneasy existence since 1944.

The Soviet youth were greatly impressed by this unique contact with those from abroad, particularly from the West. I know from personal observation, and from what the Russians told me, that many indeed had been treated to eye-opening revelations about various falsities of their propaganda. In fact, the net result of the festival may well have been harmful to the interests of the Soviet regime. The U.S. government had, however, generally discouraged attendance by Americans, although some 160 did attend. It later became known that CIA had paid the way of some participants, not of course to engage in espionage, but to observe attendees from around the world and to engage in the propaganda debate. Most important and successful in this respect was the Yale Russian Chorus, of which I had as earlier noted been among the founding members. But in 1957 I did not know that a number of its then current members had been recruited by CIA, to the extent that it was described in an internal CIA study as "an important Agency asset."[2]

---

2. "Covert Action Operations: Soviet Russia Division, 1950–1968," CIA Clandestine Services History 335, p. 30; quoted in Evan Thomas, *The Very Best Men, Four Who Dared: The Early Years of the CIA* (Simon & Schuster, 1995), pp. 62 and 362.

The festival opening had reminded me of a Cecil B. DeMille production—and Nuremburg 1936. But it was not all "show." The sincere feelings of friendship and strivings for peace of the ordinary Russian people were very impressive. The way these genuine emotions were being exploited by the regime for its own cynical purposes was equally depressing. During the festival, contacts between Russians and foreigners were of course free and frequent. But the Russian students themselves then realized, and some told me, "When it's over, they'll clamp down again, hard." I was there for some days after the festival and witnessed the tightening controls. Indeed, I experienced them. Several Russian youths with whom I talked were subsequently detained and questioned as a consequence, as I was informed by their friends and on two occasions by the students themselves after their release. The authorities wanted to know, in particular, what I might have asked them, and more generally what had been discussed. Ordinarily they would then be let go, with a warning not to mix with foreigners or (sometimes) not to see me again in particular. One young man, in Leningrad, after telling me that, said "But I am not afraid." I told him that while I would like to talk with him further, clearly he should heed the warning, and I broke off the contact.

Some of the Moscow youth I met were clearly budding dissidents. It also quickly became clear to me that they were under surveillance. (Most of the time, so far as I could tell, I was not. But I picked up a "tail" *after* meeting with them.) I limited my contact to hearing them out and answering questions about the United States and the world. I did bend a little to give them some copies of *Time* magazine they had requested that I obtain from our embassy, but nothing more. One of these young people, then twenty years old, would spend much of the next twenty years in and out of prison as a well-publicized dissident—before finally being allowed to depart for the United States in 1979. He was Alexander Ginzburg, one of the group I met at Sokolniki Park and gave the *Time* magazines. (He was not arrested for our meetings, but later for continuing dissident activities.)

On later official trips to the Soviet Union in the summer and fall of 1959, and in 1963, I had occasion also to observe the Soviet Union and people during the post-Stalin, Khrushchev era. Apart from general opportunities to observe life in the Soviet Union, those (and numerous later) visits mainly provided opportunities to learn more about trends in official Soviet thinking. But never again would there be a comparable time, or circumstances, for me to take soundings of young people or of dissidents. Most of the young people whom I met in 1957, and others like them, did not of course become dissidents. They lived normal lives within the constraints of the society and the system. For that matter, most of the people with whom I came in contact in 1957 and later trips were living with the system, without expectations that it would change in any drastic way. It had, however, already changed in important ways from the days of Stalin only a few years earlier. And as a consequence of growing contacts with the West it would change in some ways, if not yet for many years in some other respects.

The daily occasions to experience the workings of the Soviet bureaucracy in many ways were useful to complement what I had learned about the Soviet system from earlier study of its ideology, economy, sociology, and political system. The Soviet adversary in the Cold War was not an abstract monolith but a live society that could, and eventually would, change.

On my way home, I stopped over for a few days in Warsaw. There my most interesting encounter was a long conversation over coffee with two Polish journalists. We discussed mainly the thaw and the political infighting among Soviet leaders, as evident in the recent expulsion of the so-called Anti-Party Group of Malenkov, Molotov, and others. It was an interesting conversation, and as open (and informed) as any one could have in the West. One of my interlocutors, then a commentator and soon to be editor of the influential *Polityka,* was Mieczyslaw Rakowski—thirty years later to become the last communist prime minister and Party chief of Poland. I would next meet him in Warsaw some forty years later!

When I returned from the Soviet Union at the end of August, I plunged into some writing on Soviet strategy that I had begun earlier, but I was also looking forward to starting my new work at CIA. As it turned out, I had more time for writing than I had wanted, owing to a lengthy delay in obtaining my security clearance. In fact, because I was without income since leaving RAND at the beginning of July and had had to pay my own way to the Soviet Union, and had a wife and one-year-old son to support, I needed gainful employment. Bill Bundy at CIA came to my rescue, arranging for me to work in the interim at the Joint Press Research Service as a Russian-language translator. I readily passed the test and set to work translating (at home, at my own pace on piecework basis) for the three months until the clearance came through. I had taken the standard polygraph test required of all agency employees and been repeatedly grilled on any foreigners I knew—which of course I answered to the fullest of my recollection. Only much later did I learn what the problem had been. One of the Middle Eastern ambassadors I had met at the Arab League dinner in New York in 1946, to whom my mother had later written on my behalf (but without my knowledge), had sent a congratulatory telegram at my wedding. And he was suspected of communist connections. Yet I did not recall even his name, nor the telegram, much less our "contact"—the CIA interrogators never mentioned him or gave any clue as to what they thought I might be concealing. Moreover, for suspicious security investigators, there was my recent travel to the Soviet Union, even though approved by Bill Bundy. Eventually they granted the clearance.

So from September through December I wrote a book on Soviet strategy, a number of articles (including on Soviet missilery—the Soviet intercontinental ballistic missile test and *Sputnik* satellite having been launched during this period), and translated articles and a book on Soviet political affairs for the Joint Press Research Service to pay the rent. Late in December I was finally able to report for work at CIA.

4

CIA and Intelligence Analysis and Estimates

On December 27, 1957, I reported for duty at the Office of National Estimates in the complex housing the headquarters first of the wartime Office of Strategic Services, and since 1947 the Central Intelligence Agency, on the hill at 2430 E Street, NW, Washington, D.C. Below this vantage point to the south were the World War I temporary buildings that still flanked the Reflecting Pool, Lincoln Memorial, and surrounding area and housed most of the agency offices. While I was there, the old brick Christian Heurich brewery nearby was demolished, and several of us whose windows looked out on its tower adorned with large weathered copper numerals proclaiming its birth in 1894 contemplated trying to recover and rearrange the numerals on our own building to correspond with Orwell's *1984*. Our building also was occupied by the DDI—the deputy director for intelligence, Robert Amory. The DCI, the director of central intelligence himself, Allen W. Dulles, and the top administrative offices were in the adjoining buildings. In the temporary buildings below were the other elements of the DDI (a term then used to refer not only to the deputy director for intelligence, but also to the Directorate for Intelligence) and the Directorate for Plans (DDP; a euphemism for the clandestine services, in 1973 more openly renamed the Directorate for Operations, DO).

The Office of National Estimates (ONE or O/NE) comprised a Board of National Estimates (BNE), composed of a dozen or so elder statesmen, former ambassadors, generals, and professors, and a few dozen staff expert analysts who drafted the estimates, organized by geographical regions: Soviet and East European affairs (where I worked), Western Europe, the Middle East, the Far East, and "the world." The head of ONE was the assistant director (of CIA) for

national estimates, Sherman Kent; his deputy on the board (and later successor) was Abbott E. Smith, and his deputy as assistant director was William P.
Bundy. The overall office was not large, some sixty to sixty-five people in all.
(When Kent's predecessor, William L. Langer, head of the wartime Research
and Analysis Branch of the OSS, had been recalled again in 1950 from teaching history at Harvard by the DCI, General Walter Bedell Smith, to organize
ONE, Langer had been offered as large a staff as he needed; General Smith
reportedly had proposed a thousand, but Langer had said he didn't *want* more
than twenty, or at most sixty.)

CIA, like the OSS, was heavily weighted with Ivy League graduates, and for
good reasons. The eastern establishment, and Ivy League professors and graduates in particular, had not only the educational and social background, but
also language skills and experience of travel and business that made them well
able to fill diplomatic and intelligence assignments in, or dealing with, the
European countries in particular and the world at large. Moreover, the professors not only knew one another, but also their former students. History,
international relations, and area studies also had tended to be concentrated in
these universities. So there was a natural tendency to form and then to per-
petuate an Ivy League cadre of intelligence officers throughout the 1940s and
1950s.[1] In my day, this cadre included DCI Dulles, DDI Amory, DDP Richard
Bissell, Kent and Bundy in ONE, and others filling almost all the top positions
and many at all levels.

During the first ten or fifteen years of the Cold War, many young
Americans were attracted to serve in CIA on what they saw as the front line of
the struggle for freedom. This was especially true for the clandestine services,
and it was particularly the case for many of the new generation of Soviet
affairs specialists emerging from the new university area programs. It was also
true for the second generation of the White Russian emigration, the sons of
Russians who had left during and after the Russian civil war. Harry Rozitske,
not himself in this category but a wartime OSS veteran (from Harvard) who
became one of the chiefs of CIA clandestine activities directed at the Soviet
Union during the late 1940s and 1950s, later described this "younger breed of

1. In particular, see Robin W. Winks, *Cloak and Gown: Scholars in the Secret War, 1939-
1961* (William Morrow & Company, 1987). Winks has provided a fascinating and thorough
account of the major role played by the Yale alumni in American intelligence in the 1940s,
mainly in the OSS, but also in the beginnings of the CIA. Forty members of the Yale Class
of 1943 went into OSS. In the 1950s, four masters of colleges at Yale were ex-OSS or cur-
rent-CIA connected and helped steer many Yale undergraduates to CIA. So did Skip Walz,
the Yale crew coach. And at Princeton, Dean William Lippincott steered some of my class-
mates (though not me) to CIA. See also Evan Thomas, *The Very Best Men: Four Who Dared,
The Early Years of the CIA* (Simon & Schuster, 1995), especially pp. 9–16.

Russian speakers who came into CIA operations eager to take part in what many of them saw as the first battle of World War III. They were men of energy and talent, men with good prospects in civilian America who chose to fight what they saw as a threat to their ideals."[2] This was especially true of the early 1950s, after the outbreak of the Korean War.

There was less of an influx into the analytical arms of CIA because the number of political analysts remained small. Inasmuch as I was among them, I can confirm the high morale that prevailed in the Agency.[3] We saw ourselves as dedicated not only to helping to wage the Cold War, but also as members of the only arm of the government that had no institutional interests to serve other than pursuit of the truth. Allen Dulles captured that sentiment well when he had the inscription at the entrance to the new CIA building at Langley completed in 1961 (just as he, and I, were leaving the agency) read, "Ye shall know the truth, and the truth shall make you free."

The deep roots of Ivy League legacy in CIA were also marked by the statue of Nathan Hale erected in front of the entrance some years later. Nathan Hale (Yale, class of 1773) had been the first martyr of American intelligence, during the War of Independence, dying with words of regret that he had but one life to give for his country.

Allen Dulles as director of central intelligence, as well as head of the Central Intelligence Agency, was the key and commanding figure from 1953 through 1961 (and important as the deputy first for clandestine services and then overall deputy director for central intelligence from 1951 to 1953 and coauthor of a key report in 1949 that had called for establishment of a central intelligence organization). I did not know him well enough or long enough to add more than a few observations to the well-established picture of his role, but I did get to know and to respect him. He was always most interested in espionage, and he had been engaged in intelligence work as a young diplomat during World War I and at the Paris Peace Conference in 1919. (During the 1950s, he was known quite unofficially within the agency as "The Great White Case Officer.") At the same time, he also had supported the creation and maturing of analytical and estimative intelligence on the basis of integrity. He stalwartly defended "his people," specifically Bill Bundy (son-in-law of Dean Acheson), from Senator Joe McCarthy's attempts to draw blood in the early 1950s, in a way his brother John Foster Dulles did not do at the State

2. Harry Rozitske, *The CIA's Secret Operations* (Reader's Digest Press, 1977), p. 26.

3. I will often refer to CIA as "the Agency," the usual term used by those of us working in the Directorate for Intelligence (DDI), the overt analytical offices. People in the clandestine services, in the Directorate for Plans (DDP), customarily referred to CIA as "the Company."

Department.[4] Dulles, a Princetonian, was the virtual epitome of the "gentle-man spy," as his biographer correctly gauged.[5] Although not without short-comings, particularly in engaging his penchant for covert political action, he was an inspiring leader for CIA in its first full decade.

During the 1950s, in sharp contrast to recent decades, CIA was much less bureaucratic than most of the government, and at its upper reaches and inner circles was more like a club. There were plenty of tensions and very hard work, and life in CIA was generally self-contained within a shell of security, but the atmosphere inside was much more relaxed and open. To a considerable extent this atmosphere reflected the elitist Ivy League-eastern establishment back-ground of almost all of the senior people, exemplified by Allen Dulles himself. Moreover, the core of the senior staff at this time were wartime colleagues from the OSS. Even those of us who were younger, more recent recruits felt privileged by our association with "the Agency" (in the clandestine services, "the Company"), also to be at least aspirant members of this club. There was even literally a favored "club" frequented for informal social and even semi-official occasions, the Alibi Club. I was privileged to attend a few of the infor-mal get-togethers at the Alibi Club, once with Allen Dulles, featuring old clandestine services "war stories" over brandy and cigars.

I will have more to say in a later chapter about espionage, and a little about other covert operations, but my own experience was primarily in analysis and processing intelligence ("intelligence production," we called it) to service pol-icymaking and serve policy. At this point I should merely note that by far the most noted (and notorious) activities of CIA have been various covert action operations, a favorite of Allen Dulles and many (though by no means all) of the "old boys" of the club. Suffice to say that such well-known successes (at least in the near run) as the overthrow of Mohammad Mossadegh in Iran in 1953 and Jacobo Arbenz in Guatemala in 1954 were matched by some less publicized failures such as CIA support of an uprising in Tibet in 1949 and of an abortive attempt to overthrow Sukarno in Indonesia in 1958. There were a number of others. On the whole, this effort at covert political intervention was dubious at best. Finally, the disastrous CIA-managed émigré invasion of Cuba at the Bay of Pigs in April 1961 led to Dulles's retirement and marked the end of the "old boys" leadership of CIA.

Nonetheless, although covert operations later attracted public attention, as well as an undue share of attention at the time by the first leaders of CIA (and,

4. Some, even so, suffered pain and humiliation in having to defend themselves against unfounded and anonymous charges of disloyalty, including notably Cord Meyer. See his account: Cord Meyer, *Facing Reality: From World Federalism to the CIA* (Harper & Row, 1980), pp. 67–84.

5. See, in particular, Peter Grose, *Gentleman Spy: The Life of Allen Dulles* (Houghton Mifflin Company, 1994).

one may add, by others in the government, including George Kennan), the main business of CIA remained intelligence collection and production. As the latter of these was the main area of my own work at CIA, as well as the link to policy, it is to intelligence analysis and estimates that I shall turn to for the rest of this chapter.

Several broad overlapping conceptions of intelligence were at the foundation of the work of the Central Intelligence Agency. One was the concept of *national intelligence,* meaning intelligence pertaining to broad national interests, as contrasted to narrower departmental and agency interests such as, for example, *naval intelligence.* Closely related was the organizational concept of *central intelligence* in an agency or community of agencies coordinated to ensure reciprocal availability of information and evaluation relevant both to national requirements and those of individual entities (such as the U.S. Navy in this example). Third was the most basic of all because it defined not only the scope and organization of the intelligence function but also its purpose: *strategic intelligence.* Broadly, strategic intelligence is information serving the needs of national strategy, the foremost aim of which is to ensure national security. It embraces all aspects of political, military, economic, and other facets of international relations. Strategic intelligence encompasses information and evaluation of the intentions and capabilities of other countries, especially of an adversary—during the Cold War, above all the Soviet Union.

Sherman Kent laid the foundation for American thinking about strategic intelligence in a book he had first drafted even before World War II but published in 1949 in the brief interim between his service in the OSS and CIA, called *Strategic Intelligence for American World Policy.* A number of other important studies have further developed the concept.[6] So it was fitting that when a central intelligence agency was finally formed, with a body at the apex of the strategic intelligence analysis organization devoted to national intelligence estimating, Kent should guide it through most of its first two decades. Kent believed intelligence could best serve the policymaker by being objective and impartial, rather than building an advocacy case for any policy.

Kent argued that the proper role, and ultimately best service, to policymaking and to policymakers was to strive to "tell it like it is" even, perhaps

---

6. Sherman Kent, *Strategic Intelligence for American World Policy* (Princeton University Press, 1949); Roger Hilsman, *Strategic Intelligence and National Decisions* (Free Press, 1956); Harry Howe Ransom, *Central Intelligence and National Security* (Harvard University Press, 1948); and Bruce D. Berkowitz and Allan E. Goodman, *Strategic Intelligence for American National Security* (Princeton University Press, 1989). The Berkowitz and Goodman volume was intended to be an updating of the original Kent book, published by the same press. Hilsman, later to be head of the State Department intelligence office in the Kennedy years, was a fellow graduate student with me at Yale in the late 1940s, when Kent was also at Yale briefly, but was not a student of Kent's.

especially, if the conclusions of intelligence analysis are not consistent with current or proposed policy. It should not try to lead, or to follow, policy. This view prevailed in the intelligence community (particularly at CIA) in the 1950s and 1960s and was usually predominant later; it was occasionally challenged, above all in the Reagan era of the 1980s under Director William Casey and Deputy Director Robert Gates.

National Intelligence Estimates were (and are) assessments prepared by the Central Intelligence Agency with the participation of all elements of the intelligence community (as the intelligence offices of various military and civilian departments and agencies are collectively called). In the late 1950s and 1960s the coordinating body was called the United States Intelligence Board, USIB. There have been organizational changes over time. In 1973 ONE was replaced by a set of national intelligence officers, loosely organized as a National Intelligence Council. But the essential procedure remains. I shall describe it as it operated in the late 1950s and early 1960s.

Before discussing National Intelligence Estimates, I should note that the ONE staff, apart from its own expertise, relied heavily on analysis by the other offices of the DDI, and both ONE and these other offices integrated information from the full range of technical and clandestine intelligence collection. For example, one window into Soviet policy was opened by Soviet contacts with other communist parties. CIA, the FBI, and some allied or other friendly intelligence services had penetrated a number of communist parties at high levels, in one case even the head of the communist party of one Western country! This was useful not only for gauging Soviet use of international communism, but for learning sometimes important things about Soviet relations with its Eastern European allies, and notably about Soviet relations with Communist China. CIA analysts had been in the forefront in tracing the growing Sino-Soviet rift in 1958–59, and when it broke into the open in 1960–63 through penetrations of communist parties, we learned a great deal more from the polemics within the world communist movement, as the Soviet Union and China each sought to gain support by revelations of what were depicted as dastardly deeds of the other.

In analyzing Soviet political and military intentions and capabilities, however, while we had varying degrees of information, it was necessary to prepare *estimates.* As Sherman Kent would say, "An estimate is what you make when you don't *know.*"

An estimate might be prepared because it represented a standard continuing requirement prepared annually, or because it was requested by the president, the National Security Council (NSC) or the NSC Planning Board, by CIA, or another agency (usually the State Department). Terms of reference would be prepared in ONE and circulated to the other intelligence agencies (State, Army, Navy, Air Force; later also Defense). Contributions would be solicited of those agencies (and other offices of CIA) in a position to contribute on a given subject. The estimate would then be drafted by a member of the ONE staff and reviewed by the BNE. The contributions of the other agencies were drawn upon at the discretion of the ONE drafter. The draft estimate would then be circulated to all the USIB agencies, and their representatives would meet to work over the draft and seek agreement on the text. The BNE would go over the estimate as it was approaching completion. The final draft estimate would then be discussed by USIB, and any remaining dissents registered as footnotes in the final National Intelligence Estimate (NIE), which would be issued by the director of central intelligence, noting the concurrence of the other USIB members. The NIE would then be circulated to the president, vice president, secretary of state, secretary of defense, and others in the NSC and, as appropriate to the subject, other government officials (sometimes in all between two hundred and three hundred copies).[7] Often a new development or crisis would prompt a one-time Special National Intelligence Estimate (SNIE).

During my four years with the agency, there were approximately one and one-half to two NIEs per month relating to the Soviet Union, Eastern Europe, and world communism, at least half of which were on military subjects. They were, however, overlapping and most took weeks and some a number of months to complete. There was, for example, a general NIE on Soviet policy over the next five years, during the late 1950s called (for example, in 1958): NIE 11-4-58, *Main Trends in Soviet Capabilities and Policies, 1958–1963.* In 1961 the preparation of a single annual NIE document of eighty to a hundred pages or even more covering internal political, foreign policy, economic, and military affairs was abandoned. Even when it existed, it was supplemented by more detailed additional NIEs on the main aspects of military policy.

My first estimate was on a narrow subject: *Soviet Reactions to Possible United States Actions on Antarctica* (SNIE 11-3-58, February 11, 1958). It was prepared as an input to a pending NSC decision on whether to place a U.S.

---

7. A useful overall analysis of the national intelligence estimating process is the study by a former ONE staffer, Harold P. Ford, *The Purposes and Problems of National Intelligence Estimating* (Washington: Defense Intelligence College, 1989; and rev. ed. University Press of America, 1993).

For a series of informed discussions dealing with the history of ONE and national estimates, see *Sherman Kent and the Board of National Estimates: Collected Essays,* edited by Donald P. Steury, (Washington: Central Intelligence Agency, 1994); and the memoir commentaries of Ray S. Cline, *Secrets, Spies and Scholars: The Essential CIA* (Acropolis, 1976), pp. 111, 119–49; Russell Jack Smith, *The Unknown CIA: My Three Decades with the Agency* (Pergamon-Brassey's, 1995); and Willard C. Matthias, *America's Strategic Blunders: Intelligence Analysis and National Security Policy, 1936–1991* (Pennsylvania State University Press, 2001).

claim on part of Antarctica, and whether to invite the Soviet Union to participate in a planned international conference on Antarctica. My conclusion after
reviewing the evidence was that the Soviet Union, active in research in
Antarctica and like the United States not yet a territorial claimant, should be
invited. Also, it would be better not to stake a U.S. claim and thereby probably
prompt a competing Soviet one. That judgment was accepted by the BNE, the
director, and the USIB, and became the NIE. It also became U.S. policy, not in
this case and many others necessarily because of the NIE, but at least because
the NIE did not raise any new information or considerations that could have
led to a different decision. Incidentally, the 1959 Treaty on Antarctica provided for nonmilitarization of the continent and was the first arms control
agreement of the Cold War era. A few months later, I drafted the first NIE
written on the overall subject of Soviet disarmament policy (*The Soviet
Attitude toward Disarmament*, SNIE 11-6-58, June 24, 1958), which provoked
some military opposition and a strong Air Force Intelligence dissent from the
judgment that the Soviet Union would consider arms control and reduction
agreements that could curb its pursuit of military superiority.

With continuing interest in the eruptions of change and violence in Eastern Europe in late 1956, three NIEs in 1958 also examined the political
dynamics of the region: *Outlook for Stability in the Eastern European Satellites*
(NIE 12-58, February 4, 1958); *The Outlook in Poland* (NIE 12-6-58,
September 16, 1958); and *Anti-Communist Resistance Potential in the Sino-
Soviet Bloc* (NIE 10-58, March 4, 1958), the last of several estimates on that
theme during the 1950s.

Pending NATO plans for deployment of U.S. intermediate-range ballistic
missiles (IRBMs) in Europe led to a special estimate: *Probable Sino-Soviet
Reactions to U.S. Deployment of IRBMs on the Soviet Bloc Periphery* (SNIE 100-
4-58, April 15, 1958). The Quemoy crisis in the Taiwan Straits led to two estimates, *Probable Chinese and Soviet Intentions in the Taiwan Straits Area* (SNIE
100-11-58, September 16, 1958) and a contingency estimate titled *Sino-Soviet
and Free World Reactions to U.S. Use of Nuclear Weapons in Limited Wars in the
Far East* (SNIE 100-7-58, July 22, 1958). The initiation of the Berlin crisis by
Soviet leader Nikita Khrushchev's ultimatum on West Berlin led to a special
estimate, *Soviet Objectives in the Berlin Crisis* (SNIE 100-13-58, December 23,
1958), and additional estimates in each year through 1962—six on Berlin in
1961 alone. In these estimates, we at CIA correctly believed that Khrushchev
would back down, in contrast to the Department of State view.

In preparing estimates on Soviet foreign policy issues such as Berlin we in
ONE often found it appropriate and useful to resolve debates over whether
Soviet aims were "offensive" or "defensive" by combining both (as we believed
the Soviet policymakers themselves did) in estimating a range of probable
maximum and minimum Soviet objectives in any situation, especially in any

Soviet initiative. Minimum objectives tended to be defensive, and offensive ones were more opportunistic and elastic, ranging from modest to major gains depending upon what proved possible. Some military representatives, especially from the Air Force, chafed at attributing to the Soviet leaders anything but maximum offensive aims, but they acquiesced or took a footnote of dissent to reaffirm their emphasis on the threat.

Several NIE's on the Soviet missile program in the late 1950s addressed the "missile gap" alarm of 1959–61 over a possible Soviet jump on the United States in building intercontinental missile forces. An NIE on the Soviet long-range bomber force in 1958 buried a "bomber gap" controversy of 1956–58.

All of these estimates, incidentally, are now declassified and available at the National Archives. At the time, of course, they were highly secret. Although most NIEs were issued at the secret or top secret level of classification, in preparing them the key staff estimators had available more highly classified and "compartmented" intelligence, such as communications intelligence (Comint) and signals intelligence (Sigint) and U-2 and later satellite imagery intelligence (Imint). Some NIEs were issued in special, more highly classified editions as well as secret or top secret versions for usual circulation.

For example, initially I (together with almost all of my colleagues in ONE) was not cleared for "Talent" (U-2) information, until in 1959 in connection with other special duties I was cleared for it. My colleague Howard Stoertz, who was principally responsible for the main military estimates, had of course been cleared for "Talent" all along.

I vividly recall how on May 1, 1960, Howie Stoertz and I were suddenly told a U-2 was down, over Sverdlovsk in the center of the Soviet Union. We had been eagerly awaiting the results of that flight, which if it had not been shot down would in fact have confirmed only four launchers at the one operational site at Plesetsk, of the same unwieldy pattern as at the test range at Tyuratam, and would have negated two other principal suspect launch sites. In short, it would have gone a long way to disproving the missile gap more than a year (and an election campaign) before satellite photography did so. But that was not to be.

I was quite convinced that the Soviet ICBM deployment was proceeding slowly and argued for lower estimated levels than CIA, which was between the Air Force on the high side, and Army and Navy on the low side. Nonetheless, while the evidence leaned toward lower rather than higher deployment, it was not yet conclusive in 1959–60, and I could understand why some of my colleagues and ultimately Allen Dulles would hedge by taking a middle position. I was actively involved in the debate in ONE and had my say, but I was not the responsible estimates officer.

The very purpose of an "estimate" (or, as the British refer to their equivalent, an "assessment") is to go beyond a report based on information, and to assess and estimate intentions or capabilities based on the best information available from all sources, but also on what one seeks to have as the best judgments on matters that go beyond the evidence. In the case of the missile gap estimates in 1959–61, the Army and Navy intelligence offices, influenced no doubt by their institutional bias on the issue, stubbornly limited their judgment to very low estimates of Soviet missile deployment consistent with the available evidence. Air Force Intelligence, with both a mindset and an institutional interest in maximizing the Soviet missile threat, emphasized how much we did not know and estimated probable existing missile deployments and future programs as large as they could within the constraints of the evidence. The State Department estimate, based not on any institutional interest or bias but driven by the views of a few people in State's Bureau of Intelligence and Research (INR), also anticipated high levels, though not so extreme as those projected by the Air Force. As indicated above, views in ONE and CIA varied, but Sherman Kent and Allen Dulles estimated a middle range between the high and low estimates of the military agencies. As it turned out, the very low Army-Navy estimate (which I also had held) was correct.

The "missile gap" was finally dispelled between June and September 1961 by satellite photographic reconnaissance that confirmed the actual very small Soviet ICBM deployments. *All* ICBM and medium- and intermediate-range ballistic missile (MRBM/IRBM) deployment sites in the Soviet Union were first identified in satellite photography. Satellite reconnaissance provided an excellent basis for accurate short-term predictions because the eighteen-month construction cycle for missile silo launchers permitted good estimates of near-term increases in the force. Longer-term estimates remained fallible, and in the period from 1963 through 1966 the NIE estimates of future buildup were too low. Later they were again too high.

Dulles had been disinclined to challenge the intelligence offices of the armed forces in their areas of primary responsibility. And each service intelligence arm jealously guarded its own "turf" and prerogatives with respect to its counterpart in the Soviet armed forces. Consequently, through the 1950s CIA had shied away from more than a coordinating and occasionally "brokering" role in the preparation of estimates of Soviet and Warsaw Pact conventional forces. Nonetheless, when evidence of bomber production and deployment provided a direct basis requiring a challenge to the Air Force on the bomber gap, Dulles did so. Similarly, with the reservation noted, on the missile gap. The assessments of Soviet conventional forces had not provoked comparable alarms or controversy.

On January 14, 1960, I was sitting at my desk when the phone rang. "Ray, how big is the Soviet army?" It took me just a moment to recognize the voice of my boss twice above, Robert Amory, deputy director for intelligence. The call, and still more the question, was unexpected. I began to reply that the answer depended on whether certain marginal categories, such as border guards and construction troops, were counted, and did he want divisions and major arms, or manpower. Before I had gotten very far, Amory interjected impatiently, "Don't give me a dissertation, Ray, just the answer. Khrushchev has just said the Soviet armed forces total 3,600,000 men. Is he right? I've got the director [Allen Dulles] on the other line, and he wants to know." I told him that our estimate (the national estimate of the intelligence community) was somewhat higher, over 4 million, but that it was a soft (uncertain) one, and I thought Khrushchev's figure might be correct. This time I heard "Thanks," and the phone clicked off.

I quickly got a new assignment: to draft a special national intelligence estimate (SNIE) on the size of the Soviet armed forces.[8] CIA was thus charting a new course into troubled waters by attempting for the first time to "run" the estimate of conventional forces of the Soviet Army, Navy, and Air Force, insofar as these were implied by the manpower estimates. As was customary, each service prepared and submitted a draft estimate of its counterpart; as the ONE drafting officer, I was free to draw upon but also to change or even disregard those submissions—although I would of course have to defend differing estimates in the draft. The BNE chairman for the estimate was retired U.S. Air Force Lieutenant General Earl Barnes. So work on SNIE 11-6-60 was set in train, with the simple concrete task: "To estimate the [personnel] strength of the armed forces of the USSR as of 1 January 1960." Although the estimate dealt only with manpower, we took a "building block" approach, so the manpower of each component had to be estimated, and the estimate justified. This necessarily involved looking at Order of Battle of units and arms as well, and at many elements of the Soviet armed forces that had not ever been of sufficient interest to be looked at closely before.

The office of the assistant chief of staff for intelligence, U.S. Army (popularly known as G-2), had traditionally devoted most of its attention to military manpower, because the Soviet ground forces were by far the largest part of the Soviet military establishment, and manpower was a key element. But G-2's attention had also been principally on numbers of divisions and other units, and the Order of Battle composition of those units, rather than on actual manning, or on counting manpower in support, training, and other functions. The assistant chief of staff, intelligence, (ACS/I), U.S. Air Force, had counted aircraft and units rather than personnel and had sought to keep the

8. I have described the process of preparing this estimate in greater detail, and appended the text of the SNIE, in Raymond L. Garthoff, "Estimating Soviet Military Force Levels," *International Security*, vol. 14, no. 4 (Spring 1990), pp. 93–116.

Soviet aircraft totals at least even with the U.S. Air Force. The Office of Naval Intelligence (ONI) counted ships, not sailors, although it had developed a few rules of thumb for estimating Soviet naval manpower: first estimating crews on ships, then estimating personnel on duty ashore (in various support functions) equal to the number estimated as ships' complements, and finally—an unstated rule of thumb—determining that the overall Soviet naval manpower level should not be lower than that of the U.S. Navy (despite a much smaller number of Soviet ships of the line). In 1960 there was not yet a Defense Intelligence Agency (DIA).

Earlier national estimates had simply incorporated the general summary estimates of each service: the Soviet Army (ground forces) was set at 2,650,000, the Navy at 600,000, the Air Force at 500,000, and the Air Defense Forces (a separate mixed Army and Air Force service) at 400,000. The latest NIE summary estimates of the armed forces added up to some 4,265,000 men (plus 400,000 Ministry of Internal Affairs [MVD] internal security troops, Committee of State Security [KGB] border guards, and other militarized security forces not counted as part of the regular armed forces). These figures had become familiar, even traditional, changing little from year to year, and were rarely even mentioned in the annual round of meetings of representatives reviewing and coordinating draft NIEs.

The detailed breakdown of manpower estimates for each component of each Soviet service when they were submitted by the service intelligence offices suddenly added up to even *more* than the earlier unchallenged round overall service totals. In principle, there was nothing wrong with that. We were taking a new look at the subject. My own hunch that Khrushchev was giving accurate figures was not a conviction, nor of course did it represent a CIA prejudgment. But it was patently obvious that each office saw a challenge coming and wanted to provide negotiating room for a contest that was, correctly, anticipated.

The existing estimates were, as I had told Bob Amory, "soft." Some, in fact, were downright flabby. In fairness, it should be noted that no one had paid much attention to manpower levels before, and it was understandable that they had been accorded low priority both in intelligence collection and assessment. G-2, by and large, had done pretty well. They had well-established criteria for adding and deleting units from the Order of Battle. The chief weakness, as they realized, was in evaluating the manning level of individual units. Although we were able in this SNIE only to launch the process of evaluating unit strengths, we did for the first time distinguish between about a hundred divisions at "high level" strength and about seventy at much lower-level strength. Later estimates refined the distinctions into three categories, with about one-third of the divisions at 80–85 percent strength, about one third at a strength of 60–65 percent requiring augmentation, and the remaining third constituting only a cadre for essentially reserve divisions. Our estimates became much more accurate in the 1960s and later owing above all to satellite photographic reconnaissance.

By the time coordination of the estimate was completed, General Barnes and I, representing ONE, had managed to get a consensus on *all* figures (save for a mere 10,000 additional men attributed to coastal defense in a last-ditch ONI standoff). The process of producing the estimate had taken some three months. On May 3, 1960, SNIE 11-6-60, *Strength of the Armed Forces of the USSR,* was issued. The estimate concluded that Khrushchev's figure of 3,623,000 was "substantially correct" and provided a detailed breakdown with a new personnel total of 3,625,000.

The director was pleased that we had obtained a more refined estimate, and a better foundation for future estimates of Soviet conventional forces. Moreover, we had been able to do so with a consensus of the intelligence community, even though some traditional methods had been shaken up, and the overall estimate had been reduced by over half a million men.

Allen Dulles told me, beaming, in a bizarre compliment, "Ray, you've gotten rid of more Soviet divisions than anyone since Hitler!" That was not, strictly speaking, true, but we had provided a stronger basis for recognizing that many of the 175 divisions were not combat-ready, and most divisions were at reduced strength. Within a few years, with sharper analysis and new sources of data including satellite photography, it became possible to make much more accurate and useful conventional force estimates.

The NIEs on military subjects, especially those concerned with Soviet military power, were among the most influential, if only because they played such an important part in affecting decisions on American defense programs. By representing *national* intelligence, they helped greatly to discipline the military intelligence offices and still more the leaders of the military services as they pressed for their own programs. And for that reason they were bitterly contested. The military estimates also provided a mix of established facts, and best estimates of other facts, as well as judgments on future Soviet military programs and possible Soviet uses of their military power.[9]

As researchers into uses of intelligence began to discover, the policymakers and their staffs, the "consumers" of the intelligence estimates, almost all were more interested in "facts," and estimates on capabilities, than in judgments and estimates of intentions. This was hard for dedicated estimators like Sherman Kent and others of us to accept, but most policymakers believed they

9. For the most recent and complete analysis of the declassified record, see Raymond L. Garthoff, "Estimating Soviet Military Intentions and Capabilities," in *CIA's Analysis of the Soviet Union during the Cold War, 1947–1991,* edited by Gerald K. Haines and Robert Legget (CIA Center for the Study of Intelligence, 2001).

could make such "policy" judgments as well as (or better than) intelligence officers. They also often failed to attribute the same significance to estimative nuances of probability that we spent so many hours in refining. Nonetheless, the Eisenhower years of the 1950s probably represented the golden age of influence of the NIEs as a whole.[10]

In the late 1940s and early 1950s a great deal of effort was expended by the intelligence community, including CIA, on building a factual database—above all on almost everything related to the Soviet Union. The starting point had been the master files of the OSS Research and Analysis Branch, painfully built up from scratch in 1944–45. Major effort was now devoted to building a super-encyclopedia based on secret as well as open information. The National Intelligence Survey (NIS), not to be confused with the NIEs, was an enormous multivolumed secret catalogue of information, produced by the Office of Reports and Estimates, ORE (before the estimative function was split off when ONE was created in 1950), and thereafter by the Office of Research and Reports (ORR). Yet by the late 1950s and later, it fell into disuse. Air Force Intelligence, to be sure, continued to build up a massive data bank on potential bombing targets. But as basic information was assimilated, the political and military decisionmakers needed the kind of evaluations that could best be provided in national intelligence estimates.

The clandestine services were initially in the late 1940s organized in the Office of Special Operations (OSO), engaged in espionage and intelligence collection, with such veterans as Richard Helms, and the Office of Policy Coordination (OPC), engaged in covert operations, such as black propaganda, funding our friends in elections in key countries such as Italy, and the like, under Frank Wisner. (OPC was in an odd position; for several years it took policy direction from the Department of State, while being administered in CIA.) These were gradually combined under the deputy director for plans (DDP), then Allen Dulles, at the beginning of the 1950s, with functional offices for special operations and counterintelligence and geographic divisions for clandestine intelligence collection. These offices, especially the clandestine foreign intelligence service, also devoted massive efforts in the late 1940s and throughout the 1950s to building a huge stock of information needed to plan, prepare, and carry out their operations. For example, even current Soviet train and bus schedules and procedures for buying tickets were important data. Not only information, but materials of all kinds were needed—Soviet writing paper, pens, string, clothing, and everything imagina-

---

10. Even so, formal intelligence estimates were only one element in assessments of the adversary by political leaders, and not always the most important. See Raymond L. Garthoff, *Assessing the Adversary: Estimates by the Eisenhower Administration of Soviet Intentions and Capabilities* (Brookings, 1991).

ble, as well as samples of real Soviet documentation. A whole program was elaborated to acquire SOVMAT, "Soviet materials" of all kinds. And detailed information on people and places, procedures and practices, was needed.

As earlier noted, American (and foreign) travelers to the Soviet Union, rare in Stalin's day but burgeoning by the late 1950s, could supplement embassy staffs and open sources in much of this collection of information and sample materials on the basis of legal travel, observation, and collection. After my travel in the Soviet Union in 1957, while I was still awaiting clearance, I was informally (and off the record) debriefed by my friends who had also briefed me beforehand. I made a modest contribution on routine information and materials. I also had photographs of some of my young radical acquaintances in Moscow and was impressed when they were already able to identify some by name—including the later famous dissident Alexander Ginzburg.

Thus a real "intelligence gap" that had existed when the Cold War began was gradually overcome in the 1950s. In the clandestine services, CIA gained more direct experience, as well as developing liaison arrangements with a number of other friendly intelligence services, including some allies but not others and including some non-allies. In the case of Germany, the United States had sponsored a postwar resurrection of the *Wehrmacht's* Eastern Front military intelligence assets under General Reinhard Gehlen, initially taken over by U.S. Army G-2, then from 1949 loosely controlled by CIA, until the service was transferred to become the Federal Intelligence Agency, the *Bundesnachrichtendienst* (BND), the official foreign intelligence arm of the Federal Republic of Germany, in 1955–56.

The Office of National Estimates on behalf of CIA, or in conjunction with other components of the DDI, participated directly in several allied intelligence arrangements. In particular, there were in the 1950s several established joint estimates of Soviet military power produced with Britain (on a US/UK-only basis), with Britain and Canada (CANUKUS), and with Britain, Canada, Australia, and New Zealand. ONE also coordinated with the military intelligence agencies (after 1961 with DIA) on the U.S. contribution and coordination of the annual NATO military intelligence assessment (SG 152, Standing Group-152 in the 1950s; MC 161, Military Committee-161 in the 1960s). Varying degrees of sharing intelligence were involved in these ventures, least in the case of the NATO estimate, inasmuch as it was believed—correctly, as we later learned—that the Soviet Union and its allies had probably infiltrated the NATO headquarters staff and one or more NATO member governments. I participated in Washington, and one year in Paris at the SG-152 coordination session, in this exercise.

ONE had annual conferences with Britain, and less regularly with a few other close allies, on broader intelligence assessment issues. I participated in such sessions with the British in London in 1959 and Washington in 1960, and similarly with the Germans at BND headquarters near Munich and in Washington. Liaison was regularly maintained through CIA stations in capitals, and especially with these NATO allies through their senior liaison officers in Washington. I came to know most of these people well. (Shortly before my time, in the early 1950s, Kim Philby had been the MI 6 representative in Washington. I didn't know him. In one other case that I did know more closely, the hazards of liaison were exemplified when one of the senior BND officials at an intelligence conference I had attended at BND headquarters in Pullach, Bavaria, in 1960—Heinz Felfe—was discovered a year later to have been a longtime Soviet mole.)

Although British intelligence security was notoriously poor in the 1950s, the quality of British Joint Intelligence Committee intelligence analysis was unusually good. With a much smaller staff of analysts, they turned out very careful and perceptive studies. Their estimates tended to be conservative but sound. German intelligence analysis was much less impressive, and if they prepared (and shared) formal estimates similar to our NIEs I do not recall them.

One example of allied cooperation in which I participated had an amusing little sequel. Early in 1959 Australia was about to reopen an embassy in Moscow (having broken diplomatic relations after a major Soviet spy, Vladimir Petrov, defected in 1954 and disclosed espionage connections involving Australian politics). Two Australian diplomats, before proceeding to Moscow to reopen their embassy, came to Washington for briefings on the political (and security) situation in Moscow. I was one of the CIA officers who met with and briefed them, informally and at length. When we next met, just a few months later, it was unexpectedly in the Peking Restaurant in Moscow, and they were astonished and a little disconcerted to meet a CIA officer there! (I will describe what I was doing in Moscow in a later chapter.) Incidentally, the newly opened Peking Restaurant, as a restaurant serving foreign cuisine, was then unique in Moscow, although I would later joke that it was the experience of eating the poor food at that Chinese restaurant in Moscow that first led me to predict the serious rift in Sino-Soviet relations that was developing.

CIA, through ONE, also maintained a liaison arrangement of sorts with the American academic community. Ever since its inception in 1950, ONE had a panel of outside consultants, called the "Princeton Panel" from the locus of meetings, with whom a small delegation from ONE and Allen Dulles himself would meet three or four times a year. I attended quite a number of those meetings (Soviet foreign policy being a subject of abiding interest). Among the consultants were several professors at Princeton (including my mentor Cyril Black), Harvard, and Columbia, and other former officials with academic standing, notably George Kennan. (Although John Foster Dulles had failed to give Kennan even routine congratulations when he caused his early retirement, Allen Dulles remained cordial and respectful.) These consultations were somewhat one-sided, as the cleared consultants certainly learned more from reading the NIEs and having a chance to discuss them with the authors than we did in return, but it was mutually useful and interesting. Allen Dulles would regularly attend (indeed, we would fly up to Princeton with him in his private CIA plane, with its cover airline identification) and enjoyed these opportunities to talk with a cleared group informally and in a relaxed atmosphere. Over brandy and cigars after dinner, Dulles would tell (and re-tell) such true tales as his error in passing up an invitation on Easter Sunday in April 1917 in Bern to meet with a Russian opposition leader in exile about to return—Vladimir Lenin! Similarly, he would recall how at the Geneva Disarmament Conference in 1932 after long fruitless debates over how to define a bomber aircraft, someone had come up with a formula for so considering any airplane that flew higher than 10,000 feet above sea level—only to have the delegate from Bolivia, who had not said a word during the entire conference, suddenly speak up and object that any airplane using the only airport in Bolivia would have to take off above that altitude. But such stories aside, it was a chance for Dulles, members of ONE, and some of the leading academic figures in the field to further develop common understanding.

ONE, as well as other components of the DDI, was called upon from time to time to provide support to various diplomatic negotiations, apart from formal SNIEs that might have been requested. Members of ONE would sometimes brief chiefs or members of delegations, for example on disarmament, as I did several times. When a conference with the Soviet Union was held in 1958 on measures to guard against surprise attack, then an unprecedented step in arms control, CIA in addition to sending representatives from DDP and a missile expert from the Office of Scientific Intelligence on the delegation had ONE prepare an assessment. The chief CIA representative on the delegation in his later report to the director stated: "The ONE forecast regarding probable Soviet strategy and tactics, on which I briefed all the Western delegates prior to the conference, was particularly well received and proved most prophetic. Raymond Garthoff of ONE deserves special credit for this contribution."

In the spring of 1961, John J. McCloy presided over a series of panels contributing to a major new look at the whole range of disarmament and arms control issues on behalf of the new Kennedy administration. I prepared the agency comments for the director, generally supportive of the process and of proposed new positions, with a few specific exceptions. I also noted that "intelligence is one aspect of military capability" and that apart from verification, "collection of information is a legitimate element to be weighed in the balance of advantages and disadvantages to the U.S. of any particular disarmament measure." On specific issues, I noted that a provision calling for a ban on the placing in orbit or stationing in outer space of weapons of mass destruction had been carefully worded so as not to restrict satellite intelligence collection.

On the other hand, I recommended deletion of a proposal for advance notice of Arctic flights because it could impinge on intelligence collections. I also recommended that the director continue to oppose a direct telephone link between the White House and the Kremlin (and, for better or worse, the hot line agreed upon two years later was a teletype and did not include telephone communication). Finally, on a proposal for exchanges of communications and consultations in cases of communications failures or "stand downs" that could activate warning indicators and cause alarm, I noted "delicate intelligence security implications," but also "potentialities for intelligence collection and for clarification of ambiguous warning indications," and recommended that the director advise withholding this proposal pending further expert study, which he might wish to arrange.

My preparation of CIA comments on the new disarmament proposals was somewhat incestuous, inasmuch as I had been detailed to participate in the McCloy group's preparation of those very positions. It became even more so when, a few months later in a new capacity, I also prepared the Department of State position on implementing those same proposals.

The one area in which I felt that there was a greater gap than necessary was in the sharp divide between people in the DDI and those in the clandestine services in DDP. There was a security rationale and value in keeping the *work* of the DDP carefully compartmented. Although I had, from prior friendships and some special circumstances that I shall note later, somewhat more contact than most of my colleagues (except a few who had come to ONE from the clandestine services), most had no contact at all. We did receive a massive flow of intelligence reports from DDP, far more than other agencies. What I am referring to is not so much the flow of information as the interchange of experience and understanding. We had rather different perspectives, and I think both sides of the house would have benefited from more contact. But that was not to be, even many years later. I raised this matter, along with a few others, in a personal letter to Allen Dulles that I wrote at about the time I left CIA, but that was only shortly before Dulles's own departure. In some subsequent discussion and correspondence, Dulles asked for more on my views on Soviet thinking about the role of military power, but neither of us discussed further the relationship between the analytical intelligence and clandestine collection components of the Agency.

In the early 1950s, which were also the early years of ONE, the more alarmist views of Soviet militancy and aggressive policies gradually were restored to a more balanced judgment. Whether as a result of our own firm resolve in intervening to prevent communist seizure of South Korea and in building the NATO alliance as well as our own military capabilities, or as a consequence of the death of Stalin and internal problems in the Soviet bloc, Soviet actions were perceived to have become less directly threatening. Few (in government, or even outside) were inclined then to reconsider whether our judgments of 1946–52 had imputed a greater expansionist drive to the Soviet leaders than they in fact held. There was, in any case, a less strident view of the Soviet threat in the second Eisenhower administration than there had been during the Truman and first Eisenhower administrations (for example, as depicted in NSC 68 in 1950). To be sure, there was a growing concern, in many quarters even alarm, over emerging Soviet military capabilities, especially in intercontinental ballistic missiles, and implications for Soviet policy. But the difference was a more mature and nuanced evaluation of Soviet intentions. Even the Soviet pressures on West Berlin after 1958, while a cause for concern and counteraction, were not seen by most as likely to lead to war, in contrast to the jittery reaction a decade before. The Soviet leaders after Stalin's death in early 1953 were seen as politicians, not fanatics, despite their communist convictions, and not reliant on military means to pursue their objectives.

The national intelligence estimates in the mid and late 1950s reflected, and helped to bring about, this evaluation of the nature of the Soviet threat. This process was well under way when I joined ONE, but I was able to contribute to its further development. SNIE 11-14-61, for example, written just as I was leaving ONE and predicting the Soviet strategic posture for the 1960s, expressed this new understanding of the role of communist ideology in Soviet policy on the use of military power. "Soviet thinking about military policy has proceeded from a general outlook which stresses that historical forces are moving inexorably in the direction of communism." This was, however, seen as propelled by a sociopolitical movement of history "rather than by the direct use of the military power of the Communist Bloc." Moreover, the Soviet leaders were recognized as having legitimate defensive and deterrent objectives, as well as offensive ones.

> The Soviet leaders evidently believe their current strategic forces provide a strong deterrent against Western initiation of general war and are sufficient to support a more assertive foreign policy. . . .

More broadly, they saw the role of their military power

> as a means to deter Western military action against the Sino-Soviet Bloc, to inhibit the West from intervening militarily in other areas, to maintain security within the Bloc, to lend weight to their political demands and to demonstrate the success and growing power of their cause.

At the same time, we consistently held that the Soviet leaders were determined to avoid general nuclear war.

> [T]heir political outlook, their military programs of recent years, and intelligence on their current intentions, all suggest that the Soviet leaders

do not regard general war as desirable or a Western attack on them as probable. . . . There is no implication in Soviet behavior that they consider themselves in a position deliberately to attack the West, or to undertake local moves which carried with them a serious risk of bringing on general war.[11]

Today these may seem rather obvious statements. Yet when I had introduced such views in an ONE memorandum in 1959, and into the texts of several NIEs in 1959, 1960, and 1961, they were not only controversial but more than once provoked footnotes of dissent, especially from the chief of Air Force Intelligence.[12]

We recognized that Soviet policy in the latter half of the 1950s pursued a mix of offensive and defensive aims and would include elements both of negotiation and accommodation, and of pressure. As stated in NIE 11-4-59,

> we expect to see elements of both pressure and détente combined and varied as tactical advantage may suggest. . . . Whatever alternation of emphasis may occur, however, the swings are likely to fall within a range which excludes, on the one hand, the deliberate assumption of serious and uncontrollable risks of general war, and, on the other, abandonment of the concept of continuing struggle between two irreconcilable worlds.[13]

We also believed the Soviet leaders would, when necessary, retreat rather than incur "either serious risk of general war or net political loss." Nonetheless, there were risks, and we believed that "the chance of their miscalculating risks may increase if they remain convinced that their relative power is growing."[14]

> When estimating future Soviet military programs, we believed that the Soviets consider that their military policy requires a range of nuclear and nonnuclear capabilities permitting flexibility in the choice of means and the scale of operations in accordance with the political objectives sought in a particular area. The Soviet leaders probably believe that such varied capabilities become even more important under mutual deterrence from general war when, in their view, pressure and threat, maneu-

11. SNIE 11-14-61, *The Soviet Strategic Posture, 1961–1967* (November 21, 1961), pp. 3, 1, 3 (top secret; declassified 1994). See *Foreign Relations of the United States, 1961–1963*, vol. 8, *National Security Policy* (Government Printing Office 1996), pp. 198–201.

12. See Raymond L. Garthoff, *Some Reflections on the Likelihood of Soviet Intentions of War*, ONE Memorandum, August 24, 1959, 17 pp. (secret; declassified 2001); and Garthoff, "Estimating Soviet Military Intentions and Capabilities," cited in note 9 above.

13. NIE 11-4-59, *Main Trends in Soviet Capabilities and Policies, 1959–1964* (February 9, 1960), p. 2 (top secret; declassified 1994).

14. Ibid., p. 3.

vers and coups, even undeclared local wars may be undertaken with greater freedom and pushed further than in the past.[15]

Still, we did not believe the Soviet Union would *launch* limited wars with its own forces, but rather would support local wars short of Soviet military intervention.

> Soviet doctrine apparently does not contemplate conflict with Western forces in areas of contention at a distance from Bloc territory. Conflicts involving local anti-Western or Communist forces are treated under the rubric of 'national liberation wars. . . .' The Soviet support rather vaguely proffered is intended to be of a general deterrent character, but does not envisage overt Soviet military involvement.[16]

These views did not pass without controversy and dissent. On the one hand, Defense and the JCS objected to the view that the Soviet leaders would believe that they could undertake bolder actions with greater freedom, because that would require a judgment that the United States would "lack the vigor necessary to dissuade them," and they did not believe the Soviets would make such an evaluation. The chief of Air Force Intelligence, on the other hand, questioned the very idea that mutual deterrence would eventuate.[17] Beyond that, he also did not agree that the Soviets would settle for mutual deterrence. This was a basic Air Force view throughout the whole period, exemplified in the following excerpt from a footnote of dissent:

> The Assistant Chief of Staff, Intelligence, USAF, does not believe that Soviet behavior, as we have observed it, warrants the judgment that their objectives would be satisfied by attainment of only substantial deterrence and pre-emptive attack capability. Rather, he believes that the Soviet rulers are endeavoring to attain at the earliest practicable date a military superiority over the United States which they would consider to be so decisive as to enable them either to force their will on the United States through threat of destruction, or to launch such devastating attacks against the United States that, at the cost of acceptable levels of damage to themselves, the United States as a world power would cease to exist.[18]

At issue were a number of important questions: motivations and objectives of Soviet foreign policy, and prospects for American-Soviet relations, as well as objectives of military policy and programs. In addition, prospects for arms

---

15. Ibid., p. 5.
16. SNIE 11-14-61, p. 3.
17. NIE 11-4-59, p. 5.
18. Ibid., p. 9.

control (not yet in the forefront of attention in the late 1950s) were of course also involved.

I have mentioned the first estimate on Soviet attitudes toward arms control and disarmament, which I drafted in 1958. That estimate addressed positive motivations and restraining considerations in Soviet policymaking on disarmament, as well as concrete issues. It credited the Soviet leadership with genuine security concerns and a desire to reduce the risks of nuclear war, coupled with a growing confidence and belief that a positive stance would promote their "strategy of peaceful competition." Moreover, with the coming of mutual deterrence, "they might see considerable value in entering negotiations with respect to the stabilization of the nuclear balance of power at a certain level."[19] This forecast was substantiated a decade later in the SALT negotiations. Although the 1958 SNIE on disarmament as it emerged from coordination equivocated on Soviet military objectives, the Air Force Intelligence chief correctly believed the overall tenor of the estimate "suggests a Soviet willingness to curtail or limit the development of their capabilities to a level of deterrence rather than to seek the early attainment of an overpowering military superiority." He wanted the estimate to say that any Soviet disarmament agreement would be entered into only with the intention of "furthering their drive toward world domination," and would "in no way lead them to lessen their efforts to achieve an overpowering nuclear delivery capability at the earliest possible time."[20]

By the time I left ONE in September 1961, the missile gap was just ending, the Berlin crisis remained in full swing, and a new debate over the Soviet challenge in local wars under mutual deterrence was under way. Some of these issues I will refer to in other contexts in later chapters. But as I concluded nearly four years of drafting and debating assessments of Soviet policy, I felt that along with colleagues in ONE, in particular John Huizenga, John Whitman, and Howard Stoertz, I had contributed to a more sophisticated and balanced picture of Soviet capabilities and intentions. I was looking forward to entering the policymaking area.

19. SNIE 11-6-58, *The Soviet Attitude Toward Disarmament* (June 24, 1958), p. 5 (secret; declassified 1993). This estimate had not been declassified when the corresponding volume of the *Foreign Relations of the United States* (1958–1960, vol. 3) was drafted and was therefore not included in it.

20. Ibid., pp. 2, 5.

5

"Foreign Affairs Adviser" at the Pentagon

W hen I entered on duty at CIA, I did so under a "light cover," meaning that for public purposes (that is, social, banking credit, and non-CIA professional relationships) I was identified as working elsewhere. This was not then the usual arrangement for people working under the deputy director for intelligence (DDI), but Bill Bundy suggested that it might provide greater flexibility for future assignments, and I agreed. The agency made the necessary arrangements. Many CIA staff members, mainly in the clandestine services, were at that time identified as civilian employees of the Department of Defense. I was titled "Foreign Affairs Adviser" in view of my public reputation in the foreign affairs field. I did not have a physical office in the Pentagon, but I did have an office address there to which mail could be sent and received, a Pentagon telephone number that could take messages and relay calls, and of course identification credentials. I also had administrative backup if anyone needed, for example, to call for credit references, and to prepare travel orders and the like. Depending on my civil service grade (GS-14, later 15), initially I had a special passport and later a diplomatic passport identifying me as serving with the Department of Defense. In due course this became very useful.

The usual practice, and the assumption when I was given this cover status, was that it would essentially take care of routine administrative requirements. In practice, as we shall see, in my case it developed into something unexpectedly much more. The one area in which we anticipated its use (and usefulness) was in connection with my open publications. I had understood that as a CIA staff officer I would not be able freely to publish articles and books on the subjects on which I had been writing: international political and military affairs, and in particular Soviet affairs. The cover offered greater leeway, although naturally I would still have to submit everything to the agency for advance clearance for open publication.

The long delay in receiving security clearance for employment gave me the opportunity to write a great deal. I wrote and published several articles in the latter months of 1957, including one on Soviet development of satellites and intercontinental ballistic missiles that appeared just as the Soviet Union launched its first satellite, in October 1957. I also wrote an article foreshadowing military reconnaissance and possible attack missions for satellites, as discussed in Soviet publications.[1] I also had written a book on Soviet strategy and another batch of articles, in most cases submitted and accepted for publication, but not yet published, when I started work. I therefore submitted a hefty stack of manuscripts on the first day I reported for duty, so that I would not later have to submit them for clearance and so that there could be no question of my having inadvertently used any information acquired while working at the agency. For most of these later publications, as well as for all published before I began work there, I was identified simply as author of *Soviet Military Doctrine* and an authority in the field. Some, however, published later identified me as "foreign affairs adviser" at the Pentagon or a more general reference such as "Defense Department analyst."

I also continued and even expanded my regular participation as a lecturer at the U.S. National, Army, Navy and Air war colleges, the Canadian Defence College, and occasionally at the Department of State senior officer course, the U.S. Army Strategic Intelligence School, the Council on Foreign Relations, and various other official and academic institutions. I was identified by my publications, as an authority in the field of Soviet affairs, and sometimes as foreign affairs adviser at the Department of Defense. I was also so identified when I accepted an invitation to join the Council on Foreign Relations in mid-1959. One of the academic seminars I addressed in this capacity was the Harvard defense studies program run by Robert Bowie, Edward Katzenbach, and Henry Kissinger. A special graduate honors seminar at the University of California in 1958 brought me together with three former colleagues from Yale and RAND: I spoke on military strategy; Bill Fox (of Columbia, formerly Yale) on military policy planning; Bernard Brodie (of Yale and then RAND) on decisionmaking on new weapons; and Hans Speier (of RAND) on military-civilian relations.

During this period, in 1958–59 the Institute for Strategic Studies (later to

---

1. Raymond L. Garthoff, "Russia . . . Leading the World in ICBM and Satellite Development?" *Missiles and Rockets,* vol. 2, no. 10 (October 1957), pp. 72–76; and Garthoff, "Red War Sputniks in the Works?" *Missiles and Rockets,* vol. 3, no. 5 (May 1958), pp. 134–36, final portion not printed.

add the word *International* before *Institute*) was established in London. This was in part done in the aftermath of concern raised by the Soviet *sputnik* space challenge, as well as the growing general interest in strategic matters, and was initially funded by a grant from the Ford Foundation. I was not involved in the establishment of the institute, but I was an early speaker and member. In 1959 the ISS issued a pamphlet on the "military balance" between the Soviet Union and NATO. It was unfortunately replete with errors, having been put together from published sources of widely varying reliability. I called this to the attention of Alastair Buchan, the director of the institute, who was quite disturbed. A new version was issued in November 1960, much more complete and accurate, although still not up to the latest intelligence. Again, I called this to Buchan's attention, and he undertook thereafter to check out with British authorities what became annual issuances. *The Military Balance* rapidly became the most reliable and informed unofficial and unclassified source for scholars and commentators.

I mention this to note briefly something of the wide range of politico-military official and academic activities generated or sustained by the Cold War in which I participated during these years without reference to my official position at CIA. It did, however, sometimes become embarrassing. Once at the Council on Foreign Relations, soon after I had joined and was identified as foreign affairs adviser at the Pentagon, I was attending a dinner meeting in New York when Allen Dulles, also attending, called me over and asked me something—in fact, about a very secret matter involving espionage—in the company of his old friend Hamilton Fish Armstrong and one or two others, from which it was quite evident that while they might have thought (at least until then) that I was a Pentagon adviser, Allen Dulles *knew* I worked for him!

In 1958 I was invited to participate in the U.S. Army War College annual national strategy seminar (a several-day conference to which many prominent outsiders were invited, both for the intellectual exchange and to present the Army's viewpoint). The keynote speaker was Allen Dulles—but to preserve my cover, I traveled there separately and attended as a Department of Defense official.

It was not, however, always easy or even possible to keep my cover and agency affiliations separated, as evidenced by the Council on Foreign Relations encounter. One problem was that from time to time I was also called upon to lecture or participate in some conference on behalf of CIA. Bob Amory, the DDI, on occasion asked me to substitute for him in lecturing at one of the senior staff or war colleges. On one or two occasions this led to such anomalies as my lecturing to the same audience twice in a year, once as a Department of Defense expert and author, the other time as a senior CIA analyst in place of the deputy director for intelligence!

In the spring of 1959, several Democratic members of the Senate organized a study group open to all Senate Democrats, to meet informally and off the record over dinner with individual experts in the field (mostly not from the government) for discussion of various foreign policy and strategic issues. Their first guest was Henry Kissinger from Harvard. I was the second, just a week later, on April 14, 1959. I was given permission by CIA to participate on an unclassified basis, and I spoke on Soviet foreign policy and general political-military strategy. There was a lively and good discussion. Among those attending were Senators Albert Gore Sr., Eugene McCarthy, and Stuart Symington. (Senator John F. Kennedy had been planning to attend, I was told, but something came up at the last minute.) The subject of greatest interest was the "missile gap," on which I entered a spirited debate with Senator Symington. A few days later, Symington asked to see me, and we discussed it further, on a top secret classified basis, but without my being able to refer to information derived from special intelligence, such as U-2 "Talent" and satellite photography and Comint signals intelligence. Our discussion was inconclusive, as indeed were the official debates within the intelligence community at all levels of classification at that time. The agency was, understandably, skittish about this kind of unofficial discussion, but in any case it ended with that one follow-through.

My cover notwithstanding, when the agency wanted to bring me into something they did so. For instance, when the DDI, Bob Amory, wanted to have a luncheon for the visiting French strategic thinker, General Pierre Galois, he invited me as resident agency strategic commentator for a spirited dialogue on deterrence.

Often questions of cover identification, or indeed other security considerations, were ignored. Once, for example, Jack Maury, then chief of the SR (Soviet Russia) Division of the DDP, his predecessor Dana Durand (by that time sidelined to the senior research staff), and I had a long dinner conversation with visiting Professor Klaus Mehnert, who had just returned to Germany and to the United States from travels in China and Russia. During a freewheeling discussion when at one point Mehnert excused himself to go to the men's room, Jack suddenly asked, "Hey, did either of you check this guy out?" That is, had we checked to see if he had any known or suspected relationship with the German (West or East), Soviet, Chinese, or other intelligence services ? None of us had. Mehnert was well known in the field, but we didn't really know his possible connections. I don't recall who set up the dinner, but it had not been I, and as the junior participant I had not seen it as my responsibility. We weren't discussing classified intelligence information, but we were certainly reflecting knowledge and thinking in the agency. Most officers in the DDP were, by contrast, very cautious in all "outside" contacts.

Before starting at CIA, I had some friends and contacts among the press, and for them I used my new cover. A few of them and others in due course learned of my CIA affiliation, because as an intelligence analyst I sometimes participated in authorized off-the-record background briefings. One new contact was, however, rather different. At some point in 1958, news columnist Joseph Alsop called me and asked if I would come around and see him. I do not now recall if he called me at CIA or, more likely, at my home, but not at my cover phone. We met several times at his home in 1958 and 1959, for lunch or a drink. I of course fully reported these meetings. I could never understand Alsop's approach. Not only did he not try to "pump" me for information, he seemed indifferent to what little I would say and much more interested in telling me his own ideas and conclusions. In view of the fact that I was very guarded in my reactions I did not then, and still do not today, see what he found of use in our meetings. Eventually, my superiors in the agency decided that although there had been no problem, the very fact of any association if made public might be misconstrued, so we discontinued the contact. (Bill Bundy simply asked Alsop not to call me any more, and that did it.)

My public status as a foreign affairs adviser at the Pentagon received a huge boost several months after I had started working at CIA when *Time* magazine devoted an entire page to my just-published book *Soviet Strategy in the Nuclear Age.*[2] *Time* referred to me as "Defense Department analyst and specialist on the Soviet military" (and to my book as a "coldly penetrating study of modern Soviet military doctrine").[3] This was the kind of high-profile exposure that had *not* been foreseen when I was given the cover.

I had written *Soviet Strategy in the Nuclear Age* during the second half of 1957 after leaving RAND and before starting at CIA. It was well received, in reviews in the *New York Times, Washington Post,* and other leading newspapers as well as scholarly and military journals here and abroad. It was published in several foreign editions. It was a selection of the History Book Club, the Airpower Book Club, and appeared on the U.S. Army Chief of Staff's reading list, "deemed by the Chief of Staff required reading for basic military historical knowledge and understanding . . . as part of the professional preparation of Army leaders."[4] The book was briefly on the Washington, D.C., area (not nationwide) best-seller list.

A little over a year later, after writing (and clearing with the agency for open publication) several article-length manuscripts, I combined these to create a

---

2. Raymond L. Garthoff, *Soviet Strategy in the Nuclear Age* (Praeger, 1958).
3. "What the Russian Generals Think," *Time,* July 21, 1958, p. 16.
4. See "Chief of Staff's Contemporary Reading List," *Army,* September 1958, p. 60.

new sequel volume called *The Soviet Image of Future War*.[5] Lieutenant General James M. Gavin (U.S. Army, retired) wrote an introduction for it. This book, with a less well known publisher, did not get nearly as much attention as its predecessors. It did, however, anger the chief of security at CIA, responsible for clearances for open publication, because I had not cleared it as a book. I was able to demonstrate that I had cleared it, although piecemeal. It was not, however, the right way to proceed.[6]

All this open publication on Soviet and military affairs was, of course, in keeping with my cover as well as my earlier writing in the field. Moreover, one article in particular that had been published just before I started work at CIA had directly entered the interservice debate on *American* strategy. Although I had written on military and political issues other than those directly relating to the Soviet Union, that had remained the principal focus of my work. In an article published in *Army* in November 1957, I had, however, taken a public stand for the first time in the debate over American deterrence policy and military strategy. I came out for enhancing our capabilities for limited conventional warfare to meet challenges below the threshold of general nuclear war. In the article, I called for

> a return to correlation of the means with the end, the strategy with the objective. Our real objectives clearly differ in cases of, for example, a local Communist aggression against Iran or a Soviet nuclear attack on the United States. "Massive retaliation" may have been a sufficient answer to multiple challenges when we had a nuclear monopoly or even preponderance, but not as it begins to mean in fact either bluff or virtual mutual suicide. The second and related feature is a return to emphasis on destroying the enemy's military forces rather than his population or economic resources and capacity for war. . . .
>
> A strategic concept allowing flexibility of force, and providing the basis for capabilities that fit various forms and degrees of armed conflict, does not diminish the option and ability to wage total nuclear war. It does dissuade us from excessive reliance upon this strategy of last resort and restores opportunities for selecting and using effective strategies and forces in circumstances where limited objectives are better served by limited wars.

5. Raymond L. Garthoff, *The Soviet Image of Future War* (Public Affairs Press, 1959).
6. I had done the same thing, without objection, in my introduction and translation of a book by a Soviet general: Major General G. I. Pokrovsky, *Science and Technology in Contemporary War*, translated and annotated by Raymond L. Garthoff (Praeger, 1959).

It has been said, in referring to the various possible conflicts other than a general nuclear war, that 'we can't afford' them. Indeed, they are the only wars we *can* afford.[7]

These views were my own, but they were in line with the theoretical analyses emphasizing graduated deterrents, more reliance on conventional forces, and counterforce targeting expressed by others, my old colleagues William Kaufmann and Bernard Brodie in particular.[8] My approach, however, differed in that I reached these conclusions based on evaluating a *Soviet* strategy of limited challenges under cover of the strategic nuclear stalemate that, I argued, we could only deter or meet by capabilities and readiness to engage in a measured way.

In the national debate on strategy, the U.S. Army saw its institutional interests threatened and was most directly engaged in challenging the Eisenhower administration's avowed reliance on nuclear deterrence by "massive retaliation." Generals Matthew Ridgway (in 1956), James Gavin (in 1958), and Maxwell Taylor (in 1960) had all written books on this theme soon after retiring. Although I was supporting the challenge for other reasons, it was certainly in keeping with my cover allegiance. In fact, the title of my article in *Army*, "The Only Wars We Can Afford," was a direct challenge to a public statement by Secretary of Defense Charles ("Engine Charlie") Wilson, who with less subtlety than Eisenhower or Dulles had said, "We can't afford to fight limited wars. We can only afford to fight a big one." My article was reproduced for course instruction at the National War College.

In August 1960 at the annual convention of the Association of the U.S. Army, the Army's professional "alumni association" and semi-official lobbying organization, I had been asked to give the keynote address. I spoke on "The Soviet Challenge," repeating many themes of my books—and of the National Intelligence Estimates that I had been drafting, sometimes even using the same formulations. First, on Soviet objectives:

Let us begin by clarifying the aims of Soviet policy. World communism is the ultimate goal of the Soviet leaders, in the sense of their aspiration. In furtherance of this aspiration they seek to expand their influence and power beyond the Communist bloc. But they also give primary attention to maintaining the security and power of the Soviet state.

7. Raymond L. Garthoff, "The Only Wars We Can Afford," *Army*, November 1957, p. 52.

8. Brodie and Kaufmann had developed their thinking independently in the mid-1950s, although Brodie thought that Kaufmann had borrowed his views. For a good discussion, see Fred Kaplan, *The Wizards of Armageddon* (Simon & Schuster, 1983), pp. 185–201.

This statement of the Soviet objective has a number of significant implications. First, it means that the Soviet leaders have decided that deliberate initiation of general war would not be in their interest in the foreseeable future. Secondly, it means that the Soviet Union will seek to avoid serious risk of general war. Thirdly, it means that the Soviets will continue to pursue a policy of expansion of their influence and power by means short of major war. They will probably continue to attempt to identify themselves with ideals such as peace, disarmament, national liberation, and the like—ideals widely held in the world. Finally, it is nonetheless true that within this general policy they will be alert to exploit counterdeterrence (that is, the neutralization of our deterrent for certain local challenges) when they consider the risks to be low.

I took issue with the thesis of Albert Wohlstetter and his colleagues at RAND, who had argued that deterrence was "delicate" and threatened. I argued,

Mutual deterrence has already resulted from the acquisition of global thermonuclear striking power by the United States and now by the Soviet Union. Mutual deterrence has been described as a "delicate balance of terror." But while this balance is . . . by no means inevitably enduring, it is not fragile. The risks and consequences of a global thermonuclear holocaust are recognized by the Soviet leaders, and they strive to avoid any "adventurist" gamble. The importance in Soviet policy of the over-all balance of power, the "[cor]relation of forces in the world arena" as they call it, militates against a pre-occupation with purely military solutions. The Soviet leaders are not poised to unleash the terrible might of their—and our—military power as soon as a theoretical probability of military victory crosses some calibrated balance of 50 percent or 70 percent or indeed even 90 percent. In the Communist view, history cannot be made hostage to the mathematical computations of some "communivac."

Thus total nuclear war—though not necessarily other, limited, forms of war—seems ever less likely as a rational tool for the Soviet Union to advance its position.

I believed that we needed to get away from the fixation of the public debate over the threat of a Soviet surprise attack and general nuclear war. Although I did not expect *any* Soviet-American war, I did believe there was a need to prepare for possible limited wars, conventional or even nuclear, in order better to deter or to meet them. I was concerned over the growing view that the Soviet Union was turning from preparation for conventional war to preparation for launching a general nuclear war. Accordingly, I emphasized the need for countering limited military threats.

The Soviets tend in their published writings to discount or deny the possibility of local and limited wars, particularly limited nuclear war. But there are good reasons to doubt that such statements represent the real Soviet view or foreshadow future Soviet behavior. They want to deter the United States from initiating such wars, from preparing defensively for them, and from bracing our diplomatic stand by consideration of them as a recourse. In seeking to maneuver the U.S. into positions of choice between massive but mutual retaliation, or no effective response at all, the Soviets seek to deprive us of confidence that we have the alternative of limited nuclear reaction. But actual future Soviet initiative or response will be based on calculations of risk and gain. Limited wars, indeed, represent the classic form of Communist limited military action, for limited objectives, and at limited risk.

At the same time, I did not believe that the Soviet leaders were planning to launch limited wars, so I went on to say "this should not be taken as meaning that the Soviet line is likely to swerve from its general line of 'peaceful' political extension of influence throughout the world." I then turned to requirements for American strategy.

If the United States were to have a national strategy and a corresponding military and political capability primed only to deter the enemy from total war by threat of total—but mutual—destruction, the Soviets may calculate that for lesser provocation than direct attack upon the United States the total retaliation will not be made. A deterrent must be credible, and whether correctly or not, the Soviets may not always believe we would subject the United States to nuclear devastation to save a distant ally. . . . A military policy and posture is needed which provides for reliance upon local use of nuclear weapons or of conventional forces, depending upon the concrete circumstances, to meet local aggression and provocation.

American strategy today is in transition from reliance on massive retaliation to recognition of the need for more varied responses to the varied threats that face us. We are learning that balanced forces—not as an even cutting of the budget pie, but in the sense of a balance between capabilities and requirements—is an indisputable axiom and an indispensable policy. We are learning that strategy must relate the employment of military power, in any form, to the pursuit of political objectives. We are learning that the nature of the threat is highly important in determining the response. We are learning that even mutual deterrence requires us to provide a high degree of invulnerability for our strategic retaliatory forces. We are learning that we must consider requirements for effectively waging limited wars in cases of miscalculation where deterrence may fail. Finally, we are learning that strategy must be a means of achieving objectives of policy rather than merely the product of weapons development and budgetary constraint.[9]

I have cited these statements as the most economical way of recalling both the nature of the strategic debates at the time and the view I took in them as an unofficial contributor, notwithstanding my publicly undisclosed official position in an agency that shied away from involvement in the debate.

My role in this debate did not pass unnoticed in Moscow. The confidential journal of the General Staff, *Military Thought (Voyennaya mysl')*, in March 1960 described the allegedly aggressive views of U.S. Army leaders in pushing for larger ground forces and said these positions were given a theoretical foundation by a group of "rather influential theoreticians"—"R. Garthoff, General J. Gavin, General W. Wyman, W. Kaufmann," and propagandized by Hanson Baldwin. According to the Soviet author (who overstated): "The greatest popularity in American circles is enjoyed by the conception of Garthoff, the Department of Defense expert" expressed in *Soviet Strategy in the Nuclear Age* in 1958, and in the *Army* article of November 1957, which he also cited. The General Staff journal article interpreted the renewed emphasis on the U.S. ground forces as an "adaptation by the U.S. military machine to the requirements of a doctrine of 'graduated deterrence,' a supplement and development of the strategy of 'massive retaliation.' The new U.S. doctrine, assuming the organization of 'local' aggression, ascribes the main role to mobile ground forces armed with nuclear weapons."[10] Although attributing an offensive impetus to the American side, and exaggerating the success of the "graduated deterrence" view in 1960, such "counterpoint" discussions of such analyses by myself and other American commentators underscored an interactive East-West dimension of the strategic debate.

The apex of my shadow existence as the foreign affairs adviser in the Pentagon came in an unusual way. I had been invited again in 1959 to participate in the U.S. Army War College annual national strategy seminar. The keynote speaker that year was Secretary of the Army Wilber M. Brucker. The commandant of the War College, Major General William B. Ennis Jr., naturally assumed that Secretary Brucker was well acquainted with me as his foreign affairs adviser when he jocularly introduced us with a "no introductions are, of course, necessary." Brucker, who had never seen or heard of me, was polite and wary enough not to say so, and I found an opportunity hastily to explain the situation to him. He took the situation in good humor and later

9. Raymond L. Garthoff, "The Soviet Challenge," *Army*, September 1960, pp. 30–32.
10. B. Pyadyshev, "On the Socio-Political Essence of the U.S. Armed Forces," *Voyennaya mysl'* (Military thought), no. 3 (March 1960), p. 37.

kindly invited me to fly back (from Carlisle Barracks, Pennsylvania) to Washington with him in his helicopter when the conference ended. I did so, and we had a very pleasant chat. The secretary evidently enjoyed it too, because soon after he invited me to come over to his office for further conversation. Eventually, he asked if I would be interested in moving over and *really* becoming his foreign affairs adviser! I was flattered but declined the offer. Nonetheless, I still have as a memento a photograph of him that he gave me when he left office, inscribed to me as foreign affairs adviser, "for the fine work you are doing for the Country—and with best personal regards. Wilber M. Brucker, Secretary of the Army, 19 January 1961." How is *that* for cover!

6

Intelligence Excursions
in the Soviet Union

Sometime in May or June 1959 Sherman Kent asked me, "Ray, could you interpret for the vice president in Russia?" It had been announced somewhat earlier that Vice President Richard Nixon would visit the Soviet Union, but the question was quite unexpected. Yes, I replied, I could handle it, but I was not a professional interpreter and hence not the best he could have. It turned out that Marine Brigadier General Robert E. Cushman Jr., the vice president's assistant for national security affairs, was canvassing for an interpreter. Kent wanted to volunteer me for the job. In due course, I and two others were interviewed and tested as interpreters. As I fully expected, although I passed muster, I did not do nearly as well as my friend Alexander Akalovsky of the State Department's division of language services, native-born to a Russian émigré family in Yugoslavia and now for many years an American, and a professional interpreter. He, quite properly, got the job. A few days later, Kent again called me in to tell me "You're going after all!" When Nixon was told that the State Department interpreter had been selected, and learned that a runner-up had been the CIA nominee, he had said he wanted Allen Dulles's man to come along too. So I was added to the party, as an "adviser," with no specified function. (Nearly thirty-five years later, in the archives of the former Communist Party Central Committee in Moscow, I found a Foreign Ministry report of the Nixon visit that had upgraded my role by describing me as "Nixon's adviser" on the trip.)

I soon became very much involved as the CIA representative not only on the delegation but also for internal CIA and interagency preparations for the trip. Intelligence preparations for the visit covered several areas: first, briefing the vice president and other key officials and providing background information before and during the trip; second, participation in devising proposals for activities and the itinerary to present as requests to the Soviet side, and later working out a plan for the trip; participation in drafting key speeches; and finally my own preparation to support the vice president as required and to make the most of intelligence acquisition opportunities that might arise during the trip.[1]

On July 13 Director Allen Dulles briefed Vice President Nixon for some two hours, assisted by myself and senior intelligence officers on current intelligence, scientific (including military) intelligence, and economic intelligence. Then I was introduced as Dulles's representative on the delegation, and he and I alone talked with Nixon further. The briefing material had been coordinated by the Office of Current Intelligence, drawing on all elements of the Directorate of Intelligence, plus a separate briefing paper on the Soviet intelligence service and security aspects of the trip prepared by the Directorate of Plans.

Nixon showed a serious interest in being well briefed. As he himself frankly remarked, he did not know very much about the Soviet Union, but he wanted to learn. On this occasion, and subsequently, I was impressed with his evident application in listening, studying written submissions, and asking good questions. Three days later we provided follow-up notes on matters in which he had expressed particular interest, additional biographical notes, and suggested lines of response the vice president might wish to make to points and arguments likely to be raised by Khrushchev. We also responded to a request from Nixon for briefed-down summaries and analyses of interviews of Khrushchev with American and other foreign officials (eight in the preceding two years, most recently with New York governor W. Averell Harriman on June 23). On July 16 we gave the same basic briefing given to Nixon also to Milton Eisenhower, the president's brother, who was to accompany him.

Nixon in his memoir noted that he had undertaken "the most intense preparation I had ever made for a trip or meeting" and referred specifically to the briefings and papers from CIA, as well as the State Department and others.[2] And, as I have noted, I can confirm that he did indeed. He clearly was determined to do well both in his encounters with Khrushchev and in addressing the Russian people.

President Eisenhower had made it clear to Nixon that he was not on a diplomatic mission, and he had no negotiating brief, as Khrushchev also knew. Some construed Milton Eisenhower's presence as a "check" on Nixon.

1. The discussion that follows appears in a slightly expanded version in Raymond L. Garthoff, "Intelligence Aspects of Early Cold War Summitry (1959–60)," *Intelligence and National Security*, vol. 14, no. 3 (Fall 1999), pp. 1–22.

2. Richard Nixon, *RN: The Memoirs of Richard Nixon* (Grosset & Dunlap, 1978), pp. 201–14; quotation from p. 203.

Nixon's visit was a counterpart to the visits earlier in the year to the United States of two senior Soviet leaders, First Deputy Prime Ministers Anastas Mikoyan and Frol Kozlov, and preliminary to a possible exchange of visits between Khrushchev and Eisenhower. In fact, just as Nixon was leaving on his visit Eisenhower learned that through a misunderstanding Deputy Undersecretary of State Robert Murphy had extended an invitation to Khrushchev through Kozlov without conditioning it on progress in negotiations at Geneva, and Khrushchev had accepted with alacrity. When the announcement of Khrushchev's visit was made in Washington just after Nixon had left Moscow, it came as a shock to Nixon and his staff, who felt the timing detracted from the significance of his own visit.

Nonetheless, the Nixon visit was the highest-level American visit to the Soviet Union up to that time (not counting the secret wartime meeting of President Roosevelt with Stalin and Churchill at Yalta in early 1945). The main purpose of the visit was to exploit a rare opportunity for an authoritative American figure to reach the Soviet people over the head of the regime. Nixon also sought to impress the Soviet leader with American determination, and to build his own political stature. From the parochial interest that I represented, it was also seen as a rare opportunity to visit some normally unavailable areas and installations, and in general to acquire intelligence insofar as circumstances allowed, consistent with the primary political purposes of the visit.

An ad hoc committee to coordinate the "strategy" of the visit was established, comprising General Cushman of the vice president's staff, Deputy Assistant Secretary of State Foy Kohler, Colonel Charles Taylor, USAF, for the Defense Department, and myself for CIA. Themes for the vice president's speeches in the Soviet Union were reviewed by us, and the draft speeches were prepared by a working group of the Operations Coordinating Board (OCB) of the National Security Council. I submitted "CIA's comments" (some from Dulles himself, mostly my own) to General Cushman directly, and they were generally taken.

The primary intelligence target was the Soviet intercontinental ballistic missile (ICBM) program. Dulles in his briefing of Nixon had emphasized the importance of any clarification of the direction of development of the Soviet ICBM program and the nature of the Soviet missile system or systems. We had the hope, but not really the expectation, that Khrushchev might show Nixon an ICBM- or intermediate-range ballistic missile (IRBM)-launching site or factory. (With this in view, we had arranged that Kozlov see the Thor IRBM missile plant and had offered to show him—although he declined—an ICBM missile launching at Vandenberg Air Force Base or Cape Canaveral.) There was a long list of scientific and military facilities relating to the Soviet missile, nuclear, electronics, and aircraft programs that we wanted to see. Some were proposed, and a few even included on the itinerary, although not any missile production, test launching, or deployment facilities. I, and to some extent a few other members of the party, were briefed in detail by CIA intelligence analysts specializing in all these facilities, including some that the Soviet side might substitute.

The next most important intelligence target, after the missile program, was nuclear energy. Here, as the itinerary was being agreed upon, we selected two principal objects to visit, and both were included in the trip. One was the nuclear-powered icebreaker *Lenin,* then fitting out in the Admiralty shipyard at Leningrad before sea trials, and the other was a nuclear power station under construction at Beloyarsk near Sverdlovsk. To take advantage of those visits, as well as to continue talks with the head of the Soviet atomic energy program for peaceful purposes, Vasily Yemelyanov, about planned exchange visits of nuclear experts, Vice Admiral Hyman Rickover was made a member of the vice presidential party. Rickover had escorted Frol Kozlov on a visit to the Shippingport reactor near Philadelphia and to the nuclear-powered *Savannah* on his trip only weeks earlier. Rickover, as the father of the American nuclear submarine program, was especially qualified because the Soviet counterpart program was our primary interest, even though it could not of course be the object of direct observation.

In an initial contact with Admiral Rickover, the director himself, along with me and the chief of the division of our Office of Scientific Intelligence dealing with Soviet nuclear matters, met with and briefed him. I later followed through with Rickover before, as well as during, the trip.

Apart from the rather technical, albeit important, Soviet missile and nuclear propulsion programs, our main intelligence focus was on Khrushchev himself. As I noted at the time in a wrap-up memorandum on intelligence preparations for the trip, "the primary intelligence target is Khrushchev, for political intelligence on Soviet attitudes, aims, plans and even capabilities," including the ICBM program. We were also interested in his relationship to other Soviet political leaders, his own psychology, his demeanor, and his health.

Although we did not learn anything unexpected, the visit was one among a number of contacts that contributed to our overall assessments of Khrushchev and political relationships in the Soviet leadership. It was clear that Anastas Mikoyan, a member of the Central Committee since 1923 and of the Politburo since 1935 (four years earlier than Khrushchev), was on the closest basis to him, and several times interrupted and even corrected Khrushchev. The nominally second-ranking leader, Frol Kozlov, who was designated as Nixon's chief escort and host, was clearly not on such close terms. (And Yemelyanov, when asked at one point if he had taken up a certain matter with "the leadership," replied that he had not, "only with Kozlov.") As I have noted, Nixon was very attentive to biographical information on all the leaders whom he would meet, especially Khrushchev, including the records and analyses of meetings with Western leaders.

The specific occasion for Nixon's visit was to open the first official United States national exhibition ever held in the Soviet Union.[3] It was part of a U.S.-Soviet cultural exchange program signed in 1958, following negotiations launched under the "spirit of Geneva" after the 1955 four-power summit. This U.S. exhibition provided an unprecedented opportunity for visits by 2,700,000 Soviet citizens over a six-week period to see some transplanted Americana, and especially with the 75 young Russian-speaking American "guides" (selected from over 1,000 applicants, ages twenty to thirty-five, with tested fluency in Russian, and willing to work with no salary and a very modest per diem).

Among the guides was my wife, Vera, who was allowed by CIA to participate but was given special security briefings. I accompanied her to a meeting of all the guides in New York in June just before their departure, a month before the vice presidential trip. Many of them were from the second generation of the post-1917 Russian emigration. There, in a belated last-minute request, the senior United States Information Agency (USIA) representative asked me as a government official who had traveled in the Soviet Union to give a general background and security briefing to the assembled guides, none of whom had been to the Soviet Union. Perhaps imprudently, if my CIA affiliation had become known, and without authorization, I did so, and was later told it had been very useful. Later, when I arrived in Moscow with Nixon, I was of course the only member of his party who had the bonus of meeting his wife there.

Apart from coordinating intelligence aspects of the preparations for the delegation, I immersed myself in many details on localities, factories, and other things we might see. I was also briefed by the Office of Technical Services of the Directorate of Plans on concealment devices and other special equipment, almost none of which I needed. I did take a Retina camera and a Minox, and some ultrafast film then not yet commercially available. (The only use I found for the film, I must admit, was to take some color photographs in the darkened opera and ballet theaters.) I was also offered the use of CIA lightweight aluminum luggage, but when I saw a room full of identical suitcases I decided it would not enhance my cover. Incidentally, the head of technical services at the time was Cornelius Roosevelt, less well known than his cousins Archibald and Kermit Roosevelt, also serving in the clandestine services. (All were descendants of Theodore Roosevelt.) Cornelius was very proud

---

3. An extensive, informed review of the American National Exhibition in Moscow (and the Nixon visit) is contained in Walter L. Hixson, *Parting the Curtain: Propaganda, Culture and the Cold War, 1945–1961* (St. Martin's Press, 1997), pp. 151–213.

of his technical devices and eager to make them available, not unlike his fictional counterpart Q in the James Bond novels (though without proferring the lethal arsenal of the latter).

Right from the moment of arrival in Moscow (on a record nine-hour non-stop flight in the new Boeing 707) on July 23 there was a chill in the reception. This was soon translated into a diatribe by Khrushchev to Nixon in their first meeting, sharply objecting to a proclamation by the president just a few days before of a congressionally mandated annual "Captive Nations" week, in a declaration denouncing communist rule in the Soviet satellites of Eastern Europe. The timing was coincidental, but very unfortunate. Nixon had been forewarned of the Soviet reaction by Ambassador Llewellyn (Tommy) Thompson as soon as he arrived, but he could only seek to defend the measure by reiterating the implicit challenge to the Soviet Union. It was an inauspicious beginning. The verbal duel continued as the two leaders arrived together at the American Exhibition and proceeded to walk through it. Nixon at first sought to tone down the exchange but before long concluded that rather than appearing strong and steadfast as he intended, he was in danger of appearing to be weak in the face of Khrushchev's continuing diatribe. Accordingly, he too turned argumentative. Part of this continuing exchange took place in a model kitchen (being demonstrated by Vera!), so the later American press coverage dubbed it "the kitchen debate," by far the most remembered aspect of the whole trip, not least because Nixon used the exchange (and a chance photo of his jabbing a finger in front of Khrushchev's scowling visage) to claim that he had bested the Soviet leader. In fact, the "debate" was little more than a mutual exchange of epithets and one-sided claims of superiority of one or the other system. Nixon was, however, goaded into it and had to hold his own, as he did.[4]

Undoubtedly the main impact of the Nixon visit (and of the American Exhibition) was the opportunity to give millions of Soviet citizens a somewhat clearer picture of life in the United States. The unspoken but implicit underlying theme of the exhibition, also emphasized in Nixon's speech on Soviet television (that we had crafted in Washington), was not only that life in the United States was good, but also that life under capitalism was better than life under socialism. Less by design, because we took it for granted, but not less important was the evident sincerity of Nixon, and by extension of the U.S.

4. For the best general account of Nixon's visit, see Stephen E. Ambrose, *Nixon: The Education of a Politician, 1913–1962* (Simon & Schuster, 1987), pp. 515–34. When, in the course of this "debate," Khrushchev referred to the Captive Nations proclamation as "horse shit," which smelled more than anything, Nixon recalled from his CIA briefing book that Khrushchev as a youngster had cleaned pig pens and remarked that he, too, as a youth had worked on a farm, and that there was one thing that stank more than horse shit, and that was pig shit. (Nixon, *RN*, p. 207). So much for the value of thorough intelligence briefings!

leadership, on what loomed for most Russians as the most important matter: peace. While to Americans it was corny, and to Russians an echo of their own government's propaganda, still Nixon's repeated call (in passable Russian) for *mir i druzhba* ("peace and friendship") did strike a welcome and responsive chord, especially in the provincial cities of Sverdlovsk and Novosibirsk, ordinarily closed to foreign travelers. This personal identification by an American leader did much to counter Soviet propaganda claims of U.S. opposition to peace and relaxation of tensions.

In a memorandum I submitted to Nixon after the trip, at his request, I was not just playing up to his vanity when I wrote (referring to him in the third person):

> The visit of the Vice President and the American Exhibition stand as the most significant breaches to date in the curtain of denial of knowledge about the outside world. The two major addresses of the Vice President, printed and broadcast (still with limitations on dissemination, but not on content) are probably the most important messages to have reached large portions of this generation of the Russian people.

That may seem an overstatement, but bear in mind that there had been no prior appearances of American leaders—and would not be again until Nixon himself next visited some thirteen years later, as president. I continued by noting that a pro-American sentiment did not necessarily imply an anti-Soviet one, a point I was not sure he had in mind.

> The reactions of the Russians to the Vice President (based on observations made by frequently filtering through the crowds to note their attitudes and overhear their comments to one another) were heartening in their implications for better understanding of the United States. At the same time, they were not cast in an anti-Soviet manner. The same Russians could be observed, for example, at the opening of the American Exhibition, registering approval both of the remarks of the Vice President and of those of Khrushchev. A readiness to doubt many aspects of the official propaganda against the United States, and to accept the Vice President's proffered friendship as genuine, was evidently often present in people who fully accept the Soviet system and regime. Dissatisfactions of various kinds, disbelief in their own regime's propaganda, and disposition to think well of America and its intentions, can and do coexist with unquestioning acceptance of the regime. There are, of course, exceptions who do not accept the regime, just as there are exceptions who accept it so uncritically that they do not believe anything good about America. But the more complex general reaction seems one which offers us considerable opportunities for further influencing

Russian popular attitudes in competitive coexistence, though ordinarily constrained to influence short of stimulation of openly anti-regime positions.

In referring to "competitive coexistence" (a term adopted nearly two decades later by Zbigniew Brzezinski), I was in key with what years later I learned Nixon himself had stated in a memorandum to General Cushman just before the trip when we were drafting his speeches, telling him to let everyone involved know that we were never to refer to "the principle of peaceful coexistence." Paradoxically, the U.S. government never endorsed "peaceful coexistence" until Nixon himself did so as president in 1972.

In my report on the mission to Allen Dulles, I summarized my "impression that the Vice President's visit has, despite partially successful Soviet efforts to nullify its impact on the people, signally demonstrated and uniquely personified American goodwill and genuine desire for peace and friendship. The American Exhibition has complemented this by offering an unprecedented glimpse into many aspects of American life." I also noted, as I had to Nixon, that the Russian popular curiosity and genuine sympathy for, and eagerness to learn about, America did not necessarily imply lack of rapport with and support for the Soviet regime, which they believed also really wanted peace and goodwill.

I noted that this judgment was my own, but also based on the impressions of a number of the American Exhibition guides with whom I had talked. They were daily in contact with thousands of Russians. As I had noted, there were of course also dissidents, and some of the guides met some of them. CIA obtained its first underground (*samizdat;* self-published) student literature from contacts made at the exhibition.

The Soviet authorities had mounted a major campaign to offset the influence of the American exhibition. They sought to undercut it by propaganda alleging that it was a "show" display remote from the realities of American life. Hecklers were sent to keep raising issues such as lynchings in the United States. But these efforts were generally ineffective. In addition to mounting a counterexhibition of Soviet achievements at the nearby permanent All-Union Exhibition of the National Economy of the USSR, the authorities also arranged a display of wreckage from a U.S. reconnaissance aircraft shot down some months earlier (an RC-130 shot down over Armenia in September 1958) as a graphic reminder of hostile U.S. intelligence activities. Even this had little effect, and some young Russians jocularly referred to this in conversation with our guides as "the other American exhibition." Finally, many of the tickets for the American Exhibition were distributed to presumably the most loyal citizens through Communist Party and Komsomol (youth) organizations—but even this had the perverse effect of exposing many of the more influential

Soviet citizens to the exhibition, where most of them were favorably impressed.

I also told Nixon in my memorandum that I thought his public exchanges with Khrushchev had had a salutary effect.

> Khrushchev was clearly unused to being debated with by an independent authority, particularly in public. This was probably a unique experience for him, and the Soviet newspapers' distortions of verbal exchanges with the Vice President, edited to show Khrushchev at an easy advantage and the Vice President as at a false disadvantage, bear witness to the sensitivity of Khrushchev personally and to the Soviet leadership as a whole in such matters. Khrushchev cannot have been indifferent to the effect on the Russian people of having so authoritative a spokesman for the United States deliberately and unprovocatively expose the falsity of the Party's line on matters ranging from political life in America to the Vice President's own activities in Russia.

And I added my own views on the possible impact on Khrushchev's thinking:

> In seeing a gradual massive shift in the world balance of power favoring the relative position of the USSR and facilitating the ultimate success of communism, Khrushchev, in addition to seeing certain real facts of increasing relative Soviet military strength and economic growth, fuses and confuses with these developments what he believes to be evidence and confirmation of his warped ideological predispositions and preconceptions. It therefore seems necessary not only to prevent the creation of a serious actual imbalance in power in the Soviet favor, but also to deflate the swollen confidence of the Soviet leaders that they are riding with the sweep of history and of destiny. The meeting with the Vice President was an occasion which, to a unique degree, may have created cracks in Khrushchev's confidence in his own judgment of the political state of the United States—although it probably did not affect his general beliefs about the direction of history. It may have whetted his appetite to reassure himself on his visit to America—but this very process could contribute to his coming here with more open eyes than otherwise.

Apart from propaganda jousting, the one substantive discussion between Khrushchev and Nixon of intelligence interest was a long conversation at Khrushchev's dacha on July 26, the fourth day of the visit, especially over a "luncheon" that began at 3:30 P.M. and lasted until 9:00 P.M. After about a half hour of small talk, Khrushchev himself launched into a discourse on Soviet missiles. He did disclose some things of interest, including an admission that in a Soviet ICBM test just a month earlier the missile had malfunctioned and headed toward Alaska, although fortunately it fell short. Nixon noted that Kozlov had been invited to observe a missile launching, although he had not availed himself of the offer. Khrushchev said the Soviet Union didn't think the time was ripe yet for such things. Nixon also referred to Khrushchev's statement in June to Averell Harriman (as reported) that the Soviet Union had given missiles to China during the Taiwan Straits crisis the year before. Khrushchev said that Harriman had evidently misunderstood him, and that he had said that the Soviet Union *would* supply China with missiles capable of striking Taiwan *if* it were attacked. There was discussion of foreign missile and bomber bases, brought up by Khrushchev. There was also some discussion of the cost of missile systems, after Nixon had said an ICBM cost as much as 153,000 television sets (implicitly arguing for civilian consumer goods as against military missiles). Khrushchev said Soviet missiles were less expensive. He also made statements (which he would make publicly some six months later) disparaging the value of bombers and the surface naval fleet. While some of the things Khrushchev said were of interest, the intelligence yield was—not surprisingly—negligible. Nixon, I must say, did try to meet our intelligence interests.

The most important part of this long exchange began with a general observation by Nixon that he would make no public statements about the balance of power between the United States and the Soviet Union because both nations were powerful and both must ensure peace and not war. Khrushchev expressed full agreement with that evaluation. He denied that Soviet generals, unlike some American generals (whom he cited), ever declared the ability to destroy the other side. He also disclosed that he had in fact drafted a statement on the annihilatory nature of any new general war that had appeared under the signature of Chief Air Marshal Konstantin Vershinin (in *Pravda*, September 8, 1957). That fact, previously not known, was of interest to me and to our analysts. But more important by far was the implied acceptance of mutual deterrence despite a clear disparity in intercontinental forces. To be sure, in view of the fact that the disparity was in the U.S. favor—and, despite our fears of an impending missile gap, would remain in the U.S. favor for at least a decade—this was no concession by Khrushchev. Indeed, on the next such occasion, when President Eisenhower made a similar statement at Camp David in September, Khrushchev again pounced on it to claim parity. But unfortunately the fact that the imbalance of power favored the United States made it more difficult for many here to see that the Soviet leadership was aware that superiority by *any* side would be an illusory advantage in war— something that was not adequately recognized for years as we went through one alleged dangerous "gap" after another.

After the marathon Khrushchev-Nixon day in the country, the delegation made a five-day excursion to Leningrad, Sverdlovsk (now again Yekaterinburg), and Novosibirsk and some other nearby places. In Sverdlovsk in the Urals and in Novosibirsk in western Siberia, major cities and regional centers but off-limits to embassy staffs and other foreigners, the popular response was great. In Novosibirsk, for example, a huge crowd unable to enter waited outside the Opera for three and a half hours just to catch a glimpse of Nixon as he left. People lined the routes, in the countryside as well as the cities, as we visited other towns and localities in the environs.

As earlier noted, there was considerable negotiation in advance of the trip in settling on the itinerary. The Soviet side had changed many installations scheduled for visit from our first preferences, and then changed again many from those they had agreed to or even proposed, some almost at the last moment. In most cases, we eventually saw factories of little intelligence inter-est. Nonetheless, several of the visits were quite useful. For example, at Pervouralsk in the Urals we saw a major metal rolling mill that produced both small stainless steel tubing useful to their missile and nuclear programs and large pipe that we were interested in to gauge their capacity for gas and petro-leum pipeline construction. On that visit, incidentally, I told two cooperative accompanying American journalists who were aware of my affiliation the kind of questions they could appropriately ask that I could not, and we were able to elicit some useful information.

At the Beloyarsk nuclear power station near Sverdlovsk we confirmed our own estimate of a two-year delay in construction and learned also that it would have only two reactors by 1961, rather than the four originally planned for 1959. Nixon and the main party stayed only about forty-five minutes, but Rickover and I (serving as his interpreter) remained for several hours and learned more about the station and the Soviet nuclear reactor pro-gram. We confirmed that the entire Soviet nuclear power program was being stretched out.

Again at the visit to the nuclear icebreaker *Lenin* in Leningrad, the full party stayed only about forty-five minutes, mostly taken up with a twenty-minute propaganda movie about the construction of the ship and with fruit and champagne. In accordance with a previous request through Nixon to Kozlov, however, when the rest of the party left, Rickover and I remained for another three hours. That proved to be quite an experience.

With us on the *Lenin* were Captain Pavel A. Ponomarev, who was to be the skipper of the icebreaker, B. Ye. Klopotov, the director of the Admiralty ship-yard, and Chief Engineer V. I. Chervyakov, responsible for the ship's construc-tion. There also were various lesser staff and some who seemed to be superfluous, who Rickover decided must be secret police "goons"—so he began the discussion by asking who they were and demanding that they be sent away. He then demanded to see everything, particularly in and around the reactor chambers, and began to ask many detailed questions. More often than not, he would react to Soviet replies to his pointed questions by saying that what he had just been told was not correct, then repeating his question. In particular, he bored in on Klopotov, the director of the shipyard, as the man in charge. He told him that the next day he would be seeing Khrushchev (which incidentally was not true), and did he want Rickover to tell Khrushchev that Klopotov would not let him tour the *Lenin* after having permission from Kozlov (who had been there as Nixon's escort)? He told Klopotov that he had shown Kozlov everything on the *Savannah* and at Shippingport (and indeed he had shocked many American nuclear energy officials with what he had shown the Soviet delegation), and he demanded the same now. Klopotov, in particular, and the others, were sweating, in a terrible bind. They had instructions to give VIP treatment to this first visit by foreign dignitaries, but they also no doubt had instructions as well as a life-long tradition not to reveal "secrets" to foreigners. And here was an American admiral demanding more than even a Soviet admiral would. After a long, difficult standoff, someone came in and spoke to Klopotov, evidently conveying instructions from some higher authority to let Rickover see what he wanted to, but probably also reiterating not to tell him anything secret. (In the middle of his very tough pressure on the Soviet officials, Rickover jabbed me in the ribs with his elbow and happily remarked in an aside to me, "Garthoff, have you ever seen anyone handle the Russians like this?" I didn't need to confirm that indeed I had not.) The upshot was that after three hours of crawling around the reactor chambers, pipes, and turbines, Rickover had seen everything he wanted to and learned more than they wanted him to, if not everything that he wanted to know.

Without going into detail, I can say that Rickover did in fact learn some important new information on the reactor system for the *Lenin* and about the Soviet reactor program relevant to our principal interest, Soviet nuclear submarines. For example, we had known (mainly from Soviet presentations at international conferences on peaceful uses of nuclear energy that had begun in 1955) that the *Lenin* had three pressurized water-cooled and water-moderated reactors, to operate with uranium dioxide fuel, with zirconium-clad fuel elements. Rickover observed that the reactors in the *Lenin* were too large for submarines, but that the same type of reactors could be adapted for use in submarines. He also learned that the three reactors were in the same compartment, so that the others could not continue to operate while one was isolated for repairs, and any radioactive contamination could not be contained in one reactor chamber. In general, the layout was poor for maintenance. Moreover, the high pressure in the primary loop would, in his view, increase corrosion of the stainless steel piping and in due course lead to leaks. In his report on his findings, Rickover correctly foresaw difficulties that the Soviets would encounter in the operation of their nuclear submarine program.

Apart from interpreting for Rickover, there was little that I could do on this occasion, except for one stroke of luck. I was able to see from their markings that the turbogenerators on the *Lenin* had been made at the Kharkov Turbine Factory, something we had not known that would later be found useful (especially when the chief engineer of that plant visited the United States soon after in an exchange of delegations of experts on electric power). This visit to the *Lenin* was, however, to have an unanticipated sequel, as I will describe later.

The visits to Sverdlovsk, Pervouralsk, Novosibirsk, and the new "academic city" being built near Novosibirsk were of interest mainly because they were in normally closed areas. As earlier noted, the popular reaction was enthusiastic.

When the vice-presidential party returned to Moscow on July 31, waiting for me at the embassy were reports prepared in the Directorate of Intelligence on Soviet and U.S. press treatment to date of the vice president's trip. I had arranged before we left Washington to have these press summaries and analyses prepared and sent to me to give Nixon. I had been sure that he would be interested in particular in U.S. commentary on his visit. And he certainly was. The American press coverage was both extensive and quite favorable. Nixon greatly appreciated my having arranged to have such a report for him. The report was also a boost in counterbalancing the fact that he had just learned that his visit would be upstaged by imminent announcement of the planned exchange of visits by Khrushchev and Eisenhower.

The Nixon visit ended with a major television address to the Russian people, drafted by our committee in Washington, but which Nixon and his own staff, with Ambassador "Tommy" Thompson, reworked before delivery. It was a good speech, and well received.

The Nixon party then departed for Warsaw, to a remarkable massive public display of friendship for the United States in greeting him. We were in Warsaw two days before returning to Washington. The only event of interest, apart from the outpouring of public goodwill, was a discussion between Nixon and Polish First Secretary Wladyslaw Gomulka, and briefer meetings with President Aleksandr Zawadski, Prime Minister Jozef Cyrankiewicz, and Foreign Minister Adam Rapacki.

Gomulka, like Khrushchev, raised the issue of "Captive Nations Week." When Nixon advocated an exchange of ideas, Gomulka attacked Radio Free Europe as not representing an exchange of ideas, but "indirect aggression." Gomulka made clear that such matters as Polish-American trade were bilateral, and not Moscow's business. Gomulka's main interest was in urging some kind of endorsement of Poland's existing borders, pending a peace treaty with

Germany. In this respect, but also more generally, Gomulka evinced great concern over Germany (meaning West Germany).[5]

In Warsaw, I attended receptions for the delegations and some other events, but also just revisited the city (which I had seen briefly in 1957 on my way home from Moscow). I did have an interesting, if not particularly intelligence-productive, conversation with Lieutenant General Jurij Bordzilowski, chief of the Polish general staff and deputy minister of defense and last of the senior Russian-Polish (ex-Soviet Army) generals in the Polish high command after the removal of Marshal Konstantin Rokossowski and others in late 1956. I was surprised that in our conversation he disparaged his supervisor, the minister of defense and friend of Gomulka's, General Marian Spychalski, as "a political man" and "an architect by training," in contrast to himself as "an old soldier." It is now known that Gomulka had agreed with the Soviet leaders in 1956 to keep Bordzilowski as a reassurance that Poland was not embarking on an anti-Soviet course. Rokossowski was too prominent a symbol of Soviet domination, but Bordzilowski was acceptable. He remained until his retirement in 1965.

Before we had left Moscow, Nixon asked me whether I thought he should seek a meeting with Cardinal Stefan Wyczynski, the head of the Polish Catholic Church. I recommended on balance against it, on grounds different from what I believe he was weighing: the reaction in the Polish-American community. In the event, no meeting occurred because the cardinal had absented himself from Warsaw—he may have reached the same conclusion I had, that it would gratuitously accent a tie between the United States and the Polish Catholic Church.

Incidentally, our ambassador in Warsaw, Jake Beam, later observed that the great outpouring of pro-American sympathy by the hundreds of thousands of Poles who welcomed Nixon set back for some time American efforts to build American-Polish contacts and cultural relations. The Polish leaders were alarmed by the spontaneous public manifestation and were afraid of permitting more extensive ties with the United States.

After we returned to Washington, I submitted a report to the director with a résumé of intelligence acquired on the vice president's trip. In addition to what was observed or what we were told at the industrial plants, the icebreaker *Lenin*, the Beloyarsk nuclear power station, and other facilities visited, I noted our extensive photography at these and other locations. Some of these were of more than routine intelligence interest, although none directly involved our highest-priority ICBM objective. For example, I spotted and photographed a large munitions storage center near Novosibirsk not previously identified.

5. Nixon, *RN*, p. 213, referred only to the public welcome in Warsaw and did not describe these conversations with Gomulka and other Polish leaders.

Near Sverdlovsk I had seen and surreptitiously photographed from the airplane two of the new SA-2 anti-aircraft missile sites and identified one other near Moscow in addition to six of the older SA-1 sites around Moscow. One of those sites near Sverdlovsk, at Kosulino, was the very site from which an SA-2 shot down Francis Gary Powers's U-2 less than ten months later, on May Day 1960![6]

Among the incidental but valued acquisitions were local samples of soil and water and pine cones I had obtained in the Novosibirsk, Beloyarsk, Sverdlovsk, and Pervouralsk areas. These were useful for radioactivity analysis, contributing to our understanding of the pattern of Soviet nuclear activities in those key and inaccessible regions.

I quickly became involved in a series of intelligence debriefings, including one to a number of CIA and other intelligence officers (including General Pearre Cabell, the deputy director of central intelligence) in which I liberally cited Khrushchev's statements to Nixon on missiles—only to learn afterward that the vice president had just placed a complete lid on any circulation of his conversations with Khrushchev. Fortunately, there were no leaks to the press (or to the White House) on this inadvertent use of closely held information. There was excellent cooperation in debriefing information of intelligence interest from various members of the delegation.

In addition to my report to Allen Dulles, and my debriefings (some of which were disseminated as intelligence reports), at Nixon's request I also sent him a report, to which I have earlier referred. Nixon wrote to tell me that he "particularly valued having the benefit of your comments because of your background and experience in this field" and indicated he wanted to talk with me further. We did meet once, but we were both soon caught up in other things.

One of the things I was soon engaged in was planning for Khrushchev's visit to the United States, and later still more on preparations for President Eisenhower's planned trip to the Soviet Union in June 1960. We had returned to Washington from Warsaw on August 5. Two weeks later, the director asked

6. This was confirmed years later when one of Gary Powers's Soviet military interrogators disclosed that it had indeed been the air-defense complex at Kosulino, thirty-two kilometers southeast of Sverdlovsk, which I had observed and photographed as we flew into Sverdlovsk, that shot down Powers's U-2. See Lieutenant General of Justice N.F. Chistyakov, *Po zakonu i sovesti* (By law and conscience) (Moscow: Voyenizdat [Military Publishing House], 1979), p.144.

It had been reported at the time, incorrectly, that Nixon himself had seen a new type of air defense complex near Sverdlovsk. *Aviation Week,* May 16, 1960, cited by David Wise and Thomas B. Ross, *The U-2 Affair* (Random House, 1962), p. 27; and Michael Beschloss, *Mayday: Eisenhower, Khrushchev and the U-2 Affair* (Harper & Row, 1986), pp.182–83. This was a garbled leak of the sighting I had made while a member of the vice president's delegation.

me for suggestions for Khrushchev's forthcoming mid-September visit. I advised him, in a memorandum two days later, that the OCB "Special Committee on Soviet and Related Problems" had begun considering the matter and that the itinerary was pretty well set. I noted some of the specific plans for the visit. I did not make any suggestions for intelligence acquisition, which would of course only be incidental except in terms of directed conversations (and such rather specialized matters as using the opportunity to obtain a sample of Khrushchev's urine for medical analysis!).[7] Rather, I emphasized the need to seek to influence Khrushchev:

> In general, the program of Khrushchev's visit should seek to impress upon him the viability and underlying strength of the American nation, people, and economy, rather than to be focused only on specifics of industrial or military power. The freedom of political and personal expression and choice, and the basic and complete popular support of our essential political and economic system, are one major aspect of this strength. Another is the flexibility in our economic system and the many ways large and small that it differs from the nineteenth-century capitalism which, through Marx and Lenin, colors so much the false image held by Khrushchev of the Western world and especially of the United States. These crucial points will be latent in anything and everything that Khrushchev sees; the major challenge is to have them subtly pointed out to him by his escorts.

I also emphasized the desirability of letting Khrushchev reach his own conclusions, and even find his own evidence.

> Khrushchev will be suspicious of the typicality of what he is shown. He may seek to make sudden changes in his program in order to see places not scheduled and to talk with typical Americans. Unless there are special circumstances involved in any given case, I believe that this will ordinarily be desirable, and that he will be especially impressed by the reality of such observations of things which he knows have not been selected and pre-planned.

Finally, I expressed the hope the reception he received would contribute to recognition of the need to make détente a two-way street, to adopt the idiom of the 1980s.

> If Khrushchev were to be confronted by a generally reserved attitude on the part of many Americans he meets, a friendly reception but tempered

---

7. Disclosure of this acquisition of a urine sample was first made in Beschloss, *Mayday,* pp. 206–07.

to less than enthusiasm for vague generalities about "peace and friend-ship," he might come to realize that in order to stabilize a period of competitive coexistence, more would be expected of the Soviet Union by the American people than mere declarations of Soviet interest in peaceful coexistence. Hopefully, if Khrushchev initiates conversation with randomly selected Americans on the streets, at factories, etc., he will meet something of this attitude. Hostile demonstrations would, of course, be a quite different matter and highly undesirable.

I did not accompany the Khrushchev party around the country, but I did follow with great interest the course of the visit. Regrettably, Khrushchev did face considerable heckling and a hostile reception in many quarters on his visit.

In late March 1960 I sent the director a memorandum he had requested on intelligence aspects of President Eisenhower's planned nine-day visit to the Soviet Union in mid-June. I recommended he brief the president as he had Nixon, highlighting major issues likely to be raised by Khrushchev and a few key questions of intelligence interest to be borne in mind. I noted that advance intelligence briefings for some members of the official party (as well as subsequent debriefings) were very useful and should be arranged. I recommended against preparing bulky background briefing materials to be taken on the trip, as those prepared for the Nixon trip had not been used. On the other hand, brief notes on places and especially individuals the president would meet, especially away from Moscow, would probably be useful for spot briefings during the trip. I noted that the State Department, under Ambassador Charles (Chip) Bohlen's guidance, and with opportunity for our contribution, was preparing a large number of background issue papers.

I recommended two specific intelligence interests: one would be to suggest that the president request visiting "the ICBM plant," despite the fact that Nixon's written request to do so had not even been answered. I noted that even though the request might not be granted, the visit of the president might be a unique chance to induce the Soviets to give access. They had agreed to permit the president's plane to depart the Soviet Union by way of the Far East, which they had refused for the vice president. Also I recommended that even if the president decided not to request a visit to the ICBM facility, someone knowledgeable on Soviet missile production should be available in case Khrushchev decided for his own reasons to show the president a missile plant. The second intelligence opportunity I raised was the possibility of fitting out clandestinely the President's airplane (and the requested backup plane) with cameras and other intelligence sensors. Although I did not know it at the time, this recommendation was accepted, and *Air Force One* was so equipped.[8]

8. Ibid., pp. 228–29 and 452.

I also urged the inclusion of intelligence officers in the party. Aware that there was some sensitivity to the idea, I noted that "the pattern of including intelligence observers in high-level exchange visits is now well established in practice, and there is no reason to believe the President would be placed in an awkward position by including one or more intelligence officers in his party. The Soviets do so, and they expect us to do so as a matter of course." I then went on to emphasize why experienced intelligence officers with "special clearances and intimate knowledge of the state of our intelligence needs," who were capable of taking advantage of unforeseen opportunities, were needed beyond what could be conveyed by briefing others. The director obviously did not need a reminder on the value and need for intelligence officers, but I wanted him to make the case forcefully if routine objections were posed.

I hoped, of course, to be included in the president's party as I had been with the vice president, although I did not suggest myself. There was some pulling and hauling within the Agency. OCI—the Office of Current Intelligence— wanted to send its candidate, Bill Colligan, a well-qualified Russian-speaking analyst; Sherman Kent of ONE wanted me to go. The upshot was that we both were slated to be included in the party.

In April the advance party flew to Moscow. It was there when the U-2 was shot down on May 1, and the president's trip with it. The next American-Soviet summit meeting in the USSR did not occur until President Nixon visited Moscow twelve years later, in May 1972.

Before it became known that President Eisenhower would not be going to the Soviet Union, a slipup in my cover led to a bizarre encounter with a self-anointed emissary to improve American-Soviet relations. An American woman born in the Soviet Union, possessed of the idea that she could accomplish her mission if she accompanied the president on his trip, had suddenly presented herself at the administration building at 2430 E Street, NW, and asked to see me! She had seen my name in some journal as having accompanied Nixon to the USSR, and assuming (incorrectly) both that I was of Russian descent and close to Nixon and Eisenhower, had decided I was the one who could arrange for her to accompany President Eisenhower. She had gotten my CIA telephone number from Nixon's office (but did not call), and with it had then gotten my CIA address from the State Department, and was sitting in the reception office at 2430 E. As I later wrote in a memo to the director of security: "My assessment of Mrs. W_____ is that she is sincere, well intentioned, loyal, politically naive, mildly hysterical, and slightly unbalanced." Her objective was "to improve Russian-American relations by sharing the bounty of her Russian soul and her American heart." I persuaded her to give up the idea of trying to go along with the president—and not to mention our talk to anyone. There was no "fallout" from this strange encounter.

Meanwhile, soon after the Nixon trip and even before Khrushchev's visit to the United States, Sherman Kent again asked me if I could interpret, this time for John McCone, who was to lead a high-powered Atomic Energy Commission (AEC) delegation visiting an array of Soviet nuclear facilities. I hesitated, but only for a few moments, before assuring him that I could, although my knowledge of nuclear physics in *any* language was rather limited. In fact, it proved challenging but not as difficult as I feared. In contrast to the Nixon trip, however, I did have to work hard, both interpreting and observing matters of intelligence interest.[9]

Also in contrast to the Nixon trip, Soviet security escorts paid me a good deal of attention and probed others as well with respect to my role. As recounted in the next chapter, we later learned that Soviet counterintelligence knew, through a clandestine agent, of my CIA affiliation. But we did not know that at the time. Nonetheless, the trip went very well.

The head of the Chief Administration for the Utilization of Atomic Energy of the USSR, or *Glavatom*, Vasily Yemelyanov, accompanied Khrushchev on his visit to the United States. On September 15, 1959, he met with John McCone, chairman of the AEC, to discuss the latter's forthcoming visit. I attended the meeting as rapporteur. Yemelyanov offered to show McCone "everything appropriate that he would like to see" at any convenient time. They agreed that dual-purpose reactors and other facilities for the production of enriched uranium and plutonium used in military programs would not be available for visits, or for discussion or possible collaboration. Almost everything else, however, he indicated would be. McCone expressed interest in visiting research laboratories, experimental, prototype, and power reactors, and propulsion reactors such as on the *Lenin*. Yemelyanov was not only receptive, but took the initiative in suggesting also a visit to a facility where they were working on controlled thermonuclear fusion and to a uranium mine. McCone quickly expressed interest in both. Yemelyanov also suggested an exchange of data on the propulsion systems for the *Lenin* and the *Savannah*, and possible collaboration in the field of controlled thermonuclear reactions. Yemelyanov noted that Rickover had been the only foreign specialist who had been permitted to visit the *Lenin*. (He also commented in an aside that Rickover had a "difficult temperament," which McCone acknowledged was the view of some of his American colleagues as well.) Yemelyanov also expressed interest beyond their exchanges of visits and data in some joint or collaborative project, such as construction of a controlled thermonuclear reactor, although McCone did not commit himself on that idea.

9. The discussion that follows appears in a somewhat expanded version in Garthoff, "Intelligence Aspects of Cold War Scientific Exchanges: U.S.-USSR Atomic Energy Exchange Visits in 1959," *Intelligence and National Security,* vol. 15, no. 1 (Spring 2000), pp. 1–13.

In sum, as evidenced in this early meeting and later in the actual program of the reciprocal visits, the Soviet side was prepared for rather far-reaching exchanges and contacts.

The American delegation under McCone arrived in Moscow on October 9, for about ten days. It was a very full program, very rich in what we learned, and it represented a step forward in a serious exchange program by both countries, moreover in a sensitive field related to security.

At the outset, the delegation was flown from Moscow to Tallin, to board the nuclear icebreaker *Lenin*, undergoing sea trials in the Baltic Sea. About a month before, it had suddenly been launched into trials, earlier than originally planned. According to Yemelyanov, in a private comment later, they moved the date forward in order to beat the United States to the punch by having the *Lenin* at sea before its American competitor, the *Savannah*. That may well have been part of the reason, although we had other information at CIA that the launch of the *Lenin* had been rushed, and also the launch of *Lunik*, a lunar probe, to coincide with Khrushchev's visit to the United States and boost the image of Soviet technological prowess for that occasion. I don't recall that either event had much impact in the United States, but that was the Soviet expectation.

The visit to the *Lenin* for a three- to four-hour cruise under nuclear power offered nothing new to observe. We were served an elaborate dinner on board, but we did learn a few new things from briefings and especially conversations. We were interested to learn that there had been no land-based prototype reactor, and that a different reactor was being developed for submarines.

Most absorbing for me was a very unpleasant reunion with my "old friend" Klopotov, director of the Admiralty shipyard, and Rickover's "partner" in July when we had visited the ship in the yard. Klopotov remembered me and the occasion of our earlier encounter only too well, and as he drank more and more at the banquet, he gave more and more vent to his anger. For some reason, perhaps because I had been the one actually to address him in Russian in Leningrad, he attributed to me responsibility for the tough time he had had with Rickover. He finally had to be physically restrained. After we returned to Washington, I made it a point to see Rickover and tell the admiral of the impression he had left and what I had had to take as a stand-in. Rickover was simply delighted to have had that impact.

The most important institute we visited was the Institute of Atomic Energy in Moscow, headed by the renowned academician Igor V. Kurchatov (who died not long after our visit). At all of the half-dozen research institutes and laboratories we visited in Moscow and Leningrad, the scientists and engineers were reasonably forthcoming on their work, but loath to discuss broader questions where they were less sure of the guidelines for permissible disclosure.

While several other members of the delegation went to visit two nuclear power reactor complexes, McCone and a few others of us were taken to visit a uranium mine and uranium ore processing plant in Ukraine. After flying to Dnepropetrovsk we were driven the two hundred kilometers to a uranium mine near Pervomaisk, and thence to a uranium processing plant at Zhelty Vody. Although that sounds straightforward enough, there were some amusing examples of hyper-security consciousness in the trip (which Yemelyanov later indicated privately had been the subject of considerable opposition and controversy before permission was granted). First of all, when we boarded the plane in Moscow for Dnepropetrovsk, several of our escorts engaged me in conversation so that I was unable to board the aircraft until all the others had, leaving me an aisle seat. I had, however, taken the precaution of asking one of the other Americans to take a window seat away from the wing on the right side, and as I came on board he gave me that seat and sat on the aisle. As we circled to land at Dnepropetrovsk, again several Soviet escorts leaned over from the aisle and tried to engage me in conversation, impeding but not preventing me from visual observation of the huge Yuzhmash (Southern Machine-Building) Plant, which we knew to be a major Soviet missile production facility, then building the R-12 (SS-4) medium-range ballistic missile (MRBM) and the first serial intercontinental ballistic missile (ICBM), the SS-7. Later, this was the plant that produced the more advanced large ICBMs, the SS-9 and finally the SS-18.

The R-12 MRBM was a missile with a range of 1,020 nautical miles and had just become operational with deployments beginning in the western USSR. It was the same missile that the Soviets deployed in Cuba in the fall of 1962, precipitating the Cuban missile crisis. The last R-12's were destroyed in 1990 under the terms of the Intermediate-range Nuclear Forces (INF) Treaty. If we had not already known in 1959 that the Dnepropetrovsk factory was a prime intelligence target, certainly the frantic Soviet efforts to impede my observation (and successfully preclude surreptitious photography) would have told us that it was. We had, in any case, photographed it by U-2, and my main interest was in using the rare air landing in this closed city to see whether there happened at that time to be any missiles in the rail loading area adjoining the plant.

After we left Dnepropetrovsk by car, we were taken on a very long and circuitous route to the uranium mine and processing plant, intended to prevent tracing our route and destination. That effort was generally successful, but to no avail. As we arrived in the village near the uranium mill, several people, including some boys about twelve years old, gathered around to look at the strangers in their shiny black Volga cars. I went up to the boys and asked where we were. "Zhëlty Vody" was the prompt, and correct, reply.

We had been given general permission to take pictures except in certain laboratories, which were always identified. I had an Agency camera loaded with fast black-and-white film and my own personal camera with color film for slides, both of which I was using liberally. Someone in our group had just been snapping picturesque Ukrainian cottages with thatched roofs, which triggered a suggestion by one of the escorts to McCone that we should not photograph matters of "no interest" (meaning of no positive interest from the standpoint of Soviet standards of always accenting new and world-standard achievements). McCone turned to me, as the most avid photographer, mentioned the informal démarche, and suggested that I not take any pictures for a while. I remonstrated that we had not been forbidden to take photographs there, that the mine and mill were of great interest, and that I felt I must take the photographs. And I did. McCone was not accustomed to anything but full compliance with his instructions; indeed, his staff was the most cowed that I have ever seen. But I believe he saw the merit in my position. He did not say another word on the subject, and we continued to have very good relations, on the trip and subsequently.

My many photographs of the mine "tailings," taken of course from ground level, complemented very well overhead photography and permitted better definition of the height of the tailings, and I was later told this was valuable in helping our analysts to evaluate the cumulative production of the mine. At both the mine and the uranium concentration and processing plant we were given detailed information about ore concentration, the separation process, and purity of the product (uranium oxide, U^2O^8). What we were not given was any information about the quantity of production, current or cumulative or as a percentage of overall Soviet production. Yemelyanov promised to try to get additional information for us by the time of his return visit to the United States (and he did bring some).

We descended into the mine, and I suppose this gives me the highly unusual qualification for a Westerner of being able to say that I once worked in a Soviet uranium mine (although my work was interpreting, not digging).

I was kept pretty busy interpreting, but I also used opportunities to observe what my AEC colleagues could not—for example, internal administrative notices in offices and even hallways, the nature of telephones in director's offices, and the like. In other cases, as with the turbogenerators on the *Lenin*, I was able to see and note markings, origination and serial numbers on particular types of equipment. From such details our analysts could often learn things about such matters as organizational subordination of facilities that were of intelligence interest but would not fall in the scope of normal interest of the delegation. Some information I obtained this way proved quite useful.

During the preceding year there had been a major breakthrough in our intelligence on the Soviet nuclear weapons program derived directly from intelligence analysis of a completely overt source of this kind. An article published in a Soviet popular journal in July 1958 featured an interview with the director of the electrical power complex for the Ural region. Although what the director said had no doubt been carefully reviewed and disclosed nothing of interest, the journal included a photograph of him at his desk behind which hung a large wall chart that resembled an intricate mechanistic design or doodle. It was the electrical power grid for the entire Ural region. That too had been cropped and partially obscured, but by overlaying a blown-up picture of this grid over a detailed map of the region, and with laborious reconstruction of data from many sources (including balloon photography and U-2 photos), CIA intelligence analysts were able to correlate power usage with urban and industrial centers—and with the power-hungry unacknowledged secret locations of the main centers of the Soviet nuclear weapons complex in the area around the Urals from Chelyabinsk to Sverdlovsk. It was a perfect fit, confirming some centers on which we already had intelligence from other sources and pinpointing others to which attention was then directed. It was a real intelligence coup.

One of the key facilities in this area, incidentally—the plutonium production plant at Kyshtym that had provided the fissionable material for the first Soviet nuclear weapons—had been pinpointed earlier by an interesting case of intelligence historical research. CIA analysts discovered that an American mining engineer had worked with a British copper mining operation in the area before the Revolution of 1917. He was approached and gave permission to look through his papers, which had long before been given to Stanford University. The intelligence researchers found papers, photos, and a large detailed map of the entire Kyshtym area of the kind needed for mining operations. The data were extremely useful when coupled with more recent maps and photographs and helped to locate the plutonium plant at Kyshtym, as well as other nuclear facilities in the area. The retired mining engineer whose long-forgotten files yielded this valuable information was none other than former president Herbert Hoover.

After the AEC delegation returned, it prepared a report on its findings. I supplemented their report with a detailed (nineteen-page, single-spaced) memorandum that I sent to the director. Allen Dulles, in turn, sent a copy to McCone, noting that "Raymond submitted this to me to supplement your report and has oriented it to special matters of interest to the Intelligence Community." Even before receiving that report, in a meeting on October 27 with President Eisenhower (accompanied only by General Andrew Goodpaster), after briefing the president on the trip, McCone had mentioned to him that he had had "Mr. Garthoff of CIA in his party and was confident that he had obtained a great deal of information."[10]

McCone also noted to the president that the Soviet scientists in the nuclear field were quite good and had been working in that field since long before the war. Indeed, they included most of the "fathers" of the Soviet atomic bomb. As he noted, "It is quite clear that their accomplishments are by no means attributable to 'stealing our secrets' although they may have gained marginal advantage from time to time on specific details in this way."

McCone commented that as a consequence of the trip, he had "for the first time been thinking that it may be desirable to put the President's Science Advisory Committee, the AEC, the NASA and certain other laboratories into one national scientific organization." Although that did not happen, the post of science adviser to the president was later established.

Less than a month later, a Soviet nuclear delegation under Academician Vasily Yemelyanov arrived in the United States for an intensive three-week stay—visiting twenty installations across the country in as many days. It was comparable in scope but more extensive than our visit in the Soviet Union had been. The Soviet delegation included several outstanding nuclear physicists, including Academician Anatoly Aleksandrov, and several metallurgists and engineers working on nuclear reactors. I again served throughout their visit as the interpreter, with my wife, Vera, as an additional interpreter given the size of the delegation. It was an interesting opportunity to get to know some of the top Soviet nuclear scientists.

The program included visits to a number of nuclear power stations and the nuclear-powered ship *Savannah* at Camden, New Jersey, where, as in other cases, they displayed a particular interest in metallurgical aspects of the system. It became increasingly clear from their questions that they were having difficulties in reliability of precision welding, and in corrosion in their reactor pressure vessels and heat-exchangers. We correctly inferred from this that they would probably face difficulties of this nature in their nuclear submarine program.

The delegation was also taken to the National Reactor Test Center in Idaho, which resembles a moonscape with various reactor facilities scattered about. They visited ten reactors there, all in a single day—and were obviously much impressed with the scale and scope of the center, for which they had no analogue.

10. "Memorandum of Conference with the President, October 27, 1959," p. 3. Memorandum signed by Brigadier General A. J. Goodpaster, Eisenhower Library, Abilene, Kans. (declassified).

That Soviet delegation was the first to visit most facilities, but clearly the most dramatic were their visits to Oak Ridge, Los Alamos, and Argonne national laboratories, although of course only to unclassified non-weapons facilities. The work on controlled thermonuclear reactions at the Oak Ridge, Los Alamos, and Lawrence Livermore laboratories, and at Princeton University, was of great interest, especially the work under Professor Lyman Spitzer at Princeton. Yemelyanov several times suggested the desirability of a joint Soviet-American project in that field, perhaps in lieu of then planned separate American and Soviet ventures, but he did not get more than a polite hearing.

The Soviet scientists tended to be forthcoming in describing their own areas of work, where they clearly knew the limits of what they could say. They did disclose new information, although usually only when asked or even pressed to provide it. About halfway through the trip, I accidentally discovered that each of them had a prepared detailed lecture on his own specialty, but it was used only when required, that is, only if the American side pressed for a report on Soviet experience in a given area. Then it would be divulged. I made this discovery when one of the scientists inadvertently left his briefcase at a lunch table and the hotel management brought it to me. I didn't hesitate long before opening it, and after finding the report I took quick extensive notes before closing the case again and returning it to the owner. Thereafter, we made it a point at the appropriate occasion to ask each Soviet specialist for a report on his work in a given area to correspond with the reports our scientists were providing.

We also learned a great deal from the areas of Soviet interest revealed by the questions they posed. In some cases they appeared to be trying to determine who was ahead, but more often to learn about successful or unsuccessful new approaches that would help to inform their own programs—in short, to learn from our experience. Most intriguing were the questions that indirectly disclosed problems that they were facing, as they tried to find out indirectly whether we had similar problems or had found solutions. I have mentioned two important areas about which we learned this way: problems in welding reactor elements and problems of corrosion.

The Soviet scientists also pressed in a few cases to try to learn things that they realized we considered out of bounds, but that was fair game. Most notably, they sought—unsuccessfully—to learn the precise degree of enrichment of the highly enriched uranium used in some of our reactors. The only answer they got was the authorized "over 90 percent enriched." In another instance, in a conversation an American had gratuitously mentioned the place where the fuel elements for the *Savannah* were produced, which was classified information. In that instance I simply didn't interpret it, and the Soviet interlocutor gave no indication that he had heard or understood what had been said. In one case, the Soviets did obtain information beyond what was intended. Academician Aleksandrov clearly had come well prepared to learn all he could about nuclear-related biological research at Oak Ridge. At a luncheon there, he rearranged the planned seating so that he and an English-speaking member of his delegation were flanking an American scientist specializing in that work at the biological laboratory (which was not visited). Although I was occupied elsewhere and not engaged in that conversation, I was able to monitor it sufficiently to learn that Aleksandrov had probed to see what he could learn about the precise viruses being investigated, and to his surprise the American offered to provide him samples of the viruses—and did so when they met at dinner that evening. The work was not security classified, but it had not been included on the formal agenda nor had any provision of samples been foreseen. But that was a unique case.

During the trip, when the delegation was in San Francisco on November 11, as we gathered for breakfast at the hotel I noticed that the morning newspaper had a front-page article reporting that Khrushchev had just announced that the Soviet Union now had nuclear-powered submarines at sea. I immediately waved the newspaper and reported Khrushchev's assertion to Aleksandrov and another reactor specialist, Aleksandr Leipunsky. They confirmed that they did now have nuclear submarines at sea, with considerably more powerful engines than the American ones. Yemelyanov then arrived and cut off any more comments by members of his delegation. Indeed, the newspaper accounts proved to be garbled. But I had gotten confirmation from two leading Soviet reactor specialists, one of whom (Aleksandrov) had overseen the development of the power plant for the first Soviet nuclear submarine. Moreover, while the news story was spurious, the first Soviet nuclear-powered submarine *had* just gone to sea in October 1959, as we later confirmed. I had a scoop. So I went to the telephone and called the duty officer at the CIA watch office. I told him about the confirmation by the two reactor specialists that a Soviet nuclear submarine was now at sea. The next morning the story appeared in the secret daily *Central Intelligence Bulletin* and *Current Intelligence Digest.* I've sometimes wondered whether some Soviet counterintelligence analyst ever concluded that CIA had planted a false Khrushchev statement in the San Francisco press that morning in order to catch visiting Soviet scientists off guard and elicit from them information on the fact that the first Soviet nuclear submarine had just gone to sea!

In my report on the visit, I concluded that the general objectives and interests of the Soviet atomic energy delegation had been:

(1) a general assessment of the U.S. atomic energy research program, and in particular determining the extent to which published data available in the USSR reflected the real scope and areas of concentration of

the U.S. effort; (2) further stimulation of the political climate of normalization of relations and broadening of scientific contacts; (3) especial attention to engineering and metallurgical aspects of both reactor and accelerator development, both due to the fact that such aspects are naturally less fully presented in scientific reports and publications, and due to the evident difficulties which the Soviets have had in fully solving such problems; (4) probing for new breakthroughs in controlled thermonuclear research; and (5) probing for [nuclear-] related chemical and especially biological research.

I also concluded that while they had already been well acquainted with U.S. work in this field, it was my impression that they had now found that our research overall was on an even broader basis than they had realized.

I have no doubt that the exchange of atomic energy visits was mutually useful. Both sides no doubt acquired incidental intelligence, but that too may on balance have been mutually useful, and in any case I believe the United States learned more if only because our system was so much more open.

The nuclear energy exchange visits also provided some opportunity for picking up other incidental intelligence. In particular, I was able to learn some things about Soviet collaboration with China in the nuclear field (which was sharply curtailed after 1959) from a Soviet scientist recently returned from there. He was impressed with the quality of the top Chinese scientists and predicted they would have a successful program of their own.

Incidentally, about a year later in November 1960 Yemelyanov protested my presence on the 1959 AEC delegation visit to the Soviet Union, stating that "Mr. Garthoff was well known in the Soviet Union as an authority on military intelligence," and a similar unofficial complaint was registered with Ambassador Tommy Thompson soon after that. These belated protests, however, were for the record and part of a general campaign against American intelligence activities that began following the downing of the U-2 in May 1960, and had no further effect. Indeed, Yemelyanov continued to send me a personal New Year's greeting card.

At the conclusion of the Soviet delegation visit, on November 24 President Eisenhower personally received Academician Yemelyanov (accompanied by Mr. McCone, with me as interpreter). Yemelyanov said his delegation had been impressed with the scope and scale of the U.S. work on peaceful uses of atomic energy, and he invited the president to visit some Soviet facility on his planned forthcoming trip. McCone outlined the plans for further contacts and cooperation, and the president expressed his approval for such joint efforts on scientific problems of common concern. The meeting was not substantive, but it was a nice gesture by President Eisenhower, and he personally had decided to do it in part because it was a new step "up" in contacts—McCone had not been received by Khrushchev.

It had been a year of unusually interesting participation in intelligence servicing of high-level exchanges, and specifically in intelligence collection in the nuclear field. Paul Borel, the assistant director of CIA in charge of the Office of Central Reference, wrote a glowing memorandum to my boss, Sherman Kent, titled "Excellence of Intelligence Information Supplied by Raymond Garthoff." He expressed appreciation for "the unusually valuable information on Soviet scientific personalities and institutes," information "impressive in its scope and detail," particularly on the subordination of various nuclear installations on which there had been a general lack of information, as well as "the valuable intelligence information which has been published and disseminated to the intelligence community." It was nice to be appreciated, and I had found the challenge intriguing.

Allen Dulles also showed his appreciation by a personal gesture, inviting me to a luncheon at his home on Q Street in Georgetown together with other guests. While I appreciated his thoughtfulness in including me on such an occasion, I also sensed from his introduction of me as "My man, who has recently returned from Moscow" that my presence also served a useful purpose for him. Nonetheless, I was honored.

7

The Espionage Game

M ost people, when they think of intelligence, immediately think of spy-ing. In fact, espionage is but one means to acquire information, and the acquisition of information requires analysis to produce intelligence. Moreover, many experienced senior intelligence officers have observed that up to 95 percent of intelligence is obtained by various means other than espi-onage. Nonetheless, that five percent may be vital and unobtainable any other way. Espionage also has an aura of intrigue and overtones of danger that attracts attention. Never was this more true than in the time Allen Dulles was director of central intelligence.

Espionage is a very serious matter; for some, a deadly serious business. It violates international law and normal codes of civilized conduct, and yet it is virtually universal because it is considered a matter of vital national impor-tance to states. Espionage generates its own rules, and its own dynamics. As will become clearer in this chapter, espionage is therefore a game—albeit in a very serious, not frivolous, sense.

As the Cold War unfolded in the late 1940s and early 1950s, there were many reasons that the United States was led to begin building a clandestine intelligence (and counterintelligence) organization. Foremost was the grow-ing tension of confrontation with the Soviet Union and the attendant grow-ing concern over what was seen as a present threat of communist subversion and a looming future threat of war. Another contributing factor was the exist-ence and discovery of active Soviet intelligence activities (and suspected sub-versive activities) directed against us. Perhaps most important was the underlying fact that this menacing adversary maintained a closed society, and no other means seemed available to penetrate the Iron Curtain and permit us to assess the threat, and thus to prepare ourselves and to fend it off or defend against it.

The earliest CIA efforts to establish a clandestine intelligence presence in the Soviet bloc were directed primarily at building an early warning network that could alert us to Soviet troop movements westward in preparation to launch an attack on the West. In Eastern Europe, the main "assets" were the remnants of a stay-behind network left by the retreating Wehrmacht during the war, controlled by its intelligence chief on the Eastern Front, General Reinhard Gehlen. As noted earlier, Gehlen had offered his services to the United States in 1945 and had been given protection by U.S. Army Intelligence; in 1949 Gehlen, his files, and his network were taken over by CIA. But Gehlen had virtually no assets in the Soviet Union itself.

In 1949 CIA began a five-year program of recruiting and training former Soviet citizens and returning them to the Soviet Union by night overflights and air drops. Most were arrested at once, and only a few were able to establish their intended positions as "watchers" at Soviet airfields and rail junctions to report on Soviet military movements. And those few were of dubious value because most if not all were "doubled" by Soviet counterintelligence (placed under Soviet control as double agents), and all were hence necessarily suspect. CIA also supported similar British Secret Intelligence Service (SIS) infiltration of agents by sea in the Baltic states, mainly for the same purpose.

The U.S. military also began a program of peripheral and shallow penetration overflights along and over Soviet territory in the late 1940s, increased after 1950. These reconnaissance flights were used mainly to activate and thus identify Soviet radars, air fields, and other air defense installations through "Elint" (electronic intelligence sensing), and observation and photography. In short, most technical intelligence directed against the Soviet Union itself, like the dropping of agents, was for early warning and targeting for the contingency of war.

CIA did establish ties with various Russian, Ukrainian, and other émigré organizations and until 1953 provided support in efforts to harass, if not subvert, Soviet authority in the USSR. CIA placed a radio team with the Ukrainian Insurgent Army (the UPA) in the western Ukraine before its suppression in 1952, but to no real advantage either to the UPA or the CIA. In addition, attempts were made to overthrow the Albanian regime and to build an underground resistance in Poland, during the years 1949 through 1952. The dispatch of agents to foment an uprising in Albania was a complete failure, not only owing to the fact that Kim Philby, a secret KGB agent, was one of the SIS managers of that joint SIS-CIA operation. In Poland, CIA provided extensive support to a growing Polish resistance organization called WIN (Freedom and Independence Movement)—until at the end of 1952 the Polish government revealed that the whole operation virtually from the outset had been a massive provocation managed by the Polish security service.

These attempts at subversion and internal resistance were carried out primarily for political and propaganda purposes. The few attempts also to use them for espionage were never successful in producing any intelligence of value. In one instance in Latvia, for example, CIA through the SIS in 1954 attempted to learn about a suspected nuclear installation by asking an agent to provide a water sample from a river near the suspected site. He finally produced a water sample that was so radioactive it could only have come directly from a reactor coolant, not from a river—the KGB had overdone its effort to build up a double agent. We learned nothing, except that the agent had been "turned."

As earlier noted, the challenge of the Cold War not only drew upon veterans of the recent wartime covert operations, but also had wide appeal to a new generation. The wartime Ivy League connection led naturally to a postwar continuation drawing now upon the early postwar students and graduates in the field. A few of my colleagues at Yale's graduate school, and a larger number of undergraduates, in the late 1940s and early 1950s went directly into the new CIA. One, for example, was William F. Buckley (class of 1950), before becoming editor of the *National Review* and a well-known conservative spokesman and commentator. One of his mentors was Howard Hunt, of later Watergate notoriety (and earlier engaged in the failed attempt to overthrow the Albanian regime). Buckley left CIA after a few years.

Less fortunate were two fellow undergraduates of Buckley's, who also went directly into the CIA clandestine services. John Downey and Richard Fecteau (both class of 1951) were captured by the Chinese communists in 1952 when their airplane was shot down over Manchuria while on a mission to support covert operations behind Chinese lines during the Korean War. They were sentenced to life and twenty years imprisonment, respectively, and were released only in 1972 and 1973 as Sino-American relations were warming up.

Among the others who went into the CIA clandestine services for a period in the early 1950s were William Sloane Coffin Jr. (class of 1949) and Cord Meyer Jr. (class of 1942). Coffin left after three years of covert operations, dispatching Russian émigrés to be air-dropped into the Soviet Union. (Coffin had had a baptism during a wartime stint, after Russian language training, as a liaison officer with the Red Army and then, to his abiding remorse, participation in the early postwar forced return to the Soviet Union of former Soviet POWs who had served with General Vlasov's army on the German side.) Coffin went from CIA to Yale Divinity School, becoming a Presbyterian minister and chaplain of Yale and gaining notoriety in the late 1960s for civil disobedience protests against the Vietnam War. Cord Meyer, in contrast, went on to a long career in CIA, for many years heading the international organizations division of the clandestine services. Both have written of their CIA experience, providing interesting accounts of the attraction of internationalist liberals into CIA in the late 1940s and early 1950s.[1]

I have mentioned in an earlier chapter my military intelligence reserve service at Yale, in a unit headed by David Chavchavadze (class of 1950). He entered CIA and served more than a quarter of a century in covert intelligence operations directed against the Soviet Union.[2]

The work of such American intelligence officers in the field of espionage covered four functions: first, spotting and recruiting possible agents and sources of information, particularly among Soviet diplomats and intelligence officers serving abroad; second, as case officers handling such agents; third, as reports officers preparing raw data for dissemination; and finally as managers of offices in CIA headquarters in Washington (after 1961 in Langley, Virginia) and in CIA stations in foreign capitals and bases in other major cities (such as Berlin) geared to intelligence acquisition.

Apart from a few incidents in the late 1940s before tacit "rules of the game" were fully developed, there was also a mutual understanding throughout the Cold War that members of the U.S. and Soviet intelligence services would not kill one another. This rule was not applicable to (Soviet) defectors, or to third-party agents of the two sides, but it did apply to U.S. and Soviet intelligence case officers and other covert intelligence officers. Throughout the Cold War (1947–1991) CIA lost fifty-nine officers in action, but none were killed by Soviet intelligence services.

American intelligence officers, while active in "legal" intelligence acquisitions (of the kind described in the previous chapter), almost never themselves served as agents in the Soviet Union (in contrast to Soviet use of their own nationals as deep-cover "illegals" in Western countries). Moreover, even use of Americans not under diplomatic immunity for illegal intelligence observation in the Soviet Union, never extensive, was virtually abandoned after Marvin Makinen, an American college student, was arrested in 1961 while attempting to observe Soviet medium-range missile deployments in the eastern Ukraine and imprisoned for eight years. The risks were too great, and satellite photography could do the job better.

The principal intelligence, and espionage, target was secret information on Soviet intentions and capabilities. Information acquired from human sources of intelligence later came to be called "Humint," analogous to "Comint" (communications intelligence), "Elint" (electronic intelligence), and other forms of

---

1. See Cord Meyer, *Facing Reality: From World Federalism to the CIA* (Harper & Row, 1980); and William Sloane Coffin Jr., *Once to Every Man: A Memoir* (Atheneum, 1977).

2. David Chavchavadze, *Crowns and Trenchcoats: A Russian Prince in the CIA* (Atlantic International Publishers, 1990). This memoir, while interesting, is regrettably thin on clandestine intelligence service.

"Sigint" (signals intelligence), "Photint" (photographic intelligence), "Imint" (imagery intelligence), and other forms of technical intelligence. But Humint, or espionage, is dependent on access to potential sources, and throughout the Cold War, above all in the 1940s through the 1960s, access was largely limited to Soviet personnel stationed abroad. Contact with agents after their recruitment was also much less difficult abroad than when the source was in the Soviet Union. Finally, a significant share of Soviet citizens who became U.S. agents, as well as of Soviet defectors, were volunteers ("walk-ins," in CIA jargon) who took the initiative themselves in the recruitment.

For all of these reasons, there also was a heavy representation of intelligence officers among Soviet personnel targeted for recruitment, volunteering service, or defecting. These Soviet intelligence personnel abroad had the opportunity, and after serving abroad often the desire as well, to cross over.

Counterintelligence was focused on countering attempts at penetration by hostile intelligence services (as well as, particularly in the Soviet case, guarding against volunteer agents or defectors to foreign intelligence services).

One consequence of the actions launched by both the Soviet and American intelligence services against one another was a gradual shift of priorities and efforts from targeting the highest *political* or *military* requirements, to targeting the enemy's *intelligence* services. This was never acknowledged explicitly, but in practice the energies and attention of the intelligence services increasingly became absorbed in a competitive rivalry between themselves. Even the informational data bases built up by each side gave priority to learning every detail possible about the intelligence and counterintelligence services of the rival.

To be sure, strategic political and economic intelligence continued to be pursued, and military intelligence at various levels. Moreover, many sources of intelligence other than Humint were devoted mainly to those ends. The espionage-counterespionage duel between the two sides, however, "the Game," absorbed the lion's share of Humint.

Later, from the mid-1960s to the mid-1970s, deep suspicions in the counterintelligence mindset almost paralyzed CIA's secret intelligence efforts against the Soviet Union. The chief of counterintelligence from 1954 to 1974, James Jesus Angleton, carried his suspicions of a Soviet mole in CIA to the point of demoralizing the cadre of intelligence officers built up over several decades to carry out espionage against the Soviet Union and seriously undercutting its effectiveness.[3] Fittingly, this extreme suspicion found its *reductio ad absurdum* when one of Angleton's own sleuths concluded that because he had caused so much harm to the agency's work, Angleton himself must be the mole! Angleton fortunately did not deal with strategic intelligence evaluations

3. See Tom Mangold, *Cold Warrior: James Jesus Angleton: The CIA's Master Spy Hunter* (Simon & Schuster, 1992).

on Soviet intentions; his suspicions extended, for example, to never accepting that there had been a Soviet-Yugoslav split or a Sino-Soviet rift. Only after Angleton was removed by Director of Central Intelligence William Colby in 1974 did the internal situation stabilize and slowly mend in the clandestine intelligence service work directed at the Soviet Union.

In the 1950s and early 1960s, however, CIA's espionage efforts against the Soviet Union (and Eastern European communist countries) were maturing and enjoyed several notable successes, mainly from "walk-ins." One of the first was Lieutenant Colonel Pëtr Popov, serving in Soviet Military Intelligence (GRU) in Vienna in 1953, who provided much military intelligence for six years until he was arrested in Moscow.[4] In 1953–54 a whole spate of KGB officers defected in the wake of Beria's arrest and purges of the intelligence services. Later, there were other recruitments (or self-recruitments) of a number of important Soviet intelligence officers. The Soviet side, of course, also had its successes.

In November 1958 I noticed in the Soviet armed forces newspaper *Red Star* that a Swedish military delegation was visiting the Soviet Union, as part of a Soviet effort to draw the European neutrals into a less pro-Western stance. The visit included a rare observation of a Soviet military field exercise simulating use of nuclear weapons. One member of the delegation, I noted, was my old friend Colonel Stig Wennerström, from 1952 until mid-1957 the Swedish air attaché in Washington (and earlier the air attaché in Moscow). I planned to be in London in January for a U.S.-UK intelligence conference, and it seemed to me it might be worthwhile to visit Wennerström and see what I could learn about the Soviet exercise. Sherman Kent approved, and although the DDP thought they could pick up anything of interest, they posed no objection.

I wrote Colonel Wennerström in December and told him I expected to be in Europe early in the year and hoped I might see him. Without explicit connection I also noted that I had seen that he had recently been in the Soviet Union as a member of a Swedish military delegation and commented that the visit must have been most interesting. He urged me to visit and invited me to stay as his house guest. I did so from February 2 to 6, 1959. I had always found Wennerström very friendly, and although we never had extensive political discussions he had always evidenced a pro-Western orientation. He had once, in 1956 or 1957, even passed me a secret dispatch commenting on topical Soviet policy issues that had originated with the Swedish embassy in Moscow. In Stockholm, Stig and Ulla-Greta Wennerström made me feel quite at home.

---

4. See William Hood, *Mole—The True Story of the First Russian Intelligence Officer Recruited by the CIA* (W. W. Norton & Co., 1982). Hood refers to Popov as a major, but he was a lieutenant colonel.

It turned out to be a quite interesting visit. Apart from my talks with Wennerström, I met with leading figures in the Swedish Foreign Ministry, the Swedish Intelligence Service, and Swedish Military Intelligence, as well as some others. They were all familiar with my published writings on Soviet military affairs and regarded me as an expert in the field.

At the Foreign Ministry I met with Mr. Sverker Aström, the chief of political affairs, and Dr. Stellan Bohm, the chief Soviet affairs expert. Both were keenly interested in the then active question of the alleged "missile gap" and sought my view on Albert Wohlstetter's recent article ("The Delicate Balance of Terror") in *Foreign Affairs*. I dismissed the missile gap and disagreed with the idea that the deterrent balance was delicate, or that a military edge would lead the Soviets into unleashing nuclear war even if they could acquire one. The Soviet view of the overall balance of forces, I argued, was much more comprehensive, and so was American power. They agreed.

The missile gap was also the principal subject of interest with the Swedish military intelligence officers. (I met with them, at their invitation, in an intriguing private dining room of a restaurant entered through an inconspicuous panel in the wall.) They showed an amazingly detailed familiarity with all the published debate on the missile issue in the United States. They were also interested in my views on Soviet thinking about the nature of war, the recent purge of Marshal Georgy Zhukov, and other such topical matters.

Berlin was another subject of great interest. Aström, Bohm, and Wennerström separately all seemed to assume that the Soviet Union would turn over access controls to West Berlin to the East Germans, and that the West would accept. I argued the contrary, that a turnover of controls would not go unchallenged, and that the Soviets should understand that. I told Wennerström that the Soviets would be running grave risks if they assumed Western acquiescence in a turnover. Aström was clearly not sympathetic to any idea of use of force to prevent turnover of access to the East Germans. Dr. Gustav Thede Palm, chief of the Swedish Intelligence Service (whom I met courtesy of our established intelligence liaison), in contrast to Aström, Bohm and Wennerström, expressed himself very positively in favor of a strong Western stand.

A third subject was the Swedish debate over whether to acquire nuclear weapons. Wennerström had alerted me to the fact that it was then a more active issue than I had realized. Aström was particularly interested, and no doubt reflecting the internal Swedish deliberation he reviewed in detail pros and cons, without offering an on-balance conclusion. He said that Sweden was, among other things, watching to see the outcome of nuclear test ban negotiations.

I had decided to hold back for a few days and see if Wennerström would take the lead in telling me about the findings of the Swedish military delegation in the Soviet Union. On the third day he did so, while the two of us were at lunch. He gave me a thorough, detailed account of the entire visit and in particular the field exercise featuring tactical use of nuclear weapons. The Swedes had been told that they were the only foreigners to be given the information conveyed in connection with the exercise (and they were given much more than the Austrians earlier in the year) and were asked to keep the data secret. Of course, the Soviet leadership and military and security officials regarded any information given to the Swedes as compromised to the West, and might well have included some deliberate disinformation, but they also wished to convey an impression of Soviet military strength through credible disclosure.

Prior to traveling to Sweden I had checked on what we already knew about the Swedish observation of the Soviet military exercise. U.S. attachés and the embassy in Stockholm had reported very little. I learned from sources in London that the British military attaché in Stockholm had sent a report to London, "UK Eyes Only"; I was able to arrange though MI 6 that a message be sent to the attaché requesting I be allowed to see the message, and he did give me access to it in Stockholm. I also had a separate meeting with a Swedish military intelligence officer who had been on the delegation. So I had a substantial independent basis for cross-checking what Wennerström told me, and it checked out very well. Wennerström's account was, however, by far the most comprehensive and detailed.

The information is of course of little interest now, but at the time the data were of considerable intelligence value, notwithstanding Soviet control over what they would disclose to the Swedes. The information included identification of the types of small-yield nuclear weapons for tactical rocket and tactical air delivery (ranging from 2KT to 50KT in yield, with air delivery by Tu-16 "Badger" medium bombers). The exercise force, comprising the elite 2nd Guards (*Taman*) Motorized Rifle Division, had been allotted six nuclear weapons for an attack on a seven-kilometer-wide front. By far the most interesting information on strategic doctrine was a statement by the defense minister, Marshal Rodion Malinovsky, that preparation for nuclear war should not be at the expense of maintaining forces and capabilities for conventional warfare as well. He said NATO had made an error in adopting a different view. The Soviet doctrine, he said, had been approved by the Presidium (as the Politburo was then called). Malinovsky also explicitly declared, in contradiction to published Soviet military writings but as some of us had concluded was the real Soviet view, that limited wars, including limited nuclear wars, were quite possible and had to be prepared for. He said this was so despite recognition that NATO had largely committed itself to use of nuclear weapons by not having larger conventional forces.

The Swedes concluded that Khrushchev had given Malinovsky authority to decide what they would be shown and told, with two guidelines: that the Swedes must conclude that it was a militarily worthwhile visit, but that they must not be given secrets on strategic capabilities or order of battle information. Within that guidance, Malinovsky and their host throughout the visit, General of the Army M. M. Popov, deputy commander in chief of the ground forces, were forthcoming, although virtually all other officers were clearly afraid to provide any information until prompted by Popov, who had clearly been charged by Malinovsky to ensure that the Swedes were satisfied that they were being given worthwhile information.

After my return, in addition to writing a detailed trip report on my contacts and discussions in Stockholm, I prepared a separate memorandum on the information on Soviet tactical nuclear weapons, field tactics, military personalities encountered, and other military intelligence gleaned from the Swedish delegation, and this information was disseminated to the U.S. intelligence community. My memorandum was also sent up to the director, and Allen Dulles not only read it but noted a rare word of praise: "Excellent. AWD." That made my day.

A little over four years later, Colonel Stig Wennerström was arrested in Stockholm as a Soviet spy. I, like virtually everyone who had known him, was greatly surprised. If someone in the 1950s had told me that one of my friends in the diplomatic community was a Soviet spy, Stig would have been near the bottom of my list of suspects—but that is why he was so successful, and for so long. He had been recruited in 1948, just as he was beginning his second tour in Moscow as an air attaché. In fact, his dabbling in espionage had begun when he was first in Moscow in 1940 and had passed information on the Soviet Union to the Germans! After the war, he provided some information and may have given some assistance to American attachés in Moscow. For a time in the late 1940s and early 1950s he played both sides of the street, for example, taking lists of matters of interest to the Americans, providing us material on some of them, but also giving the lists with their revelation of American interests and requirements to Soviet military intelligence. While serving as air attaché in Washington from 1952 to 1957, in addition to developing many high-level contacts in the U.S. Air Force, Wennerström handled Swedish air force procurement. In that capacity, he learned a great deal from American firms eager to sell their wares. He helped negotiate purchase of the Sidewinder air-to-air missile, and was able to send to Moscow secret specifications and data on performance of that and other weapon systems. Later in Stockholm he also obtained secret information on the Bomarc missile, as well as vast information on Swedish defenses.[5]

---

5. After his trial, the Swedish government released a sanitized but extensive transcript detailing his activities as a Soviet spy (but deleting such things as his American and other

Why did he do it? First, he was attracted to the "game" of intelligence. To some extent, he worked for money. He also had a need to feel more important. His career in the Swedish air force had leveled off at a lower grade than he had expected. He also claimed to have seen a chance to play a role in helping to stabilize the East-West balance. Soviet intelligence successfully played to his vanity and his fantasies, giving him the code name "Eagle," a nominal Soviet major general's rank and medals (kept in Moscow, of course), and above all giving him the personal attention of a handler (supposedly a general) who feigned interest in Wennerström's views on matters of high policy while encouraging him to provide technical and military information, mainly on the United States and NATO, but in the later years in Stockholm on the whole Swedish defense system. Wennerström acknowledged his guilt, cooperated, and was sentenced to life imprisonment. He was released after twelve years and at this writing is (in his mid-nineties) living in the same house in the suburbs of Stockholm where I was his house guest in 1959.

Information from former Soviet intelligence archives is not yet available on the extent to which the GRU paid attention to Wennerström's political intelligence reporting or passed it to the Soviet leadership, or to confirm and perhaps enlarge on his own disclosures during his interrogation and trial. Wennerström has said that he reported whatever he learned about American thinking on the Berlin Crisis from 1958 to 1961, and that he reported that the United States was prepared to go to war over Berlin. If so, perhaps my strong expression of U.S. government determination on Berlin played a helpful role. In 1959 I had, of course, no idea that my statement to him would be reported to Soviet intelligence.

Incidentally, although I had told Wennerström of my move from RAND to my cover job in the Pentagon, he was undoubtedly advised by Swedish Intelligence at the time of my visit that I was in fact at CIA—and passed that information to Moscow. Thus by the time of my trips to the Soviet Union with Vice President Nixon and the AEC delegation later in 1959, Soviet Intelligence had information from a very good source—the chief of Swedish Intelligence to their "Eagle"—identifying me as a CIA officer.

In retrospect, notwithstanding Wennerström's Soviet allegiance, the detailed information on Soviet military developments acquired by the

---

Western contacts, and also work he did *for* Swedish intelligence). Based largely on that record was a series of articles in the *New Yorker,* subsequently published as a book. See Thomas Whiteside, *Agent in Place: The Wennerström Affair* (Viking Press, 1966). Wennerström also later wrote a memoir, subject to censorship, published only in Swedish and German. Swedish journalist Anders Sundelin has published the most comprehensive account, *Fallet Wennerström* (The case of Wennerström) (Stockholm: Norstedts förlag, 1999).

Swedish delegation and passed to me by Wennerström, graded "excellent" by Allen Dulles, was a full and valid account. Some of the information we were able to corroborate, at the time or later.

Wennerström had every incentive to provide me with a full and accurate account of what the Swedes had learned. He and his Soviet Intelligence handlers recognized that his cooperation with me—with CIA—in this matter would only bolster his pro-American reputation, whereas any equivocation, distortion, or even significant omission would have risked discovery and raised suspicions about him. So I had been given good intelligence information.

Just a month before Wennerström was arrested, another spy was convicted and executed—in Moscow. Colonel Oleg Penkovsky was a "walk-in," indeed one who took great risks to contact U.S. Intelligence through several approaches to American, British, and Canadian visitors in the Soviet Union over a period of several months from 1960 to 1961. CIA and MI 6 jointly "ran" the operation, which lasted for about eighteen months from April 1961 until Penkovsky was arrested in October 1962. Penkovsky was a senior colonel in Soviet military intelligence (GRU), assigned to conduct Soviet intelligence operations against the West from his cover assignment on the State Committee for the Coordination of Scientific Research Work, engaged in contacts with Western organizations and businesses involved with science and technology. Contact was finally secured through a British business representative, Greville Wynne, co-opted by the British SIS. It was then maintained in Moscow through contacts with British and American embassy intelligence officers.[6]

Penkovsky, like Wennerström, had a large ego and an unpromising future career. Even more than Wennerström, Penkovsky saw a mission for himself above national interests, in his case to alert the West and help stop what he saw as a dangerous drive for power by Khrushchev and other Soviet leaders. Like Wennerström's Soviet handlers, the British and American case officers (who were able to meet with Penkovsky on a number of occasions because his official work took him abroad) pandered to his ego, with uniforms of a colonel in the British and U.S. armies, and even a meeting with Sir Dick White ("C"), the head of the SIS. (They had to fend off his initial demands to meet personally

6. The main published source on the Penkovsky affair has a vastly overstated title, as the discussion will show. It is weak on evaluating the material he supplied, exaggerating its significance. Nonetheless, extensive CIA files were made available to its authors, and it tells the tale of Penkovsky's espionage for the United States and Britain in great detail and very well. See Jerrold L. Schecter and Peter S. Deriabin, *The Spy Who Saved the World: How a Soviet Colonel Changed the Course of the Cold War* (Charles Scribner's Sons, 1992). An early account issued soon after his arrest and execution was concocted from his debriefings and reports, conveying some of the information and most of the gossip he had provided, and published as though it had been a diary he (implausibly) was alleged to have kept. See *The Penkovskiy Papers* (Doubleday & Co., 1965).

President Kennedy and Queen Elizabeth!) Penkovsky's hatred for the Soviet regime, however, sometimes colored and biased his reporting.

There were other problems in evaluating the materials Penkovsky provided. For one thing, he passed along a great deal of corridor gossip from the Ministry of Defense and other questionable material. Many of his statements, for example about the location of Soviet intercontinental ballistic missiles (ICBMs), were simply wrong—although undoubtedly he believed them to be true. Yet other similar statements were valid. He provided a wealth of data on personalities, procedures, and other aspects of Soviet intelligence, particularly military intelligence. The extensive documentary material, secret and top secret military documents, was most valuable.

The question immediately arose as to what to do about information that was, if true, new and important, but was also both uncertain and often at variance with other information or our estimates. That is where I came in. In May 1961 I was unexpectedly called in to see the director. Mr. Dulles wanted me to review and evaluate some material from this new Soviet source, none of which had yet been made available beyond CIA. Specifically, Dulles wanted my recommendation whether the information from this new source was valid and should be disseminated in the intelligence community and to policymakers.

It was quite unusual for someone in the intelligence analysis business to be called on, in effect, to evaluate a live source of the operations directorate, still more so by Director Dulles personally. Thus, although I was personally on good terms with John Maury, chief of the SR (Soviet Russia) Division of the Directorate for Plans (DDP), as it was then known, there was initially a reserved attitude in that office at my involvement.

One of the key subjects on which Penkovsky provided information—or at least statements—that did not accord with the weight of judgment in Washington at the time was the state of the Soviet ICBM program. He said, in effect, that it was in great trouble and that the Soviet Union had practically no ICBM capability. Although the fears of a "missile gap" in Soviet favor were being dispelled by new intelligence from satellite photography (and would be effectively in September 1961), in the summer of 1961 there was still belief, and some evidence, that although the Soviet ICBM deployment program was proceeding more slowly than had earlier been feared, the overall ICBM program was nonetheless more serious and successful than Penkovsky suggested. Even those of us who argued that the national intelligence estimates of the Soviet ICBM program at least until September 1961 were too high could not rely on the vague and uncorroborated similar view expressed by Penkovsky.

A second important, if less critical, issue on which Penkovsky's assertions diverged from the accepted U.S. view was the status of the Soviet Army. He claimed the announced Soviet force reductions in 1960 had been a sham (which we knew from good intelligence was not true), but most striking was his claim that the Soviet Army had only about 50 divisions in its ground forces, rather than the 175 divisions held by U.S. intelligence.

The director was troubled by the discrepancy between these claims and our estimates based on other information. If true, these assertions suggested that the United States had been greatly overestimating Soviet military power. The source also claimed that the Soviet military and political leadership was unready for war, and was bluffing in its pressure on Berlin. This was a matter of great importance to national policy.

Dulles was concerned not to purvey dubious material, but also not to withhold information that could be very important. He wanted a better understanding of whether the information might be valid. The discrepancy between the new information and what we had theretofore believed raised serious questions both about the reliability of the source and the validity of his assertions. The director did not want the agency to go out on a limb by appearing to be too ready to accept the source and his information if they were doubtful. Yet the intelligence collectors were confident that the source was genuine, and the information (on these and other subjects) was important.

I concluded that the source probably was genuine, and was presenting the truth as he saw it, but that might be only part of the truth or as seen from one angle. For example, on the ICBM program his general description might be influenced by his desire to deflate what he saw as a serious Western exaggeration, and his information was not complete or always accurate, but it was consonant with the picture of a much less successful ICBM development program and much more limited deployment program than the previous CIA estimate, to say nothing of the greater Air Force estimate. It was not at variance with the Army and Navy intelligence estimates. Moreover, the new satellite photographic intelligence would remain the bedrock of our revised estimates, and it was consistent with the main thrust of Penkovsky's claims.

With respect to the figure of 50 or so divisions, I noted that it was consistent with the low side of our estimate of the number of fully manned divisions (Category I, in later parlance), and although the source had not referred to the one hundred or so other Soviet divisions, that might well have been because the Soviet military leaders regarded them in a different light from ready divisions. Many were known to be at very low, really cadre strength. By spring 1961 the number of divisions considered combat-effective was probably about 50, of a total, then, of between 140 and 150 divisions, the others requiring mobilization of reserves.

I recommended that the material be disseminated, with attention to the fact that the source probably had differing degrees of knowledge of various matters on which he was reporting, and the validity of particular assertions had to be judged with that caveat.

Dulles adopted my recommendation. A large flow of information from this source, including a wealth of documentary material on Soviet military thought, soon began to arrive. It was disseminated under more than one code-name source attribution, for security and in recognition that the validity of some of the information and even opinion that was provided was much less certain than that of documentary materials. (The documentary material on Soviet military affairs was issued under the code word "Ironbark," and the less sure military information based on Penkovsky's oral assertions or statements attributed to third parties, much of which was gossip, was issued as "Chickadee.") Much of the political information, on the Berlin crisis in particular, was issued without either code word and carefully described as coming from a well-placed source with access to senior military leaders. The source was credited as being reliable, but the reliability and validity of the information varied and was appropriately caveated.

Penkovsky's reporting on the Berlin crisis was carefully prepared and made available to the president and the State Department in July. It was taken into account in national intelligence estimates and policy deliberations, but it did not have a significant impact owing to the nature of the information and reservations about its validity. Penkovsky did not report in advance about the building of the Berlin Wall. Similarly, in 1962 he did not know about or report the Soviet decision to install medium-range missiles in Cuba. (He was unable to pass over any additional information after August, and after earlier having come under suspicion and surveillance he was arrested at the very start of the Cuban missile crisis, on October 22, 1962.)

Penkovsky supplied documentary and other information on the characteristics and the operation of a number of Soviet missile systems, including the SS-4 (R-12) missile deployed in Cuba in September to November 1962. This information proved very useful in the missile crisis. It was not, however, the crucial element permitting the identification of the missile complexes under construction in Cuba—they were spotted and identified by photo interpreters experienced in observing the same types of missile sites under construction in the Soviet Union itself from U-2 and satellite overhead photography.

The most important and extensive information Penkovsky supplied was a number of 1960–62 issues of a "special collection" of secret and top secret articles in the leading Soviet military journal, *Military Thought* (*Voyennaya mysl'*). The top secret Special Collection began only in 1960 and was restricted to Army commanders and the top echelon of the Ministry of Defense. Penkovsky enjoyed access due only to unusual high-level patronage by Marshal of Artillery Sergei Varentsov.

The first translations of these top secret articles became available in August 1961, and I wrote the first several analyses. Later, the Defense Intelligence

Agency wrote many extensive analyses of these and other like materials. The reason for starting the Special Collection was to launch a high-level debate on Soviet military doctrine in the nuclear era. The "radicals" in this debate, such as Colonel General A. Gastilovich of the General Staff Academy, argued that smaller armies, only thirty to forty Soviet divisions on the Central Front in Europe, with a large complement of tanks, could advance at a hundred kilometers a day with massive use of "hundreds" of nuclear weapons—even though NATO was credited with sixty divisions overall. The "conservatives" argued that both sides would suffer massive casualties, and therefore larger forces were needed.[7]

The few of us writing on Soviet strategy for open publication and familiar with the top secret materials could not of course refer to them in any way, but we were greatly assisted by background knowledge of them in understanding openly available Soviet military writings and in interpreting the broader debate in the Soviet Union. Internal U.S. government analyses used the materials, although except for special code-word publications they could not be cited directly. For example, the first extensive if indirect use of these materials in a discussion of current trends in Soviet military thinking appeared in a Special National Intelligence Estimate, SNIE 11-14-61, *The Soviet Strategic Posture, 1961–67*, prepared during my last months at ONE and issued on November 21, 1961.[8]

One of the most important, and least considered, aspects of such internal military (and other) discussions is what they reveal about Soviet perceptions and misperceptions of the West. The extent and significance of Soviet suspicions and fears of a NATO attack are illuminated in a startling way by some statements in the documents provided by Penkovsky. A few excerpts will illustrate the point—and the problem.

Colonel General Semën P. Ivanov, the chief of the Operations Division of the General Staff, in 1960 in a top secret analysis of the NATO maneuver "Side Step" (a large-scale exercise conducted in Europe and the Mediterranean in September 1959) wrote:

The leaders of the aggressive NATO bloc plan to launch a future world war primarily by means of a surprise attack against the countries of the

7. Those materials remained security classified until the early 1990s, when the U.S. government began to declassify its translations of the Penkovsky documents. The article cited above was the lead-off in the debate and appeared in the initial top secret issue of the Special Collection: Colonel General A. Gastilovich, "The Theory of the Military Art Needs Review," *Voyennaya mysl'*, no.1 (1960), pp. 6–20 (top secret).

8. SNIE 11-14-61, *The Soviet Strategic Posture, 1961–67* (November 21, 1961) (secret; declassified 1994).

socialist camp. One cannot rule out their launching a world war after a period of sharp political tension or local wars. They envisage carrying out preparations for an aggressive war in such a way that they will be interpreted as purely "defensive" preparations, not only by the opponent but also by the personnel of the armed forces and by the population of the member countries of the [NATO] bloc.

These are the opening sentences of General Ivanov's analysis. They sound like propaganda, but there is good reason in the discussion itself to suggest that they represented his (and his colleagues') real views. Worst of all, as General Ivanov—and his readers—understood the facts, they *supported* that conclusion.

Ivanov's analysis stated that in the exercise, Blue (NATO) gave the orders for nuclear employment at 0340 hours on September 19 [1957]—almost two hours *before* Orange (the Soviet Bloc side) launched an attack (at 0530 in the west; 0500 in the Balkans). "It follows," General Ivanov continued, that the "initial nuclear strike in the Exercise was made by the NATO forces, which is what they are indeed preparing for. This was a preemptive and not a retaliatory nuclear strike, as the NATO command was trying to show." Thus Soviet monitoring of Side Step yielded information that the General Staff interpreted as reflecting a concealed offensive first-strike plan of NATO. (Incidentally, as Ivanov noted, some 698 nuclear weapons were employed in the first six days of that exercise.) Although General Ivanov described the NATO action in Side Step as "preemptive," his general conclusion, based on overall NATO preparations and exercises, was that NATO leaders *"place first priority on a surprise attack against the countries of the socialist camp, secretly prepared in a very short time"* (italics in the original).

In another top secret analysis in 1961 General Ivanov analyzed the "Fallex-60" NATO maneuvers held in September 1960. Again, he observed that NATO "Blue" aircraft were airborne fifteen minutes *before* "Orange" launched hostilities. Thus, even though "Orange" (representing the Warsaw Pact) did start the war in the NATO exercise scenario, *in fact* Blue had preemptively launched its strike aircraft *first.*[9]

It was a very serious matter that the Soviet military and political leadership were given top secret analyses, buttressed with facts, *seeming* to support U.S. and NATO *first-strike* plans and intentions. These particular authoritative materials dated from 1960–61, but such analyses were not unique to that

9. Colonel General S. Ivanov, "Some Conclusions on the NATO Armed Forces' Exercise Side Step," *Voyennaya mysl'*, no. 2 (1960) (top secret); and "The Fallex-60 Maneuvers of the Armed Forces of the NATO Aggressive Bloc," *Voyennaya mysl'*, no. 4 (1961) (top secret).

period. It was clear from similar indications in later internal Soviet military publications that while public propaganda materials were naturally prone to distort and exaggerate, by no means all of the distortion and exaggeration was intentional or recognized to be such.

Only intelligence analysts of Soviet military thinking ever received this material, and no one even considered it from the angle of political misperception. I wrote about the general problem on a number of occasions, but I could never cite this example from the top secret Penkovsky materials. When, some years later, I attempted to get excerpts of this material declassified in order to draw attention to the dangers of Soviet misperception of NATO, I was turned down. Only now, with the Cold War behind us, has it become possible to do so.

One aspect of the handling of Penkovsky, controversial at the time between CIA and the SIS, deserves reflection. In view of Penkovsky's position in Moscow and occasional access to high-level information, CIA decided that arrangements should be made for him to sound an alert if he ever learned of a Soviet decision to launch an attack. In the light of his known hatred for the Soviet leadership and his proclivity to play a role of sounding the tocsin in the West against the Soviet danger, this might have entailed considerable risk. This was the British view, even though they had first raised the idea of an alerting system. Nonetheless, CIA insisted that such a system must allow immediate reporting without an intermediate joint U.S.-U.K. evaluation. That was logical, if indeed Penkovsky learned of some imminent Soviet military action, but it carried grave risk too.

The warning system, code-named "Distant," was simple: Penkovsky would call a specified embassy phone number and when a man answered would blow into the mouthpiece three times, wait one minute and repeat. That was all; not a word. Then, if time allowed, he would fill a "dead drop" with an explanation of what his alert was all about and leave the sign (a mark on a telephone pole) that a message was waiting in the dead drop. The CIA station chief in Moscow would report this telephonic warning signal to Washington immediately, even before checking the dead drop for a message.

On November 2, 1962, after the climax but before the full resolution of the Cuban missile crisis, the Distant signal was received, the telephone pole was marked, and attaché Richard Jacob of the CIA station in the U.S. embassy went to collect the message in the dead drop. He was detained on the spot by Soviet security officers and in due course released to the embassy. From the moment of Jacob's detention, it was clear that Penkovsky had not sent the warning call but had told the Soviet security officers about the signaling arrangement after being arrested. It is still not clear whether he told them it was a tentative alert of a possible Soviet attack, or whether he decided to play Samson and bring the temple down on everyone. In any case, the initial phone alert was fortunately not taken as a valid warning of Soviet attack. One may still wonder at the risk if this had occurred a week earlier at the peak of the Cuban missile crisis, and especially if the dead drop had not been staked out.[10]

Colonel Penkovsky had been a very productive espionage agent, providing a wealth of detail on Soviet military intelligence, a great deal of documentary material on Soviet military thinking, and information on a number of tactical and medium-range rocket and missile systems. His information on Soviet policy and on broader Soviet intentions was much less useful, owing to his biases as well as the hearsay nature of that information, reporting on what a few senior generals thought and said about Soviet policy rather than on what the political leadership was really thinking and doing.

A number of other Soviet intelligence officers and officials defected or became agents in the 1960s and early 1970s, but many of them (and some CIA officers) became the object of suspicion by Angleton's counterintelligence.[11]

I did, by chance, meet one of the major Soviet defectors, Yury Nosenko, in Geneva in April 1962, only a day before he first approached another member of our mission (a Foreign Service officer friend of mine who had served in the Bureau of Intelligence and Research, and who placed CIA in touch with Nosenko) and became an American "agent in place" in the KGB. At the time, we both were there as members of our respective disarmament negotiating delegations. He created the impression that he was a hard-liner—he said Stalin should have kept the Red Army advancing west in 1945. But that loud anti-American stance was probably defensive overcompensation for the benefit of anyone listening, at a time when he was deciding to establish contact with CIA. Incidentally, with me for part of the strange conversation in the bar was a junior but up-and-coming Foreign Service officer named Tom Pickering—later to become our most experienced ambassador and undersecretary of state. (In writing up a report on the conversation, I indicated that I thought Nosenko probably was an intelligence officer. He was, in fact, the KGB security officer for the Soviet delegation.) That was our only encounter; I never saw Nosenko after he defected two years later. He was soon the most prominent of a number of Soviet intelligence defectors who fell victim to false accusations in the tangled game of counterintelligence that reached a peak plateau that lasted a decade, from 1964 through 1974.

10. I was the first to disclose (in 1987) Penkovsky's early warning alert and its use during the Cuban missile crisis. See "Cuba: Even Dicier Than We Knew—Details of the Missile Crisis," *Newsweek,* October 26, 1987, p. 34; and Garthoff, *Reflections on the Cuban Missile Crisis* (Brookings, 1987), pp. 39–41. I was, however, in error in dating it to October 22 and in reporting that the use of the signal had not been reported to high authorities in Washington. The warning system and the incident is described most fully in Schecter, *The Spy Who Saved the World,* pp. 262, 284–87, 304–05, 346–47, and 397.

11. For a good overall account, see David C. Martin, *Wilderness of Mirrors* (Ballantine Books, 1981).

It may be useful to note briefly one other case concerning the fate of a double agent I knew. In June 1959 a promising young Soviet Navy captain, Nikolai Artamonov, defected by sea. He, too, had a wealth of information on the Soviet Navy, but little beyond that. I had occasion late in 1959 or early in 1960 to interview him on one matter that seemed both dubious and beyond his likely knowledge, a comment he had made in his debriefing about an alleged Soviet military doctrine for a surprise attack. I knew him then by the defector identification number by which he was identified on all the reports based on his interrogation, DS-3005. I confirmed that he had, in fact, probably in his own mind and certainly for the interrogator, stretched a briefing he had received on newly increased recognition of the importance of surprise in Soviet military thinking in 1955, about which we knew very well, into something that seemed far more ominous but was not. When I next met him, in 1966, he had become an American citizen with the name of Nicholas Shadrin, writing on Soviet naval affairs and working for DIA.

In December 1975 Shadrin disappeared in Vienna, where he had gone for a meeting with a Soviet intelligence contact. What had happened in the meantime was that a Soviet intelligence officer who had offered his services to the United States, Colonel Igor Kochnov, needed some successes to allay KGB suspicion. He had been assigned in 1966 to recruit Shadrin, so the FBI and CIA, working together on the case, decided to encourage Shadrin to go along with a Soviet pitch and pretend to become their agent, while serving as a double agent for the United States. He was never told that he was a pawn in a larger game involving building up a KGB agent who was secretly a double agent for the United States. Shadrin was reluctant, but finally agreed. Initially, in the United States, all went well. But on his second meeting with a Soviet agent in Vienna in 1975 he disappeared. There was no show trial, or confession of "American agent" Shadrin, or anything. The United States raised the matter of its citizen Shadrin but was told only that the Soviet Union did not have him.[12]

Ten years later, Soviet intelligence defector Colonel Vitaly Yurchenko—before he redefected to the Soviet side—reported that Shadrin had died while being kidnapped. General Oleg Kalugin and other retired KGB officers have more recently confirmed that in an attempted kidnapping of Shadrin, he was accidentally given an overdose of a drug while being hustled off from Vienna to Bratislava, an incidental victim of intrigue in a twisted struggle between the rival intelligence services in which a pawn had to be sacrificed.[13]

12. See Henry Hurt, *Shadrin: The Spy Who Never Came Back* (Readers' Digest/McGraw Hill, 1981).

13. See Oleg Kalugin, *The First Directorate: My 32 Years in Intelligence and Espionage Against the West* (St. Martin's Press, 1994), pp. 94–97.

Espionage is an inescapable element of international relations. There was, however, much more to the intelligence game than espionage in the classical sense of intelligence collection, or frustrating the adversary's attempts to collect intelligence. Especially during the Cold War it came to occupy a role not merely as an instrument of political struggle, but as a largely autonomous clandestine Cold War game waged by rival intelligence services. The pattern set in the 1950s and 1960s continued in the 1970s and 1980s on an even larger scale, as will be noted later. There is also a history of deception and disinformation, doubling agents and feeding false information to mislead and divert the adversary's attention, and even in some cases his policies. Deception and disinformation, if the consequences are sufficiently predictable and controllable, may be justified. There is, however, a serious question as to the point of diminishing or negative returns on waging an intelligence struggle to the utmost or playing the espionage game too enthusiastically to the point where it becomes the object of the activity rather than a means to serve policy.

8

Department of State:
The Kennedy Years (I)

I reported for duty at the Department of State on September 17, 1961—just three days before my old ONE office and most of CIA headquarters moved to Langley, Virginia. At first, some of my friends both at State and at CIA thought that I was changing cover. But the transfer was real. I did become a formal consultant to CIA with the approval of my new boss at State, Ambassador U. Alexis Johnson. In 1962 I helped draft the first National Intelligence Estimate on the Warsaw Pact military forces, and I occasionally met informally with the Board of National Estimates, especially after travels in the Soviet Union and Eastern Europe. Nonetheless, I was now a Foreign Service officer of the Department of State and would remain one for more than eighteen years.

Like many others, I was excited by the coming into office of a dynamic new president who promised to pursue a more active policy. And I wanted to participate in the policymaking process more directly than as an intelligence officer. Within a few months I had that opportunity.

The incoming administration not only brought a new leader and new spirit, but also a number of organizational and institutional changes. While greater flexibility and direction from the top brought some advantages, it also carried the hazard of missing some considerations that should have been brought to bear on decisions. The disastrous Bay of Pigs misadventure in landing Cuban émigrés in Cuba, although not typical, was by far the most dramatic example. More generally, in retrospect I believe it is clear that the wholesale scrapping of the national security machinery of the Eisenhower administration went too far. The routine embodied in the regular meetings of the National Security Council, its Planning Board, and its Operations Coordinating Board, although ponderous, formal, and bureaucratic, played an important role in ensuring that all relevant considerations would be brought to bear in the policymaking process. It couldn't ensure wise decisions, but it did decrease the possibility of error owing to omission of important considerations.

One of the innovations, and a good one, was the establishment in the Department of State of a small politico-military affairs staff directly under the senior officer overseeing all political, military, and intelligence matters in the department, Deputy Under Secretary of State for Political Affairs U. Alexis Johnson. This new staff was, in a sense, a much smaller counterpart of the long-established International Security Affairs (ISA) office in the Pentagon, headed by an assistant secretary of defense. Paul Nitze was named to that latter position, with several deputies, including my friends Bill Bundy, who moved over from ONE at CIA, and Harry Rowen from RAND. They had offered me a senior position slated to become head of the policy-planning division of ISA. I seriously considered that proposal, but in the end I accepted an offer by the head of the new politico-military affairs group in State, Jeffrey Kitchen. The designation for the new group was G/PM, G being the symbol for the deputy under secretary for political affairs, and PM standing for "politico-military" affairs. My title was special assistant for Soviet (initially Sino-Soviet) bloc politico-military affairs, a vague and broad term that even so only partly covered what I would soon find was my scope of activity.

G/PM had a dual role, internally coordinating among the mainly geographic bureaus of the Department of State on various political-military matters and providing staff support to Ambassador Johnson, Secretary Rusk, and other senior officers of the department, and externally representing the State Department in interdepartmental (interagency) coordination of policy. As a "seventh-floor" staff we had clout extending beyond that of a regional geographic or functional bureau in State, although of course much depended on the issue and, frankly, the competence and competitive drive of various offices and officers. In addition, in the few cases where there was an established political-military affairs role in a bureau, that role generally continued; the one such office of any significance was the regional politico-military affairs office in the Bureau of European Affairs (EUR/RPM), handling NATO affairs. G/PM developed an important contributory role too with respect to NATO affairs, but it did not displace the existing EUR position. Munitions control, checking all arms sales for compatibility with U.S. legislation and policy, quickly became a G/PM responsibility. G/PM was the home office for the "Polads," Foreign Service officers assigned as political advisers with major military commands. G/PM also became very active in overall U.S. overseas military base negotiations, in concert with the appropriate regional geographic bureau or bureaus. G/PM was the touchpoint in the State Department, working closely with ISA in Defense, to ensure that military activities were consonant with foreign policy objectives; for example, that naval ship visits or exercises did take place in various parts of the globe when we wanted them to play a reinforcing role for our diplomacy, and did not inadvertently take place when and where there were policy reasons for not wanting a U.S. presence at a given time. The State Department's role in civil defense policy and counterinsurgency programs abroad were among other responsibilities. I shall later discuss more fully several other major areas in which I carried the G/PM role—in particular, arms control and nonproliferation and military and intelligence aspects of policy on activities in outer space.

In January 1961, immediately after taking office, President John F. Kennedy had issued a directive that all public statements by generals and senior Defense Department officials were to be cleared in advance. ISA and G/PM were the clearing offices, and inasmuch as many generals made speeches or wrote articles about the Soviet threat, I found myself reviewing dozens of such statements and "censoring" them to ensure that they did not contravene policy (for example, by seeming to threaten preventive war). In retrospect, I am surprised that there were no major controversies or leakage to the press.

In October 1961 Deputy Secretary of Defense Roswell Gilpatric made a dramatic speech killing the "missile gap" once and for all. He underlined our strategic superiority by noting that even in retaliation after receiving a surprise attack by the other side, the United States could respond with a strike of at least equal power. The speech had been decided upon by President Kennedy, Secretary of Defense Robert McNamara, and Secretary of State Dean Rusk; they concluded that such a statement would be authoritative but less provocative if given by the deputy secretary of defense rather than by the president, or secretary of defense, or chairman of the Joint Chiefs of Staff. The speech was drafted in the office of the secretary of defense and ISA, but I also participated and cleared it for the State Department. (One of the principal Defense drafters, by the way, was Dan Ellsberg, later notorious for leaking the Vietnam "Pentagon Papers.")

Among the changes brought about by the new administration was abandonment of an annual overall document spelling out U.S. national security policy. Such documents had been prepared annually under the Truman and Eisenhower administrations ever since NSC-68 in 1950, since 1953 termed "Basic National Security Policy" (BNSP). Each spent about a year in gestation and constant revision before being issued, and it is true that a great deal of effort was devoted to this general policy guidance—and also that it was framed sufficiently broadly that most issues of policy remained to be hammered out ad hoc in the NSC machinery. At first, the general assumption was that preparing a new BNSP would be a priority task of the new administration. The White House NSC staff, ISA in Defense, and the Policy Planning staff and G/PM in State all contributed (not always in a coordinated manner). In the final analysis, however, the president decided (with support from the national security adviser, McGeorge Bundy) that such a paper would not give "answers" to policy issues that he would face, but could deprive him of desirable flexibility in resolving them. In short, a basic policy paper was not necessary and might be unduly constraining. Accordingly, no BNSP was issued and after 1962 the idea faded away.

There were a number of policy areas where I soon became involved. Before turning to them, I might note one example of a small initiative I sought to take but was unable to push through the internal "system" at State. For five years there had been a hiatus in direct high-level U.S.-Soviet military contacts, the last having been a visit by General Nathan Twining, then chief of staff of the U.S. Air Force, to the USSR in 1956. Various things had put off a return invitation by the United States, beginning with the Soviet suppression of the Hungarian uprising in November 1956 and continuing through the U-2 incident and recurrent Berlin crises. By 1962, as the Berlin crisis seemed to be cooling, I thought it would be a good idea to resume such high-level military contacts. ISA for Defense was in favor; so were some of the leading Soviet affairs experts, including the assistant secretary for European affairs, Foy Kohler. But in preparing a draft telegram to our ambassador in Moscow (Tommy Thompson), a usual procedure for dealing with a minor policy issue, I had neglected to clear it with the department officer most directly responsible, the head of the Soviet desk (the Office of Soviet Affairs, EUR/SOV), Malcolm Toon. I had not meant to circumvent him, but when I had an opportunity to discuss it with his boss, Ambassador Kohler, I did so, and Kohler signed off. I thought that was sufficient. But Toon objected violently, both because he had not been approached first, and because he opposed all such other-than-embassy contacts. Kohler gave in, and my little attempt to resume such contacts died. I had learned something about the way the State Department worked.

Incidentally, my years in the State Department in the 1960s gave me the opportunity to get to know much better the whole generation of senior Cold War–era Soviet experts. I worked closely with Ambassadors Llewellyn (Tommy) Thompson, Charles (Chip) Bohlen, Foy Kohler, and Jacob (Jake) Beam. Even George Kennan, out of government service since 1953 (although I knew him as a consultant to CIA), had returned as ambassador to Yugoslavia, where I visited him in 1962. I had known all of them before going to State, but now had occasion to work with them. This, of course, was also true of many other officials whom I had not known before, in the first instance my boss, Ambassador U. Alexis Johnson, and including Secretary Dean Rusk and Under Secretary George Ball.

I recall one amusing incident that evokes something of the atmosphere of those Cold War years. While preparing to go to Moscow as ambassador in August 1962, Foy Kohler paid a courtesy familiarization visit to the headquarters of the Strategic Air Command (SAC) in Omaha. I accompanied him. Among the detailed briefings was one in which an Air Force colonel, with great enthusiasm, standing next to a huge detailed map of Moscow and its environs, was pointing out the sixty aim-points for detonation of nuclear and thermonuclear weapons in greater Moscow called for in the current SIOP (single integrated operations plans). Ambassador Kohler, who had been attentive but generally silent during the briefings, interjected a question that clearly reflected a different perspective: "By the way, where is the American embassy?" He could take little comfort from being shown its central location, which of course he knew very well. Two months later came the Cuban missile crisis.

Apart from outside contact with officials at Defense, especially ISA, and to some extent at CIA, I worked with members of the White House NSC staff under McGeorge Bundy, in particular with his deputy Carl Kaysen, and with Spurgeon Keeny, a survivor from the Eisenhower era now working both for the president's science adviser and the NSC staff. Although much less flamboyant and visible than his successors in the next decade, Henry Kissinger and Zbigniew Brzezinski, Mac Bundy was better able to serve not only as an adviser but also as a channel to ensure all relevant points of view reached the president.

I began to have official contact with representatives of a number of embassies in Washington, in particular those of Britain, France, Germany, and Italy, but also of other NATO countries and some neutrals. This extended to extensive social contact with these and other members of the diplomatic corps. As I shall note in a later chapter, this came to include several diplomats from the Soviet embassy. Mainly, my contacts at the office and socially were counselors of allied or friendly embassies concerned with political and political-military affairs (including arms control and alliance relations). It also included intelligence representatives (especially British and German) whom I had known when I was at CIA, and their successors.

Finally, I also had a number of regular contacts in the press corps, mainly among correspondents covering the State Department, but also the White House and Defense Department, on a wide range of foreign policy, defense, and occasionally intelligence matters. The purpose was to help provide better informed and responsible commentary without disclosing confidential information. In one case, I realized I had said too much about a forthcoming European security diplomatic initiative to a *New York Times* correspondent. So I went to the assistant secretary in charge of public affairs and press relations and told him that the correspondent had the information (I did *not* say I had been the one to give it to him). He asked me to contact the correspondent and see if I could persuade him to hold off while the timing was sensitive in exchange for which I could fill him in with more background information on the matter. I did, and he agreed; the untimely leak was averted, and I had authorization retroactively for what I had told him and even more. I was thus able to recoup from a slip on my own part.

Very early in my State Department service, when I mentioned to a senior official an interesting conversation I had had with a correspondent of a leading weekly news magazine, he warned me that the journal in question was known to wire its stories in detail, with the names of sources, to its New York headquarters for rewrite—and these transmissions were intercepted and monitored, so I should be careful what I said. Occasionally, I learned something of interest from a correspondent, usually something he had learned elsewhere and was floating to seek confirmation or elaboration from me or others. In one case, I had a contact who proved to be a source of worthwhile intelligence. A writer for a major American news magazine, himself of Eastern European origin, he had excellent contacts with an Eastern European embassy and learned not only about their thinking but also what that embassy learned from its contacts with the Soviet embassy. I always passed this information along to our own intelligence, as well as to appropriate State Department officials, indicating my source and as precisely as possible the original source.

Bridging the period from my service in ONE to the State Department, the principal foreign policy issue was the Berlin crisis of 1961. An interagency Berlin task force met frequently throughout the year. I had attended some of its meetings as a CIA observer in the summer of 1961, so when I continued to do so representing G/PM after September at first some did not even realize my changed role. My own direct part in the Berlin contingency planning was limited, although some colleagues in G/PM became extensively involved. Soon after arriving in State, I prepared a study, titled "The Role of Military Demonstrations and Preparations in the Politico-Military Confrontation over Berlin," which I sent to Ambassador Johnson. I quickly learned that such an analytical study, thirteen single-spaced pages and not geared to any action recommendation, even if cogent, was not very useful. G/PM was an action staff for an action undersecretary.

Although most of the work of the Berlin task force and its committees had been geared to contingency planning to deal with Soviet pressures, one committee was established to consider possible East-West security negotiations that might emerge in the course of efforts to resolve the problem. Gerard Smith, a former assistant secretary for policy planning in the Eisenhower administration, was named to chair this committee. Adrian (Butch) Fisher, the deputy director of the new Arms Control and Disarmament Agency (ACDA), was its deputy head. The Department of Defense was also represented. I was the senior State Department representative. Some of our studies may have contributed to later thinking on this subject. Our work at the time, however, was peripheral as the crisis wound down throughout 1962.

The Berlin crisis was at its peak in the months after the tough exchange between President Kennedy and Khrushchev at their Vienna summit meeting in June 1961, through the building of the Berlin Wall in August, and a near clash of American and Soviet tanks at a border checkpoint in October. The confrontation of 1961 stemmed from an initiative by Soviet leader Khrushchev in November 1958 and did not really taper off until after the Cuban missile crisis of late 1962. From 1958 through 1962 the Soviet leaders sought to rid themselves of the anomaly of a Western political and military presence in the enclave of West Berlin, deep inside East Germany beyond the Iron Curtain. Indeed, Stalin had tried in an unsuccessful blockade of West Berlin in 1948–49 both to prevent the consolidation of West Germany and to rid himself of the Western presence in Berlin (what Khrushchev would later refer to in his picturesque way as "a bone in our throat" that had to be removed). Then the United States had mounted a remarkably successful air-lift of supplies to sustain West Berlin. Now, from 1958 to 1962, the Soviet threat was to turn over authority to the East Germans, in an attempt to bol-ster their authority and force the West to recognize the satellite German Democratic Republic. Khrushchev also pressed for a neutral (and neutralized) "free city" of West Berlin, with all Western military presence and political authority removed.

In the first phase of the crisis, from late 1958 through 1960, my colleagues and I at ONE in CIA estimated, correctly, that Khrushchev would back down; the State Department intelligence staff were more alarmist. In 1961, rather than a continuing standoff, both sides embarked on the more active demon-stration of politico-military determination that I have noted. Finally, the key step in resolving the crisis came with the Soviet decision to build "the Wall" sealing off the enclave in West Berlin from the East. If they couldn't expel the West from Berlin, at least they could quarantine its effect on the East and stem the costly growing torrent of East German emigration.

Most policy officials had seen the Soviet instigation of the Berlin crisis as an offensive political initiative designed not only to force the West to pull back from West Berlin, but to divide and weaken seriously the Western alliance. Every decision to take (or even contemplate) strong Western measures would tend to divide those allies and publics unwilling to take the risks from those who were prepared to do so. Moreover, to whatever extent the West did not resist and did curb its role or withdraw from Berlin, that would weaken Western European confidence in the resolve and efficacy of the NATO alliance and the American commitment.

There was, no doubt, some validity to that reading of the Soviet aim. Some intelligence estimators held similar views. Many in the intelligence estimating business, however, had a much more sophisticated picture of Soviet motivations. We had learned over the years that Soviet policymakers held a long-term perspective and pursued a strategy that included maximum, but also minimum, objectives and encompassed defensive as well as offensive aims. The maximum objectives, including offensive as well as subsuming defensive aims, were clear: they were reflected in the stated Soviet position and could be deduced from it. The real question, for intelligence estimators and policymakers, was to determine the minimum or core Soviet objectives and whether they could be reconciled with our own core objectives. The Wall answered the key question in the Berlin crisis: the core Soviet objective was the defensive interest in preventing the collapse of East Germany and weakening of the Soviet bloc in Eastern Europe, not the offensive aim of forcing the West out of West Berlin and weakening the Western NATO bloc.

The Berlin crisis lingered on as an issue through 1961 and 1962, and even thereafter on a back burner until a formal four-power agreement on Berlin was signed in 1971 as part of the creation of a structure of détente in Europe. Remaining Soviet hopes for an enhancement of their precarious standing in the strategic balance by the installation of strategic missiles in Cuba had, however, been dashed by the complete failure of that attempt in late 1962, effectively ending the Berlin crisis.

Before the Berlin crisis was completely defused, however, initial steps toward reducing tensions in the fall of 1961, above all Khrushchev's withdrawal in October of his ultimatum deadline for a change in the status of West Berlin, were suddenly overtaken by an inexplicable sharp rise in tension over a confrontation at a sector-crossing checkpoint on the border of West and East Berlin, known as "Checkpoint Charlie." On October 27, after several days of escalating U.S. rebuffs to East German attempts to get American officials to show identification documents before entering East Berlin (thus indirectly acknowledging East German sovereignty, rather than Soviet occupation authority, there) ten U.S. M-48 tanks took up position at Checkpoint Charlie, soon followed by ten Soviet tanks taking up facing position on the eastern side. This was the culmination of several days escalation of actions on both sides and the face-off of the Soviet and American tanks, with guns uncovered, the first (and only) such direct confrontation of U.S. and Soviet troops. Yet inexplicably, less than twenty-four hours later, the ten Soviet tanks withdrew, followed soon by reciprocal withdrawal of the U.S. tanks.

The Berlin crisis arose from what one may term "objective factors"—the fact that West Berlin was an anomalous Western enclave well to the east of the Iron Curtain, precipitating a clash of concrete interests of the Soviet Union and the West. The confrontation of armed tanks facing off at Checkpoint Charlie is, however, an excellent illustration of how "subjective factors" such as differing perceptions and beliefs of the two sides also contributed to tensions—and could even have precipitated war. We in Washington at the time saw the actions of the East German police at the checkpoint as an attempt by Moscow to squeeze us on indirect recognition of GDR (East German) sovereignty in East Berlin—which in turn was a threat to West Berlin because our presence and authority in West Berlin, and Soviet (not East German) authority in East Berlin, and reciprocal access to all of the city, derived from residual occupation rights of the wartime allies. Our tanks were there only to back up our rights to enter East Berlin, if necessary by breaking through any physical barrier that might be placed in the access road. The arrival of Soviet tanks was a threat to respond by force if we did so. The Soviet withdrawal of their tanks meant that the Soviet leadership had understood our determination and, recognizing the risk and its responsibility for having triggered the whole affair, had decided to back down. That was the way the whole affair was seen in the West for more than a quarter of a century.

Now, with access to much more information both on the background of the U.S. actions and especially of the Soviet actions, a very different picture has emerged. First of all, the Soviet leaders had not instigated the East Germans to press us on presenting credentials; it was an East German initiative to try to keep alive their quest for recognition. Second, when the United States began to bring up tanks to the border, including some adapted with bulldozer attachments, the Soviet leaders believed the United States was preparing to challenge the Wall by force, and they therefore sent in Soviet tanks to stand off that threat. The reason they believed that was not simply suspicion; Soviet military intelligence had observed and even photographed similarly equipped U.S. tanks in a secluded wooded area of West Berlin practicing techniques to break down a replica section of the Wall—an exercise undertaken on his own authority, and without anyone in Washington even aware, by General Lucius Clay, who had been in Germany in 1948 and had now been sent back to Berlin by President Kennedy as a symbol of our steadfastness. Finally, the withdrawal of the Soviet tanks, followed so quickly by reciprocal U.S. withdrawal, was not a Soviet retreat but a carefully prearranged action requested of Khrushchev by President Kennedy through an established unofficial channel (a Soviet military intelligence officer under cover in the Soviet embassy in Washington, Georgy Bol'shakov). That part of the story was of course known to the president and his brother Robert (the intermediary with Bol'shakov), but apparently to no one else in the administration. From the Soviet standpoint, the Soviet dispatch of tanks had deterred a *U.S.* challenge; the *United States* had backed down from plans to try to break down the Wall. Each side thus believed it had prevailed in the confrontation, and that the other had given up a significant offensive challenge. There were reciprocal, and potentially very dangerous, misperceptions. What if a trigger-happy or careless gunner on either side had opened fire? Even apart from the dangerous dynamics of such a situation on the spot, the leaders in both countries believed the other to be responsible for an offensive move that required a determined rebuff. Fortunately, that kind of direct armed confrontation was rare, and in this particular case was resolved, albeit without either side being aware of the parallel misperceptions.[1]

The Berlin crisis required us to consider possible resort to military means if needed to prevent losing our position in West Berlin. It was one of the most critical cases of the importance of politico-military inputs to policymaking in the 1960s, indeed during the Cold War.

Probably my most useful contribution to the Berlin crisis management process was a memorandum to Foy Kohler, head of the task force as well as the assistant secretary for European affairs, on January 31, 1962, outlining "Some Thoughts on Soviet Responses to Western Military Measures in the Berlin Crisis." I expressed concern over risks in the implementation of military contingency plans to meet Soviet pressure on Western access to Berlin with respect to three key elements: definition of objectives, selection of means, and communication of intentions.

> Our initial objective would be clear: to end any Soviet/GDR interference with our basic exercise of rights of access to West Berlin. The problem arises, it seems to me, in the course of implementation of any major course of action designed to serve that objective. As we undertake more and more vigorous and extensive local military demonstrations of determination, and as the Soviets meet them, not only does the level of confrontation escalate, but the *stakes* will escalate too, as each side commits its political capital in the form of prestige. Hence the *objectives* will be transformed in the course of actions and counteractions.
>
> There may also be inducements, or pressures, of other kinds leading to changes in objectives. Suppose the East Germans, or even other satellite peoples too, did rise in rebellion during a non-nuclear clash in East Germany. Would we be content to stand with our original objective of restoring the *status quo ante* on access?
>
> Finally, our objectives on maintaining access to, and even presence in, West Berlin above all serve the more fundamental aim of preserving the Western alliance. Suppose the actual implementation—even successfully—of our measures to compel an end to interference with access

1. I discovered and drew together the new information on this crisis from research and interviews in Moscow in the late 1980s and published it on the thirtieth anniversary. See Raymond L. Garthoff, "Berlin 1961: The Record Corrected," *Foreign Policy*, no. 84 (Fall 1991), pp. 142–56. Later, I published a revised and expanded account, "The American-Soviet Tank Confrontation at Checkpoint Charlie," in *Mysteries of the Cold War*, edited by Steven Cimbala, pp. 73–87 (Ashgate, 1999).

open up such deep fears in the West as to damage or destroy the alliance? This would be like succeeding in a contest to stay under water longer than anyone else, but at the cost of drowning.

Turning to the problem of selecting means, I emphasized the need for continuing *political* determination of any use of military means. Thus

> It is absolutely necessary to state the military means with a precision that cannot be derived from such terms as "expand scope as necessary" (as necessary to do what?), or "as consistent with the objective of achieving a military decision," or "as required to defeat the enemy," or even "as necessary to protect large forces." Only by making very clear the relationship between various military courses of action and the political aim can the suitability and effectiveness of the military means be judged. In *no* case should the local *initiative* in expansion of theater of hostilities or in initiating the use of nuclear weapons be left to conventional military criteria of "requirements" or "military necessity." This is important in terms of contingency planning guidance, as well as being of paramount importance in terms of decision and action in the event.

Finally, I drew attention to the problem of effectively communicating our purpose and intentions.

> Perhaps the most difficult and critical problem is the communication of our positions, and intentions, to the Soviet leaders. When we decide upon specific objectives and undertake the means designed to achieve them, the underlying premise is that we can induce, persuade or compel the other side to agree or acquiesce. If he fails to understand what we want, he can't comply. Theoretically, he might mistakenly give up more than we had thought he would and therefore had sought, but this is rather unlikely. If he misinterprets our objective and believes it to be less demanding than in fact it is, he will fail to do enough; if he believes our demands are higher than they really are, he may feel he has no satisfactory choice except to refuse even at high risk or cost.
>
> In other words, the problem of *avoiding* communication of an intention we *don't* have is perhaps the most dangerous. For example, suppose we were to launch a non-nuclear campaign on the order of several divisions into East Germany, not along the autobahn, perhaps with air operations extending all over East Germany and even into Poland and Czechoslovakia. Disturbances in East Germany might at the same time be encouraged by the West. What is our purpose? It would be to persuade the Soviets of our determination not to permit them or the GDR to impose conditions on our access to West Berlin. This does *not* touch

Soviet vital interests. But to the Soviet leaders, it would probably be seen as an effort to use the Berlin crisis as a wedge for a campaign to dislodge them from East Germany. This *would* touch their vital interests. Consequently, their reactions would probably not be the ones we desired, but rather a step up of their own military operations—nonnuclear, locally in Germany—to defeat the Western action.

I noted that there were occasions when there could be disadvantages to communicating our intentions too precisely, but military actions and reactions would not fall in that category. I also noted the problem of changing our message in cases where we *did* change our objective.

I supported the general concept of our Berlin military contingency planning of graduated increases in commitment of force, but emphasized the need to make clear our limited objectives as well as our resolve to meet them. I did question some of the higher levels of military action contemplated in the third phase of NATO's "Live Oak" Berlin contingency military plans, which involved air and land strikes into East Germany beyond the autobahn route to Berlin. I noted that while such moves might be *militarily* more feasible than an escalation of forces on the autobahn, they were *politically* more ambiguous and disadvantageous because "they blur the message we want to get to the Soviet leaders. The difference is less one of the magnitude of an operation than of its evident relationship to the cause and to the objective." My purpose was to emphasize the need for "the very closest review of all the specific plans and general guidances for Phase III operations to judge their compatibility with our basic policy objectives."

I also drew upon some of Penkovsky's materials (without directly referring to them) in noting the danger of possible Soviet misinterpretation of NATO high-alert status as a sign of impending Western initiation of war.

In retrospect, it is clear that despite all our attempts to preserve secrecy, multiple Soviet intelligence penetrations in NATO and NATO capitals had made them aware that we *would* react forcefully if necessary. This no doubt contributed greatly to Khrushchev's decision to back down from his offensive threats against West Berlin, once the Wall had dealt with his principal defensive concern and when Western determination had been demonstrated, and it illustrates the seldom appreciated fact that a failure of counterintelligence may, unexpectedly, have some positive consequences.

The greatest test of will and most dangerous crisis came in Cuba a year later, when Khrushchev deployed nuclear missiles in Cuba. That confrontation is the subject of a later chapter. The successful outcome of that crisis headed off a renewed Berlin crisis as well.

From the outset the Kennedy administration was also greatly concerned about a major Soviet challenge of a less direct kind: communist insurgencies in the Third World. According to an official present at a meeting with Kennedy after his inauguration, one of the new president's first questions was "What are we doing about guerrilla warfare?"[2] Following his first National Security Council (NSC) meeting, at which the issue was discussed, the second national security action memorandum (NSAM) instructed the secretary of defense to look into increasing counter-guerrilla resources. During the election campaign Kennedy had criticized the Eisenhower administration for failure to maintain a range of conventional as well as nuclear forces capable of "flexible response," including capabilities to deal with so-called brush-fire wars and communist-inspired insurgencies.[3]

Soviet leader Nikita Khrushchev had chosen the very eve of the advent of the new U.S. administration to deliver a speech on January 6, 1961, that seemed to promise stepped-up Soviet support for what he termed "wars of national liberation" such as in Cuba, Vietnam, and Algeria. Not mentioned by Khrushchev in his speech, but given considerable weight by President Eisenhower in a discussion with his successor, was renewed fighting in Laos. The former Belgian Congo had been in turmoil for a year. And, of course, Castro's Cuba was a bone in *our* throat. And Khrushchev seemed to be saying he would challenge us more widely. Such wars, he said, were just and were inevitable, and communists must support such wars of national liberation "wholeheartedly."

What Kennedy and his advisers (except Ambassador Thompson) did not understand was that the *more* important message in Khrushchev's speech, and indeed I later learned the reason he timed it for the incoming administration, was that *war* must be prevented, not only general nuclear war, but even local, limited conventional wars involving the great powers. "National liberation wars" and "popular uprisings" were a different matter, he held, because as indigenous actions they could not be prevented from outside, and moreover should not be interfered with. He therefore embraced them with "wholehearted support," although without promise of direct assistance, as the least he could do—and he felt compelled to show at least that much support because he was under fire from China in a major struggle within the world communist movement for not doing more to aid the advance of communism in the world. Khrushchev did believe there was a "progressive" revolutionary process under way in the world, but he was not throwing down the gauntlet in a Soviet

2. Roger Hilsman, *To Move a Nation: The Politics of Foreign Policy in the Administration of John F. Kennedy* (Doubleday, 1967), p. 413.

3. For useful reviews of Kennedy's intent, and the activities of his administration, see Douglas S. Blaufarb, *The Counterinsurgency Era: U.S. Doctrine and Performance, 1950 to the Present* (Free Press/Macmillan, 1977); and D. Michael Shafer, *Deadly Paradigms: The Failure of U.S. Counterinsurgency Policy* (Princeton University Press, 1988).

politico-military challenge to the United States and its president. It was a classic case of Khrushchev sending the opposite message from what he had intended to convey. We now know that Khrushchev indeed felt rebuffed by Kennedy and was disappointed.[4]

President Kennedy did not ignore Khrushchev's speech; to the contrary, he had it circulated to senior policy advisers and advised them to read it "and learn." But the message he took from it was that Moscow would aggressively push revolutionary activity and perhaps local wars in the Third World, and we must meet the challenge.

Throughout 1961 and 1962 President Kennedy and several of his chief advisers, in particular his brother Robert, and Walt Rostow first at the NSC staff and later heading the policy planning staff in the State Department, pressed ahead on many fronts. General Maxwell Taylor, brought back from retirement as a special military adviser to the president in June 1961, even earlier in April after the Bay of Pigs debacle had been charged with looking into requirements for limited and local wars, as well as counterinsurgency.

There was, initially, some confusion over whether the Soviet Union was likely to involve its own forces, and also some desire to broaden the problem to include "limited wars." I first became involved in this whole matter when Roger Hilsman, the new director of the Bureau of Intelligence and Research (INR) at State and a colleague from Yale (as well as a West Point graduate and wartime OSS guerrilla team leader in Burma), was asked by Secretary Dean Rusk in the first weeks in office to prepare a study of limited war in Soviet policy. Roger was of course well aware of my work in this field and decided I was the best qualified person to prepare such a study, so he arranged to "borrow" my services from ONE to prepare the study. I submitted a relatively short study (eight single-spaced pages) titled "Limited War in Soviet Policy" and also attached a fifty-page historical analysis I had earlier prepared for an academic conference on military instruments and influences in Russian diplomacy. Hilsman sent my papers to the secretary and other officers in the department on February 20, saying that INR "fully subscribed" to my findings.

I will cite here a few passages that provide the gist of some of my general conclusions. First was the general Soviet attitude toward any use of military force.

> The most basic consideration is the relation of limited war to the ideological and political worldview of the Soviet leaders, and hence to overall Soviet strategy. Warfare in general, and forms of limited war in particular, are regarded as one of many instruments of policy. The

---

4. On this point, and for a good overall account of U.S.-Soviet relations in the Kennedy years, see Michael Beschloss, *The Crisis Years: Kennedy and Khrushchev, 1960–1963* (Edward Burlingame Books–Harper Collins, 1991), pp. 60–61.

permissibility of use of this instrument depends upon calculation of relative advantage in any specific situation. Communist ideology does impart hostility, expansive impulses, and unlimited goals to Soviet policy; it does not, however, impel the Soviet leaders toward war as the primary means of satisfying these objectives. While it certainly does not erect any artificial obstacles against decisions for use of military instruments, the very existence of an expectation of eventual victory on the basis of concord with an inevitable movement of social and economic revolutionary forces of history does tend to militate against assumption of avoidable great risks and costs in the conduct of policy.

I noted, and possibly overstated, the impact that the changing strategic balance would have on Soviet thinking (although I believe it accurately portrayed Khrushchev's thinking in 1961).

The most significant development in recent years has been the Soviet emergence from strategic inferiority in intercontinental striking power. Soviet policy is constrained by the awesome consequences of general war resulting from any serious miscalculation. At the same time, however, the Soviet leaders see the most significant aspect of the new strategic situation as a neutralization of the U.S. ability to deter the bloc from unwanted actions through the threat of U.S. nuclear strength and the bloc's own growing possibilities of deterring U.S. military intervention to halt or reverse trends in the underdeveloped countries seen as favorable to the bloc. Even though the present strategic balance by no means entirely frees their hands, they believe that it does tend to bind ours.

I noted that Khrushchev's speech of January 6 had acknowledged that local wars could occur, but should be averted. As I observed, he had distinguished as a different category "national liberation wars" and "popular uprisings" which, in contrast to general and local wars, he characterized as inevitable and as deserving communist support. I noted the "Soviet sensitivity to being 'outflanked on the left'" and that the speech was an "attempt to clear themselves of Chinese Communist charges that they were against Communist revolutions and unwilling to support them." In contrast to Soviet aversion to direct involvement in local wars, I suggested that

when particular combinations of circumstances seem favorable the Soviets will probably incite or exploit local situations of unrest, violence, or civil war with material aid or even intervention covertly or by proxy. ... By and large the Soviets will probably not initiate limited wars themselves, but in instigating or covertly abetting local wars or revolutions by others they place on the West the onus, and risks, in converting internal or local hostilities into an international limited war. . . . But if the West intervenes in any local war in which the Bloc has an interest the Communists may feel more free to "match" the Western involvement than to have assumed the initiative in overt intervention.

In addition to emphasizing the critical importance of local vulnerabilities, I concluded my analysis with what amounted to an endorsement of the administration's call for enhanced military capabilities for flexible response on a global basis: "Soviet resort to limited war in any given situation is most likely to be deterred if they see sufficient U.S. and other Free World military strengths suitable for effectively waging limited warfare."[5]

One rarely knows whether such memoranda have any effect on policy-making, or indeed any effect at all. In this instance, I do know of one indirect effect my paper had. I was contacted in May at ONE by General Maxwell Taylor, then military adviser to the president, and when we met he wanted to discuss with me further some of the historical cases of Soviet involvement in limited wars, including those with Japan on the Manchurian and Mongolian borders in 1938 and 1939. He was pursuing thoroughly his mandate from President Kennedy to examine requirements for limited wars as well as counterinsurgency.

The main effort, however, was placed on both political and military preparations for counterinsurgency. G/PM was the focal point within the State Department for staff work on the problem, in the first instance to back up Ambassador Johnson. After a year of study, National Security Action Memorandum No. 124 (NSAM 124) on January 18, 1962, established a high-level "Special Group (Counterinsurgency)," or Special Group (CI), chaired by General Taylor and including Attorney General Robert Kennedy, Deputy Secretary of Defense Roswell Gilpatric, Deputy Under Secretary of State U. Alexis Johnson, Director of Central Intelligence John McCone, the chairman of the Joint Chiefs of Staff, General Lyman Lemnitzer, National Security Adviser McGeorge Bundy, and the directors of AID and USIA. The core membership (including Ambassador Johnson for State) was the same as for the longstanding Special Group on covert intelligence operations (also known at various times as the 5412 Committee, the 303 Committee, and the 40 Committee). The core membership also overlapped with a "Special Group (Augmented)" that had been established in November 1961 to monitor the most important covert operation, "Mongoose," generating subversive actions against Cuba. The Special Group (CI) was intended primarily to set overall policy, but also to ensure recognition throughout the U.S. government that

---

5. "Limited War in Soviet Policy," February 17, 1961, pp. 1–8; enclosure to memorandum with the same title from INR-Roger Hilsman to the Secretary, February 20, 1961 (secret; now declassified).

subversive insurgency (defined to include "wars of liberation") was recognized as "a major form of politico-military conflict equal in importance to conventional warfare." The NSAM explicitly directed that the Special Group (CI) ensure that organization, training, and doctrine not only of the armed forces but also of the "political, economic, intelligence, military aid, and informational programs" conducted abroad by State, Defense, AID, USIA, and CIA all reflect the new requirements for effective counterinsurgency. In practice, this generated a great deal of activity, mostly of doubtful value. Thousands of military officers went through special counterinsurgency courses, as did hundreds of senior and middle-level State Department and other government officials. The Foreign Service Institute instituted a six-week course for forty to seventy officials, repeated eight to ten times a year. This continued throughout the Kennedy administration and then rapidly tapered off, although it was not ended until 1971.

Within the armed forces, there was considerable veiled resistance to diluting traditional military training and priorities, although the Special Forces (now dubbed the "Green Berets") were greatly increased in number and prestige. Some "counterinsurgency training" usefully covered greater attention to mobility and other virtues of the parallel increased attention to "flexible response" conventional warfare training and preparation.

I had very little to do with this whole program, and even evaded the special six-week seminar on grounds of other pressing duties (an excuse that many others, mostly unsuccessfully, also sought to invoke). The whole counterinsurgency concept was a good idea gotten out of hand. To the extent that it drew attention to the problems of Third World nation-building and vulnerabilities to subversion, it may have been useful. For some in the military, it increased awareness of the need for flexibility. But the emphasis was often not on the Third World target but on Moscow and Peiping (as we persisted in calling Beijing). Concern over possible Soviet and Chinese exploitation of opportunities was appropriate, but overdrawn to the point that it tended to displace the real indigenous causes of insurgency. The big test came in Vietnam, and our counterinsurgency conditioning since 1961 may have done real harm by encouraging the belief that all we had to do was work hard enough at counterinsurgency, meeting the symptoms rather than the causes of revolutionary change. The officer in charge of the counterinsurgency policy coordination in G/PM and staff director of the Special Group (CI), Charles Maechling Jr., several years later wrote a severely critical review of the whole program.[6]

6. Charles Maechling Jr., "Our Internal Defense Policy—A Reappraisal," *Foreign Service Journal* (January 1969), pp. 19–21, 27.

Parallel to, and inspired by, the official attention to counterinsurgency, there was also some attention elsewhere in the foreign affairs establishment. The venerable Council on Foreign Relations conducted a study group on the subject in 1962. I was a member of that group and delivered a talk titled "Unconventional Warfare in Communist Strategy," later published in *Foreign Affairs*. I emphasized communist, and especially Soviet, flexibility in waging unconventional warfare. Although this meant Soviet support for insurgencies in some cases, I argued that based on their experience "the Soviet leaders generally prefer the use of subversion, or other non-violent means, to the use of guerrilla war, because the seizure of power by indigenous revolutionary forces tends to make local communist parties too independent of Moscow's control." I noted Khrushchev's statement of January 6, 1961, but cautioned that Soviet support for such wars of national liberation in practice was not unqualified or universal. I believe I put the Soviet position in proper perspective (although I overestimated future Chinese communist support for such wars). I sought to deflate both the idea that the communists had a "golden gun" in liberation wars and the idea that we could defeat them if we were just more sufficiently gung ho in meeting the challenge with our own magic counterinsurgency wand. Without putting it quite that baldly, I concluded the article by stating that:

> The future role of revolutionary guerrilla war in Communist strategy is probably more dependent on local opportunity than on anything else. . . . The most vulnerable point, then, is the local societies and polities which may be threatened. This is not a novel idea, but if our analysis of Communist thought and action brings us back to this point, we have at least discovered that there are no short cuts for either side—no basic flaws in the Communist approach, but also no secret weapons in their arsenal.[7]

My presentation was well received at the council in New York. But I don't think it had much effect in Washington, at least not on policy. It was circulated by Jeff Kitchen to George Ball, George McGhee, Walt Rostow, and Roger Hilsman. Alexis Johnson said it was "an excellent paper" and sent copies to General Maxwell Taylor and several other senior military men. Brigadier General William Y. Yarborough, commanding the U.S. Army Special Warfare Center at Fort Bragg, wrote to Alex that he had assigned it to his faculty. That was flattering. But my presentation did not do what I had hoped it would in placing the counterinsurgency issue in perspective in Washington.

Along with an exaggeration of the threat of communist insurgency around the world was a serious underestimation of the fragmentation of "World

7. Raymond L. Garthoff, "Unconventional Warfare in Communist Strategy," *Foreign Affairs*, vol. 40, no. 4 (July 1962), pp. 566–75.

Communism," and above all of what had been known as the "Sino-Soviet bloc." There was a wariness, especially among veterans of the Truman administration, over any acknowledgment of a diminution of "the Communist threat." Dean Rusk was the most prominent and influential of those who, even when recognizing the reality of the Sino-Soviet rift, underestimated its significance and consequences. He still saw Moscow and "Peiping" as inherently allies, even if now rivals and competitors for influence in the communist world.

At the same time that it embraced counterinsurgency, the Kennedy administration was giving new emphasis to building graduated deterrent capabilities, in particular conventional forces for flexible response, to deal, for example, with contingencies such as the Berlin crisis as well as possible limited wars. I had argued for this in my pre-CIA and Defense-cover writings, and welcomed it in 1961. At the same time, I became somewhat concerned at the assumption that we would be likely to face direct Soviet military challenges because of a shift in the balance of power. Too little attention was devoted to the Soviet policy of restraint from direct military engagement reflected in Khrushchev's emphasis that limited and local wars between us must be avoided, voiced in the same speech in which he had endorsed indigenous wars of national liberation. Indeed, when we did choose to engage ourselves in such a war, in Vietnam, we faced no Soviet troops but an endless requirement for more than limited American forces.

Arms control also became a factor in U.S. policymaking for the first time with the advent of the Kennedy administration. The United States and other powers had participated in disarmament negotiations for many years, and in the Eisenhower years there was negotiation toward a possible nuclear test ban. But it was the Kennedy administration that gave great impetus to a wide-ranging review conducted from March to September 1961. John J. McCloy, Republican stalwart of the eastern establishment and assistant secretary of war during World War II, just one week after the inauguration was asked by President Kennedy to examine the disarmament and arms control overall and advise the new president on policies and organization to deal with the field. From March to May nine panels of distinguished experts dealt with different aspects of the problem. For example, retired general John Hull chaired a panel on conventional arms and armed forces, in which I—borrowed from CIA—participated.

The final reports of the panels and overall report by McCloy were submitted in September (just as I transferred to the State Department). One result was the creation of the Arms Control and Disarmament Agency (ACDA), constituted as an independent agency so that it could have an independent voice of advocacy in governmental deliberations on the subject.

A Committee of Principals was established, chaired by the secretary of state, and including the secretary of defense, the director of central intelligence, the chairman of the Joint Chiefs of Staff, the director of ACDA, and the chairman of the Atomic Energy Commission. A committee of deputies was the senior working level, representing the same agencies (nominally the senior deputies to the principals, in practice often the next level), chaired by the deputy director of ACDA.

With ACDA a separate agency, the secretary of state chairing the Committee of Principals, and the State Department having many different interests in arms control and disarmament matters, some new arrangement was required in the department. G/PM was the logical touchpoint, and I was made the staff coordinator in State on all arms control affairs. I accompanied Secretary Rusk to all the Committee of Principals' meetings, as well as serving as the State Department representative at most of the deputies' meetings. It may be worth noting that as a result of the decision to center the Department of State staff responsibility for arms control matters in a politico-military office, the U.S. government went down a different path from that taken by almost all other countries, including the Soviet Union, which assigned arms control and disarmament responsibility to their respective foreign ministry offices backing up participation in the UN and other international organizations.

Of course, the parallel U.S. step, also almost unique, of creating an independent agency to have primary responsibility was even more striking. But it also made a difference in that the international organizations (IO) staffs of foreign ministries were already tied to the *international* negotiating activities they supported, while a staff like G/PM (and its later evolution into the Bureau of Politico-Military Affairs by the early 1970s) was more closely tied to balancing military and political considerations and to the *internal* interagency negotiating process and did not have the responsibility for the international negotiations that the IO staffs (and ACDA) had.[8] Of course, the IO Bureau, the Bureau of Intelligence and Research (INR), and the relevant regional bureaus of the Department of State (above all EUR/RPM handling NATO affairs, and EUR/SOV handling Soviet affairs) were also part of the process. In coordinating Department of State positions for the secretary and others in the internal policymaking process, and as part of the interagency establishment of positions and backup for negotiations, I coordinated with these and, as appropriate, other bureaus of the department. Arms control and disarmament affairs became my largest area of responsibility. Within a few years, after I left

8. In the 1950s a special assistant for atomic energy and disarmament had been named in the State Department, with a small staff, to advise the secretary on nuclear testing and other issues. In 1960 it was enlarged and called the U.S. Disarmament Administration, still within the State Department. When ACDA was established in September 1961, it absorbed the Disarmament Administration, leaving no organization in the Department of State with responsibility for arms control and disarmament matters, until I soon assumed that responsibility in G/PM.

G/PM, it was handled by a whole office; today it has a whole bureau headed by an assistant secretary of state.

The creation of ACDA in September and the working out of a comprehensive U.S. position on "general and complete" disarmament were the first tasks. But we also launched promptly into international negotiation. The important first step, incidentally, had been taken already by John McCloy in 1961, before ACDA was established or G/PM took on its role, in negotiation with a Soviet envoy (Deputy Foreign Minister Valerian Zorin) of a "joint statement of agreed principles," signed in September 1961 after four months of work, at about the same time that the McCloy panel and working groups completed their substantive and organizational recommendations. The chief value of the joint statement was its indication that perhaps at least some areas of agreement could be reached with the Soviet Union, apart from the mainly propaganda duel on general "disarmament." It also prefigured a new pattern of negotiation in which the United States and Soviet Union would often work bilaterally apart from the multilateral international negotiations.

International, multilateral negotiations were nonetheless still regarded as central, and by agreement among the many parties, a new, hopefully more productive forum than its sterile predecessor was created with neutral as well as Western and Soviet bloc representation. An Eighteen Nation Disarmament Committee (ENDC), under United Nations auspices but not part of the UN organizational system, convened in Geneva in March 1962, initially at the level of foreign ministers. The representatives of the United States and the Soviet Union were the co-chairmen of the committee. Not a great deal was accomplished, despite the unusual two-week presence of Secretary Rusk, Foreign Minister Gromyko, and the other sixteen foreign ministers, except that the new forum, and a new effort, were launched.

While Secretary Rusk and ACDA Director William Foster were in Geneva, I was responsible for one slightly embarrassing frivolity. All substantive conversations, including at dinners and similar social occasions, were written up in memcons (memorandums of conversations) and circulated for the information of others on the delegation and in Washington. As Dean Acheson once remarked, no one ever comes off second best in his memcons; there is often a tendency to remember exchanges with some bias toward one's own performance. But even apart from that tendency, there is an interesting question as to whether the understanding of each of the two sides, and still more the separately reported record, conveys properly both sides of the exchange. With that in mind, after having written up a standard memcon of a long and interesting dinner conversation that John McNaughton (Nitze's deputy for arms control) and I had had with the distinguished Polish diplomat Manfred Lachs (later to be a judge on the International Court of Justice, the World Court), I also wrote an imagined memcon as it might have been written by Lachs, giving my view of what might have been *his* perception and gloss on the same conversation, with all the trappings of a Polish document and with a note saying that this Polish memcon had been acquired surreptitiously and translated. I circulated it along with other memcons, including the real one I had written of the same conversation, but with a covering memo to hedge against a leak, stating that it was a classified American document and cross-referenced to the real Garthoff-McNaughton-Lachs memcon.

I assumed all recipients would understand the mock Lachs memcon for what it was, and almost all did. But I learned of an important exception when I was suddenly called in to see the secretary. Rusk, with ACDA Director William Foster there, handed me the mock memcon and said that Bill Foster had just brought to his attention this intriguing Polish document, and they were wondering how I had gotten it. I replied straightforwardly, before anything else could be said, that I had written it, that it was not a genuine Polish document, and that I regretted if the explanatory covering memo had been detached or was unclear. I explained why I had written it: to illustrate the difference in perceptions of the two sides and hopefully to reinforce objectivity in writing such memos. Rusk smiled, Foster looked uncomfortable, and the matter ended there.

Although the preparations for the ENDC had been under way for almost a year, and no agreements were anticipated or reached, the work leading up to the meeting had been hectic. Even in Geneva, decisions on elements of the secretary's speeches to the ENDC were sometimes reached, by Rusk or by Washington, only the night before delivery. Matters that even soon after, to say nothing of forty years later, were clearly inconsequential did not seem so to those in State, Defense, ACDA, and the White House who wrestled over whether we could use the words *general and complete disarmament* as a goal and many other equally immaterial issues.

I drafted the report that Ambassador Arthur Dean, our permanent representative to the ENDC after Rusk left, submitted to President Kennedy and to Secretary Rusk in June. I described our objectives at the negotiations as these: to protect U.S. security arrangements from any disadvantageous changes; to probe and press for any real opportunities for agreement on a basis of mutual advantage enhancing our security; and to place the U.S. position in the best light, and the Soviet position in the worst light, so far as effects on the neutral nations and general world public opinion were concerned. I said that the first of these objectives was paramount, but was only "defensive," and that the other two should be advanced as far as possible consistent with maintaining the first. I argued that we had met the first of these and would continue to do so. The second had been difficult given Soviet tactics, and was not promising, but that effort should be continued. As to the third, I believed that the United States had substantially succeeded in establishing our own readiness to seek fair agreements, and in emphasizing Soviet intransigence over verification control. (I did not, however, note that we might become less well regarded if we continued to emphasize verification controls more than disarmament objectives.)

I found that the presence of the eight nonaligned members, on balance, was favorable and had required the Soviet delegation to moderate its tactical stance and assume a more reasonable negotiating position, if not to alter its substantive position. In particular, although the United States had taken a lot of heat over resumption of nuclear testing during the conference, Soviet attempts to keep criticism directed at the United States and threats to disrupt and suspend the conference were rebuffed by the nonaligned representatives' criticism of both sides for testing and objection to any suspension of talks.

The ENDC was established, although initially both France and China declined to accept proffered seats. Eventually it was enlarged and renamed, first the Conference of the Committee on Disarmament (CCD) and later the Conference on Disarmament (CD). In some cases important multilateral agreements have been reached in the CD, and the forum has also been used for parallel bilateral and smaller multilateral contacts, as on nuclear testing.

A number of other arms control issues continued to get attention, if not yet resolution, even as the unrealistic possibility of general and complete disarmament absorbed most of the attention of the ENDC. The reality was that both the United States and the Soviet Union, and most countries, were not ready to contemplate real disarmament. Only later did some real if limited possibilities for arms limitation, and later arms reduction, become politically feasible.

9

Department of State: The Kennedy Years (II)

In its first year, the Kennedy administration had seen urgent requirements to deal with two challenges: Khrushchev's persistent pressure on West Berlin and growing Soviet-backed communist insurgencies in the Third World. The Berlin crisis spurred alliance contingency military plans, and the danger of localized conflicts led to strenuous efforts to build counterinsurgency capabilities and activities, and to the disastrous adventure of the émigré landing at the Bay of Pigs in Cuba. In terms of its own agenda, the new administration established arms control as a new instrument of policy and joined in launching new multilateral disarmament negotiations in Geneva. I have described these developments as I observed them in the preceding chapter.

The dispelling of the missile gap in revised national intelligence estimates from June 1961 to July 1962 provided a unique opportunity to review our entire politico-military strategy and requirements, particularly because the new satellite reconnaissance information could provide greatly improved intelligence on all elements of the Soviet military forces.

At an NSC meeting on July 10, 1962, a new national intelligence estimate of Soviet strategic capabilities for the next five years was discussed. It reflected the new consensus of the intelligence community on lower levels of Soviet intercontinental ballistic missiles (ICBMs) existing at the time and expected to be deployed than in earlier estimates, although it also noted expected improvements in overall Soviet capabilities in the coming years. At the meeting, President Kennedy requested a special high-level review of the implications of the new intelligence for American defense and foreign policy. A special interdepartmental committee was established, chaired by Ambassador U. Alexis

Johnson, with three working groups: one reviewing U.S. defense programs, chaired by Paul Nitze; one reviewing Soviet political and military policy, chaired by Ambassador Chip Bohlen; and one on intelligence, chaired by Sherman Kent of ONE. I was named executive secretary of the special committee, charged with overseeing the drafting of its report, and served on all three working groups.

On August 23 Secretary of State Dean Rusk submitted to the president the "Report on Implications for U.S. Foreign and Defense Policy of Recent Intelligence Estimates," signed also by Secretary of Defense Robert S. McNamara, Director of Central Intelligence John A. McCone, and Chairman of the Joint Chiefs of Staff General Lyman L. Lemnitzer.[1]

The report confirmed that planned U.S. defense programs were sufficient and that the new intelligence did not require any change in defense and foreign policy. Having served that reassuring function, the report had also served its purpose and faded from attention. At the time it was seen as a highly successful review and report, and I was proud of my role.

In retrospect, and in self-criticism as the principal drafter, I think the review failed to take an important opportunity to look beyond the minimal finding that we were doing enough and did not need to change our policies and programs. We failed to consider whether we were doing too much; whether a U.S. strategic buildup based on what we already knew then to have been grossly inflated estimates of Soviet strength and buildup should be cut back, or other policy adjustments made. Alternative policies were not debated; no disadvantages were seen in being stronger than we had thought, and any significant cutback would surely have been fiercely resisted in the Pentagon and would have become a political issue. Thus the more refined, more confident, and less threatening intelligence estimates served to confirm, rather than to challenge, the defense programs and policies established on the basis of much more threatening earlier estimates.

Our report did not highlight the fact that the United States, clearly superior in strategic forces in 1962, would *increase* its superiority throughout the five-year period of the estimate. It did not, therefore, consider the related questions as to whether and how the United States should seek to take advan-

---

1. Memorandum for the President, Subject: *Report on Implications for U.S. Foreign and Defense Policy of Recent Intelligence Estimates,* August 23, 1962 (top secret-limited distribution [now declassified]). The text of the main report is given in *Foreign Relations of the United States, 1961–1963,* vol. 8, *National Security Policy* (Government Printing Office, 1996), pp. 355–78, and see pp. 343–44, 349–51 and 379–80. The full text accompanies an analysis I prepared twenty years later; see Raymond L. Garthoff, *Intelligence Assessment and Policymaking: A Decision Point in the Kennedy Administration* (Brookings, 1984). In 1985 this study was given the National Intelligence Study Center's award for the best scholarly monograph on intelligence in 1984.

tage of that situation, which was bound to be ephemeral, either by placing pressure on the Soviet Union—or by using our strength as the foundation for diplomatic initiatives for reciprocal arms control or even political accommodation under circumstances where we could afford generosity. Nor did it consider that an American military program that increased U.S. strategic superiority could affect Soviet military programs (and political assessments) in ways adverse to our interests. The policymakers' tendency was, instead, to be relieved at the passing of the imagined missile gap and content that it would not recur during the period of their responsibility for policy. Yet even in that context the report was more concerned over whether the Soviet leaders would be more bold as their strategic capabilities increased, rather than on how they would react to the prospect of increasing American superiority— and its pursuit by the U.S. government. In short, as one looks back to the so-called golden age of American strategic superiority, it is clear that at the time we did not really know what to *do* with it.

Not once did the report refer either to the promises, or the pitfalls, of détente—either as a possible American policy from a position of strength, or as a possible Soviet (or European) policy. Nor did it refer to arms control as a possible contributing element in American policy.

The report, incidentally, was the first coordinated interagency study of Soviet or U.S. policy undertaken by the Kennedy administration, following only a few months after the president had decided to forego a basic national security policy paper. The report did provide reassurance to the administration on the eve of what would be the most trying crisis of the Cold War—the Cuban missile crisis, just two months later.

There was, however, increasing recognition that American superiority in the long run was transitory and that we needed to use this time of strength to prepare to accommodate an inexorable shift toward strategic parity between the United States and the Soviet Union. In particular, this was seen as meaning that we should modify the strategic concept and thinking of the NATO alliance. There was also recognition, although with less clear understanding, that we should reexamine our overall European policy. Least clear and least prominent was our policy interest in Eastern Europe. I shall, nonetheless, briefly turn in that direction inasmuch as I was to some extent directly involved.

The presence of foreign ministers in Geneva for two weeks in March 1962 for the opening of the disarmament talks provided the occasion for a round of courtesy bilateral meetings. In some cases, such as the meetings of Secretary Rusk with foreign ministers of the Eastern European "satellite" governments present, it was an unusual or even a first meeting. Assistant Secretary for European Affairs Foy Kohler accompanied the secretary in these meetings, as did I as "note-taker," subsequently writing up the "memcons" (memorandums of conversations) which form part of the record. (I also, unexpectedly, had to serve as interpreter—from Russian—of the meeting with the Bulgarian foreign minister.) Although nothing of great importance was discussed, these meetings (two with Polish Foreign Minister Adam Rapacki, and one each with Romanian Foreign Minister Corneliu Manescu, Czechoslovak Foreign Minister Vaclav David, and Bulgarian Foreign Minister Karlo Lukanov) were of some interest. Disarmament was of course discussed in all these meetings, but only within standard terms. Berlin was also discussed in most of them, with Secretary Rusk emphasizing our resolve to remain in West Berlin (so firmly that Rapacki seemed shaken). Rusk and Rapacki also discussed German reunification, with the Polish minister making clear that his government and, in his view, most Western governments too, were opposed in principle to German reunification even apart from the differing sociopolitical structures and alliances of the two German states. In this discussion, incidentally, in arguing that Moscow was pushing expansive aims, Rusk cited Khrushchev's speech of January 6, 1961. Rapacki countered that the real pursuit of peaceful coexistence was the main change in post-Stalin Soviet policy. Rusk and Lukanov, apart from the topical issues, discussed improving U.S.-Bulgarian relations, which the Bulgarians clearly sought. Manescu, when Rusk referred to a Soviet "bloc," responded by stressing that Romania *was,* after all, part of a socialist bloc. (Ironically, as will be noted shortly, just a year and a half later at their next meeting, Manescu was to emphasize precisely the contrary!) The Czech, David, was the most cold and hostile. David was accompanied by his deputy and later successor, Jiri Hajek, who six years later was to be one of the leading liberals in Alexander Dubcek's brief Prague Spring.[2]

As part of my responsibilities on the delegation, I was assigned to serve as our contact with the Eastern European delegations. Later, I had several brief conversations with the Romanian foreign minister and with several of the Eastern European deputy ministers who had been present at the meetings with Rusk. With two, I had occasion to renew my acquaintance in later years. I remained in Geneva (except for some travel noted below) for the full three months of the first ENDC session. During this time I came to know a number of the members of the Soviet delegation, especially Igor Usachev, with whom I had several interesting dinner conversations.

During my stay in Geneva from March through May of 1962 I also made two trips for other activities. I had arranged with Lieutenant General Francis Griswold, USAF, the commandant of the National War College, to attach

2. All of my "memcons" recording these meetings, inexplicably excepting the one with the Bulgarian foreign minister, are printed in the official record, *Foreign Relations of the United States, 1961–1963,* vol. 16 *Eastern Europe* (Government Printing Office, 1994), pp. 16–20, 110–16.

myself to the war college class visiting Central Europe at the end of their school year as a "State Department liaison officer." This was highly unusual, indeed somewhat irregular, but Griswold (a veteran of the Strategic Air Command, whom I knew from the 1958 Surprise Attack Conference) was accommodating, and Ambassador U. Alexis Johnson gave approval for State. My principal purpose was to observe and make contacts in Belgrade, which had just been placed on the itinerary. I joined the war college group as they arrived in Berlin at the end of March, and in addition to briefings there (including a meeting with General Lucius Clay), a Foreign Service veteran "old Berlin hand," Howard Trivers, took me on an unofficial tour around East Berlin—only some seven months after the Wall had gone up. Next our war college group visited Vienna, where the highlight was a very frank off-the-record session with Chancellor Bruno Kreisky, who had some interesting insights on Soviet policy in the 1950s. In Belgrade, apart from seeing my friend Ambassador George Kennan, at a dinner he arranged I met and had interesting conversations with Deputy Foreign Minister Leo Mates and with Admiral Branko Mamula, later the defense minister. Mates, well versed in international relations, discussed disarmament issues and also European security more broadly. He told me Yugoslavia was "leaving the East" on disarmament matters. We also exchanged views on developments in Soviet politics and foreign policy, and on the Common Market. The visit to the Yugoslav military academy, one reason for my going, was quite interesting, both for what the Yugoslavs had learned in Soviet war colleges prior to 1948 and their own adaptations as well as their strongly held views on guerilla warfare (and indirectly "counterinsurgency") based on their wartime experience. I continued with the war college group to Rome and then returned to Geneva. (One incidental consequence of my meetings in Belgrade was attention from the Yugoslav Embassy in Washington after my return. I began to receive lunch invitations from a member of the staff—obviously an intelligence officer—and invitations to receptions from the Yugoslav military attaché.)

Several weeks later, in early May, I again left Geneva for a brief but intense several days at the NATO ministerial meeting in Athens. This was the meeting at which the famous "Athens Guidelines" on use of nuclear weapons were advanced by Secretary McNamara. My own role at Athens was small: apart from giving a brief report to Secretary Rusk, I was there to handle disarmament and arms control issues that might arise, although that was not a focal interest of the meetings. So I had a generally relaxed time, albeit in a very frenetic atmosphere. I did, however, participate in some of the U.S. delegation meetings on NATO strategy (or more accurately, on how to handle strategic issues with our allies at the meeting), and I met with a number of colleagues from other NATO delegations. (The U.S. delegation, by the way, was by far the largest—some 130 people in all!) As I have earlier described, I returned to

Geneva before the wrap-up of the first ENDC session in late May. On my way back to Washington, I stopped to exchange views with Foreign Office, War Office, and JIC colleagues in London.

I should also mention another trip I did *not* make. The Antarctica Treaty (which I had helped come into being with my SNIE in 1958) provided for inspections for verification of nonmilitarization and other provisions. Signed in 1959, the treaty had gone into effect in 1961, and in 1963 the time had come for the first U.S. inspection of Soviet scientific installations in Antarctica. I was the natural choice as the State Department member of the team, and was initially scheduled to go. But then an objection was made by Bill Foster of ACDA (with whom I had excellent relations); he was skittish about having an ex-CIA officer participate in the first arms control inspection, given the standard Soviet arguments that our calls for such inspections masked intelligence aims. He had a point, and I did not go.

From late August to late September 1963 I visited Czechoslovakia, Poland, Romania, Bulgaria, Hungary, and the Soviet Union for consultations and discussions with officials on disarmament and related politico-military security issues. While in the USSR I also made familiarization visits to Riga and Tashkent. I had no negotiating brief, but learned about the organization and internal procedures for dealing with arms control and security issues in the Eastern Europe "satellites" (a subject to which we had not previously given attention) and learned the priority interests of each in this field. In some cases (Prague, Sofia, and Budapest) I was accompanied by an officer of the resident U.S. mission; in the others I was already acquainted with the appropriate officials in charge of disarmament affairs with whom I met (Deputy Foreign Minister Mircea Malita in Bucharest, Ambassador Manfred Lachs in Warsaw, and Ambassador Igor Usachev in Moscow, deputy for disarmament to Ambassador Semën Tsarapkin). In Bucharest I also met with Acting Foreign Minister Georgi Macovescu, whom I also knew from Geneva, for a very frank conversation.

The details were of limited interest at the time, and none today. My general conclusions were not unexpected: I confirmed that the Soviet leaders did not consult with their satellite allies, who at that time played no independent role, with the exception of Poland. Foreign Minister Rapacki had been permitted by the Soviet leaders to put forward the European security disengagement proposals that came to be known as the "Rapacki Plan" (and which had in fact been devised by Lachs). I suggested in my trip report that Romania also might begin to show some initiatives in the security field, a prescient observation as it turned out. I also concluded that the Soviet leaders were interested in some limited arms control measures not entailing intrusive on-site inspection, but in general were pushing disarmament themes not only for propaganda and possibly divisive effects in the West, but also in order to cultivate a climate of détente. I concluded that there were internal economic and even political pressures for retrenchment in military outlays, but that the Soviet leaders were at that time more inclined to create a political climate and context within which they could make some further unilateral reductions rather than reaching any major negotiated arms reduction agreements. That all proved to have been an accurate assessment. On one issue my consultations perhaps had a direct impact on events—my discussion with Usachev in Moscow on arms control in outer space, a subject to which I shall turn presently.

One incidental aspect of my visit to Budapest may be of interest. At the U.S. embassy, I encountered briefly Cardinal Mindszenty, the Hungarian prelate who had taken asylum there in November 1956 and remained until his death in 1971.

One aspect of my side visit to Tashkent may also be of interest. The embassy in Moscow suggested that I request a courtesy call on the Uzbek "Ministry of Foreign Affairs", a nominal organization. I did so, and after some delay and scurrying around I was ushered in to a small office to meet an uncomfortable and unforthcoming "representative" of the shadow ministry.

I later was to have occasion to continue my contacts with some of these Eastern European officials, in particular Ambassador Manfred Lachs of Poland. Indeed, I was having lunch with him in the delegates' lounge at the United Nations headquarters in New York on November 22, 1963, when an official there brought us first word of the radio announcement of the assassination of President John F. Kennedy.

The most significant development in U.S.–Eastern European relations in the 1960s was a remarkable secret Romanian initiative in 1963, which has only become known since I first disclosed it at a conference in Moscow in 1993. This private approach to us was the forerunner of well-known subsequent public moves in the 1960s by Romania to distance that country from full participation in the Soviet bloc, within the limits of Moscow's tolerance. But the secret approach to the United States in 1963 went far beyond anything that the Soviet leaders could have accepted had they known. It is an important unknown page of history. The priming event was the Cuban missile crisis of 1962 (discussed in the following chapter). The tensions generated by that crisis had reverberations throughout Europe. No country wanted to be brought into a war over the issue of Soviet missiles in Cuba. But while members of NATO and the Warsaw Pact dutifully gave public support to the United States and the Soviet Union, respectively, some did so with considerable trepidation. And in Bucharest, the leadership decided after that crisis that it would seek to disengage itself from any automatic involvement if their superpower alliance leader, the Soviet Union, again assumed such risks.

Romanian-American relations at that time were minimal. Nonetheless, when Romanian Foreign Minister Corneliu Manescu asked to meet with

Secretary of State Dean Rusk, when both were in New York for the opening of the UN General Assembly in the fall of 1963, a routine meeting was arranged for September 30. Manescu then arranged a private meeting with Rusk, attended only by his interpreter. It was the first opportunity after the crisis nearly a year earlier for the Romanian leadership to approach the United States government at this level.

Manescu told Rusk that Romania had not been consulted over the Soviet decision to place nuclear missiles in Cuba and was not therefore a party to the dispute. The Romanian government wanted the United States to understand that Romania would remain neutral in any conflict generated by such actions as the Soviet deployment of nuclear missiles in Cuba, and sought assurances that in the event of hostilities arising from such a situation, the United States would not strike Romania on the mistaken assumption that it would be allied with the Soviet Union in such a war.

Secretary Rusk in response indicated that the United States would take into account any country that did not participate in or permit its territory to be used in military actions against the United States or its allies. In this connection, he said that it would be important for the United States to know whether there were nuclear weapons on Romanian soil, and that if the United States were given assurance that there were none, that fact would be taken into account in U.S. targeting. When Manescu was able to see Rusk again for a return courtesy visit on October 21 in Washington, he responded that there were no nuclear weapons in Romania and offered the United States any opportunity it wished to verify that fact. (The absence of nuclear weapons accorded with U.S. intelligence, and the United States did not pursue the verification offer.)

In view of the sensitivity of the matter, any knowledge of this exchange was very closely held in Washington, and no doubt in Bucharest. When I asked McGeorge Bundy about it in 1990, he said he believed the matter had not gone beyond an oral statement by Rusk to the president. Rusk did not believe it required any action going beyond the option to "withhold" any strategic nuclear strikes against targets in Eastern Europe, which had already been provided in the single integrated operations plans (SIOP). The Romanian approach was not divulged to NATO governments. So far as is known, the Soviet leaders did not learn about it. It did not "leak" for thirty years.

Romania had, in effect, secretly repudiated its Warsaw Pact alliance obligations and promised neutrality in case of the outbreak of a war caused by Soviet actions. This stunning unilateral Romanian breach of its alliance obligations did not change history; Romania even remained a nominal member of the pact until it was dissolved in 1991. Moreover, so far as is known this was the only such break in alliance solidarity on either side—the alliances did hold up throughout the Cold War. Nonetheless, it is an important and instructive, and hitherto unknown, historical episode. When in 1990 I asked Dean Rusk, who had first told me years earlier, he agreed that with the end of the Cold War the story should be told.

Eastern European views on security and arms control was clearly in my field of responsibility, but it was far from the center of interest and activity in Washington. Policy toward Eastern Europe was in a hiatus between the confrontational period of the 1950s and a period of cautious engagement that began in the mid to late 1960s and continued through the 1970s (and is the subject of a later chapter). But during the Kennedy years it was almost forgotten. Policy toward Western Europe, by contrast, came to the fore.

Kennedy had sought to reinvigorate our NATO relationship, in part by a firm stand in defense of our presence in West Berlin, and in part by pressing a new more rational NATO strategy for deterrence and defense. The new strategy was, however, divisive—France in particular, but far from alone, had strong reservations about the strategy of flexible response and the associated program to enhance conventional military capabilities of the alliance. In addition, some unilateral American defense decisions—notably the sudden decision at the end of 1962 to cancel the Skybolt airborne ballistic missile—had disturbing ripple effects. The decision undercut British plans to rely on the missile to keep their "V" strategic bomber force viable, and the U.S. response of offering Britain our Polaris submarine ballistic missile riled the French, to whom we did not make a similar offer.

Most basically, the attempt by McNamara to impose a strategy of graduated deterrents seemed to imply a turn to a war-waging strategy, when most Europeans wanted to continue to rely on a threat of massive nuclear retaliation to deter possible Soviet bloc attack. Hence the reservations too about the Athens Guidelines in May 1962, an approach made publicly by McNamara in a speech in Ann Arbor, Michigan, a month later. McNamara's approach was exactly what I (and the U.S. Army "intellectual generals" and some other civilian strategic writers) had advocated in the late 1950s. McNamara said at Ann Arbor: "The U.S. has come to the conclusion that to the extent feasible, basic military strategy in a possible general nuclear war should be approached in much the same way that more conventional military operations have been regarded in the past." He went on to say "principal military objectives, in the event of a nuclear war stemming from a major attack on the Alliance, should be the destruction of the enemy's military forces, not of his civilian population." But far more was involved than a change in military strategic doctrine. There were important implications both for nuclear and non-nuclear (conventional) forces of the alliance, and both aspects caused divisions and controversy.

On nuclear strategy, McNamara pledged continuing commitment by the United States of its nuclear arsenal for deterrence and defense of the alliance on a whole, but he also called for the other members of the alliance—then

Britain and France, and potentially Germany and others—to give up their national nuclear forces or aspirations for such forces. He argued that "limited nuclear capabilities, operating independently, are dangerous, expensive, prone to obsolescence, and lacking in credibility as a deterrent."[3]

The allies welcomed reassurance on the U.S. commitment of its nuclear deterrent, but the French and British resented the slap at their independent nuclear forces. At Athens, the United States had advanced the idea of a possible multilateral force that could share in the nuclear delivery role (using U.S. nuclear warheads that would remain under American control), and we had been taken aback there when the Germans seemed cool to the idea.

The idea of a multilateral force (MLF), first bruited about in Washington in the Eisenhower administration, nonetheless was now pushed by the United States for several years, in the form of proposed surface ships with ballistic missiles manned by personnel of several countries (including Germany and Italy and others, as well as U.S. nuclear custodial personnel).

Other ideas for providing a European component of the alliance nuclear deterrent were already under way in terms of deployment of U.S. Jupiter intermediate-range ballistic missiles (IRBMs) in Italy and Turkey, and U.S.-supplied Thor IRBMs in Britain, all decided upon in the late 1950s after the *Sputnik*-generated missile gap scare. Some new ideas arose in 1962–63 again, of which the most imaginative was the resurrection of an idea originally dreamed up in the late 1950s, leading to a U.S. Army Engineer Studies Center paper in 1960, called *Project Iceworm*. The idea was to deploy six hundred Minuteman ICBMs under the Greenland ice cap, with mobile basing in under-ice tunnels among control centers and silos. In the 1962 version of Iceworm, the idea was to deploy NATO IRBMs under the ice cap. I don't recall that we ever raised the idea with our NATO allies, except that I believe we did informally sound out unbelieving Danish officials (since Greenland was a territory of Denmark). In any case, the idea was soon abandoned.

McNamara's Ann Arbor speech did contain the seed of an idea that successfully developed in the mid- to late 1960s in the passage cited above calling for increased allied participation in formulating nuclear policy. That is discussed in a later chapter. But from 1962 to 1965 this idea was eclipsed by the controversial MLF concept of deploying a multilateral force.

Although the MLF was the central element in the proposed new arrangement, the British were mollified by the adoption of a broader conception of a NATO or allied nuclear force (ANF) which in addition to the MLF could embrace national nuclear forces in Europe—the British, the French (if they

3. "Address by Secretary of Defense McNamara at the University of Michigan [extract], June 16, 1962," *Documents on Disarmament, 1962*, vol. 1 (Government Printing Office, 1963), pp. 625–26.

would participate, which was most unlikely), and perhaps U.S. European-based NATO-committed nuclear forces. The NATO or allied nuclear force would complement the U.S. intercontinental nuclear deterrent forces.

The idea of participation in nuclear policy was also eclipsed by a running controversy over another aspect of McNamara's new concept: the enhancement of capabilities for non-nuclear combat as reinforcement for deterrence.[4] The allies generally preferred not to undertake unpopular and costly measures to increase their conventional forces and war reserves. Moreover, many were dubious about seeming to dilute the resolute threat of all-out nuclear response to "an attack"—although, as McNamara well understood, in any actual case of aggression short of an all-out Soviet nuclear attack, the allies would certainly not have been prepared to initiate (or to have the United States initiate) a general nuclear war.

As I argued in a conversation shortly after the Athens meeting with the German army attaché in Washington, our purpose was to bolster deterrence through enhancing the range of our capability, "to avoid having to rely on our last resort as our first resort in cases where by prudent preparation we could deter or meet lesser threats by having adequate conventional strength."

In this unsettled context of some disarray in the alliance over strategy, President Kennedy at the beginning of 1963 authorized a very secret high-level internal U.S. review of European policy. George Ball, Rusk's principal deputy as the under secretary of state, was made chairman of the interagency committee. For reasons of security, the committee was obscurely called the "PR Study Group" (PR standing for "policy review," not the usual "public relations" meaning of the acronym, with the word "European" artfully omitted from the "policy" being reviewed and the usual committee called a "study group"). If there had been any leak that a U.S. overall review of its European policy was under way, it could have been very damaging, but there was none. In fact, to my knowledge this is the first disclosure of the existence of the PR group and its mandate. I was made executive secretary of the PR Study Group, for somewhat byzantine reasons. Rusk and Ball—or perhaps President Kennedy—did not want the usual NATO European experts in Washington to review their own entrenched policy, and within G/PM—the logical alternative—my colleagues Jeffrey Kitchen and Seymour Weiss, who usually dealt jealously with NATO matters, wanted to keep their distance from this review because they feared that it might prove explosive, yet they wanted G/PM in, so Kitchen advanced my candidacy. I was *persona grata* with Ball, so I was named. In addition to serving as the executive secretary of the group, I participated in a small military committee of the PR group chaired by Major

---

4. Ibid., p.627.

General Andrew Goodpaster of the Joint Chiefs of Staff that submitted a report on strategic problems and alternatives.

Notwithstanding the injunction to review our policy from the bottom up, the PR Study Group recommended essentially the policy we were already pursuing, although seeking to soften the U.S. pressures for a major buildup of conventional forces and suggesting consideration of a European nuclear force not formally subject to U.S. veto. Some members also advocated extending to France the same support for an independent nuclear force that we had accepted for Britain (although that was recognized to run counter to our efforts to prevent proliferation of national nuclear forces), but that remained controversial.

By May 1963 there was a clear clash between our objective of reassuring NATO allies through the MLF/ANF and the efforts under way since 1961 to obtain a nuclear nonproliferation treaty (NPT). The United Nations General Assembly had passed a series of Irish-sponsored resolutions on nonproliferation since 1959, the one in 1961 unanimously. Bilateral U.S.-Soviet negotiations had been launched by Secretary Rusk in Geneva in March 1962. Thereafter, while NPT continued to occupy the multilateral disarmament committee in Geneva, the really important negotiation had shifted to bilateral U.S.-Soviet talks. We kept our NATO allies (and some others) generally informed, but also maintained confidentiality with the Soviet side in order to keep the exchange from devolving into a propaganda exercise. The relationship of the NPT negotiations with the Russians, and our negotiations over nuclear defense of the alliance, would become important, and more tense, in the next several years.

I had an additional important task in 1962–63, dealing with international political and intelligence aspects of U.S. policy in outer space. Inasmuch as I am the only person who can recount much of this story, and it is of some interest both intrinsically and as a window into the inner workings of the Kennedy administration, I will go into some detail.[5]

On May 26, 1962, in National Security Action Memorandum (NSAM) 156, the president directed Secretary Rusk to establish an interagency committee to review political aspects of U.S. policy on satellite reconnaissance. The existence of the committee itself was classified information, and any reference to its function, and all of its work, was classified top secret. The deputy under secretary for political affairs, Ambassador U. Alexis Johnson, was named chairman of the NSAM 156 Committee (as it came to be called), and I became its executive secretary. The other agencies represented were Defense (Assistant

---

5. The account below draws heavily on an earlier rendition. See Raymond L. Garthoff, "Banning the Bomb in Outer Space," *International Security*, vol. 5, no. 3 (Winter 1980/81), pp. 25–40.

Secretary for ISA Paul Nitze, usually represented by his deputy John McNaughton), CIA (Deputy Director for Research Herbert P. Scoville Jr.), NRO (the National Reconnaissance Office, also a body the very existence and name of which was for years classified information, represented by its director, Under Secretary of the Air Force Joseph Charyk), NASA (the National Aeronautics and Space Agency, represented by Deputy Director Robert Seamans), and ACDA (represented by Deputy Director Adrian Fisher). The White House representatives (actively participating, but not signing the report) were Carl Kaysen, McGeorge Bundy's deputy, for the NSC, and Jerome Wiesner, science adviser to the president. The committee submitted its initial report to Secretary Rusk on July 1, 1962, and Rusk forwarded it to the president. The report was unanimous, except for the question of an arms control measure on banning weapons of mass destruction from outer space.

On July 10 the NSC discussed the report of the NSAM 156 Committee, and the president then issued NSC Action 2454, approving all but one of the nineteen recommendations of the report but referring recommendation 19 on an arms control measure back to the committee for "further study."

The main provisions of the report dealt with such matters as keeping secret the fact of U.S. space reconnaissance (intelligence collection). A ban on public disclosure that we had an operational space reconnaissance capability, instituted by President Eisenhower in August 1960, was reaffirmed. We did recommend a cautious gradual revelation of space imaging from our civilian NASA satellite programs to get the world public accustomed to the value of space observation for such purposes as mapping, surveying natural resources, and weather prediction. We opposed the idea advanced by some countries (including for a time the Soviet Union) that space should be reserved for "nonmilitary uses," since even apart from reconnaissance space was important for navigation, communications, and other uses that had military as well as nonmilitary applications. We took the position that outer space should be considered analogous to the high seas, for all peaceful purposes including military, and that all observation of the earth was allowable. These general lines of approach had many applications to international discourse and negotiation at the United Nations and in other forums, as well as in official U.S. statements by NASA, USIA, and others.

We also wrestled with the difficult question of whether, and what, to disclose about our space reconnaissance for reassurances to the American public and to our allies, and for intimidation of our adversary, the Soviet Union. There had been some limited earlier disclosures, in particular by Secretary Rusk to General Charles deGaulle in December 1961. A number of other selected allied leaders were confidentially briefed in general terms on our capability in August and September 1962 after the issuance of NSC Action 2454. Some representatives of NATO in the North Atlantic Council were given a very general briefing in September 1964. But a decision was made in NSAM 216 in January 1963 (as earlier in 1961 during the Berlin crisis, before the establishment of the NSAM 156 Committee) not to make direct disclosure to the Soviet leaders. In 1963–64 the idea of some disclosure in the context of arms control verification was considered, and while ultimately this would be very important to progress in arms limitation, it was not considered necessary to disclose a U.S. capability at that time.

After the July 10 NSC meeting and issuance of NSC Action 2454, we were left with the task of "further study" of the arms control provision, a proposal to ban weapons of mass destruction from outer space.

The United States had, in its submission to the then newly established Eighteen Nation Disarmament Committee in Geneva on April 18 of that year, included in Stage I of an "outline of basic provisions for General and Complete Disarmament" a provision banning the placement of weapons of mass destruction in orbit. (The Soviet draft treaty of March 15 had a much more vague and broad provision limiting "space devices" to "peaceful purposes.") In the NSAM 156 Committee I had drafted a paper on June 19 on the pros and cons of a separate ban on bombs in space. ("Separate" meant not as part of the pie-in-the-sky General and Complete Disarmament package.) Adrian Fisher of ACDA had submitted a memo to me a few days later proposing revised language strengthening the "pros," on which, as I recall, we largely agreed, and also suggesting shifting the forum for consideration of the matter to the Committee of Principals, which normally handled disarmament and arms control matters.

The Defense, Joint Chief of Staff (JCS), National Reconnaissance Office (NRO), and CIA members opposed a separate ban, in at least one instance (the JCS) because of a belief that the United States should keep open the option of such deployment. But in most if not in all other cases, opposition focused on the inspection measures, which it was assumed would be required, and the risk of negotiations somehow impeding our other highly important military uses of space, especially satellite reconnaissance. There was no disagreement over this latter point, but there were differing views on the effects of proposing a ban on weapons in space. The question of a separate arms control ban on weapons of mass destruction in space had been raised earlier. On September 22, 1960, President Eisenhower had proposed that, analogous to the banning of armaments in Antarctica, there should be, "subject to appropriate verification," a ban on orbiting or stationing weapons of mass destruction in outer space. The Soviet Union was not then interested, and the matter fell into abeyance.

In March 1962, in Geneva, the Canadian secretary of state for foreign affairs, Howard Green, without advance consultation and despite our last minute urgings not to do so, proposed such a separate ban, without inspection. The U.S. delegation had promptly spoken out against the measure, on the grounds that we opposed such a "declaratory measure," stressing the need for "inspection and control." This response was almost automatic, reflecting our major debate with the Soviet Union at that time over the principle of inspection and verification of disarmament. We had not, in fact, yet even studied the question of what would be needed for inspection of such a ban.

We had been continuing in the NSAM 156 Committee to study the question of a separate ban, and had largely reached a consensus. Accordingly, the very day after NSC 2454 was issued on July 10, I drafted a memorandum from Ambassador Johnson to the other members of the committee setting forth a "Recommended U.S. Position on a Separate Ban on Weapons of Mass Destruction in Outer Space," noting that with their concurrence the secretary of state would submit it to the president. With telephonic concurrence from the principals, it was sent to the president by Secretary Rusk the following day, July 12. This reply had been prepared in what for the bureaucracy was lightning speed.

The new NSAM 156 Committee report of July 12 reviewed the background briefly and recommended opposing a declaratory ban; not taking an American initiative in raising a separate ban; attempting to place the onus for rejecting such a ban on the Soviet Union; stressing the need for adequate verification controls; and, finally, noting that ACDA would "urgently" study the problem "to determine the inspection requirements for a separate ban." ACDA had favored a ban, and there had been differences of view among others. These differences had, however, now been submerged, with advocates of a ban having the opportunity later to present a proposal when inspection requirements had been determined.

Except for rather higher-ranking participation than usual at the "working level," and exceptional dispatch, it was a not untypical response by the governmental bureaucracy to a presidential request to consider an idea. But then something very unusual occurred.

About a week later, I received a call from Carl Kaysen of the NSC. He said that the president had just been discussing with him the committee's recommendations and wanted to know if the alternative of a ban relying on unilateral verification had really been examined; if so, the president was content to accept the recommendations, but if not, he wanted that possibility considered further. Kaysen considered that I was the one person who could answer. I replied that, in good conscience, I did not believe we had given the alternative a full appraisal. I did not report my conversation with Kaysen to my colleagues.

On July 23 McGeorge Bundy wrote to Secretary Rusk that the president had reviewed the memorandum of July 12 and was not prepared to accept "the total rejection of any possible declaratory ban." He expressed the view that such a ban might be in our interest if nothing better could be attained and asked for a study of national means of verification. Moreover, he questioned the general position calling for inspection in all cases regardless of possible U.S. interest in declaratory agreements in special cases. "The President hopes the matter will be reviewed in light of these comments and further recommendations presented to him soon."

At this point, I recommended to Ambassador Johnson that we accede to the ACDA desire to rechannel the matter into the normal forum for addressing arms control issues, the Committee of Principals, and he agreed. I continued to work very closely with Adrian Fisher on it.

I should also note that it is highly unusual for a president to reject a unanimous interagency recommendaticn. I am pleased to say that the bureaucracy took the president's decision exactly as it should have: not as a fiat compelling people to reverse strongly held convictions, but as a directive to consider an alternative approach.

On August 31 a draft was ready for the Committee of Deputies, "Recommendations on a Separate Arms Control Measure for Outer Space." On September 5, it was discussed by the deputies. One point that had troubled me, as well as most of my colleagues on the NSAM 156 Committee, was an ACDA-proposed call for *advance* notification of all space launchings. It would facilitate verification, but it could also facilitate interference with space reconnaissance, and we dropped that proposed element of the measure.

I drafted a memorandum signed by Under Secretary George McGhee to Secretary Rusk recommending that he support a declaratory ban as being in the U.S. interest, considering especially the political impact in the world of a nuclear sword of Damocles.

Meanwhile, a separate but coordinated NSC-State-Defense move was made. During the Kennedy administration in particular, and also in the Johnson years, there was a frequently very effective and close cooperation between the special assistant to the president and his NSC staff, and Secretaries Rusk and McNamara and their senior staffs. Much was accomplished at the "Tuesday lunches" (so called even when they were later customarily held on Thursdays) of these three men with only a few others in attendance (often the chairman of the JCS and the director of central intelligence). In this instance, it was decided to serve several policy purposes with an authoritative administration speech by Deputy Secretary of Defense Roswell Gilpatric. His speech, made on September 5, was drafted largely by Adam Yarmolinsky, then a special assistant to McNamara. I also reviewed and contributed to it. Kaysen from the White House was actively involved. In the speech, Gilpatric authoritatively stated that the United States had "no program to place any weapons of mass destruction into orbit." There was an implicit invitation to the Soviet Union to take a similar stand, as he noted that an arms race in space would not contribute to security and said that while the

United States or the Soviet Union could place such weapons in space, it would not be "a rational military strategy for either side."

On September 10, coincidentally, the Soviet Union tabled a draft space treaty in Geneva. It did not specifically address a ban on weapons in space. (It did, however, seek to ban space intelligence collection, a position that the Soviets later abandoned as they too acquired the capability for such collection.)

On September 15 ACDA Director William Foster submitted to the members of the Committee of Principals the draft "U.S. Approach to a Separate Arms Control Measure for Outer Space," prepared by "ACDA in consultation with the other interested agencies" in response to the president's request conveyed by Bundy's memorandum of July 23. It supported a declaratory ban monitored by national means of verification. There was one vigorous dissent, and one conditional support. The JCS opposed *any* separate space weapons agreement; the United States itself could not accept inspection, and should not agree to an uninspected ban; hence we should only support arms control in space in the context of a general and complete disarmament (GCD) package. Defense (ISA) supported a private informal agreement with the USSR, but a formal agreement only in the GCD context, and further preferred unilateral statements of U.S. policy, such as Gilpatric's speech of September 5.

The Committee of Principals met on September 19; Secretary Rusk was unable to be present, and ACDA Director Foster took the chair. Deputy Secretary Gilpatric, representing Defense, said that he and McNamara had no objection to a separate ban, but tactically favored a private approach. General George Decker, representing the JCS, said somewhat disingenuously that the Chiefs agreed on the desirability of the "objective" but preferred to use GCD (which meant to kill the idea). Kaysen, uneasy on the change of channels, asked me in the meeting if the 156 Committee had been brought in, and I assured him that it had. Wiesner argued on the lack of military value of large weapons in orbit; no one disagreed. Gilpatric requested, and was granted, assurance from Foster that the idea would be tried out informally on the Soviets; Fisher interjected the need for flexibility. General Decker, and Dr. Leland Haworth (AEC), remained concerned over the general principle of inspection. The meeting did not reach a decision. On September 25 the JCS submitted their comments—negative on the idea. On September 27 Foster submitted a memorandum to the president reporting on the Committee of Principals' discussion and indicating a generally favorable consensus. No other memorandums were submitted.

On October 2 NSAM 192 was issued stating that the president had reviewed Foster's memo (and the JCS comments), and that he approved the recommendations of the memo.

On October 17 Foster proposed a separate ban on stationing weapons of mass destruction in outer space to Soviet Foreign Minister Andrei Gromyko and

Ambassador Anatoly Dobrynin in New York. It is clear that Gromyko assumed that this was a variant of the longstanding Western proposals of 1957 (which covered all objects "sent through" outer space—including ICBMs—and also required inspection), and he responded with the standard Soviet counterploy to that proposal, tying it to removal of American forward bases for missiles and aircraft.

During the spring of 1963 we had observed much increased Soviet propaganda over the militarization of space. While conceivably generated by Soviet concerns over American activities in space reconnaissance and the like, it seemed more likely to reflect either Soviet misperceptions of an American interest in placing weapons in space, as alleged in the propaganda, or Soviet interest or intentions on their part to place weapons in space, masked and justified by the alleged American plans and activities.

We considered two ways to meet possible Soviet stationing of nuclear weapons in space.

On March 7, 1963, Ambassador U. Alexis Johnson submitted to Secretary Rusk a memorandum titled "Further Initiatives on a Ban on Weapons in Space," which I had drafted. It noted the increasing Soviet propaganda, recalled the several unilateral American statements that had by then been made (Gilpatric's of September 5, 1962; Senator Albert Gore's speech to the UNGA on December 3, which we had drafted in State; and a speech by Secretary Rusk on January 31, 1963), and the Soviet failure to respond to Foster's probe of Gromyko in October 1962 (and a subsequent conversation of his with Soviet Ambassador Tsarapkin in Geneva in early 1963). The memorandum raised the possibility of advancing a proposal in the Legal Subcommittee of the Outer Space Committee at the UN. Finally, it also noted that a "contingency plan for U.S. reaction to Soviet placing of a nuclear weapon in space" was being separately transmitted.

After consulting with Secretary Rusk, at his direction I wrote a draft letter from the secretary of state to the president, modifying somewhat the guidance on NSAM 192. On March 13 we sent it to some of the other principals of the NSAM 156 Committee asking for their concurrence: Nitze at Defense, Scoville at CIA, and Fisher at ACDA, as well as Richard Gardner (UN Affairs) and Leonard Meeker (Legal Affairs) in State. Revised versions were prepared, and concurrences obtained, but on April 29 Secretary Rusk decided—for tactical reasons—not to send the memorandum to the president and to "suspend for the present" further approaches to the Soviets. Johnson so advised Bundy at the White House.

On the other front, however, we moved forward. On May 8, 1963, Secretary Rusk sent to the president my revised memorandum prepared pursuant to NSAM 192, "U.S. Reaction to Soviet Placing of a Nuclear Weapon in Space," with the concurrence of the secretary of defense, the director of central intelligence, and the director of ACDA. It recommended that the United States "develop an active anti-satellite capability at the earliest practicable time, nuclear and non-nuclear." The president approved that recommendation.

On June 21, 1963, Mexico tabled a draft treaty in Geneva proposing to ban the placing of weapons of mass destruction in space. The United States neither supported nor opposed that initiative, which did not lead to negotiations.

Meanwhile, the "hot line" agreement was concluded on June 20, and negotiations in July and August on a partial nuclear test ban led to the treaty signed August 5, 1963.

It was at that juncture that I made my circuit of all the Warsaw Pact capitals, discussing arms control and security matters, but without any assignment or authorization to advance proposals. In Moscow, as earlier noted, I met with Ambassador Igor Usachev, a veteran Soviet diplomat in the field of disarmament, and with whom I was well acquainted from Geneva. I met with Usachev at the Ministry of Foreign Affairs on September 4; the Soviets, as were we, were gearing up for the forthcoming U.N. General Assembly (UNGA) session.

I asked Usachev what he saw as the prospect for a separate ban on weapons of mass destruction in space. I said it seemed to me timely, before someone would actually do it. He acknowledged Foster's probes and began by noting, as had Gromyko and Tsarapkin to Foster, the question of objects transiting outer space. Clearly, he (as they) were thinking in terms of strategic ballistic missiles. I assured him what we had in mind would not concern missiles merely transiting space, only weapons placed into orbit or stationed in outer space. Usachev accepted that clarification, but then asked about inspection—which seemed to him the main hurdle. I said that the United States would not need any inspection for this measure, which could be monitored by national means of verification. Usachev indicated that the Soviets had been very wary over what had been involved in terms of inspection and did not want to show interest and then be blamed for failure over a stalemate on inspection. (He did not say so, but the idea struck me that the Soviets had been afraid that we would "mousetrap" them into appearing to be raising obstacles to an American disarmament proposal, after which we would use their refusal to justify our own deployment of weapons in space.) In any case, he was very interested and grateful for my clarification of the U.S. proposal, its objective, and the position on inspection.

On September 19 Foreign Minster Gromyko addressed the General Assembly in New York. He reviewed a number of familiar Soviet positions, including in the disarmament field, but he also had something new and interesting to add: "the Soviet Government deems it necessary to reach agreement with the United States Government to ban the placing into orbit of objects with nuclear weapons on board. We are aware that the United States Government also takes a positive view of the solution of this question. We assume also that an exchange of views on the banning of the placing into orbit of nuclear weapons will be continued between the Governments of the USSR and the U.S. on a bilateral basis. It would be a very good thing if understanding could be reached and an accord concluded on this vital question. The Soviet Government is ready." The Soviets had put it on the line.

The next day, President Kennedy responded, favorably but cautiously: "We must continue to seek agreement, encouraged by yesterday's affirmative response to this proposal by the Soviet Foreign Minister, on an arrangement to keep weapons of mass destruction out of outer space. Let us get our negotiators back to the negotiating table to arrange a practicable arrangement to this end."

Foster urged Secretary Rusk in a memo three days later to bring the matter up again with Gromyko. He did, within a week, and confirmed Soviet readiness to proceed. The Soviets favored a treaty or some other formal undertaking.

On October 1, Fisher submitted a paper to the deputies, now referring to a "Proposed U.S.-Soviet *Arrangement* [sic] Concerning the Placing in Orbit of Weapons of Mass Destruction." The results of that meeting were reflected in a memo from Foster to Rusk setting out three alternative "arrangements": unilateral statements of intention, a U.S.-USSR agreement (probably an executive agreement), or a U.N. General Assembly resolution. I drafted a memo to Secretary Rusk from Ambassador Johnson favoring a General Assembly resolution, accompanied by a unilateral U.S. explanatory statement (so we could couch the explanation in our own careful terms, not subject to negotiation with anyone else), possibly preceded by joint or parallel U.S. and Soviet declarations of intent. I argued that a treaty or executive agreement was not desirable, taking account of possible domestic objections and the absence of escape clauses. That same day the JCS issued a paper signed by General Maxwell Taylor, opposing not only a treaty but also a UNGA Resolution and preferring a joint declaration of intent. Nonetheless, it stated: "The Joint Chiefs of Staff consider that there are no military objections to this arrangement." Two odd points were, however, raised. The JCS favored the term "weapons of mass destruction" rather than "nuclear weapons" (but did not state the reason); and they favored a withdrawal provision (hardly appropriate in a declaration of intentions).

The Committee of Principals met the next day, October 8. Secretary Rusk in the chair led off with his position: a General Assembly resolution would be best, with U.S. and Soviet supporting statements, which we could tailor to provide any needed escape clause. He also stated that we could continue to use the term "weapons of mass destruction," which must be understood to include all nuclear weapons. (I had explained to him that the reason the JCS paper wished to use the former term was to allow *later* interpretation that small nuclear weapons, for example for anti-satellite or antiballistic missile use, were not "weapons of mass destruction"—an interpretation I did not feel we could justify ex post facto; if it were desired and necessary, which I doubted, it should be faced at that time.) The JCS did not contest the point. There was general agreement, although Nitze and General Barksdale Hamlett (representing JCS) spoke in favor of declarations. Then Under Secretary Ball came into the meeting straight from a discussion with the president. The president had confirmed a separate measure, with national means of verification, but not a formal executive agreement "or anything looking like an executive agreement," or still less a treaty, for domestic political considerations. He preferred a General Assembly resolution with U.S. and Soviet supporting statements. So, by then, did we all.

One week later, on October 15, Mexico—which had "gone it alone" in June—introduced a draft resolution, the language of which had been worked out beforehand with the United States (principally), the USSR, and others. On October 16, Adlai Stevenson reiterated to the General Assembly First Committee the U.S. intention not to place in orbit or station in outer space or on celestial bodies weapons of mass destruction. On October 17, 1963, the UN General Assembly adopted by acclamation Resolution 1884 (XVIII), noting the U.S. and Soviet statements of intent and calling on all states to refrain from placing in orbit or stationing in space "nuclear weapons or any other kinds of weapons of mass destruction."

President Kennedy, simply by challenging a unanimous recommendation and a pejorative shibboleth about "declaratory" measures, caused the bureaucracy to refocus its consideration and find that by freeing itself from an assumed requirement for inspection that we ourselves wished to avoid (*not* in order to do anything prohibited by the agreement), we could more readily agree on the advantage to the United States in heading off what might well otherwise have become an expensive, destabilizing and fear-engendering, even if militarily inconclusive, arms race literally "out of this world." Moreover, by registering agreement between the United States and the Soviet Union, even though from 1963 to 1967 in a nonbinding way, the measure was effective. In the aftermath of the Test Ban Treaty debate, it is inconceivable that the Senate in 1963 would have given its advice and consent by a vote of 88 to 0, as it was prepared to do in 1967. The president effectively used his executive power to gain a de facto moratorium until the time was auspicious for a treaty. This is by no means to argue that declaratory bans, or UN resolutions, are always suitable or indeed consistent with U.S. security. But in some cases they may well be justified. Any measure must be weighed carefully and judged on its own merits.

The "declaratory ban" on weapons in space was President Kennedy's last arms control achievement, and its attainment was one of the last acts of state policy in his foreshortened administration. But it laid the basis for the arms control element of the space treaty to come under his successor in 1967.

I have recounted the story of the negotiation of the agreement to ban the placing of weapons of mass destruction in space at such length and in such detail to illustrate what I believe is a very good example (if not typical in all respects) of the internal workings of the U.S. government in the Kennedy administration, and the interrelation with negotiations with the Soviet Union (and to some extent with other countries). It was also one concrete case where I felt I had made a difference in the outcome.

One meeting on space cooperation had a curious aftermath. Sometime in 1962 or early 1963—I have lost the precise date—a Bulgarian diplomat who had developed an interest in space law and founded an International Institute of Space Law, Ivan-Asen Khristov Georgiev, set up a meeting with our deputy legal adviser, Leonard Meeker, to inform the United States of his institute and discuss the general subject. Len asked me to sit in on the meeting with him (the first such Eastern European initiative). We had an uneventful and cordial meeting, and I thought no more of it or about Georgiev until it was suddenly announced in December 1963 in Bulgaria that he had been arrested as an American spy. (In fact, he had been arrested in Moscow, in early September 1963—coincidentally at the very time that I had been there meeting on space arms control with Ambassador Usachev!) I had, in fact, been aware from CIA Clandestine Services reports that we had an agent in the Bulgarian diplomatic service, but of course I did not know it was Georgiev. To compound the coincidences, Georgiev was also alleged to have been originally recruited as an American spy by my old Princeton history professor (and later CIA consultant) Cyril Black, who had long lived in Bulgaria.

Another spy arrest at about the same time was even closer to home. In November 1963 my former Yale professor Frederick Barghoorn was arrested in Moscow as an American spy. Fred had worked in the embassy in Moscow during the mid- to late 1940s and after the war participated in a program interviewing former Soviet citizens in West Germany, so he could easily be cast as an intelligence agent, even though he was not. His arrest had been an action by the KGB to find a suitable patsy to seize and trade for a Soviet spy recently arrested in the United States. After a hue and cry in Washington, and a personal message to Khrushchev from President Kennedy, Barghoorn was released. I later learned that I was among those about whom Barghoorn was grilled by his KGB interrogators during his brief incarceration. Incidentally, the KGB officer who had picked Barghoorn as the best candidate to arrest was the same Yury Nosenko whom I had met the year before and who was already in touch with CIA and would the next year defect. The espionage game had many curious sidelights.

In looking back over the tragically curtailed three years of the Kennedy administration, there is a divide between the first two years of confrontation over Berlin and missiles in Cuba, and the last year with its incipient détente and movement on arms control. The most dramatic sign of the change was a remarkable speech by President Kennedy at American University on June 10, 1963. Perhaps the closest parallel was President Eisenhower's speech of April 1953 after Stalin's death, but that had been too tentative and offset by other signals. The American University speech was written in the White House (mainly by Ted Sorensen), along lines indicated by Kennedy himself. Ambassador Thompson was asked for his suggestions and provided useful input, but that was the only participation from the State Department. (Moreover, the speech was given to Secretary Rusk for his clearance with too little time for usual review within the department.) It was, whether owing to or despite the absence of a greater State Department role, an outstanding speech.

Kennedy called upon Americans to "reexamine our attitude toward the Soviet Union." Noting Soviet distortions in their image of us and our policies, he cited that as a warning to us "not to fall into the same trap as the Soviets, not to see only a distorted and desperate view of the other side, not to see conflict as inevitable, accommodation as impossible, and communication as nothing more than an exchange of threats." He noted our common interest in preventing war, and the "ironical but accurate fact that the two strongest powers are the two in the most danger of devastation," and that "even in the cold war . . . our two countries bear the heaviest burdens . . . caught up in a vicious and dangerous cycle in which suspicion on one side breeds suspicion on the other and new weapons beget counterweapons." He even urged that we "reexamine our attitude to the cold war, remembering that we are not engaged in a debate, seeking to pile up debating points." Although he did not yet use the word "détente," he called for a "strategy of peace" and declared that "we can seek a relaxation of tensions without relaxing our guard."[6]

It was a powerful speech, although attention focused more on the immediately operative portions announcing a moratorium on nuclear testing pending a meeting in Moscow on a nuclear test ban. The Limited Nuclear Test Ban reached a month later was the most concrete and immediate result. The potential of the address was, however, much more far reaching. It marked a particularly striking change from the assertive, even belligerent, unilateral challenges of Kennedy's inauguration and state of the union addresses of 1961 and 1962. It showed a more mature and historically expanded horizon.

Perhaps most encouraging was the Soviet response. Even years later senior Soviet diplomats told me how much of an impact it had had in Moscow. Khrushchev responded in a speech on July 2, and during their talks in Moscow told U.S. Ambassador W. Averell Harriman that they regarded it as the best speech by any president since Roosevelt.

6. "Toward a Strategy of Peace, Address by President Kennedy," June 10, 1963, in *Department of State Bulletin,* vol. 49, no. 1253 (July 1, 1963), pp. 2–6.

Kennedy—and Khrushchev—did move forward in the next months, with three important arms control agreements, as well as avoiding any serious new frictions. The first of these agreements was a bilateral U.S.-Soviet agreement on installing a hot line for crisis communication between the two governments, concluded in June 1963. The second was the Limited Test Ban Treaty (LTBT), limiting nuclear testing to underground tests, reached in trilateral talks between the United States, the United Kingdom, and the Soviet Union in Moscow in July 1963. The third, reached in October 1963, was the agreement on nonplacement of nuclear weapons in outer space, earlier discussed.

Ambassador Harriman led the small delegation to Moscow to conclude the LTBT, once it had become clear that agreement would not be reached on a comprehensive test ban treaty (CTBT). That failure had been especially unfortunate because the conclusion of a CTB at that time would have had an important effect in curtailing the arms race, and because the two sides had come so close to agreement. Indeed, it failed because of a misunderstanding. Khrushchev had concluded from several statements by American negotiators (including Ambassador Dean) that if he gave in on the principle of on-site inspection, only a few annual inspections, two or three, would suffice. Accordingly, he pushed through over resistance of some of his fellow Politburo (Presidium) members a position under which he indicated Soviet readiness to accept two or three inspections. The United States had, meanwhile, come down to ten and ultimately seven inspections. But Kennedy believed he would not be able to carry the Senate to accept so few inspections. The United States was not even willing to try to compromise on five. By July, Khrushchev withdrew his readiness to accept any inspections. So the CTB was dead for decades.

Ambassador Harriman had another important, and secret, assignment on his mission to Moscow. In the first important step taken with awareness of the Sino-Soviet rift, Kennedy asked him to convey to the Soviet leadership our growing concern over Chinese communist development of nuclear weapons. Moreover, he was to sound out the degree of Soviet concern and possible readiness to join us in countering Chinese efforts, possibly even by military action to disable their construction of nuclear facilities. Even within the U.S. government this sensitive subject was very closely held and not reported on through normal top secret communications. Harriman carried out his instructions, but despite several attempts to engage Soviet leaders on the issues, the most he could report was an apparent Soviet lack of concern and unwillingness to discuss any kind of joint action beyond the Soviet support for a nonproliferation treaty.

I did not go to Moscow with the Harriman delegation, because the secretary wanted me to help prepare to meet the possibly even more daunting task of getting an LTBT through the Senate. Eventually this was done, but only by "buying" the acquiescence of the Joint Chiefs of Staff through commitments for a number of "safeguards" to ensure a robust continuing nuclear capability. One of these safeguards was provision to ensure that if the test ban were ever terminated, the United States would be able to resume atmospheric testing without great delay. While such a hedge may have been prudent in 1963, such preparations to resume atmospheric testing continued to be funded and carried out for thirty years until someone discovered in 1993 that this wasteful activity was still continuing by inertia; everyone, including the Joint Chiefs of Staff, readily agreed that it should then cease, as it should have years earlier.

It is not too much to describe this movement forward in arms control from June to November 1963 as a significant beginning of a détente. Yet both Kennedy and Khrushchev faced some opposition to détente. Kennedy was planning to move more boldly after his reelection in 1964. In private correspondence, they exchanged expectations of advancing. In response to an encouraging letter from Khrushchev, Kennedy wrote in his last communication to him on October 20, 1963, that he was "convinced that the possibilities for an improvement in the international situation are real," but in need of their attention. Ironically, that last letter was never sent, as the result of a clerical error in the State Department not discovered until after Kennedy had been killed.[7] A year later, Khrushchev also had been driven from office.

Working at the State Department in the 1960s I was kept quite busy. Even so, I did also keep active in my outside academic contacts, activities, and writing. I participated in a number of academic conferences and contributed to a number of scholarly collaborative books. At the end of my September 1963 trip in Eastern Europe I participated in the annual conference of the International Institute for Strategic Studies in London on a study panel with Dean Acheson, whom I had previously known only slightly, and with whom I got along very well. I met with the German specialist on Soviet affairs Richard Lowenthal, whom I knew from CIA days, when I was in Berlin in 1962, and with Basil Liddell Hart at his country home in England in 1963. When the Swedish government expert on Soviet affairs Dr. Stellan Bohm visited the United States in mid-1962, I arranged for him to meet American academic figures, including Henry Kissinger and Herman Kahn. I was approached about several academic appointments, but while continuing active contact with the academic world, I was well settled into government service.

Camelot was gone, but the business of American foreign relations and security policy, above all the balance of détente and confrontation, remained. And I was eager to contribute to meeting that challenge.

---

7. See Michael Beschloss, *The Crisis Years: Kennedy and Khrushchev, 1960–1963* (Edward Burlingame Books–Harper Collins, 1991), pp. 662–63. Khrushchev's letter of October 10, 1963, is printed in the official U.S. diplomatic record, but because the last letter from Kennedy was never sent, it is not. See *Foreign Relations of the United States, 1961–1963*, vol. 6, *Kennedy-Khrushchev Exchanges* (Government Printing Office, 1996), pp. 309–11.

10

The Cuban Missile Crisis:
Turning Point of the Cold War

On the morning of October 16, 1962, President John F. Kennedy learned from National Security Adviser McGeorge Bundy that Soviet medium-range missiles had just been discovered in Cuba. This was quite unexpected (except to the new director of central intelligence, John McCone, and a few others). A recent Special National Intelligence Estimate (SNIE 85-3-62) issued on September 19 (at a time when McCone was out of the country) had considered the possibility but concluded that the Soviet leadership would probably not deploy nuclear offensive missiles in Cuba. Nonetheless, the possibility had been recognized, and indeed that is why the U-2 overflights of Cuba had reluctantly been authorized. A reconnaissance mission on October 14 had photographed missile sites under construction, and by the morning of October 15 the identification of missile emplacements under preparation for SS-4 medium-range (1,100-nautical-mile) missiles was positive. The top leadership began to be informed that night, and the president was informed early on the 16th when the finished analysis was ready to be presented.

The Soviet emplacement of strategic offensive nuclear missiles in Cuba would under any circumstances have been a serious development, all the more so that it was done surreptitiously. The fact that President Kennedy had publicly declared on September 4 and 13 that such an action would not be acceptable, and the further fact that a series of high-level deceptive Soviet assurances had been given denying that there would be such deployment, made a crisis confrontation inevitable.

By a quirk of fate, I also learned of the missiles in Cuba on the morning of October 16—although I was not among the handful of authorized officials. I was in the outer office of the CIA deputy director for intelligence, Ray Cline, on other business (in connection with an NIE on the Warsaw Pact that I was helping to draft as a consultant to the agency). I told his executive assistant that Ray had said there was "something new I should know about"—and he assumed it must be about the missiles in Cuba and informed me. (I never did learn what it was that I was *supposed* to have been told about.) A few hours later, after I returned to the State Department, when I was seeing my boss U. Alexis Johnson about something else, I mentioned the missiles in Cuba, and he turned white at the evident breach in security. By that time the president had authorized only a very limited list of officials authorized to know, and I was not on it. I explained how I had learned about the missiles and assured him that I had told no one else and would not do so. Minutes later I was called by the DDI's executive assistant and asked if I had told anyone. I said I had not. I was asked by the very worried young man responsible for having told me to tell no one, and I promised I would not do so. Several days later, I and a few colleagues were told about the new intelligence and brought into the still very secret deliberations about what to do. Alexis Johnson, along with Secretary Rusk and Under Secretary George Ball, was a member of the Ex Comm (the executive committee of the National Security Council) that handled the crisis. The Cuban missile crisis was under way.[1]

The intense thirteen-day period of the crisis in Washington had two distinct phases: the first week, from the morning of October 16 to the evening of October 22, was devoted to secret internal deliberations about how to handle the situation; the second week, from the time of President Kennedy's dramatic address to the country and the world on October 22, culminated in Soviet leader Nikita Khrushchev's acceptance on October 28 of a proposal by Kennedy for resolving the confrontation: Soviet withdrawal of the missiles in exchange for an American commitment not to invade Cuba.

There was more to the deal than was then known—the American proposal had been virtually an ultimatum, but also accompanied by a "sweetener," a secret assurance that the United States would withdraw its missiles from Turkey within five months. So both sides made concessions.

There was also less to the deal than was then known to all but a handful of top advisers—there was no common understanding about how the Soviet withdrawal of missiles from Cuba would be verified, and not even a clear agreement on what "offensive weapons" would be withdrawn. The United States insisted on withdrawal of jet light bombers as well as the medium-range missiles, and that was not agreed (or the quarantine lifted) until November

1. I have written an account of the missile crisis, on which I shall draw, but it is not my intention here to present a full history or analysis of the episode. In addition to giving first-hand impressions I will offer conclusions based on my fuller historical research. See Raymond L. Garthoff, *Reflections on the Cuban Missile Crisis,* rev. ed. (Brookings, 1989).

20. So the final phase of the crisis dragged on for another three weeks after its climax and the agreement in principle on its resolution. There was also much less to the October 28 agreement than appeared because, as the final phase of the aftermath of the crisis from November 1962 to January 4, 1963, showed, there was not even a binding U.S. commitment not to invade Cuba (as will be described later).

The "Cuban Missile Crisis," as it was immediately dubbed in the United States, was seen here as a sudden, intense but clearly defined confrontation precipitated by the secret Soviet deployment of medium-range missiles in Cuba and resolved by their removal. In the Soviet Union, it was called the "Caribbean Crisis"—a designation not only not featuring the missiles, but also implying a deeper cause: an American aggressive threat to Cuba, to which the Soviet missile deployment was a response. In the Soviet (and Cuban) view, the missiles were a product of tension, not its cause. This view was self-serving (especially with respect to the later argument that the American pledge not to invade justified the withdrawal of the missiles—an attempt by Khrushchev to put the best face-saving gloss on what was in fact a humiliating retreat, as both the Cubans and the Soviet military and political leaders well understood). But in a more significant way, the Soviet depiction of the whole affair as a Caribbean crisis generated by an American threat to Cuba did represent their view.

It is now clear that the Soviet motivation for emplacing medium- and intermediate-range missiles in Cuba was an amalgam with two principal objectives. One was to deter a feared prospective American invasion of Cuba, to defend the only "socialist" regime in the Western Hemisphere. The other was to shore up a still very weak Soviet nuclear deterrent to possible U.S. attack on the Soviet Union itself. There was a difference; while the Soviet leaders did fear that the United States would invade Cuba, they did not expect a U.S. nuclear attack on the Soviet Union. Soviet weakness in the strategic balance, however, carried over into weakness in the diplomatic and political competition of the two superpowers. The Soviet leaders were greatly concerned that without redressing the strategic balance they could be vulnerable to Western political pressures, and that their own efforts to advance their political position, notably over Berlin, would be stymied. They could not expand their own weak intercontinental nuclear force for several years, and the "missile gap" in the U.S. favor was by then embarrassingly evident. Soviet medium- and intermediate-range nuclear missiles (MRBMs and IRBMs) in Cuba, however, could redress that balance for a crucial interim few years until they could deploy a more robust deterrent in the Soviet Union with intercontinental ballistic missiles (ICBMs). Even forty MRBM and IRBM missile launchers in Cuba, the number planned in 1962, would have more than doubled the Soviet strategic missile force capable of reaching the United States.

In the deliberations in Washington in October 1962, there was relatively little attention to the question of the Soviet motivation. At first, there was consternation; the deployment had not been expected, except for a few in the intelligence and defense establishments. There was speculation, mostly assuming Soviet intention to place new pressure on the West over Berlin and perhaps also on our overseas bases in general. But the determination of Kennedy and his advisers from the first hours on had crystallized on the aim of removing the missiles from Cuba, and the debates were over how to accomplish that objective, not musing over why the missiles had been put there. There was not even agreement as to whether the missiles significantly increased the military threat to the United States. Secretary of Defense Robert McNamara and some White House aides believed it did not; Assistant Secretary of Defense Paul Nitze and General Maxwell Taylor and the Joint Chiefs of Staff (JCS) believed that it did. But that did not become an issue, because there *was* consensus that for a whole complex of political and military reasons the United States (and specifically the Kennedy administration) could not afford to let the missiles remain after the president's solemn warning in September that if there was a missile deployment "the gravest issues will arise" (September 4) and "then this country will do whatever must be done to protect its own security and that of its allies" (September 13). Moreover, the administration had been fending off a major Republican onslaught charging it with failure to recognize a threat from Cuba. The credibility of President Kennedy at home, and of the United States with its allies and adversaries abroad, was seen as being at stake. We would have to do "whatever must be done."

I have nothing to add to earlier accounts of the deliberations in the Ex Comm that developed into a debate between the "hawks," who believed we should bomb the missile sites and invade the island, and the "doves," who sought a diplomatic resolution of the conflict. From an early inclination by most members to launch an attack, the luxury of several days to deliberate led to a consensus instead to mount a naval blockade to prevent any further military buildup in Cuba, and to serve as the first step in seeking to get the missiles withdrawn. An air strike or a broader military invasion of the island remained future options if needed, and a U.S. military buildup for both alternatives proceeded apace. Diplomatic negotiation was, however, the preferred path—although only after the United States had clearly set its objective of removal of the offensive weapons and its initial show of determination by a blockade (termed a "quarantine," since technically a blockade is an act of war). Ambassador Charles (Chip) Bohlen, in particular, initially Ambassador Llewellyn (Tommy) Thompson, and several others had at the outset recommended a confidential approach to Khrushchev. I believe that would have been a mistake. More to the point, so did President Kennedy and most of the

Ex Comm members. Bohlen soon left for his new post in Paris as previously planned and announced; Thompson played an important and helpful role in the Ex Comm deliberations throughout the crisis.

While the Defense Department was gearing up to handle the quarantine and to meet various military contingencies, in the State Department we worked on the many varied diplomatic actions required. This included preparations for rallying the support of the Organization of American States (OAS) for the quarantine; for last-hour consultations with key allies; for calling a UN Security Council meeting; for key congressional consultation; and the like. For example, in the forty-eight hours from midnight October 20 to midnight October 22, the State Department transmitted fifteen separate presidential letters or messages to 441 recipients, with appropriate instructions on delivery, gave oral briefings to 95 foreign ambassadors (including Secretary Rusk to Soviet Ambassador Anatoly Dobrynin one hour before the president's speech), and drafted and dispatched the texts of U.S. proposals for the OAS and UN forums and appropriate background messages to various embassies. (This included a warning to 134 U.S. embassies and consulates to take precautions against possible hostile demonstrations after the president's address.)

These preparations were highly successful. The State Department had been confident of obtaining the support of a majority, even the two-thirds majority needed for an OAS imprimatur on the quarantine, but not of obtaining— as they did—a unanimous OAS vote on October 23 condemning the missiles as a threat to the peace and calling for their removal.

High-level diplomatic and intelligence emissaries showed photographs of the missile and other military installations to key allied leaders, and later in the UN Security Council and to the public. Convincing American evidence prevailed over Soviet denials of missile deployment, and secrecy weakened later Soviet claims of normalcy in providing military assistance to a friendly state. Two leftist African states, Guinea and Senegal, acceded on October 23 to U.S. requests that they deny use of the airfields at Conakry and Dakar to Soviet aircraft, foreclosing to the Soviet Union the option of air supply of key military equipment to Cuba.

The critical question was of course the Soviet response. While objecting strenuously to the quarantine, the Soviet Union nonetheless turned back all sixteen ships at sea carrying arms to Cuba.

For four days Khrushchev tried to maneuver for a compromise that would establish a new status quo based on American acquiescence in at least the existing missile deployment in Cuba, comprising some twenty-four MRBM launchers, with thirty-six SS-4 missiles and nuclear warheads. This was about half of the planned deployment of some forty SS-4 MRBM and longer-range SS-5 IRBM launchers, with sixty missiles and warheads in all. The SS-5 missiles were still en route to Cuba when the quarantine prevented their arrival.

By October 26 Khrushchev had become convinced that the United States would not acquiesce in the missile deployment and that time was rapidly running out to reach an agreement on their withdrawal for some quid pro quo before United States military action to destroy the missiles, and probably the Castro regime as well. There is no need to recount the story of the exchanges of messages between Khrushchev and Kennedy that led to agreement. Suffice it to say that with an enormous U.S. bombing and invasion force poised to attack (with more than 1,190 strike sorties planned for the first day, and a week of bombing before an invasion by over 140,000 paratroopers, soldiers and marines), President Kennedy picked up a vague suggestion by Khrushchev for withdrawal of the missiles in exchange for a U.S. pledge not to invade Cuba, and Khrushchev on October 28 agreed. Only years later did it become known that although the U.S. proposal was a virtual ultimatum, it was also coupled with a confidential assurance that within five months the United States would also remove its missiles from Turkey. But at the time only a handful of people in Washington knew that.

No one knows what President Kennedy would have done if Khrushchev had rejected his proposal of October 27, or what the subsequent course of events would have been. At the time, most of us working on the crisis believed President Kennedy would have authorized launch of an air attack on October 29 or 30. I now believe he would have continued to seek a diplomatic resolution, probably tightening the blockade (to interdict all oil and petroleum deliveries, putting a real squeeze on Cuba). It is now known that Kennedy was considering arranging by a back-channel for a call by UN Secretary General U Thant for the Soviet Union to withdraw its missiles from Cuba and for the United States to withdraw its missiles from Turkey. It would have been much easier for Kennedy to accede to a request from the UN secretary general addressed to both than to have publicly accepted Khrushchev's demand that the U.S. withdraw its missiles from Turkey as a quid pro quo.

One reason that it is not possible to know what might have happened is that some developments were not under the control of the leaders. On October 27 a Soviet surface-to-air missile shot down a U.S. U-2 reconnaissance airplane (causing the only combat fatality of the crisis). It is now known that the decision was made by the Soviet air defense commander in Cuba, without Moscow's knowledge or approval (and by bending his own instructions). Moreover, Castro had ordered his forces to fire on the U.S. reconnaissance airflights. I had coordinated with Defense and JCS representatives in preparing contingency plans to retaliate in a measured way for any such shootdown, and President Kennedy had approved these plans, but in the event he decided—wisely, under the circumstances—not to exercise that contingent response, while awaiting Khrushchev's reply to his proposal.

During the six days of confrontation, from October 22 to 28, the debate between "hawks" and "doves" had resumed and intensified. The quarantine had stopped the buildup, but not the completion of construction of the MRBM missile bases in Cuba, and by October 28 all 24 launchers were estimated to be operational (that is, capable of launching missiles; no missiles were ever actually prepared for launching, which might have precipitated a preemptive U.S. strike). The operative question, then, in Washington was how to move beyond the quarantine in order to persuade Khrushchev to withdraw the missiles, and if that did not prove possible, whether and when to launch an air attack and subsequent invasion in order to eliminate the missile threat.

In retrospect, it is clear that we should have devoted more attention to Soviet motivations in placing the missiles in Cuba. The SNIE in September had been wrong in concluding that the Soviet leader would decide not to place offensive missiles in Cuba. Having left the Office of National Estimates a year earlier, I had no part in the estimate—but if I had, I would have been among those incorrectly predicting the Soviet decision. There is a great deal of truth to the anguished argument advanced by some of the authors of the SNIE (Sherman Kent and John Huizenga) that it was not they, but *Khrushchev,* who had made the mistake—they had calculated how Soviet interests would be served better than he had. That, of course, was true, but it was no excuse for failing to recognize that Soviet leaders (or the leaders of any country) may make mistakes—and what counts for the policymaker is what they do, not what they should have done.

Those who believed the Soviets *would* install missiles in Cuba, as well as those who incorrectly estimated they would not, were however in error in basing their conclusions on a projection that the main Soviet objective was to support a political offensive in the world, in particular the effort to dislodge the West from Berlin. That indeed remained a Soviet objective, and Khrushchev almost certainly did intend to use the disclosure of the presence of Soviet missiles in Cuba (which he planned to make known in November) for a new push on his stalled drive on Berlin. No one in Washington, however, to my recollection or on the basis of my review of the record, recognized the extent to which Khrushchev and his colleagues were worried about shoring up their strategic position because of their perceived vulnerability and fear of *Western* pressures. I came close in a memorandum on October 23 to Walt Rostow, then chief of the Policy Planning Council in the State Department, in which I noted that "from a period of publicly anticipated and acknowledged Soviet superiority in overall military power in 1960 [the "missile gap"], the military balance had by late 1961 and since swung more and more against them, and above all this is publicly accepted." But I, too, tended to emphasize the offensive threat behind the Soviet effort to redress that balance. "It may appear in Moscow that missile bases in Cuba represent both the first, and probably the last, opportunity to place a lever under U.S. positions of strength on the Eurasian periphery."[2]

The second principal Soviet motivation had also been brushed aside in Washington during the crisis deliberations: defense of Cuba by deterrence of an expected American attack. In recent years in retrospect former Secretary of Defense McNamara in particular, but also others, have acknowledged that although the United States government had no intention to invade Cuba in the spring and summer of 1962, it is not difficult to see why Cuban and Soviet leaders at the time would have believed that we did. The United States had successfully engineered the suspension of Cuban membership in the OAS at Punta del Este in January 1962 and persuaded fifteen Latin American countries to break diplomatic relations with Cuba. The United States had pressed economic warfare, with a full embargo on U.S. trade after February 1962 and denial of entry to U.S. ports to ships of other countries en route to and from Cuba. The United States had under way a large covert action plan called "Operation Mongoose" aimed at subversion of the Castro government in Cuba, and had been conducting sabotage and attempted assassination activities. (Although the program was secret, these activities were of course well known to the Cuban and Soviet authorities.) After failure of the U.S.-sponsored Cuban émigré military landing at the Bay of Pigs in April 1961, the United States had been conducting a long series of military exercises testing contingency plans for attack and invasion of Cuba. Yet at the time we failed to see that this concerted U.S. campaign of overt and covert political, economic, psychological, subversive, and military activities directed at the Cuban regime might well lead Cuba and the Soviet Union to see a need to bolster defenses against an anticipated American attack by a Soviet military presence and a retaliatory deterrent capability.

One consequence of our failure to evaluate the reasons for the Soviet missile deployment was that the United States was unable to devise a negotiating proposal to advance from October 22 until October 27. Only after the Soviet Union had made known its interest in an American pledge against invasion of Cuba as a quid pro quo for withdrawal of the missiles did Kennedy fashion a proposal on that basis, one that was then promptly accepted.

To some extent, the differences between hawks and doves depended not only on evaluations of Soviet objectives, but also on our own objectives. Those most eager to overthrow the Castro regime, for example, were among the

---

2. Memorandum from G/PM Raymond L. Garthoff to S/P Mr. [Walt W.] Rostow, Subject: "Reflections on the Confrontation over Cuba," October 23, 1962, p. 1(top secret; declassified November 30, 1981). Cited from the text reproduced in Garthoff, *Reflections,* p. 195.

most strongly in favor of an invasion. Those most inclined to work through international diplomacy were among those most anxious to avoid unilateral U.S. military action. Those concerned over U.S. credibility with our allies wanted to show our readiness to meet our commitment not to allow missiles in Cuba, although not to display an overeagerness to resort to military action, but also to avoid any deal that would undermine our alliance commitments such as a trade of missiles in Turkey for those in Cuba. While the two Republican Ex Comm members (DCI John McCone and Treasury Secretary C. Douglas Dillon) were hawks, they both joined the consensus in favor of a blockade on October 20 and supported the final proposal for a settlement on October 27. The most unreconstructed hawk was Dean Acheson, the only non-official brought into the Ex Comm, who left it on October 20 when the decision was made to institute a blockade instead of an air strike.

Throughout the crisis, I counseled firm resolve to remove the missiles, preferably by persuasion, but if necessary by military means. In this sense, I was perhaps what can be termed a "moderate hawk." As I argued in another memorandum to Walt Rostow on October 25 in mid-confrontation, "If we maintain the original resolve to use whatever means are necessary, though not more than are necessary, to effect the withdrawal of Soviet striking power from Cuba, I believe the Soviets will in fact recognize that the United States does have the high cards." By October 25 I was concerned that we were flagging in our resolve and prematurely seeking some concession or trade-off. While acknowledging that "the terms for eventual negotiation might well include some give by the United States as well as by the U.S.S.R.," I argued it was then more important to signal our resolve. "The Soviets will simply not expect the United States to be offering concessions at a time when they have brought no counterpressure to bear on us in response to the quarantine. Any such indication (and the press is already rife with such rumors of trading off bases in Turkey, etc.), will mean to Moscow only that the United States is *not* prepared to *compel* the retraction of Soviet offensive power from the Western Hemisphere. One doesn't buy what is already his. If we concede that we must purchase the Soviet withdrawal, we undermine our right to compel it." While noting that our missile base in Turkey was not militarily important, I argued that "Berlin, too, is not *militarily* significant."[3]

I strongly opposed the idea of a trade-off of the U.S. missiles in Turkey for withdrawal of the Soviet missiles in Cuba, as both damaging in the NATO alliance and not necessary to secure the Soviet withdrawal. I was confident, by

3. Memorandum from G/PM Raymond L. Garthoff to S/P Mr. [Walt W.] Rostow, Subject: "Concern over the Course and Outcome of the Cuban Crisis," October 25, 1962, pp. 2–3 (italics in original) (top secret; declassified November 23, 1981). Cited from the text reproduced in Garthoff, *Reflections*, pp. 197–98.

October 27, that Khrushchev would withdraw the missiles without that concession.[4] I still believe he would have. The confidential assurance that Kennedy gave that he intended to remove missiles from Turkey was, however, a "sweetener" that facilitated Khrushchev's acceptance of the missile withdrawal in exchange for an assurance that the United States did not intend to invade Cuba.

On the other hand, although I was prepared to contemplate the use of military force if necessary to compel the Soviet withdrawal of their missiles from Cuba, I was not among the hawks who sought to use our overwhelming military advantage to pursue some new more far-reaching objective such as the elimination of communism in Cuba. I recall very clearly a small caucus of a few hard-line State Department officers (and Dorothy Fosdick, then chief aide to Senator Henry Jackson) with Dean Acheson, at which I was the only non-warhawk uncomfortably present.

As earlier noted, the question of the military significance of the Soviet missiles in Cuba was a controversial but not central issue in the deliberations. I was tasked after the Ex Comm meeting on October 26 to prepare an evaluation of the strategic significance of the missiles. I did so, concluding that the missiles in Cuba provided "a significant accretion to Soviet strategic capabilities for striking the continental United States." Not only would a first-strike missile salvo be increased by at least 40 percent (actually, we now know by even more), but owing to the paucity of Soviet strategic forces at that time would have permitted them to attack additional forces that otherwise they could not. I concluded that it would not upset the strategic balance, but it would dilute our existing strategic superiority.[5] I don't know whether my memorandum had any real effect, but it did enter the debate. Nitze has cited it as confirming his views; on the other hand, I was not surprised when McGeorge Bundy told me a few years ago (and has written) that it did not affect President Kennedy's or his own (or McNamara's) general judgment.[6]

During the crisis, I was engaged with representatives of the Department of Defense as well as relevant bureaus of the State Department in contingency planning for further steps in the crisis itself, and later for measures to implement the agreement. For example, I coordinated draft positions on both

4. See Memorandum (for U. Alexis Johnson from Raymond L. Garthoff), Subject: "The Khrushchev Proposal for a Turkey-Cuba Tradeoff," October 27, 1962 (secret; declassified November 20, 1981). Full text reproduced in Garthoff, *Reflections*, pp. 200–01.

5. Memorandum [for the Ex Comm], Subject: "The Military Significance of the Soviet Missile Bases in Cuba," October 27, 1962 (top secret; declassified November 23, 1981). The full text is reproduced in Garthoff, *Reflections*, pp. 202–03, and discussed on pp. 204–11.

6. See McGeorge Bundy, *Danger and Survival: Choices About the Bomb in the First Fifty Years* (Random House, 1988), pp. 451–52; Nitze is quoted in James G. Blight and David A. Welch, *On the Brink: Americans and Soviets Reexamine the Cuban Missile Crisis* (Hill & Wang, 1989), p. 150.

short- and long-term verification arrangements to monitor removal of the offensive arms in Cuba and to ensure against future reintroduction of such weapons. As the situation changed, for example the adamant Cuba refusal to allow inspection on its soil, so did our contingency plans. Moreover, we needed to draft instructions to our representatives in the United Nations, OAS, and NATO so that we could keep our allies working with us and get UN approval for various measures. One of my counterparts in this contingency planning was a bright Navy captain working for Paul Nitze, Elmo (Bud) Zumwalt, later a controversial chief of naval operations.

After Khrushchev's acceptance on October 28 of Kennedy's proposal for the United States to end the quarantine and pledge not to invade Cuba in return for Soviet withdrawal of its offensive weapons from Cuba, the height of the crisis had passed. Two major issues, nonetheless, remained, as well as several lesser ones.

First was the matter of defining the "offensive weapons" that must be removed. Clearly it included the medium-range missiles, their nuclear warheads, and associated equipment. The Soviet leaders probably did believe that these were the only weapons that the United States was insisting be removed. They were therefore taken aback when the United States soon made clear that "offensive weapons" in our view also included at least the IL-28 jet light bombers in Cuba (at first we also listed the short-range missile-carrying coastal defense craft and short-range tactical ground force rockets). The Soviet case was greatly weakened by the fact that Khrushchev, to avoid reference to the missiles, had in his message agreed to withdraw "the weapons that you consider 'offensive.'"

There were divided views among American policymakers and advisers over how strongly to stand on this issue. Some believed that because the missiles had been our real concern, it was unwise and imprudent to appear to be pushing our advantage by raising objections to the IL-28s or any other weapon system. On the other hand, some wished to press our advantage and to demand the removal of *all* Soviet military forces. Still others believed we should seek removal at least of the Il-28 bombers.

The administration had, in fact, been prepared until October 16 to accept some jet light bombers in Cuba, but once the Soviets were known to be introducing nuclear-armed medium-range ballistic missiles, the definition of unacceptable offensive arms in Cuba was drawn more tightly. On October 22 the president had applied the quarantine to "all offensive military equipment" going to Cuba, including bombers.

The debate within the administration began at the Ex Comm meeting on October 28. President Kennedy agreed we should seek to include the Il-28s, but at that point the notes of the meeting quote him as saying that "he did not want to get into a position where we would appear to be going back on our part of the deal. The Il-28 bombers were less important than the strategic missiles." This somewhat equivocal stand was, of course, known only to those few most directly involved in the crisis management. And the decision did not specify how far to press the issue, if the Soviets were adamant before deciding we were stymied. The differing views in the administration continued.

Following the Ex Comm meeting, I was tasked at the State Department with preparing a paper on the subject. I submitted a memorandum titled "Considerations in Defining Weapons Which Must Be Removed from Cuba" to Deputy Under Secretary Alexis Johnson on October 29, and he in turn cabled it to Under Secretary Ball in New York. I noted that "we would like to see the maximum military withdrawal from Cuba, but we must balance against this a reasonable interpretation." I concluded that it was not reasonable retroactively to label as offensive weapons MiG fighters, coastal defense cruise missiles, and missile-armed patrol boats that had been in Cuba, and tacitly accepted by the president when he issued his warnings on September 4 and 13. But I concluded we should insist on the Il-28 bombers as well as the medium- and intermediate-range missiles.[7] I believed we should stand firm on the bombers as offensive weapons, as listed by the president on October 22, as a matter of principle, but also that we should not attempt to broaden our demands once the Soviet side was prepared to accept them.

That is the position the president decided on. I was confident Khrushchev would give in on withdrawal of the bombers. More important, so did Tommy Thompson, and his judgment carried great weight with President Kennedy, who had initially equivocated on the bombers. Eventually the Russians persuaded Castro to accede. Accordingly on November 20, President Kennedy announced Soviet agreement to remove the bombers and ended the quarantine. Both sides ended their military alerts. By then the crisis was really over.

Subsequently, the United States did seek to persuade the Soviet leaders to remove the four regiments of Soviet ground troops we had identified in Cuba during the crisis. One of these, incidentally, was commanded by Colonel Dmitry Yazov, some thirty years later the Soviet defense minister and in August 1991 co-conspirator in the failed coup d'etat against President Mikhail

7. Telegram no. 1133, State Department to the U.S. Mission to the United Nations (hereafter, State to USUN), Eyes Only, Under Secretary Ball from Alexis Johnson, October 29, 1962, pp. 1–2 (secret; now declassified). This telegram, via State Department "backchannel," transmitted the full text of the memorandum I had prepared titled "Considerations in Defining Weapons Which Must Be Removed from Cuba." It is reproduced in Garthoff, *Reflections,* pp. 212–13. The entire Il-28 issue, and other matters noted here and on the pages following, are discussed more fully in Garthoff, *Reflections,* pp. 97–129.

Gorbachev! Within a few months three of the regiments returned to the Soviet Union. Castro persuaded the Soviet leaders to leave one, re-designated a brigade, but the issue then faded away—until it reemerged in 1979 in a brouhaha precipitated by the belated U.S. discovery of a Soviet combat brigade in Cuba and incorrect initial assumption that it represented a new deployment.

One important matter did remain after November 20, one that the Soviet side continued to pursue for another month and a half: formulation of a U.S. pledge against invasion. Agreement could not be reached, and eventually the matter was left to rest on the exchange of letters between Kennedy and Khrushchev on October 27 and 28, 1962, and oral assurances by President Kennedy. While the United States was quite prepared to affirm an assurance that it had no intention of invading Cuba, it was not prepared to give a blank check to Cuba and the Soviet Union. If circumstances changed—for example, use of Cuba as a base for aggression against some neighboring country—the United States insisted on retaining its right to take military action against Cuba in accordance with its rights and obligations under Article 51 of the UN Charter on individual and collective self-defense and under the Rio Treaty. From a practical point of view, since the United States would unilaterally determine whether the situation had changed and warranted military action (and, indeed, the invasion contingently prepared for in October–November 1962 before the crisis was resolved had been justified under the Rio Treaty), such an assurance was very hollow. Reluctantly, the Soviets decided they were better off leaving the vague assurance rest on President Kennedy's letter (even though that had been hinged on several conditions that had not been met—UN verification of withdrawal of the offensive arms and "lasting safeguards" against their re-introduction).[8]

President Kennedy understood very well that while the outcome of the missile crisis had been a triumph, and while his entourage capitalized on that outcome as his triumph and that of the United States, it was not the kind of success he wanted to repeat. The burden and the risks, and the uncertainties of chance, were far too great. The resolution of the crisis had involved more of a mutual compromise than the public then knew; the successful outcome was not the fruit of a newly found and proven tool of coercive diplomacy, even if his political standing at the time benefited from the widespread view that it had.

President Kennedy's speech at American University in June 1963, as noted in the previous chapter, set exactly the right tone of a new approach in American-Soviet relations, seeking a mutual move toward improving relations. I had nothing to do with the decision on the speech, although I had par-

---

8. Garthoff, *Reflections,* pp. 125–27.

ticipated in the post-crisis policy planning under Walt Rostow's direction that I hope contributed to its thrust. As noted in the previous chapter, several arms control agreements were reached in 1963 and a broader détente did begin to emerge. Both sides, however, continued to be very cautious about détente. Moreover, Khrushchev's position had been weakened by his errors in the Cuba venture, and in two years he was removed. President Kennedy was assassinated just one year after the crisis ended. And new issues arose, above all Vietnam.

Nonetheless, the Cuban missile crisis had a profound impact on both the United States and the Soviet Union and their future relations. Strong and even sharp differences from time to time arose, and conflicting interests caused continuing recurrent tension and even confrontation. Yet never again did a crisis threaten war. In that sense, while the Cold War continued, the missile crisis was a turning point.

There were greatly diverging views among participants in the crisis at the time, and among them and historians ever since, as to how great the danger of war had been in October 1962. While there were many reasons for individuals to have reacted differently and to have judged the danger differently, there also appears to have been a significant divide between the top leaders and the senior professional experts in the State Department, CIA and the military. President Kennedy, Under Secretary of State Ball, and Secretary of Defense McNamara, as well as some senior White House aides such as Ted Sorenson, felt that the risk of war had been very great. I am not sure if Secretary Rusk was in the same category. (The hawks, on the other hand, such as Nitze, McCone, and Dillon, by and large did not.) But most of us at the level of expert adviser, especially analysts of Soviet policy, believed the risk of war, while heightened, remained low. President Kennedy soon after the crisis made an off-the-cuff estimate that the danger of war had been between three in one or even chances. Most of us would have said it was never more than one hundred to one, and probably much less.

One reason for the discrepancy no doubt was the heavy burden of responsibility felt by the president and some of his closest top associates. As advisers, others had less responsibility, as well as more readiness to rely on our judgment of the Soviet reaction (notwithstanding the fact that most of us had been wrong on the question of whether Khrushchev would put the missiles in Cuba in the first place). Undoubtedly, the prudence shown by both President Kennedy and Chairman Khrushchev was crucial, but it was equally fitting whether the odds of war were seen as even or "only" a hundred to one.

Divergent judgments remain to this day over how the Soviet leadership would have responded to an American air attack and invasion of Cuba. McNamara and Sorenson, for example, believed in 1962 and believe today that the Soviet leaders would have felt compelled to make a military response somewhere. The hawks, such as Nitze, McCone and Dillon did not. Nor did I or most other professional experts. Russian veterans of the crisis are also divided—some, particularly military men like General Anatoly Gribkov, believe (or purport to believe) that there would have been some military response. Others, including Khrushchev's foreign policy aide at the time, Ambassador Oleg Troyanovsky, believe there would not have been. Although the archival record is only partly open, there is no evidence of any contingency plans for a Soviet military response. Also, we now know that during the crisis Khrushchev told several other Soviet leaders and advisers that under no circumstances could they permit war, and he angrily rejected a suggestion by Vasily Kuznetsev to take even nonmilitary countermeasures against Berlin— one of the principal concerns of American policymakers.

Many of us conducting research on the crisis in recent years have been struck by the number of incidents in which the top leaders failed to control events despite extraordinary efforts to do so, and the risk from uncontrolled actions was no doubt even greater than realized at the time. Still, the strong resolve and prudence shown by both leaders was even more important.

The most significant conclusion probably is that whatever the risk of war was in 1962, even if it was considerably lower than the top leaders then believed, there was a fundamental underlying determination on both sides not to permit war. Moreover, that determination was reinforced by what McGeorge Bundy has termed "existential nuclear deterrence" that was more important than deterrence based on calculating the strategic balance. It is not surprising that Khrushchev would have been deterred from escalating to war because of the overwhelming U.S. strategic superiority at the time. What is surprising to those who have thought in traditional terms about nuclear deterrence is that President Kennedy, despite that overwhelming superiority, was equally deterred by the prospect of taking actions that might escalate to nuclear war.

I vividly recall the enthusiasm of a senior Air Force planner, a three-star general, who told me at the peak of the crisis that we had a 90 percent chance of destroying 99 percent of Soviet strategic forces, and a 99 percent chance of destroying at least 90 percent of the Soviet forces, in a U.S. first strike. Leaving aside whether that was an accurate estimate (it was credible), clearly at no other time before or since did either side have a higher degree of superiority. The United States at the end of October 1962 had a first-strike salvo of over three thousand strategic nuclear weapons (with many nuclear bombs remaining). The Soviet Union, if it had marshaled all of its forces with even a marginal intercontinental capability, could not have placed more than three hundred weapons on the United States in a first strike. But even if the United States had attacked first—an option President Kennedy never considered—

under the optimum estimate of the Air Force planner the Soviet Union might have been able to place some three to thirty thermonuclear weapons on American targets. In terms of war-gaming theory and deterrence-based strategic calculus, the United States would have won handily—three thousand weapons delivered versus thirty. But no president, no responsible political leader of the United States or the Soviet Union, would have ever chosen such a victory if there were a choice and war could be avoided. The common nuclear danger was a far more potent force in constraining the crisis than all the calculated criteria of the military balance and deterrence. Kennedy preferred to make some concessions in a negotiated settlement rather than take military action far less risky then initiating a nuclear war even from a position of overwhelming strength.

There was a general recognition after the Cuba confrontation, above all by responsible political leaders on both sides, that nuclear war or any action seriously risking nuclear war must be avoided. That cardinal lesson of the crisis was learned.

The second principal lesson that should have been learned, but regrettably was not, was that deterrence could rest on a relatively modest secure and assured capability for retaliatory devastation. It did not require arcane calculations of who would have the largest surviving force after several rounds of thermonuclear "exchanges" involving thousands of warheads and millions of lives. The United States as well as the Soviet Union failed to recognize and apply this lesson. Instead, the two superpowers engaged in pursuit of deterrence based on a war-waging capability and engaged in a fruitless, costly, and tension-engendering strategic arms race for more than a quarter of a century. Parity and a strategic balance and stalemate was achieved and preserved, but at a needless cost in quantitative and qualitative "enhancements" of deterrence that yielded no strategic or political gain to either side, as they should have realized would be the case.

Although my thinking on strategic matters was influenced by the experience of the crisis at the time, I certainly did not then draw so clearly the conclusions that I present now. I shared in the general elation that we had succeeded in turning back a Soviet challenge. I drew the conclusion that "firmness in the last analysis will force the Soviets to back away from rash initiatives," and that the outcome demonstrated that "the Soviets are not prepared to risk a decisive military showdown with the U.S. over issues involving the extension of Soviet power." I also speculated that "over the long run, one effect may be to make the Soviets far more responsive to our efforts at finding peaceful solutions to the whole range of world problems," although I emphasized that prospect was at best over the long run. At the same time, I argued that even in the near run, the United States should "take the initiative in offering to negotiate on major issues between East and West."[9] This is why I so welcomed President Kennedy's American University speech and its openness to improving relations with the Soviet Union to the extent the other side was prepared.

Some time later, I was surprised and proud to be awarded the Department of State's Superior Honor Award with silver medal for my contribution during the Cuban missile crisis.

In 1962, as I lived through the missile crisis, I could never have imagined that thirty years later I would have the opportunity to discuss the crisis with Fidel Castro, Andrei Gromyko, and leading Soviet and Cuban military and intelligence men whom we had then been facing at a distance in fateful confrontation. The conjunction of the melting of the Cold War and the passing of a quarter century led some of us by 1987 to launch a unique experiment in a joint look back at the missile crisis by surviving American and Soviet participants and historians. A large number of U.S. documents being declassified at that time supplemented (and often modified) the plethora of memoir and participant-inspired accounts of the 1960s and 1970s that had previously provided the basis for popular and historical writings. Very little had yet appeared from Soviet sources, although a trickle had begun. Sergo Mikoyan, son of the Soviet leader who had had the unenviable task of bringing Castro around to accept the settlement Khrushchev had made in 1962, in 1986 asked me to write an article on the crisis for the journal *Latinskaya Amerika,* of which he was editor. I agreed to do so provided he too would write one based on his father's recollections (as earlier told to Sergo). He agreed, and decided also to commission an article by a leading Cuban analyst. That little symposium in a Soviet academic journal was a "first" in several respects—a first U.S./Soviet/Cuban collaboration on the subject, a first recounting based on Anastas Mikoyan's memoirs, and a first exposure to a Soviet journal audience of American views.[10]

I subsequently decided to write a book with a fuller account and reflection on the crisis, drawing on my own experience but also all available sources, Russian as well as American, including declassified U.S. documents. My

9. Memorandum for U. Alexis Johnson, Subject: "Significance of the Soviet Backdown for Future U.S. Policy," October 29, 1962 (secret; declassified June 10, 1977); from the full text in Garthoff, *Reflections,* pp. 214 and 216. I was the drafter of this memo, sent by Jeffrey C. Kitchen.

10. Raymond L. Garthoff, "The Caribbean Crisis (Cuban Missile Crisis) of 1962: Reflections of an American Participant," Rafael Hernandez, "The October Crisis of 1962: Lesson and Legend," and S. A. Mikoyan, "The Caribbean Crisis in Retrospect," *Latinskaya Amerika* (Latin America), no. 1 (January 1988), pp. 40–80.

account also gave more extensive attention to Cuban aspects of the crisis then had previous American studies.[11]

Meanwhile, a conference of American participants and historians met in Hawk's Cay, Florida, in March 1987, under the auspices of Harvard University, and a second follow-on conference in Cambridge in October 1987 included Soviet representatives too, including Sergo Mikoyan, although none were direct veterans of the Soviet 1962 crisis. Several other conferences continued to expand participation and to spur more disclosures and releases of declassified documents. The next three conferences in Moscow (1989), Antigua (1991), and Havana (1992) included Cuban veterans of the crisis as well.[12]

The Moscow conference brought a large number of Soviet veterans of the crisis and other political observers and historians into the process. Andrei Gromyko and Anatoly Dobrynin, as well as the 1962 Soviet ambassador in Havana, Aleksandr Alekseyev, were among the Soviet participants (which also included the KGB *Rezident* in Washington in 1962, Aleksandr Feklisov, and the GRU military intelligence go-between in the back-channel Kennedy-Khrushchev exchanges of 1961–62, Georgy Bol'shakov). Several leading Cuban figures from Castro's entourage in 1962 were also there. Declassified documents were, however, still slow to appear.

The Havana conference in January 1992, only a few weeks after the dissolution of the Soviet Union, included active participation by Fidel Castro. I had the opportunity to ask Castro several specific questions about the crisis and its aftermath, and in general what he had to contribute was quite interesting (including the fact that he had not known at the time, and indeed not until I noted it in Havana, how weak the Soviet Union was in strategic intercontinental forces in 1962). Castro seemed to welcome the opportunity to discuss the crisis with us, particularly with Bob McNamara. He also enjoyed some out-of-conference conversations with Ray Cline, who had been the deputy director for intelligence in CIA, and me. I presented him with a large chart with color photographs of all of the then current members of the Cuban leadership prepared by CIA that I had brought along. He was intrigued and asked to be sure he had understood that he could keep it. Raul Castro, his brother

11. Raymond L. Garthoff, *Reflections on the Cuban Missile Crisis* (Brookings, 1987). A later revised edition (1989) has been cited earlier in this chapter.

12. For accounts, including edited transcripts, of the Hawk's Cay and Cambridge conferences, see Blight and Welch, *On the Brink;* for the Moscow conference, see Bruce J. Allyn, Blight, and Welch, *Back to the Brink: Proceedings of the Moscow Conference on the Cuban Missile Crisis, January 27–28, 1989* (University Press of America, 1992); and for the Havana conference, Blight, Allyn, and Welch, *Cuba on the Brink: Castro, the Missile Crisis, and the Soviet Collapse* (Pantheon, 1993). There have been several other international conferences on the Cuban missile crisis under various auspices.

and the defense minister, one evening took several of us, including McNamara, General William Y. Smith, Ray Cline, and Sergei Khrushchev (Nikita Khrushchev's son), to his office and showed us a special chamber with his hot line to Moscow. He wanted Sergei to pick it up and say in Russian "This is Khrushchev speaking," but Sergei, somewhat intimidated by the whole scene, declined. Raul went on at some length about the extensive preparations (currently in 1992, not in 1962) to meet any U.S. invasion and seemed somewhat nonplussed that the only reaction from McNamara and the rest of us was to deplore the waste of resources.

The key question, of course, is what have we learned from opening the archives and exchanging views from both sides of the crisis (or really all three sides, to give the Cubans their due). As I have indicated in my review of the crisis, we have clarified the Soviet motivations for deploying the missiles in Cuba, and Khrushchev's decision during the crisis on withdrawing them. The American determination to have the missiles removed, one way or another, was confirmed, but we have learned that President Kennedy would have continued to seek a negotiated solution and if necessary probably made further concessions; resort to military means would have been only a last resort. Both leaders, and most but not all of their advisers, were keenly aware of the risks of uncontrolled escalation if hostilities were begun. We have learned that Castro advised Khrushchev that if the United States invaded Cuba he should not lose the strategic initiative but preemptively strike the United States first with the nuclear weapons of the Soviet arsenal—but that this advice only reinforced Khrushchev's determination to end the crisis promptly on the terms offered by the United States. Castro might have thought that the fate of Socialism, of Cuba, and the Soviet Union was inextricably linked, but Khrushchev did not and was resolute that Soviet security not be made hostage to any outcome of the crisis over Cuba.[13]

We have confirmed that the nuclear warheads for the missiles were in Cuba, which had been prudently assumed in 1962 when it could not be established. On the other hand, only recently have we learned that there were also about a hundred tactical nuclear weapons in Cuba available to counter an invasion force. While the possible presence of tactical nuclear warheads for dual-capable weapons was not excluded by cautious U.S. military planners, Kennedy and other policymakers (and intelligence estimators) did not really believe they were there. If an invasion had been undertaken, some of the tactical nuclear weapons would probably have survived the seven-day air bombardment planned to precede the invasion, and with or without authority from Moscow those weapons might have been used against the U.S. invasion

13. See Blight, Allyn, and Welch., *Cuba on the Brink,* pp. 360–64, on Castro's urging of a preemptive Soviet nuclear strike on the United States if Cuba were invaded.

force. So the risks in that event would have been greater than expected, even though both Kennedy and Khrushchev would almost certainly have prevented any escalation of nuclear hostilities beyond Cuba.[14]

The answers to many intriguing secondary questions about the crisis have also received clarification or revision. For example, an initiative by the KGB chief of station in Washington (Aleksandr Feklisov, then known as Fomin) through an American newsman, given some credence and even importance by U.S. policymakers in evaluating Khrushchev's terms for settling the crisis, has now been determined to have been an unauthorized probe, misrepresented to Moscow, and not involved in the actual decision by Khrushchev to resolve the crisis. On the other hand, only now has it become known that Robert Kennedy, no doubt with his brother's authorization, had early in the crisis through another unofficial but established back-channel (a Soviet GRU military intelligence officer, Georgy Bol'shakov, under Soviet embassy cover as a public affairs officer, also through American newsmen) first hinted to the Soviet side that a deal could be arranged to trade a discreet withdrawal of U.S. missiles from Turkey for the withdrawal of the Soviet missiles from Cuba. Such details about the crisis were not central to it, but they illustrate the complexities and uncertainties in historical reconstruction of events.

One central conclusion that remains is the importance of the Cuban missile crisis not only as the most dangerous confrontation of the Cold War, but also as a turning point in focusing the leaders of both countries on the absolute priority of avoiding nuclear war. The geopolitical rivalry would continue another quarter of a century, as would the arms race, and each side would continue to seek advantages when opportunities arose, but never again would any leader of either country pose a situation in which there was as great a danger of direct hostilities or use of nuclear weapons.

14. See Raymond L. Garthoff, "U.S. Intelligence in the Cuban Missile Crisis," in *Intelligence and the Cuban Missile Crisis,* edited by David A. Welch and James G. Blight, pp. 18–63 (Frank A. Cass, 1998).

11

Department of State: The Johnson Years

President Lyndon B. Johnson, entering office through the tragic death by senseless assassination of a dynamic young president suddenly cut down in his prime and at the height of his popularity, sought at once to emphasize continuity of the administration and its policies at home and abroad. He could not fit the mythical image of Camelot that then prevailed, but he could continue at least initially with essentially the same leadership team and policies. After election as president in his own right a year later, Johnson did set his own distinctive imprint on Washington and on American domestic policy working toward a Great Society, and in foreign policy through inclinations to seek a détente in the Cold War, although both were soon overshadowed and eclipsed by war in Vietnam.

In foreign policy, the triumvirate of Secretary of State Dean Rusk, Secretary of Defense Robert McNamara, and National Security Adviser McGeorge Bundy remained in place, and when changes were later made they were mostly transfers within the team that had come into office with Kennedy, as when Walt Rostow three years later succeeded Bundy. The first year of the Johnson administration (or last year of the Kennedy administration under his successive leadership) saw little initiative and change in foreign policy, but did involve responses to the situation in Vietnam that moved toward greater involvement. No one knows whether Kennedy would have taken the same course. In any case, Vietnam later came to dominate virtually all else and ultimately to bring down the president himself from even seeking a second term.

The war in Vietnam, even though it was so important to the fate of American policy and the Johnson administration, will scarcely figure in this account because I was not involved in policy on Vietnam and have little to contribute on the subject. The only time I was briefly brought into deliberations on policy over Vietnam was in early 1965 when the first crucial decisions on bombing the North and introducing American troops were made. Contrary to what was often said later, there *were* knowledgeable experts on Vietnam in the U.S. government, and their advice was uniformly against direct U.S. intervention, and even more important against seeing the war there as a test of U.S. will and capability to resist the advance of World Communism. This did not, however, fit the preconceptions of most decisionmakers, so such advice (and in the future the experts) was ignored. I was among the government experts on Soviet affairs, and experts on China, who were consulted before the crucial decisions on intervention and escalation were made, but the wrong questions were posed. Political decisionmakers wanted to know if the Soviet Union or China would directly enter the war in Vietnam against us if we intervened. My answer, and that of most if not all of us, was that they would not. But at least some of us went on to say that was not the most important question: the real issue was whether we could prevail and achieve our objectives (a free and viable anticommunist South Vietnam) by American military intervention, and we did not believe that we could. Of course, that issue did transcend whatever expertise we had on Soviet, Chinese or Vietnamese affairs and involved also questions of U.S. will and capabilities. But the critical input on the nature of the situation in Vietnam, and on the nature of the ideological/geopolitical "Communist" challenge, was brushed aside. Policymakers saw a need and a duty, some perhaps even an opportunity, to demonstrate American power and resolve. The belief that the United States was faced with a challenge that it must meet was also sustained by the view of many policymakers, including Dean Rusk, and probably Lyndon Johnson, that the Chinese and Soviet leaders saw Vietnam as a test of a policy of communist expansion through "wars of national liberation" in the Third World. If the communists won in South Vietnam, not only might there be a falling dominos effect in Southeast Asia, but the leaders in Moscow and Beijing might be more tempted to launch or exploit more "wars of national liberation" around the world. While most experts on Soviet and Chinese policy did not share this view, the new experts on "counterinsurgency" and old experts on "World Communism" did. The political leadership, that is to say the president, was most moved by his own beliefs that the United States—with himself at the helm—was being challenged and must respond. The war in Vietnam was permitted to become the overriding element in American policy, despite the fact that the Johnson administration wished to concentrate on the Great Society in domestic affairs and a détente in East-West relations.

None of the few histories of American foreign policy in the Johnson administration have taken note of President Johnson's desire, especially after his own election to the presidency, to meet his Soviet counterpart and develop a détente in relations with the Soviet Union. Most accounts do acknowledge his efforts to carry forward the Kennedy administration's efforts in 1963 to develop arms control and other cooperative security arrangements with the Soviet Union. A pause in possible high-level contacts was of course to be expected as Lyndon Johnson settled into the presidency. There were early Soviet steps to develop relations with the new president and his administration, and by the Johnson-Kennedy successor administration as well. Deputy Prime Minister Anastas Mikoyan had come to the funeral of President Kennedy, and he and Johnson had exchanged reassurances. On November 26, Johnson wrote to Prime Minister Alexsei Kosygin repeating assurances of a desire to improve relations. There was, however, no occasion to do more, and the new American administration faced other tasks.

The Johnson administration did undertake to carry forward the new search for arms control agreements with the Soviet Union that the Kennedy administration had launched in 1963.[1] The first major initiative was an attempt to get agreement on a "Strategic Nuclear Delivery Vehicle (SNDV) Freeze," that is, a cap on the existing numbers and characteristics of strategic bombers and missiles. President Kennedy, some months earlier, had decided on such a step as easier than reductions, particularly given the U.S. superiority in strategic delivery systems. President Johnson, in January 1964, now made this his first presidential arms control initiative. It was conservatively fashioned from the standpoint of a suspicious and very cautious American government establishment and Congress, and the proposal had no attraction for the Soviet leaders: it would have introduced prying verification machinery into the closed Soviet society, and most important it would have frozen the Soviet Union into strategic inferiority.

In addition to representing the State Department in the deliberations leading up to this proposal, I went to Geneva where the proposal was introduced into the disarmament committee. There I had ample opportunity not only to hear the Soviet arguments against our proposal (mainly directed to the verification aspects), but also to sense the gradually evolving thinking on arms control as the Soviet side began to move beyond mere propaganda about "general and complete disarmament." Other variants we tried failed for the same reason as the freeze, for example a proposal for a "bonfire" of medium bombers

1. By far the most thorough account of arms control in the Johnson administration, in particular on nuclear testing and nonproliferation, is the detailed memoir of the former chairman of the Atomic Energy Commission, Glenn T. Seaborg, with Benjamin S. Loeb, *Stemming the Tide: Arms Control in the Johnson Years* (Lexington Books, D. C. Heath, 1986). Many of the key documents are in *Foreign Relations of the United States, 1964–1968*, vol. 11, *Arms Control and Disarmament* (Government Printing Office, 1997); hereafter *FRUS, 1964–1968*.

by the two sides. The proposal that the two countries destroy such bombers on a one for one basis was obviously a non-starter, since it was well known that the United States had decided to phase out its B-47 bombers, while for the Soviet Union its equivalent Tu-16 medium bombers were the mainstay of its bomber force. (The only reason the proposal was made was because it was the sole one to which the JCS and military services would agree—and even then they would agree only to propose reductions exactly on the scale and timetable that the U.S. had already decided upon for unilateral action.) Talk continued in Geneva, but it was to be three years before the United States government was to propose a serious strategic arms control proposal.

The Johnson administration also picked up the idea of informal mutual parallel actions, agreed upon but not formally negotiated obligations. Limits on military expenditures had been mentioned by the Soviet Union as a possible "separate measure" in the summer of 1963. President Kennedy had then taken the initiative with Ambassador Dobrynin in August in suggesting "mutual example," rather than a formal agreement, on limitation in military expenditures. Most of us were very wary of this approach because we knew the Soviet published defense budget was neither comparable to our own nor a reliable indicator of Soviet defense spending. Nonetheless, it was decided that because we were planning to reduce our own defense budget, we might as well try to get some Soviet commitment to do so as well. In late November 1963, shortly after President Kennedy's assassination, Rusk told Dobrynin that we would unofficially advise them of our planned reduced defense budget level, and in early December we did so. A few days later, Dobrynin replied that the Soviet Union would make a cut by almost precisely the same amount. Khrushchev took a public initiative on December 16, 1963, declaring that they had decided to reduce their military budget and suggesting that it would be a good thing if other states did so as well. Johnson and Rusk then publicly noted U.S., and announced Soviet, plans to reduce defense spending, but without referring to any direct relationship or coordination. In February Ambassador Foy Kohler suggested to Gromyko continued reciprocal unilateral budget cuts, and Gromyko endorsed the idea of "mutual example." The next year, in November and December 1964, Gromyko and Rusk again privately advised each other of planned cuts in the next year's budgets, and Kosygin in December in addressing the U.N. General Assembly referred to reductions in military budgets as contributing to détente.

A hazard of this approach became more clear, however, when the next year the United States began again to increase its defense budget owing to Vietnam. In June 1965 Kosygin bitterly complained to former Swedish Prime Minister Tage Erlander, and in July to Averell Harriman, that the United States had reneged on an unwritten "commitment" on reducing military expenditures. In September Gromyko complained to Rusk. Rusk argued that the United

States had only made a unilateral statement of intentions barring unforeseen developments that had later arisen, and it was not an "agreement." But the Soviet leaders were not assuaged. The experiment in mutual example in defense budget reductions had come to an unhappy end.

One other example of this approach was tried. In his State of the Union message in January 1964, President Johnson announced a cutback in U.S. production of enriched uranium and plutonium for nuclear weapons and called on other powers to do the same. He followed this with a private message to Khrushchev in February informing him of such cuts by twenty-five percent. Khrushchev replied that the Soviet Union was also ready, although in an oral message he indicated it would not necessarily be by the same percentage. President Johnson personally told Ambassador Dobrynin in April that he wanted agreement on a mutual example so that he could refer to it in a speech on April 20. The Soviets agreed, and both countries made such declarations on April 20 (followed a day later by Prime Minister Alexander Douglas-Home of the United Kingdom, whom the United States had notified only at the last moment). Our later intelligence was ambiguous; the Soviet Union did cut back production at some facilities, but apparently boosted it in other new facilities. In any case, the U.S. action had been undertaken because we had more fissionable material for weapons than we needed, irrespective of what the Soviets did. The idea of approaching the Soviet leaders to seek a parallel move had originated with Secretary McNamara, and then been vigorously pushed by William Foster of ACDA. Although the subject continued to be discussed in Washington over the next year, there was no further follow-through action along this line for three decades.

I continued to serve as the State Department representative at the Committee of Deputies meetings, and as Secretary Rusk's aide at the Committee of Principals meetings on arms control. I also regularly participated in the meetings of arms control and disarmament experts at NATO headquarters in Paris, attending seven meetings from 1963 through 1967. Apart from the several weeks in Geneva in early 1964 for the SNDV freeze discussions, I did not attend further meetings of the disarmament committee there.

After the failure of the ill-conceived strategic freeze proposal in 1964, there was little to do on bilateral arms control with the Soviet Union. I and most of my colleagues in the State Department did not believe it was useful just to go through the motions if we had nothing serious to propose. For example, when in December 1964 ACDA Director William Foster suggested a general high-level approach to the Soviet leadership on disarmament and arms control even though we had no new substantive proposals, I drafted a memo from Deputy Under Secretary Foy Kohler to Secretary Rusk recommending he sign an enclosed memorandum of reply to Foster turning down the idea, which he did. By this time, while my more hard-line colleagues (including Jeff Kitchen and Sey Weiss in G/PM, and some in the Pentagon) regarded me as an "arms controller," my most dedicated arms control friends in ACDA and some quarters in State (and even Defense) considered me rather conservative on the subject.

The most important arms control issue in the mid-1960s was nuclear nonproliferation, especially following the first Chinese nuclear weapons test in October 1964. The United States had advance intelligence on preparations for the test. Although some aspects of available information were unclear, Secretary Rusk responded to a press question (from a reporter who had been primed to raise the subject) on September 29, about two weeks before the test, in a maneuver intended to deflate the impact of the Chinese test on public opinion by making clear in advance that the United States knew the test was coming and was not alarmed about it. On October 18, two days after the test, President Johnson referred to Rusk's "timely warning" of the test. Those of us who had helped prepare for Rusk's statement anticipating the forthcoming test were pleased that we had been able to put advance intelligence to a useful policy purpose.

A special interagency committee under the auspices of the Policy Planning Council in the State Department, informally called the "Johnson Committee," had been studying the problem of how to deal with the emerging Chinese nuclear program for nearly two years. There remained, however, uncertainty as to what the consequences would be in other countries. Among options it had considered (but rejected) was a U.S. preemptive strike on Chinese nuclear facilities. An even earlier (September 1961) Policy Planning Council proposal to consider helping India acquire a nuclear testing capability prior to Communist China had been rejected by Rusk as contrary to our general nonproliferation interests (although, curiously, he did consider this idea in 1964). Another higher-level interagency committee on nonproliferation had been established in August 1964, chaired by Ambassador Tommy Thompson, and I served as its executive secretary. We too had considered a wide range of possible responses to Chinese development of nuclear capabilities, including a preemptive strike.

After President Johnson's election to the presidency, one of his first initiatives was to establish in November 1964 a special blue-ribbon "Task Force on Nuclear Proliferation," chaired by former Deputy Secretary of Defense Roswell Gilpatric and better known as the "Gilpatric Committee." The task force included such luminaries as my old boss and former director of central intelligence Allen Dulles, John J. McCloy, former NATO supreme commander General Alfred Gruenther, former White House science adviser George Kistiakowsky, and others of similar caliber and reputation. A senior staff for the committee was chaired by Spurgeon Keeny of the NSC staff; I was named to coordinate for the Department of State.

As the State Department representative for the committee, I provided advice and information and wrote a number of memorandums on different aspects of the problem. My main function, however, was to serve as a conduit, arranging to gear the expertise of a number of bureaus of the department into providing full support for the work of the committee. I was given primary responsibility for four of the six main "problem areas": those relating to Europe (mainly the NATO nuclear-sharing arrangements); issues relating to other regions (especially India, Japan, and Israel); possible multilateral agreements (mainly a comprehensive test ban, a nonproliferation agreement, denuclearized zones, no first use policy, and strategic arms control); and policies toward existing nuclear powers (the USSR, China, France, and Britain, especially China and France). Defense dealt with U.S. nuclear weapons policies and practices; ACDA and AEC (Atomic Energy Commission) had principal responsibility for peaceful uses of atomic energy, technical aspects of nuclear weapons, including safeguards and inspection, transfers of technology, and availability of fissionable material. We also arranged briefings by leading experts and officials, as well as briefings for senior officials in our respective departments and agencies. Notwithstanding some spirited differences of judgment, we worked well together.

After nearly three months of intensive work, the Gilpatric Committee submitted its report to the president on January 21, 1965. The Gilpatric Report (fully declassified only in 1996) was treated as very secret, and with good reason. We had considered a wide range of possible antiproliferation measures, including support of nuclear-free zones, military guarantees to India, a broadened commitment to Japan, pressures on Israel, and even rollback actions intended to deprive China of its nuclear capability and to place pressure on France to give up its nuclear weapons program. The more extreme measures were not recommended, but the report did urge giving higher priority to nonproliferation and combining inducements (such as security guarantees) with pressures (including threats to withdraw security commitments).[2]

There were few identifiable concrete results of the work of the Gilpatric Committee. Yet its endeavors were, I believe, fruitful. It helped us all better understand what was, and what was not, feasible. Although I generally supported the conclusions of the report, I did have reservations about some of the conclusions, especially as they could affect our alliance relationships, and I expressed them in an informal memorandum to Secretary Rusk. He, in turn, not only discussed my concerns (which he fully shared), reassuring me, but invited me to join him in a relaxed tête-à-tête lunch in his private back office (where he often dined alone), and we talked candidly at length about a num-

2. See *FRUS, 1964–1968*, vol. 11, pp. 121–82; the text of the report appears on pp. 173–82.

ber of things. I had worked fairly closely with Dean Rusk for over three years at that point, but even more senior officers in the department rarely had such opportunities to chat (when they did, as George Ball and Alex Johnson did most frequently, it was usually over a whiskey at the end of an always long day). We were on an appropriate first-name basis: he called me "Ray," while I always addressed him as "Mr. Secretary."

In late 1964 someone discovered that there were half a dozen different interagency committees engaged or dealing with the implications and consequences of the Chinese nuclear test. In addition to the Thompson and Gilpatric committees, and the Johnson Committee (under Policy Planning Council auspices), there was also a "Fisher Committee" chaired by ACDA Deputy Director Adrian (Butch) Fisher, and an "Ad Hoc Committee on the Chinese Communist Nuclear Detonation" under an interdepartmental psychological-political working group chaired by Under Secretary W. Averell Harriman. I was the only person serving on all these committees and had the additional duty of ensuring that all relevant offices in the State Department were engaged or at least informed. There was also an internal JCS study under way on military implications of the Chinese test that I was responsible for monitoring for State.

The long road to a nuclear nonproliferation treaty, although by no means the only element of our counterproliferation strategy, as I have indicated, remained a central element from 1961 to its conclusion in 1968 (and ratification in 1970). The United States and the Soviet Union shared an interest in nuclear nonproliferation, and the main impediment in reaching an accord was the difficulty in finding a formulation that would reassure the Soviet side that our NATO allies—and above all Germany—would not obtain a nuclear weapons capability, while reassuring our allies—above all Germany, but also Italy—that they were not being frozen into a position of permanent inferiority. The key, of course, was bolstering not only American commitments to our allies, but also allied participation in nuclear deterrence sufficient to reassure them without seeming to Moscow to create a new threat to the Soviet Union.

The main NATO effort to find a solution to its own problem of reassurance from 1962 through 1964 was the attempt to reach agreement on a multilateral nuclear force (MLF), with a seaborne nuclear force with mixed national manning but no individual national control. At first the Johnson administration made a renewed strong effort to rally flagging support for the MLF, but by the end of 1964 Johnson and most of his advisers (especially McGeorge Bundy) had decided the MLF would never work. It was not abandoned, however, until late 1966. Meanwhile, negotiations between the United States and the Soviet Union continued. The key turning point came in December 1966, when we and the Soviets reached tentative agreement—tentative because we still had to obtain allied acceptance before we would proceed.

I was not directly involved in the nonproliferation treaty negotiations with the Soviet side, and only in a limited way in the parallel negotiations with our NATO allies. I was, however, of course directly involved in the internal Washington deliberations including in the Committee of Principals (as well as in such directly related exercises as the work of the Thompson, Gilpatric, and other committees). It was a taxing ordeal.

I believe that Dean Rusk has not been accorded the credit that he is due for persistent if cautious support for the nonproliferation treaty. The most able and active advocate was Adrian (Butch) Fisher, the deputy director of ACDA, more bureaucratically adept than Director William Foster and more ingenious than anyone else in finding ways to resolve difficulties in Washington, with Moscow, and with our NATO allies. But Rusk, like Defense Secretary Robert McNamara, was never so enamored of the MLF as to give it priority over all other objectives, and contributed to ultimately reaching both a better resolution of the issue of shared NATO nuclear planning and a nuclear nonproliferation agreement with Moscow.

I had frequent discussions of nonproliferation, as well as other arms control matters, with allied diplomats in Washington. I remember particularly a vivid comment by an irate Italian diplomat saying that we were still trying to punish the Axis powers (Germany, Italy, and Japan) by keeping them from having nuclear weapons, while the wartime allied powers (the United States, Great Britain, the Soviet Union, and and France) had them. I also had discussions of the NPT with Soviet diplomats.

Along with my continuing work as the State Department focal point on arms control, I continued also to serve as the executive secretary of the NSAM 156 Committee dealing with intelligence aspects of outer space activities. The direct work of this committee, however, although it continued until the end of the Johnson administration, was increasingly routine. The one area in which the committee continued to perform an important function was in reviewing again in 1964 the question of disclosure of satellite photographic reconnaissance capabilities. In September 1964 the North Atlantic Council in Paris was given a briefing, although still one that held back from disclosing the capabilities of our operational systems. There was also discussion in the NSAM 156 Committee, but no recommendation, on possible disclosure of such capabilities for purposes of arms control and disarmament verification. The later resolution of this question was simply to rely, to the extent feasible, on generally acknowledged but not specifically identified "national technical means of verification."

The Policy Planning Council of the State Department included, as one of about twenty ambitious major interagency studies set in train by Walt Rostow in 1963, a study titled "National Security Policy Planning Implications of Outer Space in the 1970s." I was chairman of the committee that prepared the study. We completed it late in 1963 (it was issued on January 30, 1964). It was, incidentally, the only one of the twenty-odd commissioned studies to be completed—all the others fell by the wayside, and formal interagency policy planning faded away.

Even at the time, and still more in retrospect, most of the findings and conclusions of our study (on which there was complete consensus) seem unexceptional. Nonetheless, they helped to establish consensus "boundaries" on various issues that were, and others that could have been, controversial and less informed. We were agreed that the United States should "pursue vigorously the development and use of appropriate and necessary military activities in space, while seeking to prevent extension of the arms race into space." We interpreted national security broadly, including matters of political prestige, and endorsed international cooperation in space activities, while preserving and protecting necessary national military and intelligence programs. We endorsed a ban on deployment of nuclear and other weapons of mass destruction in space.

One of the main conclusions of the study, much less obvious in 1963–64 than today, was that military uses of space would, although of great importance, continue to be "contributory to more fundamental elements of the military balance on earth. . . . We should face squarely the likelihood that military developments in space will not be 'decisive.'" We also discounted alarmism about Soviet ambitions and capabilities in space, still widespread in the mid-1960s.

The main positive contribution of the study was to demonstrate that space weapons for attacking targets on earth were, although feasible, not a cost-effective alternative to earth-based missiles, and neither an attractive option nor a serious danger. The main shortcoming of the study was our failure to oppose the development of anti-satellite systems, space-borne or earth-based. Worse, we endorsed pursuit of such weaponry. We did urge careful consideration of arms control limitations, but we did not specifically press for limitations on anti-satellite weapons. In retrospect, I find that a serious lapse in our forward vision.

The main development in the field of policy on outer space was the negotiation of the Outer Space Treaty of 1967. Among many other things, its terms protected our important military support and reconnaissance (intelligence collection) activities, and it incorporated the language of the 1963 U.N. General Assembly resolution banning deployment in space of weapons of mass destruction. The NSAM 156 Committee monitored the negotiation to assure those objectives, but the actual negotiation was handled by the specialists in the legal and international organization offices.

I was among the officials gathered in the East Room of the White House with President Johnson on January 27, 1967, on the happy occasion of the signing of the Outer Space Treaty. Later that same day we learned that the crew of Apollo I had died in a tragic accident at Cape Kennedy, and our joy turned to ashes.

Among my responsibilities as a "special assistant on Soviet bloc politico-military affairs" I kept up an active interest in Soviet military, and especially strategic and political-military, developments. Ambassador Llewellyn (Tommy) Thompson occasionally asked for my views on current developments in that area (which I would also usually provide to Alex Johnson, Jeff Kitchen, and Tom Hughes, chief of INR, the Bureau of Intelligence and Research). But as I had learned early in State, my role was not as an intelligence or even policy analyst, but as a policy adviser, coordinator, and staff officer. I have noted but some of the many committees on which I served, in a number of cases as the executive secretary or director. There were also other ties to the politico-military field, as on visits to the Strategic Air Command (SAC) and other major commands. I attended a special refresher course on nuclear weapons in Albuquerque, New Mexico, in 1965 (having attended similar week-long courses earlier, in 1955 and 1961). I also participated in a conference on tactical nuclear weapons in 1969.

During this period I continued to take part in a number of war games, including some managed by the Joint Chiefs of Staff "SAGA" (Studies, Analysis, and Gaming Agency). Some of these included several days of play by midlevel officers such as myself, and less extensive participation by senior military officers and officials. Playing a war game to test out nuclear war management with hard-hitting Air Force General Curtis LeMay was surely the most memorable. Such gaming tested not only military contingency planning and political-military coordination, but also conditioned at least most of those who played these simulations to a keener appreciation of the need for close ties between our foreign policy and military planning and operations, and included players who also dealt with these matters in real-life crises. By far the most interesting, and unusual, was service literally "in the field," in one of the largest and most important U.S. field exercises, "Desert Strike."

Alexis Johnson called me in one day in the spring of 1964 and asked if I was ready to take part in a *real* war game. He told me that I didn't really have any choice, because General Paul Adams, CINCSTRIKE (commander in chief, U.S. Strike Command), had asked for me by name to be assigned for a pioneer test of the use of national political, as well as higher military, command in a large joint field-exercise testing concepts for the tactical employment of nuclear weapons. There had, of course, been a number of field exercises with the simulated use of nuclear weapons, but this one would engage national "war cabinets" of the two contending sides to make decisions on when and how to authorize the military commanders to use nuclear weapons, and to decide other issues guiding the military. Finally, although the two sides would represent hypothetical adversaries I would serve on the "Red" side, not so designated but intended to represent the Soviet-Warsaw Pact side. General Adams later told me that he had asked Ambassadors Chip Bohlen and Tommy Thompson as to who could best serve in that role, and each had independently and promptly named me. So I was off to the Mojave Desert.

Desert Strike lasted for two weeks, May 17–30, 1964, with over 100,000 men, 780 aircraft, 1,000 tanks, and 7,000 other vehicles ranging over 150,000 square miles of California, Nevada and Arizona, and with simulated air strikes reaching to Washington State and Texas. Four Army divisions and three Army Reserve and National Guard brigades, and fifteen tactical Air Force squadrons, took part. It cost $60 million, and there were 33 accidental deaths.

Two mythical countries, Nezona and Calonia, went to war. Nezona bore closest resemblance to the Soviet Union and opened the war with an offensive (although after a blundering Calonian provocation in seizing two key dams over the Colorado River border). Nezona had an initial two-to-one superiority on the ground, while Calonia, defending, had a two-to-one nuclear superiority. The "war cabinet" of Nezona was composed of General Jacob L. Devers, USA, Ret., as prime minister, General Ira C. Eaker, USAF, Ret., as defense minister, and myself as foreign minister. For Calonia, the prime minister was General Nathan Twining, USAF, Ret., General Clyde Eddleman, USA, Ret., as defense minister, and Hank Ramsey, the political adviser at STRICOM, as foreign minister.

Among the specific military objectives of the exercise, the most important were to test initiation of tactical nuclear warfare, control of escalation, and tactical operations on the nuclear battlefield. The two war cabinets had to decide whether and when to use nuclear weapons; once initiated, how to control escalation; and how much, if any, delegation of authority to give the field commander once the tactical nuclear war was on.

Nezona preferred not to initiate use, for mutually reinforcing political and military reasons. Calonia did not use them for three days, during which Nezona brought the entire Second Armored Division, Fifth (Mechanized) Infantry Division, and two infantry brigades across the Colorado River in the face of Calonian conventional air and ground opposition. When Calonia first used nuclear weapons, it employed only four strikes on distant airfields and three on battlefield and interdiction targets. Nezona responded with tactical nuclear strikes on airfields, but for nearly a week the Nezona field commander elected not to use his battlefield weapons. The field commanders on both sides chose to use their nuclear weapons sparingly. Half-way through the exercise, some control-umpire intervention was required in order to turn things around and let the "good side"—the Calonian armor, reinforced, supported by airborne landings—take the offensive and drive the Nezonans back to the river along most of the line.

In my postaction critique I observed: "There is a real problem of defining the proper line between the province in which the national government should reserve decision to itself, and that in which the military command should have full command authority. Probably the key specific question was how to balance necessary measures to prevent or control escalation on the one hand, against crippling restraints on the conduct of military operations on the other." As I noted, "both War Cabinets delegated considerable authority on the use of nuclear weapons to the field commanders, who could . . . have expended ten times as many nuclear weapons on the first day of use, had they wished."

One "political-military" aspect of the exercise proved particularly interesting. The existence of war cabinets provided an opportunity to relate the application of military means to political objectives. Our Nezona cabinet set an ascending scale of objectives, ranging from a minimum of restoring the old status quo on the dams (a UN-type administration of a demilitarized zone), to our own full control over the dams, on to a political foothold in the Mojave province of Calonia, and at maximum to annexation of the whole of Mojave. We were mindful of such things as the political significance of exploiting our "liberation" of the major part of the territory and population of "Mojave," and instituted appropriate propaganda and political measures to this end. (For example, our "psywar" teams actually printed and distributed propaganda leaflets.) A sharp disagreement arose in the Nezona war cabinet between General Eaker and myself, however, over whether it was justified to "interfere" with a field commander's plan for redisposing his forces in order to meet a political objective: in this case, holding a key disputed point (Davis Dam) at a time when a cease-fire was being negotiated. Our field commander had planned for military reasons to abandon the dam and fall back across the river. I finally prevailed in gaining General Devers's support in overriding that decision, and Nezona continued to hold that key asset when the exercise ended. For General Eaker, the principle of noninterference by political authorities with the decisions of a field commander took precedence over pursuing a political purpose calling for a different military action.

There were a few senior British and German military observers (no others were invited). I was struck by the fact that the main conclusion by the German generals (one of whom was General Heinz Trettner, chief of staff of the Bundeswehr) was that nuclear weapons must be used promptly and decisively (a conclusion they felt was bolstered by the need for the exercise control umpires to "adjust" the exercise to allow the Calonian forces to regroup and be reinforced so that they could drive the Nezonan forces back to the river). I was disconcerted over that, and I did get General Trettner to agree at least that it was necessary first to determine whether an armed clash was a local incident or a major conventional offensive, but he remained firm in his conviction that only nuclear weapons could stop a major Soviet conventional attack, and that they must be used early.

Desert Strike was regarded as quite successful, but despite the recommendation of the participants, simulating national war cabinets in major field exercises was not continued.

I continued to lecture on Soviet political and military affairs and U.S. policy toward the Soviet Union at the National War College, all the service war colleges, and those of Canada and NATO. I also engaged in various Defense projects; for example, in 1966 Paul Nitze, secretary of the Navy, placed me on a study group on "War at Sea."

In May 1966 I again became a formal consultant to CIA on the interpretation of Soviet strategic policy and its effect on Soviet military plans and programs. The CIA request to the State Department for my services said they would be "significant" and have "important national security implications," no doubt an exaggeration, but I was happy to assist my old colleagues in the agency.

On occasion I was also consulted informally by colleagues in the clandestine services of CIA. For example, in late 1968 or early 1969, as one of the most avid consumers of the clandestinely acquired Soviet General Staff journal *Military Thought (Voyennaya mysl')*, I was asked how valuable it really was. They did not want to raise the matter with DIA (the Defense Intelligence Agency) or others but needed a candid evaluation because their sole Soviet source had been jacking up his price unreasonably. The journal was a useful source on Soviet strategic thinking but not comparable to the top secret version acquired earlier by Colonel Penkovsky. I expressed the hope we could continue to obtain it but said that I did not think it was of the highest importance. A few months later, in the summer of 1969, the collectors dropped the source and did not find a new one able to provide delivery to us until a year and a half later.

In August–September 1966 I made a far-reaching trip in Europe, combining half a dozen different conferences and activities on one extended visit. I repeated visits to Vienna, and to Bucharest and Prague to discuss arms control and European security issues with officials in those countries. In London, I talked with Foreign Office and Intelligence colleagues. I also stopped in Bonn and talked with German foreign ministry officials, and in Munich met informally with German Intelligence (BND) officers and with Klaus Ritter, a former BND officer now heading a newly established Institute for Science and Policy dealing with national security affairs. I thus had an opportunity to gauge thinking in Germany at the beginnings of a more active West German role in Eastern Europe. They were preparing to move toward establishing diplomatic relations with the Eastern European states (which they had previously denied themselves because these countries had extended diplomatic recognition to East Germany). I also discussed the rapidly moving work toward a nuclear nonproliferation treaty (NPT) with German officials.

In Bucharest, my main interlocuter was Corneliu Bogdan, then head of the North America Department of the Ministry of Foreign Affairs and soon to become the Romanian ambassador in Washington. He was, as I was aware, also affiliated with Romanian Intelligence—all in all, an interesting and influential figure. (Later Bogdan was dismissed, and in 1988 placed under house arrest. Only a few weeks after the fall of Nicolae Ceauçescu, in January 1990, at a time when Bogdan seemed likely to assume a role in the new post-communist government, he died.)

On this trip I also attended an international conference on the Northern Cap sponsored by the Norwegian Institute of International Relations, including an interesting visit to northern Norway. In Oslo I also discussed security matters with Norwegian officials, including Under Secretary of Defense Arne Lund. (I also had an opportunity to discuss evolving Swedish thinking about nuclear weapons with a senior official present at the Norwegian conference.)

In early September I participated in the Sixth World Sociological Congress in Evian, as a scholar specializing in political-military affairs. I crossed swords there with a number of Soviet military sociologists and historians, including Lieutenant General Pavel Zhilin. A year later at a conference in London on armed forces and society, I renewed my acquaintance with General Zhilin and other Soviet and Eastern European military "academics."

Along with questions of possible European security arrangements, the matter of U.S. troop levels in Europe began in 1966 to become an issue. The primary factor was not, however, East-West considerations so much as a rising question in the United States, with U.S.-allied frictions as well. Senator Mike Mansfield introduced the first of a series of resolutions that would continue for six years to place pressure on the U.S. government to reduce troop levels in Europe. Also, to meet American budgetary pressures, the United States pressed its allies (especially Germany) for financial assistance through "off-setting" payments for services in support of U.S. forces in Europe. Senior statesman John J. McCloy was asked to study the issue and make recommendations, and I was one of several people who provided him assistance and advice. In a memorandum to him on October 14, 1966, I advised against any sizable reductions but in accordance with his request reviewed the pros and cons of various rationales (for example, that the troops were needed in Vietnam; that the threat, the opposing forces, had been overestimated; or that our allies had not provided sufficient forces to justify maintaining a strong American component that would be vulnerable if the allied flanks remained weak, and that the nuclear threshold would therefore need to be lowered despite our aversion to that outcome). The outcome was a decision in April

1967 for a modest reduction in U.S. forces in Europe, by placing some on a "dual-based" rotational basis. This arrangement, called "Reforger" for the Army forces and "Crested Cap" for the Air Force, worked well over the following years.

I was concerned about a growing tendency to exaggerate the Soviet strategic threat. It was true that in the late 1960s the size of the Soviet strategic arsenal was growing and the Soviet Union was moving toward numerical parity in strategic delivery systems. I did not, however, believe that this development would weaken the strategic balance, as it did not threaten the continuing American strategic deterrent. Moreover, with the advent of multiple independently targeted reentry vehicles (MIRVs), the U.S. superiority in the number of strategic warheads would not only remain but would grow. Nonetheless, there were serious concerns in some circles in Washington and in Western Europe over a possible Soviet impression that "parity" in strategic forces could undermine American commitment to continue to use its deterrent to protect its allies from limited threats below the strategic threshold.

Even within the State Department, among a few of the Atlanticists who were worried not so much as to what the Soviets might do but about the concerns of our allies, and among a few hard-line colleagues in my own politico-military staff (G/PM), were those who favored emphasizing the threat and opposing moves toward détente in East-West relations. Jeff Kitchen and especially Seymour (Sey) Weiss in G/PM held this view. Sey and I were often at loggerheads, and advocating opposite positions. Moreover, as someone remarked at the time, U.S. policy in action often depended on "whether Ray Garthoff or Sey Weiss was the last to gain Alex Johnson's ear" before a policy decision was to be made.

If I was a "dove" to some, I was still regarded as a "hawk" by some others. For instance, in a meeting of the Gilpatric Committee in January 1965, I had warned against "exchanging good relations with our allies for an uncertain détente" with the Soviet Union, when some of my colleagues proposed pressing our allies hard to meet Soviet terms for nonproliferation.[3] I believed we could maintain our own strength and strong alliance and on that basis meet the Soviet Union in improving relations in a context that would serve our respective security interests.

In 1967 I wrote a top secret memorandum using the most complete intelligence to illustrate that depending on the terms used the strategic balance (or imbalance) could be described in radically different ways. The strategic relationship could be depicted as either very reassuring or very dangerous even with the same intelligence information and estimates, depending on how one selected the forces to be compared. My memo was considered very dangerous

3. Ibid., p. 167.

by some in the Pentagon, in particular Lieutenant General Berton Spivey, director of the Joint Staff of the JCS, and even by a few of my colleagues in State, in particular Sey Weiss, not only because it could be used to construct comparisons that would support complacency, but also because it tended to undermine the rather alarmist comparisons that *were* used to support Defense budget programs. I did not know at the time, but recently I have seen a declassified internal White House memorandum of August 28, 1967, that *did* transmit my memo to National Security Adviser Walt Rostow with the comment that this "excellent memo by Ray Garthoff underscores the danger of categorical statements on the U.S.-Soviet strategic balance" and urged that a proposed presentation by Secretary McNamara that emphasized U.S. superiority be reconsidered. I argued in my memorandum that rather than claim superiority in terms that might not be sustainable in the future, "we should emphasize not our strategic superiority but our very high level of confidence in the reliability of our deterrent under any circumstances." I also noted that this would be the best position to have taken if we did get into strategic arms negotiation with the Soviets, as we hoped to do. A similar State Department memorandum dated December 18, 1967, based on an internal study of the implications of parity to which I had contributed, recommended to Secretary Rusk that he write to McNamara and urge that we avoid references to "superiority" or "parity" and instead emphasize the sufficiency and sturdiness of our deterrent. Gradually McNamara and others did this.

I also sought to contribute to a public debate on this issue and understanding outside the administration. For example, my old friend and former boss as deputy director for intelligence at CIA, Robert Amory, in 1968 contributed to writing a Republican Coordinating Committee paper, "U.S. Relations with the Soviet Union," and asked my advice. I thought the final paper was generally good, except that it still called for seeking military superiority. Accordingly, I wrote to Bob on July 18, 1968, commenting on the paper:

> There is only one point to which I would pose any objection: the references to a need to maintain "decisive arms superiority" and "paramount military strength." It would, of course, always be desirable for us to have a margin of superiority, but—as I am sure you agree—it is no longer feasible to have anything that can really be called "decisive arms superiority." By contrast, I think the statement that "our nuclear deterrence must be unequaled and unassailable" correctly identifies the bedrock of our security interests. "Decisive arms superiority" probably represents something that we no longer have or can reacquire, but it also represents more than we really need in order to deter Soviet resort to arms. I am particularly concerned about this point in terms of its implications for future attitudes toward the U.S. position in the upcoming talks with the Russians on strategic arms limitations.

Negotiations with the Soviet Union on strategic arms limitations became the most important politico-military, strategic, and political development in U.S.-Soviet relations from the late 1960s for at least a decade. After the sterile debates over competing proposals on "general and complete disarmament" in the 1950s and 1960s, and the one-sided arms control proposals that were occasionally advanced (such as our strategic "freeze" proposal of 1964), a *real* negotiation began by the end of 1969. Our launching of a major effort in this direction had begun at the end of 1966. This was the first real attempt to engage the Soviets in a serious negotiation on the strategic arms race. And I found myself in the center of it from the outset.

The key mover behind a new initiative was Secretary of Defense Robert McNamara. He had always been prepared to consider realistic arms control, but his driving purpose was to head off a U.S. decision to deploy antiballistic missile (ABM) defenses. He was sure such a move would develop not only its own momentum, but would spark a major new upturn in the strategic arms race between defensive and offensive arms on both sides. And he was determined to try to prevent that from happening.

Although McNamara took the initiative in raising the idea of seeking negotiated limitations with the Soviet Union, Secretary Rusk and others in State, William Foster and Butch Fisher at the Arms Control and Disarmament Agency (ACDA), and Walt Rostow and Spurgeon Keeny on the NSC staff in the White House, all strongly supported the effort.

The United States and the Soviet Union had both been developing ABM systems for years, and the Soviet Union had recently begun to deploy a limited defense around Moscow. The question posed in the Defense budget review in late 1966 was whether, as the Joint Chiefs of Staff now wished to do and McNamara did not, to announce and seek funding for a major U.S. deployment. In several meetings at the LBJ ranch in Texas in November, culminating in a meeting in Austin on December 6, McNamara obtained President Johnson's agreement to announce only a contingent funding request coupled with an attempt to get Soviet agreement to ban or limit ABM deployment, in which case of course the United States would not proceed. By the time the president announced his budget on January 24, 1967, initial soundings had brought a cautious Soviet agreement to consider limitations on ABMs and strategic offensive arms. The budget message merely announced the intention to hold discussions with the Soviets on limiting ABMs. After a further reply from Kosygin on February 28, by March 2 the president was able to announce Soviet agreement in principle to discuss limitations on the arms race in strategic offensive and defensive arms.

The initial approach to the Soviet side had been made by Ambassador Thompson to Ambassador Dobrynin in Washington on December 6 and 7, 1966. Thompson, who arrived in Moscow in late January as the American ambassador, continued to carry the brunt of the repeated efforts to get Soviet agreement to open negotiations mainly through Foreign Minister Andrei Gromyko. Secretary Rusk and Deputy Under Secretary Foy Kohler (who had earlier served as ambassador in Moscow) continued contact with Dobrynin in Washington. I drafted the telegrams of instructions to Thompson, and initially the position papers in Washington. Soon the subject was put in the regular Committee of Principals (and Deputies) channel, and a triumvirate prepared most of the papers: in addition to myself for State, Butch Fisher of ACDA and John McNaughton of Defense (he had succeeded Nitze as assistant secretary for international security affairs), until McNaughton's tragic death in an air accident in June 1967, after which he was succeeded by Paul Warnke.

In the very first draft strategic arms position paper (on January 13, 1967), which I drafted and which was then circulated to the Deputies Committee, I proposed a freeze on construction of additional strategic offensive and defensive missiles launchers (allowing completion of those then under construction), to be verified by unilateral national means of verification (mainly photographic reconnaissance satellites). Land-based medium and intermediate-range ballistic missiles (MRBMs and IRBMs), of which the Soviet Union had hundreds mostly facing Europe, and the United States had none, were included along with land-based intercontinental ballistic missiles (ICBMs). Land-mobile ballistic missiles were to be banned to meet JCS concerns over ability to verify numbers. In my draft, there was also a general ban on testing and deploying *any* "new systems"—which would include multiple independently targeted reentry vehicles (MIRVs) on ballistic missiles, although MIRVs were not explicitly mentioned. These provisions, with some modification, essentially remained the U.S. position throughout 1967 and 1968, except for early removal of the ban on technological improvements, above all MIRVs, on which the United States enjoyed a significant lead and which the Pentagon was determined to deploy.

This initial proposed position was worked over, modified and elaborated into a proposal discussed by the Committee of Principals on March 14. General Earle ("Bus") Wheeler, chairman of the Joint Chiefs of Staff, objected to a freeze on ABMs, noting that it would close out for the United States the option of an ABM defense against China, as well as against the USSR. He also considered it extremely unlikely that the Soviet leaders would give up such an option, saying it was "inconceivable" to him that they would settle for an ABM defense only of Moscow, the only place deployment was under way. Most others tended to agree. (As the negotiations would reveal, they were wrong.) Possible MIRV limitations were not an issue at the March meeting of principals only because McNamara had decided it would be better for the time being to set aside the issue of a ban on testing and deployment. Rusk, on the recommendation of Kohler and myself, agreed. So MIRV was not even brought up. Even so, no agreement on a strategic arms limitation position for the U.S. government could be reached at the March meeting.

Even before the March meeting of principals, it was decided that the United States must consult (or at least advise) its NATO allies. The allies had shown an intense interest in the prospective U.S.-Soviet negotiations from the time they had learned that the United States—without first consulting them—had raised the matter with the Soviet Union. Throughout the whole year a constant stream of counselors of the NATO embassies in Washington came to see me, as the State Department "point man" on the issue. We decided to use the already scheduled semi-annual (and usually routine) NATO "disarmament experts" meeting on March 7–8. Accordingly, I drafted and cleared with the other agencies a sketchy presentation that Ambassador Harlan Cleveland, chief of the U.S. Mission to NATO, could make to the Permanent Representatives of the North Atlantic Council (NAC) in Paris. The instructions to Cleveland laid out what little could be agreed upon (prior to the meeting of the principals, it will be noted), with the rather cryptic comment "Garthoff prepared [to] clarify questions with respect to above presentation," rather than the usual guidance on answers to questions likely to arise. This presentation on March 7 would then be followed by a two-day session of experts. For that discussion, I was accompanied by Herbert (Pete) Scoville, formerly of CIA but then assistant director of ACDA, and Art Barber, McNaughton's deputy for arms control at Defense. We fielded many questions, and inadvertently in discussion made the first disclosure to the allies of the U.S. MIRV program! The main allied concern was whether U.S. weapons in Europe would be included in the U.S. proposal (they were assured they would not), and whether Soviet MRBMs and IRBMs facing Europe would be included as well as missiles capable of striking the United States (and they were assured they would). But there was an underlying unease over two more basic questions that were never directly posed: would such U.S. negotiation with the Soviet Union impinge on the U.S.-allied relationship, and would a possible agreement diminish or end U.S. strategic superiority, and if so, would "parity" weaken the extended nuclear deterrence that they regarded as the bedrock of their security? At the same time, a number of members welcomed the prospect of arms limitation and curbing of the arms race, and none wanted openly to object to it. All in all, the frankness, as well as the substance, of our responses at least helped to dispel some concerns, and it inaugurated what would become a very extensive and highly successful pattern of alliance consultation when SALT later came into being.

Notwithstanding the divergence of views in Washington at the March 14 meeting, on instructions Ambassador Thompson did tell the Soviets on March 18 that we were ready to open talks on April 12. (In fact, the delegation had been named; Thompson was to head it, I was to be the Department of State member of the delegation.)

Efforts to get Soviet agreement to a time and place for negotiations, or clarification of their position, continued not to be successful. The first opportunity for a high-level approach came when Prime Minister Kosygin came to New York for a UN Security Council session in June. After a curious Alphonse-Gaston routine over location, Kosygin agreed to meet President Johnson at Glassboro, New Jersey, almost exactly half way between New York and Washington. (Kosygin could not be seen going to Washington while the Vietnam War was heating up, and Johnson could not go to New York as a supplicant to talk with Kosygin.) The meeting lasted two days (June 23 and 25, with Kosygin taking the day between to return to the Soviet mission in New York for secure-phone consultations with his colleagues in Moscow). The main subject of discussion was the just ended Arab-Israeli war. Johnson, however, was determined to try to persuade Kosygin to enter into strategic arms talks and authorized McNamara to make the pitch.

Kosygin clearly was uncomfortable and determined not to go beyond his brief in the talks. He kept pushing on the open door of including strategic offensive as well as ABM weapons in the talks and seemed impervious to McNamara's explicit rejections of arguments that Kosygin kept attributing to him, such as that offensive weapons were good and cheap, while defensive weapons were bad. In retrospect, and with information now available, it would seem that the American clarifications did help, but not sufficiently to lead to an early Soviet agreement to begin talks. Not only was the Soviet Union still far behind the United States, but it was still building up, while the United States had completed its buildup (of launchers, with the next stage to be a vast increase in the number of warheads through MIRV deployment).

Meanwhile, preparations continued in Washington, although there was understandably a general inclination not to make the most painful choices before it was necessary to do so. Finally, in September, Deputy Under Secretary Kohler obtained Rusk's authorization to circumvent the deadlocked Committee of Principals machinery in order to facilitate staff work among three key parties. He proposed that I work with Butch Fisher from ACDA and Paul Warnke from Defense in modifying the unagreed March positions in order to be prepared in case the Soviet leaders suddenly agreed on talks. We did so, also keeping the White House NSC staff informed. In effect, we cut out the JCS. The most important change we made, however, was not one that any of the three of us wanted: to abandon an ABM freeze (still at zero ABMs for the United States) and substitute a proposal for some equal agreed number of ABM launchers for each side. I originally drew up a position allowing 1,000 ABM interceptors, or some other agreed number, to each side. That would accommodate the planned U.S. Sentinel ABM system (which called for a total of 672 interceptors). When Warnke presented the draft position paper to McNamara, however, he objected to the 1,000 figure and preferred simply saying "an agreed number"—deferring the issue and allowing the possibility of an agreed number of zero (or, of course, more than 1,000). I recommended to

Rusk that he agree, and the position paper was so amended. In the absence of talks, this position paper remained in the files, and although many modifications were made the next year, it still formed the basis for the position adopted in August 1968 (including the deferral of the question of limiting MIRV and of an unspecified "agreed number" of ABMs).

Notwithstanding the Soviet agreement in principle to consider strategic arms limitations, there was a very long delay before they were in fact ready to open negotiations—not, in fact, until mid-1968. One reason, I was sure then and now, was that the Soviet Union was still far inferior to the United States in numbers of strategic weapons, and they did not want to put themselves in the position of having to reject U.S. proposals for a "freeze" in levels of forces that would limit them to inferiority. And, in fact, our proposals in 1967 and 1968 *would* have sought to do just that. Although the U.S. freeze on building up additional missile launchers would have yielded approximately equal overall numbers in 1967, and even a larger number for the Soviet Union in 1968, that was true only because it included seven hundred Soviet MRBMs and IRBMs; in intercontinental weapons (ICBMs and SLBMs) capable of striking the United States and the Soviet Union, the United States would still have retained quantitative as well as qualitative superiority in 1968.

By September 1967 President Johnson felt that he must proceed with authorization of an ABM deployment. He did, however, permit McNamara to couch the justification in terms of meeting a light Chinese attack and possible accidental launchings, rather than a full-scale Soviet attack. I and some other colleagues at State who had the opportunity to review McNamara's ABM speech in advance tried to soften the Chinese attack rationale, although we strongly supported keeping the deployment limited. McNamara in his speech, and President Johnson in a message to Kosygin, explicitly reaffirmed interest in negotiating limitations with the Soviet Union. The American decision to begin ABM deployment, together with an increasing Soviet offensive force level approaching that of the United States, finally led the Soviet leaders in mid-1968 to agree to begin talks. (At about that time, the acronym SALT—for Strategic Arms Limitations Talks—was coined by Bob Martin, a colleague from the State Department serving at NATO, and began to be used to describe the process that continued for the next decade.)

There were many indirect signs of a continuing controversy in Moscow over both the general question of serious negotiations with the United States over strategic arms, and specifically over the question of what ABM defenses the Soviet Union should deploy. A number of influential Soviet scientists were beginning to take seriously the arguments of some American scientists favoring a ban on ABMs in order to prevent an escalation of the strategic arms race. CIA learned that in October, after the U.S. announcement of ABM deployment, Academician Mikhail Millionshchikov, vice president of the Academy of

Sciences of the USSR, was granted permission to invite some of the American scientists to Moscow for unpublicized talks. There had earlier been some such bilateral talks between these Americans (informally called the "Doty group," after MIT Professor Paul Doty) and their Soviet counterparts, including Millionshchikov, on the occasion of larger multinational "Pugwash" meetings (so termed after their first meeting place in Pugwash, Canada, in 1957). The scientists met in Moscow December 28–30, 1967, but before the meeting, Doty and several of his colleagues went to Washington for an off-the-record background meeting with U.S. officials from State, Defense, the White House, and CIA. I was one of the members of this group of officials. We filled in the American scientists on U.S. thinking on ABM and strategic arms limitations, and on what we knew of Soviet thinking and the Soviet weapons programs. They also met briefly with McNamara. The meeting in Moscow seemed to go very well, as the American participants reported back to us. We also learned that the Soviet scientists regarded it as very successful and important, leading to a "conceptual breakthrough" in thinking about ABM limitation in Moscow. Among the Soviet scientists was Academician Aleksandr Shchukin, a key link between senior Soviet scientific-technical specialists and the very important Military-Industrial Commission (the VPK), which oversaw Soviet military programs. Shchukin was later to be the VPK representative (though never so identified) on the Soviet SALT delegation when the negotiations eventually took place. There were a few new members of the American and Soviet groups, in particular two later influential political scientists, Henry Kissinger from Harvard and Georgy Arbatov, the recently named director of a new Institute of USA Studies under the Academy of Sciences of the USSR, each making his debut in unofficial contacts with representatives of the other superpower.

On June 21, 1968, Kosygin finally wrote to Johnson expressing the hope that talks could begin. On July 1, on the occasion of the opening for signature of the Nonproliferation Treaty (NPT), parallel announcements were made in Washington and Moscow that the talks on "limitation and reduction of offensive strategic nuclear weapons delivery systems as well as systems of defense against ballistic missiles" would begin soon.

Work in Washington on SALT had continued in the first half of 1968, with my draft of January 1967 being elaborated by my successor in G/PM, Jack Shaw, and with Warnke's deputy Morton Halperin, as well as ACDA and NSC staff representatives. The center of gravity however shifted from State to Defense, and Mort Halperin took a lead in forging a consensus in the Pentagon, with Major General Royal Allison representing the JCS. I returned from Brussels to participate in July and August on behalf of the yet undesignated SALT delegation.

In July an "Executive Committee" (ExComm) of the Committee of Principals began to meet with a much smaller membership, essentially Rusk for State, Clifford (who had replaced McNamara at Defense in early 1968), Foster of ACDA, Rostow for the White House, and General Wheeler of the JCS. A working group, again smaller than the Committee of the Deputies, was chaired by Butch Fisher of ACDA, on which I (representing the SALT delegation, although at that point I was its only designated member!) sat along with the State representative. The ExComm of the Committee of Principals met on August 7 and again on August 14 to discuss and agree on a U.S. position for the talks. (At the August 14 meeting Walt Rostow asked whether I or some other Sovietologist had drafted likely *Soviet* proposals—we had not, but we had of course postulated what the Soviet positions on the issues would be.)

The August SALT Basic Position and other related documents spelled out the U.S. position for the negotiations. The heart of our proposal was cessation of construction of additional launchers for ICBMs, IRBMs and MRBMs, SLBMs (and SLBM-launching submarines), although allowing completion of land- and sea-based launchers and submarines already under construction. Mobile land-based ballistic missiles, and mobile land- and sea-based ABMs, would be banned. No limits would be placed on bombers or air defenses. There would be an agreed equal number of fixed ABM interceptor launchers. Finally, there would be no prohibition against improvements in existing weapons systems (implicitly including MIRVs).

The controversial issue of ABM limitations had been finessed by drafting the U.S. proposal to specify merely an agreed equal number—a number that could be zero, 1,000, or 10,000. (McNamara had been prepared to accept a freeze allowing the Soviet Union to keep its 48–64 launchers/interceptors at Moscow with none for the United States, but most of us believed it would be politically too disadvantageous as a matter of principle to allow such a disparity, even though strategically that small Soviet ABM deployment was insignificant.) The other major issue was never really joined: a ban on MIRVs. Although Bill Foster wanted to press for such a ban, Butch Fisher and Dean Rusk got him to join those of us in State, Defense, and the White House who strongly supported a MIRV ban but did not want to make it an issue with the JCS and others in Defense who felt just as strongly that the United States should keep its MIRV program. We did not yet know the Soviet position, although they of course knew we were ahead in MIRV development and would almost certainly have agreed to a ban. Even on the question of deferring MIRV flight testing, due to begin in August, it was decided not to press for a delay.

Several years later, Dean Rusk told me that if the SALT summit had gotten under way in 1968 as planned, President Johnson had told him that he was prepared to propose a complete ban on MIRVs and on ABM. Awareness of the president's view explains why Rusk, Clifford, and Rostow were prepared to put aside the MIRV issue in developing the formal August 1968 position rather than raise it prematurely. They all regarded it as essential that SALT be launched with Pentagon support and without a politically damaging divergence on such a key matter.

Literally on the day before a planned announcement in Washington and Moscow on August 21 of a forthcoming summit meeting in Leningrad to begin on September 30, at which President Johnson would himself launch SALT talks (that would begin simultaneously in Geneva), the Soviet Union intervened militarily in Czechoslovakia. Although initially Johnson equivocated, he had no alternative but to cancel the planned announcement and put off the talks. Nonetheless, throughout the remaining four months of his term, President Johnson still hoped he could proceed with a summit meeting and initiation of SALT. By November, the defeat of his party's standard-bearer, Hubert Humphrey, by Richard Nixon made the possibility of a summit remote. Even then, Johnson toyed with the idea and had Ambassador Thompson in late November propose a mid-December summit in Geneva. The Soviet leaders, however, after ascertaining through the president-elect's transition team that Nixon opposed the idea, naturally let it die.

I believed, as did Secretary Rusk and most of us in the State Department, that much as we wished to begin SALT as soon as possible, in the period after August 20 it would not have been appropriate to do so in the light of the Soviet intervention in Czechoslovakia. After November 6, and the election of Richard Nixon, there was a major additional reason not to proceed. Rusk declined to send a recommendation to the president to open bilateral talks, as proposed by ACDA in October. Both Rostow at the White House and Clifford at Defense did urge that talks be opened at a summit, even after the election, and as noted above President Johnson tried to do so, but it was not feasible.

A couple of weeks after the invasion of Czechoslovakia, convinced that the talks could not proceed and with no further SALT work to do in Washington, I took it upon myself to return to my post at NATO headquarters in Brussels. I told both Deputy Under Secretary Chip Bohlen and Assistant Secretary for European Affairs John Leddy that if SALT did revive they knew where to find me, but NATO was agitated by the aftermath of the Czechoslovakian events, and I thought I should return. They agreed. Leddy requested that I brief the key American ambassadors so that they would be aware of the U.S. position if and when SALT was revived, and for reasons of security it was not considered desirable to send our position by telegram. Accordingly, I briefed my boss, Ambassador to NATO Harlan Cleveland, when he was in Washington on September 6, and then Ambassador David Bruce in London on September 10, Ambassador Sargent Shriver in Paris on September 12, and Ambassador Henry Cabot Lodge in Bonn on September 13. All were very interested in learning about the proposed talks, and especially our plans for consultation with our allies. (Lodge also was emphatic in his belief that it would be a serious mistake to begin talks before the election. I told him that there was no decision on whether to do so, but that in my personal view it was highly unlikely.) I reported to Leddy on my discussions with the ambassadors and resumed my duties in Brussels.

Even as President Johnson reluctantly gave up the idea of a summit meeting or beginning of SALT negotiations, he did take two unpublicized steps. In mid-September he proposed (via Rostow through Dobrynin) agreement on "principles and objectives" for SALT, to which the Soviet leaders did reply a few weeks later. The primary objective was to "maintain stable strategic deterrence." The Soviet reply accepted that objective, and indeed several subsidiary additional ones, and added an emphasis on the interrelationship of strategic offensive and defensive arms and also called for "equal security" and no military advantage to either side.

The second step taken by the administration, literally in the last week of its tenure in January 1969, was to present a revised draft of principles and objectives for SALT to the NAC in Brussels, in hopes of gaining allied support that would help lend impetus to early talks and make it harder for the incoming administration to ignore those principles. I was back at NATO headquarters at the time and faced the incredulity and confusion there at a last minute initiative of an outgoing U.S. administration on such an important subject. Moreover, not all of the allies liked all of the "principles," and the representatives were suspicious that the objectives, if not of Soviet origin, at least had been prenegotiated with the Soviet side before allied consultations—as indeed was the case, although we had not been so informed and did not confirm those suspicions. The whole idea of agreed principles and objectives was dropped by the new administration, both in NATO and with the Soviet leadership.

The attempt in 1967 and 1968 to launch SALT, although unsuccessful for that time, did lay the foundation for the subsequent successful SALT negotiations that began under the Nixon administration in late 1969 (and which will be the subject of a later chapter).

In addition to negotiation of the NPT, and efforts to launch SALT, unsuccessful efforts to negotiate a more comprehensive nuclear test ban continued. This was, however, a much lower priority in the United States and in the Soviet Union as well. In 1966 a "threshold" test limitation, banning all tests above a certain low and readily verifiable level, was considered but never agreed upon in the U.S. government, owing to the strong interest in the Defense Department to conduct further weapons tests that would be constrained. In the meantime, we had some problems over implementation of the 1963 Limited Test Ban Treaty.

The 1963 treaty had banned all except underground tests. It had been recognized that even underground tests vented small amounts of radioactive particles into the atmosphere, so the treaty set as the limit any test that "causes radioactive debris to be present outside the territorial limits" of the testing state. It was recognized at the time that even that standard might cause problems because of the growing sensitivity of detection devices and the possibility of minute particles entering the upper atmosphere and being carried beyond national borders. NSAM 269 had established a "NSAM 269 Committee" chaired by the national security adviser to ensure that the vigorous program of underground tests planned would conform to the treaty obligations. Alexis Johnson was the State Department member, and a technically qualified G/PM officer served as his staff man. When problems later arose between the United States and the Soviet Union, I became involved too.

During 1965 and 1966, at least two Soviet tests, and at least two U.S. tests, did cause small quantities of radioactive particulate matter ("debris") to be detected beyond our respective national borders. Within the government there was no desire to do more than make a minimum complaint to the Soviets about their tests and state a defense of our own. It was clear that neither country was willfully or significantly violating the treaty. But there were congressional and editorial outcries when Soviet technical violations occurred and became known, especially by opponents of arms control. We had to walk a fine line between not appearing to ignore Soviet violations, but also not arguing for standards that we too were violating.

Participation in policy on a wide range of Cold War strategic, space, arms control, nonproliferation, and European security issues during the years of the Johnson administration did not often bring me into matters concerning the Third World. The Indo-Pakistani war of 1965 did, however, give added momentum to internal studies of counterproliferation measures to restrain India from acquiring nuclear weapons. Both the Thompson and Johnson committees devoted considerable attention to this problem in 1965–66. One scheme that was considered envisaged providing an aircraft carrier to India; another was to assist India in demonstrating prowess in some non-nuclear scientific-technological area, such as in outer space.

The most important Third World crisis in this period was the Arab-Israeli Six-Day War of June 1967. We monitored Soviet activities closely, but the only incident in the crisis directly involving either the United States or the Soviet Union was the attack on the U.S. signals intelligence monitoring ship U.S.S. *Liberty* by Israel. Our military and intelligence agencies were unanimous in finding it to have been a deliberate and unprovoked Israeli air and sea attack, but President Johnson was determined to accept belated Israeli apologies and claims that it had resulted from misidentification of the U.S. ship no matter how lacking in credibility those excuses were. The hot line was used during the incident to let the Soviet leaders know that American naval aircraft sent to the scene were not going to participate in the war or threaten Soviet ships in the area.

Toward the end of the Six-Day War, as Israeli forces turned north and were threatening Damascus, the Soviets did warn the United States through several channels that they could not just stand by and see Syria completely defeated, but before any Soviet intervention became a real possibility Israel accepted a cease-fire on that front as well. Before that occurred, however, a diplomat in the Soviet embassy in Washington known to be a KGB agent, with whom I had become acquainted (as I shall describe later), had urgently called and asked to meet with me on Saturday, June 10. He had conveyed the Soviet warning (as did at least one other Soviet intelligence contact to another American official). He made clear that any Soviet military intervention would be limited to defending Damascus, and that they hoped such intervention could be avoided through Israeli acceptance of a cease-fire on existing lines of engagement. I had promptly reported the warning to Deputy Under Secretary Foy Kohler, and through the executive secretariat of the department to Secretary Rusk. Fortunately, as noted, the question became moot that same day.

After the June War, McGeorge Bundy at the NSC asked Paul Warnke, the new assistant secretary for international security affairs at Defense, and me at State to prepare a study of what the United States could do to seek limitations on arms supply by the United States and the Soviet Union to both sides in the Arab-Israeli confrontation. We did prepare some recommendations, but the subject was swept up in a broader review of what could be done in the aftermath of the war, and soundings with the Soviet government did not lead to anything.

My only other contact with that region in this period was a visit in December 1968 to Cairo, Egypt, as a tourist, for the first time since I had left there with my parents as an infant. I found the visit most interesting. One small vignette on changing times: the former Anglo-American Hospital on Gezira Island in the Nile, where I had been born, was in 1968 an officers club for Soviet military advisers. Yet four years later they would be gone.

Meanwhile, by 1967 I had been thinking more and more about expanding my experience by seeking assignment to the field. I explored several possibilities, most interesting of which was in the U.S. Mission to NATO, then in Paris but slated to move to Brussels. Ambassador Harlan Cleveland, our representative at NATO, urged me to join him in a new senior position as counselor for political-military affairs. We knew each other well, from his previous service as assistant secretary of State for UN and other international affairs. I agreed, and was assigned to the U.S. Mission to NATO as of February 1968.

As I have earlier noted in passing, during my six years plus in G/PM from late 1961 to early 1968 I increasingly came to have many contacts with representatives of the embassies of most NATO and some other allied and neutral countries. This was especially the case in 1966–67, when a number of arms control and Soviet political-military developments arose, including discussions of the U.S. position or views on the NPT and SALT, information and U.S. thinking on various Soviet military developments, on the Soviet role in the June 1967 Middle East war, and the like. Most embassies, of course, sought to develop useful contacts in the State Department. What brought me into this process more actively was the increasing interest in arms control and Soviet developments that were more in my sphere of responsibility than of the Soviet Desk or the NATO affairs or other offices in any of the geographic bureaus. I also had extensive social contact with many of these counselor-level embassy officers. Incidentally, a remarkably large number, at least half a dozen, returned to Washington by the 1980s as ambassadors.

The main gap in such contacts in the 1960s was vis-à-vis the Soviet and East European embassies, which tended to restrict themselves to strictly necessary business with their respective counterpart desks in the bureau of European affairs. I had contact with several officers of the Soviet Embassy, albeit occasionally and not very usefully until 1967. I did, however, come to know some officers with whom I would later have more substantial dealings. Among these were Georgy Kornienko, Viktor Komplektov, Yuly Vorontsov, and Aleksandr Bessmertnykh, all counselors and deputy chiefs of mission under Ambassador Dobrynin in Washington in the 1960s and early 1970s, and later all deputy ministers of the Foreign Ministry in Moscow (Kornienko for many years Gromyko's senior deputy), one (Bessmertnykh) even foreign minister briefly, and the latter three also all serving as Soviet (or Russian) ambassadors in Washington.

I might recall one small contretemps. In 1967 Komplektov had complained to me that he didn't know any other people in the State Department except the SOV (Soviet Desk) officers, and he wanted to meet "someone interesting." So I invited him to lunch with a colleague whom I was sure he would find interesting, and who might like to meet him: Zbigniew Brzezinski, then a professor who had been serving a term on the Policy Planning Council in the Department of State. Komplektov had been riled by some articles by Brzezinski describing the Soviet Union as a regional, rather than a global, power and tried to stir up an argument by contending that the United States was not a "European power," NATO notwithstanding, and the like. The lunch was sufficiently lively, though Brzezinski and I didn't get a great deal out of it. Years later, long after Brzezinski had returned to Washington as President Jimmy Carter's national security adviser, two officials in the Soviet Foreign Ministry told me that after Brzezinski had been named, a group of them in the Foreign Ministry had been speculating on Brzezinski's likely role in U.S. policy toward the Soviet Union, and Komplektov had volunteered that he knew Brzezinski, and he wasn't so bad or so tough. Later, as the Soviets assessed Brzezinski as both bad and tough, his colleagues had chided Komplektov on his poor forecast.

The most interesting Soviet embassy officer whom I met and saw frequently in the late 1960s was a junior officer by rank, a second secretary, named Boris Sedov. As I ascertained from our State Department intelligence and security offices soon after first meeting Sedov in the fall of 1966, he was in fact a KGB (state security) intelligence officer. That fact was no reason for me not to continue to see him, but I of course kept it in mind and fully reported on all my meetings with him—which totaled some twenty-six from late 1966 through 1970 (and, as I shall describe in due course, others later). At most of these meetings one subject of persisting interest was SALT, especially in the prenegotiation years 1967–68 when twenty of these meetings occurred. Other subjects of interest also arose, and Sedov as an intelligence officer not only had questions of interest to Moscow, but also occasionally messages to convey and relative leeway in discussing matters. I, of course, reported Sedov's conversations in detail in memorandums of conversation that were distributed, depending on the subject, to appropriate officers in the department (and to CIA). In fact, Sedov's conversations proved of sufficient interest that the executive secretariat kept a file of them for Secretary Rusk. Sedov was the officer who transmitted the warning on contingent limited Soviet intervention during the Arab-Israeli war in June 1967 to which I referred earlier. He also gave me a report on the Soviet side's impressions of the Glassboro summit meeting in June 1967, based on talks with his friend Viktor Sukhodrev, who had been the Soviet interpreter. Of course, one had to weigh in any given case whether Sedov was relaying information, misinformation, or gossip or personal speculation. For example, in May 1967 Sedov told me that one reason the Soviets, especially the Soviet military, had opposed the MLF was that *their* Warsaw Pact allies would be encouraged to seek something of a role with respect to Soviet nuclear forces. Sedov had interesting things to say about the deteriorating state of Sino-Soviet relations and sought to elicit from me official U.S. thinking on China. I had published the text and written a commentary on an interesting polemic against China that had appeared in the closed Soviet journal *Military Thought,* and Sedov was obviously curious about how I had obtained access to it. (I had sought, and obtained, permission from CIA to release it; of course I did not tell Sedov, but he assumed as much.)

When Communist Party Secretary Yury Andropov was named to head the KGB in May 1967, Sedov remarked that it seemed to be a demotion for him. I suggested that perhaps instead it marked a promotion for the KGB. Sedov then commented that "he and his friends" in the embassy had in fact been speculating on that possibility. A month later when Andropov was named a candidate member of the Politburo, he remarked that he and his friends had been surprised (but obviously were pleased). I met in passing one or two of his friends (from the KGB), including on two occasions his boss, the KGB *rezident* (or station chief) in Washington, Boris Solomatin (then a colonel, later a major general, in the KGB). At receptions in the Soviet embassy on the occasion of Soviet Armed Forces day (February 23, 1967) and the fiftieth anniversary of the Bolshevik Revolution (November 7, 1967), Sedov introduced me to Solomatin. It became clear in the conversation that Solomatin was irked by the fact that regular Soviet diplomats (such as Vorontsov) were increasingly in contact with State Department officers (in my case, on SALT in particular), diluting the near monopoly that his KGB officers such as Sedov had enjoyed.

In my discussions of the proposed strategic arms talks with Sedov and Vorontsov I was able to some extent to see what issues were of greatest interest to the Soviet side (and occasionally to distinguish particular interests of the KGB differentiated from those of the professional diplomats developing an interest in arms control). I was able to help persuade them in 1967 that the United States would rely to the maximum possible on unilateral national means of verification, allaying their persistent suspicions of U.S. interest in embarrassing them over demands for on-site inspection that they would not accept. I was also able to make clear that we were not going to press them to the wall for a simple freeze of the status quo of U.S. superiority (in view of the fact we were willing to allow completion of launchers under construction, although I did not become that specific). I told them, in response to queries, that the United States would propose inclusion of Soviet MRBMs and IRBMs facing Europe. In turn, I learned that they would seek to include bombers (which we, having a decisive superiority, were inclined to leave out), and most important that they would press to include U.S. "strategic" forward-based systems (FBS) in Europe. Sedov told me that as early as June 1967, and of course I fully reported it along with everything else, but it still came as a surprise to most Americans when from the outset of SALT in 1969 and 1970 they pressed that issue.

Vorontsov (with whom I met on SALT and related matters five times in 1967–68, and more frequently later) discussed with me in January 1968 the interesting and important work of the unofficial and unpublicized Doty-Millionshchikov group in Moscow a few weeks earlier, not only confirming the role of those talks in influencing the still forming official Soviet views, but permitting reference to the positions taken in those discussions without committing either of us to raise points not officially decided in our respective governments. After Glassboro, Secretary McNamara also had his newly designated assistant secretary for international security affairs, Paul Warnke, begin a series of parallel informal meetings over lunch with Vorontsov, so the latter had both State and Defense Department unofficial contacts on SALT.

In 1968, when most American officials believed the Soviet Union would want a significant ABM deployment, Vorontsov told me that the outcome would probably be agreement on no more than a small, thin ABM defense on each side rather than zero ABM or a large deployment. Again, most in Washington nonetheless were surprised when SALT began in late 1969 and the Soviet side showed a preference for small ABM deployments.

When I was back in Washington for SALT preparations in the summer of 1968, Vorontsov first informed me (and my colleague Jack Shaw) at a luncheon on August 19 that we would be receiving the reply the next day setting the date for SALT, as we did.

My talks, especially with Sedov, covered a wide range of subjects. We also developed a social contact apart from our business lunches. Once, shortly after the defection of Stalin's daughter Svetlana Alliluyeva to the United States in 1967, Sedov commented with amusement that his five-year-old daughter Olga was all excited by television coverage of the "Miss America" pageant, and how he had tried to explain why she could not become Miss America when she grew up. I rejoined, "Why not? If Stalin's daughter can, anyone can." Sedov found that less amusing than I did, but took it in good humor. That was the closest I ever came to hinting to Sedov that he might defect, and he was careful never even to hint at asking me to do anything improper.

Apart from my official activities, during the four years of the Johnson administration before my departure to Brussels in early 1968 I continued to be fairly active in outside writing for publication and attendance at academic and think-tank conferences. At a conference at Stanford University commemorating fifty years of communism in Russia, at which I delivered a paper, I met Alexander Kerensky, the aging prime minister of the short-lived Provisional Government of Russia in 1917. I had heard him give a lecture in New York in the early 1950s, but this was the only occasion I had to meet and talk with him, a living page of Russian history.

I published a book on Soviet military policy in 1966, based largely on a number of essays I had written earlier, and in the same year edited another volume on Sino-Soviet military relations. In addition to writing, I also did some part-time evening teaching first at the Institute of Sino-Soviet Studies of George Washington University in 1962–63, and then at the School for Advanced International Studies of Johns Hopkins University in 1963–67. I taught evening courses on Soviet politics, Soviet foreign policy, and Soviet strategy.

In 1965 the slow-moving wheels of bureaucracy yielded the State Department's Superior Honor Award to me for my work on the Cuban missile crisis. Soon after, I was honored with the Arthur S. Flemming Award, granted annually to the "ten outstanding young men in federal government service." Needless to say, I was gratified by these honors, but much more by the exhilarating work in the State Department, the prospect of SALT, and the challenge of dealing with new aspects of foreign diplomatic service "in the field," at the U.S. Mission to NATO.

12

The Diplomacy of East-West Relations

The Cold War always involved measures by the United States and its allies directed against the Soviet Union and its bloc—military measures to deter, and if necessary to defend, against hostile pressures, incursions or attack; political and economic measures to strengthen the West and indeed other countries of the non-communist "free" world to prevent Soviet bloc and other communist encroachment; and political, psychological, economic, and sometimes covert measures to weaken the enemy. Sometimes these were unilateral U.S. actions, sometimes collective Western (mainly NATO) moves, and they varied greatly in their nature, but they shared the characteristic of being measures unilaterally generated by the West in order to more effectively wage the Cold War against the adversary.

The Cold War also involved another set of political, economic, cultural, and eventually military measures that, although also directed at least in part toward strengthening our side and weakening the opponent, involved a different characteristic: they were measures adopted together with the adversary, requiring at least tacit but often explicit and negotiated terms that each side saw as serving its interests. The most important common interest by far was in preventing the Cold War from overheating into an unprecedented nuclear catastrophe for the world. But many other elements of tacit or limited cooperation coexisted with the continuing confrontation of the two blocs. Every trade transaction, indeed even sitting together and arguing at the United Nations, marked recognition by both sides that there were considerations that made such dilutions of the confrontation serve common or at least congruent interests of both sides. Moreover, there were active diplomatic contacts and exchanges throughout, although these had been at a nadir in the period from the late 1940s to the mid-1950s. The diplomacy of East-West relations thus involved pursuit of congruent interests as well as efforts to wage the Cold War.

Although the Cold War was global, its "central" front remained in Europe. In contrast to the Western alliance, the Soviet bloc in the east was rigidly controlled by the Soviet leaders in Moscow. The communist states of Eastern Europe were seen as mere puppet regimes under Moscow, and were called "satellites" by the West. This term was actually more apt than was generally understood, as the local leaderships were not mechanical puppets, but retained interests of their own and some leeway for pursuing their own interests, although to be sure within orbits sharply circumscribed by basic Soviet interests. Two of these countries did, in fact, escape from the orbit of Soviet control; Yugoslav president Marshal Josip Tito in 1948 successfully broke out from the Soviet bloc, followed later by geographically isolated Albania.

The Western powers welcomed the defection of Tito's Yugoslavia, although it remained a communist regime and did not join the Western alliance. The West (especially the United States and Britain) also sought to weaken, and if possible to break, the Soviet bloc by a wide range of covert and propaganda activities in the 1950s. There was also much political rhetoric, particularly in the United States during the presidential campaign of 1952, about going beyond containment of communist expansion to a "rollback" or liberation of Eastern Europe from communist dominion. Yet when the first major local popular uprising occurred, in East Germany in June 1953, the West did not give assistance to the demonstrators, and the opposition was quickly suppressed. After a major national uprising in Hungary in October–November 1956 was bloodily suppressed by Soviet troops, again with no Western support to the "freedom fighters" (as the rebels were termed in the West), it was generally recognized that the Soviet bloc would not be overthrown by internal insurgency alone, and that the West would not risk general war to come to the assistance of popular uprisings in the East. When in 1968 even a liberal communist regime in Czechoslovakia, not challenging the authority of the Soviet bloc, allowed a degree of internal freedom that the Soviet (and other bloc) leaders saw as dangerous, it was removed by a Soviet-led Warsaw Pact military intervention.

Early Cold War militant ideological anticommunism was thus tempered by practice and became more pragmatic and realistic. The threats of communist subversion in the West, and of Soviet attack on the West, receded. So, too, did prospects for Western-supported subversion in the East, as failures of the late 1940s and early 1950s demonstrated. Direct Western intervention to liberate the East had never been contemplated, and this was confirmed in 1953 and 1956. The division of Europe was the new reality in the Cold War world.

For roughly the second half of the Cold War, from the mid-1960s to the late

1980s, the West sought to encourage the gradual evolution of the countries of the Soviet bloc, including the Soviet Union itself, through normalization of relations. By treating the "satellite" countries as genuine states rather than merely as puppets of Moscow, while avoiding any provocative steps that would precipitate Soviet suppression, it was hoped that they would in fact become more autonomous actors. By including them in pan-European institutions, such as the Conference on Security and Cooperation in Europe (CSCE), they would to some extent become European, and not merely Soviet bloc, states. This approach appealed to the Western European states.

The United States sought to encourage both internal liberalization and greater independence from Moscow through a policy of "differentiation," rewarding those states deemed to be more liberal (such as Poland) or more independent (especially Romania) from the others. The objective of the policy was sound, but in practice it was weak because our leverage was so limited. The main element was trade relations, in particular granting or withholding nondiscriminatory most favored nation treatment, but it was also applied to cultural exchanges and other aspects of normalization of relations. The Western Europeans relied more on the effects of normalization, rather than leverage to bargain for those desired effects. There was more rhetoric about bridge-building between West and East in the United States, but more real building of contacts and bridges by the Western Europeans. To the United States, the Soviet bloc was an alliance appendage to the Soviet Union; to Western Europeans, while the countries of Central and Eastern Europe were under communist rule, they remained part of Europe. There was no sharp difference in policy objectives between the United States and its European allies, but the difference in practice did lead to some frictions arising from greater European interest in détente and in building an architecture of pan-European security cooperation.

For the United States and its allies, the diplomacy of East-West relations to an important extent thus embraced the internal diplomacy of the NATO alliance as well as relationships with the communist bloc countries of Eastern Europe.

At the time I went to Brussels in early 1968, the NATO alliance was approaching its twentieth year. More important, at the December 1967 ministerial-level NATO meeting a report on the future tasks of the alliance, the so-called Harmel Report, had been adopted, establishing formally for the first time explicit recognition that the alliance rested on two "pillars": defense and détente. While defense was rooted in the military capabilities of the alliance members, it also embraced the political will and political control on which deterrence and defense rested. Its bedrock role was to reinforce the defensive military element of the Cold War confrontation. Détente, on the other hand, while consistent with defense, went beyond it to comprehend the diplomacy of East-West relations, to ameliorate the dangerous rough edges that a purely military confrontation would entail, and to complement effective deterrence and defense by continuously seeking to find areas of congruent interest with the adversary. The minimal aim of détente was to keep the Cold War from becoming "hot"; the maximal aim was to mitigate and erode the confrontation of the Cold War. Both served the purposes of containment of the Communist threat, but the new emphasis on détente reflected a cautious optimism that the diplomacy of East-West relations could help to attenuate the Cold War.

The military or defense pillar of the alliance was modernized at the same time. Also at the December 1967 NATO ministerial meeting a revised Military Committee guidance for NATO military planning was adopted, under the designation "MC-14/3." This new guidance, which the United States had been pushing for since 1962, formally shifted the basic NATO military concept from in effect massive nuclear retaliation in response to any Warsaw Pact attack to "flexible response," a response geared to the nature of any attack and relying initially on conventional forces to meet any conventional attack. The United States did not envisage waging a lengthy non-nuclear World War III in Central and Western Europe, nor did the European allies really want the United States to start dropping thousands of nuclear weapons if there was a limited Warsaw Pact incursion. But the Europeans felt that the threat of immediate (or at least early) use of U.S. nuclear weapons would best deter Soviet attack of any kind, while the Americans were more concerned that a limited breach of deterrence could precipitate a nuclear holocaust that could have been avoided by persuading the Soviet leaders to discontinue a limited aggression. Flexible response, as well as an appropriate supporting military posture, was exactly what those of us in the late 1950s had been urging and what Robert McNamara had worked for so tirelessly ever since 1961. Fittingly, McNamara was present when MC-14/3 was adopted, at his last NATO meeting before leaving the Defense Department. "Flexible response" in MC-14/3 was a compromise that left unclear the precise allied response, but reaffirmed readiness to take whatever measures were necessary to defeat an attack. Most Europeans believed that the new concept precluded graduated escalation, while Americans had precisely that in mind, but the compromise remained the mainstay of the defense pillar until the Cold War ended in 1990.

Even today in retrospect it is much too much to say that NATO's (and the U.S.) deterrence doctrine "worked." The burden of all the available evidence from Soviet archives and memoirs confirms the view that some of us had at the time, that *no* Soviet leadership *at any time* during the Cold War ever contemplated a military attack on the West. So deterrence at most reinforced Soviet recognition that the risks and costs of war far outweighed any possible advantages. To be sure, that reinforcement may have been prudent. And it helped to deter possibly more risky Soviet behavior in situations short of a Soviet attack, in particular in such crises as over Berlin and missiles in Cuba. But almost certainly the principal benefit of the policy of deterrence was not dissuading Soviet attack, but reassuring the Western countries.

I have noted in the previous chapter that in 1966–67 the United States had wrestled with the problem of maintaining our own share of conventional forces in Europe, which was needed not only for its intrinsic contribution to a flexible response posture, but also to keep our allies, ambivalent over the concept, from undercutting it by their own force reductions. There was no way to make up fully for the damage to such a posture incurred by the French withdrawal of its own territory as well as its participation in NATO military planning, although French forces remained in West Germany, and France remained a member of the alliance. (Also, only French withdrawal from the Military Committee made possible adoption of MC-14/3). Later in this chapter I shall discuss the conjunction of military and political factors that led to bringing this issue of military force levels into the new diplomacy of East-West relations.

Another important political-military development concerning the defense pillar of NATO was the final demise of the MLF by the end of 1966 and the rise instead of the Nuclear Planning Group (NPG). It was McNamara's idea to create a consultative body that could meet the allies' interest in participation in nuclear planning and, not less important in his view, provide a forum in which he could inform and educate their representatives. (Initially, it was widely referred to as "the McNamara Committee.") The British and Germans took a keen interest in the NPG soon after its inception, and when the ticklish problem of keeping it small by rotational representation for smaller interested members was worked out, it was a great success.

McNamara attended the first two meetings of the NPG, in Washington in April and Ankara in September 1967. I participated in the preparation and attended some sessions of the Washington meeting, at which McNamara went all out to provide new and interesting (for some, overwhelming) detailed information on U.S. and Soviet nuclear weapons and planning. Three important studies were launched. One dealt with nuclear mines (atomic demolition mines, ADMs), which could be deployed (or have prepared facilities for rapid deployment in time of crisis or war) along frontier zones. The Turks were initially interested; the Germans were too, but did not want anything done that would convey an impression of a permanent border between West and East Germany. A second study, dealing with the problem of timing, extent, and targeting of a limited number of tactical nuclear weapons, was central to flexible response and controlled escalation. Not surprisingly, this study continued over several years (including my time in Brussels) and was never fully resolved. The allies would not even study scenarios involving extensive tactical employment of nuclear weapons and were skittish over anything but very limited initial "demonstrative" use to show resolve. Eventually we listed a number of options in general terms, without defining what would be done in any given situation.

The third NPG study dealt with possible ABM deployment in Europe. Launched at the Washington meeting, and discussed at Ankara, this study was concluded in time for adoption at the third NPG meeting in The Hague in April 1968. I participated in this study, initially in 1967 as an expert, and in 1968 as part of the U.S. NATO mission. British Defense Minister Denis Healey took the lead in this one and helped guide it to the conclusion that an ABM defense for Europe under foreseeable technological conditions was "not at present politically, militarily or financially warranted."

The NPG study on possible European ABM deployment was also important to the U.S. consideration of ABM deployment for the United States, and potentially to SALT negotiations. McNamara and those of us on the U.S. team in the NPG were of course keenly aware of this connection, and used it not only to obtain our preferred NATO decision, but also to bolster the positions we favored in Washington. The NPG group decided the reasons leading the United States to decide upon a light ("thin," in U.S. parlance) defense against China as announced by McNamara in September 1967 would not be "relevant" in the case of European defense (despite a showing by a Norwegian representative, to the surprise of virtually all of the rest of us, that China was closer to Scandinavia than to the United States!). The NPG concluded that the deployment of ABMs by the two superpowers would "not be likely to upset the overall strategic balance between them," and if kept "light" it should not have seriously adverse political effects, such as on possible arms control negotiations. But most important for McNamara, the NPG concluded that a "heavy" ABM deployment by the United States could stimulate pressure in NATO for a European system, which would be controversial and "a misuse of resources," or alternatively could cause resentment if the United States enjoyed such protection while Europe did not.

After McNamara's departure, for the third and fourth NPG meetings (at The Hague in April and Bonn in October 1968) Secretary of Defense Clark Clifford represented the United States. Then, for the fifth and sixth (in London in May and Warrenton, Virginia, in November 1969) the succeeding secretary of defense was Melvin Laird. I was present as part of the U.S. delegation at the meetings in The Hague, Bonn, and London, before leaving the NPG and most other NATO functions for SALT. The NPG had proved itself, under different U.S. administrations and secretaries of defense, to be a useful element of NATO's "defense pillar," along with the flexible response concept in military planning.

I found the NPG ministerial meetings interesting, especially for the byplay around defense ministers and staffs, who shared a protective interest in their domain vis-à-vis the foreign ministries. I enjoyed conversations with Denis

Healey (not merely because he had once written a favorable review of one of my books!). He was much less mechanistic than our Defense officials on the nature of deterrence and East-West political-military relationships.

With respect to the new second pillar of détente, NATO moved cautiously. Movement had been under way, and continued, in a number of Western countries. President Charles de Gaulle had launched a bilateral effort to stimulate an East-West détente in 1966, in parallel to his distancing from NATO's military alliance. After the formation of a broad political coalition in West Germany in late 1966, a détente-oriented Ostpolitik began there as well.

In the United States, too, President Johnson had launched a détente directed at the communist countries of Central and Eastern Europe beginning in 1964, but more consistently in 1966. On May 25, 1964, Johnson had included in a speech a call for "building bridges" to the countries of Eastern Europe, but without elaboration or follow-through. There was yet no U.S. policy toward Eastern Europe. Only more than a week later, on June 3, was NSAM 304 issued, calling for a study of criteria for differentiation among the countries of Eastern Europe as a basis for policy. The policy was not, however, articulated until more than a year later in NSAM 352 on July 8, 1966. This time the policy had been developed, and a speech drafted (largely by Zbigniew Brzezinski, serving on a tour with the Policy Planning Council in State). President Johnson's speech, on October 7, 1966, while harking back to bridge-building, now called for "a shift from the narrow concept of coexistence to the broader vision of peaceful engagement" with the countries of Eastern Europe and the USSR.[1]

The call for peaceful engagement and building bridges with the countries of Eastern Europe by no means represented a soft line. The Soviets immediately reacted negatively to what they perceived, correctly (despite U.S. disclaimers), to be a challenge to their hegemony in Eastern Europe. It was waging the Cold War by détente. Nonetheless, the new U.S. policy did not preclude a lessening of tensions with the Soviet Union as well, and at least indirectly it countenanced that possibility. Although the speech did not include these words, the secret policy NSAM had set as an objective of U.S. policy to "help create an environment in which peaceful settlement of the division of Germany and of Europe will become possible." In his State of the Union message, on January 10, 1967, President Johnson boldly set as an objective an end to the Cold War.

NATO was thus building on a growing consensus when it had commissioned the report proposed by Belgian Foreign Minister Pierre Harmel. As

1. On U.S. policy toward Eastern Europe, including the texts of the two NSAMs cited here, see *Foreign Relations of the United States, 1964–1968*, vol. 17, *Eastern Europe* (Government Printing Office, 1996), pp. 1–79; NSAM 304, p. 12, NSAM 352, pp. 54–55.

earlier noted, the final report, usually referred to simply as the "Harmel Report" (although it had been collectively drafted and titled "The Future Tasks of the Alliance") was approved on December 14, 1967. The Harmel Report recognized that in the nearly two decades since the alliance had been established "the international situation has changed significantly and the political tasks of the Alliance have assumed a new dimension." While reaffirming the need for deterrence and defense, the other task of the alliance was now articulated as "to pursue the search for progress towards a more stable relationship in which the underlying political issues can be solved. . . . to further a détente in East-West relations" and ultimately a European settlement.[2]

I arrived in Brussels to assume my new duties just as we were turning from the lofty rhetoric of the twin pillars to face the question of just what we had meant and what the alliance was now to do. As I have indicated, important new steps on the further development of the pillar of defense were well under way. But initial steps on the new path of détente were by no means clear or agreed upon. I also faced the mundane task of finding or defining my role as head of a new "political-military section" between the long established political and military sections of the mission—no less difficult in view of the fact that the work of the whole mission was really political-military affairs. Ambassador Cleveland had only a sketchy idea of what I and my new section should do, so we worked things out in a pragmatic way. The NPG staffing role, while political-military in some aspects, was clearly in the domain of the defense adviser, Tim Stanley (who, moreover, held an additional hat as "Representative of the Secretary of Defense in Europe"). So he continued formally to represent the United States on the NPG Working Group, and his staff handled most of the work, while I served as the alternate U.S. representative and my staff also actively participated. Most "disarmament" issues, as a subject of consultation in the Committee of Political Advisers, initially remained with the Political Section. The new major action subject in this area, however, was assigned to my section: working on an alliance position on mutual reductions of conventional forces in Europe (initially termed MFR, for mutual force reductions, but after a year or so MBFR, mutual balanced force reductions, to emphasize allied determination that any cuts must be "balanced").

I had been involved in initial U.S. studies of this subject in Washington, and a paper had been prepared in October 1967. But there was no authorized U.S. position or proposal to put forward to the alliance. Our work at NATO, which had just begun in the first months of 1968, was given impetus when the NATO ministers meeting in Reykjavik, Iceland, in June 1968 decided, in the absence of other initiatives, despite the limited preparation to date to call for initiation

---

2. The Harmel Report is available in many sources; for example, *NATO Final Communiqués, 1949–1974* (Brussels: NATO Information Service, 1975), pp. 195–202.

of "a process leading to mutual force reductions." Work continued, but slowed after the Soviet-led intervention in Czechoslovakia.

There were hopes by some, and lingering concerns by others, in the alliance as to whether the Soviet Union had an interest in negotiating mutual reductions. This prospect was not, however, the only reason for alliance attention to the issue, indeed not the main reason for many. The U.S. government, and some of the allies, saw advocacy of mutual reciprocal reductions as the main objective, whether this led to negotiations, and whether negotiations led to an agreement, or not. The reason was that alliance support for reciprocal reductions could be used to fight off growing American calls for unilateral reduction of U.S. forces in Europe. Indeed, many who championed the idea of mutual force reductions for this purpose hoped that the Soviet Union would *not* agree, because they believed commensurate Warsaw Pact reductions would still not warrant any significant NATO, and especially U.S., reductions. Our NATO studies in 1968–69 were based on proportional reductions; larger on the Warsaw Pact side only to the extent the existing Pact forces were larger. By the early 1970s, NATO shifted to proposals for still larger Warsaw Pact reductions to make up for such factors as geographical advantages for reinforcement on the Pact side. The calculus, however, remained stubbornly tied to narrow quantitative military considerations—what was sometimes called "bean counting."

Some three months after the Soviet-led Pact invasion of Czechoslovakia, on November 20, 1968, I wrote a memorandum to Ambassador Cleveland in which I tried to indicate a more bold conception of the role negotiations over mutual force reductions could play in the diplomacy of East-West relations— or at least could have played if pursued earlier:

> The general tendency has been to regard this subject as at least slightly tainted with disarmament do-goodism. Our analyses of the subject (especially, but not only, the military analyses) have focussed on essentially minor risks, while totally ignoring possible major gains. There has been very little awareness that the two traditional ways of affecting the relative military balance—increasing one's own forces, or destroying those of the enemy—are not the only ways of affecting relative forces ratios. Soundly considered negotiated agreements are at least a conceivable third way. Whether there is any realistic possibility for such agreements does not depend on us alone, and the prospects are not very encouraging; but the only way to find out whether there is a realizable possibility is to try. I think it is just barely possible that there was such an opportunity in the middle 1960's. Without, for the moment, arguing that point, *if* we could have agreed on modest reciprocal force limitations in Central Europe, the Soviets could not have built up an invasion

force or entered Czechoslovakia without violating an international agreement with us, and the risk of confrontation with the U.S. might have been enough to tip the scales against the armed intervention in Czechoslovakia. To put it another way, even if we had added a few divisions to NATO's central front, it would have made no difference whatsoever in Soviet calculations with respect to intervention in Czechoslovakia; no kind of unclear or even clear signal before the invasion would have been credible to Moscow; but an agreement freezing the numbers of Soviet troops in each country, including none in Czechoslovakia, would have played a role. Now, of course, it is too late for MFR for some considerable time—perhaps for the 1970's—because the Soviets now certainly see all too clearly that they cannot afford to give up the option of use of force within their bloc if they are to hold it together. If we had hard-headedly looked at MFR as a way of curbing Soviet freedom of action, as well as stabilizing the East-West balance, we might in fact have been able to serve those objectives; instead, MFR was generally regarded—by most advocates, as well as by most skeptics—as being nice to the Soviets and reducing our own theoretical freedom of action to build *up* forces the Alliance will never build up.

Over the next several years, MFR/MBFR "studies" in the alliance continued, but there was no real movement until 1972–73. Then we embarked on a fruitless confrontational negotiation over MBFR from 1973 to 1989. I do not suggest that a more forthcoming Western position would necessarily have led to agreement; probably it would not. The Soviet Union was more interested in keeping a quantitative edge in conventional forces in Europe and in keeping Eastern Europe out of any collaborative security arrangements with the West. But NATO also was too wary.

Most of the "political-military" matters of attention in NATO in the late 1960s did not yet concern the diplomacy of East-West relations, but the diplomacy of internal Western relations and support for the defense "pillar" of the alliance. Although the flexible response doctrine enshrined in MC 14/3 was newly confirmed, it had been (and continued to be) a gradual process rather than an immediate action matter. The withdrawal of France from the integrated military command of NATO did require a great deal of logistical, infrastructural, military planning, and psychological adaptation. (The forced transfer of NATO's political headquarters from Paris to Brussels also required structural and psychological readjustments. I arrived just after the move, but also felt the impact. As one of my European colleagues astutely remarked on the psychological adjustment of the move from the city of Paris to Brussels, "It's like moving in to live with the sister of the woman you love.") My own direct role in dealing with this adjustment was very limited and prosaic: one "political-military" issue that I inherited was working on the NATO financial claims against France for the forced move. Other such political-military areas included routine civil emergency planning, NATO exercises, and the challenging task of devising better crisis-consultation procedures (soon to be tested by the crisis over Soviet intervention in Czechoslovkia). I assumed responsibility for the U.S. role in new studies of the Mediterranean security problem, given renewed attention after the June 1967 Arab-Israeli war and subsequent new Soviet practice of keeping a naval squadron on permanent station in the Mediterranean. The issue of U.S. troop levels in practice concerned the NATO–Warsaw Pact balance much less than balance-of-payments offsets by our European allies to justify keeping up American troop levels in Europe. I was also involved in policy on negotiations within the alliance on such matters as basing rights. Above all, political as well as military "consultations" were central.

All the members of the NATO alliance, including the United States, had a mixed record with respect to advising our allies of what we were doing or planning to do in our foreign relations and military activities. Sometimes, though not in most cases, we truly consulted our allies in advance in order to obtain their reaction and advice before we took some decision, and (more often) in order to gain their support or at least acquiescence in what we then decided to do. When we (again, I am speaking of the United States, but also all the other allies) failed to consult, the next best course of action was to inform our allies of some unilateral U.S. decision in advance of an action. Least satisfactory was to explain some decision or action after the event or even to evade an explanation. Despite numerous shortcomings and frictions over flawed or failed "consultations," the overall pattern in NATO was still much more forthcoming than most bilateral relations without it.

One of the most keen issues during the mid- and late 1960s, for example, was the negotiation of the Nuclear Nonproliferation Treaty (NPT). As earlier discussed, the negotiation took place on several planes, a broad multilateral negotiation at Geneva in the disarmament committee was the most conspicuous but least important. There were inter-allied consultations, partly in NATO but largely bilaterally among a few key NATO countries (including the United States with Germany in particular, but also with Britain, France, and Italy), and East-West negotiations (essentially between the United States and the Soviet Union, supplemented in a limited way by talks of the Germans and some other NATO countries with the Soviet Union, but not with the other Warsaw Pact countries). The core remained U.S.-Soviet negotiations between ACDA Director Bill Foster and Ambassador Aleksei Roshchin in Geneva, and Secretary Rusk with Ambassador Dobrynin in Washington, and infrequent meetings with Foreign Minister Gromyko. The United States kept NATO informed in a general way, and the Germans and British much more fully, throughout. Nonetheless, the United States did not really consult our allies on the key formulations relating above all to possible future European nuclear relationships until we had essentially reached agreement with the Soviet Union in December 1966 (coincident with our decision to abandon the MLF). Consultations within NATO as well as bilaterally were then close until final agreement and signature of the NPT in July 1968.

I certainly do not cite the case of consultations in NATO over the NPT as a model case, but it was an important example of the practical combination of unilateral and consultative actions feasible in the real world of East-West diplomacy. The course of consultations on the NPT was often rocky, with frictions and suspicions on occasion that the United States was not telling all (which was true) and might not protect European interests (which was not the case), but above all because the Europeans naturally wanted themselves to define their interests and how to protect them. Yet the United States was the only feasible interlocutor for serious negotiations with the Soviet Union. The overriding Soviet concern was that indirectly the West Germans might acquire control over nuclear weapons, if not through the MLF then in some other way. The principal German concern was not to be the subject of permanent discrimination vis-à-vis its nuclear European partners, Britain and France. The general European concern was not to foreclose conceivable Western European unification, including succession to a nuclear status already enjoyed by two of its members. The United States wanted to tie the Soviet Union and others into a firm agreement not to proliferate nuclear weapons. All of these concerns were met in the final compromise resolution of the issue in agreement on the multilateral NPT.

The second major icebreaker in cutting through East-West relations frozen by the Cold War was the flagship of détente in the late 1960s and early 1970s: the Strategic Arms Limitation Talks (SALT). It was of course understood that only the United States and the Soviet Union could negotiate about their respective strategic arms, and a SALT agreement if reached would be bilateral. Nonetheless, the NATO allies of the United States, seeing their security dependent above all on the U.S. strategic nuclear deterrent, regarded SALT as affecting them as much as it did the United States itself. The ultimate strategic deterrent to Soviet attack on the United States was certain to be sustained, but the European allies' concern was that agreed limitations might somehow impinge on the extended deterrence on which *their* security was seen to depend. Thus the Europeans saw their security interests in the conduct of SALT as at least if not more in need of assured protection than the security interests of the United States. In addition, the very SALT negotiation process tended to imply recognition of emerging strategic nuclear parity, even if no agreements were reached. And while strategic analysts and far-seeing political leaders had long foreseen a parity in effective deterrents, and mutual deterrence, as inevitable, Western publics and many officials had not yet accustomed themselves to the idea that the U.S. strategic superiority on which they had so long been able to rely was a fading reality. This was true of course with or without SALT, but SALT reflected an American acceptance of this shift and thus seemed to acknowledge an enhanced Soviet strategic position.

The NATO allies did not oppose SALT. Indeed, most welcomed it because if the Soviet Union was prepared to reach agreement, SALT offered the prospect of real arms control—that is, a constraint on the arms race and a stabilization of deterrence. Some also saw SALT as the strategic East-West component of détente to complement what they hoped to see in European security arrangements. Finally, some were pleased to see the United States as ready to do its part, if the Soviet Union would as well, to begin a process of arms limitation and reductions. While the span of allied sentiment ranged from mere acceptance of SALT to enthusiastic support, virtually all wanted to be included in the process through real consultations. The NPT depended ultimately on acceptance of the European countries, some of whom were essential parties. There had to be alliance consultation and consensus. A SALT agreement, however, would be bilateral. The United States could reach and implement a SALT agreement without the allies. It did not, of course, wish to do so, but the extent of alliance consultation on SALT depended wholly on what the United States would decide to do.

That is why SALT became the key test of alliance consultation. I have mentioned the well-received initial experts' briefing at the North Atlantic Council in March 1967, when SALT was first proposed. Planned consultations in August–September 1968 had been held up pending completion of the U.S. position and agreement on a time and place to begin the talks, and then were suspended after the Czechoslovak crisis and postponement of SALT. I have also noted the odd consultation on SALT "principles and objectives" in January 1969 during the final week of the outgoing Johnson administration, abandoned by its successor. Thus the initial phases of consultation on SALT were a mixed bag. As the U.S. government worked out SALT studies and initial positions during the summer of 1969, in June and July SALT and the strategic balance were discussed at three meetings of the North Atlantic Council, and I conducted two full-day experts' meetings with senior political advisers as well. Then, before the opening of the preliminary talks with the Soviet side in Helsinki in November 1969, the senior members of the U.S. delegation, led by Ambassador Gerard Smith, flew first to Brussels to brief the North Atlantic Council. The NAC permanent representatives welcomed our consultation, or rather frank exposition of the exploratory position of the U.S. side for the forthcoming talks, but also wished to obtain more detailed information on many points. To meet this interest, I conducted an additional experts' meeting. Following the initial Helsinki session, the delegation sent a report, and later Ambassador Smith and I went to Brussels to brief the NATO representatives on the outcome, and I again fielded questions from NAC political advisers and visiting NATO experts. That pattern of briefings prior to and following each of the seven SALT sessions, and on other occasions when the nature of the negotiations warranted, continued. From June 1969 through June 1972 after the signing of the SALT I Interim Agreement and ABM Treaty the SALT delegation provided forty-five oral or written communications to the NAC, conducted twenty-two briefings of NAC by senior SALT delegation members, and held six detailed experts' meetings. I participated in all these briefings except one, served as the senior SALT delegation representative for two of the NAC briefings (including the final briefing after the SALT I agreements were signed), and conducted all of the experts' meetings.

The SALT consultations were highly successful, and similar exchanges were later held for SALT II in the 1970s, and the negotiations on intermediate nuclear forces (INF) and the Strategic Arms Reduction Talks (START) in the 1980s and early 1990s. By this time, the process was routine. But between 1969 and 1972 it met an important need to establish allied confidence in the United States. On matters of particular interest to the allies, the U.S. position was in fact set or revised to reflect their preferences. For example, initially we sought to include Soviet MRBM and IRBM missiles facing Europe, as well as ICBMs and SLBMs threatening the United States. More important, we rejected persistent Soviet attempts to include U.S. forward European-based systems (and, with allied concurrence, in support of this stand dropped our own effort to include Soviet medium-range systems).

Consultation was (and is), of course, a two-way street. Neither the United States nor its NATO allies were prepared to consult on all matters or to commit themselves to reach agreement before acting. But the readiness to consult on a wide range of matters, above all those most central to the purposes of the alliance, was important and contributed to the continuing vitality and success of NATO. As I wrote in a memorandum on consultation to Ambassador Cleveland in December 1968: "NATO . . . may well be unique. With all of its faults, including shortcomings in the area of consultation, it is surely marked by a higher degree of achievement than any other international, multilateral, political organization."

There was a recurring question as to whether, or to what extent, NATO should expand consultation beyond the North Atlantic Treaty area. From early times in the 1950s, it was agreed that NATO would not include the colonial empires of those members having such possessions, either in terms of the protective area of the alliance or in terms of consultation. Nonetheless, it was clear that involvements of NATO members, not least the United States, around the world were relevant to NATO. Vietnam became a prime example. The

Middle East was another important area because it engaged the often divergent positions of several NATO countries, and the Soviet Union as well. I was
often struck by the fact that many American political figures, especially but
not only hard-liners, would believe that all that was needed was "American
leadership" and activism to bring a more vigorous alliance into play around
the world beyond the European area, in order to wage the global Cold War
more effectively. What these people did not understand was that the
Europeans did not want to become involved in a global crusade, or in
Vietnams, or in becoming American satellites, to put it a bit harshly. Efforts
during the Cold War to expand NATO's role beyond the European area more
often than not had a weakening effect, rather than a strengthening one, on
alliance solidarity.

I observed that in addition to the formation of "NATO policies" and a spirit
of shared alliance views (as well as a corps of professional "NATO specialists"
in various allied foreign ministries, including our own), there tended to be a
less evident and less conscious projection of NATO solidarity into views
attributed to the Soviet adversary. There is no question but that the Soviet
leaders sought to stimulate and to play upon differences among NATO members and wished to weaken the organization. But these were a standard Soviet
tactic, rather than the central Soviet objective. Their objectives were to
enhance their own security, and to expand their power. NATO was an adversary, a major extension of American power, and frequently an obstacle to
Soviet courses of action. But "splitting the alliance" was not itself the overriding Soviet objective. And sometimes NATO was seen as the lesser evil, for
example, preferable to an autonomous nuclear armed West Germany or even
a U.S.-German alliance.

One of NATO's concerns was its own internal security. This concern,
shared by the U.S. government and other NATO member governments, as well
as the alliance organization, was well founded. As time went on, a number of
Soviet and other Warsaw Pact intelligence penetrations of NATO headquarters, as well as of individual NATO governments, were discovered. This necessarily put a certain restraint on providing sensitive intelligence or policy
information to the alliance as a whole, although not so seriously as to impede
consultation and development of common positions or the operation of
alliance organizations.

In due course a number of Soviet and other Warsaw Pact intelligence penetrations of NATO were uncovered (apart from numerous penetrations of the
governments of NATO members). For example, in the early 1960s a U.S. Army
sergeant, Robert L. Johnson, working at the Armed Forces Courier Center at
Orly Airport in Paris where NATO headquarters was then located, had passed
over everything that came through, including Berlin contingency plans and the
locations of U.S. nuclear weapons in Europe. Later, another U.S. Army ser-

geant, Clyde Lee Conrad, in the period from 1975 to 1985 again passed over many secret NATO military documents. The access to documents available to these low-ranking military personnel was the key to their importance as agents.

At the time I was in Brussels, a Turkish national, Imre Nahit, chief of the financial department of NATO headquarters, was able to obtain many documents from NATO central files and pass them to his Romanian intelligence handlers. When he was arrested in September 1968, he had 1,440 secret NATO documents in his briefcase! I participated in both the U.S. and NATO formal "damage assessments," evaluations of the nature and scale of his disclosures, and of the consequences. In the course of reviewing the materials passed by Nahit for our assessment, I was struck by the fact that although by definition we would have preferred they not be made available to the Warsaw Pact, individually and as a whole the compromised political and military documents clearly showed that NATO was indeed planning only defensive actions. The same was true of the even more sensitive military documents passed by Conrad to his Hungarian and Czechoslovak handlers. In 1990 General Janos Kovacs, the new head of Hungarian military intelligence, noted that the latter penetration had in fact contributed to better East-West relations. "The interesting paradox," he said, "was that Conrad's information helped prove that there are no offensive NATO plans and this led sober-thinking people to reassess the situation and to develop a new approach."[3]

Soviet intelligence placed great stock in documentary materials, and was able to cross-check by virtue of its control not only over a variety of agents, but also through different East European communist intelligence agencies, against targets not only in NATO headquarters, but in most if not all governments of NATO countries. They thus had a very good system for redundant and cross-confirming information, and were able to have confidence in it.

I am not in a position to say whether the United States ever conducted successful disinformation operations through NATO channels, using multiple channels to provide false confirmation. I can, however, say that we often provided true information to our allies with awareness that it would almost certainly become known in Moscow. That is to say, we sometimes provided information that we were certain would leak to Soviet intelligence because we *wanted* the Soviet leaders to know how much we knew or what we were planning or prepared to do. We also understood that the Soviet leaders placed much higher value on information, especially valid documentary materials, that they acquired by clandestine means.

There was, of course, two-way traffic in secret information and disinformation. We relied much more on technical intelligence collection, including

3. Cited in "Spy Credited with Improving East-West Ties," Associated Press release, *Washington Post*, June 20, 1990.

overhead aircraft and later satellite reconnaissance, and less on espionage (though not for lack of continuing efforts, with varying success). In the nature of things, we had far less, and less certain, information on Soviet and Warsaw Pact intentions as distinct from their military forces and capabilities.

I found after my return from Washington to Brussels in September 1968, that in the aftermath of the Soviet-led Pact invasion of Czechoslovakia there was concern over possible further Soviet military interventions in Eastern Europe. It was, of course, appropriate to consider the contingencies of further Soviet interventions in Romania and Yugoslavia, even if we deemed such action unlikely. In addition, Secretary Rusk and other senior officials warned Ambassador Dobrynin and others that such action would adversely affect U.S.-Soviet and East-West relations. I participated actively in such contingency planning and consultation in NATO. Although most NATO officials and their governments were reasonably balanced in their assessments of the possibility of such Soviet interventions in Eastern Europe, some were excessively alarmed and even feared possible Soviet military actions in Austria or to the West. This was excessive overreaction to what had happened.

In a memorandum to Ambassador Cleveland on November 19, 1968, I decried this tendency to alarmism. As I noted to him, at the then recent meeting at ministerial level of the NATO Defense Planning Committee, the defense minister of one of the NATO countries had said: "More importantly [than an increase in Warsaw Pact capabilities], the sudden, even reckless manner in which the final decision to invade appears to have been taken causes deep concern for the future. We now perceive, I think, a greater risk of an impulsive, irrational thrust by the Soviets which would have grave consequences for all of us." I took sharp issue with such an evaluation, which I characterized as "wrong with respect to the decision to invade Czechoslovakia, and misleading with respect to future Soviet behavior." The "intervention in Czechoslovakia was the result of a reluctant, agonizing, carefully considered Soviet decision. It may have been a mistake from the standpoint of long-term Soviet interests, but it was certainly not reckless, impulsive, or irrational." I noted that the consensus of NATO ambassadors in Moscow, as well as American intelligence analysts in Washington, was that the new Soviet doctrine of intervention in the Socialist Commonwealth (the "Brezhnev Doctrine," as it soon came to be called) was "an effort, after the fact, to justify the action against Czechoslovakia, and not a guide to future Soviet plans and actions." I argued that the "Soviet leaders today, as in the past, show every indication of being rational, prudent, cautious and deterred." In a more sarcastic tone than usual, I commented further, "We can, of course, intentionally overstate the Soviet threat, and then when it does not materialize, claim the credit for having prevented it . . . but if this is our purpose we, or at least *some* of us, ought to know that this is what we are doing."

Threat estimates of Soviet and Warsaw Pact military capabilities also continued to be exaggerated. This was less serious than the tendency to impute dangerous intentions, but it contributed to overall exaggeration of the threat. In part, it resulted from a tenacious grip on maximizing the threat that some of our NATO partners held and others cultivated in order to assure support for military budgets. It also stemmed from prudent withholding of certain U.S. intelligence information that could reveal sensitive collection capabilities and would not be accepted by our allies unless we risked compromising such sources to persuade them.

Soon after I had arrived in Brussels, before the Czechoslovak intervention, I had tried to get some relevant useful intelligence released for circulation to our NATO allies, on a secret basis, but was rebuffed. Specifically, I wanted to pass along some information obtained from intelligence debriefings of a senior Czech defector, Major General Jan Sejna, who initially provided reliable information. (Later, as often happens, in an effort to prolong interest in his revelations, especially after he had been publicly "surfaced," he exaggerated or invented things sought by eager Western interlocutors.) I knew the odds did not favor release even of the limited information I sought, but I thought the effort worth making (although I may not have enhanced the prospects by my choice of cable subject caption: "Cashing a Czech").

Within a few months NATO was back to business as usual, and as earlier noted was launching studies of mutual force reductions. Incidentally, that was one case where Nahit's treachery may have misled the Soviets, at least for a time. The 1968–69 mutual force reductions studies, positing proportional reductions, were among the documents he passed over, but well before MBFR began in 1973 proportional reductions had been abandoned. I am sure, though, that the Warsaw Pact continued to obtain materials disclosing the changed NATO position.

About mid-way in my tour, at a time when Ambassador Cleveland and his deputy and some others were at the NATO ministerial meeting in Washington in April 1969, I served as chargé d'affaires ad interim in charge of the mission for about ten days. Perhaps it was the relatively inactive tempo of NATO headquarters while most senior officials were away celebrating the twentieth anniversary of NATO, coupled with the opportunity presented by being in charge, but in any case I used the occasion to send an inventive cable, reporting in detail on imaginary exchanges at a NATO "Temprep" meeting (the ambassadors were permanent representatives to NAC, "Permreps" in usual cablese). In the several-page cable I bestowed caricature names on identifiable representatives, with clever repartee and a considerable dose of satire and mockery of ourselves, our colleagues, and our usual work. It was, if I may say so without undue immodesty, rather well done. Whether it was appropriate and proper to do it at all was another matter, and I must admit it was highly questionable. I sent the cable straight, signed it as acting chief of mission addressed in the first instance to Ambassador Cleveland, but pro forma to the secretary of state (as are all cables to the department), with copies to all U.S. embassies in the capitals of NATO countries. The cable was captioned "USNATO Is Alive and Well, Living in Brussels." I sent it "Limited Official Use" and "NOFORN" (meaning not for foreign nationals) in order to prevent the temptation of leaking an unclassified cable to the press or to our allies, some of whom no doubt would have been offended at my mocking of individual and national peculiarities and biases. Amazingly, it did not leak (although the fact of its existence did become known to some NATO colleagues in Brussels).

I never received a reprimand, although Ambassador Cleveland was very unhappy at the light tone I had taken with respect to our serious work, and I know a few senior officers in the Department of State were not appreciative. Numerous junior- and middle-ranking Foreign Service officers, and some senior ones, on the other hand, were delighted at it. Many congratulated me, and referred to it even many years later.

In retrospect, I must acknowledge that it was probably not the right (or wise) thing to do, although I believe it had redeeming features in placing our usually serious efforts in perspective. In any case, while I may have exercised less than the best judgment in sending that message, I believe I made up for it in another action I took as chargé. One of the officers in the defense adviser's office came to me with great concern over a technical, but not minor, problem. Unless we could get authorization from the secretary of defense, who was then traveling in Europe, and take action ourselves within the next few days, the United States would lose $25 million. The money had been provided for a NATO infrastructure program for construction of aircraft shelters on air bases—a program we put in place after the Israeli Air Force had shown the vulnerability of the Egyptian Air Force in 1967—but was not ready to be expended, and the United States would recover those funds only if we acted immediately. But for the U.S. mission to directly contact the secretary of defense on the matter, and both obtain his approval and then act on it without going through the usual prescribed channels, would be highly irregular. I would be considered in some quarters as exceeding my authority. I didn't hesitate on that one: I arranged to get the matter to the secretary of defense by courier for his approval, and then acted upon at NATO. We made the deadline and saved the U.S. government 25 million dollars. For that initiative, I was later commended.

Meanwhile, the twentieth-anniversary meeting of NATO in Washington was the occasion for renewal of the North Atlantic Alliance, and this time rather than specifying a ten- or twenty-year renewal term the extension of the alliance was for the indefinite future. Even France had no objection. In retro-

spect, it seems natural that there should have been such a unanimous reaffirmation of NATO in 1969, but in fact there had been some uncertainty in
between 1966 and 1968 as to whether the partial "defection" of France and
new stirrings of détente would lead to a much more tentative endorsement of
the alliance for the future. In any case, the Soviet intervention in Czechoslovakia dispelled any remaining doubts and ensured solidarity on the smooth
and indefinite renewal of the alliance.

I had found rewarding my assignment at NATO, even though it was interrupted by my being called away for SALT in 1968 and again in 1969.
"USNATO," as the U.S. mission to NATO headquarters was called, was a fringe
actor in Washington policymaking, notwithstanding Harlan Cleveland's
activism and despite being more influential in the policy process than most
embassies. It was thoroughly involved in all aspects of NATO activities, except
direct military planning at Supreme Headquarters, Allied Powers in Europe
(SHAPE) in Mons, and completely separate even socially from the U.S.
embassy to Belgium and the rest of the non-NATO diplomatic corps in
Brussels. I found it interesting working with representatives of the other allies,
a daily diplomacy more extensive than in a bilateral embassy. In later years, I
would see many of my NATO colleagues in other assignments, including several as ambassadors in Washington. I also had occasion (especially because of
SALT) to work directly with NATO Secretary General Manlio Brosio. As I have
indicated, the mission (and I) were involved in a wide range of matters, some
of them interesting and a few quite important.

Although policy was made in Washington, it was useful to get a feel for
implementing policy in the field. The central issue was the diplomacy of East-
West relations, even though the exigencies of intra-Western alliance relations
consumed most of our attention (in Brussels and in Washington). The new
challenge that had presented itself by the late 1960s, and would dominate the
1970s, was the role of détente, now formally the "second pillar" of the NATO
alliance. I wrote a memorandum to Ambassador Cleveland on November 20,
1968, titled "Delusions About Détente: Some Lessons from the Czech Affair,"
that set out my thinking. My memo had no role in stimulating the détente that
was soon to blossom, although it described rather well the approach that
President Nixon was to adopt, and later to call "hard-headed détente." I believe
it bears quoting rather extensively.

> Détente has been set back. But what *is* détente, and what does it *mean*
> for us that it has been "set back"?
> Any illusions about Soviet devotion to détente as a goal have been, or
> should have been, dashed by the brutal Soviet intervention in
> Czechoslovakia. There were some over-eager and over-optimistic expec-
> tations about early progress in improving East-West relations. Indeed,

we have occasionally heard statements across the [North Atlantic] Council table which seemed to reflect such misbegotten expectations. No doubt these illusions will resurrect themselves.

But the most pervasive delusion about détente, it seems to me, has been the tendency to identify it with a warm and friendly glow on the part of all concerned. From that perspective, it is quite proper to view with some alarm the risk of being taken in by the Soviets. There was, and remains, a real danger—if that is the way *we* approach the matter. But if we appreciate the fact that so-called détente measures can be coolly contracted between adversaries, rather than necessarily being the embrace of friends, we could do much to avoid such risks.

There also have been, and remain, opportunities for us in détente quite apart from the vague possible cultivation of improved attitudes and relationships. Indeed, I believe we have seriously, and unnecessarily, restricted ourselves from vigorously waging détente in such a manner as to push the East off balance. Fundamentally, the foundation on which the Soviet empire has been constructed is much more precarious than is the basis for the NATO community.

The Soviets have seen this much more clearly than have we. They have blasted the concept of bridge-building with a ferocity that betrays their fear. They have attributed various cynical designs to us where, alas, our horizon has been much more limited. We have, in general, been too guarded in our outlook to see the real possibilities for the offensive potential of a policy of détente. We have failed to exhibit the self-confidence we should have had in pushing détente. We have over-estimated Communist political strength and cunning, and short-changed ourselves. For example, the West Germans have (despite some recent tendency to change) been excessively defensive and backward on contacts with the East Germans, where they should have taken all opportunities for contact and swamped the East Germans. One sees the same hyper-defensiveness in self-consciously erecting verbal barriers against splitting our own Alliance, rather than getting down to the business of splitting the really fragile Warsaw Pact Alliance.

I do not, of course, mean that we should raise again the banner of a paper crusade to roll back Communism in Eastern Europe. The less said about that sort of thing the better. What I have in mind is, first of all, to clarify our own understanding of what détente *can* mean, and then quietly but vigorously to go about pursuing a broad course of mutually supporting policies which would lead to results favorable to our long-term objectives.

Of course, the Soviets will react keenly against our efforts, and in a sense the repression of Czechoslovakia represented just such a reaction to the national (not Western-manipulated) trends in Eastern Europe. But we can at least try to inspire, cultivate, and assist trends toward independence from Moscow, and liberalization, in ways least likely to bring forceful repression. . . . A *strategy* of détente has been called for, and still is. By this I mean acting on the basis of an overview relating various developments to one another. . . .

I have attempted above to sketch out a way of looking at détente differently from the generally prevailing view. Our effort to get people [in NATO] to look at SALT as an effort to strike a mutually advantageous business deal between two sharp-eyed and coldly calculating adversaries, and not as an elevated Pugwash love-in of the nuclear superpowers, is one big step along this path. I hope we can do more.

This was the vision of a rather tough détente I then held, with particular reference to Eastern Europe, but not excluding possible mutual accommodation with the Soviet Union, especially in the field of strategic arms control.

Two months later, on the eve of the new administration in Washington, I carried my thinking about the relationship between détente with the Soviet Union and the diplomacy of East-West relations in the aftermath of the suppression of Czechoslovakia a considerable step further. This time I also prepared it as a telegram for Washington, dispatched on January 13.

As we reexamine the prospects, and even the meaning, of détente in 1969, we are likely to be led to give predominant attention to Western (and above all American) relations with the Soviet Union itself, rather than with the Eastern European Communist countries. This is not to say that we should abandon our efforts to influence the situation within and among the countries of Eastern Europe; it is merely to recognize that since Moscow is evidently determined to put a strong governor on the rate of political movement in Eastern Europe, perhaps the best way to influence that movement is by influencing the regulating power.

To the extent that Moscow is determined to keep the Warsaw Pact members tied fairly closely to its own political forms and policy line, we can best influence the development both of the Soviet Union itself and of the other European Communist countries by doing things that will encourage evolution in the Soviet Union itself, rather than directly challenging its hegemony. Our policy has never posed a choice between the USSR or the East European Communists, and should not do so now, but these are questions of priority. We cannot abandon our efforts to cultivate better relations with the Eastern European Communist countries, but this effort will now, in practice, be more of an adjunct to our efforts to affect the Soviet Union rather than in an attempt to pry them away from the Soviet Union. Developments in Eastern Europe within Moscow's tolerance level have in many cases come sooner and gone further than in the USSR, and there seems to be some feed-back from such developments within the Soviet Union. However, it now seems likely that Soviet reactions against successful evolution in Eastern Europe would retard progress in both those countries and the Soviet Union, so long as Moscow viewed the more rapid pace of movement in Eastern Europe as a divisive threat.

It will be very difficult to develop meaningful détente relations with the Soviet Union. But it is likely that one of the most effective ways to work toward this will be by dealing with things that can really have important effects on the security environment in which the Soviet government and people live. SALT would appear to be the most eligible and significant of these just now.[4]

I also used this cable to press for a beginning of SALT, discussed in the following chapter.

When SALT began in the fall of 1969, indeed beginning several months earlier, I was again in Washington as part of the SALT delegation. From then on, I was rarely in Brussels (and then usually for SALT consultations). By 1970 I was fully engaged in SALT, and the range of other active issues in the political-military field also attracted me to return that fall to Washington as deputy director of the Bureau of Politico-Military Affairs (PM). PM had developed into a full-fledged bureau from the small cadre of experts, of which I had been one, assembled a little less than a decade earlier on Alexis Johnson's staff as G/PM. It was from that vantage point that I observed the development of détente with the Soviet Union, as well as becoming deeply engaged in SALT, for the next three years.

---

4. "SALT and Détente," USNATO 0130 to SecState, Washington, January 13, 1969 (confidential, 2 pages, declassified February 1, 1996). The telegram was of course sent over the name of the chief of mission, Ambassador Harlan Cleveland.

13

Negotiating on Strategic Arms: SALT and the ABM Treaty

The single most ambitious undertaking of the détente experiment was the attempt by the two superpowers in the Strategic Arms Limitation Talks (SALT) to control their strategic military competition. For adversaries even to attempt to deal together with the most sensitive and critical issues of their national security marked a significant step forward.

President Nixon had called in his inaugural address to move from an era of confrontation to one of negotiation, and SALT was in time to become the "icebreaker" negotiation. Nixon did not, however, want to forgo what he (and his National Security Adviser Henry Kissinger) believed to be the leverage that SALT talks could provide on other issues. The Soviet leadership had promptly made clear its interest and readiness to proceed with SALT, but rather than encourage an early start of talks, Nixon and Kissinger saw Soviet eagerness for SALT as something that could be exploited by linkage of SALT to Soviet assistance in negotiation on other issues—above all, Vietnam. Accordingly, at his first press conference on January 27 Nixon spoke of steering a "middle course" between arms talks irrespective of progress on political settlements on the one hand, or withholding arms talks or agreements until political settlements were reached. "What I want to do," he explained, "is to see to it that we have strategic arms talks in a way and at a time that will promote, if possible, progress on [resolving] outstanding political problems at the same time." On that public occasion he mentioned as an illustration progress on the stymied issue of peace in the Middle East, but his paramount interest was Vietnam. This was made crystal clear when Kissinger bluntly told Ambassador Anatoly Dobrynin in early April that Nixon was ready to send a negotiator to Moscow promptly

to agree on principles of strategic arms limitations *provided* there was a con-
current meeting in Moscow with North Vietnamese officials empowered to
negotiate on that problem. Apart from the important fact that Nixon and
Kissinger had an exaggerated impression of Moscow's influence over the
North Vietnamese, the Soviet leaders were not prepared to enter SALT as sup-
plicants. The proposal was not even given a reply, but the Soviet leaders from
then on bent over backwards to emphasize that they did not need SALT any
more than did the United States.

On the home front, the Nixon administration in 1969 had a different concern. Although prepared to negotiate, including SALT, it did not wish to appear
to its conservative constituency as soft on relations with the Soviet Union.
Accordingly, when Secretary of State William P. Rogers spoke on October 25
about prospective initiation of SALT, he went to pains to disassociate it from an
American interest in improved political relations with the Soviet Union, saying,
"We are not talking about détente or anything else"—just strategic arms control.

This was the position taken at the time by most of us who believed that U.S.
interests in strategic stability could be served by SALT. In my cable from
Brussels in January 1969, I had emphasized the value of SALT in the absence
of improvement of political relations.

> Our efforts in the last two years to engage the Soviet leaders in a discus-
> sion of possible strategic arms limitations, and more generally to pro-
> voke a high-level dialogue on crucial global strategic matters, were
> predicated on the assumption that the existing state of our relations
> with the Soviet Union through the years of intensified embroilment in
> Vietnam would not preclude consideration of ways to dampen down the
> strategic arms race. The problem has been seen as essentially one of
> inducing the Soviet leaders to recognize the futility and risks of an
> uncontrolled strategic arms race apart from—and even despite—the
> international political context. We have sought to persuade the Soviet
> political leaders that it was necessary to seize the moment in order to
> control an increasingly expensive and dangerous competition in which
> neither side could hope to gain any kind of real dividends, a state of
> affairs not dependent upon greater or lesser degrees of hostility or
> détente.
>
> Strategic arms limitations remain an extremely important objective
> to pursue, and for these reasons. But the new political context of the
> post-Czechoslovakia world, and the advent of a new administration in
> Washington, now add new dimensions of relevance. Strategic arms
> limitations—and, in paler degree, even negotiations about such limita-
> tions—would represent renewed efforts by both sides to engage in a
> common effort to serve the common interests even of adversaries. In

short, SALT can represent a realization of the pursuit of a safer world order even during continuation of political conflict.[1]

The problem with this approach was that Nixon and Kissinger had relatively little interest in strategic arms control and, as noted above, were pursuing a stratagem of linkage in the hope of getting leverage on Moscow. Only much later, when it had become clear that the pursuit of leverage was in vain, and the prospect of a SALT agreement had become a political asset in American politics, did Nixon and Kissinger press ahead in 1971–72 to reach an agreement.

The new administration had at the outset launched a series of calls for studies, called National Security Study Memorandums, "NSSMs." Among the very first was a study of military posture (NSSM-3). Although such priority for a military policy review was entirely appropriate, by contrast the first such study on SALT was not launched until March in NSSM-28, after the military program, including a new ABM (antiballistic missile) program, had already been decided upon. It would have been better to study both in conjunction.

I had returned from Brussels to Washington on short visits in June–July and August–September 1969, during which I was involved in SALT, having been slated to become the executive officer of the yet unformed delegation. In October–November I was back as the delegation prepared for preliminary talks in Helsinki in November–December 1969. In the fall of 1969 I resumed informal conversations on SALT both with Boris Sedov, my KGB contact at the Soviet embassy, and with Yuly Vorontsov, deputy chief of mission under Ambassador Dobrynin. I had a few general reciprocal explorations of possible SALT positions with Sedov before the first two SALT sessions in late 1969 and the spring of 1970. Sedov left Washington soon after, but by then I had in any case turned more to official contacts with Vorontsov, with whom I met fourteen times before and after SALT sessions over the period from November 1969 to July 1972. We each probed on substantive issues and also handled official business concerning SALT (such as exchanges of tentative delegation lists and discussions of procedure, and later conveying official positions on some issues that had arisen in the SALT talks).

The first round of talks was held in Helsinki, November–December 1969. Six subsequent rounds were held alternately in Helsinki and Vienna, concluding with the SALT I agreements signed at the first Nixon-Brezhnev summit in Moscow in May 1972. Over half of the time during this two-and-a-half-year period we were at the negotiating table.

---

1. "SALT and Détente," USNATO 0130 to SecState, Washington, January 13, 1969, pp. 1–2 (confidential, declassified February 1, 1996).

I will not review the two and a half years of negotiation of SALT I in any comprehensive way. Most of the record of the exchanges is now available.[2] What may be of greatest interest would be an inside look at the negotiations (in Washington among the competing interested parties, as well as in Helsinki and Vienna between the U.S. and Soviet delegations, and in direct back-channel Washington-Moscow exchanges).

The first and most far-reaching SALT proposal for consideration was advanced in May and June 1969, by Gerard Smith, the director of the Arms Control and Disarmament Agency (ACDA). It was the essence of simplicity, but also potential effectiveness: Stop Where We Are (SWWA). The United States and the Soviet Union had a rough parity, at about 2,200 strategic delivery vehicles on each side, and a SWWA agreement was judged by the intelligence community to be verifiable. But both the civilian leadership of the Pentagon and the Joint Chiefs of Staff were strongly opposed to stopping the competitive advance of military technology, in particular a big step forward with multiple independently targeted reentry vehicles (MIRV), which the United States was about to deploy in large numbers and which the Soviet Union did not yet have.

In retrospect, it would surely have been in the interests of all if some such agreement could have been reached. Today the hope is that a START III treaty early in the twenty-first century might return us to the levels of 1969–70, some 2,000–2,500 warheads, after more than three decades during which both sides built up from a few thousand to levels of over 10,000 strategic warheads on each side by the time the Soviet Union expired. But SWWA was rejected, even though it might well have provided the basis for agreement.

Guidance for the initial exploratory talks was approved by the president only on November 12, the day before the delegation departed for Helsinki (several of us stopping en route at Brussels to brief the North Atlantic Council, the NAC). As noted in the preceding chapter, consultation on SALT at the NAC, initiated in 1967 and 1968, assumed considerable importance in allaying possible concerns of our allies as we negotiated with our common adversary concerning our common nuclear deterrent. I played a very active part in these alliance consultations, accompanying Ambassador Smith and on two occasions substituting for him. I also conducted a series of additional experts' meetings, usually held in conjunction with the NAC briefings, for more detailed discussions.

At the first round of SALT each of the sides was cautiously sounding out the other, and no proposals were advanced. We later learned from members of

2. See John Newhouse, *Cold Dawn: The Story of SALT* (Holt, Rinehart & Winston, 1973); Gerard Smith, *Double Talk: The Story of SALT I* (Doubleday, 1980); Henry A. Kissinger, *White House Years* (Little, Brown & Co., 1979); and Raymond L. Garthoff, *Détente and Confrontation*, 2nd ed. (Brookings, 1994). Many of the actual records of the negotiation are now being declassified and available to scholars.

the Soviet delegation that it was only after they had reported back to Moscow following that initial exploratory round that the Soviet leadership decided that the United States was interested in serious negotiation and that SALT would continue. We passed a test we had not even been aware we were undergoing. Our government had assumed a continuing SALT had been decided and agreed upon earlier.

By the time the SALT negotiations began, decisions in Washington on policy and positions to be taken in the negotiation had been effectively concentrated in Henry Kissinger's hands in the White House, supported by his National Security Council (NSC) staff. The interested departments and agencies of the government had diverse, often conflicting, interests and positions that had to be taken into consideration, if only because eventually any agreements reached would have to be sustained by Congress and the public, and there were vocal and politically powerful constituencies supporting various defense and arms control objectives. The NSC, although only advisory to the president and subject to whatever role he assigned it, was the traditional highest-level body for consideration of such issues. The NSC formally met on SALT half a dozen or so times, but it was not an effective forum for the consideration of detailed issues involved in the negotiation. It was the forum in which the secretaries of state and defense personally participated, and occasionally its meetings were important. The key continuing body that met frequently and had the major responsibility for airing, debating, and influencing SALT positions was, however, a bureaucratically ad hoc creation called the Verification Panel, initially established in July 1969 to consider diverging views of the agencies on the important question of requirements for verification of compliance with any arms control provisions of agreements. But it soon displaced completely the nominally logical body, the Undersecretaries Committee, comprising the under or deputy secretaries of the NSC departments, chaired by the under secretary of state. The reason was simple: the Verification Panel was chaired by Henry Kissinger and had essentially the same membership: the under secretary (after July 1972 deputy secretary) of state, Elliot Richardson, and later John Irwin, the deputy secretary of defense, David Packard, the chairman of the Joint Chiefs of Staff, Admiral Thomas Moorer, the director of the Arms Control and Disarmament Agency, Gerard Smith, the director of central intelligence, Richard Helms, and (for reasons never clear) Attorney General John Mitchell.

The Verification Panel met much more frequently than the NSC; in 1971, for example, the NSC met on SALT only two or three times, but the Verification Panel twelve to fifteen times. I regularly briefed Richardson and later Irwin before these meetings and served as the staff officer accompanying them at the Verification Panel meetings. It was a great pleasure to work with both of those gentlemen.

A Verification Panel Working Group, composed of representatives of all of these agencies (except the Justice Department) at the assistant secretary level, was the real working-level body. It met frequently, hashed out and prepared positions, and identified alternatives and conflicting positions for the consideration of the Verification Panel. I participated in the Verification Panel Working Group from September 1969 to September 1970 in my capacity as the executive secretary of the SALT delegation, and thereafter until January 1973 also representing the State Department. When the delegation was abroad, engaged in negotiation, another interagency body called the Backstopping Committee, chaired by the deputy director of ACDA, Philip Farley, handled the daily stream of communications from the delegation.

The SALT delegation was unusual in that it was a collegial group appointed by the president, and its head was "chairman" of an interagency delegation, rather than being *the* negotiator with a single integrated staff. Gerard Smith, the chairman of the delegation, was also the director of ACDA, and his nominal deputy as chairman of the delegation was Philip Farley, although he rarely attended the negotiations (remaining in Washington to head the Backstopping Committee and serve as the delegation's direct link to Kissinger and the Verification Panel and its members, as well as to administer ACDA).

The other delegates or members of the collegial delegation were all seasoned senior representatives of key agencies: Ambassador Llewellyn (Tommy) Thompson and later Ambassador J. Graham (Jeff) Parsons, representing State; Paul Nitze representing Defense; Lt. General Royal Allison, USAF, representing the Joint Chiefs of Staff (JCS); and Dr. Harold Brown, defense scientist and a former high Defense official (and future secretary of defense), as an expert not affiliated with any agency.

I was selected to serve as executive secretary or chief of staff of the delegation, as well as senior adviser from State. My deputy or alternate was Sidney Graybeal of ACDA, and our main delegation staff was composed of experts from the State Department, ACDA, and CIA (analysts under nominal cover). Reflecting the unusual nature of the delegation, there were autonomous staffs from Defense for Nitze, from the JCS for Allison, and one officer from State to assist Thompson (later Parsons). Administrative support was provided by ACDA.

Notwithstanding the unusual character of the delegation, we worked together quite effectively. The four senior delegates and I met with Ambassador Smith usually every morning at 10:00 to review new instructions and other information, and when meetings were scheduled with the Soviet delegation to review our presentations, and of course we met frequently each day as required and usually ate lunch together. All our meetings were in confining plexiglass inner rooms specially constructed to preclude electronic eavesdropping. Sid Graybeal handled the task of coordinating preparation of materials within the compartmented delegation staffs.

The U.S. delegation numbered nearly a hundred people, about half in secretarial and other support roles, including a detachment of Marines borrowed from various embassy guard details. Our staff was larger than that of most embassies (including those in Vienna and Helsinki).

The quality of our SALT delegation staff was very high, as evidenced by the fact that it included as then junior officers two future deputy national security advisers (David Aaron, in the Carter administration, and Robert Gates, in the Reagan administration) and two future directors of central intelligence (again Gates, in the Bush administration, and R. James Woolsey, in the Clinton administration).

The fact that the SALT I negotiations were held in alternating sessions in Helsinki and Vienna gave us some variety, but this shuttle arrangement was an administrative burden and inconvenience. It arose from our having proposed several locations, including Helsinki, which the Soviet side accepted, but with a later preference in Washington for Vienna, so we ended up agreeing on both. Both the neutral Finns and Austrians were delighted to host negotiations between the superpowers on strategic arms control and competed to provide hospitality (and such amenities as external security; for example, each of the senior delegates and I were assigned individual cars with plainclothes police drivers for the whole duration of the sessions.) But we routinely had little reason for contact with anyone but the Soviet delegation.

As a small gesture to our Finnish hosts, as well as to superpower cooperation, our administrative officer came up with the idea of a commemorative necktie bearing the Finnish, Soviet and American national coats of arms. I liked the idea and told him to go ahead. I didn't even think to mention it to Gerry Smith, who only learned of it when the boxes of ties arrived. We then learned that Gerry didn't care much for the idea. But we had the neckties. I decided that we could probably get the Finns to present the ties to the two delegations as if the entire idea had been theirs. The Finns indeed were delighted to take the ties, and to assume responsibility and take the credit. The presentation was a great success; among others, the head of the Soviet delegation, Vladimir Semenov, often wore his tie, although Smith never did (nor did General Allison or his Soviet counterpart).

In Helsinki our delegation, vastly larger than the embassy, was housed in a relatively isolated modern lakeside hotel called the *Kalastajatorppa* (Fisherman's Hut), and we leased an isolated building for our offices. In Vienna we stayed in hotels, but our offices were in the *Strudelhof*, a seventeenth-century palace near the American embassy. Our conference room had a plaque commemorating the fact that on July 19, 1914, Count Leopold Berchtold had signed there the ultimatum to Serbia that touched off World War I. That of course provided material for a toast to the prospect that our deliberations would have a more favorable impact in history.

The Soviet delegation was roughly similar to ours in composition. In part this was owing to the nature of the task, and to similar constituencies in the two governments. In addition, they had asked us in advance about the composition of our delegation, and I had kept them informed through Yuly Vorontsov, who advised me of their delegation. There were some interesting variations, including a more prominent and direct role for the Soviet military-industrial complex, represented by the deputy chief of the powerful Military Industrial Commission (VPK), Academician Alexander Shchukin, and the deputy minister of the Radio-Technical Ministry, Peter Pleshakov. The chief of the Soviet delegation was Deputy Foreign Minister Vladimir Semenov, a senior diplomat but not experienced in arms control issues. The most influential member of the delegation clearly was Colonel General Nikolai Ogarkov, first deputy chief of the General Staff, accompanied by another senior officer, Colonel General Nikolai Alexeyev. The senior Foreign Ministry officials initially included Georgy Kornienko, Oleg Grinevsky, Victor Karpov, and later Roland Timerbaev. My counterpart as general (executive) secretary of the Soviet delegation was a Foreign Ministry official (but identified GRU, Soviet military intelligence, officer), Nikolai Kishilov.

Early in our first encounter, in Helsinki in November 1969, members of Paul Nitze's staff brought to his attention what they and he regarded as an ominous sign: about a dozen of the Soviet delegation members had been identified as having, or were suspected to have, intelligence affiliations. I checked and noted that our own delegation had about the same proportion of current or former intelligence officers, beginning with myself and my deputy Sid Graybeal, both formerly CIA officers. Only Paul remained somewhat suspicious. There was one, and only one, incident that illustrated the fact that such negotiations were setting a new pattern that not everyone at first understood. Again, in the earliest days in Helsinki, one junior intelligence officer listed as an adviser in the Soviet delegation approached a member of the U.S. delegation who was of Russian descent and bragged about knowing details of his biography, a gratuitous implication that "they" had their eye on him. Nothing more. When I reported the incident to our senior delegates, they were rightly incensed. I, too, felt it was important that we make the ground rules very clear, and immediately complained to Kishilov and said that I expected there would be no more suggestions of playing games with my delegation. Kishilov was taken aback, agreed, and said he would look into the matter at once. The offending "adviser" was never seen again, and there were no further incidents in SALT.

All official delegation reporting to Washington came through my executive office, and no cables could be sent without my signature or Sid's. In addition to reports on formal plenary negotiating sessions (which in due course diminished in frequency), informal meetings of various kinds including individual conversations by delegation members with their counterparts at a social hour after formal sessions were all reported to Washington in MemCons (memorandums of conversation) sent by diplomatic pouch, in all some one thousand in the two and a half years of SALT I. Highlights of conversations and key formal statements were sent daily by cable.

All official communications were sent through State Department channels, signed off by me or Sid (most important matters were also cleared by Ambassador Smith and as appropriate other senior delegates). The Defense Department and JCS elements routinely (and State, ACDA, and CIA elements occasionally) also transmitted back-channel messages to their own home offices, but this created difficulties only in a few cases when over-zealous Defense Department representatives tried end-runs in Washington to circumvent the delegation.

In addition to advice and support to Gerry Smith, managing (with Sid) the delegation staffwork, and reporting to Washington (including nightly conversations by secure telephone), my other principal function was handling contacts with the Soviet delegation. This included from the outset such routine matters as coordinating with my counterpart, Kishilov, on the format, time, and place of meetings. Very soon it extended to cautious exchanges on the substance of the discussions, to negotiation of a "work program," and later to exploration and negotiation of virtually the full range of substantive issues. I also accompanied Gerry Smith on all his meetings with his counterpart, Vladimir Semenov, even most of the occasional dinners or other social encounters.

As my meetings with Kishilov and with Oleg Grinevsky, a senior Foreign Ministry official and closest adviser to Semenov, and in that sense also my counterpart, began to get more and more into substance (and the formal meetings of delegates became more and more statements for the record), there was some resentment of my role, especially by some of the harder-line Defense and JCS staff members, and even General Allison (though we were personally on very good terms). We offset this to some extent by my usually meeting with Kishilov and Grinevsky accompanied by another member of our delegation (Jack Shaw of State, or Larry Weiler of ACDA, later Ambassador Jeff Parsons) so that I was at least somewhat protected against speculation that I might be exceeding my mandate. There would have been even more concern had it been known (as it was only to Ambassador Smith) that rather early on, on May 21, 1970, Minister Semenov had approached me directly and, expressing concern over the sluggish course of the negotiations, had asked me with whom I wished to carry out private exploratory talks: Kishilov? Grinevsky? I had replied either or both as he saw fit. The next day Kishilov came to me and said he and Grinevsky were ready to meet with me at any time; the minister had so instructed them. This was one of the very few things

I did not think it appropriate to note in a circulated MemCon but only in a memorandum for the record (and for Ambassador Smith). Semenov was wary about personally conducting such private explorations, to Gerry Smith's dismay, but he recognized they were essential, that I could do it for the American side, and that he could rely on (but if necessary repudiate) Kishilov and Grinevsky. So we became the point men in the SALT I negotiations, entering first on new terrain or seeking a path through known obstacles. Semenov would refer to us, in talking with Smith, as the "shadows" of the delegation chiefs, and the "wizards," because we could get difficult things done. This informal, but authorized, element of the negotiation was highly productive. I found these encounters the most fascinating part of our work.

Gerry Smith sought to engage Semenov's interest and understanding by giving him a copy of Francis Walder's book *The Negotiators,* a wonderful account of the negotiation between ideological (religious) adversaries, Catholics and Huguenots in sixteenth-century France. (Kishilov complained to me about the heavy burden this placed on his delegation to translate the whole thing into Russian!) Semenov frequently quoted the Bible, the Koran, Greek mythology, or Goethe. Once I had to come to the rescue of our excellent interpreter when he was stymied by Semenov's reference to *empedokl',* which I recognized as Empedocles. Semenov's point in claiming that Empedocles believed in a bizarre theory of biological evolution through chance combinations was never clear to us. Gerry Smith later proposed a toast to Zeus for felling Phaëthon with a thunderbolt when the impetuous youth almost atomized the Earth by losing control of the chariot of the Sun, suggesting we should seek to draw on the wisdom of the ancient Greeks in our endeavors to harness the runaway chariot of the nuclear arms race. I was not content to leave Empedocles to Semenov, and when we were arguing for a comprehensive agreement, I drafted a statement for Gerry claiming (I hope correctly) that Empedocles had said the universe was composed of four elements: earth, water, air, and fire, and in terms of our (SALT) universe this obviously meant including land-based missiles, sea-based missiles, bomber aircraft, and megatonnage firepower. Obviously such philosophical banter did not affect the negotiations directly, but it did contribute to developing rapport between the delegations.

More formal working groups were set up in 1971 and 1972 to work on ad hoc technical matters and to prepare joint drafts, initially with many bracketed alternatives reflecting points of disagreement. Even formal meetings of the delegates were usually changed to smaller "mini-plenaries," as we referred to them. After all of the formal meetings, plenaries or mini-plenaries, the usual pattern was to break up into small conversation groups among delegates and among attending selected staff officers over drinks. (We managed to assure that the few press references referred to these as "tea breaks," although the standard beverages were Jack Daniels Black Label and Stolichnaya vodka. After the delegation was replaced in early 1973, the successor U.S. delegation did switch to coffee and tea to assure no press speculation about incautious or overly friendly personal encounters, although we had had no difficulties.) The informal exploratory talks I held with Kishilov and Grinevsky in 1970–71, apart from our postmeeting discussions, were usually over luncheon or dinner; by 1972 they were usually morning and afternoon negotiating sessions. I learned only twenty-five years later, from Oleg Grinevsky, that from the outset he and Kishilov were "wired" with recording devices for all of our meetings. That was a security measure to ensure that Grinevsky and Kishilov had not disclosed any security classified information, not to ensure an accurate record of the discussions.

One of the peculiarities of prolonged international negotiations is that "transnational," "transdelegation" partnerships of interest develop, whereas unanimity of views may be lacking within a delegation (and among the home offices of a delegation). For example, certain American and Russian negotiators wanted to ban "futuristic" types of ABM systems, as we eventually did; others, on both sides, did not. To my knowledge, there were no instances on either side of disloyalty to a delegation or its instructed position. But there were issues on which some delegates and advisers sought earnestly to persuade members of the other delegation, while others did not.

I developed a very good working relationship with Kishilov and Grinevsky, with whom by 1971 and 1972 I was in virtually daily contact. Although they had much less leeway than I, we were able to work out solutions to many problems ad referendum to the chiefs or full delegations. In fact, by 1972 in the final months most of the negotiation was conducted in what was called the "Group of Four," Jeff Parsons accompanying me while I negotiated with Kishilov and Grinevsky. The outline of all the remaining key elements of the ABM Treaty was worked out in a breakthrough package that I presented to Kishilov and Grinevsky on a Finnish-hosted jaunt of the two delegations to Rovaniemi, Lapland, on the Arctic Circle in April 1972 in what became known as the "Tundra Talks." In that instance, although we did not know it at the time because our delegation had been kept in the dark, I preempted a meeting taking place secretly in Moscow between Henry Kissinger and Leonid Brezhnev in preparation for the first Nixon-Brezhnev summit. We later learned that Semenov, kept informed by his government and brought back to Moscow, had taken an uncharacteristic initiative and presented the position I had advanced in the Tundra Talks as an authoritative U.S. proposal and obtained Soviet government agreement. Although I (and the delegation) had not been authorized, and I had not presented, a formal proposal, it was in line with what

Washington was ready to accept (as I knew from back-channel exchanges between Kissinger and Smith). Accordingly, when Brezhnev presented the compromise package to Kissinger it was accepted.

I have mentioned some semi-official but off-the-record back-channel communications within the U.S. government. Although much of the SALT I negotiation was carried by our exchanges away from the formal negotiating table, it was still between delegations and subject to delegation and Washington interagency approval and confirmation. An extraordinary feature of the SALT I negotiation without precedent (although with later descendants) was the secret initiation in January 1971 of a back-channel correspondence between Nixon and Prime Minister Alexsei Kosygin, followed by extensive meetings and negotiations between Kissinger and Ambassador Anatoly Dobrynin, leading to a suddenly disclosed agreement in May that would recast the whole framework of the SALT I negotiations and agreements. This "breakthrough" involved abandonment of the effort to reach agreement on a comprehensive treaty embracing limitations on strategic offensive and defensive arms, and substitution of a more readily attained separate ABM treaty and certain (ill-defined) interim measures to limit offensive strategic missiles. This scaling back of the SALT objective was necessitated by a deadlock over defining which offensive arms were to be considered "strategic" and hence subject to limitation.

The agreement was made public on May 20, 1971, with great fanfare as a breakthrough. In one sense it was, although it was only procedural and marked a retreat or lowering of our sights as to what we now expected to achieve. Worse still, it had been sloppily negotiated, with several premature U.S. concessions that had to be retrieved with great difficulty over the next year (in particular to regain inclusion of submarine-launched ballistic missiles) or given up. Most remarkable, this back-channel White House negotiation over five months, as well as the flawed result, was not known to the U.S. delegation, or even to the secretaries of state and defense, until the day before the public release. I had picked up from guarded comments by Kishilov and Grinevsky that there was a back-channel negotiation under way, and some indications as to the content, but being uninformed officially and limited by our own restrictive guidance, we on the delegation were unable to contribute to the outcome.

Nixon and Kissinger justified bypassing the delegation and the whole of the government beyond the White House as necessary to obtain the result and to "save" SALT. Yet the cause of the deadlock in the negotiation was an adamant U.S. (and Soviet) position, and if the acceptability of a May 20-type outcome had been made known, and the normal channels of policy decision and negotiation used, the negotiation of the interim agreement on offensive arms over the next year would not only have been greatly eased, but the resulting agreement would have been better and less subject to the objections later raised to the one negotiated on the basis of the May 20 guidance. Nixon and Kissinger found it much easier to change the U.S. position so radically by avoiding what would have been a bruising fight in the executive branch, but the outcome may not have justified that convenience.

The back-channel was used again in the spring of 1972, now with Brezhnev rather than Kosygin, again mainly Kissinger with Dobrynin (and in April directly with Brezhnev), and most critically in the final days of negotiation in Moscow at the summit itself. In May 1972 Nixon unwisely decided to keep the U.S. delegation in Helsinki while he and Kissinger negotiated in Moscow, supported only by their own aides. The result was predictably less satisfactory than it could have been. Kissinger did bring in the delegation to some extent by back-channel, but with delays and less satisfactory communication than if we had also been in Moscow. At one point, on May 24, Ambassador Smith had to point out in an urgent cable to Kissinger that a draft the presidential delegation in Moscow was about to approve would inadvertently have prevented the United States from proceeding with its highest priority program for converting Minuteman I single-warhead ICBMs to Minuteman III MIRV warhead missiles by banning any increase in volume of existing ICBM missiles. The U.S. negotiators in Moscow, with no expert military advisers, had been so intent on limiting Soviet missiles that they had overlooked that effect! Only after agreement had been reached were we summoned quickly to Moscow.

The principal agreement reached in SALT I was the ABM Treaty. The initial aim of both delegations had been to negotiate a comprehensive strategic arms limitation agreement embracing both strategic offensive and defensive arms. Indeed, it was the Soviet side that in January 1967 had insisted on including strategic offensive arms, as well as ABM, which had initially been the focus of American concern and interest. At the time the SALT talks began in November 1969, as earlier noted, the two sides had rough numerical parity in terms of the number of strategic nuclear delivery vehicles (SNDVs), as we referred to the mix of ICBM launchers, SLBM launchers, and strategic bombers (about 2,200 on each side). The Soviet total included more ICBMs, and the United States had larger numbers of SLBMs and heavy bombers. If it had been only a matter of leveling off these central strategic forces, there would probably have been little difficulty in agreeing on an equal level somewhere between 2,000 and 2,500 SNDVs. There was, however, a significant discrepancy in defining "strategic forces," to which we shall return. In addition, levels of SNDVs was not the most important problem.

It was generally recognized in 1969–70 that the two most important issues in SALT were whether limitations could and should be placed on multiple warheads for strategic missiles, MIRV, and on antimissile defenses, ABM systems. The maximum arms control contribution to strategic stability would have been agreement on a verifiable ban on further development and any deployment both of MIRV and ABM. Even without reductions, each side would be limited to a few thousand deliverable strategic warheads, and in the absence of antimissile defenses, that would continue to provide both ample assured retaliation and mutual deterrence.

The first issue for some was whether the Soviet Union would be content with mutual deterrence and give up prospects for gaining strategic superiority. For others, the first issue was whether *the United States* should be prepared to do so. There were large questions as to both propositions. Theoretically, those most concerned about a possible Soviet quest for superiority should have been most eager to tie them down, if possible. But in fact those most alarmist as to Soviet intentions and capabilities usually also sought maximum U.S. defense efforts and counted on the U.S. lead in advanced technology to give us an edge, if indeed not decisive superiority. More logically, those that favored arms control were prepared to give up possible American advantage in an arms race, provided the Soviet side were limited comparably.

There were of course many serious (and other contrived) questions as to possible enhanced capability to nonlimited systems, circumvention of limits, and verifiability. In addition, there were the direct interests of constituencies. The U.S. military had been counting on MIRV and was just launching a massive deployment program that would increase our absolute and relative strategic striking capability over the next decade. To give up MIRV would mean to settle for mere parity in numbers of strategic forces. (To be sure, in the longer run the Soviet Union would also acquire MIRV, and with a larger force of larger ICBMs could be expected to have as great or greater MIRV capability— but that was at least a decade away and much could change by then.) There was a much weaker constituency for ABM. With available technology, in which the United States also enjoyed a lead although the Soviet Union had first deployed a modest defense for Moscow, an ABM system would be costly and of doubtful effectiveness. ABM alone offered no prospect of undercutting deterrence. It would, however, further stimulate the offensive arms race. In conjunction with known (and yet unknown) advances in strategic offensive forces it could be destabilizing. The maximum arms control approach would, to repeat, ban both MIRV and ABM. Banning, or sharply limiting, ABM would reduce instability and reduce incentives for the strategic arms race. Whether ABM limitations alone would really dampen the arms race would, however, depend on restraint by the two countries. Marginal constraints on offensive arms would help, but only marginally.

In the spring of 1970 the U.S. government set out to establish its position on what offensive and defensive strategic arms limitations it wanted. As Henry Kissinger later described the situation, even after five meetings of the Verification Panel and a meeting of the National Security Council, "there was no consensus; there was a babble of discordant voices." Nixon, never very interested in the substance of SALT, left the sorting out of options and a position to Kissinger, who on March 27 issued a directive in the president's name "asking the agencies to reduce the chaos to four options for Presidential decision." But the existing machinery was too bulky, and it was decided that some one person had to formulate the main options. I was designated to perform that task. I had been given the bare bones of four options by the presidential directive, but I had to work out full positions and coordinate the result so that those agencies that favored one or another option would support it. The four options were: (A) MIRV, and a nationwide ABM defense, were allowed; (B) MIRV would be allowed, but ABM would be limited to defense of the National Command Authorities (NCA, that is, Washington and Moscow); (C) MIRV would be banned, and ABM limited to NCA defense or banned; and (D) MIRV would be allowed, but with substantial reductions in strategic offensive delivery vehicles (especially large—Soviet—ICBMs), with ABM limited to NCA defense or banned. Option A entailed minimal arms control and was favored by the JCS. Defense, and especially Paul Nitze, favored Option D. Gerry Smith and I, and in general the State Department, ACDA, and CIA favored Option C, with maximum arms control. Without anyone seeming to favor Option B, it was everyone's second choice. The president (in reality Kissinger) decided that the delegation would propose *both* Options C and D to the Soviets in Vienna in April. In fact, as presented, both were almost certain to be rejected by the Soviets, and indeed Kissinger expected Option B to emerge—everyone else's second choice, but his first choice.

I had worked night and day for three days (sporadically resting in a hotel room across the street from the State Department) preparing the eighty-two-page document presenting in detail the four options. The four options were presented to an NSC meeting on April 8, in a session aptly described by Kissinger as a "Kabuki play"—"All this feinting and posturing was performed before a President bored to distraction. His glazed expression showed that he considered most of the arguments esoteric rubbish; he was trying to calculate the political impact and salability of the various options, of which only the broad outlines interested him." Kissinger admits that he then made the decisions (to proceed with Options C and D, and to modify some aspects from my draft). Kissinger has also admitted that he was "swayed by bureaucratic and political considerations more than in any other set of decisions in my period of office," although elsewhere he had said with pride that "our negotiating position would reflect not bureaucratic compromise but careful analysis of consequences and objectives," and providing "clear choices" for presidential decision.[3]

---

3. These quotations are from Kissinger, *White House Years*, pp. 541–43 and 149. See also Smith, *Doubletalk*, pp. 117–20; and Garthoff, *Détente and Confrontation*, pp. 154–62.

At a meeting in the White House cabinet room of the senior SALT delegates with the president that summer, I was struck by the extent to which Nixon was not well aware even of the main aspects of our negotiating position. I don't believe he had any interest in whether MIRV was banned or not, except that he understood the military leadership was strongly opposed, and he didn't want to be undercut by them on the Hill when it came time to get the necessary support for ratification.

Kissinger's reformulation of my draft made two important changes. First, the proposal for a complete ABM ban was dropped, leaving a limited NCA defense in Options B, C and D. Second, for Option C, he added on-site inspection of a MIRV ban. Moreover, the MIRV ban provision was formulated to prohibit testing, development, and deployment of MIRVs, but not their production. Both of these changes made it certain that the Soviet side would reject our MIRV ban proposal, as Kissinger intended. The Defense and JCS representatives had wanted an on-site inspection requirement, but I had not included it because CIA, State, and ACDA were confident that a MIRV ban prohibiting developmental testing would be adequate for verification. The Soviet Union had not yet begun such testing, which we could monitor with confidence. The United States, on the other hand, had completed such testing and was in production and about to start large-scale deployment of MIRVs. Later, when the Soviet side objected strongly to our omission of a ban on production of MIRVs, the delegation sought but could not obtain authorization to *add* that element—without weakening any other provisions, including even on-site inspection. The Soviet side was suspicious that the United States would produce and stockpile MIRVs, just stopping short of deploying them; because they had not yet tested and developed MIRV, they were unable to do that. In reality, the reason Kissinger had excluded a production ban, and added the onsite inspection provisions, was simply to ensure that the Soviets would reject the proposal, as they did.

I well recall how my counterpart, Oleg Grinevsky, listened as we presented our MIRV ban proposal, then put down his pen and stopped taking notes. He told me after the meeting, "We had been hoping you would make a *serious* MIRV proposal." No one knows whether the Soviet leaders would have agreed to a fair MIRV ban, because we never proposed or showed interest in one.

The "reductions option," Option D, was also so loaded that it fell of its own weight. The Soviet side was not interested in reductions disproportionately cutting their most effective and potentially MIRVable ICBMs while the United States could make its reductions in mothballed B-52 bombers and proceed at full pace with its planned MIRV buildup. The Soviet side did not necessarily object to reciprocal reductions, although many in Washington failed to recognize this fact and simply saw a negative Soviet reaction to "reductions."

With the rejection of Options C and D, the delegation devised a "Vienna Option" variant of Option B and in late July 1970 was authorized to present it. But we remained at loggerheads especially over offensive forces limitations (to be discussed presently) until the abandonment of negotiating a comprehensive agreement in May 1971 earlier described.

The ABM Treaty was of course concluded, and was a major achievement. Its negotiation, however, while never perhaps at hazard, was a tortuous path. When SALT began in late 1969, in accordance with the administration's defense policy enunciated in March 1969 before the SALT preparations were seriously under way, a flat statement in our guidance reaffirmed a presidential commitment to a thin nationwide ABM defense system capable of defending the country against small attacks or accidental launchings. By the time I was asked to draft the four options in March 1970 Kissinger was responsible for introducing the defense of NCA (national capitals) as an option, and when Options C and D were revised for presentation to the Soviet side, the alternative zero ABM (a complete ban) was withdrawn. Accordingly, when in April 1970 we presented the alternative MIRV ban or reduction approaches, both contained the same ABM proposal of a limited NCA defense.

There are indications that both Kissinger (who later was unhappy with the NCA defense proposal that he had fathered) and Nixon believed the *Soviet* side would propose a thin nationwide defense (with China in mind), thus taking the onus on themselves for a more extensive ABM system and shoring up slipping support in the U.S. Senate for our own deployment. But as those of us who followed the matter understood, an NCA defense, ABM defense of Moscow and Washington, was the first preference of the Soviet leaders. It allowed them to keep the defense they had already deployed at Moscow and would hold us to a minimum. The main reason that Kissinger and Nixon were prepared to give up a nationwide ABM defense, and eventually to settle for very limited ABM defenses, was that Congress had shown it would not support extensive, much less nationwide, deployment.

The Soviet delegation accepted the proposal to limit ABM to NCA defense within a week after we proposed it in April 1970. The U.S. delegation was then required, by a bewildering stream of changing instructions, to spend the next two years trying to walk away from our own proposal. To be sure, the first step was to introduce as an "alternative" a possible zero ABM. The Soviet side had made clear at the first encounter in Helsinki that they were prepared to consider a complete ABM ban, but once we had offered to let them keep the Moscow deployment it was clear that it would be difficult to get them to agree to eliminate it. When Semenov later did privately indicate Moscow's interest in considering an ABM ban, we were instructed by the White House to drop the idea. Then we were instructed to try to get Soviet agreement to a lopsided deal: *four* U.S. ABM sites for defense of ICBM fields to the *one* Soviet site at Moscow, soon abandoned for three to one, then two to one. The only purpose of those feckless proposals was that the White House could say on the Hill that the funding it was requesting for three or four ABM sites was consistent with the U.S. position in SALT.

It soon became quite clear that the final ABM limits would either be two for two, or one for one. Finally, the ABM Treaty signed in 1972 allowed two sites for each side, one for NCA defense and one for ICBM defense. And in a protocol amending the treaty signed in 1974 (after the Nixon administration had found it could not get support on the Hill for an ABM defense of Washington) this was cut down to one site on each side.

As earlier noted, there was a serious problem from the outset in defining "strategic" forces for purposes of SALT. The Soviet side was adamant on defining "strategic" for purposes of bilateral U.S.-Soviet arms control as meaning weapons capable of striking the Soviet Union and the United States. They insisted on counting, or taking into account in some meaningful way, the large number of U.S. forward-based systems (FBS) with nuclear munitions capable of striking targets in the Soviet Union. Most Americans tended to shrug off the "FBS problem," as it was called—to see it at first as a mere distraction or negotiating ploy, and at worst as a Soviet attempt to stir up trouble with our allies and gain a strategic advantage. The United States initially had sought to include Soviet medium- and intermediate-range ballistic missiles (MRBMs and IRBMs) in SALT, but we dropped that in 1970, with the consent of our allies, largely to strengthen our case for omitting our own FBS. But the FBS issue was not a negotiating tactic. The Soviet side had a case: the United States had about a thousand nuclear delivery vehicles, mostly bombers and fighter-bombers, located on air bases abroad or on aircraft carriers within striking range of targets in the Soviet Union, and capable of delivering a powerful punch. Indeed, a U.S. Department of Defense study in 1972 concluded that these FBS forces *alone* could destroy 25 percent of the Soviet population, or 90 percent of all Soviet MRBMs and IRBMs, or 20 percent of the combined Soviet ICBM and MRBM/IRBM force, in an initial strike.[4] This was *not* the intended employment of those forces, but it shows why Soviet military planners were loath to omit consideration of such forces from the strategic balance.

We rejected the Soviet arguments on the perfectly reasonable grounds that to limit U.S. FBS, without limiting Soviet theater nuclear forces facing those FBS and our allies in Europe and Asia, their real counterpart, would mean to

---

4. Department of State, Memorandum for the Verification Panel Working Group, "FBS and Other Non-Central Systems in SALT TWO," October 20, 1972, pp. 28–29 (secret, declassified December 31, 1980).

grant a major advantage to the Soviet side. The problem was not Soviet intransigence, but a real issue on which both sides had valid considerations that made agreement very difficult, if indeed possible at all. The result was that the Soviet side in 1970 suggested putting the impasse over strategic offensive forces aside and agreeing in the first instance on an ABM treaty, which then appeared much closer to agreement.

The U.S. side, the SALT delegation as well as the agencies in Washington, was not eager to agree to an ABM agreement alone because we would lose leverage on the offensive issue. The delegation was instructed to "stand fast" on our latest comprehensive proposal, and did so from August 1970 to May 1971. Then, suddenly, the earlier described May 20, 1971, agreement reached by the White House back-channel negotiations was unveiled, calling for an ABM agreement, to be accompanied by "certain measures," unspecified, to limit offensive arms.

Before the agreement of May 1971, the Soviet side showed its impatience at the impasse and long delay on dealing with offensive arms by starting construction of eighty new launchers for ICBMs, including thirty for large ICBMs, the first since a unilateral and unannounced Soviet moratorium on additional ICBM launchers had begun in the fall of 1969. They may have hoped this would prompt us toward some agreement. After May, construction of those eighty launchers continued, but no new additional ones were started. Thus as a result of unilateral Soviet restraint during the two and a half years of SALT I negotiations only 80 additional Soviet ICBM launchers were added, as compared to 650 in the preceding two and a half years. There were of course none added after the SALT I Interim Agreement was signed. Construction of submarines with SLBMs, in which the Soviet Union was still behind the United States, continued during the negotiations, and thereafter within the limits set by the Interim Agreement.

The vagueness of the understanding on the "certain measures," including above all whether SLBMs were to be included along with ICBMs, and if so limited at what levels, and even the form the agreement would take, were thorny issues for the next year.

Suffice it here to say that Kissinger's casual agreement in negotiating the May 20 accord to omit SLBMs, as Smith and Nitze were able to discover when given access to a hastily sanitized file of the exchanges, was not made known to the U.S. government (almost certainly including President Nixon). Thus when, to Kissinger's surprise, there was virtually unanimous agreement in the U.S. government to include SLBMs, it became a very uphill battle in the negotiations. The Soviet side was confident that Kissinger's earlier commitment meant they could continue to stand fast. Finally, Kissinger persuaded the Soviets that the U.S. government *had* to include SLBMs, but that it could be done in such a way that the limitation would not really impinge on whatever

SLBM buildup they intended; it would, in short, be a contrived limitation to satisfy officials in Washington without really limiting what the Soviets planned to do. Kissinger took the highest estimate of Soviet SLBM buildup of several alternative programs in the latest NIE (rounded off at 950 SLBMs) and presented this to Brezhnev as a notional limit, at the *highest* level they could build, then presented the same thing in Washington as a Brezhnev proposal that he had wrung out of him, that would satisfy the U.S. requirement for inclusion of SLBMs, at a *lower* level than they otherwise could build (using inflated projection of past buildup, higher than the NIE estimates, to which he had gotten Admiral Moorer's assent, thus using the military penchant for overestimating the potential threat to his advantage). It was fast footwork, and left many hanging issues, but it worked.

The ABM Treaty was the centerpiece of the successful conclusion of the SALT I negotiation. The more controversial but less important Interim Agreement has usually been referred to loosely in later years as the "SALT I agreement," inasmuch as its successor, the SALT II Treaty, was intended to succeed it as a more extensive limitation on strategic offensive arms.

The "Interim Agreement on Certain Measures with Respect to the Limitation of Strategic Offensive Arms" was an executive agreement of five years duration, in contrast to the ABM Treaty of indefinite duration. It essentially froze the level of strategic missile launchers, with a limited trade of older ICBMs for SLBMs. It was certainly not disadvantageous to either side, but it also was not a very significant limitation. In view of the fact that it only covered ICBM and SLBM launchers, and not strategic bombers (or FBS), the numbers were unequal to U.S. disadvantage, 1,710 on the U.S. side to 2,258 on the Soviet side. This was appropriate because it was just a freeze of the prevailing levels of missile launchers, but the impression caused by the unequal numbers prompted criticism in the United States.

Undoubtedly the greatest shortcoming of the SALT I negotiation was the failure to ban MIRV or to limit in any meaningful way a continuing competition in strategic offensive arms. The United States was above all to blame for not even making a serious attempt to limit MIRV. Both countries, however, in SALT I and in the subsequent drawn-out SALT II negotiation, failed even to attempt to agree on balanced far-reaching constraints of a kind that should have been seen as being in their common interests. On both sides there was too much deference to keeping open options and efforts to gain an advantage. A key lesson that should have been learned from the Cuban missile crisis, that advantages on the margins of the strategic balance were not militarily usable or politically worth the effort, was never applied. Strategic arms control became a reality in the 1970s and was resurrected in the latter half of the 1980s, but it never made the contribution it could have made to moderating the costs, tensions, and risks of the Cold War because leaders on both sides were not ready to give it a chance—even with prudent verification assurances of reciprocal compliance.

Two specialized agreements were also reached in the framework of SALT I. An agreement on Measures to Reduce the Risk of Outbreak of Nuclear War, usually referred to simply as the "accident measures agreement," seeking to prevent accidental causation of an unintended nuclear war, was negotiated by the two delegations, mainly by Ambassador Parsons on our side, and signed on September 30, 1971, by Secretary Rogers and Foreign Minister Gromyko. Another agreement, the Agreement on Measures to Improve the USA-USSR Direct Communications Link, was signed at the same time, modernizing the technology for implementing the direct communications line established in 1963. This more technical agreement was negotiated by specialists from Washington and Moscow, under the auspices of our SALT delegations. These agreements made a modest but useful contribution to strategic stability.[5]

Perhaps the most important contribution of the SALT negotiations was the very fact that they took place. SALT I showed the recognition by the Soviet leaders, as well as by those of the United States, of the futility of an unconstrained arms race. SALT did not create strategic parity, but it did reflect its existence. It also involved the beginnings of a strategic dialogue that I believe has been undervalued, and to which I shall return presently. But even apart from the specific terms and effects of the formal agreements, strategic arms control entered the national security planning of both countries. It involved top-level political and military leaders, and lower-level political-military staff cooperation in consideration of many new issues, breaking new ground in this respect in Moscow and enhancing such cooperation in Washington. SALT reflected a political decision by both countries that the risks of negotiation and agreed constraints could be less than the risks (and costs) of unrestrained competition. It imposed some restraint, though not enough, on the strategic arms competition. The ABM Treaty was a major achievement, but the failure to curb MIRV undercut much of the value of that treaty as well as devaluing the weak limits placed on offensive arms.

The SALT I negotiations were a political achievement in helping to reduce tension and reinforce strategic stability, although it became clear in the late 1970s and early 1980s that strategic arms control alone could not sustain détente. The SALT I agreements were oversold politically in 1972, then undervalued especially after 1979, when the pendulum of public support had swung away. Indeed, over time the SALT agreements even engendered some negative

---

5. For the most complete discussion of these agreements, see Raymond L. Garthoff, "The Accident Measures Agreement," and Sally K. Horn, "The Hotline," in *Avoiding War in the Nuclear Age: Confidence-Building Measures for Crisis Stability,* edited by John Borawski, pp. 56–71 and 43–55 (Westview Press, 1986).

consequences, as real, ambiguous, and imagined circumventions and violations fed suspicions of the adversary and of strategic arms control. Nonetheless, the SALT negotiations made an important positive contribution to
U.S.-Soviet (and East-West) relations in the era of détente.

I have mentioned the role of SALT in contributing to a strategic dialogue,
albeit one the potential of which (as with strategic arms control) was never
fully realized. As early as 1967–68 unofficial and confidential official pre-SALT
talks had opened a limited dialogue, as noted in an earlier chapter, although
one that was not continued under the Nixon administration. Nixon and
Kissinger were in fact opposed to strategic dialogue, both because they
thought it would distract attention and because they did not believe in
"abstract" ideas in a dialogue between adversaries. When they did agree to
such statements, above all in the Basic Principles of Mutual Relations between
the United States and the Soviet Union signed at the 1972 summit, and the
Prevention of Nuclear War Agreement signed at the succeeding 1973 summit,
it was only to placate a Soviet interest with what they regarded as harmless,
but essentially valueless, rhetoric.

At the outset of SALT, I and a few others had tried to generate support for
a strategic dialogue. Our principal "success" was an address that Secretary
Rogers delivered on November 13, 1969, just as our delegation left for
Helsinki. He affirmed the existence of mutual deterrence and noted that "a
capacity for mutual destruction leads to a mutual interest in putting a stop to
the strategic arms race." He called for a "dialogue" about managing the strategic relationship between the two superpowers. And he emphasized that ultimately "the question to be faced in the strategic arms talks is whether
societies with the advanced intellect to develop these awesome weapons of
mass destruction have the combined wisdom to control and curtail them."[6]
It was a good speech, but it had little resonance or impact—above all in the
White House.

Our delegation contributed its share to launching a dialogue, and most
important so did the Soviet side. Minister Semenov's very first presentation
was an eye-opener for many on the American side. He explicitly endorsed
mutual deterrence:

> Even in the event that one of the sides were the first to be subjected to
> attack, it would undoubtedly retain the ability to inflict a retaliatory strike
> of annihilating power. Thus, evidently, we all agree that war between our
> two countries would be disastrous for both sides. And it would be tanta-
> mount to suicide for the one who decided to start such a war.

6. "Strategic Arms Limitation Talks," address by Secretary Rogers, November 13, 1969,
Department of State Bulletin, vol. 61, no. 1588 (December 1, 1969), pp. 465–68.

This statement, as Semenov privately confirmed, had been cleared by the highest political and military leaders in Moscow.

Incidentally, after that very first substantive meeting of the two delegations, I passed a copy of the text of Ambassador Smith's remarks to Kishilov, and he gave me Semenov's. Thereafter, to ensure precise and accurate reporting, we exchanged such prepared statements by the chiefs of the delegations. Our statements were routinely classified *secret,* and hence so was the copy I provided to the Soviet delegation. Their first statement had not borne any classification, but from then on all were also marked *sekretno.* Ambassador Tommy Thompson later told me I had "escalated" our practice; the U.S. Embassy in Moscow routinely labeled *confidential* papers that it passed to the Soviet side, even though most carried the higher *secret* classification in the U.S. handling. U.S. security classifications had long included special captions for documents shared only with certain close allies, such as "U.S. and U.K. Eyes Only." We joked that we now needed a new category, "U.S. and USSR Eyes Only."

After the first two weeks of preliminary talks in Helsinki, Gerry Smith invited each of the four other senior delegates and myself to prepare memos on our personal initial impression of the talks and future prospects. Apart from a number of more specific impressions and conclusions, I also addressed the underlying Soviet recognition of mutual deterrence and some implications for SALT of our respective approaches to strategic stability. I think it is worth noting here what I said then, as it bears on the strategic themes I had been expressing for some time and have referred to elsewhere in this account, as well as providing a clearer picture of some of the initial exchanges we were having in SALT.

> I regard the Soviet affirmations accepting the concept of mutual deterrence as serious, and as a significant step forward in providing an underpinning for SALT. Unlike most of our colleagues, I do not find this position surprising or a radical new departure in Soviet thinking.
>
> A similar point of departure does not always mean we will reach a similar destination. It does not mean that they will always draw the same conclusions with respect to particular possible or desirable limitations, as we have already had occasion to see. But I do not believe it is disingenuous, or a sham, or a trap. In fact, I would conclude that the Soviet position is probably predicated on expectation of a more durable situation of mutual deterrence than is our own, given the high American concern with vulnerability of the land-based ICBM force. Hence, it is we who will be the more reserved and "difficult" with respect to some limitations on offensive forces. . . .
>
> On doctrinal matters, it is also clear that the Soviet approach to questions of peace and war is predicated more on the domination of political

judgments than on mechanistic calculations, and that these political judgments are very conservative. They are able to understand our concerns with vulnerabilities prompting "incentives" to strike, and have even begun, in cases where it supports their position, to cite such arguments—always (correctly) attributing them to our prior reference to the possibilities. But I do not believe that Soviet policy makers are inclined to believe that rational great powers, such as the U.S. and USSR, are led to weigh slide-rule derived "incentives" to strike as important factors in unleashing thermonuclear war. (The Soviet concept of preemption is a much more limited and precise one than ours—it relates directly to a last minute seizure of the tactical initiative before the enemy has succeeded in striking, but when there is no way to head off the war—it does not extend to more general "incentives" to strike in a crisis because of a degraded assured destruction quotient. Of course, we may educate them to be more trigger-happy, if only because they may draw the conclusion that we are.)

I do not, of course, quarrel with our prudent weighing of potential risks to integrity of our deterrent, nor with our effort to find negotiable limitations which will reduce such risks, but there is a certain hazard in persuading the Soviets that we are over-concerned with such matters. On balance, I think, so far, we are succeeding in supporting our attention to factors contributing to crisis instability without raising alarms about an American propensity to overact in a crisis. But it is we who are back to 1959 talk of "delicacy of the balance of terror"; the Soviet position is solidly in the tradition of the 1960s adumbrated in the SALT context by Robert McNamara at Glassboro and McGeorge Bundy publicly more recently. We are probably the more sophisticated military technical analysts; despite general ideological distortions, on this point they may well be the better political historians.

Both delegations of course emphasized sources of potential stability and instability in relation to our preferred limitations (which were usually the product of more mundane institutional interests and technological or geostrategic advantages). Nonetheless, overall the discourse and debate in terms of strategic stability gave additional weight to it, even if our specific positions were often "loaded" to the advantage of the presenting side. There were surprisingly few real divergences over strategic considerations. Two are worth noting, one concerning a matter of strategic doctrine and practice, the other a highly political issue.

On April 27, 1970, Semenov in a plenary address referred almost in passing at one point to improvements with respect to early warning systems "owing to which silos containing ICBMs may be empty at the moment when the enemy attempts to strike them, while the ICBMs that had been in the silos would already be en route." This was a clear reference to what is called in American parlance "launch on warning," a concept for preventing success of an enemy attack by firing one's own missiles before they can be destroyed. The risk, of course, is that the warning system may be in error, in which case an intended defensive measure could become an inadvertent and unintended first strike by the side that had erroneously believed it was under attack. Two weeks later, Ambassador Smith brought up Semenov's remark and asked if he had in fact been describing a launch-on-warning concept, which we believed to be dangerous. Semenov replied at the next session (on General Ogarkov's whispered advice, he did not reply immediately), lamely claiming he had been referring to U.S. discussions of such a concept. We were able to cite a very recent statement by Secretary of Defense Melvin Laird rejecting reliance on launch on warning and asked the Soviet side whether they could supply a similar official assurance. They ignored that invitation and later closed the discussion by thanking us for clarification of the U.S. position on the subject.

Some later published accounts of SALT have referred to an alleged complaint by General Ogarkov to General Allison that specific military information should not be discussed in front of civilians. In fact, the occasion for his comment was on this subject, launch on warning, and what he said was that such questions should not be brought up in the SALT talks, and that General Allison "as a military man, should have known the answer to that question" about launch on warning. In fact, while both countries recognized the risks of inadvertent war from launch on warning, the military establishments of both countries continued throughout the Cold War to develop concepts if not for launch on warning, then for "launch under attack," perhaps after the first detonations to be sure an attack was in progress, but still to fire the missiles (and launch bombers and take other measures) as soon as it could be ascertained that an attack was being made. It remained a very risky business, and to a lesser extent does to this very day.

The other case of a sensitive political issue arising in the SALT dialogue concerned possible measures to head off a "provocative attack" by a third party, masquerading as one (or both) of the superpowers to embroil them in a nuclear war that neither had sought. The arch villain of such a scenario, with motive, means, and opportunity, was Communist China. Both delegations had from the outset of SALT referred to dangers from accidental, unauthorized, or third-party provocative attack, in particular as one consideration in weighing the desirability of ABM defenses, but also in considering other possible strategic arms constraints. As earlier noted, an agreement on a number of measures to make less likely such an attack or incident was incorporated in an accident measure agreement signed in September 1971.

Soviet probing on measures to prevent a provocative attack (by China, but never explicitly named in formal sessions) in July 1970 caused great alarm to some, above all Henry Kissinger, then maneuvering for the spectacular opening to China in 1971–72. Semenov raised this sensitive issue first of all with me alone, and later with Gerry Smith, before raising it in a formal meeting of the delegations. Suffice it to say that Kissinger flatly rejected the idea at once in the Dobrynin back-channel, but did not inform the rest of the U.S. government, which proceeded with studies finally recommending its rejection, a formal White House decision on rejection in November, and finally authorization for the delegation to reject the proposal (which the Soviet side had not raised again) on the record in December.[7]

In only one other case did the Soviet side raise a "political" issue, a suggestion by Semenov in private talks with me and then Smith in December 1970 for a reciprocal pledge not to be first to use nuclear weapons. Gerry and I each rejected it on the spot. Again, Kissinger rejected it in the back-channel but did not inform the rest of the government. I knew from my talks that the Soviet delegation would not pursue the matter. Also, I had told Vorontsov that we rejected the idea (which he undoubtedly knew from Kissinger's talks with Dobrynin). At a Verification Panel meeting, Kissinger raised the subject and declaimed that if the Soviet side pursued the matter we must be prepared firmly to oppose it. I spoke up to assure the panel that the Soviet delegation would not raise the subject again (and they did not). Kissinger was flabbergasted that I could confidently know that they would not. It was a sign to him that the front channel, and I in particular, were becoming *too* involved. Of course, he said nothing, but he gave me an odd look. Only too late did I realize that he had only been posturing, taking a strong stand on an issue that he, but no one else (except me) knew was dead in order to demonstrate his toughness. Unintentionally, I had spoiled the effect he was seeking.

This was only a very small incident in what developed as a very odd and one-sided rivalry and even jealousy between the Nixon White House and the SALT delegation. In his memoir, Henry Kissinger, himself a major contributor to this phenomenon, provided testimony to the recurring suspicion of President Nixon that somehow Ambassador Smith and the SALT delegation were going to be given the credit for SALT that he felt he deserved, and even that we were seeking to do so. This was a very peculiar attitude, since we were of course a part of his administration, had been charged by him to conduct the negotiation, and whatever we accomplished would be to the credit of the Nixon administration. We were not some independent rival entity, nor did we ever do anything or even think of doing anything that would or could take away from the responsibility and credit to President Nixon himself.

7. The full story on the provocative attack issue is more complex, and interesting. It is spelled out in Garthoff, *Détente and Confrontation*, pp. 198–205.

It is true that in the hectic final weeks of frantic negotiation to complete the SALT I agreements in time for their signature at the Nixon-Brezhnev summit in Moscow in late May 1972 there was a good deal of crossed and tangled lines in the parallel negotiations being carried out by the delegations in Helsinki, and first by Kissinger alone with Brezhnev in late April and then above all in the frenetic negotiations by Kissinger and Nixon and a few aides with the entire Soviet leadership team and experts in Moscow at the summit.

The determination by Nixon and Kissinger to leave the U.S. SALT delegation in Helsinki, still negotiating on myriad details and a few major issues, while they undertook in Moscow to resolve these same issues, was an error of the first magnitude. And it stemmed primarily from Nixon's desire not to have to share the limelight with Ambassador Smith and the delegation, and even to make it appear that he and his White House team could resolve remaining issues that we could not. In the event, what it did was to contribute to the confusion and result in some undesirable and unnecessary problems (as well as an unimportant but highly disadvantageous concession by Nixon personally, in writing, in a secret understanding that the United States would not exercise its "right" to trade in older ICBM launchers for SLBM launchers, as the Soviet side was intending to do). I will not review here, however, the complex tangle of issues, which I have done elsewhere in detail.[8]

I will comment briefly on the summit. Gerry Smith, Paul Nitze, General Royal Allison, and I were finally given permission to fly to Moscow (with the Soviet delegation) on May 26, only hours before the agreements were to be signed. We were still at work confirming English and Russian texts of the agreements on the plane en route. (In fact, we later discovered two small technical errors, requiring retyping and nonceremonial re-signing the next day.)

There were many amusing, or at least unpredictable, aspects of our arrival and activity in Moscow. First of all, except for a car meeting Ambassador Smith and whisking him away alone, and the U.S. air attaché escorting General Allison, there were no arrangements to meet and transport Paul Nitze and myself. I went with some of the Soviet delegation directly to the Ministry of Foreign Affairs, in order to get last-minute corrections in the texts to be imminently signed, unaware that Nitze had been left to fend for himself. He got into the city, but then was unable to enter the U.S. embassy residence, where a formal banquet being given by President Nixon was just ending. Finally an official from the Soviet Ministry of Foreign Affairs recognized the former U.S. deputy secretary of defense and helped him get to the Kremlin for the signing. Meanwhile, I found that the Ministry of Foreign Affairs had no

8. See Garthoff, *Détente and Confrontation*, pp. 176–95; and Smith, *Doubletalk*, pp. 364–440.

electric contact for an electric typewriter I had brought along, and no English typewriter that a young lady from the U.S. embassy staff, whom I had coopted, could use. So the corrections could not be made, and we had to dash off to the Kremlin with the texts as they were.

The signing ceremony itself, in the St. Vladimir Hall, went without any further incident, following a reception with the entire Soviet leadership. That reception itself was of interest, especially since at least one Politburo member (Pëtr Shelest) had opposed going ahead with the summit meeting after the United States escalated bombing of North Vietnam on the eve of the planned summit. I recall shaking hands with Shelest along with the other Politburo members at the reception, but he initially refrained from joining in a toast to the SALT agreements until his colleague Aleksandr Shelepin talked him into it.

Gerry Smith had been asked by Kissinger to hold a hasty press conference upon arrival, but Kissinger was not satisfied with Smith's cautious and, he thought, insufficiently enthusiastic answers and held a major *ex promptu* press conference at the Moscow Intourist Hotel restaurant night club after the ceremony.

Gerry Smith was thoroughly disgusted with the whole way in which the delegation and the conclusion of SALT I had been treated and decided on an early departure for us the next morning. So SALT I ended on a far less than satisfactory note, although the main purpose had been served. Gerry Smith thought about retiring after SALT I, but I believe he hoped the president would urge him to stay on, and he would have done so. But after the way that Nixon and Kissinger had handled SALT and the SALT delegation, climaxing in the chaotic last-minute Moscow negotiation and farcical hours surrounding our last minute call to Moscow and treatment there, he had had enough. Gerry told the president, through Kissinger, that he planned to resign, but would be willing to remain on through the first session of SALT II that fall (that is, until after the presidential election). The president did not ask him to stay longer.

SALT I did not, however, end with the signing of the ABM Treaty and Interim Agreement in Moscow. The U.S. Senate had to advise and consent to the ratification of the ABM Treaty, and both Houses had to approve the Interim Agreement as a congressionally approved executive agreement. A few senators had visited the SALT delegation in Vienna, but congressional interest throughout SALT I had been slight. Senator Henry Jackson had held informal hearings during SALT, in particular in March 1971 when it appeared that the administration might agree to an ABM Treaty alone. Jackson had specifically asked that I participate in that hearing and had pressed me on whether I found "the Soviet ABM-only proposal" acceptable, and whether I supported going ahead with our Safeguard ABM deployment and "hard-site" defense for our ICBM sites. I responded that I favored research and development of hard-site defense, supported continuing with Safeguard subject to future SALT developments, and did not favor acceptance of the Soviet ABM-only proposal at that time. (Jackson, whom I knew slightly and who had earlier regarded me as a knowledgeable Soviet affairs expert, had been put up to grilling me by friends of his staff aide Richard Perle in the State Department, in particular Sey Weiss, who strongly favored ABM deployment and regarded me as vulnerable on this issue.)

When the administration made its initial presentations of the SALT agreements to Congress, no one from the SALT delegation had been asked to participate. Ambassador Smith, chief of the delegation and director of the Arms Control and Disarmament Agency, was not even able to get a seat for his wife in the Senate gallery. Later, the administration made a secret deal with Senator Jackson to accept a version of an amendment he had introduced implicitly critical of the SALT I Interim Agreement by calling for nothing less than equal levels of intercontinental strategic forces in the follow-on (SALT II) treaty.

In the hearings on the SALT I agreements, Senator Jackson again called on me on a point concerning Soviet large ICBMs, on which we clashed but with no particular consequence. I had also been asked by the assistant secretary of state for public affairs to speak with certain senators in support of the SALT agreements, and I did so, all above-board. Again, Jackson's staff complained of this to General Alexander Haig in the White House as though it had been somehow improper for an official to support the administration.

The SALT I agreements were of course finally approved by Congress in September and ratified. Incidentally, at a White House reception celebrating the ratification of the SALT I agreements, I was engaged in conversation with Yuly Vorontsov, Ambassador Dobrynin's deputy, and Spurgeon Keeny of ACDA, when we were joined by Henry Kissinger. Henry made some complimentary comment on my contribution to SALT, but when Vorontsov joined also with some words of praise for my role, Henry mischievously added that "he wasn't always sure which side I was on." Vorontsov rejoined that "*they* always knew which side I was working for" with a tone conveying that they had no doubt that it was the U.S. side. Having enjoyed his own barbed joke, Henry moved along.

Meanwhile, soon after our return to Washington, I was asked by Ambassador Smith to go to Brussels to present the final report of the SALT delegation on the now completed SALT I negotiations and agreements. I was honored and pleased to do so. As I have mentioned earlier, I had participated in all the delegation reports to NAC on SALT (with the sole exception of one by Ambassador Parsons on the Accident Measures Agreement), and I had represented the delegation in briefing NAC at the end of the fifth session in October 1971. In addition to the report to the NAC ambassadors on June 16, I held another experts' meeting where the discussion was more detailed. Both went very well, and I believe the straightforward and candid reports on SALT I that we provided did a great deal to reassure our NATO allies and ensure their support.

We prepared for the first round of SALT II over the early fall months. I arranged through Yuly Vorontsov at the Soviet embassy that all SALT II sessions would take place in Geneva, ending the earlier rotation between Helsinki and Vienna.

During the preparations for the first SALT II meeting, Secretary Rogers had named me the Department of State delegate, replacing Ambassador Jeff Parsons, who had retired. The position carried ambassadorial rank as a presidential appointment. But before that was arranged, although after announcement of my appointment by the State Department, an unusual thing occurred: Alexander Haig called the department to say that the president did not want to make any changes in the delegation before the election. At the time it all seemed very odd, although a few months later the reason would become quite clear. In any case, I went to Geneva as the Department of State delegate, less the presidential designation and ambassadorial rank.

The Swiss were much more blasé about having SALT in Geneva, which had long hosted many, many conferences and permanent international organizations. We were but one small fish in the diplomatic Lake Geneva. Vera and I enjoyed being there again, if only for a month.

The two delegations, little changed in composition, met in Geneva from mid-November to mid-December 1972. It became clear that the obstacles to reaching a comprehensive limitation of strategic offensive arms remained formidable. We did establish the Standing Consultative Commission called for in the SALT I agreement. (The first U.S. commissioner was my colleague Sid Graybeal; the Soviets chose a general.)

My old KGB acquaintance Boris Sedov showed up in Geneva, renewing acquaintance with me and with SALT, both in abeyance since the spring of 1970. I met with him twice, the second time after being encouraged to do so by the CIA base in Geneva. Our conversations were as usual lively, but not very productive.

Soon after we returned from Geneva and work was about to gear up for the next round of SALT II, a number of things suddenly happened. First of all, as planned, Ambassador Gerard Smith resigned from the SALT delegation (and ACDA) on January 4, 1973. My old boss in State, Ambassador U. Alexis Johnson, was named to succeed him. Alex was very competent, but also very careful, and it was clear that the delegation would be on a tight leash. Second, virtually the entire delegation was replaced. I first learned that I would be leaving the delegation when Alex Johnson called me in for a chat and told me that for the good of my own career I should move on from SALT. He made clear that personally he would very much like me to stay on, but that I needed to get into a more regular diplomatic career. He did not then tell me, but I soon learned, that the White House had ordered that the entire senior SALT delegation be replaced, specifically including me. It was to be a thorough "purge."

President Nixon had startled his own staff immediately following his second inauguration on January 20, 1973, by coldly demanding written resignations from his whole cabinet and senior White House staff. Although most were kept on, he had flaunted his power and their vulnerability. A purge of the upper reaches of the entire executive branch was planned and initial steps were taken before the Watergate scandal began to open up and Nixon called off the general purge. The SALT delegation and "SALT community" in Washington, and the Arms Control and Disarmament Agency, were however priority targets and were purged in January. Of the seventeen top positions in ACDA, only three incumbents remained a few months later. Kissinger was not the originating source, but when asked who should remain at ACDA he recommended only one person, Deputy Director Phil Farley. Phil, however, uncomfortable at remaining when all his colleagues were being ousted, also retired and left. ACDA was cut in budget and size and placed under a conservative leadership.

The decision to replace the entire SALT delegation was a separate but parallel action, as was the reassignment of some of the key officers who had worked on SALT backstopping in State and elsewhere. Although I remained as a deputy director of the Bureau of Politico-Military Affairs for about six months until I went on to an new assignment, from mid-January on I was not only off the delegation but also withdrawn from all work on SALT.

At least Alex Johnson had promptly informed me that I was leaving SALT, even though initially he did not say why. I had learned that the intention was to field a whole new delegation, and Alex confirmed that the White House thought it would be a good idea to field "a new team." When I became aware a few weeks later that General Royal Allison was still making travel plans and giving work assignments to his staff for the next round of SALT II, unaware that he was being removed, I told Phil Farley who advised Roy to check with the chairman (of the JCS), who then belatedly informed Roy that he was being replaced. Allison was offered another position not commensurate with his rank, and retired. Harold Brown had made a very useful contribution to the delegation, but because he represented no constituency in Washington, he was overlooked and not on the "hit list" to be removed. Paul Nitze, on the other hand, was initially told by Alex that he could play a useful role in backstopping, but was being replaced on the delegation in order to field the new team. Paul, however, fought the decision, rallied support from friends on the Hill, and finally was permitted to remain. He had not personally been a target of the purge, as had Smith, Allison, and myself.

Nixon may have had his own reasons for wanting a "new team" in SALT, as Kissinger too may have had. The impetus for the wholesale SALT purge, however, had come from Senator Scoop Jackson. In a private conversation with Jackson in the Rose Garden, Nixon had agreed to replace the SALT delegation with a new team, as he had accepted a version of Jackson's amendment on equal strategic force levels in SALT II, in exchange for Jackson's support not only for the SALT agreements but also for the Trident submarine program, which Jackson had threatened to kill. In the final analysis, Jackson got even more: one of the two Trident submarine bases was moved from the Navy's preference for California to Jackson's state of Washington. But the purge of the SALT team and weakening of ACDA were also part of the deal.[9]

There was more to the purge, including collusion between Sey Weiss and some others in State with their friends Richard Perle on Jackson's staff, Fred Malek in the White House personnel office, John Lehman in the White House legislative office, and probably Alexander Haig, chairman of a White House committee on NSC-legislative relations. Senator Jackson and the hard-liners knew what they were doing. The long-run effect was to weaken the arms control constituency and make it harder—and ultimately impossible—for Kissinger to maneuver between hard-line and soft-line alternatives; he could no longer occupy the center fulcrum balancing position but had to face, and lose, to the hard-line views on SALT of Defense secretaries James Schlesinger and then Donald Rumsfeld in the Ford administration in 1975–76.

Just a year after the SALT I agreements were signed, in mid-1973, a rather remarkably well-informed book appeared detailing SALT I, *Cold Dawn* by John Newhouse. It was a balanced, well-grounded study, although tilted toward the Kissinger–White House perspective on the negotiations because its author had been given extraordinary access to information on the negotiations, and above all the decisionmaking in Washington. The source of this largesse on what for everyone else was still found only in highly classified documents was Henry Kissinger, primarily through members of his staff, as Newhouse later confirmed to me. We were aware during the negotiations that Newhouse was writing a book on SALT and had received reminders from Washington on secrecy of the negotiations. Gerry Smith was punctilious in avoiding any contact with Newhouse (and the press), and the delegation as a whole also avoided any contact. Paul Nitze and I, however, individually, did help provide some balance to the book by contributing what we felt we could on the delegation's perspective. Incidentally, there were a number of leaks to

---

9. The purge of SALT and ACDA has been partially told in several published accounts, including Peter J. Ognibene, *Scoop: The Life and Politics of Henry M. Jackson* (Stein & Day, 1975), pp. 199–216; and Elizabeth Drew, "A Reporter at Large: An Argument Over Survival," *New Yorker* (April 4, 1977), pp. 109–12.

the press during SALT, a few from Defense, a few from us in State, but all the most serious ones from Kissinger's office in the White House.

January 1973 marked the end of a six-year period from our initial proposal of strategic arms talks in December 1966–January 1967 to the successful conclusion of SALT I in May 1972 and launching of SALT II late in that year. The SALT experience included the most intensive, exciting, and pathbreaking negotiations since the Cold War had begun, and I believe was to retain that distinction. To be sure, the high-level leadership contacts and negotiations on a far broader range of subjects was overall of highest importance, and also went through its most intense development at this same time in the development of détente. SALT, in this perspective, was but one element in a much larger mosaic, and was so regarded by the leaders on both sides. But from the standpoint of direct involvement in coming to grips with the political-military issues at the heart of the Cold War confrontation, SALT was a unique and important part of that mosaic. It was particularly important in its impact on Soviet thinking, although that was not adequately appreciated in Washington.

The SALT negotiation provided the most intense and direct role in diplomatic negotiation, policy implementation, and bureaucratic maneuver of my career. It was the highlight of my experience in terms of real (not nominal) responsibility and in making a definite contribution. It was exciting, even exhilarating. And although rather suddenly removed, I and my colleagues had at least been able to launch and carry out the first stage of the negotiations successfully.

I was deeply moved by personal recognition of my efforts by Secretary of State William Rogers in a letter to me on June 8, just after the conclusion of the agreements. He wrote:

> With the signature in Moscow of the strategic arms limitation agreements, I wanted to send you a personal note of recognition for your outstanding contribution to the work which led up to this historic event.
>
> Your colleagues in the Department of State have admired your virtuoso performance over the past three years as General Secretary of our SALT delegation. Your disciplined dedication to a successful outcome, your mastery of the complex detail of the subject matter, your ingenuity in seeking and finding solutions to negotiating impasses, your facility with the Russian language and unique ability to develop a relationship of candor and confidence with your Soviet counterparts contributed significantly to the end result in Moscow.
>
> You have every right to an immense personal satisfaction in knowing you were a principal architect and builder of these agreements, which will surely stand among the major achievements of our time.

Ambassador Gerard Smith also wrote me a similar letter expressing "the very high appreciation I have for your unique contribution to the SALT outcome. . . . no one in the Delegation made a greater contribution to these negotiations. . . . There is hardly a provision of the agreement that does not reflect your handiwork." My immediate boss, Ron Spiers, director of PM, together with Gerry Smith, later proposed to the secretary that I should be given the highest Department of State merit award, the Distinguished Honor Award, and he agreed. I knew nothing of that proposal until I was informed that I had been selected to receive the award. Ironically, I was informed of this high honor for my contribution to SALT in the same week in January 1973 that I was advised I was being shifted away from SALT! Alex Johnson, then still under secretary for political affairs, hastily arranged to confer the award himself so that Secretary Rogers and the department would be spared the embarrassment of the incongruity of the secretary of state granting me its highest honor for my work in SALT at the same time that the White House was pulling out the red carpet from underneath. Two weeks later, Rogers presented Ambassador Smith, now retired, with the ACDA Distinguished Honor Award.

The secretary of state's citation for the Distinguished Honor Award read:

> For exceptional service in the cause of peace, as Executive Secretary of the United States Delegation to the Strategic Arms Limitation Talks.
>
> At every stage of SALT, Dr. Garthoff, through personal initiative, quick insight, thorough analysis, and sound judgment, has made singular contributions to the development of possible United States positions for the President's decision. His untiring persistence has been exceptionally effective in negotiating and supporting our positions in consultations with the North Atlantic Council which led to acceptance of the SALT process.
>
> His mastery of the highly technical and sensitive issues, vast knowledge of United States and Soviet strategic policy and doctrine, fluency in the Russian language, and shrewd and innovative negotiating sense assisted materially in reaching the historic SALT agreements between the United States and the Soviet Union.

I was proud to have had the opportunity to serve in a key role in the SALT I negotiations, and to have had my contribution appreciated at least in some quarters.

14

Developing Détente in
U.S.-Soviet Relations

As we have seen, the course of the Cold War oscillated between periods of greater and lesser tension, between confrontation and détente. The first significant lessening of tension had come after the death of Stalin, in the period from 1953 to 1956. The Soviet suppression of the Hungarian uprising and renewed pressures on Berlin worsened relations, and the Berlin crisis of 1961 and the Cuban missile crisis of 1962 ensued. A new détente had emerged in 1963–64, but the war in Vietnam and Soviet intervention in Czechoslovakia in 1968 again brought tension.

President Richard Nixon, with a reputation as a hard-line anticommunist ever since he entered politics in the late 1940s, nonetheless came into office in 1969 calling in his inaugural address for an "era of negotiation" to replace an era of confrontation, and with the avowed goal of building "a structure of peace."[1] Later, Nixon championed "a new strategy of peace," knowingly or not echoing President Kennedy's American University speech of June 1963.

Nixon did not use the word "détente" in his inaugural address, or indeed for more than a year, but the concept was clearly there. There was an interesting insider feature of that first presidential public statement. Included in Nixon's address was a seemingly routine reference that "all nations" should

1. "Inaugural Address of President Richard Milhouse Nixon," January 20, 1969, *Weekly Compilation of Presidential Documents*, vol. 5, January 27, 1969, pp. 152–53. I have examined the American—and Soviet—conceptions of détente, and the entire course of U.S.-Soviet relations in the period from 1969 through 1980, in some detail in Raymond L. Garthoff, *Détente and Confrontation: American-Soviet Relations from Nixon to Reagan*, rev. ed. (Brookings, 1994).

know that "our lines of communication will be open." While innocuous, this phrase had been inserted by the president's new assistant for national security affairs, Henry Kissinger, to send a secret signal to Moscow. As Kissinger disclosed in his memoir many years later, since he had been in Governor Nelson Rockefeller's entourage he had remained in occasional touch with a Soviet embassy officer, Boris Sedov. Sedov was, in fact, a KGB officer, as Kissinger was aware (and as the reader may recall had also been a regular contact of mine since 1966, and continued to be.) It was Sedov who had urged Kissinger to have Nixon include in his inaugural address some such statement about keeping the lines of communication to Moscow open, saying that would be well received in Moscow. (It had the additional advantage to Kissinger of showing the Soviet leadership his own ability to influence the president, and to Sedov of demonstrating to Moscow his ability to serve as a conduit through Kissinger to the new president.) On the occasion of President Nixon's first meeting with Ambassador Dobrynin on February 17, he again referred to keeping open lines of communication and privately informed him that matters of special importance and sensitivity should be taken up only with Kissinger, not the Department of State. A Kissinger-Dobrynin back-channel was established as the main connection between the Nixon administration and the Soviet leadership.[2]

There was uncertainty and great interest in the policy orientation of the new American administration not only in Moscow, but also in allied capitals and at NATO (and, indeed, in the State Department and U.S. missions abroad as well). President Nixon made it a point to arrange that his first trip abroad, and only a month after his inauguration, was to Western Europe, and his first stop was NATO headquarters in Brussels. His speech there was well received.

Amidst the bustle of the presidential visit, Henry Kissinger called me aside and asked whether I would be interested in working with him in Washington. There was little time for conversation, and he asked me to discuss it further with his aide Larry Eagleburger, with whom he had spoken about it. Larry was straightforward about the job, although not in a position to answer all my questions. Nor did he tell me, if he knew, that the reason Henry was seeking to recruit me was because he had had a falling out with his old friend Helmut (Hal) Sonnenfeldt, already brought on to the staff to handle Soviet affairs. By the time I wrote to Henry and he replied, he and Hal had composed their differences and there was no opening.

Meanwhile, even earlier I had been contacted by my old friend Gerry

2. See Garthoff, *Détente and Confrontation*, pp. 30–31 and 79–82. Sedov of course was dropped; neither Kissinger nor Dobrynin wanted a competing channel. Incidentally, one consequence of Kissinger's disclosure of Sedov's role and KGB affiliation in his 1979 memoir was to "burn" Sedov as a publicly identified KGB officer, barring him from further assignment in the West.

Smith, the new head of the Arms Control and Disarmament Agency. He asked me to join him as assistant director for international affairs, a position equivalent to an assistant secretaryship of state. I accepted, but suddenly Gerry called me to apologize that he found he could not offer me the position because Bill Rogers had told him he needed me for something important in the State Department. Rogers and I, at that point, had never met, and I never learned what (or who) it was that led him to block my ACDA assignment. Perhaps Alexis Johnson had told him that I should be their man on SALT; in January Johnson had told me that I should plan to serve on the SALT delegation, as had been expected in 1967 and again in 1968.

As related earlier, I remained at USNATO formally until August 1970, but in effect not much after mid-1969, as I served on the SALT delegation. Then, in September 1970, I assumed my new duties as one of the two deputy directors of the Bureau of Politico-Military Affairs (PM) under my old colleague Ronald Spiers (and with Tom Pickering as the other deputy).

My principal duties in PM were handling preparations for SALT in Washington whenever the delegation was in Washington, and managing the delegation under Gerry Smith whenever negotiations were under way, as discussed in the preceding chapter. Here I shall note the broader development of the détente in U.S.-Soviet relations as I observed it from 1970 into 1973 in PM, and from 1973 to 1975 from the vantage point of other assignments in those years.

The problem of extricating the United States from Vietnam dominated most aspects of policy during the years 1969 to 1972, as had Vietnam for the preceding four years under President Johnson. Nixon and Kissinger had relied heavily on "linkage," leverage on issues where we had power, to move events in areas where we had less capability. This was not a new technique of policy (and, incidentally, I had recommended it in my 1968 memorandum calling for a strategy of détente). But both Nixon and Kissinger had exaggerated expectations of what they could do with that approach. In particular, they hoped to use Soviet interest in relaxed tensions, SALT, and trade as levers to induce the Soviet leaders to press North Vietnam into meeting our requirements for dignified disengagement with honor. The first problem was that the United States also wanted relaxed tensions, strategic arms limitations, and trade, so there was not that much leverage to move the Soviets to do much more than deal with those issues on their merits, with mutual concessions to reach agreements to mutual advantage. The second problem was that the Soviet leaders had only limited influence over the Vietnamese. Linkage was more successful, including as applied to the problem of extricating ourselves from Vietnam, when we were able in 1971–72 to play the China card in triangular diplomacy with the Soviet leadership. PM was involved in the Vietnam imbroglio, but thankfully I was not and was absorbed in SALT.

There were several other Third World flashpoints on the road to détente over the period 1969–72. In 1970 alone four events primed confrontations: our retaliatory invasion of Cambodia, a PLO-Syrian-Jordanian fracas, an Egyptian-Israeli "canal war" in the air over the Suez Canal, and a subcritical confrontation with the Soviet Union over a submarine base in Cuba. In 1971 an Indian-Pakistani war erupted, also involving Soviet-American tension. The only one of these that involved direct Soviet responsibility and direct U.S.-Soviet relations was a limited confrontation over construction for a Soviet submarine base at Cienfuegos in Cuba in 1970.

In mid-September 1970 U.S. U-2 aerial reconnaissance detected construction under way for a submarine base at the Bay of Cienfuegos in Cuba, confirming suspicions aroused by the recent arrival from the Soviet Union of submarine support equipment. A leak to the press and background briefings by the Pentagon and Kissinger (as an anonymous "White House source") converted the matter into a mini-crisis in Washington on the eve of a visit to Europe by President Nixon, before there had even been any opportunity to raise the matter with the Soviet side. The political crisis was averted by a Soviet assurance conveyed through Ambassador Dobrynin that there would be no Soviet submarine base in Cuba, and by public reaffirmations by an authorized TASS statement in Moscow and by the State Department spokesman in Washington that the 1962 understandings reached at the conclusion of the Cuban missile crisis would be observed.

The Soviet Union had indeed tested the limits of the "understanding" and concluded that they should not proceed with a submarine base in Cuba. But another development also underlay the whole affair and its resolution. Unknown even in the U.S. government beyond a few officials in the White House, shortly *before* the American detection of the construction at Cienfuegos, Soviet chargé d'affaires Yuly Vorontsov had called on Kissinger in early August and unexpectedly raised the question of reaffirming the Kennedy-Khrushchev understanding of 1962 with respect to Cuba. Kissinger was somewhat perplexed (even years later when he first revealed the Vorontsov démarche in his memoir) as to why the Soviets should want to raise a matter that tended to tie their hands. In any case, Kissinger did discreetly ask Under Secretary of State U. Alexis Johnson to provide him with the 1962 record, and he in turn asked Ray Cline (the CIA deputy director for intelligence in 1962, now chief of the Bureau of Intelligence and Research in the State Department) and me to do so. We were not told why. We did, and as Kissinger learned and informed Nixon, the understanding had "never formally been buttoned down" in 1962. "It emerged that there was no formal understanding in the sense of an agreement, either oral or in writing." That was indeed the case, and we had been careful over the years following *not* to tie down the vague U.S. commitment against invasion of Cuba. But Kissinger and Nixon, without consulting the secretaries of state and defense or anyone else, decided to take this unexpected opportunity to tie down the Soviet commitment through new reciprocal assurances, which they did in August. These new assurances formed the basis for the public assertions of an understanding in October at the end of the Cienfuegos flap.

Why did the Soviets raise the matter in August? Kissinger remained perplexed because he saw it as a gratuitous Soviet offer to reaffirm their commitments. Years later I asked Vorontsov, and he explained it. Castro was again concerned over a possible attack by the new Nixon administration. Soviet intelligence did not confirm that danger, but the Soviet leadership decided to try to elicit an American reaffirmation, as they succeeded in doing, in order to be able to reassure Castro that the Soviets had taken the matter up with the Americans and been able to obtain reassurance that the United States would not attack.

Kissinger and Nixon had not "reaffirmed," "clarified," and "amplified" an existing 1962 understanding; they had reached a new agreement that had deliberately not been concluded in 1962. Perhaps it should have been done. In any case, the Soviet Union would never again attempt to deploy missiles in Cuba, and the United States would not invade. But the considerations that had led the Kennedy administration not to formalize such a commitment were not even raised and reconsidered under the new back-room, back-channel diplomacy.

There were several reverberations of these 1970 events in 1972. First, early in the year, probably with an eye to the forthcoming summit meeting, Kissinger formally requested in NSSM 144 an interagency policy study on Soviet naval deployments in the Caribbean. The study was assigned to the Interagency Political-Military Group (IPMG), a formal working group of the NSC at the assistant secretary level. I chaired the IPMG for this study. Yet for this top secret NSC study, we were denied any access to the 1970 exchanges. I objected strongly, and suffered General Alexander Haig's anger for persisting in my request for the record, and still more when I submitted the unanimous final IPMG report noting that we could not determine whether subsequent Soviet actions violated the 1970 understanding without access to the exchange.

The Soviets did, in fact, test the boundaries of the agreed limitations by sending a G-class diesel missile-launching submarine to Cuba for the first (and last) time soon after the IPMG study and shortly before the Moscow summit. President Nixon did not raise the matter there, but there had been an even more clear indication of the firmness of the U.S. position. Throughout the brief stay of the Soviet missile submarine in Cuba (at Nipe, not Cienfuegos), U.S. surveillance ships had remained just six miles off-shore, and when the submarine departed, those ships and P-3 naval patrol aircraft repeatedly made sonar contact and forced the Soviet submarine to surface and resurface, a procedure continued until the submarine was well into the Atlantic. Undoubtedly the Soviet leaders were aware of this unusual assertive U.S. naval action, but remarkably Nixon and Kissinger were not, even after the event. The episode was, among other things, a striking example of inability to exercise complete control over policy.

Also in the fall of 1972, and again in early 1973, Secretary of Defense Melvin Laird wrote to Secretary of State Rogers urging protests against a new Soviet practice of sending two Tu-95 D *Bear* turboprop naval reconnaissance aircraft from Murmansk to Cuba, then flying missions from Cuba in the Caribbean before returning to the Soviet Union. In State, we did not find any basis for charging the Soviet side with violation of the understandings of 1962 or, so far as it was known, of 1970. We did not, however, present that case and respond. Kissinger orally instructed Under Secretary Alexis Johnson to just "sit" on Laird's requests, and that was done. The Soviet reconnaissance *Bears* thus never became an issue between the United States and the Soviet Union, although the State Department took the blame from Defense for failing to act, and confidence in the system of coordinating policy suffered.[3]

The first two summit meetings between President Nixon and General Secretary Brezhnev, in Moscow in May 1972 and in Washington in June 1973, marked the high points of the new détente between the two countries. In both countries, especially in the United States, the elaboration of a concept and program for détente came after the process had gotten well under way. Moreover, despite his initial call for opening an "era of negotiation," Nixon had even been prepared on the eve of the first summit to jeopardize it by initiating a bombing of Hanoi; the stronger Soviet interest in détente led them to go ahead notwithstanding that sign of Nixon's priorities.

The SALT negotiation had been the pathbreaker for political détente, and the ABM Treaty and Interim Agreement on strategic offensive arms were the focal point for attention at the 1972 summit, as well as representing a significant step in arms control. The other principal product of the meeting was agreement on a document called the "Basic Principles of Relations between the United States of America and the Union of Soviet Socialist Republics," signed on the last day of the summit. It represented a kind of charter for détente. The Basic Principles had been a Soviet proposal, and they regarded it as a major achievement. Nixon and Kissinger, and the American government and public, gave far less attention and attributed far less significance to the document. It had, in fact, been negotiated secretly by Kissinger and his staff at Nixon's behest without the knowledge even of the secretary of state and was regarded by them as merely a harmless concession to persistent Soviet importunity.

---

3. For more on these Cuba-related events of 1970–72, see Garthoff, *Détente and Confrontation*, pp. 87–95, and 338–41, although I have added a few details here.

The Basic Principles represented more an aspiration than a realistic basis for a code of conduct by the two powers. The provision most criticized in official circles in the United States was acceptance of "peaceful coexistence" as a basis for conducting relations, not of course because anyone wanted war, but because it was a long-standing Soviet propaganda slogan. Most cynical was a commitment by each of the sides not to seek to "obtain unilateral advantage at the expense of the other." Both powers constantly sought to do just that, and continued to do so. Subsequently, each could (and occasionally did) accuse the other of violating the Basic Principles when it saw actions by the other as seeking unilateral advantage as its expense. Nonetheless, the agreement on Basic Principles at least expressed a recognition that the two sides could and should seek to behave with some restraint and in a civilized way in their mutual relations. Regrettably, differences in understanding as to what each side saw as admissible behavior on its own part, and as inadmissible behavior by the other, were not pursued. If they had been, the Basic Principles could have played a more useful role than merely serving as additional justification for criticisms of the other side when it failed to live up to the unrealistically high ground of the rhetoric of the agreement.

At the second summit meeting a year later, in Washington in June 1973, the main new accord was in a sense an elaboration of some of the Basic Principles, an agreement between the two countries on the prevention of nuclear war. Again, the agreement stemmed from a Soviet initiative and persistence in its pursuit, and the absence of any other broad political accord to underpin the summit which the leaders on both sides were determined to depict as a new success in developing relations. The purpose of the agreement, and its provisions, were unexceptional and clearly laudable: to prevent nuclear war by acting in such a way as to prevent its outbreak. The two countries each undertook to refrain from the threat or use of force against the other or its allies and other countries, and to consult over any situation that would "appear to involve the risk of a nuclear conflict." As with the Basic Principles, because the agreement dealt with intentions and purposes, it could mean a great deal or very little, depending upon how it was interpreted and applied. Soviet sponsorship of the Agreement on the Prevention of Nuclear War and high praise for it again contrasted with reluctant American agreement and modest evaluation. It also caused considerable pain to NATO allies who had not, with a few exceptions, been consulted or advised in advance about an agreement that seemed to some to impinge on American alliance commitments and to represent a move toward a superpower "condominium."

There was, perhaps surprisingly, less concern articulated at another aspect of the new superpower "era of negotiation" and its concrete embodiment in SALT. The U.S.-Soviet détente in the 1970s was predicated upon strategic parity and mutual deterrence. This was a realistic recognition of the existing condition, when each side had the capability to destroy the other even if the other side had struck first. Nixon, to his credit, understood and accepted this reality. Kissinger had it in mind when he said that "the challenge of the time is to reconcile the reality of competition with the imperative of coexistence." It was, of course, easier for the Soviet Union to acknowledge parity because it marked a major advance over the previous period of American superiority. For the same reason it was more difficult for U.S. leaders to do so (and easy for domestic political opponents to criticize). But as envisaged by Nixon and Kissinger, their task was to "manage the emergence of Soviet power." To a certain extent that implied adjustment by the United States to the reality of increased Soviet power and strategic parity. But it also meant to pursue a U.S. strategy aimed at containing and harnessing Soviet power. And to do this, détente was expected to enmesh the Soviet Union in a web of relationships with the West, and above all with the United States, which the White House would weave. In this new interdependent relationship, the Soviet leaders would be faced with "incentives for moderation and penalties for intransigence."

The Soviet leaders, of course, had their own interpretation of détente, and expected to "manage" a transition for the United States from American dominance to a parity in political as well as military standing of the two superpowers.

The agreements on Basic Principles on Mutual Relations and on Prevention of Nuclear War, in retrospect, cannot be said to have played any substantial role in affecting the course of the Cold War and its final settlement. They did not have any weakening effect on U.S. or Western resolve or behavior, as some critics had feared, nor can it be demonstrated that they moderated the pursuit of advantage and calculation of risk by either side as both continued to wage the Cold War. Nonetheless, on balance the attempt to establish some charter for détente relations that would constrain risks of war was probably sound and may have been more useful than can be ascertained. It did, however, underline that détente could not be prescribed in rhetoric and proclamations, it had to represent the actual policies of the powers. And in the 1970s, while there was a preference on both sides for détente over unbridled confrontation, it remained in the framework of the Cold War. Détente was a more sophisticated and less belligerent way of waging the Cold War, rather than an alternative to it.[4]

The competitive relationship continuing between the superpower rivals under détente was well illustrated by President Nixon's actions following the

4. See Garthoff, *Détente and Confrontation,* especially chapters 1, 2, 9, 10, and 28. Détente as understood and practiced by Nixon and Kissinger in the 1970s was very much akin to détente as I had described it in my memorandum of November 20, 1968, cited above, pp. 239–42.

first summit in 1972.[5] Nixon flew directly from the Soviet Union to Iran, where he sought to establish the shah as, in effect, American proconsul in the region, in keeping with the Nixon Doctrine. The shah was promised virtually any American arms he wanted. A contributory reason for the shah's deputation that was not apparent was to follow through on some confidential conversations with the Chinese and to signal to them U.S. intention to build regional positions of strength around the Soviet Union, détente notwithstanding. In addition, while in Tehran the president accepted the shah's proposal covertly to arm the Iraqi Kurds. (Iraq had just signed a treaty of friendship with the Soviet Union.) Thus the Kurds became proxies of the United States and Iran (and of Israel, which joined in providing support). And there was a later chapter to this American initiative: the shah of Iran induced President Mohammed Daoud of Afghanistan during the period 1975–78 to move away from his previous close alignment with the Soviet Union, to improve relations with Pakistan, and to crack down on Afghan leftists. It was Daoud's arrest of communist leaders Taraki, Karmal, Amin, and others in April 1978—not some plot concocted in Moscow—that led the Khalq military faction to mount a coup and depose him, turning the government over to the People's Democratic (Communist) Party, and setting in train the developments within Afghanistan that led to an Afghan civil war and eventually Soviet intervention.

From Iran President Nixon flew to Poland, where he was again greeted by stirring public acclaim (as he had been in 1959), demonstrating not only that the United States would support more or less nonaligned communist regimes (Nixon had visited Romania in 1969 and Yugoslavia in 1970, as well as China in 1972), but also that no part of the Soviet alliance was out of bounds to American interest under détente.

As a direct result of the U.S. handling of the Middle East question at the détente summit meeting, Anwar Sadat—who was already secretly in touch with the United States—six weeks later expelled the 20,000 Soviet military advisers (and Soviet reconnaissance aircraft) from Egypt.

Only a few months later, in September 1972, China and Japan—with American encouragement—renewed diplomatic relations. And in December new armed clashes occurred on the Sino-Soviet border.

Further, upon President Nixon's return to Washington from the 1972 summit he urged not only ratification of the SALT I agreements, but also an increase in strategic arms. Secretary of Defense Laird even conditioned his support for SALT on congressional approval of new military programs, which he justified as necessary so as to be able to negotiate "from a position of strength," wittingly or not invoking a key early symbol of the Cold War.

5. The paragraphs that follow are drawn from Garthoff, *Détente and Confrontation*, pp. 1135–37.

I would not argue either that the Soviet perception of American responsibility for the subsequent decline and fall of détente was justified, or that the United States was wrong to compete with the Soviet Union. But it is necessary to recognize that not only the Soviet Union but also the United States was vigorously "waging détente" in the 1970s—and that the Soviet Union was not violating some agreed, clear, and important standard to which the United States in practice adhered. Each of the sides applied a double standard in judging its own behavior and that of the other with respect to the Basic Principle (as enunciated in the 1972 agreement) of not seeking "unilateral advantage at the expense of the other." Each saw its own actions as compatible with pursuit of a *realistic* policy of détente. Each, however, sought to hold the other side to its own *idealized* view of détente. As a result, each was disappointed in and critical of the actions of the other.

Problems in articulating the meaning of détente were not only to be found in discordant applications in policy. There were also difficulties (on both sides) in explaining within the respective political establishments and to the broader national publics pursuit of a strategy of reducing tensions with the rival superpower coupled with affirmations of strength and vigilance in continuing competition with that adversary. There was no inherent or logical contradiction between keeping up one's strength and guard while seeking to reduce tension, but for many there seemed to be. Moreover, opponents of détente could and did argue that at the very least by blurring the image of an enemy, national resolve would be eroded.

The Nixon administration sought to meet this challenge, as well as to claim political credit and seek to build its reputation in the general field of foreign relations, by issuing an unprecedented series of annual reports on its foreign policy strategy and achievements. The idea was good, and on the whole the reports were well done. The reports were drafted by Kissinger's staff and reviewed by him; although signed by President Nixon, in fact he played virtually no direct role in their production. Nonetheless, they did embody his foreign policy strategy, in which he played an important role notwithstanding his substantial reliance on Kissinger. Four reports were issued, the first on February 18, 1970, and the others early in each of the succeeding three years. (A fifth, planned for early 1974, was drafted but never issued because of the press of Watergate.) All were given the superhead of "U.S. Foreign Policy for the 1970s," and each had a title emphasizing peace: "A New Strategy for Peace," "Building Peace," "The Emerging Structure of Peace," and "Shaping a Durable Peace." The détente strategy was spelled out, although the word itself was not used to describe U.S. policy until the 1973 report. This caution in avowing détente, and the self-serving nature of many of the characterizations of American policy, undercut the role the reports had been designed to play. The public impact of the reports was minimal, and they did not succeed in building a real understanding of détente strategy.

As noted above, Kissinger jealously controlled the drafting of these reports. Only reluctantly were they "cleared" with the departments of State and Defense. I had occasion to be one of the few in State to participate, and I can attest that Kissinger's staff was most reluctant to make changes except where there were demonstrable errors of fact.

The Department of State, or to be more precise some senior officials in State, had long felt that it was wrong for the only major report on U.S. national security policy to be the annual reports of the secretary of defense, which covered politico-military policy as well as the activities of Defense. With the advent of the White House reports on foreign policy strategy this was no longer the case—but the Department of State was further marginalized. So an effort was made to develop in the State Department a more comprehensive report on U.S. foreign relations. By the time the second White House report was issued, in late February 1971, it was followed in a few weeks by the first of a new series called "United States Foreign Policy, 1969–70: A Report of the Secretary of State," submitted to the chairman of the Senate Foreign Relations Committee (more or less paralleling the practice of the secretary of defense's annual reports). It was four times the size of the White House report, over six hundred pages, but it was essentially a catalogue of our foreign relations — almost an appendix to accompany the policy and strategy report of the president. The second and third State Department reports also followed the White House reports in 1972 and 1973. But after Rogers's replacement by Kissinger in 1973, the series—which had never lived up to expectations—was discontinued.

Although the seeds of disillusionment with détente had been present from the beginning, in 1972–73 there was still a strong interest by the leaders of both countries in accenting the positive and claiming credit for the popular idea of reduced tensions.

The first of several blows to détente was the serious weakening of President Nixon's position in 1973–74 as a result of Watergate. Although the détente policy was not even indirectly involved, Nixon's weakened political position meant that he could not actively pursue détente or prevent actions that would later undermine it, such as growing congressional efforts to manage relations with the Soviet Union. The efforts of Senator Henry ("Scoop") Jackson to control policy both on trade and arms control beginning in 1972–73 had by 1974–75 prevented successful pursuit of SALT II under the Nixon and successor Ford administrations, and had killed the U.S.-Soviet trade agreement through the Jackson-Vanik amendment preventing normalization of trade. The October 1973 Arab-Israeli war also turned some away from support for improving U.S.-Soviet relations. Still more, applying again a double standard, the administration depicted Soviet support for one side in the Angolan civil war in 1975–76 as inconsistent with détente behavior (even though the United States too had been involved, in supporting the other side, which, however, turned out to be weaker). There were other important aspects of the decline of the U.S.-Soviet détente, which is the subject of a later chapter.

Only in European-centered, multilateral détente was there continuing success. The Western Europeans had taken the initiative in pursuing an East-West détente in Europe, sparked first by President Charles de Gaulle in the late 1960s and then by Chancellor Willy Brandt of Germany in the early 1970s. That had an impact on American policy. Nixon and Kissinger wanted to carry out their own brand of détente with linkage in relations with the Soviet Union and China, but they were very wary of Western European initiatives in détente, mainly because they could not control it. An ill-conceived palliative advanced publicly by Kissinger in early 1973 declared that that year would be the "Year of Europe." The Europeans were not amused to be assigned a "year" by the Americans, and the whole initiative collapsed. Nixon and Kissinger then realized that they had no alternative, and reluctantly accepted an East-West détente in Europe in order to play a major role in it and better manage the process. Later in the 1970s, however, Ford and Carter could no longer manage the process. By the late 1970s, as the U.S.-Soviet détente weakened and collapsed, European détente flourished.

American policy toward Eastern Europe throughout this period (and indeed from the late 1950s to the late 1980s) was based on a pragmatic acceptance of the reality of communist control. A policy of "differentiation" among the countries of the Soviet bloc in Eastern Europe sought to give marginal trade and other incentives to those countries that showed some signs either of internal liberalization or of lessened dependency on Moscow. The leeway for those countries, and the means available to the United States for leverage, were so limited as to make exercise of linkage marginal at best. Western European countries, more inclined to normalization of trade and other relations without such great attention to efforts at fine-tuning "differentiations," did more to build slowly an underlying recognition that Europe, even if politically divided, remained Europe.

Multilateral diplomacy also helped. In the early 1970s, paradoxically as things turned out, the United States and NATO pressed for reciprocal force reductions (MBFR), while the Soviet Union and Warsaw Pact championed a conference on security and cooperation in Europe (CSCE). At the 1972 summit Nixon agreed to CSCE negotiations if the Soviet side would agree to MBFR negotiations. Later, after the successful conclusion of a CSCE signed at a multilateral summit meeting in Helsinki in 1975, and failure to break a continuing MBFR impasse, the West came to see MBFR as a burden and the CSCE as a success in East-West diplomacy.

When MBFR preliminary talks began in January 1973, I had just left SALT, as described in the preceding chapter, but remained deputy director of the Bureau of Politico-Military Affairs and was given the task of chairing the interdepartmental MBFR working group backstopping our delegation in Vienna. There I had to hammer out a consensus of the Washington agency representatives, and then help our delegate at the Vienna talks, Jonathan Dean, to force through a consensus among reluctant NATO representatives in Vienna, to acquiesce in the Soviet desire to omit Hungary from the area of putative limitations. There were sound reasons for that position, but it was not easy to argue that we should not press for a maximum area for reductions on the Warsaw Pact side. The real reason was that in preliminary talks not disclosed to our allies (or even to the agencies in Washington) Kissinger had already conceded the point to Ambassador Dobrynin. (Some of our allies suspected as much, but it was never confirmed to them, or indeed to anyone else until I first disclosed it in 1985.)

My association with MBFR was, however, to prove short-lived. I had overseen preparations in State since 1970. A few weeks after assuming the backstopping role in Washington in early 1973 I made a brief visit to the MBFR delegation in Vienna (stopping off on a personal, almost clandestine, visit to see also the new SALT delegation in Geneva). But shortly after, when Deputy Secretary John Irwin was unable to attend one of the Verification Panel meetings on MBFR at the White House, I had to represent the State Department. I had attended such meetings earlier as Irwin's staff adviser, but when I appeared as the interim State Department principal, Kissinger was miffed (as he always was when forced by circumstances to deal with anyone other than his own staff at lower than the under secretary level). Whether Kissinger then acted, or whether he merely mentioned my presence and General Al Haig acted, I don't know. But the upshot was quick and clear: the department was advised that Garthoff was not only off SALT, but also MBFR and anything else dealing with East-West issues.

Accordingly, I was no longer able to function as the deputy director of PM overseeing the work and representing the State Department on SALT, MBFR, and other East-West issues. I expected a new assignment that summer in any case, but now I needed not only a new assignment but something to do for the next few months. First of all, I took up a long-standing United States Information Agency (USIA) request for some knowledgeable U.S. official to visit Japan and talk about the SALT accords and political and strategic implications of SALT with Japanese officials, academic figures, and press representatives. There was considerable interest and some disquiet in Japan over SALT and the

U.S.-Soviet strategic relationship. I had never been to Japan, and so I went in April for several weeks, speaking to small groups in several cities. After I returned, I arranged to take a couple of months of refresher French language training at the Foreign Service Institute. Meanwhile, after a brief and unsuccessful search for a suitable deputy chief of mission assignment, the Foreign Service had come up with a solution: the Senior Seminar. An under secretary of state (no longer Alexis Johnson, who was now the SALT delegation chief) called me in for a chat and explained that it would be good to "take me out of the line of fire" (from the White House) for a while, but not to worry, because they would not forget me and in a year things would have cooled off so that I could resume a more active and appropriate role. I had misgivings, but no real choice.

The Senior Seminar had been started in 1957, as an equivalent for the Foreign Service of the military services' war colleges, providing an academic year of advanced training for mid-level future senior officers. It is a remarkably well-conceived institution, providing an opportunity for rising mid-level Foreign Service officers, typically after somewhat over twenty years of service in missions abroad and the State Department at home, to spend ten months studying the broad picture, not diplomacy or foreign policy, but American society at large as well as the U.S. government in its overall relationship to foreign relations. It is a wonderful experience, and an excellent way to keep Foreign Service officers attuned to our own changing society. A number of field trips around the United States permit seeing at first hand factories, farms, research laboratories, prisons, universities, and military installations and talking with business and labor leaders, farmers, judges, local officials, newsmen, and many others from a wide range of society. All of us have had varied past experience, but no one could fail to have a greatly broadened view as a result of such exposure. I was elected president of the Sixteenth Senior Seminar, 1973–74, simply because I was the senior member, the only FSO-1 in the class.

I will note only one additional feature of the seminar. Each member also had an individual research project. I chose to write a comparative study of policy planning in the foreign ministries of five countries, entailing visits to Paris, London, Rome, Bonn, and Moscow to meet with foreign policy planning officials of those countries. It turned out to be an interesting and useful exercise. I knew many of the officials directly involved. In the case of the Foreign Ministry of the USSR, I had previously learned a great deal from a member of that policy planning staff (who had, indeed, told me much more than he should have), so I had a good basis to build on. Incidentally, the Soviet staff was called the "Directorate for Planning Foreign Policy Measures," reflecting the Soviet view that national policy *objectives* were decided at a higher level, but that particular foreign policy *measures* were an appropriate subject for attention in the ministry. It would be too much of a digression to go into the substance of my findings, but they were of interest in the Department of State, and to CIA as well.

My transfer "out of the line of fire" to the Senior Seminar was of little consequence to anyone but me, but it reflected in a small way a curious phenomenon of the détente engagement with the Soviet Union. The expert SALT delegation from the first negotiation had been replaced by a capable but non-activist implementation team under Alexis Johnson. In Moscow, after Ambassador Jake Beam (who had been shamefully ignored) returned in early 1973, it was more than a year before a successor was sent there (Walt Stoessel, an experienced but cautious professional), so that the United States had no ambassador in Moscow during the Washington Summit or the October Arab-Israeli War. By October 1973, of course, William Rogers was gone and Henry Kissinger had become secretary of state as well as assistant to the President for national security affairs. The "back channel" had displaced the normal channels of policy making and policy implementation.

Détente was under way, but it rested on the shoulders of two men, and in 1973–74, in the wake of Watergate, President Richard Nixon went down and out, leaving Kissinger under siege and in a greatly weakened position notwithstanding the support of his successor, President Gerald Ford.

15

Inspecting the American Conduct of Foreign Relations

During the mid-1970s I had an unusual opportunity to examine the role and operations of the Foreign Service in these Cold War years. It came about as an outcome of the Foreign Service assignment process. Inasmuch as assignments are usually decided well in advance and among competing aspirants for positions, the "search" for an appropriate onward assignment was under way throughout the year I was at the Senior Seminar. Kissinger had become secretary of state, and the under secretary who had assured me that I "would not be forgotten" was gone. But he was right about one thing, I was not forgotten. When the director general of the Foreign Service proposed my candidacy as ambassador to Mauritania, and later for another small embassy, negative responses came back from the secretary's office. It was quite clear that I would not be approved for any chief of mission post by Kissinger. Meanwhile, I had by chance encountered an old acquaintance, Jim Sutterlin, then serving as the inspector general of the department. He asked whether I might be interested in serving as a senior inspector, which he said—rightly—was a much more interesting job than most officers realized. I merely replied politely that I would think about it. But some months later I *did* begin to think about it, and it seemed increasingly appealing. I followed through and in 1974 was assigned to the office of the inspector general (S/IG).

My first assignment in S/IG was what was called a "special inspection," not part of the usual pattern of checking on missions abroad, but close study of a particular aspect of the department's work, in this case the procedures within the top echelon of the department for assigning tasks and ensuring their implementation. The executive secretariat in the office of the secretary of state (known as S/S-EX, for Secretary/Office of Secretary-Executive Secretariat), S/S for short, is the key central link for ensuring vertical and lateral communication in the department between "the Principals" (the secretary, deputy secretary and under secretaries) and "the Bureaus" (the geographical and functional operating units, such as European Affairs and Politico-Military Affairs, respectively, each headed by an assistant secretary of state or equivalent). The deputy under secretary for management had asked the inspector general to check on the process of work assignments by the principals and S/S-EX to the bureaus and responses from them, evidently because he was aware that the system was not working as well as it should. He may also have sensed that one reason for shortcomings was a disregard for use of the established procedures by some principals, not least the new secretary, Henry Kissinger. It would be easier to raise this matter if such a conclusion was reached and presented by the office of the inspector general. In any case, that was one of the principal findings of my inspection of the process.

Action memorandums and staff studies requested by the principals, and those originating in the bureaus addressed to the principals, totaled nearly 100 items a day, or some 35,000 a year. The problem addressed in this inspection was the handling of these internal assignments within the department. (This did not include the thousands of telegrams received daily from over a hundred embassies and missions, all addressed to the secretary and requiring decisions on distribution and action assignment in the department, and a similar number of outgoing cables daily requiring drafting, clearance, and authorization for transmittal. In 1974 over one million telegrams were sent or received by the Department of State, all in the name of the secretary.)

S/S could direct or monitor work assignments and ensure that those with a need for participation were involved, and that assignments were fulfilled, only if it was itself aware of the assignment in order to enter it into its monitoring computer. The system worked well when it was used, but the more the system was bypassed, the more likely were failures to ensure the best result. In the worst case, a request outside regular channels could result in a decision being made by a principal and acted upon without that fact being known to the central command and control system or to other principals—and even to diverging decisions by two principals. Regular channels also were often not used because of urgency and a belief that shortcuts would save time. An oral request or direction by the secretary (or any other principal) to some assistant secretary (or to anyone else) would not become known to S/S unless someone informed them. Moreover, oral requests were often imprecise or unclear, sometimes by telephone, and were handled in a variety of ad hoc ways within bureaus. Oral requests were also sometimes deliberately used to curtail participation by others and to control and minimize knowledge of some matter. Bypassing the secretariat was regularized in some cases (for example, on

China policy), but was ad hoc and inconsistent in other cases. Similarly, the use of special categories of restrictions on circulation, intended to keep information to a minimum of personnel, had quadrupled in the year mid-1973 to mid-1974 under Secretary Kissinger.

There is no need to dwell here on my report. A number of procedural recommendations were acted upon, but those dealing with the most sensitive issues, above all the tendency of the secretary to bypass the department's system, were dealt with more gingerly, mainly by leaning on the bureaus to ensure they made S/S aware of such assignments except in cases where the secretary clearly intended secrecy to be maintained.

Following this interesting excursion into evaluating one important aspect of the department's management function, I spent the next three years carrying out eight "conduct of relations" inspections. The objective was to provide evaluation of U.S. policy and its management and implementation for a given country or area. An inspection team began work in the offices or country directorates of the geographic bureau responsible for the country scheduled for inspection, familiarizing itself with the work and problems of the area, relevant policy papers, interagency and internal State coordination, and the relationship between the department and the posts in the field. Next would come up to two or three months inspecting posts in the country or countries covered by the bureau office. The result was an inspection and evaluation of all aspects of the U.S. conduct of relations with a given country: policy formulation and articulation, internal coordination in the State Department, coordination between State and other agencies, coordination between the home bureau in the department and the embassies in the field within its area of responsibility, management within the missions abroad by the ambassador and his staff, and policy implementation by posts in the field.

Each inspection team was composed of a senior inspector who headed the team and usually three to five other inspectors. A "senior inspector" was, according to department regulations, considered equivalent to a chief of mission. In view of the fact that he had to make evaluations of the performance of ambassadors serving as chiefs of mission at embassies inspected, it was preferable if he too had previously served as a chief of mission, although not all of us had. The senior inspector was of course responsible for the work of the entire team, and for the full set of inspection reports prepared on each post inspected. All functions of each post had to be evaluated, so some degree of experience and expertise was required on political affairs, economic affairs, consular operations, and administrative operations. One inspector was always qualified as a financial auditor, and often experienced also in other administrative functions. For some posts, expertise in commercial relations, economic assistance programs, or politico-military affairs was also necessary. The number and qualifications of each team were therefore tailored to the nature of the posts to be inspected.

The eight conduct of relations inspections I conducted from 1974 into 1977 included three of our largest embassies at the time (Paris, Manila, and Bangkok), each with about five hundred Americans and up to fifteen hundred local nationals. Medium- to large-size embassies (fifty to a hundred or more Americans) included Rome, Ottawa, Tel Aviv, Madrid, Lisbon, Lima, Quito, and Rangoon. We also inspected a number of smaller embassies in the Middle East and Africa, and more than two dozen consulates in those countries.

This overview gives a general idea of the global geographical range of my inspections and suggests the wide range of issues entailed. For example, I was in Bangkok during the spring of 1975 at the time our neighboring embassies in Saigon, South Vietnam, and Phnom Penh, Cambodia, were overrun. Both in Thailand and the Philippines there were large questions at that time as to the future of the extensive U.S. military presence in those countries. The inspection of our embassies in Israel, Jordan, and Syria and the U.S. office in Iraq in 1976 came during a hiatus in shuttle diplomacy on the peace process in the Near East. In Italy, France, and Portugal a shift to the left, and even some local communist political resurgence, in those NATO countries had by 1976 raised concerns in Washington and questions for the U.S. conduct of relations.

There were many interesting aspects of the inspection process, but I shall limit myself to a few observations relevant to the context of the Cold War.

Several small posts in central Africa were the subject of my first inspection. The problems of small posts in that area were vividly exemplified by something that had occurred not long before our inspection. The United States had maintained a two-man skeletal embassy in Malabo, Equatorial Guinea, accrediting our resident ambassador in next-door Cameroon. The pressures under a particularly arbitrary dictatorship had led most foreign missions to leave the island capital of that small country, but we had decided to leave the two-man listening post. Then suddenly we heard nothing from them, and upon dispatch of an officer to check on the situation we learned that one of our two men there had gone berserk and killed the other. No replacements were sent. I concluded, not merely from that one incident, that in general we could probably cut back on our policy of having a resident ambassador and embassy staff in virtually every country, and do instead as many other countries did and accredit one ambassador to several small African countries. But in 1974 the United States wanted to have a full presence everywhere, as befit the leader of the Western world, and also in particular to keep an eye on Soviet representatives. The Soviet Union, for prestige and penetration, also then had resident embassies almost everywhere in Africa (most of which were closed down in the early 1990s in the last years of the Soviet Union and then by its successor Russia). From the 1960s through the 1980s the chief priority of U.S. intelligence in the area was to monitor the activities of Soviet diplomatic (often intelligence) officers there, and if possible to recruit them. The Soviet Union had a parallel reciprocal interest.

During the Cold War, CIA also had ties and paid retainers to several African dictators, most notoriously to President Mobutu Sese Seko of Zaire (now the Democratic Republic of Congo). At the time of our inspection, CIA had begun to close some of its smaller stations in Africa (including prematurely in Luanda, just a few years before Angola became independent and an area of competition in the Cold War). But it still had an extensive presence. (Incidentally, most central African capital cities are located on rivers, the main transportation lines, and often forming borders as well. I was surely not the first to observe that the identity of our CIA station chiefs was usually quite transparent, among other reasons because they were in each country the sole owners of identical *Swift* class high-speed motor launches.)

The consulate at Chiang Mai in northwestern Thailand near the borders of Burma and Laos was an interesting post. This area had been the seat of CIA support of former Kuomintang generals, who had become local warlords engaged in the heroin trade of the "Golden Triangle." The original belief that these irregular military forces could be useful for harassing Communist China had dissipated and American covert intelligence support for paramilitary actions had, if belatedly, ended years before our inspection, but the massive local drug traffic and interplay of rival warlords, tribes, and armies in Burma, Thailand, and Laos continued. I observed heroin poppy fields by helicopter. Our consulate was by 1975 primarily engaged merely in monitoring such activities in the area (as was our parallel consulate across the mountains in Mandalay, Burma, which we also inspected).

My son Alexander, who turned nineteen in Chiang Mai, accompanied me for part of my Thailand-Burma inspection trip. He returned to the States after several weeks, with a stopover with friends at our embassy in Saigon, just a few weeks before the fall of South Vietnam. He had a close call. Flying from Bangkok to Saigon he could either have taken a direct flight or a less direct route with a brief stop in Vientiane, Laos; he finally decided on the direct flight. The very plane he would have been on, had he taken the other route, was shot down over South Vietnam with all aboard killed, the only civilian passenger liner downed in the war. We didn't mention this close call to Vera until much later, long after he was back home.

In preparing for the inspections in Thailand and the Philippines I had arranged briefings in the Pentagon, as well as the State Department, and on both inspection trips I stopped over in Honolulu to consult with the commander in chief, Pacific, and his staff, in view of the importance and large U.S. military presence then in those countries. In both cases, especially Thailand, I recommended ways to cut the U.S. presence, more or less in line with expectations and plans of the Defense Department and the U.S. military command. In Thailand, a new government soon after made its own decision for a much more precipitous and virtually complete U.S. military withdrawal. A similar, but much less sudden, course was taken later in the Philippines.

In the Philippines, I discovered that the U.S. military wished to withdraw the nuclear weapons that were stocked at our two principal bases there, but had unaccountably been held back by Washington. I did not address this sensitive and non-foreign service matter in my inspection report, but after returning to Washington I looked into the matter and found that Kissinger as national security adviser had put a hold on Pentagon plans to withdraw the weapons, believing that somehow we should be able to get something from President Ferdinand Marcos in exchange for "agreeing" to withdraw our nuclear weapons. In fact, Marcos preferred they stay, because he believed it made the Philippines more useful to the United States and that we would therefore pay more to keep them there. A little over two years later we did remove the weapons, with no particular extraneous gain or loss by either party.

Occasionally incidental to my inspection trips unanticipated opportunities arose to pursue other interests. Most intriguing was an unusual approach from a Soviet diplomat with whom I was previously acquainted. I will not mention the time or place, nor the subject of my interest other than that it concerned Soviet policymaking. But the extraordinary, even bizarre, aspect of this meeting was that it occurred on the initiative of this Soviet diplomat *through* the local CIA station! A CIA station officer told me that the Soviet diplomat, with whom they were in contact, had learned of my presence (no doubt from CIA) and asked the station whether they could arrange for him to meet with me to resume our earlier conversations. The station obviously was cultivating this contact in the interest of recruiting the diplomat. They encouraged me to meet with him, which I was only too happy to do, both to assist them and because I had found him to be forthcoming and interesting in our earlier meetings. The upshot was that the Soviet diplomat and I had an excellent dinner, alone (except presumably for a listening device), arranged and paid for by CIA. In terms of my interests, it was a productive conversation. I subsequently reported on the content of our discussion, but the interest of the CIA station was in developing its relationship with the Soviet diplomat, rather than in whatever he had to tell me about Soviet policymaking. I do not know what happened subsequently; I have not heard anything further about the diplomat, and I presume he is now retired from Soviet (and American?) service.

Although I did not inspect our embassy in Tehran, I did spend a couple days there in 1975 en route home. I was graciously received by Ambassador Richard Helms, the former director of central intelligence, who had been given the assignment as a consolation award by President Nixon after his removal as director (and subsequent to reconsideration of Nixon's initial but ill-conceived offer to make Helms our ambassador to Moscow!). He made it possible for me to get around. I did not foresee the explosion in Iran to come just four years later, but from my observations it did not surprise me.

Other agencies in Washington, and the personnel of other agencies represented in missions abroad, were of course directly involved in "the conduct of relations" as well as the Department of State and Foreign Service. Although we did not evaluate the operations of other agencies in the field, we did evaluate their coordination and relationship to the respective embassies and to overall direction by the U.S. ambassador. Although the ambassador was responsible for all U.S. official activities in the country to which he was the accredited representative of the president, the extent of his control and even awareness of all activities of other agencies varied in practice. For example, in one country, the ambassador assured me that he was fully aware of the activities of the CIA station, yet within a few days I discovered from my interview with the CIA chief of station himself that this was not the case.

Apart from U.S. military bases in those countries where we maintained such facilities (such as Thailand and the Philippines), and separate U.S. missions accredited to international organizations (as in Paris and Brussels), all other agencies were normally part of the U.S. embassy. In most countries, the Foreign Service (including support staff) constituted less than half of the total personnel, the others including then the offices of the United States Information Service (USIS, the overseas arm of the United States Information Agency, USIA; now integrated again into the State Department), the Defense attaché, CIA stations, in many Third World countries Agency for International Development (AID) offices (now again integrated into State), Drug Enforcement Administration (DEA) offices, and occasionally attachés from other U.S. departments and agencies. There were in all about 23,000 Americans serving in U.S. missions abroad in the early 1970s, of whom only about 5,000 were from the Foreign Service of the Department of State—about an equal number were from AID, one and a half times as many from Defense, about 1,400 from USIS, and the remainder from a wide array of agencies, including CIA personnel, most of whom were under cover of the Departments of State and Defense and thus counted above in those totals.

The contribution of the men and women of the Foreign Service to the well-being and security of the country is not sufficiently appreciated. The former image of the diplomat as a striped-pants cookie-pusher, as caricatured by some malevolent critics, has now been largely replaced by the image of bureaucrats serving abroad. Both characterizations have some foundation, but both profoundly misunderstand and underrate the role of the Foreign Service officer in representing and serving American interests, from negotiation of important political, security, and economic agreements and reporting on developments around the world, to routine tasks of helping out Americans in trouble abroad. The Foreign Service of the United States is composed of many very intelligent and tough men and women who have to meet a wide variety of challenges, including dangerous assignments.

The Foreign Service was on the front lines of the Cold War, along with our military and intelligence services. Few may realize it, but in fact during the whole of the Cold War more ambassadors were killed in the line of duty than generals. Of five ambassadors killed, three were personal friends of mine— Rodger Davies, shot in the Embassy in Nicosia, Cyprus, in August 1974; Francis Meloy, kidnapped and murdered in Beirut, Lebanon, in June 1976; and Adolf (Spike) Dubs, kidnapped and killed in a shootout in Kabul, Afghanistan, in February 1979. And of course there were many others of all ranks.

I will not review here the findings of our various inspections, except that it may be useful to take as one example some aspects of the 1976 inspection of our "conduct of relations" with countries of Western Europe.

Our policy was at a critical juncture after three years of turbulence in relations with our Western European allies. After a leftist military clique seized power in Portugal in July 1974, Secretary Kissinger became quite pessimistic as to the possibility of preventing the communists from coming to power. Indeed, his main effort was placed on warning other NATO countries that might also turn left, and in insulating Portugal from full access to and participation in NATO affairs. (Kissinger's contingency planning even extended to discreet American contact with putative separatists prepared, for their own reasons, to declare the Azore Islands independent if a communist government established itself in Lisbon, to assure the United States continued control of the important U.S. Air Force staging base at Lajes in the Azores and denying it to the communists.) Our ambassador in Lisbon, Frank Carlucci, was far less inclined to write off Portugal, and fortunately Western European socialists weighed in to strengthen a noncommunist alternative. Shortly after my inspection, in July 1976, a moderate government under Antonio Ramalho Eanes stabilized the situation. Meanwhile, in November 1975 Generalissimo Francisco Franco of Spain died, raising concern over the stability of the successor government there. And in Italy, in elections in 1975 and 1976 the communists gained a third of the vote. The rise of less sectarian and more popular "Eurocommunism" in Spain, Portugal, and Italy made American (as well as Soviet) leaders nervous (although, as I later quipped, the European Left was "more gauche than sinister"). This posed a number of questions concerning our conduct of relations with those countries in the mid-1970s.

These questions as to the substance of our policy and relationship intersected with a question as to our mode of conduct of relations. Among other things, it meant that as crises in internal developments in Spain, Portugal, and

Italy (and other countries, including Greece and Cyprus) arose, or on important matters with a country such as France even in the absence of crises, direct control was assumed by the secretary and his closest aides. Thus, our inspection found that the WE bureau in the State Department and our embassies in Western Europe were hampered in their work because they were "not always kept advised of high-level contacts, exchanges, and decisions, including those of the Secretary of State." As we noted, "This does not contribute to a smooth and consistent conduct of relations, or permit most effective use of the Department's action offices or Embassies, despite other advantages that may be found in the practice."

I did not challenge the authority of the secretary of state to make and to execute policy as he deemed fit, but I did believe it should be done with recognition and awareness of the costs, and consideration of modifying practices in ways to mitigate disadvantages while preserving the desired secrecy and control over policy. Accordingly, my report continued:

> The Department's top management has evidently decided that there is a higher premium on secrecy than on full participation in policy formulation and on sharing information on policy among agencies concerned. This is a command decision. We would, however, recommend that the basic policy assessment and refinement process be brought to full cycle with a cleared, interagency-approved policy instruction based on Washington review of the Embassy Assessments, supplemented as necessary by additional confidential guidance to the Ambassadors.

The tight control by the secretary and a few trusted aides put an additional burden on them, and on others, that could be mitigated. "[S]ince some important aspects of our policy and its implementation are closely held even within the Department by senior officers, a large volume of messages covering wide ranges of subjects must be cleared by Seventh Floor principals conversant with the intricacies of policy and high-level exchanges. If more of this knowledge were shared with the Office Director, he could clear such [message] traffic without the burdens and delays on the entire system caused by the present arrangement."

I also found that the process of keeping high-level exchanges secret had a negative impact on the ability of other officers to function as productively as they could. For example, "our officials are sometimes placed at disadvantage in gaining information through interchanges with their French counterparts, and both the European Bureau and Embassy Paris are impeded to some degree in providing Department principals with staff support on important issues."

Finally, the absence of formal guidance made implementation of policy difficult. For example, in France in 1976 we found it was unclear to the embassy to what extent—if any—embassy officers should maintain contact with members of the Socialist Party; even the draft guidance in Washington waffled over an objective of "doing everything possible to drive a wedge between the Socialists and the Communists," while acknowledging that "we lacked ways in which to do so," and that we must be wary because "any such efforts could boomerang against us." That was hardly clear policy guidance.

One might, of course, question whether a Foreign Service inspector should note negative effects of practices of the secretary of state. The question could have a real, as well as a philosophical, answer. At the next annual inspection conference after my Western Europe inspection, the secretary made known that he wished inspections to concentrate more on the effectiveness of the implementation of policy, and less on its formulation. His close aide Larry Eagleburger, later himself briefly secretary of state in 1991, let me know privately that Kissinger's initial reaction to my report had been to go through the ceiling and call for abolishing the office of the inspector general! By contrast, only a few months later the next administration, looking over the record, bestowed the department's Superior Honor Award on the office of the inspector general for our work in the two years from April 1975 to March 1977.

Having by now gone around the world a couple of times inspecting, I felt I had learned what it meant in practice when Henry Kissinger had, in a more friendly earlier encounter, once told me, "You will go far, Ray, you will go far." In any event, serving as a senior Foreign Service inspector had been an extremely interesting and rewarding experience. In his evaluation report on me, the inspector general, Ambassador Bob Sayre, noted that "Mr. Garthoff was not given the easy ones, but those [inspections] which we were certain would require a high degree of tact, tenacity, professional judgment and not just a little bit of courage. It was out of admiration for this unusual performance that I strongly recommended his assignment as an Ambassador in an Eastern European country."

And that is what happened.

16

Ambassador to Bulgaria

I had just recently returned from my inspection of our embassy in Canada when, in mid-April 1977, I received a call advising me that the secretary of state had recommended me to become our ambassador to Bulgaria. I knew this meant that not only the secretary had approved, but also the White House, although there would still be a process of confirmation lasting several months.

I was delighted, and so was Vera. On my brief visit to Sofia in 1963 I had been charmed by the country, especially the unspoiled turn-of-the-century architecture of Sofia. I was interested in the history of the small Slavic Balkan country, as well as in the current political situation in the Soviet bloc in Eastern Europe. Bulgaria was, of course, an "Iron Curtain" country, and relations were constrained by the general parameters of Cold War realities.

The Senate hearing on my nomination, July 25, was brief and routine. Only Senator Clifford Case of New Jersey had questions, designed to elicit that I was reasonably knowledgeable on Bulgaria and that U.S. policy was wary but not belligerent. Some staff aide had probably quickly drawn up logical questions about Bulgaria, its history and economy. I answered the questions easily, but I had the distinct impression that I could have said anything and, unless it had been politically outrageous, no one would have known the difference or even noticed. I was sworn in by Deputy Secretary Warren Christopher on August 5.

Meanwhile, my formal preparation in July and August consisted mainly of a crash seven-week course in the Bulgarian language at the Foreign Service Institute, undertaken on my own initiative. I also reviewed EUR/EE office files on Bulgaria, familiarizing myself with the record of exchanges with

Embassy Sofia and the range of continuing tasks and problems, and visited other agencies with an interest in Bulgaria and in some cases a presence in the embassy staff.

A routine request to meet with Secretary Cyrus Vance was never acted on. I asked George Vest, the assistant secretary for European affairs, what policy guidance he had for me. He replied, "Ray, you know the country and the issues better than I do. I don't have any guidance for you." That was the whole of my policy guidance from the department (and none from the White House, although I touched base with the NSC staffer on Eastern European affairs). Just as I was leaving for Sofia in September, a new formal policy guidance on Eastern Europe was approved, Presidential Directive (PD)-21. It had scarcely been referred to in my briefings.

PD-21 did not mark a sharp change from the policy of "differentiation" in dealing with the communist-ruled states of Central and Eastern Europe, depending on the two criteria of their relative independence of international action, and internal liberalization, each to the extent feasible within the constraints imposed by the existence of the Soviet bloc.[1] The aim was to encourage somewhat greater independence (as exhibited by Romania) or liberalization (as exhibited by economic reform in Hungary). Some had advocated requiring change in both respects (Romania, for example, was among the least liberal internally), but it was recognized that that would unduly constrain any leeway in American steps to encourage change. In addition, the new guidance relaxed what had been an unduly rigid hierarchy or rank order of these states; the old guidance had prevented any step with those such as Bulgaria or Czechoslovakia, which ranked low, until a comparable step (such as, for example, a cultural exchange agreement) had been taken with *all* of the states ranked above the one in question. In practice, the only change by the Carter administration was to raise Hungary to join Poland and Romania in the ranks of those favored by the United States. The principal inducement was a return of the Hungarian royal crown and jewels (turned over to the U.S. Army in 1945 for safekeeping by Hungarian officials fleeing Soviet occupation of the country), followed by a grant of most favored nation nondiscriminatory trade status to Hungary in 1978.

Zbigniew Brzezinski, Carter's national security adviser, was the principal author of the revised policy. It was intended to carry further the idea of

1. For background on the evolution of U.S. policy toward Eastern Europe, a concise review is given in my chapter "Eastern Europe in the Context of U.S.-Soviet Relations," in *Soviet Policy in Eastern Europe,* edited by Sarah M. Terry, pp. 315–48 (Yale University Press, 1984), and for detailed accounts dealing with the 1970s and 1980s, see the relevant chapters in my *Détente and Confrontation: American-Soviet Relations from Nixon to Reagan* (Brookings, 1994) and *The Great Transition: American-Soviet Relations and the End of the Cold War* (Brookings, 1994), respectively.

"peaceful engagement" that he had advocated when serving briefly in the Johnson administration, although in a less confrontational manner than some of the earlier pronouncements on "bridge-building." Kissinger had sought to rely mainly on involving the Soviet Union in a web of ties increasing the Soviet stake in maintaining, rather than disrupting, the status quo, and relations with the countries of Eastern Europe were given low priority. Brzezinski placed more emphasis on prompting positive change in the Soviet Union, in part through encouraging peaceful change in Eastern Europe, which was a parallel objective. Secretary Vance and the Department of State tended to see internal change and liberalization as a desirable fruit of détente, rather than the aim of a more active American effort to press for internal change, given our very limited leverage.

Brzezinski, incidentally, opposed the one positive step taken, the improvement in relations with Hungary. In particular, he opposed the long overdue return of the Hungarian crown so long as that country remained under communist rule and attempted unsuccessfully to derail the initiative sponsored by Secretary Vance and supported by Vice President Walter Mondale and former Vice President Hubert Humphrey.[2]

In any event, the limited scope for application of American policy in Eastern Europe kept changes, and indeed any American influence, to the margin. In practice, even the abandonment of a rank order, not having ever been publicized, was hard to see. The Czechoslovak foreign minister, in an informal conversation in 1978, jocularly inquired of me whether American relations with Czechoslovakia, or with Bulgaria, were at the bottom of U.S. priorities in Eastern Europe. Similarly, the Bulgarians by 1979 were sensitive to the fact that Secretary Vance had met at least briefly on the fringes of the annual UN General Assembly meetings with every Eastern European foreign minister except the Bulgarian. That was, incidentally, the result of unplanned spot decisions in several cases, but even though true, that explanation was hardly convincing to the Bulgarians.

As I departed for Bulgaria, the concrete opportunities for improvement in relations were not great, but at least specific conflicting interests were also minor, apart of course from the major reality that we were on opposing sides of the barricades in the Cold War.

I arrived in Sofia on September 14, 1977, and was received by Todor Zhivkov, chairman of the State Council (as well as first secretary of the

2. For discussion of the difficulties in returning the crown, and incidentally a good example of the occasional helpful role of an active political appointee as ambassador, see the memoir of the American ambassador in Budapest at the time: Philip Kaiser, *Journeying Far and Wide: A Political and Diplomatic Memoir* (Charles Scribner's Sons, 1992), pp. 266–92.

Communist Party), to present my credentials as ambassador within forty-eight hours, rather than waiting the usual week or so. The ceremony was colorful, with an honor guard of tall Bulgarian soldiers dressed in late nineteenth-century Balkan uniforms—not proletarian at all, but very Bulgarian. We exchanged brief formal prepared statements expressing our reciprocal desires and those of our governments for good and improved relations, and then had a reasonably relaxed conversation. The most notable thing in Zhivkov's remarks was an unexpected provocative statement that I was well known to be an expert on Russian missiles, but that I wouldn't find any in Bulgaria. I assured Zhivkov that I would be looking for ways to improve U.S.-Bulgarian relations, not for anyone's missiles. U.S.-Bulgarian relations were not bad, but despite the exchange of polite assurances of reciprocal desires to improve relations, it was clear there would be little change under prevailing conditions. Zhivkov assured me he would be available as required, but that was a routine courtesy. I had few occasions over the next two years for brief conversations with him, and no real discussions, but that was to be expected. My few serious exchanges of view, and the few times I had real issues concerning our relations to bring up, were with the foreign minister.

The key officials with whom I had most to deal were Foreign Minister Petur Mladenov, already six years in that post although only forty-one years old, and recently raised to be also a member of the Party's Politburo; Deputy Foreign Minister Boris Tsvetkov; Deputy Prime Minister Andrei Lukanov, then recently named to that post and only thirty-nine, overseeing all Bulgarian foreign economic relations; and Ambassador Lyuben Gotsev, the very able head of the Fourth Department of the Foreign Ministry (dealing with the United States, Canada, and Western Europe). I developed good rapport with Foreign Minister Mladenov. With the Gotsevs and Mladenovs, Vera and I also enjoyed a pleasant social relationship (frequently seeing the Gotsevs, and naturally less often the Mladenovs). Mladenov, for example, did not fail to send Vera roses on her birthdays, a gesture we of course did not mention to our colleagues in the diplomatic corps, none of whom (except of course the Soviet ambassador) enjoyed social relations with the foreign minister and his wife.

The U.S. embassy in Sofia was a fairly small mission, with a staff numbering only some sixty-one people, of whom twenty-six were Americans and thirty-five were local Bulgarians. The key person on my staff was my very able deputy chief of mission (DCM), Charles Magee. I was pleased with the embassy staff, who performed their tasks well and worked well together. There were no serious frictions or shortcomings within or among the various components of the mission.

Just prior to my arrival, Embassy Sofia (along with half a dozen others in Eastern Europe and a number elsewhere) had been reduced from class-III to class-IV status, an internal State Department categorization that did not affect the actual complement of our embassy, but was made in recognition of existing realities. This relatively routine recommendation for downgrading the administrative level of these posts did occasion an interesting policy intervention. Officials in the Bureau of European Affairs of the State Department had accepted an inspection report recommendation for this change, but requested one amendment: to leave Embassy Bucharest as a class-III post, in the expectation that improving relations with Romania might justify a modest enlargement of the post there. There was no disagreement in the department, but because it did mark a change from an inspection recommendation it was flagged on the action memorandum that went to the National Security Council (NSC) staff for routine information and concurrence. On the NSC staff, the officer responsible for Eastern European affairs brought the matter to the attention of his boss, Zbigniew Brzezinski. Zbig, who was eager to encourage any sign of independence from Moscow in Eastern Europe, decided Romania should be accorded yet greater attention in our relations, despite its oppressive internal rule. He therefore proposed that rather than being kept at its current level, Bucharest should be raised to become a class-II embassy, like Belgrade and larger than Vienna. Now the European Bureau, which had wished not to reduce the status of Bucharest, also did not wish to raise it. Brzezinski, however, was adamant and the department did not choose to carry its objection to a higher level (never taking the matter up with Secretary Vance). So Embassy Bucharest was raised to class II, while the others were lowered to class IV.

Although the embassy was fairly small, and our work fairly routine, during the one year 1978 we sent 3,200 telegrams to the Department of State (nearly ten a day), and received 11,000 from the department, for a monthly average of nearly 1,300 cables received or sent. If more than 3,000 telegrams in a year from quiet Sofia seems like we were flooding the department, bear in mind that in any given month, say March 1978, the department received 106,478 telegrams from its several hundred posts in the field.

One administrative subject may deserve brief comment, and that was the matter of security for an American embassy in a communist country during the Cold War. On the one hand, the tight internal controls in such societies meant that security against such things as criminal or terrorist acts was generally quite good (we did receive some threats and warnings, to which the Bulgarian authorities gave full attention). The main problem was of course security of our operations *from* the Bulgarian secret services. Some forms of surveillance were routine and merely had to be kept in mind. We never regarded our offices as secure (except for a special secure conference room or "tank"), although the chancery and residences were periodically "swept" by specially equipped visiting American security personnel. It was taken for granted that our local Bulgarian employees might disclose anything they observed or learned. For example, I had a Bulgarian chauffeur, Simeon, who invariably drove Vera and myself to all official and social occasions, and on our travels around the country. I had no secret meetings or reasons to conceal any of my comings or goings, so we never gave second thought to the fact that he was undoubtedly reporting routinely on all of my movements.

Yet there were security risks. We encountered none (or at least became aware of none) during my tour in Bulgaria. But in other countries in Eastern Europe in the same general time frame, one American ambassador's shoes were found to have been tampered with and a microphone hidden in the heel of one, so that he could have carried it into the "secure" conference chamber. The wife of the American ambassador in one of the Eastern European countries was seduced and compromised by the local-national chauffeur, who was of course suspected of being a security service employee, although whether any classified information may have also been compromised was uncertain (and there was no blackmail attempt in this case, as there had been in Moscow with a French ambassador and several other Western diplomats over the years). But for virtually all practical purposes we simply had to live and operate in a fishbowl, but not pay too much attention to that fact and go about our business.

The ambassadors of the NATO countries in Sofia formed a kind of social core within the noncommunist diplomatic corps. We had a monthly luncheon, taking turns as host, but the paucity of real political discourse leads me to term it largely a social association. For some, however, the social whirl of Western and Western-oriented diplomatic colleagues, and with virtually no contact with Bulgarians or others, constituted the focus of their activity in Sofia. There were few real professionals on Eastern Europe or communist affairs, the principal exceptions being French Ambassador Christiane Malitchenko, whom we knew from a tour in Washington; Austrian Ambassador Dietrich Bukowski, a linguist who had earlier served in Moscow and Beijing; and Yugoslav Ambassador Radovan Urosev, who was better keyed into internal political developments in Bulgaria than anyone else except the Soviet ambassador. Britain, Germany, and Italy were also well represented, if not by experts in the area.

My Soviet colleague was Vladimir Basovsky, typically for Soviet ambassadors to allied communist countries of Eastern Europe a career Party functionary rather than a professional diplomat. My Western colleagues in the diplomatic corps (and my predecessors) had only the most cursory distant contact with him and his embassy. I, however, found him a pleasant and useful contact, and Vera and I, speaking Russian, became close enough that we occasionally met alone socially. I learned more about Soviet-Bulgarian relations, and internal Bulgarian developments, from him than from anyone else (except from my Yugoslav colleague on internal Bulgarian affairs). Basovsky was a friendly, thoroughly Soviet but jaded apparatchik. His wife, by contrast, was an enthusiastic idealist-communist, one of the very few in my experience, and I believe one of very few at all, left in the Soviet Union by the 1970s. I also got to know one of the counselors of the Soviet embassy, Boris Pyadyshev, with whom I shared an interest in Soviet and American political-military affairs and with whose work (mostly published under a pseudonym, Boris Dmitriev) I was familiar—including a critical review of one of my books. (Today he is editor-in-chief of the respected Russian journal *International Affairs*.)

During our stay, in early 1979, Soviet leader Brezhnev visited Sofia on one of his periodic visits. He was accompanied by two colleagues, Konstantin Chernenko, newly raised to the Politburo and on a first visit to Bulgaria, and another more junior newcomer, Mikhail Gorbachev, recently raised to the Party secretariat. The diplomatic corps was not invited to meet with Brezhnev, as we were with most visiting foreign heads of state, and could only follow the visit from the press. From my conversations with Basovsky, however, it was clear that both he and Zhivkov were giving very close attention and deference to Chernenko, whom they had not known personally, but who they knew to be a close companion to Brezhnev and saw as a potential successor. It was also clear that as a consequence they paid almost no attention to Gorbachev. (I was curious enough to ask Washington for some reference material on him, as we had none in the embassy.)

Basovsky was overdue for a transfer, having been in Sofia for seven years, and during the visit Brezhnev told him that he would be returning to become deputy head of the International Department of the Central Committee, a very influential position. Basovsky told me this confidentially, only to have to tell me sheepishly a few days later that he would be the deputy chief of the Cadres Abroad Department, not the International Department. The Cadres Abroad Department vetted and handled high-level personnel matters such as ambassadorial and other foreign assignments. Brezhnev, well past his prime, was simply confused and careless about such a second-level appointment. Basovsky's successor, who arrived only a few weeks before my own departure, was Ambassador Nikita Tolubeyev, recently ambassador to Cuba, with whom I had only one real conversation, about Soviet-Cuban relations.

Ambassador Basovsky, as the Soviet representative in Bulgaria, had a unique position. He not only had great influence, but even acted virtually as an adjunct member of the Bulgarian leadership. He was not a colonial viceroy, but he was obviously more than just the envoy of a powerful "fraternal" ally. He even appeared in public along with members of the Bulgarian Politburo flanking Zhivkov on the reviewing stand for parades, rather than occupying a place in the much less prominent position reserved for the diplomatic corps.

(That only reflected a parallel anomaly of the parades; along with individual portraits of members of the Bulgarian Politburo on placards held aloft by paraders, and sometimes with those of Marx, Engels, Lenin, and their own Georgy Dimitrov, were portraits of the members of the current *Soviet* Politburo.)

There were a few members of the diplomatic community with whom we had no contact: those representing Albania, Cuba, the PLO, and until the end of 1978, the People's Republic of China. We were not the only ones to hold some colleagues at arm's length. An illustration of the extremes of Albanian diplomatic distancing, at the time from both the United States and the Soviet Union, occurred when the Albanian chargé d'affaires promptly departed from a dinner party hosted by the Pakistani ambassador immediately after learning that my deputy was present. His chancery had taken the precaution of inquiring in advance whether any Soviet diplomats would be there, but had neglected to ask if there would be any Americans.

As soon as it was publicly announced that the United States and the People's Republic of China would exchange diplomatic recognition on January 1, 1979, my Chinese colleague, Ambassador Meng Yueh, demonstratively approached me at a reception. I formally called on him (because he had seniority in the corps) on January 5. We met a few times at dinner, but had no real professional exchanges, with one small exception. Having learned of a forthcoming trip to Vietnam by Foreign Minister Mladenov before it was publicly announced, and having in mind that the United States now wished to cultivate relations with China, I passed that tidbit of information to him. He seemed to be more grateful than I thought it deserved, but that was fine. It became clear from our conversations that the Chinese had very poor connections in Sofia, even in the diplomatic corps. After U.S. recognition of China, my friend Boris Pyadyshev in the Soviet embassy told me: "It's your [the U.S.] turn—good luck!"

One indirect and peripheral example of representation was occasionally provided when the diplomatic corps in Sofia would be invited to meet a visiting head of state. By far the most interesting were Shah Reza Khan Pahlevi of Iran in August 1978, only months before having to flee his country, and Muammar Qaddafi of Libya. I had a brief conversation with the shah, which I used to speak well of his ambassador in Sofia (who had been terrified that all should go well on the visit, and that the expensive gifts he had for the shah and empress and other members of the royal delegation would be appreciated). The shah responded dryly, "Well, he does at least speak Russian, doesn't he?" that apparently being the chief attribute he had in mind. I assured him that his ambassador indeed was fluent and represented the shah and Iran most effectively. (The ambassador later managed to escape Iran with his family, if not with most of his possessions, and at last word I have had was managing a restaurant in California.) My meeting with Qaddafi did not go beyond the obligatory handshake in the reception line. I watched his eyes go steely as I was introduced as the American ambassador.

Apart from the relatively few American visitors, official and unofficial, and these fleeting visits of foreign dignitaries, we saw few other visitors. I did, however, have brief encounters with two of the numerous Soviet visitors to Bulgaria. Twice in 1979 my old KGB interlocutor from years past in Washington, Boris Sedov, came to Sofia and contacted me. He seemed interested mainly in renewing our contact after seven years. In August he also asked what the Soviet side could do to help the U.S. government to get the SALT II Treaty ratified; the treaty was clearly in trouble in the Senate, and at that time the brouhaha about a Soviet brigade in Cuba was making the prospect of ratification ever more doubtful.

The other Soviet visitor was someone I had not previously met, although I knew a good bit about him and would see him frequently in the years following. Georgy Arbatov had headed the Institute of USA (later, and Canada) Studies of the Academy of Sciences of the USSR since its founding some twelve years earlier. He was, I knew, well connected in senior official circles, including with Politburo member (and KGB chairman) Yury Andropov. Boris Pyadyshev had worked briefly with the institute, and when the Arbatovs visited Bulgaria for a seashore vacation, he suggested that we meet. I welcomed the suggestion, and Vera and I invited the Arbatovs and Pyadyshevs to luncheon in early September 1979. We had a pleasant visit, although my efforts to persuade Arbatov that the serious contretemps over the Cuban brigade had arisen from bad luck and poor handling in Washington, rather than representing a deliberate effort by enemies of détente to derail détente and the SALT II Treaty, were clearly not entirely successful.

Turning to the central focus of my assignment, U.S.-Bulgarian relations, the first thing to note is that it was of course far from the center of American foreign policy, or, for that matter, Bulgarian policy. That is, to be sure, true of U.S. relations with the vast majority of countries in the world. Yet international relations is a complex weave of relationships, and even minor elements are nonetheless part of a larger whole. Accordingly, the professional approach is to try to do well whatever one's limited responsibility requires and opportunity allows.

As for U.S.-Bulgarian relations, there had been little movement for years and would not be for years yet to come. There had been gradual normalization of relations. Relations had been severed by the United States in 1950 after the Bulgarian government had accused the U.S. minister of being a spy and contact for a Bulgarian political opponent who was executed. Relations were restored only in 1959. Our last few "legations" (an anachronism in the post–World War II world)—including Bulgaria—had been raised to the status of "embassies" only in 1966. A consular agreement was concluded in 1976. A cultural exchange agreement had been signed shortly before my arrival.

A few months after I arrived, in November 1977, I was able to sign an agreement reciprocally lifting discriminatory travel restrictions on the movement of American diplomats in Bulgaria and Bulgarian diplomats in the United States. This was the last of a series of such agreements with Eastern European Soviet bloc states removing this vestige of a harsher era, leaving such travel restrictions only between the United States and the Soviet Union. (Incidentally, it was the United States that had first imposed such travel restrictions on the Bulgarians and other Eastern European diplomats a decade earlier, in view of the fact that East European defense attachés and diplomats were serving as proxies for Soviet diplomats long denied free travel in response to Soviet restrictions on U.S. diplomats.) The Helsinki Accord of the Conference on Security and Cooperation in Europe (CSCE) reached in 1975 had called for free movement of peoples, and it was in keeping with that major step in European détente that these residual restrictions on movement of diplomats were removed.

A second situation that posed a new challenge to our relations arose almost immediately after the favorable removal of travel restrictions. Also in line with the then forthcoming Helsinki CSCE summit meeting, Bulgaria had stopped jamming broadcasts of the Voice of America (VOA) three years earlier. Now, inexplicably, we detected in November and December 1977 that Bulgaria had resumed systematic jamming of VOA broadcasts. I first reported this development to the department on December 14, after we had confirmed our own monitoring with U.S. monitors in Belgrade and Vienna as well. I wrote that I intended "to request an urgent meeting with the Foreign Minister to protest jamming as unexpected, unwarranted, retrograde step in U.S.-Bulgarian relations, and at variance with content and spirit of Helsinki Final Act." The department wired its concurrence, including specific reference to the Final Act. I met with Foreign Minister Mladenov on December 22 and made my démarche. It seemed to me that Mladenov, although a member of the Politburo, had been unaware of the jamming when I told him about it. He cautiously promised an early response. On December 28 I was called to the Foreign Ministry and told that there would be no more jamming. My cable to the department that same day was captioned "Subject: On the Fourth Day of Christmas . . . Cessation of Bulgarian Jamming of VOA."

As part of the U.S. program to curb the global narcotics trade, the United States had approached the Bulgarians and found them receptive to cooperation. Bulgaria was astride the main truck route from Turkey to Central and Western Europe, used by millions of Turks and other international travelers, so it could play a key role in interdicting the narcotics trade. Initially held confidentially to our respective customs services, this cooperation blossomed into

closer Customs and DEA ties with the Bulgarians and to international conferences held in Bulgaria in September 1977 and September 1978, cosponsored
by the United States and Bulgaria. I opened the conference in 1978. There
were also indications of new Bulgarian cooperation in combating international terrorism, including Bulgarian cooperation in the arrest and extradi-
tion of four suspected German terrorists to the Federal Republic of Germany.

The Bulgarian record on cooperation in curbing the narcotics trade, terrorism, and clandestine arms shipments was, however, mixed. Although there
was new cooperation, and that was a welcome development, there also was
evidence of covert Bulgarian involvement in those same activities. Their cooperation in curbing narcotics traffic could even cynically be interpreted as getting rid of the competition. A Bulgarian export company, Kintex, secretly
controlled by the Bulgarian security service, was known to be involved in the
illegal arms trade and probably the narcotics trade as well.

As for support for terrorism, Bulgarian support for Third World national
liberation movements had long included some financial backing, paramilitary
training, and sanctuary for PLO and African radical opposition movements
that sometimes engaged in terrorism. Beyond that, the Bulgarian security
service (*Durzhavna Sigurnost*, DS) was responsible in 1978 for assassinating
the Bulgarian anti-communist émigré Georgy Markov in London with a poi-
son pellet administered by contact with an umbrella, and for a second similar
attempted assassination in Paris. Bulgarian responsibility for these actions (in
fact, Zhivkov's) was evident at the time, and it has been confirmed in the post-
communist period from the Bulgarian security archives and former Bulgarian
and KGB security personnel.

Although the attempted assassination of Pope John Paul II in May 1981
occurred after I had left Bulgaria, I might note that despite claims (subsequently retracted) by the attempted assassin, Mehmet Ali Agca, of Bulgarian
responsibility, judicial proceedings in Italy and post-communist searches of
the Bulgarian security service archives have convincingly established that
there was no Bulgarian (and hence no KGB) conspiracy to assassinate the
Pope. Agca may, through his ties with a right-wing Turkish terrorist group
called the Grey Wolves, earlier have had contact with the Bulgarian DS—but
not in the assassination conspiracy.[3]

What did move forward were implementation of the cultural exchange
agreement and humanitarian steps to resolve cases involving divided families.
There were relatively few divided family cases involving Bulgaria, two to three
dozen (the number kept changing as old cases were resolved or dissolved and
new ones appeared). In some countries of Eastern Europe they numbered in
the hundreds. But we gave them full attention.

3. See Garthoff, *The Great Transition*, pp. 92–95.

One incident illustrates both the wide range of things that become involved in assisting Americans abroad and the sometimes out-of-channels way they can be resolved. One evening I was called by our consular officer to alert me that an American tourist transiting Bulgaria on his way home from a big game hunting trip in Mongolia had been detained at Sofia airport because he was carrying with him a high-powered hunting rifle and ammunition. I knew just whom to call. Vera and I had gotten to know an interesting Bulgarian, Lieutenant General Khristo Ruskov, and his wife. They, too, were ardent opera-lovers. Ruskov was retired from the army and was chairman of the Bulgarian Hunting and Fishing Union. He was also an old personal friend of Zhivkov's from wartime partisan guerrilla days, which was why I had cultivated him, apart from the fact that he and his wife, a medical doctor, were charming social acquaintances. General Ruskov was only too glad to help out a fellow hunter, and me, by quickly arranging the release of the American and his gun and ammunition (the only thing the hunter didn't get back were some copies of *Playboy* magazine, also confiscated, that had mysteriously disappeared).

My most sophisticated and productive general discussions of Bulgarian economic and trade matters were with the very able young deputy prime minister overseeing all foreign trade matters, Andrei Lukanov. He was the son of former foreign minister Karlo Lukanov, whom I had known in Geneva in 1962. Andrei Lukanov was very capable, and after the ouster of Zhivkov in 1989 and transformation from communist to socialist rule, Lukanov became prime minister (as Mladenov had become president). I was to see Lukanov again after many years on a visit to Washington he was planning to make in early 1997, but just a few weeks before that planned trip Lukanov was assassinated (or simply murdered, it was not clear) in Sofia.

Vera and I did have one extraordinary experience in discussions of the subject of trade. In a relaxed informal luncheon in mid-1978 with Ambassador Gotsev and Deputy Minister of Foreign Trade Atanas Ginev, Vera made an impassioned and convincing case for the prospects for selling Bulgarian cosmetics in the West. We had visited one of the leading Bulgarian cosmetic plants, in Plovdiv, and seen what they had. They had excellent materials and even products that they were selling in Bulgaria, the Soviet Union, and Eastern Europe very cheaply, but that could be sold for much more and in hard currency if they were marketed properly. In the nonmarket Bulgarian economy, they didn't understand requirements for market targeting, packaging, and advertising. Suddenly, Ginev very seriously proposed that Vera take on the responsibility. He could arrange to give her a franchise to market Bulgarian cosmetics in the West. He was clearly not joking. We were a bit taken aback. I was not certain as to the legal restraints on my wife, who was not an employee of the United States government, but I was sure that it would at least be an impropriety for the wife of the American ambassador to engage in commercial activity with the Bulgarian government. We let it drop. Incidentally, on a visit to Bulgaria in 2000, I learned that the cosmetics plant was the sole profitable business enterprise in Plovdiv, and was being privatized.

There had been no special American political consultations with Bulgaria. Of course, as ambassador I would occasionally be instructed to lobby for an American position (as in seeking to persuade Bulgaria to oppose, or at least abstain on, UN resolutions that would, for example, call upon the United States to "decolonize" Puerto Rico). But that was hardly political consultation. On a few occasions I discussed political affairs with Foreign Minister Mladenov in an attempt to explain the U.S. position. But that too was not official consultation. The first such instance came in early 1979, when Deputy Assistant Secretary for European Affairs Jim Goodby visited Sofia (and other Eastern European communist capitals) for the express purpose of consulting and exchanging views in preparation for the CSCE meeting in Madrid in 1980. This practice of treating the Eastern European communist states as independent countries worth reasoning with and exchanging views was long overdue and I believe very desirable. It may not have changed the positions of the Bulgarians or others on any concrete issue, but it helped pave the way for their return a decade later as truly independent countries. We had not held such consultations before the Helsinki CSCE meeting in 1975, or the Belgrade meeting in 1977, but after 1979 it became the new practice to do so.

As for keeping in touch with Washington, apart from our regular cable and pouch correspondence, there were a few visits from officials in the State Department. In mid-1978 there was a meeting of all American ambassadors to European countries, attended by Secretary of State Cyrus Vance and other leading officials. Such meetings, held every two or three years, are a useful way to keep in touch. The last previous such meeting, with Secretary Kissinger in 1976, had led to an unfortunate leak of remarks by Counselor Helmut Sonnenfeldt allegedly calling for American acceptance of the existence of an "organic relationship" between the countries of Eastern Europe and the Soviet Union, termed the "Sonnenfeldt doctrine." He had not, of course, advocated American acquiescence in a permanent Eastern bloc, and was even a conservative on policy toward the region, but the ambiguity of the phrase gave rise to misinterpretations that some were only too ready to attribute. The misinterpretations were rebutted, but perhaps the most incisive repudiation of a new "Sonnenfeldt Doctrine" was made by Kissinger, who remarked, "If we had really been announcing a new doctrine, do you think I would have let Sonnenfeldt take the credit for it?"

Nothing dramatic was said at the London Chiefs of European Missions Conference in June 1978, and there was no leak. We were, however, told of some new developments under way, including the likely establishment of diplomatic relations with China later in the year. I also visited Washington for a month or so in the fall of 1978, and again in the summer of 1979, for consultations. There was, as I was not surprised to find, very little interest among policy-level officials in consultations on our relations with Bulgaria. State Department INR and CIA analysts of Bulgarian, Balkan, and Soviet bloc affairs, on the other hand, were enthusiastic recipients of our extensive reporting and active in meetings with me when I was in Washington.

Most of our activities in the embassy, apart form the consular, cultural, and commercial support roles described, involved what are called representation and reporting. "Representation" means simply representing the United States in the host country, in the first instance handling the business of the U.S. government with the local government, but more broadly serving as the representatives of our country. It includes standing in lines for one's turn to shake hands with the local chief of state, or a visiting chief of state of another country, on behalf of the government of the United States, and of course greeting others at our annual reception on the Fourth of July and attending national day receptions of other countries and numerous ceremonial occasions hosted by the local country. Sometimes it is possible, even convenient, to carry on a productive conversation with a local official or diplomat of a third country.

Similarly, representation is carried out by taking the United States flag, so to speak, even literally on the ambassador's car, on visits to other cities and regions of the country to which one is accredited. In two years, I made eleven official visits to parts of Bulgaria outside Sofia. In Vidin, for example, a historic city on the Danube in the northwestern corner of Bulgaria near both Romania and Yugoslavia, and the home town of then Foreign Minister Mladenov, the mayor told me I was the first American ambassador ever to visit the city. Official visits were sometimes interesting, always something new. On such official visits, we would learn a lot about the country, not only local history and production statistics, but also about the interests and mood of the people. I always found the conversations with local newspaper editors more revealing of public interests than what local officials had to say (and *much* more than what was printed in their own newspapers). Thus even while engaged in representation, we also found some grist for reporting.

We did much more representational visiting around the country than most, if not all, of our diplomatic colleagues (and my predecessors). My Soviet counterpart, who did travel around, did so in effect as an adjunct member of the Bulgarian leadership rather than as a foreign ambassador (except for one thing: in seven years in Bulgaria, he did not learn the language). I could converse and deliver toasts in Bulgarian, and the Bulgarians appreciated the effort by a foreign ambassador to learn their language as well as to visit them.

Reporting was a major part of our work. There was, of course, inevitably a substantial gap between what we would like to know and report (for example, on frictions between Bulgaria and its neighbors, or within the Politburo, or on

Bulgarian or Soviet bloc plans and activities in foreign affairs), and what we were able to learn and therefore did report (mostly on internal political and economic developments of little real interest or use in Washington).

The embassy's reporting was largely self-generated and dependent on what we could learn. There were also annual reports and spot reporting on subjects that the department had specified (occasionally for our embassy, but mainly in broad guidance to all embassies or at least those in Eastern Europe). We therefore submitted reports on economic performance, trade, human rights, foreign policy, relations with the Soviet Union and other Eastern bloc countries in particular, and on more specific subjects such as religious activities, the public mood, current developments within the Bulgarian government, and the like.

In Bulgaria in the 1970s there was virtually no discernible political dissidence. Any sign of it was promptly quashed, but even that was rare. There was greater artistic and literary leeway in Bulgaria than in the Soviet Union, but not with respect to political expression. Only several years later did the first signs of expression of discontent appear. A single dissident Bulgarian proclamation was published in Vienna in April 1978, called "Declaration 78," but we could not find any sign of roots for it in Bulgaria, and I am unaware of any later revelation of successfully hidden dissidence. The one self-proclaimed dissident who descended on the embassy was evidently unbalanced. We did not, of course, conclude from the lack of evidence that there was necessarily an absence of political dissatisfaction, but we could not evaluate it. It would be another decade before such signs began to appear, initially keyed mainly to ecological concerns.

Despite the tight clamp on political dissidence, as in most authoritarian states there was a lively underground in humor aimed at the political system. For example, one anecdote went as follows: Todor Zhivkov's aged peasant mother comes to Sofia to visit her son, who proudly shows off his Mercedes car, his super-dacha estate at Boyana, and the like. His mother is impressed but seems worried. When he asks why, she replies: "Well, this is all very fine, Tosho, but what if the Communists ever come to power?" The ambassador of Romania, then one of the most internally repressive of the Soviet bloc countries, once told me such a political anecdote, following which he commented: "One gets five years for telling that joke." And when I smiled, he added: "And three years for listening to it." That was not of course literally true, but it was not prudent for Bulgarians to give voice to too much such lightly veiled criticism. Nonetheless, letting off steam through subversive humor continued, even among Bulgarian officials.

Bulgarian foreign policy was one subject on which we were able to provide some useful analysis. Bulgaria was closely aligned with the policy of the Soviet Union, and most observers were content to leave it at that. In reality, the

Bulgarians chose to align themselves closely with the Soviet Union and were loyal allies, but they did have their own priorities and interests. No other country was so dependable and close an ally to the Soviet Union, nor so close in cultural tradition, economic integration, and political association as Bulgaria. Yet Bulgaria was not a mere puppet. Moreover, there were differences and divergences between the two countries, especially as to economic relations, although these differences were little recognized, in part because both Bulgaria and the Soviet Union had an interest in not making them known. I became aware of this facet of relations, and of a number of concrete instances of friction, mainly from my conversations with Ambassador Basovsky, who was relatively open in our talks, and by confirming them in guarded discussions with Bulgarian officials. The Soviet leaders sought to restrain Zhivkov from some of his desires to industrialize (for example, in industry utilizing petroleum products, the raw materials for which Bulgaria obtained largely from the Soviet Union at below-world-market prices and balanced with trade in Bulgarian products below world trade standards). Zhivkov himself, on two occasions in private remarks to Western leaders, boasted that Bulgaria should be regarded as a colonial power because it drew its resources from its colony (the Soviet Union) and sold back the manufactured product. I learned of at least two cases where the Soviet Union had declined to provide the capitalization for a Bulgarian industrial plant that they considered unwise, but Bulgaria persevered and obtained capital from Japan and Germany.

Bulgaria ran a heavy trade imbalance with the Soviet Union, made up for by a positive balance with other members of the Council for Mutual Economic Assistance (CMEA or CEMA). Bulgaria in the late 1970s imported 70 percent of its energy resources, 90 percent of which came from the Soviet Union. Bulgaria had nearly 80 percent of its foreign trade with CEMA members, but it managed its economic dependence well, receiving far more in technical assistance, credits, and raw materials than it extended, mostly from the Soviet Union.

Thus in contrast to Romania, Bulgaria trumpeted—and exploited—its alignment with the Soviet Union, rather than chafing and resisting it. And they quietly went ahead on their own on concrete matters where they differed that did not challenge the overall relationship. In short, although the relationship was one of close alignment between a major power and a small satellite, they were two distinct countries with individual national interests, notwithstanding common cultural and ideological ties, a political and military alliance, and substantial but not complete economic dependency of one on the other. Foreign and national security interests of the two countries were seen as basically the same, but the range of active interest and engagement of the Soviet Union was global, and for Bulgaria was European- and Balkan-centered.

In historical terms, although Bulgaria had over the past century since regaining national independence veered between Russian and German tutelage, there were deep Bulgarian roots of solidarity with its Slavic "big brother," Russia, even preceding but especially after the Russo-Turkish War and liberation of Bulgaria in 1878. Many thousands of Russian lives were lost in that campaign in Bulgaria, although to be sure they were serving Russian as well as Bulgarian interests. The centenary celebration of that event in 1978 evoked genuine popular enthusiasm. A commemorative medal was struck, and many officials wore it at the time.

In a rather curious incident, I was given the medal too, as had been only one of my diplomatic colleagues--the Russian ambassador. This was in fact one time that it made eminent sense for him to be so honored while the rest of us were not, but in a playful mood when he was wearing his newly acquired medal at a public commemorative meeting on the anniversary, I mock-complained to him that I had not been given comparable opportunity to join in displaying my respects for the historic occasion. Ambassador Basovsky immediately called over a Bulgarian official and told him I too should receive the medal. And in due course I did! It was a bizarre little episode, above all in the Cold War, for an American ambassador to be given a Bulgarian medal by direction of the Soviet envoy!

The second essential strand of Bulgarian foreign policy after its close relationship with the Soviet Union, and with deeper historical roots, was its Balkan policy. There was, however, to put it mildly, little interest in Washington in Balkan affairs (except the different case of Greek-Turkish-Cypriot relations). Late in 1977 I had submitted a cable on developments in Balkan diplomacy, and colleagues in Embassy Bucharest and Embassy Belgrade joined in a "round-robin" of spirited exchanges, mostly keyed to speculation on what would happen in Yugoslavia and the region after Josip Tito died. Our judgment that there would be no immediate crisis internally or from Soviet or Bulgarian initiatives was later borne out. In our longer-range speculations, I cannot say that we then foresaw what would occur more than a decade later. That, however, would have meant foreseeing the fundamental changes in the political environment, above all the end of the Cold War and the collapse of communist rule first in Eastern Europe and then in the Soviet Union, and finally the disintegration both of Yugoslavia and of the Soviet Union. While we in the three Balkan embassies (and some colleagues in Moscow and others where we tried unsuccessfully to generate participatory interest) enjoyed our exchanges of view, there was no sign that anyone in the department (or elsewhere in Washington) was the slightest bit interested.

In the spring of 1979 Embassy Sofia came due for inspection. I had of course read carefully the most recent previous inspection report before going to Sofia, as well as drawing on my own experience in conducting inspections, so unlike some of my colleagues I actually looked forward to the experience. The inspection went very smoothly, as we had no real problems apart from those inherent in the circumstances. The inspection report was very favorable and evaluated my performance in these terms:

> Capable and experienced in Eastern European affairs, the Ambassador provides excellent substantive leadership for the Mission. He is admired by the staff for his intelligence, analytical ability and integrity. He sets high standards of performance through his own excellent representations and reporting and expects top quality in the style and content of work of other members of the staff. The Ambassador prefers to lead by example and establishment of general principles, correctly leaving to the energetic DCM [Deputy Chief of Mission Charles Magee] the task of daily Mission coordination. The Chief of Mission and the DCM complement each other effectively. Post representation is performed graciously and generously and the handling of official visitors is exemplary.

The inspectors also found the embassy's reporting (our main function) to be "surprisingly comprehensive" and observed that in addition to the reporting by our combined political-economic section, "output of quality reporting is substantially augmented by other Embassy officers, notably the Ambassador." The inspectors did not note (as I might have had I been conducting the inspection) that there was much more reporting by Embassy Sofia (and the other EE posts) than the department was really interested in.

In June Vera and I returned to Washington for consultations and home leave. By that time I had learned that the department wanted to recycle a number of career officers serving as chief of mission after two-year tours of duty, in order to give a larger number of senior career officers a chance to serve in such posts. As a consequence, I would be leaving Sofia later in the year.

In late May, shortly before my departure for Washington consultations, Foreign Minister Mladenov received me for what I assumed would be a normal exchange of views before my departure, something we both thought would be useful. It was that, but also much more. For more than three hours (in Russian, obviating the need for interpretation, and with only Ambassador Gotsev in attendance), Mladenov and I had a wide-ranging discussion, including a fuller than usual *tour d'horizon* of current world affairs, as well as Bulgarian-American relations.

Our review of U.S.-Bulgarian relations was thorough and productive. Mladenov of course emphasized what Bulgaria had done and what the United States could do, and I the obverse, but we each also made constructive responses and advanced some new possibilities. Mladenov's main concrete interest was in advancing commerce, but he also gave some emphasis to the fact that in political relations, notwithstanding a number of ministerial-level

Bulgarian visitors to the United States, there had been none from the United States in recent years. Mladenov emphasized Bulgarian desire to resolve all outstanding humanitarian consular cases and presented me with five newly approved ones. When I expressed surprise and regret at rejection of a proposal to accredit a nonresident science attaché (we had wanted our new science attaché resident in Bucharest also to be accredited to Bulgaria and to visit from time to time), it turned out that Mladenov was uninformed on the matter—as in the case of jamming of VOA radio in 1977, clearly a case where Mladenov as foreign minister and even as a Politburo member had been kept out of the loop on a decision by security authorities. Gotsev lamely explained to Mladenov that the Foreign Ministry had been uninformed of the whole matter until after a decision had been made not to increase the number of non-resident diplomats. Similarly, when I raised the matter of unavailability in Sofia of any Western non-communist newspapers, Mladenov was annoyed that it had not yet been taken care of, telling Gotsev it should be. I also complained that the militia (police) guard outside the embassy intimidated some Bulgarians from visiting our small embassy library open to the public.

We also had a good, open discussion of a number of current international issues, including European security, the Mid-East peace process, U.S.-Chinese relations, the recently signed U.S.-USSR SALT II Treaty (which Bulgaria warmly welcomed), and the Macedonian issue. I shall not review the discussion of these issues except to state that Mladenov was unusually candid. Gotsev later commented that Mladenov had high confidence in me and scarcely ever had such frank discussions with any ambassadors, and never before with an American ambassador. (I have recently obtained from the Bulgarian state archives the declassified *Bulgarian* record of our conversation, in which Mladenov noted that he had told me that in the whole twenty-year period since reestablishment of Bulgarian-American diplomatic relations, I was the American ambassador who had played "the most constructive role" in developing U.S.-Bulgarian relations. I appreciated the compliment but did not include it in my report of the meeting, not wanting it to appear to anyone in Washington that I was suffering from what we termed "localitis," identifying *too* closely with the local country of one's assignment.)

The important thing was not that Mladenov and I had developed a good rapport, or even that he had taken a balanced and forthcoming approach on the whole range of issues relating to U.S.-Bulgarian relations, encouraging and welcome as that had been. As I learned in a subsequent tête-à-tête arranged at the initiative of Ambassador Gotsev, Mladenov had discussed his forthcoming meeting with me in advance with Zhivkov and had been specifically authorized to seek closer political and economic ties with the United States. Gotsev told me that after his meeting with me, Mladenov had remarked to him: "I hope the Americans realize that I have extended my hand, and grasp it."

Gotsev commented that "the United States is of course the most important country in the world." He noted that Bulgaria enjoyed very close ties with the Soviet Union and had no desire to change that relationship. At the same time, some Bulgarian leaders, including Zhivkov and Mladenov, wished to increase the Bulgarian role in world affairs, of course without illusions as to the limited role of a small country. He remarked that in extending their contacts with the West, they had enjoyed greatest success in improving political and economic relations with West Germany and Japan. As a result, there were German and Japanese "lobbies" within the Bulgarian leadership, but no foundation yet for an "American lobby." Gotsev remarked that whenever a major trade deal with a Western country was being considered, Zhivkov would inquire about the quality of the technology as compared to that of the United States.

Gotsev frankly reviewed the Bulgarian effort to obtain most favored nation (MFN) nondiscriminatory trade status from the United States. He said flatly that Bulgaria hoped to get MFN status before Czechoslovakia or East Germany. It had resolved all the issues we had raised, such as a settlement with American bondholders, and was resolving all the divided family cases. There were no financial claims or other disputes. There was no emigration problem with a Jewish or other minority (as in the Soviet Union). I noted that Romania and Hungary had qualified for MFN status on the basis of existing U.S. legislation. I asked Gotsev what I acknowledged was a blunt "undiplomatic" question: had Bulgaria consulted with the Soviet Union before hiring an American law firm (Morse) to investigate MFN requirements and prospects, and before expressing interest to me and other American officials in a possible "Hungarian solution" to obtain MFN status for Bulgaria?

Without responding directly, Gotsev did answer my question: the expressions of interest were based on the judgment of the Bulgarian leadership that MFN status from the United States, "for economic and political reasons," would serve Bulgarian interests. At the same time, they wished to proceed "discreetly and deliberately" and did not want to display their interest and then have it rebuffed by the United States "in front of the other socialist countries" (clearly meaning the Soviet Union). He said the "Hungarian solution" (which had annoyed the Soviet Union by accepting the Jackson-Vanik criteria) was *not* out of the question. But in 1978 the Bulgarian reading from me after my 1978 consultations, from the visit to Washington by Tsvetkov and himself, and the "Morse report" had all suggested that the United States was not yet ready to grant Bulgaria MFN. Now they hoped that a changed international situation might make it possible. Gotsev noted that frankly Bulgaria had little to bargain with, having agreed to virtually all of the admittedly minor issues we had earlier cited, and he said some in the leadership believed this had been a mistake.

Gotsev made clear that Mladenov believed, and Zhivkov had agreed, that my return to Washington for consultations at this juncture was the best opportunity to probe the American reaction, and Mladenov was awaiting with interest whatever I could bring back as a response.

After reporting both the Mladenov and Gotsev approaches (I described the latter as an "evidently orchestrated informal elucidation," saying "explicitly what a foreign minister and Politburo member could not say in such a direct and open way"), I noted that together they constituted "a clear signal and request for an American response." I withheld my own comments and recommendations, inasmuch as I was returning imminently to Washington for consultations.

I was afraid that I knew what the American response would be: we would not grasp the extended hand. Although we had virtually nothing to lose, and potentially something to gain, there was no prospect of a publicly exploitable anti-Soviet step either in greater Bulgarian independence from the Soviet bloc, or internal liberalization, to justify raising Bulgaria from the lower tier to the favored ranks in U.S. relations with the countries of Eastern Europe under PD-21. I believe there were untapped possibilities, not for prying Bulgaria away from close alignment with the Soviet Union or from Zhivkov's authoritarian grasp, but for example in diluting Bulgarian support for Third World national liberation movements and in shifting the balance on such matters as interdicting the drug trade to a more constructive path. But those were not possibilities that could be advanced with any assurance, and not at the beginning of a process of improving and developing relations.

I raised the matter with George Vest, the very able and savvy assistant secretary of state for European affairs, but as I expected he did not think the time was ripe to raise the question of upgrading relations with Bulgaria. It was not even a question to pose to Secretary Vance. I accepted George's judgment on the situation in Washington (then floundering over the Soviet brigade belatedly "discovered" in Cuba), with regret.

The negative response was left to me to convey as I saw fit. It marked, in substantive terms, the end of my two-year effort to improve U.S.-Bulgarian relations within the narrow confines imposed by the general East-West political situation, by the Bulgarian government, and now it turned out even more by the U.S. government. That the latter proved the most limiting factor was the only somewhat unexpected, and I believe unfortunate, element. U.S.-Bulgarian relations would continue to coast without any significant change for another decade until the end of the Cold War.

When I returned to Sofia at the end of July, I made an appointment to see Gotsev, not Mladenov. That was the first signal. I told him I could report, on the basis of my consultations, that the United States government would continue as before to seek to improve relations. Gotsev's face fell; "continuing as before" was clearly not grasping the extended hand that Mladenov had proffered two months earlier. I also informed Gotsev, confidentially, that I would be leaving that fall after a little over two years in which I would have done what I could to advance our relations.

I saw Foreign Minister Mladenov several times, and toward our departure he and his wife honored Vera and me at a most pleasant private luncheon for just the four of us at their apartment. Our personal relations remained excellent, and although we did discuss the general political situation when I paid a farewell call in late September, there was no basis for a renewed real dialogue on U.S.-Bulgarian relations.

Curiously, it was a planned meeting of Mladenov with my successor several times removed just ten years later that was the spark provoking a sharp argument and rift between Mladenov and Zhivkov, leading to Mladenov's resignation and soon thereafter Mladenov's successful challenge to Zhivkov in the Politburo and Zhivkov's ouster. Mladenov succeeded him as "president" (chairman of the State Council), Andrei Lukanov was made prime minister, and my friend Lyuben Gotsev became foreign minister, in the first short-lived post–Cold War transitional government in Sofia in 1989–90.

As I was preparing for my departure, I was advised that the Bulgarian authorities wished to present me with the highest degree of their principal medal granted to distinguished foreigners, the Order of the Horseman of Madara, First Class. This Order was frequently (though not always) bestowed on departing ambassadors, but not often "First Class" (my predecessors, for example, had received this Order, Second Class). I was naturally pleased that they would wish to do this. As required by regulations, I informed the department and requested authorization to accept the award. Such approval is normally routinely granted, but time began to slip by with no response from Washington. I made discreet back-channel inquiry and learned that some unidentified office (the NSC staff?) was withholding clearance of the cable of approval, on the grounds that U.S. agreement to accept the honor might imply too much "normal" friendly relations with Bulgaria. I thought this was ridiculous, and so did my home office in the department. I wanted to receive the Order, but more important, it would be a gratuitous slap to the Bulgarians to refuse. Well, I reasoned, if a cable of approval was hamstrung (no one wanted to buck it up to a senior level to resolve), then so would be a cable of rejection. So I sent a new telegram noting that time was now short, and that if I did not receive an instruction to decline the award, I would assume approval was granted. Again, no word from Washington, so I accepted the Order. (This advance forewarning of assuming approval unless denied is a technique for back-door authorization that I had employed in arms control negotiations, as no doubt have other activist envoys and negotiators.)

After all the usual departure calls on Bulgarian officials, farewell calls, and parties in our honor in the diplomatic corps (and a few with Bulgarians), we departed Sofia on October 9. During the three months until I retired at the end of the year, I prepared a report on U.S. relations with Eastern Europe, essentially for my own catharsis on the subject and a few friends, as I knew it was destined for "the files" of the department.

My tour as ambassador to Bulgaria thus capped my career in the Foreign Service and in general in direct government service, although I was by no means retiring from the field of international relations, as I will describe in a later chapter.

17

The Decline and Collapse
of the Détente of the 1970s

The U.S.-Soviet détente of the 1970s, as shown in an earlier chapter, did not emerge early in the Nixon administration, notwithstanding Nixon's inaugural call for a turn to an "era of negotiations," or as a well-developed conception. Détente was, however, launched with considerable fanfare by the time of the May 1972 Moscow summit meeting and the June 1973 Washington summit. Despite the convergence of a number of reasons for a détente policy on the part of both the American and Soviet governments, and widespread public support, the policy soon began to face difficulties. For one thing, although congruent, the reasons for a détente in Washington and Moscow were not entirely the same, nor was the very conception of détente itself. Most important, both governments oversold détente to their constituencies and interpreted it in terms that placed the burden of fulfillment of high expectations on the other side. When reality did not meet these overblown expectations, each side blamed the other for failing to meet idealistic commitments while justifying its own behavior by more modest realistic standards.

Opponents of détente naturally were even more critical of the performance of the other side, and in the United States also criticized their own leadership for having been taken in by the other side in adopting détente in the first place. There was a difference, reflecting the different political systems. Opponents of détente in the United States freely and loudly made their case and pressed it to replace the leaders in power. In the Soviet Union, those who were wary of détente could not openly criticize their own leadership, or even détente, but argued instead for particular policies that were not supportive of détente, while directly attacking the United States for alleged failures to abide by détente. Thus in the Soviet Union détente itself remained in favor, although some policies were pursued that in practice tended to undermine it, while the United States was blamed for the decline of détente. In the United States, however, the very idea of détente was attacked and eventually discredited, with blame placed not only on the Soviet Union but also on the U.S. leaders who had supported it.

The first stirrings of doubt over détente were present even as its greatest apparent successes were being reached in 1972: the U.S.-Soviet agreement on "Basic Principles of Relations," a kind of code of conduct, under which the two countries pledged not to seek advantages at the expense of the other side (never a realistic, or for that matter sincere, commitment by either side), and the first strategic arms control (SALT) agreements. At the time, however, these were accepted as real achievements by all but a small group of skeptics.

Ironically, most early misgivings over détente were really concerns stemming from its successes. Although the constraints imposed by the SALT accords of 1972 were insufficient to prevent a continuing arms race, they did place some limitations on the freedom of action of the two countries, and that was enough to make uneasy those who preferred to keep all of their own options open, even if that meant the other side also kept its freedom of action. Real steps in arms control were not welcomed by those wary of the very process, as well as of the Soviet Union.

The first significant stirrings of disenchantment with détente came with the October 1973 war in the Middle East. Although détente had not prevented the United States and the Soviet Union from initially aiding their traditional allies in the Arab-Israeli conflict in 1973, the two powers had cooperated in obtaining a cease-fire. The most dramatic event, to be sure, was a pseudo-crisis when Soviet words and actions were misconstrued in Washington as possibly threatening a unilateral military intervention to impose the cease-fire, and prompted an unnecessary worldwide U.S. military alert. But the more important development was Soviet-American cooperation in imposing a cease-fire. Yet this very success of détente caused many American supporters of Israel to presage a Soviet-American condominium that could bring pressure on Israel to settle the dispute with the Arabs.[1]

Other actions by both sides undercut détente. Vigorous U.S. efforts from the very outset to curtail Soviet influence in the world and to expand U.S. influence were noted in the earlier chapter on developing détente. The same was true when opportunities presented themselves to the Soviet Union in Africa in the mid- to late 1970s (Angola in 1975–76, Ethiopia in 1977–78), to

1. See Raymond L. Garthoff, *Détente and Confrontation: American-Soviet Relations from Nixon to Reagan,* rev. ed. (Brookings, 1994), pp. 404–57, esp. pp. 454–57.

Soviet allies (North Vietnam taking the South in 1975), and to local communists pressing a challenge (in Nicaragua in 1979 and some other places in Central America and the Caribbean). Yet far more important than the Soviet adventures in Africa and elsewhere in the Third World was the U.S. establishment of full relations with China in 1978 on the basis of an avowedly anti-Soviet strategic partnership. Both sides justified their own actions and criticized the actions of the other as inconsistent with détente.

The United States Congress, by imposing its own "linkage" on Soviet emigration restraints, had undercut the Nixon and Ford administrations' efforts from 1972 to 1975 to provide the economic dividends of détente promised to the Soviet leaders by Nixon and Kissinger.

Finally, probably the most important element in the decline of détente in the United States was a growing fear that the Soviet Union was gaining and the United States losing in the strategic arms competition. In part this was a belated realization that strategic parity had displaced the superiority that the United States had enjoyed throughout the nuclear age. And belief that arms control could stabilize the balance was diminishing. In the public perception there was a growing threat of a "window of vulnerability" for the United States and a "window of opportunity" for the Soviet Union to exploit politically or even militarily to our peril.

This rising American concern over the strategic threat was stimulated by a number of strategic analysts and others, most of whom opposed détente and arms control and wanted the United States to seek to restore its strategic superiority. No doubt many of them to one or another degree believed their own dire predictions of a growing Soviet threat, but such warnings also were seen as the only way to generate political support for a higher U.S. defense effort. Some political figures also saw that line of attack as the best way to unseat the proponents of détente—Nixon, Ford, and Kissinger, and later Carter and Vance.

There is no need here to detail the long list of events from 1975 to 1980 that reflected and spurred on this trend. By 1976–77 public opinion polls showed the American public for the first time believing that more should be spent on defense. In January 1976 President Ford had still defended détente, but in March (after challenger Ronald Reagan had done well in early primaries) he banned the very word from his campaign. Even the Democratic challenger, Jimmy Carter, was ambivalent on détente during the campaign (and indeed later as president).

An influential Committee on the Present Danger was established in November 1976 and pressed the case for the next decade. The committee had in fact been forming since early in the year, but as a bipartisan coalition the founders decided to wait until after the election to announce formally and publicly the establishment of the committee. The committee was led by a distinguished group of prominent "cold warriors," many of whom had served in the cabinets of various presidents, including Paul Nitze, Eugene V. Rostow, Ronald Reagan, C. Douglas Dillon, Dean Rusk, David Packard, Henry H. Fowler, James Schlesinger, Admiral Elmo Zumwalt, J. Lane Kirkland, William Casey, Jeane Kirkpatrick, Richard Perle, Max M. Kampelman, Ben Wattenberg, Richard Pipes, Norman Podhoretz, and Richard V. Allen. It was drawn from various quarters, including Republican conservatives, Democratic "neo-conservatives," the "military-industrial complex," and others who were simply wary of détente and the Soviet Union. Some, including Dean Rusk, soon dropped out, but Paul Nitze, Eugene Rostow, and others began a major drive directed mainly toward defeating SALT II and building American power for confrontation with the Soviet Union.[2] Many would rise, or return, to high office in the Reagan administration five years later, although others would continue to criticize even that administration for not doing enough to boost defense efforts.

Coincident with the launching of a public campaign against détente and strategic arms control was a leak to the press of the result of a bizarre "experiment in competitive analysis" in estimating the threat. A "Team B" was constituted, made up of "outside experts," to critique the official National Intelligence Estimates of strategic capabilities and objectives and present a more alarmist alternative view of the Soviet threat.

The Team B episode originated in the dissatisfaction of some hawkish members of the President's Foreign Intelligence Advisory Board (PFIAB) with what they believed to be too complacent an estimate of the threat from Soviet strategic capabilities presented in the National Intelligence Estimates (NIEs). PFIAB proposed that a panel of outside experts with a more hard-nosed view of the threat be given access to the same intelligence information as the official estimators and given a free run at preparing a less sanguine alternative assessment. When first proposed, in 1975, then Director of Central Intelligence William Colby deflected the proposal, but in early 1976 his short-term successor, George Bush, authorized the unusual procedure. The idea of outside experts offering alternatives to test was not without merit, but at the least the terms of reference should have been clear, and there should have been two alternative teams and viewpoints, one more pessimistic but the other more optimistic, Teams B *and* C.

Team B was composed of ten former officials and academic figures as members and advisers, selected because of their "more somber" view of the Soviet threat, chaired by Professor Richard Pipes of Harvard University. Some specific issues dealing with Soviet strategic forces were addressed, but the

2. A compilation of most of the alarmist publications of the committee has been published; see *Alerting America: The Papers of the Committee on the Present Danger*, edited by Charles Tyroler (Pergamon-Brassey's, 1984). The main theme was reflected in one early paper titled "Is America Becoming Number 2?"; they argued it was, and to our peril.

main thrust of the report was to castigate the NIEs on the matter of Soviet objectives and intentions and to offer a more dire picture.

In 1992 the Team B report and the official NIE on Soviet strategic forces (the Team A estimate) were declassified and released. It is clear in retrospect that Team B was wrong on almost every count, although divergent views on long-range Soviet objectives in the 1970s still remain as an academic issue.

On several important specific points it wrongly criticized and "corrected" the official estimates, always in the direction of enlarging the impression of danger and a threat. For example, the range of the *Backfire* medium bomber was considerably overestimated, contributing to a serious impasse in the SALT negotiations, inasmuch as the Soviet side *knew* that it was not an intercontinental bomber and naturally resisted U.S. attempts to include it. Moreover, Team B overestimated by more than 100 percent the number of *Backfire* bombers the Soviet Union would acquire by 1984 (estimating 500 when the real figure was 235). Team B seriously overestimated the accuracy of the SS-19 ICBM, feeding the unwarranted fears of a "window of vulnerability" for the U.S. ICBM deterrent. Team B estimated the Soviet Union would field a mobile ABM system, which it did not. It regarded as ominous, rather than reassuring, that no intelligence information had been acquired on Soviet development of nonacoustic antisubmarine warfare capability, again raising concerns over a looming threat that did not arise. It saw as a "serious concern" possible upgrading of mobile intermediate-range missiles (the SS-20) to become ICBMs and criticized the draft NIE for estimating that the SS-16 mobile ICBM program would remain small. In the event, *no* SS-16s were deployed and *no* SS-20s upgraded to ICBMs. With respect to exotic technologies for ABM defense, Team B castigated the NIE for failing to draw more attention to the threat of Soviet development of charged particle beam directed energy interceptors, stating that it would be "difficult to overestimate" the magnitude of the Soviet effort, yet by those very alarmist words it did so. (Indeed, this is one area where the Soviets may have intentionally sought to feed our fears through a deception campaign, unwittingly abetted by Team B.) The large-scale but ineffective Soviet civil defense efforts were also depicted as an important part of a Soviet design to be able to fight, and win, a nuclear war, and Team B even suggested incredibly that the ABM Treaty helped the Soviet leaders "to pursue a goal of achieving assured survival for the USSR and assured destruction for its major adversary."

The Team B reported "an intense military buildup in nuclear as well as conventional forces" and criticized the official NIEs for failing to describe adequately the scale of the Soviet military effort. Yet precisely at that time the official NIEs had changed to describe an increased buildup with a growth in military expenditures of 5 percent per year. Moreover, as the intelligence community concluded in 1983, by then it had become known that from 1976 on, the rate of growth had fallen to 2 or 3 percent, with no increase in the rate of growth in procurement of military hardware. Thus while Team B was estimating a relentless continuing buildup at a growing pace, in fact the Soviet leaders had just cut back their military effort and would not increase it for at least the next seven years. To be sure, the Soviet Union continued to spend a great deal on its military programs, but it was not the limitless buildup in pursuit of a war-winning capability that Team B ascribed. Team B went even further, arguing that there was *no* constraining effect of the requirements of the civilian economy. The NIEs were attacked for even suggesting economic considerations might limit Soviet military growth, and Team B itself asserted that "Soviet strategic forces have yet to reflect any constraining effect of civil economy competition, and are unlikely to do so in the foreseeable future."[3] With leaks by Team B members, and no official rejoinder, the whole exercise contributed at the time to the growing public impression of an ominous mounting Soviet threat.

During the years of the decline of détente, from 1974 through 1979, while I was serving as a Foreign Service senior inspector and then as ambassador to Bulgaria, I was an interested (and dismayed) observer of what was going on. There were bound to be continuing conflicts of interest between the United States and the Soviet Union, and the United States needed vigorously to serve its interests. But clearly much of the increased tension was unnecessary and not in our interests. In particular, the alarmist exaggeration of a military threat was pernicious, not only in spurring an unnecessary arms race but in distorting public understanding and national policy.

Although I was not in a position to participate directly either in the intragovernmental maneuvering or the public debate over the military threat and necessary U.S. countermeasures, I did what I could on the margins. First of all, while in the inspection corps, I resumed writing for publication after nearly a decade. Between 1975 and 1978 I published four major articles on the SALT I negotiation and agreements. Without directly entering the public debate over intelligence assessments of the threat spurred by the Team B exercise, I did publish an article in *International Security* ("On Estimating and Imputing Intentions") that sought to place the problem in perspective and provide some guidelines to understanding the issues.

I demolished the shibboleths that forces and capabilities are "objective" and easily compared, that all that matters are "capabilities" rather than "intentions," and that one can infer and impute intentions from capabilities. I noted,

3. See Intelligence Community Experiment in Competitive Analysis, *Soviet Strategic Objectives, An Alternative View, Report of Team "B"* (Washington: CIA, December 1976), 55 pp. (top secret, declassified October 8, 1992). This quotation is from p. 22; other references throughout. For an excellent review in depth of the Team B episode, and the context of strategic alarms in the 1970s, see Anne Cahn, *Killing Détente: The Right Attacks the CIA* (Pennsylvania State University Press, 1998).

for example, that in discussing the U.S.-Soviet strategic nuclear balance, it was equally correct to state *each* of the following "facts": the Soviet Union has more missile megatonnage; the United States has more strategic megatonnage (including bomber as well as missile loadings); that the Soviet Union has greater missile throw-weight; that the United States has greater missile accuracy; that the Soviet Union has more submarine-launched ballistic missiles (SLBMs); that the United States keeps more SLBMs on station within range of their targets; that the Soviet Union has (some) SLBM missiles with the greatest range; that the United States has the SLBM force with the greatest range (on average its SLBMs have greater range); that the Soviet Union has more strategic delivery forces (then about 2,500 to the United States' 2,150); that the United States has more individually targetable warheads and bombs (then over 9,500 to the Soviet Union's 3,500); and so forth. To cite but one other illustration of the flexibility of "the facts," I noted that the Department of Defense had recently stated that from 1965 through 1975 the Soviet Union had built 205 "major combatant ships" to only 165 for the United States. That statement was correct in its own terms, but misleading; it did not make clear that the definition of "major combatant ships" had been stretched to include all ships of over 1,000 tons; even if one raised that low definitional threshold to only 3,000 tons, the United States led by 122 to 57 ships since 1960 (inasmuch as the Soviet Union, with a coastal defense requirement we did not have, had built 83 small ships of 1,000 to 3,000 tons while the U.S. had built only two). Similarly, it was noted that the Soviet navy, with 253 submarines in 1975, had "the largest submarine fleet in the world." True, but it also would have been correct to say that the Soviet submarine fleet in 1975 was only half as numerous as it had been in 1955. Of course the Soviet submarine fleet in 1975 was more capable than it had been twenty years earlier, even though smaller, but less capable than *our* smaller submarine force. Numerical comparisons of forces are less relevant than they seem, less "objective" facts, and more subject to deliberate distortion of their significance than is commonly appreciated.[4]

Many of the alarmist U.S. depictions of the Soviet threat in the 1970s and 1980s referred to it in terms of a "relentless buildup," "unprecedented," and "unparalleled." The Team B report, for example, said "the intensity and scope of the current Soviet military effort in peacetime is without parallel in twentieth century history," except perhaps in Nazi Germany.[5] The Committee on the Present Danger constantly preached the same message, with particular emphasis on the buildup of Soviet strategic missiles. The Soviet strategic buildup *was* substantial. Over the five years ending with the freeze of levels

---

4. Raymond L. Garthoff, "On Estimating and Imputing Intentions," *International Security*, vol. 2, no. 3 (Winter 1978), pp. 22–32, esp. p. 30.

5. *Report of Team "B,"* p. 46.

imposed by the SALT I Interim Agreement in 1972 the Soviet buildup in ICBM and SLBM missile launchers was 1,050. Yet it was not an unprecedented or unparalleled buildup. The U.S. buildup of ICBM and SLBM launchers in the preceding five years, 1963 through 1967, was 1,060. Similarly, the Soviet buildup of MIRV warheads by the late 1970s at its peak was about 1,000 a year—but it was not enough to affect the U.S. buildup in MIRVs, which had begun five years earlier. Thus by 1980 the United States enjoyed a quantitative superiority in strategic bombs and warheads of 9,200 to 6,000. Indeed, despite its "relentless buildup," the Soviet Union *never* equaled the United States in strategic warheads. The closest it came was by September 1990 when the START I Treaty was signed, just a year before the collapse of the Soviet Union. By then, the official totals (using START I Treaty counting rules that under-counted strategic bomber loadings favoring the United States) were 10,563 for the United States to 10,271 for the Soviet Union. Actual figures by 1990–91 were about 12,700 for the United States to about 10,700 for the Soviet Union. So much for the "unparalleled" Soviet buildup of the 1960s, 1970s, and 1980s.[6]

Questions of intentions are of course even more difficult to estimate and more liable to deliberate or unintended subjective distortion and error than are evaluations of forces and capabilities. The main Team B report had focused on Soviet objectives and intentions and had presented an unjustified ominous picture. Team B gratuitously and without foundation asserted that the Soviet arms buildup "certainly exceeds any requirement for mutual deterrence," which implicitly raised the question of why then the United States, with such a deterrence objective, should have built up even larger strategic forces. Team B sought to make a case for a uniquely dangerous Soviet pursuit of world domination and readiness to countenance the use of its growing military power. It asserted, in a demonstrably untrue statement, that "there is no evidence either in their theoretical writings or in their actions that Soviet leaders have embraced the U.S. doctrine of mutual assured destruction or any of its corollaries. Neither nuclear stability, nor strategic sufficiency, nor 'parity' play any noticeable role in Soviet military thinking." Moreover, it asserted that "while hoping to crush the 'capitalist' realm by other than military means, the Soviet Union is nevertheless preparing for a Third World War as if it were unavoidable." Military power, it was alleged, was seen by Moscow as "an instrument by means of which, in the decisive moment in the struggle for world hegemony, the retaliatory power of the United States can be preventively neutralized, or, if necessary, actively broken." Finally, in the judgment of Team B, in a conclusion set in italics for emphasis,

---

6. See Raymond L. Garthoff, *Perspectives on the Strategic Balance* (Brookings, 1983), p. 8, for the figures above, excepting those for 1990–91, which are given in *Arms Control Today,* December 1994, p. 29, and November 1995, p. 30.

Within the ten year period of the National Estimate the Soviets may well expect to achieve a degree of military superiority which would permit a dramatically more aggressive pursuit of their hegemonic objectives, including direct military challenges to Western vital interests, in the belief that such superior military force can pressure the West to acquiesce or, if not, can be used to win a military contest at any level.[7]

There was room for debate as to Soviet objectives and predictive estimates in 1976, but it was evident at the time, and all the more so with benefit of hindsight, that National Intelligence Estimates were not the place to argue for hard-line, or any other, policy. As it was, the NIEs in this period and later generally erred on the side of overstating the military threat.

Team B was so bold as to suggest a crucial military confrontation with the Soviet Union within the ten-year span of the estimate. Yet ten years later we saw not a Soviet Union threatening or launching global nuclear war for world domination, confident of its superiority, but an ever weakening Soviet Union with a radically revisionist leadership under Mikhail Gorbachev urging radical disarmament and launching a mix of concessionary negotiations and unilateral measures to decisively turn down the arms race and end the Cold War.

Again, it is clear in retrospect that what had been needed in 1976 was not a hard-line Team B, but a more imaginative and far-seeing "Team C." It was not beyond even contemporary understanding at that time that the Soviet Union had accepted the fact of inescapable mutual deterrence, and was experiencing the economic burdens of the arms race, and for both reasons saw value in arms control restraints to turn down the arms competition.

The Soviet Union, and the United States, were pursuing the strategic arms competition at levels far beyond the real needs of mutual deterrence. Both powers were too cautious to accept more than fringe arms control limitations. And the political climate in the United States in the mid- to late 1970s would not sustain more. As the fruits of détente seemed sparse or sour in both countries, cooperative measures were given less and less leeway, rather than more.

I had, of course, no direct part in the Team B exercise. Some time before, however, in November 1975, my services as a consultant on Soviet strategic objectives had been requested by CIA and approved by the State Department. Accordingly, I was involved both before and after the Team B episode in advising CIA. (Incidentally, the nominal "Team A" was not a team at all; it was the normal interagency intelligence estimating committee and included such hawks as the representatives of Air Force Intelligence under Major General George Keegan.) In June 1977 CIA wrote to thank me for "the thoughtful and informative discussion you had with us about estimating Soviet intentions,"

7. *Report of Team "B,"* pp. 14, 46–47.

which provided in particular a "useful corrective" against the idea that overestimates were merely hedging on the side of prudence.

Professor Pipes published an article in *Commentary* in July 1977 titled "Why the Soviet Union Believes It Could Fight and Win a Nuclear War," a preposterous idea that he had introduced into the Team B assessment. I could not openly enter into a debate with Pipes on the matter, but I had already been working on a study of Soviet military thinking on nuclear war. With no reference to Pipes's article (or, of course, the top secret Team B report), I cleared with the State Department and published in the summer 1978 issue of *International Security* an article titled "Mutual Deterrence and Strategic Arms Limitation in Soviet Policy," using previously classified Soviet military writings as well as other sources to demonstrate that Soviet political and military thinking did *not* support Pipes's (or the Team B) contention of Soviet belief that it could win a nuclear war.[8] "Team A" had chosen to ignore, rather than argue, the contentions of Pipes and his collaborators that the leaders of the Soviet Union were intent on gaining a war-winning capability and did not accept mutual deterrence, strategic parity, or strategic stability. I took Pipes on, citing in refutation precisely the kind of confidential Soviet military sources that he had claimed supported his contentions. My article was well received in academic security studies circles, and in its original and later revised versions was reprinted in several books on Soviet strategic thought, but it had little impact on the general public.

Curiously, Pipes chose to prepare a polemical attack on my article four years later, after I had retired and as he was completing a two-year tour on the NSC staff of the Reagan administration. It was so polemical that *International Security* declined to print it. The editor of the conservative journal *Strategic Review*, to which Pipes had then submitted his article, contacted me and said he would publish Pipes's article only if I agreed to his reprinting my original article (abridged somewhat) and to writing a rebuttal. I was delighted, and the resulting package of my article, Pipes's critique, and my rebuttal was published under the supertitle "A Garthoff-Pipes Debate on Soviet Strategic Doctrine" in the fall of 1982. (In contrast to an unexpected sharp oral exchange at a Council on Foreign Relations study group in 1981, at which Pipes had caught me off-balance and I did not do well, I am confident that I "prevailed" in this written debate, as even a number of hard-liners have reluctantly conceded.)[9]

Returning to 1977, as the general debate on the nature of the Soviet threat and consequently the role of arms control and détente was under way, the

8. Raymond L. Garthoff, "Mutual Deterrence and Strategic Arms Limitation in Soviet Policy," *International Security,* vol. 3, no. 1 (Summer 1978), pp. 112–47.

9. "A Garthoff-Pipes Debate on Soviet Strategic Doctrine," *Strategic Review,* vol. 10, no. 4 (Fall 1982), pp. 36–63.

Carter administration came into office, and my tour in the inspection corps was drawing to an end. My first preference was return to strategic arms control, perhaps as the chief SALT negotiator, or in some other responsible role. Les Gelb, the new director of the Bureau of Politico-Military Affairs at State, suggested that I serve as the State Department representative on the SALT delegation, picking up where I had left off four years earlier. But all such possibilities faded as Paul Warnke was subjected to a grueling fight before being confirmed (with less than the two-thirds Senate majority that an arms treaty would require). It was no longer thought wise to consider me for any position in the arms control field, especially one that would require Senate confirmation.

Before going to Ottawa in February 1977 for an inspection, I did urge colleagues in the State Department to stick to completing the modest SALT agreement based on the Vladivostok accord of 1975 and not to try for something more ambitious. But while my thinking was in line with the working level in State, the matter was not addressed until later at the level of senior policymakers. There the decision was to try for a much more far-reaching agreement, and even the fallback envisaged was not in line with what the Soviet side had been led to expect. The March 1977 Vance mission to Moscow on SALT failed, and negotiations were put back a year.

Zbigniew Brzezinski, the new national security adviser, whom I had known for many years, suggested that while I was awaiting a suitable position I might want to join him on the NSC staff to help run a major reevaluation of the strategic relationship. This study, set in train in February 1977 under Presidential Review Memorandum 10 (PRM-10), eventually led in August to a Presidential Decision (PD-18) on strategic policy. Although keenly interested in the subject, I was dubious that I would be able to influence the outcome and quite wary of any temporary assignment that would permit the personnel chiefs in the department to conclude that I was "taken care of" and could be omitted from early decisions. So I declined that offer.

As I have earlier noted, in April 1977 I was offered the position of ambassador to Bulgaria and was delighted to accept. I had also been sounded out on another position that might have interested me, had I not been offered the Bulgarian post. The position of national intelligence officer for the Soviet Union at CIA was coming open as my colleague from ONE days, John Whitman, was retiring. A return to intelligence assessment would have completed a circle in my government service, but I was more interested in the diplomatic assignment.

I had few opportunities while serving in Sofia to become engaged in either official or unofficial analysis of the U.S.-Soviet strategic relationship. I did participate in two Defense Department war games, one in Germany in 1978 and one in Washington while there on consultation in the summer of 1979. I also to some extent kept in touch with friends in Washington more directly involved. On the whole, however, as I have described in the preceding chapter, I was absorbed in the world as seen from Sofia. That included an awareness that U.S.-Soviet relations were sliding downhill, despite the Vienna Summit meeting of President Jimmy Carter with Soviet leader Leonid Brezhnev and SALT II Treaty signing in June 1979, in what proved to be a last gasp of détente.[10]

While I was still in Sofia in the spring of 1979, I received a letter from John Steinbruner, the head of the Foreign Policy Studies program at the Brookings Institution in Washington, inquiring whether I might be interested and available to join them at some time, either on a leave of absence from the State Department or otherwise. I had just recently reached fifty years of age which, together with over twenty years of U.S. government service, made me eligible for early retirement. And I soon learned that the department wanted to shift a number of Foreign Service chiefs of mission after two-year tours, including me, so I had a natural juncture for choice ahead.

Brookings was the premier think tank, not only in seniority but in stature and quality, and I was interested. When I returned to Washington for consultations and home leave in June, I met with John Steinbruner and Bruce MacLaury, the president of Brookings. Brookings's interest in my undertaking research on American-Soviet relations and security policies coincided perfectly with what I wanted to do, and I agreed to go to Brookings, perhaps at the start of the next year, as a senior fellow in Foreign Policy Studies.

I did not, however, inform the Department of my intention to retire until somewhat later. Several positions were suggested for possible new assignment, including vice president of the National Defense University (better known for its central institution, the National War College), a post traditionally held by a senior Foreign Service officer; and of course with my past career in political-military affairs it would have been a natural, and a pleasant assignment. Only later did I learn that George Vest had also advanced my candidacy for the post of ambassador to Vienna, but that position was given to an experienced political appointee (my friend Phil Kaiser, recycling after spending the past two years while I was in Sofia as our ambassador to Budapest). I did not seek out a new assignment and proceeded to prepare to retire at the end of the year.

Just as I was retiring at the end of December 1979, the Soviet Union mounted its military intervention in Afghanistan. President Carter reacted to that event and the ominous threat it seemed to many to represent by dismantling the whole weakened edifice of the détente of the 1970s. So my departure from government service and turn from participation to reflection and study of the Cold War coincided with a major turning point in the Cold War itself, a shift from détente to renewed confrontation.

---

10. For a fuller treatment of the decline and fall of détente in the latter half of the 1970s, see Garthoff, *Détente and Confrontation*, chapters 11 through 29.

18

Witness to the Cold War Endgame: 1980-90

My retirement from government service at the end of 1979 did not mean retiring from the arena of the Cold War. Although my direct participation in governmental policymaking and policy implementation in general came to an end, I remained very active in the broader activities of the academic and political establishment concerned with East-West relations and the Cold War. Formally I served as a consultant to the Department of State for two years, 1980 and 1981, although not actively, but I did continue thereafter to serve informally and on an ad hoc basis as a consultant to the State Department and CIA.[1] Now, however, after thirty years of service within the American national security system, I was in a new position with a quite different role and relationship to official policy. As a private citizen and scholar I sought to contribute to policy debate through my research and published studies, direct contributions to the media, congressional contacts and testimony, participation in public organizations, direct contacts with Russians visiting the United States and especially on my own frequent visits to the Soviet Union, and in many other ways.

The Brookings Institution is one of the oldest and most respected private research institutes dedicated to enhancing public understanding of foreign

1. My formal security clearances for access to classified information lapsed after the expiration of my formal consultancy with State at the end of 1981, but from time to time I was granted clearance to participate in classified discussions or to consult on particular matters, in particular by CIA. I also was no longer required to obtain clearance for public statements or publications, except on intelligence matters and in cases where my previous access to classified information might have raised a question.

policy and other issues of public policy. In contrast to the RAND Corporation, when I was there in the 1950s, and most other post-war think tanks, Brookings does not conduct security classified research, or in general contract research for the government. Relying on its own endowment and foundation grants, it seeks to stimulate and elevate public understanding of issues through independent scholarship. It proved a most congenial and attractive place to work and provided support for independent thinking on a nonpartisan basis. I remained at Brookings as a senior fellow in Foreign Policy Studies throughout the final phases of the Cold War (indeed, until 1994, and even thereafter as a senior fellow retired). But before discussing my activities relating to the Cold War while I was based at Brookings, it may be useful to set the stage by recalling briefly the course of events in those years.

As earlier noted, the weakened edifice of U.S.-Soviet détente had collapsed in the wake of the armed Soviet intervention in Afghanistan in December 1979 and the American reaction. President Jimmy Carter promptly launched a punitive political counteroffensive against the Soviet Union. The Soviet intervention was unwarranted and deserved the condemnation it got from the Carter administration, sparked by Carter's own reaction and with Zbigniew Brzezinski in the lead. At the same time, the administration misconstrued the causes of the Soviet action, proclaiming the "Carter Doctrine" and throwing a mantle of protection over the Middle East, supposedly threatened by a Soviet drive beyond Afghanistan. It is now clearly established by materials in the Soviet archives that the decision to intervene was reluctant and the commitment limited to bracing local communist rule in Afghanistan, already beset by civil war, in fear of American intervention and advance to Soviet borders. (The motive of the post-Soviet Yeltsin administration in Russia in releasing the archival documents was to castigate the Soviet leaders of 1979 for their action, but the record also clearly shows how mistaken was the official American characterization of the Soviet perception and intention.)[2]

I note the sharp turn in American-Soviet relations at the beginning of 1980 because it not only marked the virtual shelving of the relationship for the remaining year of the Carter administration, but given the strong anti-Soviet posture of the succeeding Reagan administration marked postponement of any attempt to restore relations for the following four years as well. Only in the second Reagan administration, and especially after the advent of a remarkably different Soviet leader, Mikhail Gorbachev, was it possible to advance to a renewed détente by the late 1980s and beyond to an end of the Cold War by the close of the decade.

2. For a full examination, see Raymond L. Garthoff, *Détente and Confrontation: American-Soviet Relations From Nixon to Reagan,* rev. ed. (Brookings 1994), pp. 977–1046; and on the American reaction, see pp. 1046–75.

Recently retired and newly ensconced at Brookings, in early 1980 at the request of the U.S. Information Agency (USIA) I wrote a commentary that supported the U.S. position indicting the Soviet intervention in Afghanistan but challenged the argument that it was part of a major offensive thrust. I also argued for not throwing détente overboard; that a rise in tensions, even one prompted by a Soviet move that we condemned, did not "eclipse the value of a continued effort to reduce tensions; on the contrary, while it may make the task of détente more difficult, it also makes it more necessary." "Should not," I argued, "actions which contravene détente be vigorously rebuffed, rather than jettisoning détente itself?" I also argued that "while Soviet motivations for the military occupation of Afghanistan and direct interference in its political processes do not justify those actions or mitigate the offense, they may be relevant both to the appropriate response and to the question of whether détente can have a future." Finally, noting the much more restrained response of most of our allies and irritation in Washington, I argued that we should "make every effort to concert our actions to the extent possible," not only to maintain alliance solidarity and to make sanctions more effective, but also because "consultation may help to identify the best courses of action," and because "common interests can usually be best served by a common stand." I concluded my analysis with the following:

> 'Détente' as a general relaxation of tensions is manifestly at odds with the heightened tensions which have been generated by this engagement of Soviet military power. Nonetheless, the pursuit of enhanced security through diplomacy and negotiation, seeking to control and limit arms competition and the spread of tension, clearly remains a real need. If we were not adversaries, we would not need détente.
>
> The dilemma—and challenge—of statesmanship, and of public understanding and support, is to combine firm and strong Western resolve to deter or to counter any recurrence of Soviet resort to force with a recognition that if détente as a banishment of tensions was a misconception, and détente as a general relaxation of tensions at this time no longer prevails, détente as a containment and constraint on tensions is more necessary than ever. While success in sustaining détente in this sense remains to be achieved, to abandon the effort would serve the interests of no one and could jeopardize the interests of all.

In retrospect, this evaluation would be given more credit than it was at the time. But it didn't fit the mood in the United States in 1980. Somewhat to my surprise, USIA did circulate my essay to its posts abroad, and it was given wide dissemination; a number of my European friends applauded its message. The essay was included in a widely used text on Soviet foreign policy.[3] USIA did not, however, ask me to write any more commentaries.

I was queried, and occasionally cited in articles, by reporters and appeared on several television programs with the same message. All this marked quite a new departure for me, as throughout my career i had avoided public comment on issues of current policy.

Another unaccustomed public role was testimony in congressional hearings. The first came only a few weeks after I began to work at Brookings, a hearing on Soviet strategic forces held by Representative Les Aspin's Subcommittee on Oversight of the Permanent Select Committee on Intelligence of the House of Representatives in February 1980. Richard Pipes also testified at that hearing, and despite our very different evaluations of Soviet strategy, we were not far apart in believing intelligence estimators should give greater attention to the more difficult "soft" intelligence on Soviet military thinking rather than rely so heavily on what could be learned from technical intelligence collection on military "hardware," weaponry, and forces.

Six months later I testified before the Subcommittee on Asian Affairs of the House Committee on Foreign Affairs on the implications for U.S. policy of the Soviet perspective on Sino-American relations. Former ambassador to Moscow Malcolm Toon also testified. Although we had not always seen eye to eye on relations with the Soviet Union, we both advanced the same caution: that the United States should develop its relationship with China on its own merits, and not on a common anti-Soviet platform, because to do so would prejudice our future relations with China if and when our strained relationship with the Soviet Union, or China's, were to change. On these and subsequent occasions (altogether I testified at some eleven congressional hearings during the 1980s) I was called as an expert based on my past experience. On most later occasions I testified on arms control issues.

I also began intermittent correspondence and occasional meetings with several members of Congress throughout the 1980s, always on their initiative, including Senators Albert Gore Jr. and Edward Kennedy, and Representative Aspin, mainly on arms control matters.

Most extensive was participation in a large number of academic conferences in Washington, at universities, and abroad. I participated actively in many study groups convened by the Council on Foreign Relations, the Atlantic Council, and other such forums of the unofficial establishment. The themes of most of these conferences and seminars were U.S.-Soviet relations, Soviet policy, and East-West arms control issues, including strategic arms reductions, intermediate-range missile deployment and later arms talks,

3. As a chapter titled "Afghanistan and Détente," it appeared in *The Conduct of Soviet Foreign Policy,* edited by Erik P. Hoffman and Frederic J. Fleron Jr., 2nd ed. (Aldine, 1980).

antiballistic missile (ABM) and space (anti-satellite) arms control. I also fairly frequently gave guest lectures or seminars on such subjects at universities, as well as at official institutions such as the National Defense University (and its National War College) and the Senior Seminar and occasional conferences sponsored by the Foreign Service Institute of the Department of State. Among international conferences in which I participated were several annual conferences of the International Institute for Strategic Studies (IISS), Pugwash conferences of international scientists, and international congresses on Soviet and East European studies.

I participated in a few organizations such as the Arms Control Association and the American Committee on East-West Accord (later renamed to focus on American-Soviet relations). And I occasionally spoke to groups such as the Women's Leadership Conference and the Women's National Democratic Club in Washington. I even participated in a panel of the annual meeting of the American Psychiatric Association in 1985 (on American-Soviet relations). The most high-profile meeting was one on U.S.-Soviet relations at the Carter Center in Atlanta, cosponsored by former presidents Jimmy Carter and Gerald Ford in the spring of 1985.

Brookings welcomed such outside activities, to which I contributed and from which I gained contacts as well as some broader understanding. My central function as a senior fellow in Foreign Policy Studies, however, as well as my principal interest, was in my research. I had proposed, and John Steinbruner and Bruce MacLaury had approved, my undertaking a comprehensive research study of U.S.-Soviet relations in the preceding decade of the 1970s, marked by the rise of détente and then its decline and fall in the Nixon, Ford, and Carter administrations. In a little over five years, *Détente and Confrontation: American-Soviet Relations from Nixon to Reagan,* a 1,147-page book, was published in 1985.

My main focus, then, in my research at Brookings for the first half of the 1980s was on all aspects of U.S.-Soviet relations in the period from 1969 through 1980, including rivalries and involvements around the world and political, military (including arms control), economic, propaganda, and intelligence interactions. It also of course included the domestic roots and facets of policymaking in Washington and Moscow and the relations of the two powers with their allies and client states.

The basic methodology was simply a careful and thorough collection and analysis of all the available facts relating to the many aspects of the subject. This included efforts to expand the database beyond the written record of publicly available facts. It was obviously too soon after the events to be able to draw upon the large record of security-classified documentation in the two governments, with a few exceptions. Nonetheless, I had two considerable advantages: First, I had, although without then having in mind a project of research and writing about it, lived through and been intensely interested in the subject throughout that decade within the U.S. government. I was thoroughly informed of the full record on some aspects of the subject, and aware of a great deal on most others. Second, I also knew many of the principal actors and the supporting personnel in both countries. Accordingly, I had a substantial advantage in interpreting the public record and in interviewing knowledgeable sources previously, or still, in government service. To a certain extent, this was true with respect to the Soviet side as well as to our own. In addition, most of the principal American participants (including Nixon, Kissinger, Ford, Carter, Brzezinski, and Vance) had written memoirs of the period that were very useful sources and helpful in digging into matters beyond their direct disclosures.

In addition to my research and study of the 1970s, throughout the 1980s I was also engaged in constant "contemporaneous research," collecting materials and pondering what was occurring during that decade as well. This work served as the basis for my follow-on major project, a sequel volume to *Détente and Confrontation* dealing in depth with the years 1981 through 1991, titled *The Great Transition: American-Soviet Relations and the End of the Cold War* and published in 1994. Although I no longer had the advantage of having worked on the subject directly within the government, I sought to compensate by continuing close contact with those who were, as part of my research. I also prepared and published, in 1994, a revised and updated edition of *Détente and Confrontation.*

The advent of the Reagan administration in 1981 brought many changes in Washington and greatly affected American-Soviet relations, even though the Carter administration in 1980 had abandoned détente. Ronald Reagan himself, I am convinced, and some of his entourage, really believed that the United States had fallen behind the Soviet Union in military power, and in political activism and initiative. Many members of the Committee on the Present Danger, about fifty of whom were named to senior positions in the new administration, believed their own propaganda that the United States had become "number two" in military power, although others knew this to be an exaggeration. Reagan believed a boldly confrontational stance was needed to mobilize America (and the "Free World") to make greater efforts not only to stop but to roll back the juggernaut of Communism in the world. Much of this new advocacy of strength was rhetorical posturing, but not without significance. The sustained major military buildup in the first Reagan administration, however, was much more than rhetoric, if less in capability than the tremendous cost incurred, doubling the national debt and turning the United States from being the world's largest creditor into the world's greatest debtor nation.

I need not recall here the avalanche of rhetoric about the "evil empire," in the early 1980s, much of it by Reagan himself. But this campaign had, among other things, an adverse effect on internal government assessments and policy. The most notorious example of poor policy based on a "fight fire with fire" dictum were the illegal activities revealed in the Iran-Contra scandal in 1986. I had become aware in 1981 of an indicative early example.

Secretary of State Alexander Haig launched a campaign against alleged Soviet support of "international terrorism," beginning in his Senate confirmation hearings. I knew that he had been advised by the director of the State Department's Bureau of Intelligence and Research that intelligence reporting did not support his contention, and he agreed to request a formal national intelligence estimate (NIE) by the whole intelligence community. Both Haig and William Casey, the gung-ho new director of central intelligence, were viscerally sure that the Soviets must be backing international terrorism, and both cited the recent book by Claire Sterling, *The Terror Network.* They were then advised that CIA had supplied concocted misinformation to Sterling for public propaganda and that the book was not only unreliable but "tainted." Casey nonetheless rejected a draft NIE that declared, on the basis of intelligence information, that the Soviets "do *not* encourage the use of terror by their third world clients." Finally, after a bruising battle and several drafts, an NIE was issued that fudged the issue and said the Soviets were "engaged in support of revolutionary violence worldwide," and that in turn national liberation movements and insurgencies that the Soviet Union "directly or indirectly" supported, but did not control, often "carried out terrorist activities as part of their larger programs." It was disheartening in the intelligence community, and to those of us aware of the story, to see intelligence estimating, which is supposed to inform and support policy formulation with the best possible objective forecasts, bent to serve policy and propaganda purposes.[4]

One avenue of approach to my study of U.S.-Soviet relations in the early 1980s was to establish or reestablish contacts with Soviet officials knowledgeable of their country's perspective and actions in the relationship. One resource was my own acquaintance with most Soviet diplomats involved in relations with the United States in the 1960s and 1970s, to the extent that I could contact them and that they would feel free to discuss the subject. A second, and the most appropriate and useful for my research contacts, was the Institute for USA and Canada of the Academy of Sciences of the USSR, headed by Academician Georgy Arbatov.

As earlier noted, I had met Arbatov shortly before in Bulgaria, but I had known his deputy Vitaly Zhurkin and several other members of the institute staff for several years from IISS meetings. Aware of my retirement and move to Brookings, Arbatov soon sent a formal invitation to visit the USA Institute,

---

4. See Garthoff, *The Great Transition: American-Soviet Relations and the End of the Cold War* (Brookings, 1994), chapter 1, especially pp. 23–25 on the NIE.

offering also to help arrange meetings with others in Moscow (and to arrange travel in the Soviet Union). Such invitations to American scholars and sometimes former public figures were a standard part of the institute program. Many U.S. officials were leery of Arbatov and his institute as purveyors of "the Soviet line," which of course they were. Visits of qualified American specialists on the Soviet Union, however, also offered an opportunity to convey the American perspective. To be sure, American academic and other visitors were not disciplined or instructed to carry an official "American line," but the variance in American viewpoints helped to create a more healthy awareness by Soviet "Americanists" of pluralism in American life, and in the long run a more accurate picture of America in Moscow was in *our* interest. Moreover, while Arbatov (who had ties to the KGB) and his institute served Soviet propaganda interests, through their publications as well as contacts, they also gave increasingly realistic internal assessments of U.S. policy to the Soviet leadership as a result of their own growing sophistication. It was by no means a one-way street, and I believe on balance it was in the interests of better understanding and relations between the two countries. These contacts also contributed indirectly to the "new thinking" that later brought the Soviet leadership under Gorbachev to hasten the end of the Cold War.

On my first visit to Moscow in September–October 1980, in addition to meeting many Soviet scholars at the USA Institute and the Institute for the World Economy and International Relations (IMEMO), I had good conversations with several senior officials at the Ministry of Foreign Affairs, including Gromyko's senior deputy, Georgy Kornienko, whom I knew from his service in Washington in the 1960s, Viktor Komplektov, whom I had also known in Washington and at SALT, and Oleg Grinevsky from SALT. Our ambassador, Thomas J. Watson Jr., arranged a luncheon in honor of my visit where I met a number of Soviet officials and scholars. (I appreciated Tom Watson's gracious hospitality; at the same time, I knew that in those years our embassy welcomed the opportunity afforded by visitors to invite appropriate Soviet officials and others whom they did not otherwise have a good reason to see.) Arbatov also arranged for me to meet with Vadim Zagladin, the first deputy chief of the influential International Department of the Central Committee of the Communist Party. I found my exchanges with Kornienko and Zagladin especially useful, and those meetings became the first in a series of recurring encounters with them both on later trips throughout the 1980s and early 1990s.

My son Alex, engaged in graduate studies at the University of Pennsylvania, accompanied me. We also were given quick trips to Leningrad, and to Tashkent and Samarkand. For me it was interesting to revisit those places, and for Alex it was all new. We met Arbatov's son Alexei, who was about the same age as my Alex, and worked at IMEMO. Later, in the 1990s, he became an important member of the Russian Duma and its Defense Committee.

One unexpected and somewhat unwelcome sidelight of my 1980 visit to Moscow was the reappearance of my long-time KGB acquaintance, Boris Sedov. While Sedov never made any direct recruitment approach, in 1980 and 1983 (on my second visit) he seemed to be testing whether I would go beyond discussion of current events (which I was quite ready to do with him as with any Soviet official). The furthest that Sedov went was to suggest that I write a paper on current thinking about U.S.-Soviet relations, allegedly for the Soviet press agency, for which I would be paid by one of his colleagues in the embassy in Washington. I was quite prepared to write articles for the Soviet press (as indeed I did some years later) and even to be reimbursed in a normal way, but I was not prepared to write anything for an under-the-table payment from the KGB. (I also knew that it was a KGB technique to start someone writing innocent papers and then escalate into raising more sensitive subjects.)

After returning to Washington I reported the fact that Sedov had contacted me in Moscow to the Office of Security at the Department of State (where I was still a cleared consultant), but on their decision I transferred future contact on such meetings to the FBI. The FBI dutifully took note, but there was never anything out of order. My FBI contacts occasionally found of some use keeping in touch on some of my meetings with diplomats from the Soviet embassy, which I regularly reported to them. I also discussed findings from my Moscow conversations with friends and former colleagues in the Department of State and at CIA.

The visit had been useful, primarily to establish many new contacts with Soviet scholars and to resume contact on an unofficial basis with some Soviet diplomats and officials with whom I was already acquainted. Their mood on Soviet-American relations was somber. Virtually all officials and scholars, not surprisingly, supported the official Soviet line that the severe deterioration in relations was the fault of the United States, although some evidently did so without enthusiasm or conviction, and a few privately and guardedly acknowledged Soviet mistakes (in particular in intervening in Afghanistan). I learned little new information, but the visit helped establish a foundation in contacts that in the years ahead became more fruitful.

There was little movement in U.S. relations with the Soviet Union in the first three years of the Reagan administration, and most of that was adverse. Arms control was for all practical purposes in abeyance even before Reagan formally disavowed the SALT II Treaty in 1986, and especially after he announced in 1983 a new initiative to develop and deploy a space-based antiballistic missile (ABM) system, popularly dubbed "Star Wars," threatening the ABM Treaty.

The most prominent development in those years was the unfolding of the program to deploy U.S. intermediate-range ballistic and cruise missiles as part of NATO's theater nuclear forces (TNF) in Europe. I wrote a few op-ed newspaper articles and journal articles on both the Soviet decision to deploy SS-20 intermediate-range missiles and the NATO TNF decision and testified before two congressional committees. I was concerned about an unnecessary spiral in the arms competition, but what troubled me even more than the drift of arms control onto new shoals was the absence of any strategy for managing U.S.-Soviet relations.

The Soviet Union also exhibited no constructive strategy for managing relations, but instead mounted a major propaganda campaign in Western Europe to try to prevent the NATO TNF deployment, an attempt that predictably failed. The Soviet Union then cut off the desultory strategic arms reduction talks (START) as well as parallel intermediate-range nuclear forces (INF) talks, in the fall of 1983.

That junction was the low point in U.S.-Soviet relations. Notwithstanding that fact, indeed partly owing to it, I chose that time again to visit Moscow, in September–October 1983. I went under the auspices of Arbatov's Institute of USA studies, and in addition to talks in Moscow I traveled to Volgograd (formerly Stalingrad), Armenia, and Georgia, accompanied by Sergei Rogov, slated to be assigned to the Soviet embassy in Washington as the representative of the institute (a decade later he succeeded Arbatov as director of the institute).

In Tbilisi, I was invited to address a large conclave of the Georgian Academy of Sciences on the current state of Soviet-American relations. I spoke in Russian (apologizing for being unable to do so in Georgian) and was frankly critical of many positions taken by both the Soviet and the American governments. There were many questions, especially on the then recent KAL-007 incident. The whole occasion, which was a rarity if not unique, went very well. Later, a Russian professor with close ties to friends in Georgia told me that my lecture had been the "talk of the town" in Tbilisi for some time.

I again met with many of the same scholars and officials as I had in 1980, as well as new ones, including Colonel General Nikolai Chervov, chief of the General Staff directorate responsible for arms control. Despite the negative climate, he engaged in a long, serious detailed discussion. I met again with the senior deputy minister of foreign affairs, Georgy Kornienko, and Vadim Zagladin of the International Department, who had played a major role in the failed Soviet attempt to stop the NATO TNF deployment.

While I was in Moscow, Soviet leader Yury Andropov issued a famous declaration on September 28 saying, "If anyone had any illusions about the possibility of an evolution for the better in the policy of the present American administration, recent events have dispelled them once and for all."[5] Principal

---

5. "Statement by the General Secretary of the CC of the CPSU, Chairman of the Presidium of the Supreme Soviet of the USSR Yu. V. Andropov," Pravda, September 29, 1983. For a more full account of the heightened tensions in relations in 1983, see Garthoff, The Great Transition, pp. 85–141.

among the recent events to which he referred were the American reaction to the Soviet shootdown of South Korean airliner KAL-007 that had inexplicably strayed deeply into Soviet territorial airspace, and the initiation of deployment of American intermediate-range missiles in Europe. But earlier that year there had also been President Reagan's characterization of the Soviet Union as an "evil empire," and indeed "the focus of all evil," and his call for a "crusade" against the Soviet Union, soon followed by a further pitch to extend the major military buildup already under way and to develop space defenses, "Star Wars." The American invasion of Grenada followed the KAL incident.

In a talk with a deputy editor of *Pravda*, Sergei Vishnevsky, he candidly informed me that the Party set a "quota" on the frequency of favorable references to the United States to be published in the paper, and that the quota had dropped from between 60 and 80 percent during the heyday of détente in the 1970s to zero. Whether literally true or not, that did reflect the general change. I found my contacts in the Foreign Ministry, Central Committee, and academic institutes very discouraged, and some alarmed, at the course of events.

In chance meetings with ordinary Russian citizens I encountered real concern. Most striking was the mood in Kvareli, in rural Georgia, where the local Party chief told me how, for example, he had just been approached by a woman in tears fearing her son would be called to war. After my return I wrote an article for the *Washington Post* on this unusual official-level and public alarm.[6]

The fall of 1983 was not only a low point in U.S.-Soviet relations, but also a high point in tensions. Later we were to learn that a NATO military command exercise in early November 1983 was the climax to this growing tension, provoking a high intelligence alert in Moscow over the possible U.S. initiation of nuclear war. When the United States learned of this (through a British spy in the KGB, Colonel Oleg Gordievsky), it contributed to a new more restrained and moderate policy line launched by President Reagan in a speech on January 16, 1984.[7]

Meanwhile, after I returned to Washington in October 1983 I again briefed my friends in CIA and the State Department. Now, in addition, the Office of Domestic Contacts in CIA established a more systematic relationship to debrief me on matters of interest to the various elements of the intelligence community. That office, with several changes of name, was (and is) responsible for obtaining information of foreign intelligence value acquired by cooperating American citizens traveling abroad. I continued over the years following to meet with representatives of that office after each of my more or less annual trips to the Soviet Union and on other occasions when I had access

6. See Garthoff, "Now Get Ready for the Real Crisis," *Washington Post*, November 6, 1983; *International Herald Tribune*, November 7–8, 1983.

7. See Garthoff, *The Great Transition*, pp. 139–42.

to information of intelligence interest. Knowing the interests of the intelligence community, and with contacts at senior levels in the Soviet government and Party, I was able to provide a good deal of useful information. I also continued to meet informally with CIA analytic offices to discuss various aspects of Soviet internal and foreign policy.

In Moscow in 1983 I also had unusual success in obtaining Soviet military publications. I acquired, and brought back, over 100 issues of the confidential General Staff journal *Military Thought* (*Voyennaya mysl'*), dating from the early 1960s through the mid-1970s. More than half of these were not previously available in the United States. It was quite a coup. Although the material was somewhat dated, it was still of considerable interest to analysts of Soviet military affairs. To note but one example, we learned for the first time about Soviet thinking as early as 1970 on possible limited use of nuclear weapons in response to limited NATO initial use, seeking to avert escalation to all-out nuclear war, contrary to the public Soviet position.

Most of my time, despite all of the many conferences and other activities, was of course devoted to extensive research on the many aspects of U.S.-Soviet relations. After completion of my book *Détente and Confrontation,* the nature of changes under way in the Soviet Union and later in U.S.-Soviet relations as well led to more frequent visits to the Soviet Union in the latter half of the 1980s, and to a more active role in Washington as well.

I had become aware in 1984–85 both from subtle changes in some Soviet writings, and even more from contacts with some Soviet academic visitors, of the development of "new thinking" eroding the stereotypes and ritual rhetoric of Marxism-Leninism. I was amazed when several younger Soviet academics visiting the United States in June 1985 had eagerly advanced many new, and even radical, themes, particularly because two of them were sons of prominent orthodox Party figures. Several senior academic figures in 1984–85, even before Gorbachev's selection as the Party leader, had written somewhat more cautiously about what they already called the "new thinking." This truly new thinking then began to appear in statements of Mikhail Gorbachev and a few other leaders.

The turning point, for me, was Gorbachev's address to the Twenty Sixth Congress of the Communist Party of the Soviet Union at the end of February 1986, which made elements of new thinking the accepted Party line. Gorbachev's speech, and even more the revised Party program on which work had been under way for several years under his predecessors, still contained positive references to Marxism-Leninism (although rejecting "ossified prescriptions" in its name), and sharp criticisms of "imperialism," but what was significant was not that there remained remnants of old ideological thinking, but that there were also bold, even startling, new pronouncements. Most important was an abandonment of the central Marxist-Leninist-Stalinist tenet that underlay the Cold War: the idea that two worlds or systems, capitalism and socialism (communism), were historically destined to remain in conflict until the eventual triumph of the latter. This ineluctable struggle of two worlds imparted the zero-sum nature to their relationship: gains for one could only be at the expense of the other. Even the post-Stalin recognition of the necessity in the nuclear age for peaceful coexistence and avoidance of war, of greater importance than was recognized in the West at the time, was regarded as modifying but not displacing the imperative to wage the basic class struggle in the international arena through all other means. But now Gorbachev was saying something entirely different: he spoke not about two contending camps but about an "interdependent, and in many ways integral, world that is taking shape." One world, not two. Moreover, he went beyond a recognition of global interdependence to call for "creation of a comprehensive system of international security"-military, economic, political, humanitarian, and ecological. Moreover, Gorbachev argued that no country could any longer find security in military power, either in defense or deterrence. Rather, security could only be found through political means and on the basis of mutual security among states.[8]

These were remarkable ideas to be advanced by a Soviet leader, and not surprisingly they were not welcomed by many of the other Soviet leaders who did not share Gorbachev's enlightened new thinking. But they provided the foundation on which rested not merely further policy pronouncements, but actual policy and concrete actions taken over the next five years. I visited Moscow for two weeks shortly after the congress, and now my Soviet friends and contacts opened up and further elaborated the new thinking.

Soon after my return to the States, I attended a conference of many leading Soviet affairs specialists and was surprised to find that very few of my colleagues had paid much attention to the address, and none seemed to me adequately aware of the dramatic change. (This led me to consider writing an article on "Gorbachev's Secret Speech," laying out all the startling new statements as if they had been spoken in a secret address and only at the conclusion identifying them as excerpts from his publicly available report to the Party Congress. It was a good idea, but regrettably I didn't follow through and do it.)

My earlier discussions with some of the now emerging "new thinkers," and especially in the wake of the Party Congress, certainly helped me to recognize the significance of this step along a path that only gradually and belatedly became clear to everyone. Meanwhile, I continued my now developing dialogue with a number of academic scholars and officials. Again, I had long discussions with Georgy Kornienko and others at the Foreign Ministry

---

8. See ibid., pp. 253–65, for further discussion and the source references to questions above.

(including Deputy Minister Vladimir Petrovsky, one of the "new thinkers"), Vadim Zagladin at the Central Committee (whose son Nikita, incidentally, was one of the young "new thinkers" I had met in the pre-Gorbachev period), and General Nikolai Chervov at the Ministry of Defense. I found a growing pragmatism, including awareness that some hostile (and from their standpoint incorrect) Western perceptions were grounded in Soviet actions, in particular in the Third World—a step forward. Some had even begun to see the United States and the Soviet Union as rivals, but with some important common interests, rather than as the leaders of two irreconcilable ideological camps. Others, while accepting a new conception of security, continued at least for form or cover to give it an ideological justification (for example, finding signs that Lenin had seen or foreseen growing international interdependence and the need for peaceful coexistence). Significant change was clearly under way.

While I was in Moscow, on March 13, 1986, two American warships in the Black Sea (to which periodic visits were made to show the flag) broke with past behavior patterns and deliberately entered Soviet territorial waters within six miles of the coast of the Crimea, ignoring Soviet warnings and signals to withdraw. The purpose was to assert a new (and dubious) interpretation of the right of innocent passage. It was clear from my conversations that senior Soviet officials (including General Chervov, who briefed me in detail) regarded the action as a provocative slap in the face (all the more so as, it so happens, Gorbachev was resting at a dacha for Soviet leaders in the vicinity— something presumably not known by the U.S. Navy when it planned the excursion). I was of course quite uninformed but argued that, if deliberate, it might have been a tactical decision; I was sure it was not a sign of a harder political line. (Today, having since learned that in the early 1980s the U.S. Navy deliberately sent attack aircraft toward Soviet territory from silent fleet incursions close off shore in order to "spoof" Soviet coastal air defenses, I am less sure.) Pentagon officials readily confirmed to news reporters that one purpose of the penetration of Soviet territorial waters had been to exercise innocent passage, and that the other purpose was to collect intelligence (which, incidentally, is inconsistent with "innocent passage" under international law). They also said that the U.S. Navy would within a few days carry out "similar" excursions in the Gulf of Sidra off Libya. On March 24 a U.S. naval movement into the Gulf of Sidra (the lead ship was the U.S.S. *Caron,* a special intelligence-collection destroyer, freshly arrived from the Black Sea where it had been one of the two Crimean intruders) led to a clash with Libyan patrol vessels and retaliatory U.S. air strikes on Libya. Soviet suspicions of the provocative nature of the Crimean incursion were hardly allayed.

The major part of my discussions in Moscow was of course directed to the key question of whether there were possibilities for an improvement in U.S.-

Soviet relations, a question Soviet officials and scholars all saw as most properly directed at Washington. They were ready. There was particular interest in the prospects for meaningful arms control.

Vera had accompanied me this time. In Leningrad and Moscow we could see a few signs of Gorbachev's internal *perestroika* (literally "restructuring," although "reformation" is a better translation of what it constituted). For example, an art exhibition displayed imaginative paintings that were forbidden in the days of "socialist realism" in art, and a few young soldiers in uniform were self-consciously attending church services with their families. But the visible signs of budding openness were still limited.

Among the things that were changing but slowly was the pervasive presence of the security authorities. In my own case, soon after our arrival in Moscow I had received a telephone call, this time not from Boris Sedov but from one of his KGB colleagues, picking up the contact. It was getting a little tiring, but I did meet "Anatoly." He sought to be helpful, for example, in my rounds searching for hard-to-find books. We would then get into a competitive dance as he tried to pay for my book purchases before I could do so. But I began thinking about whether there was some more productive way to take advantage of this unwanted attention, and I came up with an idea. As I have mentioned, in 1983 I had been able to make a one-time windfall acquisition of a large back file of the confidential General Staff journal, *Military Thought*. Now, when Anatoly was pressing to be of some assistance, I put it to him: Could he help me get current and recent issues of that journal? Anatoly solemnly said he would see. And within a day or two he brought back a reply: he could not get me full original issues (each monthly issue had about eight articles and totaled around a hundred pages—and was stamped "Only for Generals, Admirals, and Officers of the Soviet Army and Navy"), but he would get me xerox copies of articles on subjects in which I was interested. He brought a few from a recent issue. I told him it was too difficult to define the subjects of my interest and I really needed to see at least the tables of contents for current issues, and for past years the comprehensive annual index in each December issue. Sure enough, he brought me tables of contents of the most recent issues and the annual index for 1985. I took extensive notes on the annual index (which was itself valuable) and marked the most interesting articles I wanted. Before I left I had a file of articles and had marked several recent annual indexes for the future. This rather unusual arrangement continued through meetings on my next three visits to Moscow in 1987, 1988, and 1989.

After my return to Washington, in addition to my now standard meeting with representatives of the CIA Office of Domestic Contacts to report on matters of intelligence interest, I also contacted directly the chief of the Soviet and East European Division of the Directorate of Operations. As I knew, the

Military Thought materials were of considerable interest to CIA and military analysts in the intelligence community, which lacked many issues of the journal, and so too was the prospect of continuing access. I made available the materials I had obtained and clarified priority interests for future acquisition. In exchange, in order that I could focus future acquisitions on materials of greater interest to the analysts and avoid duplicating issues already available, I was permitted to use and cite in my own writings issues of the journal already in CIA's possession. It was a mutually useful arrangement, although of course I had made clear that I would provide such materials as I obtained without a quid pro quo.

My next visit to Moscow, in February 1987, was under different auspices. Gorbachev decided to hold an international forum, "For a Nuclear-Free World, for the Survival of Humanity," which he personally addressed. It was an ambitious initiative in public diplomacy. It was distinguished from previous Soviet-sponsored peace propaganda extravaganzas such as international youth "festivals" in two important respects: first, while Gorbachev was indeed using the forum to propagandize internationally the new thinking on international affairs, he was also using it to advance the process in the Soviet Union, for the first time characterizing the developments under way in the Soviet Union as "essentially revolutionary changes . . . of immense significance" not only for Soviet society but for the world. Second, an effort was made to assemble not only inveterate optimists and peace seekers but people reflecting a wide spectrum of views, including skeptics and critics of *perestroika* and disarmament, and cultural as well as political intellectuals, in all about a thousand people. I received an invitation not from Arbatov (who did extend some of the invitations), but from Evgeny Primakov, then director of the Institute of the World Economy and International Relations (and a decade later the Russian prime minister). In his address to the forum, Gorbachev declared, among other things, that the Soviet Union was prepared to give up its status as a nuclear superpower and to rely on mutual international security—in line with his first major disarmament proposal in January 1986 seeking a nuclear-free world and with his near-agreement with Ronald Reagan on abolishing all nuclear weapons at their summit in Reykjavik in August 1986.

At the Kremlin reception for the forum after Gorbachev's address, as people mobbed Gorbachev, his close Politburo colleague Eduard Shevardnadze, and others, I noticed alone off on the sidelines, fittingly, two of the old-timers retired at the Party Congress the year before from candidate membership on the Politburo, Vasily Kuznetsov and Boris Ponomarev. So I went over and chatted with them. Kuznetsov in particular was showing his age. Ponomarev, for so many years head of the International Department of the Central Committee, was also clearly living in the past tense, so I decided to "visit" him there and asked a few questions about the dissolution of the Comintern in

1943. He brightened up and began to recount with animation how, when the former Comintern head Georgy Dimitrov left for Bulgaria in 1944, he and Dmitry Manuilsky had picked up the action with respect to the handling of ties with the other parties of the world communist movement in the newly constituted International Department.

Incidentally, I was struck by the incredibly weak security for Gorbachev and the other leaders, especially with 1,000 foreigners of various persuasions turned loose in the Kremlin.

While in Moscow for the forum, I had opportunity to continue my series of conversations with active officials as well, including several generals, and including again Kornienko, now however as senior deputy to Dobrynin in the International Department, and with Valentin Falin, making a political comeback and in a year or so to take over that department from Dobrynin.

I also, of course, had further opportunity to observe the course of Gorbachev's *perestroika*. The most striking example in February 1987 was the first public showing of a remarkable film called *Repentance* (*Pokayaniye*), filmed a few years earlier in Georgia with the quiet approval of Shevardnadze, then still the Georgian Party leader. But although he had permitted the film to be made, it could not yet be shown. Now released, it was showing at a Moscow theater, and the evening I attended with a young Georgian friend, the audience (including myself) was spellbound; when we left the theater, in vivid contrast to the usual noisy chatter of the departing crowd, there was an eerie silence as people were absorbed in their own thoughts provoked by the film. The plot was the odyssey over several generations of people caught up in a dictatorship that immediately brought to mind the worst of the Stalin terror (but with Georgian, Nazi, and Italian Fascist symbolism as well). It also had clear religious overtones. The film was artistically interesting, but the greatest impact was political and for a Soviet audience in a sense personal as well.

While Gorbachev's *perestroika* was beginning to make its mark in the Soviet Union and in pronouncements about world affairs, in Washington in the mid-1980s many aspects of American-Soviet relations were being considered still in familiar terms of variations on Cold War experience.

During 1985 and 1986, for example, I participated in a number of "crisis simulations," or politico-military games, along with a number of retired senior officials and generals, some sponsored by the Center for Strategic and International Studies (CSIS). As in the RAND and MIT political games in the 1950s, and in the real war game Desert Strike in 1964, I found it was still difficult to get even highly experienced military and political figures to focus on making decisions and strategies keyed to attaining political objectives. In 1987 I participated in two simulations of Soviet foreign-policy making at the State Department's Foreign Service Institute (FSI), playing the role of general secretary (with others in appropriate military and political positions in my

"Politburo"). Most experts were, however, still not ready to accept a Gorbachev/Garthoff Soviet foreign policy line as real. In 1986 I also participated in a large FSI conference on summitry, presenting an analysis of the role summit meetings play as one among many diplomatic instruments. In a smaller FSI symposium on negotiation, elaborating a number of characteristics of American negotiating style, I shocked some members of the symposium by observing that although the entire discussion was predicated on the assumption that negotiation was a means to reach agreements, as usually it should be, there were times when one or another party would engage in negotiation with no intention to reach agreement but for some other reason. This seemed to me to be elementary, so it was my turn to be shocked when I found this was a novel idea to some of the participants whom I had assumed knew better.

Among many other conferences, symposiums, and projects in which I participated in these years I should also mention two working groups sponsored by the Atlantic Council that met over the years 1985–87. One was on U.S. policy toward the Soviet Union, chaired by General Andrew J. Goodpaster, and finally published in mid-1988 as *U.S. Policy Toward the Soviet Union: A Long-Term Western Perspective, 1987–2000.* A companion study by a working group on strategic stability and arms control and looking to the future, co-chaired by General Brent Scowcroft and R. James Woolsey, titled *Defending Peace and Freedom: Toward Strategic Stability in the Year 2000,* was also issued in mid-1988. Both studies involved many discussion meetings and drafts, participation by many experienced people, and produced solid, thoughtful analyses. But both failed utterly to foresee even the possible consequences of what was already occurring in the Soviet Union. I even considered withdrawing from them, and finally wrote a dissent published with the second study:

> The Policy Paper is a balanced, middle-of-the-road assessment and prescription for strengthening stability through strengthening deterrence. It makes many sensible observations and recommendations. With minor changes, it could have been written any time in the past decade, and we would undoubtedly have been better off by far if American policy had been carried out on the basis it prescribes.
>
> My dissent stems from the fact that the framework for the study was focused on the year 2000, not 1965 or 1975 or 1985. I believe that it fails to recognize the pitfalls of resting on familiar deterrence doctrine, and the potentialities offered by significant change under way in the thinking of the new Soviet leadership. I would not state that a sharp improvement in American and Alliance security is assured by new thinking in Moscow, nor that we should entrust our security to hope that it can be. . . . Still, unless we start soon to make a major effort to determine the

extent to which the Soviet Union is prepared to work seriously toward shared security, we will never know the potential for enhancing our common security. That effort should be made, in arms control and in development of political relations, naturally with prudent safeguards in our position as we pursue the possibility.

The paper is a solid, conservative platform; regrettably, it does not raise our horizons to the potentialities for the year 2000.[9]

Even I was very conservative, in hindsight, and of course no one then foresaw that the Soviet Union would cease to exist within a few years. But this study was completed by late 1987 and published in July 1988 and it should have been much more open to the emerging realities and further possibilities of change.

The principal issue in American-Soviet relations in the mid-1980s was the American pursuit of ballistic missile defenses under Reagan's Strategic Defense Initiative (SDI), or "Star Wars." Raised in 1983, just as the issue of NATO TNF was being resolved with the deployment of American intermediate-range missiles in Europe, SDI became the central new element in the U.S. military buildup. Controversial in the United States and only reluctantly and minimally supported by U.S. allies, SDI nonetheless had captured President Reagan's imagination. To the Soviet leaders, SDI represented a major escalation of a growing American military-technological challenge that the Soviet Union would be very hard pressed to meet. To some of them it seemed to pose a threat of possible American military attack or at least hard political pressure. And it was seen as foreclosing, even more than the US. refusal to ratify SALT II and the tough U.S. position in the strategic arms negotiations (START) since 1981, the possibility of any continuing strategic arms control. The Soviets in vain argued, using the same arguments *we* had advanced in the late 1960s, that there was an inescapable link between strategic defense and strategic offense. The ABM Treaty of 1972 had not been able to stop the continuing competition in strategic offensive arms, but it had helped to keep it in check. Now SDI was predicated on abandoning the ABM Treaty and gave a major impulse to retaining and building up strategic offensive capabilities in order to preserve mutual deterrence. Moreover, while Soviet (and Western) scientists almost unanimously rejected the idea of the feasibility of a defensive shield capable of preventing all attacking nuclear missiles from arriving on target, Reagan's dream, military planners *did* see the possibility of strategic defenses believed capable of coping with a ragged retaliatory strike by missile survivors of a powerful surprise first strike by the other side. SDI was thus

9. See *Defending Peace and Freedom: Toward Strategic Stability in the Year 2000*, edited by Brent Scowcroft and R. James Woolsey (University Press of America, 1988), pp. 47–49.

seen as increasing strategic instability, as well as precluding strategic arms control and reductions in offensive arms.

Some Soviet leaders were more alarmed than others as to American intentions and as to the potential capabilities of SDI. Just as the U.S. program began to pick up momentum, the new Soviet leadership under Mikhail Gorbachev came to power and began to wrestle with its response. Gorbachev was determined to end the arms race and the confrontation of the Cold War, but SDI loomed as the biggest obstacle even to taking new steps along this path. After the summit meetings at Geneva in December 1985 and Reykjavik in August 1986, Gorbachev decided that Reagan was indeed committed to his Star Wars vision. Only dramatic new approaches and Soviet concessions could circumvent the obstacle of SDI. Hence the major Soviet concession leading to the INF Treaty in 1987 eliminating all intermediate- and lesser-range ballistic missiles (of which the Soviet Union had many more than did the United States).

In the final analysis, Gorbachev overrode more conservative elements in the leadership and proceeded not only with the INF Treaty but strategic and conventional arms reductions. But from 1985 to 1987 this was a difficult passage. One important element was the role of leading Soviet scientists in evaluating SDI and devising a response. In the past, the Soviet response would have been predictable: to emulate the United States with a "Soviet SDI" (they had been conducting research, of course, as had the United States), and to increase their offensive missile force as a hedge to ensure a surviving retaliatory capability.

Contrary to the hopes and expectations of some advocates of SDI, and the continuing impression of many Americans, however, SDI did not force the Soviet Union into major new defense expenditure and thus increase the heavy burden of defense spending on the strained Soviet economy. There were Soviet concerns that SDI might have that effect, but although studies of the Soviet response were undertaken, new military programs were not. Based on the findings of the Soviet scientists, the sensible decision was made to meet any SDI programs if and as a concrete military threat became real though appropriate, less costly, offsetting "asymmetrical" countermeasures. As a concrete military-technological challenge, SDI was never sufficiently defined to require, or even to permit, creating and procuring appropriate countermeasures. "Star Wars" as a priming element to increase the Soviet military burden never got off the ground, much less did it bleed them dry. Nor did it force Gorbachev to make political concessions in arms control or otherwise contribute significantly to ending the Cold War.

In these years, 1984–87, many of these same Soviet scientists (notably Evgeny Velikhov, Roald Sagdeyev, and Andrei Kokoshin) began to participate in semi-official and unofficial meetings with American counterparts under the auspices of such American organizations as the Federation of American Scientists and the National Academy of Sciences. I participated in many of these meetings and observed the interesting and important interaction of these Soviet scientists with Western scientists and arms control specialists.

The Reagan administration's efforts to push SDI among other things led to an ill-conceived attempt to free the program from the constraints of the ABM Treaty by a unilateral "reinterpretation" of the provisions of the treaty banning the development and testing of space-based ABM systems or components. By misreading the negotiating record and distorting the text, the administration argued for what it called a "broad interpretation" that would permit such development and testing if the systems were based on new physical principles. This self-serving interpretation was not thoroughly examined or agreed upon within the administration before it was prematurely surfaced by National Security Adviser Bud McFarlane in October 1985 in a television appearance. The controversy within the United States raged for the next two years and was not fully set at rest until the Clinton administration formally repudiated the so-called broad interpretation in 1994.

I had personally negotiated much of the relevant text of the ABM Treaty in 1971–72 and was able to refute the claims of those who devised the complaisant broad interpretation. The matter was hotly debated in the Senate, which resolved the matter in 1987 by a resolution reaffirming the traditional interpretation as the basis for the SDI development program. I testified in joint hearings held by the Committee on Foreign Relations and the Committee on the Judiciary of the U.S. Senate on March 11, 1987. I noted that the testimony before the Senate in 1972 in the ratification hearings on the ABM Treaty, as well as the negotiating record, unequivocally supported what was now termed the traditional interpretation, and not the new so-called broad interpretation. All members of the SALT negotiating team except one were agreed that the traditional interpretation was the correct one. The one exception was Ambassador Paul Nitze, who had previously held the same view as the rest of us but was persuaded by members of the administration in which he now served that there was sufficient uncertainty in the record on the Soviet view to justify the broad interpretation. Neither he nor any other administration spokesman explained why, if there were a question as to the Soviet interpretation, or as to the correct interpretation, the United States failed to raise the matter with the other treaty signatory before announcing unilaterally a new interpretation.

I joined with other ABM Treaty negotiators in several letters and articles supporting the treaty against SDI and in particular denouncing the contrived new "broad" interpretation. A number of us (including four former secretaries of defense) mounted a National Campaign to Save the ABM Treaty.

I wrote a short book, extensively drawing on the negotiating record, demonstrating the insubstantiality of the new interpretation. The book, *Policy versus the Law: The Reinterpretation of the ABM Treaty* was hard-hitting, but this was appropriate in view of the fact that the flagrant efforts to distort the historical record and undercut U.S. legal commitments were very serious.[10] As Bruce MacLaury, president of Brookings, wrote in his foreword to the book "the ABM Treaty reinterpretation poses profound questions as to the functioning of American political and governmental decisionmaking processes, and as to compliance with the law of the land and international obligations. It is clearly a matter that should receive the most careful scrutiny and public discussion." I had access to much of the negotiating record and cited a number of key documentary sources from the ABM negotiation that had been omitted from the official State Department analysis submitted by Judge Abraham Sofaer, the legal adviser of the department. Sofaer had Paul Nitze's endorsement for the reinterpretation but had failed to contact any of the other negotiators, or even to research the full negotiating record. It was a shabby performance on a matter of highest importance.

When my book appeared, Judge Sofaer remonstrated threateningly. Bruce MacLaury invited him to lunch, and we discussed the matter with him. Sofaer was unable to cite a single instance in which my thoroughly documented analysis rejecting his interpretation was in error. He did not again repeat his threats of court action.

I also wrote an article for the *Washington Post* in the spirit of investigative journalism, noting some of my findings on the reinterpretation process in 1985.[11] I had learned that the "anonymous government official" cited by the Heritage Foundation in the first public surfacing of such a reinterpretation (in April 1985, six months before McFarlane's unveiling of it as a new official interpretation) was Bretton C. Sciaroni, the counsel of the president's Intelligence Oversight Board. (Sciaroni's only earlier public identification had been in connection with the Iran-Contra scandal, as the author of the official—and faulty—ruling that the NSC staff was exempt from compliance with the Boland Amendment barring any U.S. government official involved with intelligence activities from participating in providing military assistance to the Nicaraguan contras.) I had checked my information with Bruce Weinrod, the director of research at Heritage, who declined to identify their anonymous source. Then I called Sciaroni himself—whom I had never met, but who confirmed to me that he had indeed been the author of the Heritage report. What followed was completely unexpected; a day or so after my disclosure in the *Washington Post*, Sciaroni was fired from his position with the Intelligence

10. See Garthoff, *Policy versus the Law: The Reinterpretation of the ABM Treaty* (Brookings, 1987).

11. See Garthoff, "The Making of the ABM Uproar: How Opponents Managed to Stir up a Tempest over a Treaty," *Washington Post*, September 20, 1987.

Oversight Board. I had not intended my disclosure to be punitive; I was simply disclosing the full record.

I returned to the Soviet Union in April–May 1988, again this time under the auspices of the USA Institute. I made the usual rounds of consultations with officials and scholars. There had, to be sure, been some changes; for example, as earlier noted, Dobrynin and Kornienko were now the head and senior deputy of the International Department of the Central Committee; and Arbatov's former chief deputy, Vitaly Zhurkin, was now head of a new Institute of Europe. One interesting change was that most academic international affairs specialists were now most interested and excited to discuss fast-moving internal developments in the Soviet Union.

Local television continued to show both propagandistic and well-made educational and artistic programs, but both now had to compete with American soap operas. On stage, in addition to seeing some contemporary Soviet plays, I saw a rendition of *Biloxi Blues*. In a quite new Moscow divertissement under *glasnost'* (openness), a contest was under way to select "Moscow Beauty, '88" (by 1990 there were a whole series of such contests, "Miss Moscow," "Miss USSR," even "Miss KGB"!).

I went to several of the new private "cooperative" restaurants, where service, ambience, and the food were all much superior to standard Soviet institutional restaurants. My favorite, *Aist* (the Stork), featured background music ranging from Alexander's Ragtime Band to Tina Turner, and excellent trout. Once when I was dining alone at the *Aist,* an attractive young woman asked if she could join me, a common phenomenon in often crowded Soviet restaurants. Our initially lively conversation tended to fade as our divergent interests became more clear; my main interest was professional, learning more about attitudes and thinking of young Soviet citizens. Her interest was professional too, but it was a quite different profession, so after a while she excused herself and went on to seek a restaurant patron more interested in collaborating on her specialty.

The most interesting occasion for seeing change under way was the May Day celebration. The traditional disciplined (and formerly heavily military) parade across Red Square was replaced with a much less regimented one that was more a participatory demonstration. All the expected slogans were there: Peace, Labor, even Solidarity of Workers of the World, and also *Perestroika, Glasnost', Demokratizatsiya,* and the like. Replacing long-standard denunciations of the West were not only calls for "New thinking in the nuclear age" and "Elimination of nuclear weapons," but also U.S. and Soviet flags together with "Nyet" to crossed missiles of the two countries, and "Da" to clasped hands of friendship and cooperation.

I had a pass giving me access to a privileged area of stands near the Lenin mausoleum, but of course of far lower station than the assembled leaders on high. To my surprise, among those near me was Boris Yeltsin, removed from the top leadership the previous fall.

For me, the highlight of that visit was a unique opportunity to see life really at the grass roots, hundreds of miles from Moscow, in the heart of Russia. With Arbatov's assistance, I arranged to go to Ulyanovsk (pre-Revolutionary Simbirsk) on the Volga and there to visit the locations of the ancestral estates of Vera's mother's family. In Ulyanovsk, I was met by local officials, had the inescapable briefings on the achievements of the Party and local government, and was interviewed by the local newspaper (which later published an article that bore little resemblance to what I had said). But they also provided the local museum curator and a vehicle and driver able to handle the very poor roads I had to traverse to reach one of the locations. I say locations because both estates had long ago been completely destroyed, although I could see the remnants of the foundation of one. The dying villages were not greatly different from what they had been at the time of the Revolution seventy years earlier, except for deterioration and the replacement of serviceable horses with a few mostly unserviceable trucks and tractors. I was received with curiosity and respect. I was not only the first visitor from America to come to these remote villages—it turned out I was the first visitor from *Moscow* for many years! The village heads each proffered the best hospitality they could muster, in their homes, showed off the pitiful local library (mostly dusty volumes of Lenin), and eagerly sought a few words of encouragement. It was very moving, and I rose to the situation as best I could, but what could I say? They had never heard of *perestroika,* and if one were to return today I wonder whether they would even be aware of the dissolution of the Soviet Union! (The Ulyanovsk region, incidentally, has been one of the least progressive and most communist-voting areas of Russia.) I had traveled widely in the Soviet Union over forty years, but never so deeply into the real backwaters that constitute the vast part of rural Russia. It was quite an experience.

Back in Moscow, in addition to my professional discussions and observation of the changes under way there, as earlier mentioned I continued to meet with Anatoly and to place new requests and receive articles from *Military Thought.* Now, in addition, I had independently found a new source through whom I could obtain these articles, increasing coverage.

In Washington, there continued to be a flow of Soviet visitors, mostly academics. In November 1988 there was an interesting "U.S. and USSR Emerging Leaders Summit," a panel of which met with me and some colleagues at Brookings. In general, the expansion of American-Soviet unofficial contacts, particularly among scholars, had been growing since the mid-1980s. A series of "Dartmouth conferences," in addition to earlier and continuing Pugwash meetings and disarmament talks, with unofficial but often well-connected Soviet and American academic figures, played a not inconsequential role, especially in stimulating the "new thinking" in the Soviet Union. Some of these meetings even dealt directly with problems of mutual perceptions.

Before describing my next visit, and conference, in Moscow in early 1989, I must recall the earlier beginnings of what was to become the most ambitious and extensive attempt to reconsider a major crisis of the Cold War on a joint U.S.-Soviet basis. The Cuban missile crisis of 1962, discussed in an earlier chapter, was the most intense and probably the most dangerous confrontation of the Cold War. As I noted, with the twenty-fifth anniversary in 1987, a series of international conferences on the crisis began. In all, a core series of five major conferences, and three others under other auspices, extended over some ten years. It happens that I am the only one to have attended *all* of them. The process of bringing together actual participants, from all the key countries, and historians from all three countries, and increasing archival documentation, has not only made the Cuban missile crisis the most thoroughly studied such event, but also has illustrated the continually revised historical picture as new information has become available, and the importance of bringing together participants, analysts, and historical documentation. Some of the key participants have since died, including Andrei Gromyko, only months after the 1989 Moscow conference, and Dean Rusk and McGeorge Bundy more recently.

Participation in the Moscow conference in early 1989 also gave me an opportunity to renew and expand contacts on other subjects. I again saw General Chervov, and through him Marshal Sergei Akhromeyev, for most interesting discussions. In addition, I met at the conference and saw later at his institute Colonel General Dmitry Volkogonov, then the director of the Institute of Military History.

This Moscow visit in early 1989 also marked the end of my KGB contact (and the flow of Soviet military writings through that channel). Boris Sedov reappeared along with Anatoly, obviously reassessing the whole contact. Although I assume Sedov had been aware of the arrangement to give me articles from *Military Thought*, he seemed surprised perhaps at the scale of the transfer when Anatoly brought me what I had previously requested. Although I submitted another request list, I heard nothing more about it. Indeed, that meeting in early February 1989 marked the last contact of any kind with Sedov and Anatoly. On each of my visits beginning in 1980 I had been contacted soon after my arrival, about which they were evidently informed by KGB monitoring of visa issuances. From my next visit in mid-1990 on, there were no further contacts. What had surprised me was that they bothered to waste their time and hospitality on six visits from 1980 to 1989, and still more that from 1986 to 1989 I had been milking them for hundreds of confidential Soviet military articles, and without their even asking for anything in return. So termination of the contact was less surprising than its earlier continuation.

The mood in Moscow had deteriorated in the year from early 1988 to early 1989. My driver was sharply negative on the Soviet leadership as a whole, and all the leaders individually—except Boris Yeltsin; he even suggested the rest should all be lined up against a wall and shot. While that was more extreme than most comments, there were many remarks showing popular fatigue with infighting in the leadership and the failure of *perestroika* to lead to greater prosperity. True, there was an election campaign atmosphere for the first time, and some looked forward to real elections to the new legislature, but others were apathetic. The optimism that had begun in 1985 and 1986 and flowered in 1987 and 1988 was now on the wane.

In addition to the potentially revolutionary changes in the Soviet Union itself (and, although not yet evident, in Russia and other successor states beyond), the most important change was of course in the overall transformation of the relationship to the United States and to the world. As I have noted, I understood rather early, by March 1986, that radical change in the Soviet Union and potentially leading toward the end of the Cold War was under way. Central among the elements in this change was the security relationship, including military and arms components. Although these were not the driving elements, they were the most visible. Arms control, as we have discussed, was dependent on mutual decisions and agreements, and was initially stymied by the U.S. stand on SDI, until Gorbachev found a way around that obstacle. Radical change in arms control, and radical change in military doctrine and strategy, also required "new thinking" and acceptance of these bold changes by the Soviet military leadership.

One of the first steps was in correcting the record on the recent past. For seven years, from 1977 to 1983, Defense spokesmen for the Carter and Reagan administrations had been sounding an alarm about a "relentless Soviet military buildup" and a resultant "military spending gap" as evidenced by a Soviet annual rate of increase in military spending of some 4 or 5 percent, far more than the United States and NATO. Secretary of Defense Caspar Weinberger in 1982 and 1983 even replaced the customary comparisons of the strategic *forces* of the two sides with graphs depicting overall military *spending* outlays. This "supply-side" defense analysis emphasizing expenditure inputs, rather than capabilities outputs, was questionable in any case, but it only highlighted a more basic error. All these comparisons, apart from their significance, rested on intelligence *estimates* of Soviet military spending. And, to the discomfort of the Reagan administration, by the fall of 1983 the intelligence community—DIA as well as CIA—had to report that based on new information and reanalysis it now turned out that ever since 1976, just when CIA had boosted its estimates to a 4–5 percent annual increase in growth, in fact it had been only 2 percent—*less* than the United States and NATO, and weapons procurement had even leveled off. To be sure, Soviet military expenditure and procurement remained high. But it now had become clear that the "relentless

Soviet buildup" to an important extent reflected U.S. error in estimating Soviet outlays, rather than being what Secretary of Defense Harold Brown had termed "a disquieting index of both Soviet capabilities and Soviet intentions." Brown had been widely quoted, especially by hard-line defense advocates, for the quip that "when we build [our military capabilities], the Russians build; when we stop, the Russians build." That aphorism, however, incorrectly implied there had been a time when the United States had stopped. The experience of the mythical "spending gap" suggested a more apt aphorism: "When the Russians build up, we say they build up; when they don't build up, we still say they build up."

The reluctant acknowledgment that there was no spending gap was not used to modify the U.S. buildup—the next U.S. defense budget called for a 13 percent real increase, while the Soviet increase was still 2 percent. The only change was that comparisons were no longer made to the Soviet rate of military spending. Moreover, the striking news was slipped into routine testimony and not highlighted, so that initially it received no public notice at all. I alerted Steve Rosenfeld of the *Washington Post*, who promptly wrote a column that first drew the change to public attention. I followed with an article of my own for a somewhat different readership in the *Bulletin of the Atomic Scientists*.[12]

During all this period, and continuing, while the intelligence community and three successive administrations had overstated the growth of Soviet military expenditure, the military burden on the Soviet economy was being underestimated (at 15 to 16 percent of gross national product) because the size and productivity of the overall Soviet economy was considerably overestimated.

Deflating the spending gap only helped to clear the decks a little. The main questions concerned changes under way in the Soviet political leadership's thinking about military power and in Soviet military policy, doctrine, and strategy. Here, too, there was need for some important revisions of what had been understood about Soviet military doctrine in the pre-Gorbachev period, as well as the changes being made. So I began to collect and review new material from all sources, including some newly declassified Soviet materials in the United States, and my new growing files of *Military Thought*, and to begin work on a book on the changes under way in Soviet military thinking. One of the newly available sources was the "Voroshilov papers," nearly verbatim notes on the 1974–75 course of the Voroshilov General Staff Academy in Moscow taken by an Afghan colonel admitted to the secret-level courses, which he had spirited out of the country. These were eventually published in 1989–90 in

12. See Central Intelligence Agency, Office of Soviet Analysis, *USSR: Economic Trends and Policy Developments*, Joint Economic Committee Briefing Paper, September 14, 1983, pp. 8–11, 18, presented to a subcommittee of the Joint Economic Committee of Congress, September 20, 1983. See Garthoff, "The Spending Gap," in *Bulletin of the Atomic Scientists*, vol. 40, no. 5 (May 1984), pp. 5–6; and Stephen Rosenfeld, "Knockdown of a Soviet Buildup," *Washington Post*, November 18, 1983.

two volumes by the National Defense University, together with interpretive introductions that I had been asked to write for them.[13]

At a conference of experts on Soviet military affairs sponsored by the Center for Strategic and International Studies in 1987, I presented a paper on "new thinking" in Soviet military doctrine, based on all available sources, including some key articles from recent issues of *Military Thought,* and this paper was later published.[14] (Some of my colleagues, at the conference and after the article was published, grumbled over what they assumed was favored treatment by CIA in giving me access to these articles; they could not, of course, realize that in fact it was I who had provided the articles to CIA—or still less that they had been given to me by the KGB!)

There was great resistance in some quarters, particularly in the military agencies and above all in the Defense Department's top echelons, to the idea that the Gorbachev leadership—that *any* Soviet leadership—*could* remove the pursuit of military power (in their view, the pursuit of military superiority) from a central place and priority in overall Soviet policy. In July 1988 I participated in a "workshop" at the National Defense University, not a simulation or game but a discussion titled "Thinking Red in Wargaming." Unfortunately, most of the military participants were still thinking "dark Red," leading to a spirited exchange with a Defense Intelligence Agency (DIA) expert on the Soviet military. I argued that Gorbachev was pressing ahead with important changes in military doctrine and policy and predicted a major unilateral reduction of forward-deployed Soviet forces in Europe. This prediction was angrily rejected by my DIA colleague, and when I argued that my sources in Moscow said that withdrawal of a tank army from East Germany was under consideration, he was scornful. Five months later, Gorbachev announced an overall reduction of 500,000 men, including the unilateral withdrawal and disbandment of six tank divisions in Eastern Europe, including four (a tank army) from East Germany. DIA was obviously so mired in "old thinking" that it couldn't even see new evidence (surely the intelligence community had better sources, and in any case I had promptly passed my information along to the intelligence community after my visit in April–May 1988).

I brought my renewed research and study of the changes in Soviet military doctrine to a conclusion with the publication in mid-1990 of *Deterrence and the Revolution in Soviet Military Doctrine.*[15] As the title indicates, I devoted particular attention to analysis of Soviet (and by comparison American)

13. *The Voroshilov Lectures, Materials from the Soviet General Staff Academy,* vols. 1 and 2 (National Defense University, 1989 and 1990); introductions by Raymond L. Garthoff.

14. Garthoff, "New Thinking in Soviet Military Doctrine," *Washington Quarterly,* vol. 11, no. 3 (Summer 1988), pp. 131–58.

15. Garthoff, *Deterrence and the Revolution in Soviet Military Doctrine* (Brookings, 1990).

thinking about deterrence, and on the prevention and ending of any war that should occur, as well as on doctrine for waging war. Although I focused on the changes in Soviet thinking and doctrine from 1986 to 1990, I also reexamined the main developments of the preceding decades, all now further informed by access to a full file of *Military Thought.*

In mid-1989 the Soviet authorities removed the restrictions on circulation of *Military Thought,* previously having banned even any reference to the name of the journal from open publication. From January 1990 it was available for open subscription. In 1989–90 I had encouraged an enterprising graduate student at Columbia, Kent Lee, whose interest in Soviet military affairs had brought us together and who had asked my advice on directly approaching the editors of the journal. He did so successfully, and later obtained not only declassification and release of the entire back file of *Military Thought,* but also of a number of other formerly classified Soviet military publications, including publications of the General Staff Academy.

On my visit to Moscow in the summer of 1990, I myself met with Major General Aleksei N. Bazhenov, the chief editor of *Military Thought,* and urged his support for Lee's initiative. In the spring of 1991, Bazhenov visited the United States for the first time, and I hosted a dinner seminar for him at Brookings with a dozen or so Russian-speaking specialists on Soviet military affairs. (The group included several from CIA, whom I so introduced—with their permission, albeit over the objections of one of my colleagues who believed it would embarrass and constrain General Bazhenov, a needless worry rapidly dispelled; he liked the attention of the Washington experts.) General Bazhenov had earlier invited me to contribute to his now open journal, and my article on deterrence (presented as "views of an American expert on problems of contemporary security") was published in the August 1991 issue of *Military Thought*—the first article by an American ever to appear in the journal. (This was, incidentally, only the most striking of about half a dozen of my articles published in several Soviet journals in the late 1980s and early 1990s, notably *International Affairs,* in most if not all cases the first by an American author.)

My summer 1990 visit to Moscow, under auspices of the U.S. Department of Defense, was primarily to attend a conference of American, British, and Soviet specialists on the subject of "the emerging strategic future," although the main discussion concerned military reform in the Soviet Union—a subject recognized as overdue on the agenda, but on which little concretely had been done (and on which too little has been done at the time of this writing over a decade later). Among the Soviets attending were some of the new radical military reformers, some older conservatives, a number in the middle just trying to feel their way. It was a sign of the changing times that foreigners should be welcomed to discuss such controversial security issues.

Although the conference was interesting, I found my most useful and productive meetings were alone with individual Soviet military men, including some at the General Staff Academy. I held some such meetings that summer, some on another visit to Moscow a few months later, and others later as some Soviet military men visited the West. Some were well-known Soviet military theoreticians, such as Major General Valentin Larionov, a retired professor of the General Staff Academy, and General of the Army Makhmut Gareyev, long head of the Military Science Directorate of the General Staff and later deputy chief of the General Staff. Colonel General Georgy Mikhailov, a retired air defense and later military intelligence officer, had personally participated in debriefing Francis Gary Powers when his U-2 was shot down on May Day 1960.

As the old political ideology was rapidly being transformed, and military doctrine as well, in the latter 1980s Soviet military men who thought about policy, doctrine, and strategy (in every country always a small minority) had a particularly difficult time in adjusting their thinking. Some, such as Major General Vladimir Slipchenko, chief of military-scientific research at the General Staff Academy, tried to weigh the great changes under way in the military-technological revolution in terms of the evolving political changes. He saw a future generation of advanced nuclear and space weapons as decisive, and in our discussions in July 1990 he proposed joint consideration of what he saw as destabilizing factors in the military-strategic picture possibly leading even to a *combined* Soviet-Western military doctrine. Others, including Major General Ignaty Danilenko, chief of the department of military "politology" (until late 1989 called the department on Marxism-Leninism and war) at the General Staff Academy, saw as the great challenge the need to reinforce stability in a destabilizing world. He saw the key problem as re-ensuring the non-use of military force to meet new challenges such as changing world demographic situations (which he posed in neo-Malthusian terms). A few months later, in November, I had another long talk with him in which he expanded on his concerns about military policy—but he was still seeking some overall theory (in place of Marxism-Leninism); as he put it, he wanted to devise a military-political framework like the periodic table of chemical elements. But this was not a question of mere abstractions. Danilenko believed the United States, with the Soviet Union in support, would need to meet future crises like the one then unfolding in the Gulf over the Iraqi seizure of Kuwait. General Danilenko had completely discarded Marxism-Leninism. He saw the Cold War as a result of Stalin's world revolutionary and power ambitions, and the American possession of the atomic bomb, and a resulting "logic of confrontation" between the two rivals. He recognized egregious Soviet errors in the Cold War. He also believed that American military intellectuals had been responsible for many errors—and then were unhappy with the consequences.

Thus while some Soviet military strategists and theoreticians, unleashed for new thinking, continued to project fears of a World War III space war, more of them worried increasingly about the implications of their own dissolving empire in 1989–91, and thereafter in their retraction to seventeenth-century Russian borders. Increasingly, military concerns were refocused on regional replays of World War I and the Great Game of the nineteenth century.

The *ideological* geopolitics of the Cold War thus dissolved into a new *realist* paradigm of geopolitical rivalry. Some hoped for an American-Russian partnership, but many saw the United States as the main rival—and some even as the main obstacle to Russian achievement of its legitimate national aims. One of General Danilenko's prescient concerns expressed to me in November 1990 was that the United States would continue to seek stability primarily through NATO, rather than a broader European framework that would embrace the Soviet Union (Russia) as well. He also opined that our two countries would be doomed if we remained locked in confrontation while the rest of the world developed.

I was not involved in policymaking in Washington even peripherally in these years. I did, however, continue to be consulted and engaged to some extent on assessing Soviet affairs, as in my inclusion in the Department of Defense visit to Moscow in July 1990 for informal talks with the Soviet military.

From time to time I would be invited to special seminars or conferences by CIA. Some of these were unclassified forums for discussions between agency analysts and academic specialists on the Soviet Union. Occasionally, I would be given a one-time clearance in order to attend a classified CIA conference for consultation. On one occasion, I was given a top secret briefing based on materials on military strategic thinking provided by a highly placed source on the Soviet General Staff. (So, too, was Richard Pipes, so that there was no basis for claiming that only adherents of one view of Soviet strategy were being favored; predictably, we interpreted the materials quite differently.) I did not know at the time, nor did the CIA analysts, that the source of those materials was by then suspect of having been "turned" by Soviet counterintelligence. He was in fact one of the sources compromised by CIA officer Aldrich Ames, who had become a KGB mole. When this situation later became publicly known, CIA was heavily criticized for having disseminated material without warning recipients of the possibly tainted source. The Soviet and East European Division chief in the Operations Directorate who was responsible for that decision was certain that the General Staff materials in question were genuine, and from what I was shown I believe that to have been a correct evaluation. A doubled agent is often given valid information to supply in order to build his credibility. Nonetheless, the likelihood that the agent was being controlled and the possibility that the material might be adulterated should certainly have been flagged when the material was disseminated.

My visit to Moscow in November 1990 was really the first "post–Cold War" visit, even though the Soviet Union was still alive. While I was in Moscow, the Paris summit meeting adopted a "Charter for Europe," and the members of NATO and the Warsaw Pact (the latter soon to dissolve) declared they were "no longer adversaries" and solemnly proclaimed "the end of the era of division and confrontation" that had been the Cold War. This consolidated the effect of the year since the dismantling of the Berlin Wall, the end of communist rule in Eastern Europe, and then the reunification of Germany.

The occasion for this visit was a U.S.-Soviet joint conference on the Eisenhower era sponsored by the Institute of USA, so it also served (as had the one in January 1989 on the Cuban missile crisis) to look back at one part of the Cold War history we had shared. My paper prepared for the conference was later expanded and published as a monograph titled *Assessing the Adversary: Estimates by the Eisenhower Administration of Soviet Intentions and Capabilities.*[16] In it I drew upon declassified National Intelligence Estimates and other documents, supplemented by my recollections. My earlier affiliation with CIA was publicly unveiled for the first time in the Soviet Union in the Moscow discussions. At a dinner given by our host, Georgy Arbatov, as a number of toasts were made to Eisenhower, Khrushchev, and others, I decided to expand the scope of post–Cold War openness by proposing a toast to Allen Dulles. Some of my colleagues, American historians in Moscow for the first time, obviously from the horrified looks on their faces thought I had gone too far. But as I continued with the toast it was evident that it carried an appropriate message for joint post–Cold War history. I recalled how Khrushchev, when he visited Washington in 1959, had been introduced by President Eisenhower to a number of assembled cabinet members and other leading members of the administration, including Allen Dulles. Khrushchev, after a moment's pause, had remarked: "I know who you are. You pay a lot of people to spy on us, and we pay them to spy on you. We ought to get together and only pay them once." Dulles had amicably agreed. Intelligence, I suggested, if not always successfully, had played a valuable role in the Cold War in helping to assess the opponent more or less realistically. Now, we historians could benefit from joint efforts, and with access to the archives in both countries, in assessing both sides in the Cold War more realistically than before.

Arbatov, in conversations with me later, alluded (albeit guardedly) to this subject in saying that although he had to meet certain requirements, he had succeeded in keeping his institute independent. He did not refer to the fact that he had just recently dismissed one of his deputies who we knew had been a senior KGB officer, Radomir Bogdanov (who, by the way, I had found an

16. Garthoff, *Assessing the Adversary: Estimates by the Eisenhower Administration of Soviet Intentions and Capabilities* (Brookings, 1991).

interesting discussant in our conversations at the institute). Similarly, neither of us ever referred to the fact that at least three members of his institute staff had been uncovered as agents recruited by American intelligence.

In this connection, I should note that one of the members of the Institute of USA whom I had met and found interesting and astute in our discussions in 1983 and 1986, Sergei Federenko, was later disclosed to have been a source for U.S. intelligence since the mid-1970s. Federenko was the adopted son of a high-ranking Ministry of Foreign Affairs official, Ambassador Nikolai Federenko, who had served as Soviet representative to the United Nations in New York in the mid-1970s, and Sergei was there at the same time as a junior officer on the UN disarmament staff. The curious aspect of the story is that Sergei Federenko's CIA case officer in New York was Aldrich Ames. Moreover, the two of them developed a genuine friendship. By the time Ames began to spill all he knew to Soviet intelligence in the mid-1980s, Sergei was back in Moscow at the USA Institute. Ames, notwithstanding his friendship with Sergei Federenko, did accurately inform the KGB that he had served as a "source," although not a recruited and controlled "agent," for CIA since the mid-1970s. Sergei had, wisely, made as a condition of his collaboration with U.S. intelligence that he would only do so while abroad, not in Moscow. The KGB of course put him under surveillance, but there was no clandestine activity to discover, and as the son of a senior official they required more than just the word of their agent Ames to arrest him (and Ames had said he was a source, not an agent). Federenko was not permitted to travel abroad, and was kept under watch, but was not arrested. Only under *perestroika*, in 1989–90, was he again permitted to travel, and after the collapse of the Soviet Union in 1992 he decided to stay in the United States and was given asylum. Yet even after Ames's arrest, and the discovery of his disclosures about Sergei, Federenko has continued to regard him as a friend. Some American counterintelligence specialists continue to be suspicious of the fact that Federenko was never arrested, although others accept Federenko's explanation. The whole relationship is, under any interpretation, one of the most curious of the small mysteries of the Cold War espionage game.

Although the Cold War had ended, the revolutionary changes in the Soviet Union were still very much under way. It was fascinating in 1990 in the evenings to see hours of replay of the day's Supreme Soviet political debates on Russian television. The tired slogan used by the Bolsheviks in 1917, "All Power to the Soviets [Councils]," was now again displayed, with an entirely new significance from what it had meant in the intervening seventy years during which the Supreme Soviet (and all soviets) was a toothless tool of the Communist Party. While I was there, the Supreme Soviet of the *Russian* Republic (followed by almost all the others) refused to accept a law of the USSR Supreme Soviet (on price increases)—and prevailed.

Again, I observed the seventy-third—and last official—anniversary of the Bolshevik Revolution on November 7. Gorbachev and other Soviet leaders were there (including Yeltsin, but he departed to lead a separate "people's parade"). Gorbachev spoke for a civil society and a law-governed state, democracy, and the market. But it was a strange kind of celebration, by some of the October Revolution, by others of its virtual demise. Even the TV commentator referring to the occasion remarked, "Some see it as a triumph, others as a tragedy." There were separate small demonstrations by various splinter groups; I saw about forty "Young Monarchists of Russia" marching in tattered pre-revolutionary uniforms. The Democratic Union carried the pre-revolutionary Russian tricolor, "the white, blue, and red" (as the Russians denominate it). One former worker, a thirty-eight-year-old Leningrad man, at the edge of Red Square fired an automatic rifle, apparently aiming at the leadership tribunal. (I observed the commotion but did not at the time realize what had happened.)

There were signs of the new freedom from the constraints of the old Soviet authoritarian regime. People were freely buying and selling almost anything. All the former taboos were gone, as evident in the availability of books and journals featuring such disparate new subjects as religion, sex, capitalist management, and pre-revolutionary Russia (including photographs of the imperial family and even of officers of the White Army). Soon bookstores that previously had displayed *Fundamentals of Marxism-Leninism* (if few were sold) were showing (and rapidly selling) *Fundamentals of Marketing*. Western fashion and cosmetics stores opened.

Change was unmistakably under way, but whether it was under control, or could be controlled, was an open question. Gorbachev tried to steer the course of events, but eventually was unable to control even his own government. The leaders of the abortive coup of August 1991, in their failed attempt at least to preserve the Union and some semblance of socialism, were most immediately responsible for precipitating precisely what they had feared. Gorbachev has been blamed by most Russians for the failure of his *perestroika,* and in contrast to his stunning success in moving to bring about the end of the Cold War, he did suffer a stunning defeat of his attempt at internal reformation of an enlightened socialist Union. After the failure of the conservative coup, Gorbachev was never able to regain control of the situation or defeat the countercoup led by Boris Yeltsin, who successfully used his power base in Russia to overcome Gorbachev's reforming Soviet Union, at the cost of also destroying whatever chances there were for a looser voluntary union of most of the republics.

I was in Washington as the Soviet Union expired at the end of 1991. I attended a Christmas party on December 19 given by Soviet Ambassador Viktor Komplektov (whom I had known for thirty of the forty-five years of the Cold War). It was the first Soviet-sponsored Christmas celebration ever—and the last reception ever of a *Soviet* embassy in Washington. On December 25, the Soviet flag was replaced over the Kremlin by the white, blue, and red tricolor that I had seen just a year before carried only by a small splinter group of demonstrators—and that several years earlier would have brought about instant arrest.

I returned to Moscow, to Russia rather than the Soviet Union, six times over the rest of the 1990s, three times in conjunction with conferences on the Cold War, and on five occasions to use former Soviet archives for research on the Cold War. I also participated in a number of other international conferences abroad (in Prague in 1994 revisiting the Soviet suppression of the Prague Spring of 1968, in Budapest in 1996 reliving the Soviet suppression of the popular 1956 uprising, in Warsaw in 1997 examining the crisis of 1980–81 that ended in martial law, in Budapest again in 1999 on the tenth anniversary of the 1989 revolution, in Berlin in 1999 on the intelligence Cold War in that city from 1945 to 1961, and in Plovdiv, Bulgaria, in 2000 on the Balkans in the Cold War). In all of these, and other conferences in the United States, Russian colleagues—historians and former Soviet officials—have also participated actively, and we have all been seeking more of the record to the extent access can be gained to formerly secret archives and documents, as well as recollections of participants. It has been most interesting to see again former antagonists and colleagues, such as my counterpart in the SALT negotiations a quarter century earlier, Ambassador Oleg Grinevsky, former Foreign Minister Aleksandr Bessmertnykh and First Deputy Foreign Ministers Georgy Kornienko and Yuly Vorontsov, former aides of Gorbachev such as Anatoly Chernyayev and Georgy Shakhnazarov, and to meet and talk with former leaders including President Mikhail Gorbachev, Foreign Minister Eduard Shevardnadze, and others. In 1999 I was even able to meet with most of the leaders of the abortive 1991 coup.

Incidentally, in this connection my last acquisition of particular interest to CIA came in 1994 when, doing research in the archives of the former Communist Party Central Committee, I found and obtained copies of the top secret annual reports of the KGB to Soviet leader Mikhail Gorbachev for the years 1985, 1986, 1988, and 1989—a fascinating and still valuable source of intelligence.[17]

My post–Cold War travels and research have also extended farther afield. As noted in an earlier chapter, by coincidence only days after the dissolution of the Soviet Union, another in the series of tripartite conferences on the Cuban missile crisis of 1962 was held in Havana, Cuba, in January 1992. Some

---

17. I subsequently published an account of these reports: Garthoff, "The KGB Reports to Gorbachev," *Intelligence and National Security,* vol. 11, no. 2 (April 1996), pp. 224–44.

of my American colleagues had some qualms about going to Havana, although I cleared it with Under Secretary of State Larry Eagleburger, and it was quite rewarding. Our visit was too short and busy with the working conference to do more than get a glimpse of life in Cuba in 1992. It was too early to see the full impact of the withdrawal of Soviet (then Russian) subsidized trade, further compounding the decades of denial of American trade on any basis. But Castro made clear the determination of his regime to carry on. Incidentally, one interesting feature of the Havana waterfront tied our past historical interest to the present. At a prominent site on the beach in Havana stands an erect seventy-five-foot-tall SS-4 medium-range ballistic missile of the kind secretly deployed to Cuba in 1962. (This missile was not, of course, capable of being fired, nor one that was overlooked in 1962, but an inert museum exhibit allowed under the 1987 U.S.-USSR INF Treaty that provided for the elimination of that category of missiles from active arsenals of the two countries.)

My first visit to China followed a few weeks later in early 1992. I have not mentioned earlier that throughout the 1980s I had participated in a number of conferences and meetings with Chinese officials, beginning with a Brookings conference in 1981. (I also had several private meetings with the Chinese military representative to the United Nations in the mid-1980s, arranged discreetly by my old friend Cyril Black at Princeton.) The visit to China was arranged by the National Committee on U.S.-China Relations, which brought four Soviet affairs experts, including Marshall Shulman and myself, to meet with Chinese experts on the Soviet Union (Russia). My visit to China was interesting not only because it was my first direct contact with the country and important changes were under way, but also because of the reverberations of the collapse of the Soviet Union only a few weeks before. I met with Chinese officials and academic experts on Russia (the Soviet Union) in Beijing and Shanghai, and we exchanged views on what would emerge in Russia. The Chinese were of course vitally interested for both geopolitical and ideological reasons. They were not alarmed, but they did exhibit concern over uncertainties in the future political course of Russia and the existence of newly independent Central Asian states as neighbors to their own Central Asian province of Xinjiang (Sinkiang). Most fundamentally, they could not but wonder what were the lessons for themselves from the sudden collapse of communist rule in Russia and Eastern Europe. They believed the outcome of the Soviet experience under Gorbachev justified their own course of gradual economic change coupled with continuing tight political control by their Communist Party, but uncertainties (and probably divergent preferences) about their own future evolution evidently lay below their surface reassurance. I was by chance in Shanghai for a celebration dinner on the twentieth

anniversary of the Shanghai Communiqué marking President Nixon's opening to China.

The Cold War years thus passed into the post–Cold War era, opening two
major challenges to us all. First, naturally, is to look forward to the future and
seek to determine what paths the United States, Russia, Europe, and the world
would—and should—take. Particularly in the case of Russia (and Ukraine
and other post-Soviet newly independent states) this involves difficult questions of identity and internal development, as well as relationships to the rest
of the world. The second challenge, while less consequential, may also be significant: to look back at the past with the benefit of more information and
hopefully more insight, to reexamine the Cold War. I shall have a little more
to say on that in the concluding chapter.

In wrapping up this rapid review of the closing period of the Cold War as
I traveled through it to the conclusion of my journey, I shall close by proudly,
if immodestly, quoting from the citation that accompanied presentation to me
of the Wilbur Lucius Cross Medal by my graduate alma mater, Yale University,
in May 1992.

> Scholar and diplomat, foremost authority on what was the Soviet
> Bloc, your career combines academe and government service. Your
> more than 40 books and over 100 articles cover such subjects as Russia's
> military security policies, military tensions between the USSR and
> China, the rise and fall of détente in U.S.-Soviet relations during the
> 1970s and 1980s, re-evaluation of intelligence assessments made by the
> Eisenhower and Kennedy administrations, and your efforts to shield the
> ABM Treaty from "Reaganite" misinterpretation designed to promote
> the SDI. . . .
>
> The Cold War in which you were an eminent participant-observer
> may have ended but not the greatness of your humane, objective schol-
> arship as a pre-eminent contemporary historian.

19

Reflections on the Cold War

U ltimately, there is but one Truth, one objective History. But if there is no subjective truth, there surely are subjective as well as objective approaches to comprehension and appreciation of the truth, including history—experiencing and feeling a historical phenomenon, as well as analyzing it.

The Cold War is now the subject of historical analysis, and that means analysis of what happened and why, what decisions were made, by whom, for what ends, and with what consequences, and what factors influenced or even determined the course of events. Subjective considerations—including the aims, perceptions, and values of key participants in the historical process—are (or at least should be) recognized as part of the phenomena to be objectively analyzed. At best, empathy for historical actors (and not merely for those with whom the historian most comfortably and implicitly finds identification) may be sought.

Yet there is more. The Cold War, as very recent history, was experienced by all of us who lived through it. That, of course, means all of us above the age of about twenty-five, but in widely varying degrees and ways. Not only do we all differ in the span of our life lived during the Cold War, but in our exposure to and awareness of its influences. Some of us not only lived through the period of the Cold War, but personally and professionally played roles as participants or observers. This memoir has been written in the belief that one man's journey through the entire span of the Cold War could be of interest to those who had not traveled the same path—and none of us has taken precisely the same path even when in greater or lesser degree we shared the journey.

The Cold War was experienced by the generation that was "present at the creation" of the postwar world, in Dean Acheson's famous characterization, as an unavoidable challenge, a gauntlet thrown down that could not be ignored, a challenge in which we were fated to be a protagonist, and on the side of Right. There were very few Americans who then doubted the reality of that challenge or our predestination to pick up the gauntlet. There were even fewer, of course, who imagined that the other protagonist might at the same time see the challenge as addressed to himself and originating with us.

To some extent American leaders in the Cold War saw a political necessity to oversimplify the relationship deliberately (beyond unconscious and unrecognized biases and distortions); in Acheson's telling phrase, a need to be "clearer than the truth" in depicting the threat.[1] But American leaders saw a real challenge and a real responsibility to meet it by containing a real threat.

Revisionist historians since the 1960s have challenged the traditional view that the United States led the West from the late 1940s on in meeting and containing (and ultimately defeating) a Soviet quest for world domination. Indeed, they have often posited virtually the reverse: an American quest for hegemony that rallied a grand alliance against a mythical Soviet threat conjured up to justify that mobilization of the Western world in support of American aims, in short, to wage a Cold War that need not have occurred.

Today a "post-revisionist" generation of historians, increasingly with the benefit of fuller access to the documentary record and the advantages of retrospection, see the Cold War as a much more complex phenomenon, and more difficult to ascribe entirely to either Soviet or American designs.

In considering the history of the Cold War it is necessary to strive for a nuanced and balanced depiction of a very complex reality. "Balanced" does not of course mean equal apportionment of historical responsibility, but efforts to weigh considerations on all sides.

I have no doubt that the myth of a Free World, led by the United States, rallied to counter an aggressive Evil Empire, was too simple and clear. It was not a completely accurate or adequate description of the ensuing contest. Yet it was more correct than the revisionist reversal of responsibility of the protagonists. Most important, in my mind, is that undergirding the geopolitical contest of the Cold War was an ideological foundation.[2]

---

1. See Dean Acheson, *Present at the Creation: My Years in the State Department* (W. W. Norton, 1969), p. 375, referring to NSC-68 in 1950. Acheson had earlier been responsible for the broad depiction of the threat in the Truman Doctrine in 1947.

2. I have written several articles and chapters in collective books dealing with the origins, nature, and end of the Cold War. Portions of the discussion in this chapter are based on my "Why Did the Cold War Arise, and Why Did It End?" in *Diplomatic History*, vol. 16, no. 2 (Spring 1992), pp. 287–93, reprinted in *The End of the Cold War: Its Meaning and Implications,* edited by Michael J. Hogan (Cambridge University Press, 1992); and from my chapter "Who Is to Blame for the Cold War?" in *Statecraft and Security: The Cold War and Beyond,* edited by Ken Booth (Cambridge University Press, 1998).

The fundamental underlying cause of the Cold War was the reinforcing belief in both the Soviet Union and the United States that confrontation was unavoidable, imposed by history. Soviet leaders believed that communism would ultimately triumph in the world and that the Soviet Union was the vanguard socialist/communist state. They also believed that the Western "imperialist" powers were historically bound to pursue a hostile course against them. For their part, American and other Western leaders assumed that the Soviet Union was determined to enhance its own power and to pursue expansionist policies by all expedient means in order to achieve a Soviet-led communist world. Each side thought that it was compelled by the very existence of the other side to engage in a zero-sum competition, in which the interests of one side were ineluctably against the interests of the other. And each saw the unfolding history of the Cold War as confirming its views.

The prevailing Western view was wrong in attributing a master plan to the Kremlin, in believing that communist ideology impelled Soviet leaders to unrelenting advance, in exaggerating communist abilities to subvert the Free World, and in thinking that Soviet officials viewed military power as an ultimate recourse to achieve their ideological goals. But the West was not wrong in believing that Soviet leaders were committed to a historically driven struggle between two worlds until, ultimately, theirs was destined to triumph. To be sure, other motivations, interests, and objectives played a part, on both sides, including national aims, institutional interests, and even personal psychological considerations. But these influences tended to be expressed in terms designed to enhance the ideological framework rather than to weaken it. Moreover, the actions of each side were sufficiently consistent with the ideological expectations of the other side to be so interpreted as to sustain their respective worldviews for many years.

The Cold War was, to be sure, waged as a geopolitical struggle extending to all aspects of international relations and to many parts of the globe. Nonetheless, it was conceived and continued to be seen as being waged within an ideological framework. A Manichaean communist worldview spawned a Manichaean anti-communist worldview. Each side imputed unlimited objectives, ultimately world domination, to the other. In addition, each side's operational code looked to the realization of its ambitions (or its historical destiny) over the very long term and thus posited an indefinite period of conflict.

Even though both sides envisioned a conflict of indefinite duration, and even though policy decisions were pragmatic and based on calculation of risk, cost, and gain, there was always the hazard of a miscalculation. That could be especially dangerous, given the historical coincidence of the Cold War and the first half-century of the nuclear age. Nuclear weapons, by threatening the existence of world civilization, added significantly to the tension of the epoch; the stakes were utterly without precedent and beyond full comprehension. This is not to deny that nuclear weapons also helped to keep the Cold War "cold," to prevent a third world war in the twentieth century. In the final analysis, and notwithstanding their awesome power, nuclear weapons did not cause, prevent, or end the Cold War, which would have been waged even had such weapons never existed. The arms race as well as geopolitical competition in the superpower rivalry were, however, both driven in part by underlying ideological assumptions.

While the Cold War and the nuclear arms race could be attenuated when opportunities or constraints led both sides to favor a relaxation of tensions or détente, they could not be ended until the ideological underpinnings had also been released. This occurred under Mikhail Gorbachev's leadership, with a fundamental reevaluation of the processes at work in the real world, a basic reassessment of threats, and finally a deep revision of aims and political objectives.

"Victory" in the Cold War did not come through Western geopolitical containment and military deterrence alone. The Cold War was certainly not won by the Reagan military buildup and the Reagan Doctrine, as some have suggested. The Cold War expired only when a new generation of Soviet leaders realized how badly their system at home and their policies abroad had failed, and above all that their ideological worldview did not reflect reality. Western containment did successfully stalemate Moscow's attempts to advance Soviet hegemony. Over four decades it performed the historic function of holding Soviet power in check until the internal seeds of destruction within the Soviet Union and its empire could mature. At that point, it was Gorbachev who brought the Cold War to an end.

I am *not* arguing that history depended on Mikhail Gorbachev, or *could* have depended on any individual leader on either side. What *was* a matter of historical determination was that *only* a Soviet leader *could* have taken the decisive step in ending the Cold War. Why? Because the Cold War rested squarely on the belief, on both sides, that two ideological and geopolitical world systems were locked in an inescapable struggle to the finish. And that belief in turn rested on the Marxist-Leninist worldview positing an inevitable struggle for world hegemony between two irreconcilable contending socioeconomic (class), political, geopolitical, and military systems. *Only* when a *Soviet* leadership was able to recognize that such a worldview was false, and to act on the basis of rejection of that worldview, could leaders of the United States and the West accept (at first cautiously) the possibility of moving, in President George Bush's words, "beyond containment." The guiding U.S. Cold War conception of containment of the Soviet and world communist threat was derivative of and dependent on the *Soviet* belief in inescapable conflict between two systems. Only when a Soviet leader—it happened to be Gorbachev in the latter half in the 1980s—saw and repudiated by word and deed the fallacious foundation for the Cold War could Western leaders see that containment of a no longer extant communist threat to the Free World no longer had meaning.

This excursion into the origins, nature, and end of the Cold War represents my current conclusions, but provides appropriate background for discussion of my reflections on the Cold War as I experienced it, especially in the early years.

It *was* a Soviet threat, in part real and in part imagined, that generated the American dedication to waging a Cold War. From this stemmed the policy of containment and deterrence. I shared this view at the time (in the late 1940s and early 1950s); in an article written shortly before Stalin's death in 1953, I argued that "the Soviet view of international politics, of the relation between the Soviet-dominated and free worlds, conceivably may change in time. But . . . the only way in which Soviet policy may in time be altered is by consistently firm, unprovocative, but resolute determination of the free world to permit no communist aggression in any form, and to build and maintain the strength to give that determination meaning."[3]

The ideological underpinning of the policy of the Soviet Union made it essentially different from pre-Soviet—and post–Soviet—Russia. I noted in several writings over the years the fundamental distinction from the acceptance by pre-revolutionary Russia of the world political order. As I wrote in 1966, "the revolutionary drive of Bolshevism has subsided—and may yet alter in its nature—as the Soviet state continues its coexistence with the rest of the world; but so far the Soviet outlook has not accepted reconciliation with the world [order]."[4] I had made the same point in a letter to a member of the faculty at the Army War College in 1960 when asked my views on why the Soviet Union was different from a noncommunist Russia (earlier, or in the future). I emphasized the Soviet nonacceptance of the basic state system and belief in a historical world change, unlimited expansion of communism, and hence the greater risk of war.

But my principal observation on the origins and early years of the Cold War, specifically from the late 1940s through the period of Stalin's rule ending in March 1953 and with diminishing but continuing effect thereafter, is that virtually all of us engaged in official responsibility or academic study of U.S. security interests, and world affairs, as well as of the Soviet Union, believed we had no choice but vigorously to wage the Cold War as the preferable alternative to a nuclear war.

3. Raymond L. Garthoff, "Ideological Concepts in Soviet Foreign Policy," *Problems of Communism*, vol. 2, no. 5 (September–October 1953), p. 8. It was written in late 1952.

4. Garthoff, *Soviet Military Policy: A Historical Analysis* (Frederick A. Praeger, 1966), p. 27.

Thus for those of us completing our formal education (many after an interruption for service in World War II) in the late 1940s and early 1950s there was a strong magnetic attraction to joining in one or another way in the effort to meet the looming challenge of the emerging Cold War. Most of course went on to traditional careers in business or the civil professions for traditional reasons. But many of us with a bent toward international affairs or national security as a calling or a career eagerly turned not only to postwar renewals of traditional diplomatic or military service, but also to burgeoning new Cold War opportunities for service, ranging from academic study of communism and the Soviet Union to classified political, intelligence, or military research and analysis, or to clandestine intelligence collection and covert operations, including propaganda and political warfare.

This of course was the path I chose, from academic research on Soviet political and military affairs through classified research and analysis at the prototypical Cold War think tank, the RAND Corporation, with close ties to the U.S. military, to the Office of National Estimates at CIA, and on to a variety of positions in the Department of State focused on relations with the Soviet Union and the "Soviet bloc." Most of my colleagues tended to stay with one or another chosen career, with the Foreign Service or the clandestine services of CIA or one of the military services, or in academia, although the varied nature of Cold War activities came to occupy such a broad span of American policy that there were frequent overlapping and cross-assignments. Moreover, many Cold War activities involved private enterprises (especially but not only defense industries) and the academic world as well as government service.

In short, my journey through the Cold War, while unique (as was that of each of us), was not so atypical as it may seem. And above all in the 1950s and first half of the 1960s, there was a solid consensus and broad public support for waging the Cold War in whatever ways the government found necessary. This consensus was later challenged, and public support eroded, from the mid-1960s through the 1970s after Vietnam, military disillusionment, revelations of CIA assassination plots and other excesses, and public withdrawals of support from every president after Kennedy—Lyndon Johnson for Vietnam, Richard Nixon for Watergate, Gerald Ford for ineffectiveness, Jimmy Carter for perceived irresolution and the hostages in Iran, Ronald Reagan for Iran-Contra.

This is a very incomplete sketch of the changing political picture in the United States, drawn merely to evoke awareness of the later change from public satisfaction and support with U.S. Cold War policy in the 1950s and early 1960s. Another reason for this change, of course, is that the nature of the relationship with the Soviet Union was changing too. To be sure, every president from Eisenhower through Reagan and Bush in practice combined with containment attempts at mitigating the confrontation of the Cold War with détente. So, too, did every post-Stalin leader of the Soviet Union. But neither side was able to find a basis for stable détente, and both continued also to seek advantage in a continuing geopolitical competition. The first sustained effort with any notable success was in the Nixon-Ford years, but that too failed. The final effort came in the later Reagan-Bush years, and owing to the decisive change of ideological orientation by a Soviet leader, Mikhail Gorbachev, led beyond détente to an end of the Cold War.

There are still controversies among historians as to relative responsibilities for the origins and rapid generation of the Cold War in the late 1940s, and even more as to the credit for the rapid dissolution of the Cold War in the late 1980s. More attention needs to be directed also to study of the relative responsibilities for the long continuation of the Cold War from the mid-1950s to the mid-1980s. Given the dynamics of the political and arms competitions, and especially the processes in both countries that were generated by the rivalry of the Cold War, I doubt that there were any major missed opportunities to have brought the Cold War to an end earlier, though some tensions could—and should—have been averted or alleviated. As I have noted, it required above all a profound change of worldview by a Soviet leadership to end the fundamental ideological belief in a historically destined conflict of two world systems. One key element of such a change, however, was in perceptions of the adversary, and both sides could and should have been more open in their own outlook and perception, and could and should have pursued policies that might earlier have modified the perceptions held by the adversary.

In my own case, as scholar, researcher, and intelligence analyst and estimator in the 1950s and early 1960s I combined a firm belief in the validity of the prevailing conception of a hostile Soviet design and requirement for resolute American containment with a conviction that the foundation for our policy should rest on the most accurate and complete understanding of the adversary. Political warfare might justify propaganda that exaggerated the shortcomings of the enemy and overstated the threat from him, but policy should rest on the closest approximation of reality, the truth, that we could make. Gradually over the 1960s and beyond I saw increasing possibilities in Soviet policy for building on common interests, at the same time that we continued to compete with the Soviet Union and to confront it where it posed a direct challenge. Hence my stand in the Cuban missile crisis, to do what it took to remove the missiles from Cuba, by military action if necessary, but if feasible by diplomatic pressure. Similarly, because we had put down a marker on bombers as well, they too must be removed—but I opposed the idea of changing our objective in midcrisis to demand more, with respect to Soviet presence in Cuba or Castro's rule. I welcomed the small steps toward détente in the 1960s, and Nixon's détente in the 1970s, without expecting it would mean an end to the rivalry of the Cold War.

The Cold War was an amalgam of confrontation and cooperation, with one or the other rising or falling in relative importance, but neither ever fully absent. That is why this memoir has been about both competition and co-existence.

In the late 1940s and 1950s there was a strong tendency for internal policy deliberations and pronouncements to reflect the public rhetoric of confrontation. NSC-68 in 1950, the U.S. "charter" of the Cold War, was the cardinal example (as George Kennan and Chip Bohlen objected at the time). There may not have been opportunities for doing much to mitigate the confrontation of the Cold War at the time, owing to the even more ideologically ingrained hostility in internal policy discourse in the Soviet Union, as well as in its public rhetoric. But later throughout the Cold War, notably reaffirmed in the early 1980s, the U.S. concentration on political warfare against an "evil empire" made even the limited détente of the 1970s unsupportable. Détente in the 1970s did not prevent Richard Nixon and Henry Kissinger (or the Soviet side) from pursuing geopolitical competition and containment. But as a legacy of the 1950s the priority given to political warfare even in later decades led to concentration of efforts to take advantage of every opportunity to weaken the enemy—and often to denying or ignoring opportunities for building on common interest. Thus in the Truman administration the central body for coordinating policy was a Psychological Strategy Board (in the Eisenhower administration the successor Operations Coordinating Board, with a broader coordinating role and more neutrally named, had a similar priority). Psychological warfare and covert operations were only the most sharp-edged examples of instruments to weaken and subvert the adversary. Economic denial, isolation by surrounding alliance blocs, and other means of political warfare were vigorously pursued.

One of the driving elements behind the militancy of the early Cold War years was the fear of war. From 1948 through 1953, the last years of Josef Stalin's rule, the communist takeover of Czechoslovakia, a "war scare" over Berlin and then the Berlin blockade, Soviet testing of an atomic bomb, and the outbreak of the Korean War all stimulated great concern. The rapid shift from wartime alliance to Cold War conflict in the latter half of the 1940s, and flood of revelations of Stalin's tyranny, raised popular fears that Stalin might soon launch a war. Professional concerns in the government establishment generally focused on a somewhat later period when Soviet military power would have been increased. (Fortunately, that period of greatest danger always seemed to recede a few years as the earlier predicted dangers did not materialize.) Even those of us less inclined to see war on the currently visible horizon did not doubt its possibility at some time, nor did we see any alternative to a long, tough confrontation and need for containment of the threat.

There was, of course, also a connection between official (and officially inspired) warnings and mobilization of public support for containment, and public fears—not only of military dangers from the Soviet Union, but of communist subversive dangers within.

In the post-Stalin years of the 1950s, there was some attentuation of the public fear, but there remained both real and overstated alarms over Soviet military advances—the "bomber gap" of the mid-1950s and "missile gap" of the late 1950s to 1961 being only the most prominent. I and others professionally analyzing these threats were disturbed by the exaggerations, even as we sought to determine the real political and military challenges. Some of us even recognized that the Soviet leaders, aware of their own capabilities and shortcomings, could only believe the United States was consciously exaggerating Soviet capabilities (as well as militarist intentions) in order to justify its own pursuit of growing military superiority. There was, in fact, considerable truth to that view, although the causes of American concern were by no means reducible to that one consideration. Both sides pursued (and justified) military programs to deter the other and to ensure as favorable a position in the strategic relationship as possible. Impact on the evaluations made by the adversary were singularly lacking.

The same important aspect of our assertive waging of political warfare was completely ignored at the time, and has even now been too little reflected upon. No one really considered the effect of such aggressive U.S. actions in the late 1940s and early 1950s as overflights, dropping agents, and supporting guerrilla separatist movements in the western USSR on the perceptions of U.S. policy objectives by Soviet leaders and their national security establishment. Consideration of this factor could not have been the only or even the governing factor in policy determination, but it could and should have been taken into account. I was not in the policy process at the time, but I was in contact with friends serving on the staff of the Psychological Strategy Board, State, CIA, and the Pentagon who were. Moreover, we now have extensive (if still incomplete) declassified records of high-level deliberations. It is clear that the widely prevailing view was simply that we were waging a defensive Cold War against an enemy who would use any means to advance his position and that we were compelled to do the same.

In a top secret *Report on the Covert Activities of the Central Intelligence Agency* prepared by Lieutenant General James Doolittle at the request of President Eisenhower in July 1954, this Cold War philosophy was spelled out in frank clarity. The report stated:

> It is now clear that we are facing an implacable enemy whose avowed objective is world domination by whatever means and at whatever cost. There are no rules in such a game. Hitherto acceptable norms of human conduct do not apply. If the United States is to survive, long-standing American concepts of "fair play" must be reconsidered. We must

develop effective espionage and counterespionage services and must learn to subvert, sabotage and destroy our enemies by more clever, more sophisticated and more effective methods than those used against us.[5]

While recognizing that this was a "fundamentally repugnant philosophy" for Americans, the report did not shrink from concluding that we must pursue "aggressive" covert action, "if necessary, more ruthless than that employed by the enemy." This approach also, if less sharply, pervaded all aspects of American policy, especially during the early years of the Cold War.

Virtually no consideration was given to the fact that we were also influencing *Soviet* perception of *our* aims. No matter how justified our actions seemed and indeed may have been, we failed to realize that we were, for example, in fact going beyond what the adversary was doing in paramilitary and covert operations violating sovereignty and challenging the legitimacy of the Soviet Union. More important, when we were resorting to the same means, did we want the Soviet leaders to see our objectives as a mirror reflection of what we believed were theirs?

To be sure, the Soviet leaders were predisposed by their Marxist-Leninist ideological worldview to see the Western imperialist powers as bent on their destruction. Sometimes, later, when it was argued that we should not provoke the Soviet side, the ready retort was that they were already as hostile to us as they could be, and doing everything they could to weaken us. No consideration was given to the fact that they not only had an ideology but also a policy, one that was subject to some correspondence to varying exigencies of the Cold War. In particular, no consideration was given to the fact that a Western policy of unremitting hostility could only seem to confirm their ideological predispositions, and that we should seek to lead them to question their ideology as well as to constrain their behavior.

In retrospect it is of course easier to be critical than it was at the time, and I am convinced the main lines of containment policy *were* justified and successful. It is still not easy, even in retrospect, to reconsider whether and when there could have been more balance in our policy. In the late 1940s and early 1950s, indeed, there was virtually no opportunity for any constructive engagement with the Soviet Union. Later, in the late 1950s and 1960s there was, if somewhat tardy and understandably wary, a growing acknowledgment by some in both countries of the possibility and desirability of lessening tensions and engaging in limited cooperation. When the Nixon and Brezhnev administrations turned to détente, they were both unable to do so without a one-sided depiction of the process and raising of excessive public

---

5. Cited by John Ranelagh, *The Agency: The Rise and Decline of the CIA* (Simon & Schuster, 1986), pp. 276–77.

expectations that led to later disappointment and disillusionment in the late 1970s and early 1980s.

Nonetheless, although on a rocky path, there was from the 1960s on gradual exploration of possible limited collaboration between the United States and the Soviet Union even as we remained adversaries.

I and some colleagues in the Office of National Estimates had sought even in the 1950s to establish through our intelligence estimates of Soviet policy that there were foundations for coexistence and even limited cooperation, as well as a continuing need for containment and deterrence. We noted that Soviet leaders also saw requirements for security as well as inclinations for expanding their influence. Above all, they too recognized the need to avoid nuclear war and would temper their policy actions accordingly. Such views, now commonplace among students of the Cold War, were anathema at the time to those who believed we must bend all efforts to maintain (or, later, it was argued to "regain") military superiority and to wage an unremitting Cold War and painted a picture of unalloyed Soviet pursuit of superiority and ultimate military victory.

Among the most steadfast proponents of a constantly growing Soviet military threat were many in the armed services, including many (not all) in the military intelligence organizations. Some stressed the Soviet espionage and subversive threat, including deception. Virtually any Soviet diplomatic or other policy measures that contradicted a picture of unremitting Soviet hostility and threat could be, and they were, dismissed by these advocates of confrontation as deceptive and dangerous disinformation.

Within CIA, there were differences. For those in the clandestine services who were engaged constantly and exclusively with the "game" of espionage, and saw only sharp rivalry with their counterparts, there was naturally an overriding focus on the elements of competition in the U.S.-Soviet relationship. So, too, for those devoting their lives to political warfare and covert operations. Intelligence analysts and estimators faced a much more variegated reality. Military planners and commanders and their staffs naturally concentrated on preparing for potential military conflict and meeting the most threatening contingencies. Diplomats had yet another perspective, often involving hard competition with the Soviet adversary in third countries and in multilateral diplomatic forums, and frustrations in our bilateral relations, but also sometimes engaged in negotiation and a difficult diplomatic pursuit of common objectives.

All of us were pursuing the national interests of the United States—in military, intelligence, economic, political, propaganda, and diplomatic arenas—but the nature of interaction with the Soviet side differed, sometimes greatly, and so did the image of the adversary. Moreover, the global political context, and the positions of both Soviet and American leaderships, changed. I was privileged to have the opportunity to gauge these diverging perspectives from various vantage points in my government service over the years of the Cold War.

One of the most important areas in the gradual development of limited cooperation between the two superpowers was the field of arms control and disarmament. In fact, that term covered at least three different common objectives of the two powers. First, at least in point of time, was the effort to curb nuclear proliferation by other powers through the pursuit of a nuclear test ban and a nonproliferation treaty, a common interest of the United States and the Soviet Union. The second objective was to reduce the risks of the strategic arms competition between the two protagonists. In addition to the "hot line" and a series of agreements in the 1970s and 1980s on avoidance of accidental or unintended war, the principal achievement was the ABM Treaty of 1972 that sought through assured mutual deterrence to reduce incentives for pursuit of strategic superiority. Contrary to the argument of opponents of the treaty, it did serve that function. It did not, however, by any means end a continuing buildup of more advanced strategic offensive arms, as many of its advocates had hoped. Although the leaders of the United States and the Soviet Union could agree to head off a future competition in ABM systems, they were not prepared to curb their existing programs for perfecting and building strategic offensive arms.

Initially, in the late 1950s and early 1960s, I had been skeptical of the possibilities for arms control, and still more on disarmament. Nonetheless, I believed there was a basis for limited steps based on mutual interests and had so indicated in the first national intelligence estimate on the Soviet attitude toward disarmament and arms control, one that I drafted in 1958. This understanding developed throughout my work in this field in the State Department throughout the 1960s.

By the end of the 1960s, with emerging parity and the prospect of a destabilizing and costly competitive pursuit of ballistic missile defenses, both sides were ready to begin, if cautiously, serious reciprocal probing of the possibility of agreement. I was an early staff participant and advocate in this process and later had the opportunity to play a key part in the ensuing Strategic Arms Limitation Talks (SALT), leading to the ABM Treaty and initial strategic arms agreement in SALT I. I will not repeat what I have described earlier, but I want here simply to note that the opportunity not only to participate but to make a real difference in the formulation of American policy on SALT from 1967 through 1972, and especially in the conduct of negotiations with the Soviet side, was in many ways a high point in my government service. Subsequently I was on the periphery, but during the breakthrough stage of strategic arms control I was fortunate to be in the center of the arena.

Strategic arms control played a certain modest but positive role in contributing to stability during the latter half of the Cold War and to fostering a limited détente in the 1970s and again in the mid-1980s. It was not pursued with sufficient consistency or confidence to play the larger role it could have played in these two respects. In a broader sense, arms control efforts had a more ambiguous influence on the course of the Cold War. Tough, conservative arms control positions held by both sides, while justified at least in part as sound negotiating technique in dealing with an adversary, also tended to reinforce prevailing conceptions and perceptions of the adversarial relationship and to some extent even to accent misperceptions exaggerating the tendency of the adversary to seek advantages and to maximize power for the continuing competition characteristic of the Cold War.

I mentioned earlier two of three common objectives of arms control. The third objective was to turn down the arms race, reduce arms, and engage in partial disarmament. This was the objective most sought by many nongovernmental public advocacies in the United States and most of the world (except the Soviet Union and its bloc, where such public interest was channeled into propaganda denunciation of Western "imperialists" as the obstacle to disarmament). But in practice, as noted, there was no success—or even real efforts—by the United States and the Soviet Union until the mid-1980s, when both Presidents Ronald Reagan and Mikhail Gorbachev actually sought such reductions and succeeded at least in launching the process with the INF Treaty in 1987. This treaty was important in helping to wind down the Cold War, as well as providing new impetus to arms control.

Thus only in the transitional end game of the dissolving Cold War from 1987 through 1990 were serious strategic arms reductions (START I in 1990), and conventional arms reductions (CFE in 1990) treaties achieved, mainly through disproportionate Soviet concessions in negotiations and unilateral reductions. This process continued after the Cold War in 1991–92 by mutual concessions (START II in 1992) and unilateral actions by both sides (on tactical and seaborne nuclear weapons in 1991). Only at the end of the Cold War did strategic arms control unambiguously contribute to political accord.

Arms control was notable because it required the two sides, above all the two principal adversaries, to address jointly at least some aspects of the military competition, touching on a sensitive security area. And, as noted, it came to play a role in U.S.-Soviet political relations. Nonetheless, it remained peripheral to the overall geopolitical arena of the Cold War.

The Cold War had arisen as the postwar political order in Europe settled in the mid to late 1940s into a sharp division of the continent. As the "Iron Curtain descended," in Churchill's phrase, the Soviet Union consolidated its hegemony in Eastern Europe, and the United States joined the Western powers in creating an unprecedented peacetime military alliance, NATO, later incorporating also West Germany. The United States also moved to create several other regional as well as bilateral alliances in Asia and the Middle East.

Initially, the Soviet Union under Stalin extended its alliances to China and North Korea, but otherwise shied away from involvements in what came to be called the "Third World." Subsequently, in the latter 1950s, the 1960s, and the 1970s the Soviet Union ventured further in establishing ties with a number of countries of the Third World and seeking local clients.

With the situation in Europe essentially "settled" by the late 1940s, and in Northeast Asia (after the Korean War confirmed the early postwar lines), the area of greatest fluidity and change shifted to Southeast Asia, the Middle East, postcolonial Africa, South and Southeast Asia, and the Caribbean Basin. Shifting opportunities led to greater or lesser Soviet or Western initiative, as well as to shifting geopolitical and political priorities. Although always secondary or tertiary in real significance, the flareups and gains or losses in individual cases made the Third World seem to occupy a more important role in the Cold War than was warranted. I would not argue that all of the Third World conflicts were of no consequence for the United States or the Soviet Union, but the more general observation is that the impact of the Cold War on the Third World was more important than the impact of the Third World conflicts on the Cold War. The Cold War led to a gross oversimplification of our views of world politics (and national and regional politics in the Third World in particular). Today in the post–Cold War world, it has become more clear that there are many complexities in world (and Third World) politics. That has always been true, but during the Cold War we made international politics seem more simple by seeing everything through Cold War lenses, focusing only on effects on the U.S.-Soviet global rivalry.

Afghanistan is a good example. Once the Soviet Union intervened directly in December 1979, U.S. policy in the 1980s was reduced to the single aim of bleeding the Soviet Union in Afghanistan and pillorying the Soviets in world forums, without regard to the role of Pakistan (our ally) or others, without regard to the internal political dynamics of Afghanistan, and without regard to what would follow when the Soviet Union had withdrawn. One consequence has been a no less bloody civil war (which had begun well before Soviet intervention and continued after), emergence of an even more repressive regime in Afghanistan, and the spillover effect of many terrorists whose arming and training we abetted but who now threaten U.S. interests and the general world order.

Even in Europe the oversimplification of the Cold War led to American politics geared to leading the Atlantic Alliance in an anti–Soviet bloc policy even when that alone was no longer appropriate. Fortunately, our allies were less hampered by this approach than the United States itself when it came to East-West relations in Europe and took the lead on such important steps as the Conference on Security and Cooperation in Europe (CSCE). The European lead in seeking East-West détente in the 1970s was a major element in inducing the United States reluctantly to join in, in order not to lose all leverage and influence on the process. Ironically, the United States and the Soviet Union shared an antipathy and even fear of the Eurocommunist movement in the 1970s, because it threatened the clean dividing lines underlying Cold War Europe.

The North Atlantic Alliance and NATO were a great success. So, too, was the economic recovery stimulated by the Marshall Plan, and the later Western European movement to a European Union. Eastern Europe was fated to remain under Soviet hegemonic control until a Soviet leadership encouraged real independence and was prepared to accept the consequences even when that led to a complete collapse of communist rule and the Eastern military alliance, economic coordination, and political bloc. The East-West détente of the 1970s and 1980s did not directly bring about change, but it contributed to it more than even its strongest advocates had anticipated. NATO had given vital reassurance to Western Europe when it was weak and the Soviet Union appeared to be strong and threatening. But it could not do anything when popular uprisings or manifestations of independence occurred in East Germany in 1953, Hungary in 1956, Czechoslovakia in 1968, and Poland in 1980–81. It took a political development in Moscow, transcending and ending the Cold War, to free Eastern Europe.

I observed and was involved in a small way in the evolution of Western European, and Eastern European, movement toward détente, especially while working at the NATO Council in Brussels in the late 1960s and in Bulgaria in the late 1970s. But the thing that was most clear to me, and increasingly to colleagues, was that the key rested in U.S. and Western relations with the Soviet Union, and above all with developments in Moscow. That would indeed be the key to ending the Cold War.

I strongly supported the main policy line of détente in the 1970s and 1980s, recognizing that even in a continuing Cold War, along with firm defense of Western interests against Soviet challenges, there were also areas of congruent interest and opportunities for ameliorating the confrontation. Although I was critical of some of the means of conducting policy in the Nixon-Kissinger years, I believed (and believe now) that the policy was essentially correct. I was particularly dismayed at the attacks on détente based on unfounded or overstated concerns as to the military balance and alleged Soviet abuses of détente. This line of attack frustrated both the Ford and Carter administrations and was triumphant in the first Reagan administration. I decried the application not only in propaganda but in policy too of a double standard that made impossible a course of action that would best serve our interests. I welcomed the return of détente (not so christened, of course) in the second Reagan and Bush administrations to meet the extraordinary initiatives of Mikhail

Gorbachev and accept a basic transformation of relations that would end the Cold War by 1990, even before the collapse of the Soviet Union.

It has been fascinating to observe the differences in viewpoint today among former American officials who played a part, in some cases major roles, in U.S. Cold War policy. On the one hand are the vindicated Cold Warriors who are sure their uncompromising support of containment and deterrence won the Cold War, and that there was no other path that might have ended the Cold War even earlier. Paul Nitze, principal author of NSC-68 in 1950, is a prime example (although "ultras" would disown him because he favored cautious arms control). On the other hand there are those who take a more critical reading of the complexities of history and wonder if reexamined history may not show some other paths that may have been taken. The late McGeorge Bundy was, in my view, a good example of this other kind of Cold Warrior.[6]

There is a general agreement among Cold War veterans, including myself, that containment and deterrence were a necessary and appropriate American policy for meeting the perceived Soviet challenge and threat in the Cold War. That view is shared by most, but by no means all, scholars and historians of the Cold War. With the benefit of experience and retrospective vision, however, many of us who lived through those decades now believe that the military threat was greatly exaggerated. So, too, was the threat of an ominous global communist movement and the danger from subversion. There was a worldwide communist movement with most elements subject to Moscow direction and control. But the reaction of McCarthyite hysteria in the United States, to note but one prominent example, was obviously grossly exaggerated. Later, too, the evidence of serious fissures after the excommunication of Marshal Josip Tito's Yugoslavia in 1948 and the Sino-Soviet split by 1960 should have disabused us of the fear of a Sino-Soviet Bloc and of International Communism as a monolithic movement. Above all, although the Soviet Union as a Marxist-Leninist state may have been ready to do "anything" to expand its power, it was plainly not prepared as a matter of prudent policy to do "everything." That should have been clear to all by the mid-1950s after Stalin's death.

6. For Nitze's reaffirmation of his ominous threat evaluations from the early years of the Cold War (NSC-68 in 1950 above all) on through the Committee on the Present Danger in the 1970s, and his equally strong call for highly developed deterrent capabilities through the 1980s, see Paul H. Nitze, *From Hiroshima to Glasnost: At the Center of Decision, A Memoir* (Grove Weidenfeld, 1989), and my review of it in Garthoff, "Nitze's World: A Broad Interpretation," in *Arms Control Today*, vol. 20, no. 1 (February 1990), pp. 21–26. For Bundy's reevaluation and conclusion on the efficacy of a general "existential deterrent," see McGeorge Bundy, *Danger and Survival: Choices about the Bomb in the First Fifty Years* (Random House, 1988), and my review in Garthoff, "Existing and Coexisting in the Nuclear Age," *Arms Control Today*, vol. 19, no. 6 (August 1989), pp. 33–34.

It is ironic that increasingly only the most hard-line fringe of communists, and the most hard-line fringe of *anti*-communists, still believed in the 1970s and 1980s that communism (and the Soviet Union) was really on the path to victory in the Cold War. When Soviet communists would tell me in the 1950s and 1960s that "history would decide," I would readily agree that we should let History decide. And so we did, and History has decided.

One of the most dangerous aspects of the Cold War was its increased militarization after the Korean War, and the later grip of the arms race. The danger was not, however, that the Soviet Union would gain superiority and attack us (nor, after the mid-1950s, that we might be tempted to use the great superiority we did then have before it was eroded by the ineluctable advance of mutual deterrence). The danger was that the dynamic of the arms race and the concomitant fears on both sides could lead to rash moves and miscalculations. Fortunately, the experience of the Cuban missile crisis inoculated leaders on both sides against any further attempts by either side to risk war for any acquisitive geopolitical advances. Nuclear weapons did serve as an existential deterrent to war or even to assuming great risks of war.

A lesson regrettably *not* learned from the Cuban missile crisis or any other episode in the geopolitical rivalry was that the continuation of an arms race was not necessary for deterrence of war. Instead of recognizing that leaders on neither side had an incentive to launch a war strong enough to lead to consideration of deliberate initiation of war in the nuclear era, deterrence theory elaborated justification for infinite expansion and perfection of strategic nuclear weapons to meet "requirements" generated by completely unrealistic scenarios of "prevailing" in second or third "exchanges" of tens of thousands of thermonuclear weapons. *Any* weapons program could be justified by the argument that it would "enhance deterrence." To be sure, sanity in political judgment was not lost, and we survived the Cold War. But risks, as well as costs, were raised unnecessarily by excessive militarization of the rivalry, excessive reliance on fallible technologies of warning and communication, and substitution of mechanistic "requirements" of deterrence (in such coin as missile "throw-weight") for strategic and political thinking.

Maintaining the military (and deterrent) balance was demanding, especially because there always existed a margin of uncertainty that each side wanted to assure to itself and deny to the opponent. But the reality of a military-deterrent balance was not deemed enough. Perceptions of the military balance and of the power relationship were also seen as crucial. Deterrence is predicated on an adversary's recognition of capability for retaliation. Reassurance to one's allies as well depends on their perceptions of both strength and will to use it in their behalf (the latter feature again pressing for a margin of superiority). Thus under deterrence doctrine in addition to meeting requirements for assuring a real military-deterrent power, it was held that perceptions of that power by both friend and foe must also be assured in order to maintain credibility, and effectiveness, of deterrence of the enemy and reassurance of one's allies. Yet capabilities sufficient to survive an enemy attack and retaliate in similar measure are, perforce, so powerful as to be threatening if used in a first strike.

Even when the threat of war had clearly diminished in periods of political détente, the "threat" always remained because it was defined in terms of "capabilities" rather than "intentions," and capabilities on both sides, justified by unrealistic alleged requirements for deterrence, did indeed continue to rise virtually to the end of the Cold War. Born from considerations of prudence, deterrence grew to engender very imprudent consequences.[7]

Although the military deterrent relationship was central to the containment policy, it was far from encompassing it. Military, political, and economic power was also engaged around the world. The same factors were at work. For example, credibility of the will of the United States to deter or contain a Soviet challenge in Europe was instrumental in leading the United States into two large wars in Korea and Vietnam. To reassure allies, as well as to deter even "proxy" communist expansion, it was deemed essential for the United States to commit its own conventional military power.

In reflecting on the major decisions of the geopolitical contest of the Cold War, probably few of the major confrontations could have been avoided. Stalin's decision to unleash the North Korean army in 1950 was, we now know, based on a mis-estimate that the United States would not intervene and the North could win a quick victory. And Truman's decision to intervene with the armed forces of the United States was based at least in part on a mistaken judgment that Stalin was testing Western resolve. Nonetheless, given those flawed perceptions, the Korean War was probably unavoidable. The consequences, on balance, were to Western advantage, successfully strengthening the NATO alliance and containment, and leading to a major increase in U.S. military strength. In contrast, the U.S. direct involvement in the war in Vietnam from 1964 to 1973 was based on errors widely recognized at the time, and while understandable was not inevitable. The consequences were also clearly disadvantageous for the West, and the intervention almost certainly much more costly than the loss of Vietnam in the mid-1960s would have been. Neither allies or adversaries would have considered American resolve on containment or deterrence of the Soviet Union to be weak if Indochina had been let slip under local communist rule in the 1950s or 1960s. Nonetheless, neither the Korean War nor still less the war in Vietnam, nor any or all of the other so-called "proxy" wars in the Third World, had a decisive impact on the course

---

7. For a more extended discussion, see Garthoff, *Deterrence and the Revolution in Soviet Military Doctrine* (Brookings, 1990), pp. 6–16 and 24–38.

and outcome of the Cold War. Indeed, the most important impact of the geopolitical contest (given the realities of stability in Europe) was probably the psychological fueling of the ideological underpinning of the global political and military confrontation.

If my judgment on these two examples is correct, it suggests that many lesser battles of the Cold War were also not necessary, even given the reality of the Cold War contest. Still more, it raises questions as to whether there may have been earlier opportunities to bring the Cold War to a close. On the other hand, there remain many indications that until the mid-1980s Soviet leaders continued to see the world through an ideological prism that precluded their ability to envisage a real end to the Cold War. When a Soviet leader, Gorbachev, *did* see the world differently and seek to end the Cold War, it was only after repeated and significant unilateral actions and concessions that the Western leaders were prepared to accept that fact.

It is only with the end of the Cold War that it has become clear that this underlying ideological foundation mandating an adversarial relationship was what prevented any of the periods of détente from becoming a stepping-stone to a post–Cold War world. Détente was a way of cushioning the risks to permit continued competition and the workings of the historical forces that would ultimately determine the outcome of the struggle. And it did perform that historic service. But détente was still seen on the one side as a means of the class struggle, as the Soviets openly avowed during the détente of the 1970s, and regarded on the other as a veiled form of containment, as the record of American policy in the 1970s closely observed clearly shows (and as Kissinger and Brzezinski boast in their revealing memoirs).

The reality of the geopolitical competition provided each side with ample real grounds not only to confirm its own judgment that it was right, and on the side of Right, but also to have real suspicions and fear of the other. It is important to realize that not only did this process feed vicious propaganda and public perceptions, but also that it influenced and sometimes dominated real assessments and beliefs of the leaders. This was the most insidious aspect of the process of reciprocal prejudgment and projection of blame. Moreover, while reality could be interpreted (sometimes easily, sometimes only by feats of unconscious legerdemain) as supporting the image of the enemy and of permanent conflict, there was an underlying ideological conception that established the essential foundation for the whole Cold War—the Marxist-Leninist conception of world class struggle as an objective phenomenon, rendering inevitable and inescapable a global geopolitical conflict. That such a Marxist-Leninist worldview underlay Soviet thinking and policy was, if sometimes misunderstood in terms of its operational role, obviously recognized by Western leaders, who tirelessly drew attention to World Communism as the enemy. What was not reflected upon, although it would not have been denied, was that the attribution of this worldview to the leaders of the Soviet Union and "World Communism" *also underlay the Western policy of anti-Communism.* Containment of Soviet and communist expansion was seen as necessary because that was seen as the driving force behind the concrete adversary: the leaders of the Soviet Union and all at their command.

Acts of state policy that might have been taken even if the communist ideology had never existed were nonetheless taken by both sides in the belief that they were sanctioned, respectively, by communism and by anti-communist containment. Moreover, while Western policy (in alternating phases of confrontation and détente) remained essentially one of containment, many in the West went an important step further. Why, was their argument, should the West continue a policy of mere containment that could, even if successful, last indefinitely, and moreover might some time fail. Why not extirpate communism, defeat and destroy the Soviet empire and the Soviet Union, and not merely contain its further expansion. Why not roll back and defeat and destroy communism? Although sometimes rhetorically powerful in domestic political propaganda, especially in the United States, and sometimes inhibiting palliatives such as détente, this logical embrace of ultra anti-communism never became state policy in the West. But the Manichaean ideological underpinning was there for the containment version of Western policy that *was* the heart of operative ideology and policy from the late 1940s to the late 1980s.

If only briefly, note must also be taken of the fact that the ideologically driven dynamic of the Cold War also had serious repercussions and impact on the internal life of each country, more pervasively in the case of the Soviet Union (above all in Stalin's day), but reaching far beyond obvious excesses such as McCarthyism in the United States as well. Some have characterized the result as the rise of the "national security state."

In the final analysis, the shared ideological worldview of communism/anti-communism, imputing an ineluctable contest, was the distinguishing feature defining the Cold War. In Western analytical terms, the Cold War was a zero-sum game in which the gains of one side were automatically losses to the other, ruling out genuine compromise, reconciliation, shared interests, and conflict resolution by any means but prevailing over the other. In Marxist-Leninist terms, this was encapsulated in the phrase *Kto kogo?* Who will prevail over whom? In analytical terms, the communist version posited a "correlation of forces" between adversaries, a version of the balance of power with the important distinction that while the given relationship at any moment would be in flux, the ultimate objective and result would be not an equilibrium balance, but victory for the side that prevailed when the correlation ultimately tipped decisively. This conception was rarely recognized in the West, and when it was it was almost always interpreted in terms of the military balance of forces, which was *not* the Marxist-Leninist conception (military power being an important factor, one crucially important not to neglect, but neither the driving force of history nor the ultimate arbiter, and hence not the foundation of Soviet policy).

The shared view of the ideology of "communism/anti-communism" was an amalgam of myth and reality. Neither side was set on "world domination" with the clarity, intensity, consistency, or malevolence imputed by the adversary. Yet leaders on both sides did foresee and seek to counter efforts of their adversaries in the belief that the enemy was foreordained (or believed he was foreordained) to carry the struggle to the end. Moreover, leaders on both sides *did* hold ideologies that foresaw and sought to further global hegemony of their own system. Although the Marxist-Leninist ideology was most explicit, the American-led counter-communism ideology was not guided only by containment of communism. There was a strong belief in the Wilsonian and Rooseveltian themes of "making the world safe for democracy" and assumptions about the nature of democracy that excluded any place for an ideology opposed to pluralism, human rights, and other attributes of a "world community." (Moreover, as *Time* magazine had dubbed it, the world was now living in "the American Century.")

The global rivalry spawned by the communist/anti-communist shared worldview also meant that other aims and values were perforce subordinated "for the duration" to the supreme task of waging and winning the Cold War. This meant, as earlier noted, even certain curbs on normal freedoms at home in the interests of security. It also meant subordinating other considerations in relationships with other countries, overlooking some rather large anomalies in depicting the anti-communist coalition as the "Free World." Many of its members lacked human and political rights no less or even more than did citizens of some communist countries.

This was one major distinction of the ideologically undergirded Cold War that distinguished it from earlier geopolitical rivalries such as the Great Game played between Great Britain and Russia over Southwest and Central Asia in the nineteenth century. But there were others. The ideologically based zero-sum game approach to the global rivalry in a bipolar world also subordinated the leavening influences of the balance of great powers in the eighteenth and nineteenth centuries.

One Cold War legacy that is particularly pernicious is the denunciation of those accused of judging actions of the two sides in terms of "moral equivalence." The Soviet Union and the United States each covertly provided funds to opposing sides, for example, in the Italian elections of 1948. From a Cold War standpoint, as we saw it, the Soviet Union was aiding communist subversion in Italy, while the United States was reacting to support democracy. To suggest that both sides were engaged in similar activities, it was said, would be to suggest moral equivalence of the Soviet and U.S. actions. Similarly, to regard NATO and the Warsaw Pact as counterparts was seen as equating an alliance of free countries and a Soviet-dominated bloc of satellites; to be guilty of according moral equivalence to the latter. Because the aims, the moral ends, of the two sides were seen as wholly different, it was regarded as careless (or worse) to suggest any equivalence in the means employed. Yet there were many similarities in the geopolitical waging of the Cold War. Hopefully, in the climate of a post–Cold War world it will be possible to be more objective in our judgments.

There was no moral equivalence of the two systems implied by a similarity or even identity of many means of *waging* the Cold War. There was a vital moral distinction (and, it turned out, a practical advantage) to a system based on choice versus one based on dictatorship in the struggle of the Cold War. At the same time, this does not necessarily mean that everything the West did was right and everything the Soviet side did was wrong, as was usually depicted during the Cold War.

With the growing access in recent years to formerly secret documentation in the archives of the United States, and now of the former Soviet Union, as well as other countries, it is becoming possible to examine many episodes of the geopolitical contests of the Cold War with much greater awareness both of the situation as known and perceived by various parties at the time, and of actions taken. "The facts," however, rarely speak for themselves; there is, for example, need to consider context and the extent of contemporary knowledge of various facts by decisionmakers. There is also need to look objectively at the evidence and not prejudge actions by either side in terms of Cold War viewpoints or long-assumed views.

Reflections on the Cold War concern recent history but are also relevant for the future. I hope this account of one man's journey through the Cold War may stimulate the reader's reflections too.

Epilogue:
A Personal Reminiscence

With the exception of the first chapter, on my formative years, coinciding with the formative years of the Cold War, I have omitted personal, autobiographical discussion not directly relating to my passage through the years of the Cold War. References even to my wife, Vera, my constant companion through the journey, and my son, Alex, have entered only rarely, inasmuch as I have focused on my professional activities and observations. I will not, in this brief epilogue, seek to fill in my personal history and that of my family, but I think it is not inappropriate at least to mention here my closest companions and a few words on how they too have been affected by our shared experience of the Cold War period, as well as to add a few closing personal ruminations.

To start at the end, I will note that as I write today, a decade after the end of the Cold War, Vera and I are enjoying retirement—although I continue to be fairly active in research, writing, and participating in conferences and "oral history" projects, mainly focused on aspects or episodes of the Cold War. At the present time, for example, I am working on the underexamined role of intelligence in the history and historiography of the Cold War. Nonetheless, I am "retired." In addition to our home in Washington and weekend home (in a two-hundred-year-old manor of a one-time thousand-acre tobacco plantation in nearby Maryland), we have recently acquired a classical eighteenth-century château in France as a summer residence. Our son, Alex, and his family (wife Ellen and two wonderful adopted Chinese boys, Nicholas and Andrei) live in Hong Kong, now for over a decade, where he is active in investment banking.

My youngest brother, Douglas, who followed me in Russian studies at Princeton, has recently retired after thirty years' service in intelligence—three years as an officer in military intelligence in Germany and Vietnam and twenty-seven in the Central Intelligence Agency, serving in both the Intelligence and Operations directorates. He is now engaged in historical studies related to the Cold War. (His wife, Paulette, continues to work at CIA.) My other brother, Stanley David, has retired after a career in private industry in the Midwest, not directly related to the Cold War (save for two years of military service in Army Intelligence). All of my two brothers' four sons, like ours, are engaged in nongovernmental professions (ranging from advertising design to postgraduate studies in philosophy). So two-thirds of my family's Cold War generation, but none of our progeny, have chosen government service.

My wife's careers (in real estate renovation and sale of period houses, and later as a stock investor) had to be interrupted and curtailed by frequent travel and residence abroad, although she continues to be active now in our semiretirement. She of course shared directly in the important social dimension of diplomacy and foreign service. The role of Foreign Service wives has been underappreciated—certainly under- or unrewarded even by the Foreign Service, even though until the 1960s wives were "graded" in the annual personnel performance evaluations of all officers. Ambassador Harlan Cleveland at the U.S. Mission to NATO added a personal note saying of Vera that her "combination of brains and femininity has adjusted well to the special requirements" of service abroad as a Foreign Service wife. And his successor, Ambassador Bob Ellsworth, commented even on the official evaluation that I was "ably abetted" by Vera, whom he characterized as "charming, cultivated, a pleasant hostess who enjoys life overseas."

Our son, Alex, experienced life in a family deeply interested in international affairs. In fact, we generally spoke Russian at home in his early years to help him acquire it as a second native language. Later, of course, he lived abroad and traveled widely with us. He was first influenced toward East Asia when at age 18–19 he accompanied me to Hong Kong, Bangkok, and Rangoon. Of course he experienced the disadvantages, as well as the advantages, of change of domicile and school. After Groton prep school, he graduated from the University of Pennsylvania.

Our immediate and extended families suffered no ill consequence from the tensions of foreign service in the Cold War, but we know others who did. Especially in the clandestine services of the CIA there were special stresses stemming from the need for officers to shut their wives and families out from most of their own lives, to a far greater extent than Foreign Service or military families. Military and civilian foreign service families have, however, also often found the strains of overseas life, frequent moves, and long unpredictable hours of government service stressful, sometimes even too much to bear. Many, of course, have adapted well, and some have thrived on this life. But it was not for all.

The question that perhaps *should* have been asked by government personnel engaged in foreign service, especially in the stresses of the Cold War, I believe surely was: Was it worth it? Did whatever First Secretary X, or Lt. Colonel Y, or clandestine Case Officer Z was doing really matter? More precisely, did it count for enough to be worth the hard work and often sacrifices involved? Yet in my observation very few ever posed that question even to themselves. There was always a job to do. Many saw it as a challenge and rose to meet it. Some, to be sure, burned out and either left or carried on minimally until early retirement. But most saw his or her tasks as important parts of a larger mosaic, perhaps more important than would a detached objective observer, and worked hard to accomplish these tasks.

On reflection in retirement, many who think back on this question may conclude that what we worked so hard at, and indeed what we accomplished, was less important than it seemed at the time. And usually that is true. On further reflection, however, a recognition that while the contributions of any individual, indeed of *every* individual, even highly placed, may be less than one wishes it to have been (and probably once thought it to have been), that very fact bears witness that the collective contributions of many *did* accomplish whatever was achieved—and that gives meaning and value to the efforts of all.

Along with virtually all my contemporaries in the late 1940s and early 1950s I saw the emerging Cold War as the great challenge of our time, and the Soviet Union under Stalin's Communist worldview and dictatorial control as constituting an inescapable and implacable adversary. With distance of time and historical hindsight it is easier to take a more detached perspective and see more readily that the actions of both sides and interactions between them contributed to generating the Cold War and to its subsequent pursuit. Nonetheless, I continue to believe there *was* a great challenge to which we were obliged to respond. Whether our response was always necessary or wise is another, and important, matter. Also, the initial consensus of support for extraordinary measures to meet what was perceived as an extraordinary threat later changed, as (I believe) the nature of the adversary and the threat in the post-Stalin era changed.

For many, the Vietnam War was a turning point in public acceptance of the view that American leaders were to be entrusted with judgments and decisions on waging the Cold War. The postwar consensus on foreign policy was shattered. From the outset, in the early 1960s and especially the critical years 1964 and 1965, I strongly opposed our increasing involvement in Vietnam (although, as I have noted, I was not involved in the policymaking). I could understand the argument that it was necessary to display resolute resolve both to adversaries and allies, but I did not see either American alliance commit-ments or the geostrategic balance as requiring us to intervene there. For me, Vietnam was a terrible mistake, costly in lives and treasure, because I believed that it was unnecessary to meet the real requirements of waging the Cold War. But I did not identify myself with the active protest movement, even psycho-logically.

My own greatest divergence from official thinking in the 1970s and 1980s concerned the military requirements for deterrence. As I have indicated in this memoir, I believed that our official estimates, and still more the political rhet-oric and military programs, greatly exaggerated both existing and prospective Soviet military strategic capabilities and ominous Soviet strategic intentions. This is, I believe, now even more convincingly demonstrable, but it was clear enough then. The various political, military, military-industrial—and psycho-logical—incentives for overstating the threat were too handy to permit clear-eyed assessments. I have noted many examples, and my efforts to moderate some of them, in this account, and I may on another occasion seek to do so more systematically. More broadly, the subject of the influence of reciprocal perceptions (and misconceptions) of the adversaries requires much more attention.

For my own part, while not wishing to sound (or to be) too self-satisfied, I am grateful for the opportunity to have served throughout the Cold War and at least to have done what I could do to contribute to the overall achievement. I would not for a minute wish not to have served in any of the varied analyti-cal, staff, advising, and diplomatic roles that I had the good fortune to hold for thirty years of the Cold War. Nor do I regret spending the last ten years of the Cold War and the years since principally as a diplomatic historian and scholar of the Cold War. This memoir represents my recollection and reflection on that experience in the hope it will be of interest to at least some others who may have shared the journey through these years in similar or differing ways, and also to those too young to have had the opportunity to do so.

Index

Aaron, David, 249

ABM. *See* Antiballistic missile system

ABM (Antiballistic Missile)Treaty, 233, 255, 259, 262, 263, 270–71, 282, 329, 355, 357, 373, 385; "reinterpretation" of, 357–59, 373

Absolute Weapon, The (Brodie), 6

Accident Measures Agreement, 263, 271, 285

ACDA. *See* Arms Control and Disarmament Agency

Acheson, Dean, 41, 140, 167, 175, 177, 374, 375

Adams, Paul, 198–99

ADMs. *See* Atomic demolition munitions

Africa, 295–96, 326, 387

Aesopian language, 17

Afghanistan, 285, 336, 338, 339, 345, 387

Agca, Mehmet Ali, 312

Agitator's Handbook for the Festival (Moscow, 1959), 34

AID (Agency for International Development), 135, 136, 298

Air Defense Command, 10

Air War College, 14, 62

Akalovsky, Alexander, 72

Akhromeyev, Sergei, 361

Albania, 101, 102, 221, 309

Aleksandrov, Anatoly P., 95, 97

Alekseyev, Aleksandr, 185

Alekseyev, Nikolai, 250

Alibi Club, 42

Allen, Richard, 328

Alliance consultations, 230–34. *See also* NATO

Allied Nuclear Force (ANF), 152–53

Alliluyeva, Svetlana, 219

Allison, Royal, 210, 248, 249, 251, 267, 269, 273

Alsop, Joseph, 65

American Committee on East-West Accord, 341

American National Exhibition in Moscow (*1959*), 76–80

American Red Cross, 25–28

American University speech (John F. Kennedy, *1963*), 165, 180–81, 184, 277

Amerika journal, 35

Ames, Aldrich, 367, 369

Ames, Iowa, 26, 28

Ames Daily Tribune, 26

Amin, Hafizullah, 285

Amory, Robert, 39, 40, 48–49, 50, 63, 204

"Anatoly," 351, 360, 361

Anderson, Orvil, 15

Andropov, Yury V., 217, 310, 346

Angleton, James Jesus, 104–05, 117

Angola, 288, 296, 326

Ankara (NPG meeting), 224, 225

Antarctica, 45–46, 148, 156

Antigua conference, 185

Antiballistic missile systems, 205–11, 218, 225, 245, 253, 341, 345, 355–56. *See also* Strategic Defense Initiative (SDI)

"Anti-Party Group," 30, 37

Anti-satellite systems (ASAT), 197

Arab-Israeli War of *1967*, 207, 214–15, 217, 230, 238; of *1973*, 291, 326

Arbatov, Aleksei, 344
Arbatov, Georgy, 210, 310, 343, 344, 346, 352, 359, 360, 368–69
Arbenz, Jacobo, 42
Arctic, 55, 253
Argonne National Laboratory, 96
Armenia, 79, 346
Arms control and disarmament, 55, 60, 138–40, 141–42, 147, 207, 385–86, 390–91; Soviet view, 46, 60, 142
Arms Control and Disarmament Agency (ACDA), 125, 138–40, 156, 158, 192, 194, 206, 207, 208, 210, 211, 212, 245, 246, 248, 258, 272–74, 279
Army journal, 66, 67
Arnold, Henry H. ("Hap"), 9
Artamonov, Nikolai (Shadrin, Nicholas), 118
Asia, 386, 387, 397
Aspin, Leslie, 340
Assessing the Adversary: Estimates by the Eisenhower Administration of Soviet Intentions and Capacities (Garthoff), 368
Association of the U.S. Army, 67
Aström, Sverker, 106
"Athens Guidelines" (NATO), 147, 151, 152
Atlantic Council, 340, 354–55
Atlas (ICBM), 20
Atlee, Clement, 24
Atomic bomb, 2, 37, 95, 366. *See also* Nuclear weapons
Atomic demolition munitions (ADMs), 224
Atomic Energy Commission (AEC), xii, 90, 93, 95, 98, 109, 139, 194
Austria, 106, 236, 249

B-*47*, medium bomber (U.S.), 191
B-*52*, heavy bomber (U.S.), 258
Backfire, medium bomber (Soviet), 239
Badger, medium bomber (Soviet), 106
Baker, James, 2
Baldwin, Hanson, 70
Balkans, 115, 302, 305, 317–18, 371
Ball, George, 123, 137, 153, 163, 169, 179, 181, 195
Ballis, William, 17
Ballistic missile defense (BMD). *See* Antiballistic missile systems
Baltic States, 101
Barghoorn, Frederick, 6, 164
Barber, Arthur, 207
Barmine, Alexander, 13
Barnes, Earl, 49, 51
"Basic Principles" Agreement (U.S.-Soviet), 264, 282–83, 284, 326
Basovsky, Vladimir, 307–08, 308–09, 317

Bay of Pigs (Cuba), 42, 120, 133, 143, 175
Bazhenov, Aleksei, 365
Beam, Jacob, 85, 123, 291
Bear heavy bomber (Soviet), 282
Belgrade, 147; U.S. embassy, 306, 318
Beloyarsk, 75, 82, 85, 86
Berchtold, Leopold, 249
Beria, Lavrenty, 105
Berlin, 371; blockade (*1948–49*), 2, 6, 33, 126, 381; crisis (*1958–62*), xiii, 46, 60, 109, 113, 123, 125–31, 143, 170, 171, 174, 175, 176, 182, 224, 234, 277; East Berlin, 18, 127–28, 147; Four Power Agreement (*1971*), 127; Wall, 126–28, 368; West Berlin, 46, 106, 126–31, 146, 151
Bessmertnykh, Aleksandr, 216, 371
Bissell, Richard, 40
Black, Cyril E., 5, 22, 54, 164, 372
BND (Bundesnachrichtendienst) (FRG), 53, 54, 201
BNSP (Basic National Security Policy), 122–23
Board of National Estimates (BNE). *See* Central Intelligence Agency, Office of National Estimates
Bogdan, Cornelius, 202
Bogdanov, Radomir, 368
Bohlen, Charles ("Chip"), 88, 123, 171, 172, 199, 212, 381
Bohm, Stellan, 106, 107
Bohr, Niels, 3
Boland Amendment, 358
Bol'shakov, Georgy, 128, 185, 187
Bolshevik Revolution (*1917*), 360, 370
Bomarc missile, 108
"Bomber Gap," 47, 382
Bonn, 20, 290; NPG meeting, 225
Borel, Paul, 99
Borkenau, Franz, 17
Bowie, Robert, 15, 62
Brandt, Willy, 288
Brezhnev, Leonid, 253, 254, 255, 262, 282, 308, 336, 383
"Brezhnev Doctrine," 236
Brodie, Bernard, 6, 20, 62, 67
Brookings Institution, xiv, 336, 337–38, 339, 340, 341, 343, 358, 360, 365, 372
Brosio, Manlio, 239
Brown, Harold, 248, 273, 363
Bruce, David, 212
Brucker, Wilbur M., 70–71
Brussels, 212, 213, 215, 219, 222, 229, 232, 233, 235, 237, 238, 239, 244, 245, 271–72, 278, 298, 388
Brzezinski, Zbigniew, 79, 124, 216, 226, 303–04, 306, 335, 338, 342, 392

Buchan, Alastair, 63

Bucharest, 148, 149, 201–02; U.S. embassy, 306, 318

Buckley, William F., 102

Budapest, 31, 148–49, 304, 371; U.S. embassy, 149, 304

Bukowski, Dietrich, 307

Bulgaria, xiii, 146, 148, 164, 302–24, 343, 371; author as U.S. ambassador, 302–24, 330, 335, 388; foreign policy, 316–18, 319–23; internal affairs, 315–16; Politburo, 309, 311, 315, 320, 322; relations with Soviet Union/Russia, 316–18; trade, 313–14, 317, 319, 321

Bundy, McGeorge, 123, 124, 135, 150, 155, 157, 159, 160, 168, 177, 182, 195, 215, 266, 361, 389

Bundy, William P., 22, 23, 37, 40, 41, 43, 61, 121

Bunker, Ellsworth, 25

Bush, George H. W., 328, 377, 379, 380

Bush administration, 249, 388

"C," 110. See also Secret Intelligence Service

Cabell, Pearre, 86

Cairo, 2, 4, 215

Cambodia, 280, 295

Camp David, 81

Canada, 53, 156, 302

Canadian Defence College, 62, 201

Cape Canaveral, 74

Cape Kennedy, 198

"Captive Nations Week," 77, 84

Caribbean, 281, 327, 387

"Caribbean Crisis," 170. See Cuban missile crisis

Carlucci, Frank, 299

Caron U.S.S., 350

Carr, Edward H., 4

Carter, Jimmy, 216, 288, 303, 327, 336, 338, 341, 342, 379

Carter administration, 249, 303, 334, 338, 341, 342, 362, 388

"Carter Doctrine," 338

Case, Clifford, 302

Casey, William, 328, 343

Castro, Fidel, 132, 173, 179, 180, 184, 185, 186, 261, 371, 380

Castro, Raoul, 185–86

Central America, 327

Central Asia, 148–49, 344, 372, 394

Central intelligence (definition), 43

Central Intelligence Agency (CIA), xii, 3, 6, 8, 17, 22–23, 35, 37–38, 39–60, 77n, 97, 99, 103, 120, 136, 156, 185, 248, 250, 257, 258, 272, 291, 296, 297–98, 315, 333, 345, 347–48, 362, 364, 367, 368, 379, 382, 397; Deputy Director for Intelligence (DDI), 39, 63, 169; Directorate of Intelligence (DDI), 22, 39, 41n, 44, 56, 73, 84; Deputy Director for Plans (DDP), 39, 52; Directorate for Plans (DDP), 39, 41n, 55, 56, 64, 73, 76, 105; Directorate of Intelligence (DI), 397; Directorate of Operations (DO), 351, 367, 397; Division, Soviet Russia (SR), 11, 64; Division, Soviet/East European (SE); 351, 367; Central Reference, Office of (OCR), 99; Current Intelligence, Office of (OCI), 73, 89; Domestic Contacts, Office of, 347, 351; National Estimates, Office of (ONE), xii, 22, 39–60, 120, 126, 335, 379, 384; Policy Coordination, Office of (OPC), 52; Research and Reports, Office of (ORR), 52; Scientific Intelligence, Office of (OSI), 55, 75; Special Operations, Office of (OSO), 52; Technical Services, Office of (OTS), 76–77

Center for Strategic and International Studies (CSIS), 353, 364

CFE Treaty. See Conventional Forces in Europe Treaty

Charyk, Joseph, 155

Chavchavadze, David P., 5, 103

"Checkpoint Charlie," 127–29

Chelyabinsk, 94

Chernenko, Konstantin, 308

Chervov, Nikolai, 346, 350, 361

Chiang Mai, 296

"Chickadee," 113

Chikalenko, Nikolai, 25–26

China, 7, 44, 64, 98, 132, 142, 166, 189, 194, 195, 206, 217, 225, 285, 294, 309, 340, 372–73, 387; and SALT, 259, 267–68; relations with United States, 309, 327, 340, 370–72

"China card," 279

Christopher, Warren, 302

Churchill, Sir Winston, 1, 24, 74, 386

CIA. See Central Intelligence Agency

CINC STRIKE, 198

Civil defense, U.S., 25, 28, 122; Soviet, 25–26

Clandestine services (CIA), 23, 40, 52, 56, 101, 102, 164, 201, 397. See also Central Intelligence Agency; Espionage

Clay, Lucius, 128, 147

Cleveland, Harlan, 207, 212 215, 227, 228, 233, 236, 237, 238, 239, 242n, 397

Clifford, Clark, 211, 212, 225

Cline, Ray, 22, 169, 185, 186, 280

Clinton administration, 249, 357

CMEA (Council on Mutual Economic Assistance), 317

Coffin, William Sloane, Jr., 102

Colby, William, 105, 328

Cold Dawn (Newhouse), 274

Colligan, William, 89

Columbia University, 4, 12, 13, 16, 17, 54, 365

"Comint." *See* Communications intelligence

Comintern, 352–53

Commentary journal, 334

Committee on Disarmament, 42

Committee on the Present Danger, 327, 331, 342, 389n

Committee of Principals, 138–39, 158–59, 162, 206, 210–11, 192, 196, 206, 210–11

Committee of State Security (KGB). *See* KGB

Common Market, 147. *See also* European Union

Communication, 56, 130–31, 278, 293–94, 300–01

Communications intelligence ("Comint"), 47, 64, 103. *See also* Signals intelligence

Communist Bloc, 57, 389. *See also* Soviet bloc and Sino-Soviet bloc

Communist insurgencies, 131–38, 189, 387

Communist Party of the Soviet Union. *See* Soviet Union

Comprehensive Test Ban Treaty (CTBT), 166. *See also* Nuclear testing

Conference on Disarmament (CD), 142. *See also* ENDC

Conference on Security and Cooperation in Europe (CSCE), 222, 288–89, 311, 314, 387–88

Congo, 132, 296

Congress, U.S., 270–71, 287, 327, 340, 357

Conrad, Clyde Lee, 235

Containment, 1, 189, 220–21, 375–77, 378, 380, 381, 383, 389, 393

Conventional Forces in Europe (CFE) Treaty, 386

"Correlation of Forces," 393–94

Council on Foreign Relations, 62, 63, 137, 334, 340

Counterinsurgency, 131–38, 189

Counterintelligence, 104–05

Covert operations, 35, 42, 52–53, 101–02, 135, 175, 221, 343, 381, 382–83, 384

Crawford, William, 6

Crimea, 28, 350

CSCE. *See* Conference on Security and Cooperation in Europe

CTBT. *See* Comprehensive [Nuclear] Test Ban Treaty

Cuba, 1, 20, 132, 280–282, 308, 372, 380; Cienfuegos confrontation, 280–82; Soviet brigade in, 180, 310, 322

Cuban missile crisis (*1962*), xiii, 92, 113, 116–17, 127, 131, 145, 149, 168–87, 262, 277, 280–82, 361, 368, 380, 390

Cushman, Robert E., Jr., 72, 74

Cyrankiewicz, Jozef, 84

Czechoslovakia, 130, 146, 148, 235, 237; *1948* coup, 33, 381; *1968* crisis and intervention, 212, 221, 228, 229, 230, 236, 239, 241, 277, 303, 304, 388

Dakar, 172

Dallin, Alexander, 30–31

Danilenko, Ignaty, 366–67

Daoud, Mohammed, 285

Dartmouth Conferences, 360

David, Vaclav, 146

Davies, Rodger, 299

Davis, Richard, 6

DEA (Drug Enforcement Administration), 298, 312

Dean, Arthur, 141, 166

Deception, 199, 235–36, 329, 384

Decker, George H., 159

Defending Peace and Freedom: Toward Strategic Stability in the Year 2000 (Atlantic Council), 354–55

Defense, Department of, xii, 121, 125, 136, 172, 173, 177, 213, 251, 257, 258, 260, 296, 297, 331, 335, 364, 365

Defense Intelligence Agency (DIA), 53, 118, 201, 364

de Gaulle, Charles, 155, 226, 288

"Demonstration" use of nuclear weapons, 225

"Desert Strike," 198–201, 353

Détente, 145, 165, 167, 181, 188, 189, 222–23, 226–27, 239–42, 243–44, 264, 275, 277–91, 325–26, 338, 339, 380, 381, 383, 386, 387–88, 392; in Europe, 226, 288, 388

Détente and Confrontation: U.S.-Soviet Relations from Nixon to Reagan (Garthoff), 341, 342, 348

Deterrence, 10, 57–70, 151–52, 182–83, 204, 207, 223–24, 226, 332, 354, 364–65, 377, 378, 389, 390–91, 399; existential, 182, 389n, 390; graduated, 70, 183, 223; mutual, 58–60, 66–70, 256, 264, 265–66, 283, 332, 334, 389, 390; NATO, 151–52, 208, 231–32; Soviet, 57–60, 332, 384. *See also* Flexible response

Deterrence and the Revolution in Soviet Military Doctrine (Garthoff), 364–65

Devers, Jacob L., 199, 200
Dillon, C. Douglas, 175, 181, 182, 328
DIA. *See* Defense Intelligence Agency
"Differentiation," 222, 288, 303
Dimitrov, Georgy, 309, 353
Disarmament. *See* Arms control and
    Disarmament; Arms Control and
    Disarmament Agency
Disinformation, 119, 235–36, 329
Dissidents: in USSR, 36, 53, 78, 79; in
    Bulgaria, 316
"Distant" (signal), 116–17
Dmitriev, Boris (Boris Pyadyshev), 308
Dnepropetrovsk, 92
Dobrynin, Anatoly, 160, 172, 185, 191, 192,
    205, 216, 230, 236, 243, 245, 254, 255, 268,
    271, 278, 280, 289, 353, 359
Doolittle, James, 382
"Doty Group," 210, 218
Double agents, 101, 103, 118, 119, 297
Douglas-Home, Alexander, 192
"Doves," 171, 203
Downey, John, 102
DS (*Durzhavna Sigurnost*), Bulgarian State
    Security, 312
Dubs, Adolf ("Spike"), 299
Dulles, Allen, xii, 13, 16, 39, 40, 41, 42, 47, 48,
    49, 51, 52, 54, 55, 56, 63, 73, 74, 75, 79, 86,
    94, 99, 100, 108, 110, 111, 112, 113, 193,
    368
Dulles, John Foster, 41, 42, 54, 67
Dunn, Frederick, 6
Durand, Dana, 64
Durzhavna Sigurnost. *See* DS

"Eagle," 109
Eagleburger, Lawrence, 278, 301, 372
Eaker, Ira C., 199, 200
East Berlin. *See* Berlin
East Germany. *See* Germany
Eastern Europe, 6, 7, 14, 18, 25, 27, 33, 39, 44,
    45, 46, 77, 101, 105, 120, 125, 145–46,
    148–51, 167, 201–02, 216, 221–22, 226,
    236, 240–42, 288, 302–24, 364, 386, 388
Eddelman, Clyde D., 199
Eddy, William A., 4
Egypt, 2, 4, 215, 285
Egyptian-Israeli "canal war" (*1971*), 280
Einstein, Albert, 3
Eisenhower, Dwight D., 14, 15,16, 24, 26, 27,
    74, 81, 84, 86, 88–89, 94, 98, 132, 155, 156,
    165, 368, 379, 382
Eisenhower administration, 14, 52, 57, 120,
    122, 125, 132, 138, 152, 368, 373, 381
Electronic intelligence ("Elint"), 101, 103

Elizabeth II (United Kingdom), 111
Ellsberg, Daniel, 122
Ellsworth, Robert, 397
Empedocles, 252
Emigrés, Russian and Soviet, 101, 250
ENDC (Eighteen Nation Disarmament
    Committee), 140–42, 148, 156. *See also*
    Committee on Disarmament
Erlander, Tage, 191
Espionage, 100–19, 164, 234–36, 384
Eurocommunism, 388
European Union, 388
European security, 147, 148–49, 151, 201, 202
Ex Comm (Executive Committee of the
    NSC), 169–79
Ex Comm (Executive Committee of the
    Committee of Principals), 210–11

Falin, Valentin, 353
"Fallex-*60*," 115
Far East, 39, 46, 88
Farley, Philip, 248, 273
FBI (Federal Bureau of Investigation), 44,
    345
FBS (Forward-Based [nuclear delivery]
    Systems), 218, 233, 260–62
Fecteau, Richard, 102
Federenko, Nikolai, 369
Federenko, Sergei, 309
Federation of American Scientists (FAS), 357
Feklisov, Aleksandr, 185, 187
Finland, 3, 249
First strike, 15–16, 114–16, 182, 266. *See also*
    Preventive war; Pre-emptive attack
Fisher, Adrian ("Butch"), 125, 155, 156, 158,
    160, 195, 205, 206, 208, 211
"Fisher Committee," 195
"Flexible response," 132, 138, 151, 223, 224,
    229
Fomin, Alexander (Aleksandr Feklisov), 187
Ford, Gerald, 288, 291, 327, 341, 342, 379,
    380
Ford administration, 327, 341, 388
Foreign Broadcast Information Service
    (FBIS), 17
Foreign Service, 289–99, 397. *See also* State
    Department
Foreign Service Institute, 136, 290, 302, 341,
    353–54
Fosdick, Dorothy, 177
Foster, William C., 140–41, 148, 158, 159,
    161, 162, 192, 196, 205, 211, 230
Fowler, Henry, 328
Fox, Colonel, 5
Fox, William, 6, 62

France, 4, 24, 34, 124, 142, 151, 152, 194, 224, 228, 230, 231, 238, 239, 252, 295, 300–01
Franco, Francisco, 299
"Free World," 342, 375, 394
Fundamentals of Marketing, 370
Fundamentals of Marxism-Leninism, 370
Funston, Keith, 26

G-class Soviet submarine, 281–82
G-*2. See* Intelligence, U.S. Army
Galois, Pierre, 64
Game theory, 10, 15, 18–19, 182–83
Gardner, Richard, 160
Gareyev, Makhmut, 366
Garthoff, Alexander, 11, 296, 344, 396, 397
Garthoff, Andrei, 396
Garthoff, Douglas, 397
Garthoff, Ellen, 396
Garthoff, Nicholas, 396
Garthoff, Paulette, 397
Garthoff, Raymond L., 55, 70, 94, 95, 98, 99, 141, 203, 204, 207, 275, 276, 289, 301, 303, 334, 354
Garthoff, Stanley David, 397
Garthoff, Vera, 11, 25, 76, 77, 272, 296, 302, 305, 307, 310, 313, 319, 323, 351, 396, 397
Gates, Robert, 44, 249
Gavin, James F., 22, 66, 67, 70
Gehlen, Reinhard, 53, 101
Gelb, Leslie, 335
General Staff (Soviet), 114–16, 347, 348, 367
Geopolitical conflict, 1, 187, 284–85, 338, 347, 376, 381, 386, 390, 391–92, 395
Geneva (conferences), 24, 55, 74, 117, 140, 141, 143, 145–48, 154, 156, 159, 160, 190, 191, 192, 212, 230, 256; SALT II meetings, 272, 289
Georgia, 28–29, 346, 347, 353
Georgiev, Ivan-Asen Khristov, 164
Germany, 3, 34, 53, 54, 85, 128, 152, 164, 195, 196, 201–02, 224, 226, 230, 231, 234, 240, 288, 307, 312, 317, 318, 335, 368; East Germany (GDR), 106, 126, 127–28, 129–31, 202, 221, 224, 240, 364, 388; Nazi Germany, 3, 331
Gilpatric, Roswell, 122, 135, 158, 159, 160
"Gilpatric Committee" (nonproliferation), 193–98, 203
Ginev, Atanas, 313
Ginzburg, Alexander, 36, 53
Glassboro summit conference (*1967*), 207, 217, 266
Goethe, Johann W. von, 252
Gomulka, Wladyslaw, 84–85
Goodpaster, Andrew J., 94, 154, 354

Goodby, James, 314
Gorbachev, Mikhail S., 179–80, 308, 333, 338, 344, 348–49, 350, 351, 352, 353, 356, 362, 364, 370, 371, 372, 377, 380, 386, 388–89
Gorbachev administration, 364
Gordievsky, Oleg, 347
Gore, Albert, Sr., 64, 160
Gore, Albert, Jr., 340
Gotsev, Lyuben, 305, 313, 319–23, 323
G/PM. *See* State Department, Politico-Military Affairs
Graybeal, Sidney, 248, 250, 251, 272
"Great Game, The," 367, 394
Great Society, The, 188, 189
Great Transition: American-Soviet Relations and the End of the Cold War (Garthoff), 342
Great Britain. *See* United Kingdom
Green, Howard, 156
Greenland, 152
Gribkov, Anatoly, 182
Griffith, William, 16
Grinevsky, Oleg, 250, 251, 252, 253, 254, 258, 344, 371
Griswold, Francis, 146–47
Gromyko, Andrei A., 140, 159, 160, 161, 184, 185, 191, 206, 230, 263, 344, 361
Grover, Colonel, 14
GRU (*Glavnoye razvedivatel'noye upravleniye*), Soviet military intelligence, 3, 105, 110, 185, 250
Gruenther, Alfred, 193
Guzenko, Igor, 3

Hague, The, NPG meeting, 225
Haig, Alexander, 271, 272, 274, 281, 289, 343
Hajek, Jiri, 146
Hale, Nathan, 41
Halperin, Morton, 210
Hamlett, Barksdale, 163
Hamel Report (NATO), 222, 226–27
Harriman, W. Averell, 73, 81, 165, 166, 191, 195
Harvard University, 12, 13, 17, 40, 54, 62, 185, 210, 328
Havana Conference on Cuban missile crisis, 185, 371–72
"Hawks," 171, 174, 203
Hawks Cay Conference on the Cuban missile crisis, 105
Haworth, Leland, 139
Healey, Denis, 225, 225–26
Helms, Richard, 52, 247, 297–98
Helsinki (SALT meetings), 232, 245, 246, 249, 250, 255, 264, 265, 269, 288
Heritage Foundation, 358

Hilsman, Roger, 43n, 133, 137
"Historicus" (George Morgan), 6, 14
Hitch, Charles J., 10
Hoover, Herbert, 94
Hot line (direct U.S.-Soviet communications
    link), 56, 161, 214, 263, 385
How Russia Makes War (Garthoff), 21
Hudson Institute, 10
Hughes, Thomas, 198
Huizenga, John, 22, 60, 174
Hull, John, 138
Human intelligence ("Humint"), 103–04.
    See also Espionage
Humphrey, Hubert, 212, 304
Hungary, 148, 235, 303, 304, 321; uprising of
    1956, 16, 18, 25, 31, 33, 221, 277
Hunt, Howard, 102

ICBM. *See* Intercontinental ballistic missiles
"*Ice worm*," 152
I Chose Freedom (Kravchenko), 3
Ideology in the Cold War, 3, 57–58, 67–68,
    221, 375–77, 383, 392. *See also* Marxism-
    Leninism
IISS. *See* International Institute for Strategic
    Studies
Iklé, Fred C., 10
IL-*28* Soviet light bomber, 178–79
"Illegals," 103. *See also* Espionage
Imagery intelligence ("Imint"), 47, 104
India, 193, 194, 214
Indochina, 391. *See also* Vietnam
Indo-Pakistani War of *1965*, 214; of *1971*, 280
INR (Bureau of Intelligence and Research,
    Department of State), 133, 139. *See also*
    State Department, intelligence
Institute of Atomic Energy (Moscow), 91
Institute of Europe (Moscow), 359
Institute of Military History (Moscow), 361
Institute for the Study of the USSR
    (Munich), 16
Institute of USA and Canada (Moscow), 210,
    310, 343, 344, 346, 359, 368, 369
Institute for the World Economy and
    International Relations (IMEMO),
    Moscow, 344, 352
Intelligence, Cold War, 368, 371, 384; esti-
    mates, xii, 44, 126–27, 328–33, 362–63,
    384; State Department, 4, 12, 43, 46, 48,
    117, 126, 133, 216, 280; U.S. Air Force, 11,
    12, 13, 47, 48–49, 59, 60, 112, 333; U.S.
    Army, 5, 11, 12, 13, 21, 48–49, 53, 101,
    112, 397; U.S. Navy, 48–50, 112, 350;
    Warsaw Pact, 234–35. *See also* Central
    Intelligence Agency; KGB.

Intercontinental ballistic missiles (ICBMs),
    10, 19, 20, 47, 48, 62, 74, 80–81, 88, 92,
    111–12, 143, 170, 209, 211, 233, 255, 261,
    262, 269, 271
Interim Agreement on Offensive Arms (SALT
    I), 233, 261, 262, 270–71, 282, 332
Intermediate-range ballistic missiles
    (IRBMs), 19, 46, 48, 74, 152, 170, 172,
    206, 207, 209, 211, 218, 233, 260, 345
Intermediate-range nuclear forces (INF)
    negotiations, 346, 356; treaty, 92, 233, 356,
    372, 286
International Affairs journal, 308, 365
International Institute for Strategic Studies
    (IISS), 62–63, 167, 341, 343
International Communism, 389. *See also*
    World Communism
Iran, 42, 66, 285, 298, 309, 379
Iran-Contra scandal, 343, 358, 359
Iraq, 285, 295, 366
IRBMs. *See* Intermediate-range ballistic
    missiles
Iron Curtain, 1, 25, 127, 302, 386
"Ironbark," 113
Irwin, John, 247, 289
Israel, 194, 214–15, 280, 295, 326
Italy, 4, 123, 195, 196, 230, 295, 298–99, 307,
    312, 394
Ivanov, Semën P., 114–15
Ivy League (and CIA), 12, 40, 102

Jackson, Henry ("Scoop"), 177, 270, 271, 274,
    287
Jackson-Vanik amendment, 287
Jacob, Richard, 116
Japan, 1, 2, 135, 194, 285, 289, 317
JCS. *See* Joint Chiefs of Staff (U.S.)
JIC. *See* Joint Intelligence Committee
    (U.K.)
Joint Chiefs of Staff (JCS), 122, 139, 144, 156,
    158, 159, 162, 163, 166–67, 171, 173, 191,
    195, 204, 205, 206, 209, 210, 211, 251, 257,
    258, 273
Joint Intelligence Committee (JIC) (U.K.),
    54, 148
Joint Press Research Service (JPRS), 37, 38
John Paul II, 312
Johnson, Lyndon B., 188, 189, 190, 192, 193,
    197, 205, 208, 209, 210, 211, 212, 213, 214,
    226, 279, 379
Johnson, Robert L., 234
Johnson, U. Alexis, 120, 121, 123, 125, 135,
    143–44, 147, 154, 157, 158, 160, 162, 169,
    179, 195, 198, 203, 214, 242, 272–73, 276,
    279, 280, 282, 290, 291

Johnson administration, 188, 189, 190, 191, 195, 213, 219, 232, 304
"Johnson Committee" (nonproliferation), 193, 195, 214
Jordan, 28, 295
Jupiter MRBM, 152
Justice, Department of, 247

Kahn, Herman, 10, 16, 167
Kaiser, Philip, 304n, 336
KAL-*007* (Korean Airlines *007*) incident, 346, 347
Kalugin, Oleg, 118
Kampelmann, Max M., 328
Karmal, Babrak, 285
Katzenbach, Edward, 62
Kaufmann, William, 10, 67, 70
Kaysen, Carl, 123, 155, 156, 158
Keegan, George, 333
Keeny, Spurgeon M., Jr., 124, 193, 205
Kennan, George F., 1, 6, 16, 43, 54, 123, 147, 381
Kennedy, Edward, 340
Kennedy, John F., 64, 111, 120, 122, 126, 128, 131–34, 135, 138, 141, 143, 149, 151, 153, 162, 163, 164, 165, 166, 167, 168, 171, 173, 175, 177, 179, 180, 181, 184, 186, 187, 190, 191, 277, 280, 379
Kennedy, Robert F., 128, 133, 135, 187
Kennedy administration, 55, 120, 122, 131, 138, 143, 145, 151, 154, 158, 164–65, 171, 188, 281, 373
Kerensky, Alexander, 219
KGB (*Komitet gosudarstvennoi bezopasnosti*), Committee for State Security (Soviet), 50, 102, 105, 117, 188, 164, 185, 187, 215, 217–18, 278n, 310, 312, 344, 345, 347, 351, 361, 371
Khrushchev, Nikita S., 23, 27, 28, 29–30, 31, 46, 49, 50, 51, 73–84, 86–89, 91, 97, 100, 126, 128, 131, 132–34, 137, 138, 143, 146, 164, 165, 166, 167, 169, 170, 171, 172, 173, 174, 177, 180, 181, 182, 186, 187, 191, 192, 280, 286, 342, 368
Khrushchev, Sergei N., 186
Kintex, 312
Kirkland, J. Lane, 328
Kirkpatrick, Jeanne, 328
Kishilov, Nikolai, 250, 251, 252, 253, 254, 265
Kissinger, Henry A., xiii, 21, 62, 64, 124, 167, 210, 243, 244, 245, 247, 248, 253, 254, 255, 256, 257, 258, 261, 262, 264, 268, 269, 270, 271, 274, 275, 278, 279, 280, 281, 282, 284, 286, 288, 289, 291, 292, 294, 297, 299, 301, 314, 327, 381, 388, 392

Kistiakowsky, George, 193
Kitchen, Jeffrey C., 121, 137, 153, 192, 198, 203
"Kitchen Debate" (Nixon and Khrushchev), 77
Klopotov, B. Ye., 82–83, 91
Kochnov, Igor, 118
Kohler, Foy D., 74, 123, 129, 145, 191, 192, 206, 208, 215
Kokoshin, Andrei, 356
Komplektov, Viktor, 216, 250, 344, 346, 349, 353, 359, 371
Korea, South, 56; North, 387, 391
Kornienko, Georgy, 216, 250, 344, 346, 349, 353, 359, 371
Kosygin, Aleksei N., 190, 191, 205, 207, 209, 210, 254, 255
Kovacs, Janos, 235
Kozlov, Frol R., 74, 75, 81, 82, 83
Kreisky, Bruno, 147
Kremlin, 56, 269–70, 352–53, 371, 376
"Kremlinology," 7, 17
Kurchatov, Igor V., 91
Kurds, 285
Kuwait, 366
Kuznetsov, Vasily V., 182, 352

Lachs, Manfred, 140–41, 148, 149
Laird, Melvin, 225, 267, 282
Langer, William L., 40
Laos, 132, 296
Larionov, Valentin, 366
Latvia, 5, 102, 148
Launch on warning, 266–67
Lawrence Livermore National Laboratory, 96
Leddy, John, 212, 213
Lee, Asher, 21
Lee, Kent, 365
Lehman, John, 274
Leipunsky, Aleksandr, 97
Leites, Nathan, 6, 7
Le May, Curtis, 198
Lemnitzer, Lyman, 135, 144
Lenin (icebreaker), 75, 82–84, 85, 90, 91, 93
Lenin, Vladimir I., 27, 55, 87, 309, 350, 361
Leningrad (St. Petersburg), 29, 30–31, 36, 75, 81, 82, 91, 212, 344, 351
Liberty, U.S.S., 214
Libya, 309, 350
Liddell Hart, Basil H., 21, 167
Limited [Nuclear] Test Ban Treaty (LTBT), 163, 165–67, 213–14; violations, 214
Limited war, Soviet policy, 68–69, 107, 133–35, 138; U.S. policy, 66–70, 133–35
"Linkage," 279, 284, 288

Lisbon, 295, 299
"Live Oak" (NATO military contingency planning), 131
Local war, Soviet policy, 60, 133–34, 138
Lodge, Henry Cabot, 212
London, 105, 107, 201, 290; U.S. Chiefs of Mission conference, 314–15
Los Alamos National Laboratory, 96
Lossky, Nikolai O., 5
Lowenthal, Richard, 167
Lukanov, Andrei, 305, 313, 323
Lukanov, Karlo, 146, 333
Lund, Arne, 202
Lunik (Soviet lunar probe), 91

McCarthy, Joseph, 41
McCarthy, Eugene, 64
McCarthyism, 3, 21, 41, 42n, 389, 393
McCloy, John J., 55, 138, 140, 193, 202
McCone, John, xii, 90–99, 135, 144, 168, 175, 181, 182
McFarlane, Robert C. ("Bud"), 357, 358
McGhee, George, 137, 158
MacLaury, Bruce, 336, 341, 358
McNamara, Robert S., 10, 122, 144, 147, 151, 158, 159, 170, 175, 181, 185, 186, 188, 192, 196, 204, 205, 209, 210, 211, 218, 223, 224, 225, 266
"McNamara Committee" (NPG), 224. *See also* NPG
McNaughton, John, 141–42, 155, 206, 207
Macovescu, Georgi, 148
McSweeney, John, 6
Maechling, Charles, Jr., 136
Magee, Charles, 305, 319
Makinen, Marvin, 103
Malek, Fred, 274
Malenkov, Georgy M., 17, 29, 37
Malinovsky, Rodion, 107, 108
Malita, Mircea, 148
Malitchenko, Christiane, 307
Mamula, Branko, 147
Manchuria, 102, 135
Manescu, Corneliu, 146, 149–50
Manhattan Project, 3, 15
Mansfield, Mike, 202
Manuilsky, Dimitry, 353
Marshall Plan, 3, 388
Marcos, Ferdinand, 297
Markov, Georgy, 312
Martin, Robert A., 209
Mates, Leo, 147
Marx, Karl, 87, 304
Marxism-Leninism, 348–49, 366, 370, 377, 383, 389, 392–94, 398

Massachusetts Institute of Technology (MIT), 12, 13, 16, 18, 210, 353
"Massive retaliation," 66–70
Matthews, Francis, 15
Maury, John ("Jack"), 64, 111
MBFR. *See* Mutual Balanced Force Reductions
MC-*14/3*, 223, 224, 229
MC-*161*, 53
Meeker, Leonard, 160, 164
Medium-range ballistic missiles (MRBM), 48, 92, 103, 113, 168, 170, 172, 174, 178, 179, 206, 207, 209, 211, 218, 233, 260, 372
Mehnert, Klaus, 64
Meloy, Francis, 299
Meyer, Cord, 3, 16, 42n, 102
MI 6, 107, 110. *See also* SIS; United Kingdom, intelligence
Middle East, 37, 39, 234, 285, 295, 326, 338, 386, 387
Mikoyan, Anastas I., 74, 75, 184
Mikoyan, Sergo A., 184, 185
Mikhailov, Georgy, 366
Military Balance, The, 63
Military balance. *See* Strategic balance (U.S.-Soviet)
Military-Industrial Commission (VPK) (Soviet), 210
"Military spending gap" (U.S.-Soviet), 362–63
Military Thought journal, 12, 70, 113–15, 201, 217, 348, 351–52, 360, 361, 363, 364, 365
Millionshchikov, Mikhail, 209, 210, 218
Mindzenty, Jozef Cardinal, 149
Minuteman ICBM, 152, 255
MIRV (multiple independently-targeted reentry vehicles), 203, 206, 207, 208, 211; in SALT, 246, 255–59, 262, 263
"Miss America," 219
"Missile Gap," 47–48, 60, 11, 122, 143, 174, 382
Mitchell, John, 247
Miterev, Georgy, 25–28, 30
Mladenov, Petur, 305, 309, 311, 313, 315, 319–23
Mobutu, Sese Seko, 296
"Moles," 104–05, 367
Molotov, Vyacheslav M., 30, 37
Mondale, Walter F., 304
Mongolia, 135, 313
"Mongoose" (covert operation), 135, 175
Moorer, Thomas, 247, 262
"Moral equivalence," 394–95
Morgan, George, 6, 14
Moscow, 108, 109, 110, 124, 206; author's visits, 28–37, 76, 77–84, 91–92, 129n,

148–49, 344, 353, 355, 360, 361, 367–68, 371; conference on the Cuban missile crisis, 185, 361; Moscow State University, 31; SALT, 243, 247, 253–54, 255, 269, 270, 278, 282, 290; U.S. embassy, 318; CIA station, 116; "Moscow Beauty '88," 359
Mossadegh, Mohammed, 42
MRBMs. *See* Medium-range ballistic missiles
Murphy, Robert, 74
Mutual balanced force reductions (MBFR), 227–29, 237, 288–89
Mutual deterrence, 58–60, 66–70, 231, 256, 264–65, 283
Mutual example, in arms control, 191–92

NAC (North Atlantic Council), 230–34, 246, 271–72, 276. *See also* NATO
Nahit, Imre, 235, 237
Narcotics trade, in Golden Triangle, Southeast Asia, 296; in Bulgaria, 311–12
NASA (National Aeronautics and Space Administration), 155
National Academy of Sciences (NAS), 357
National Committee for Free Europe, 16
National Committee for the Liberation of the People of the USSR, 16–17
National Defense University, 336, 341, 364
National intelligence, 43, 51
National Intelligence Council (NIC), 44
National Intelligence Estimates (NIE), 43–52, 328–33, 343. 368; NIE *11-3-58, Soviet Reactions to Possible United States Actions on Antarctica,* 45–46; NIE *11-4-58, Main Trends in Soviet Capabilities and Policies, 1958–1963,* 45; NIE *11-6-58, The Soviet Attitude Toward Disarmament,* 46, 60, 385; SNIE *11-6-60, Strength of the Armed Forces of the USSR,* 49–51; SNIE *11-14-61, The Soviet Strategic Posture, 1961–1967,* 57–58, 114; NIE *85-3-62, The Military Buildup in Cuba,* 168, 174
National intelligence officers (NIOs), 44
National Intelligence Survey (NIS), 52
National Security Council (NSC), 14, 44, 45, 121, 123, 124, 126, 131, 143, 155; Ex Comm, 169–179; IPMG, 281; National Security Action Memoranda (NSAM): NSAM-*124,* 135; NSAM-*156,* 154–64, 196; NSAM-*216,* 156; NSAM-*269,* 214; NSAM-*304,* 226; NSAM-*352,* 226; National Security Study Memoranda (NSSM): NSSM-*3,* 245; NSSM-*28,* 245; NSSM-*144,* 281; Operations Coordinating Board (OCB), 14, 16, 74, 87, 121, 381; Planning Board, 14, 44, 45, 121; Staff, 208,

306, 323, 334, 335, 358; SALT role, 247, 256, 257
NATO (North Atlantic Treaty Organization), 6, 25, 53, 54, 56, 107, 114–16, 124, 126, 131, 147, 150, 152–53, 176, 178, 192, 194, 195–96, 207, 213, 222–39, 278, 288, 295, 299, 307, 345–46, 347, 355, 367, 368, 386, 388, 391, 395; Athens Ministerial Meeting (*1962*), 147; intelligence, 53, 235; State Department office, 121, 139, 153; U.S. Mission to, xiii, 207, 209, 213, 215, 227, 239, 279, 397. *See also* NAC
NATO War College, 21, 62, 67, 146–47, 201
Negotiation, 252, 354, 384, 386
Negotiators, The (Walder), 252
Newhouse, John, 274
"New Thinking" (Soviet), 344, 348–50, 354–55, 362
New Zealand, 53
Nicaragua, 327
Nicolaevsky, Boris, 17
NIE. *See* National Intelligence Estimates
Nineteen Eighty Four (Orwell), 39
Nitze, Paul H., 121, 141, 155, 160, 163, 171, 177, 181, 182, 201
Nixon, Richard M., xii, 72–86, 88, 109, 212, 239, 243, 244, 245, 254, 255, 257, 258, 259, 261, 264, 268, 269, 270, 273, 274, 277, 278, 279, 280, 281, 282, 284, 285, 286, 287, 288, 291, 298, 325, 327, 373, 379, 380, 381, 383, 388
Nixon administration, 213, 260, 286, 327, 341
Nixon-Brezhnev summit meetings. *See* Summit meetings (U.S.-Soviet)
"Nixon Doctrine," 285
NKGB, 13. *See* KGB
North Korea. *See* Korea
North Vietnam. *See* Vietnam
Norway, 202, 225
Novosibirsk, 78, 81, 84, 85, 86
NPG (Nuclear Planning Group, NATO), 224–25, 227
NPT ([Nuclear] Non-Proliferation Treaty), 154, 196, 202, 210, 213, 230–31
NRO (National Reconnaissance Office), 155
NSC. *See* National Security Council
NSC-*68,* 57, 122, 381, 389
NSC-*5440,* 15
Nuclear nonproliferation, 193–96, 203, 385. *See also* NPT
Nuclear-powered submarines, U.S., 75; Soviet, 75, 83–84, 97
Nuclear testing, 142, 163, 165, 166, 213. *See also* Comprehensive [Nuclear] Test Ban Treaty, Limited [Nuclear] Test Ban Treaty

Nuclear weapons. Cold War, 376–77; China, 98, 166, 193; Sweden, 106, 202; U.S., 115, 152, 198, 199–200, 224; Soviet, 94, 107, 108, 114, 186, 381. *See also* Atomic bomb
Nuclear Weapons and Foreign Policy (Kissinger), 21

Oak Ridge National Laboratory, 96, 97
OAS (Organization of American States), 172, 175, 178
Office of Strategic Services (OSS), 3, 13, 17, 39, 40, 43, 52, 133
Ogarkov, Nikolai V., 250, 267
One Million Random Digits with 100,000 Normal Deviates (RAND), 20
"Open Skies," 24
Operations Coordinating Board (OCB). *See* National Security Council
Organization of Ukrainian Nationalists (OUN), 17
OSS. *See* Office of Strategic Services
Outer space, 154–64, 197–98
Outer Space Treaty (*1967*), 197–98

Packard, David, 247, 328
Pahlevi, Shah Reza Khan, 309
Pakistan, 285, 309, 387
Palm, Gustav Thede, 106
Paris, 207, 229, 234, 290, 298; Summit (*1960*) 368
Parity. *See* Strategic parity
Parsons, J. Graham ("Jeff"), 248, 251, 253, 263, 271
Paxson, Edward, 15
PD-*18*, 335
PD-*21*, 303, 322
"Peaceful coexistence," 79, 283
Perceptions, xiv, 114–115, 170, 286, 325–26, 338, 344, 345–47, 374, 380, 381–383, 386, 390–91, 399
Perle, Richard, 271, 274, 328
Perestroika, 351, 353, 360, 362, 369
"Petofi Circle," 31
Petrov, Vladimir, 54
Petrovsky, Vladimir, 350
PFIAB. *See* President's Foreign Intelligence Advisory Board
Philby, Harold A. R. ("Kim"), 54, 101
Philippines, 296–97
"Photint" (photographic intelligence), 104
Pickering, Thomas, 117, 279
Pipes, Richard, 328, 334, 340, 367
Pleshakov, Pëtr, 250
Plesetsk, 47

PLO (Palestinian Liberation Organization), 280
Plovdiv, 313, 314, 371
PM. *See* State Department, Politico-Military Affairs
Podhoretz, Norman, 328
Polads (political advisers), 121, 199
Poland, 41, 84–85, 130, 140–42, 222, 285, 303, 388; author's visits, 37, 85, 148; crisis of *1956*, 18, 25; U.S. subversion, 101–02
Polaris (SLBM) missile, 151
Policy planning, xii, 123, 174, 193, 196–97, 290–91
Policy Versus the Law: The Reinterpretation of the ABM Treaty (Garthoff), 358
Politburo. *See* Soviet Union, Politburo
Political games, 18–19, 353–54
Political-military affairs. *See* State Department, Political-military affairs bureau
Political warfare in Cold War, 14–15, 16–17, 380, 381, 382–83, 384
Politics Among the Nations (Morgenthau), 4
Ponomarev, Boris N., 352–53
Ponomarev, Pavel A., 82
Popov, M. M., 108
Popov, Pëtr, 105
Portugal, 295, 299
Potsdam, conference (*1945*), 24
Powers, Francis Gary, 86, 366
"PR Study Group," 153
Prague, 148, 201, 371
Pravda, 27, 32, 81, 347
Pre-emptive (anticipatory) attack, 59, 114–16, 186, 266
President's Foreign Intelligence Advisory Board (PFIAB), 328
President's Intelligence Oversight Board, 358
Press relations, 124–25, 274–75
Prevention of Nuclear War agreement, 264, 283, 284
Preventive war, 15–16
Primakov, Evgeny, 352
Princeton Panel, CIA consultants, 54–55
Princeton University, xii, 1, 2, 3, 4, 5, 10, 22, 40n, 96, 164, 372, 397
PRM-*10*, 335
"Project Control," 14–15
Propaganda, 16, 116, 190, 200, 283, 342, 343, 344, 380, 386, 393
Psychological Strategy Board (PSB), 14, 16, 381, 382
Psychological warfare, 13, 14, 200, 381
Psychological warfare division (PWD), U.S. Air Force, 14

Pugwash conferences, 210, 241, 341, 360
Pullach, Bavaria (BND headquarters), 54, 201
Pyadyshev, Boris, 308, 309, 310

Qaddafi, Muammar, 309–10

R-12 (SS-4 in NATO designation) MRBM, 92, 113
Radford, Arthur, 14
Radio Free Europe (RFE), 16, 84
Radio Liberty, 16
RAND Corporation, xii, 7–8, 9–23, 121, 338, 353, 379
Rapacki, Adam, 84, 146, 148
"Rapacki Plan," 148
Rakowski, Mieczyslaw, 37
Ramsey, Henry, 199
Reagan, Ronald, 327, 328, 342–43, 345, 347, 352, 355, 377, 379, 380, 386
Reagan administration, 44, 249, 328, 334, 338, 342, 345, 357, 362, 377, 388
"Reagan Doctrine," 377
Reconnaissance, air (U.S.), 101. See also U-2
Reconnaissance, satellite (space) (U.S.), xiii, 10, 47, 48, 51, 55, 62, 111–12, 113, 197, 206
Red Cross, American, 25–28; Soviet, 25–28, 30
Report on the Covert Activities of the Central Intelligence Agency, 382
Reykjavik, 1968 NATO meeting, 227; 1986 U.S.-Soviet summit, 352–56
Richardson, Elliot, 247
Rickover, Hyman, 75, 82–84, 91
Ridgway, Matthew B., 67
Rio Treaty (OAS), 180
Rockefeller, Nelson, 278
Rogers, William P., 263, 264, 272, 275, 276, 279, 287, 291
Rogov, Sergei, 345
"Rollback," 221, 240, 293
Romania, 146, 148, 149–51, 201–02, 222, 236, 285, 303, 315, 316, 317
Roosevelt, Archibald, 76
Roosevelt, Cornelius, 76–77
Roosevelt, Franklin D., 74, 394
Roosevelt, Kermit, 76
Roosevelt, Theodore, 76
Rosenfeld, Stephen, 363
Roshchin, Aleksei, 230
Rostow, Eugene, 328
Rostow, Walt W., 133, 137, 174, 175, 181, 188, 196, 204, 205, 211, 212, 213
Rowen, Henry ("Harry"), 10, 121
Rozitske, Harry, 40
Rumsfeld, Donald, 274

Rusk, Dean, xiii, 121, 122, 123, 133, 139, 140–41, 143, 145–46, 147, 150–51, 153, 154, 155, 157, 158, 162, 165, 169, 181, 188, 189, 191, 192, 193, 194–95, 196, 204, 205, 206, 209, 210, 211, 212, 217, 236, 328, 361
Ruskov, Khristo, 313
Russia, 373, 378; archives, 338, 371; Duma, 344; Supreme Soviet, 369

SA-2, Soviet air defense missile, 86, 173
Sadat, Anwar, 285
Safeguard ABM system, 270–71
SAGA (Studies, Analysis, and Gaming Agency, JCS), 198
Sagdeyev, Roald, 356
Saigon, 295, 296
SALT (Strategic Arms Limitation Talks), xiii, 100, 207, 217–19, 231–33, 242, 243–76, 282, 289, 335, 385–86; ABM limitation, 256–60; definition of strategic forces, 255, 260–62; and détente, 243, 264, 275; MIRV limitation, 246, 255–59, 262–62; no first use of nuclear weapons, 268; origins, 205–213; provocative attack by third parties, 267–68; "purge" of SALT activists, 272–74; SALT I agreements, 263, 269, 270–71, 272, 285, 326, 385; SALT II negotiations and treaty, 233, 262, 270, 272–75, 287, 310, 320, 328, 335, 336, 345, 355; SALT (I) delegation, 248–53; strategic dialogue, 264–65; strategic stability, 244, 263, 264; the "Tundra talks," 253; the "Vienna Option," 259; Verification Panel (VP) and VP Working Group, 247, 248, 256, 268. See also ABM Treaty; Accident Measures Agreement; Hot line; Interim Agreement on Offensive Arms (SALT I)
Samizdat, 79
Satellites, earth, 10, 19, 20, 62, 196–97. See also Reconnaissance, satellite (space)
Savannah, 75, 83, 90, 91, 95, 96
Sayre, Robert, 301
Schlesinger, James, 274, 328
Sciaroni, Bretton C, 358
Scoville, Herbert P. ("Pete"), Jr., 155, 160, 207
Scowcroft, Brent, 354
SDI. See Strategic Defense Initiative
Seamans, Robert, 155
Secret Intelligence Service. See SIS
Sedov, Boris, 216–19, 245, 272, 278, 310, 345, 351, 361
Sejna, Jan, 237
Semenov, Vladimir, 249, 250, 251, 252, 264–65, 266, 267
Senate, U.S., 64, 270–71, 287, 302, 357

Sentinel ABM system, 208
SG-*152*, 53
Shadrin, Nicholas (Artamonov, Nikolai), 118
Shakhnazarov, Georgy, 371
Shanghai, 372–73
SHAPE (Supreme Headquarters Allied
    Powers Europe), 239
Shaw, John ("Jack"), 210, 219, 251
Shchukin, Aleksandr, 210, 250
Shelepin, Aleksandr, 270
Shelest, Pëtr, 270
Shevardnadze, Eduard, 352, 353, 371
Shulman, Marshall, 373
Shultz, George, 2
Shriver, Sargent, 212
"Side Step" (NATO exercise), 114–15
Signals intelligence ("Sigint"), 47, 104, 214.
    See also Communications intelligence;
    Electronic intelligence
Sikorsky, Igor I., 5
Sino-Soviet bloc, 7, 46, 57,121, 138, 389. *See
    also* Soviet bloc
Sino-Soviet relations, 44, 54, 98, 105, 132,
    134, 138, 166, 217, 285, 309, 340, 372, 373,
    389
SIOP (Single Integrated Operations Plan,
    U.S. nuclear war plan), 150
SIS (Secret Intelligence Service) (U.K.), 54,
    110
Skybolt missile, 151
SLBMs. *See* Submarine-launched (or sea-
    launched) ballistic missiles
Sleeper, Raymond, 14–15
Slipchenko, Vladimir, 366
Smith, Abbott E., 40
Smith, Gerard C., 125, 232–52, 257, 261,
    265–72, 276, 278
Smith, Walter Bedell, 40
SNIE (Special National Intelligence
    Estimate). *See* National Intelligence
    Estimates
Sobolev, Arkady, 27
Sofaer, Abraham, 358
Sofia, 302–04. *See also* Bulgaria
Solomatin, Boris, 217–18
Sonnenfeldt, Helmut ("Hal"), 278, 314
"Sonnenfeldt Doctrine," 314
Sorenson, Theodore, 165, 181
Soviet bloc, 57, 67, 149–51, 22, 303, 316, 373,
    379
Soviet embassy, Washington, 215, 216,
    370–71
Soviet Image of Future War, The (Garthoff),
    65, 70
Soviet Military Doctrine (Garthoff), 21, 62

Soviet Strategy in the Nuclear Age (Garthoff),
    65, 70
Soviet Union, 1, 13, 14, 23; air forces, 12, 21,
    28, 49–50, 107; archives, 18, 72, 129n, 223,
    338, 371; arms control, 59–60, 161,
    243–76, 346, 351; army, 48–51, 111–12;
    author's visits, 23, 28–37, 53, 76, 128n,
    148–49, 344–53, 360, 361, 367–68, 371;
    bases abroad, 280–82; Communist Party
    (CPSU), 25, 34, 308, 347, 348–49, 371;
    demise of, 370–71, 389; economy, 17, 330,
    363; foreign policy, 18, 44, 46–47, 59,
    67–69, 295–96, 340, 341, 343, 378;
    General Staff, 114–16, 347, 348, 367;
    International Department, Central
    Committee of the CPSU, 308, 344,
    352–53, 353, 359; Komsomol, 32, 79; lead-
    ers, 30, 37, 57, 75, 308; military policy and
    doctrine, 57–59, 67–69, 107, 113–16,
    264–65, 332, 334, 362, 363–67, 384;
    Ministry of Foreign Affairs (MID), 161,
    269, 290, 344, 347, 249–50; Ministry of
    Internal Affairs (MVD), 33, 50; missiles,
    47–48, 74–75, 80–81, 111–13, in SALT,
    206–11, 218, 233, 255–62, 269, 271; navy,
    50, 281–82, 331; nuclear propulsion,
    74–75, 83–84; nuclear weapons, 94, 107,
    108, 114, 186, 352; Politburo (Presidium),
    18, 29–30, 75, 107, 166, 217, 270, 308;
    SALT, 248, 257, 258, 275–76; society,
    24–37, 77–80, 82, 347, 351, 353, 359–60,
    362, 370; Supreme Soviet, 369; Twenty-
    Sixth Party Congress, 348–49, 352; views
    of U.S., 114–15, 325–26, 344, 345–47,
    380–83. *See also* KGB and GRU
Sovietology, 17
SOVMAT, 53
Space reconnnaissance, 154–56, 196–97. *See
    also* Reconnaissance, satellite (space)
Space weapons and arms control, 149,
    156–63, 196–98, 341
Space Treaty. *See* Outer Space Treaty
Spain, 299
Special Group, 135; Special Group
    (Augmented), 135; Special Group
    (Counterinsurgency or CI), 135–36
Speir, Hans, 10, 19, 20, 62
Spiers, Ronald, 276, 279
"Spirit of Geneva," 24, 75
Spitzer, Lyman, 96
Spivey, Berton, 204
Sputnik, 20, 38
SS-*4*, 92, 113, 168, 172, 372
SS-*5*, 172
SS-*9*, 92

SS-*16*, 329
SS-*18*, 92
SS-*19*, 329
SS-*20*, 329
Stalin, Josef V., 1, 7, 14, 15, 24, 25, 26, 27, 30, 56, 74, 117, 165, 219, 353, 378, 381, 386
Standing Consultative Commission (SCC), 272
Stanford University, 94, 219
"Star Wars," 345, 347, 355, 356. *See also* Strategic Defense Initiative (SDI)
START (Strategic Arms Reduction Talks), negotiations, 233, 346, 355, 386; START I Treaty, 332, 386; START II Treaty, 386
State Committee for the Coordination of Scientific-Research WORK (Soviet), 110
State, Department of, xii–xiii, 17, 22, 41–42, 44, 52, 62, 72, 88, 121–22, 123, 139, 165, 172, 177, 179, 238, 275, 276, 278, 282, 287, 289–91, 292–94, 300–01, 304, 306, 314, 335, 337, 345, 366, 391, 393, 398; AID, 298; European Bureau, 306; Executive Secretariat (SIS), 293; Foreign Service, 298–99, 397; Foreign Service Institute (FSI), 136, 290, 302, 341, 353–54; Inspector General (S/IG), xiii, 292–301; intelligence (OIR; INR), 4, 12, 43n, 46, 48, 117, 126, 133, 216, 280, 315, 343; International Organizations Bureau (IO), UN affairs, 139; Legal Affairs (L), 358; NATO affairs (EUR/RPM), 121, 139, 153; policy planning (S/P), 123, 174, 193, 196–97, 216, 226; politico-military affairs (G/PM), 121–23, 125, 139, 203, 242, 273, 279, 289, 334, 385; Security, Office of, 345; Senior Seminar, 290–91, 292, 341, Soviet affairs (EUR/SOU), 123, 139, 216; Undersecretaries Committee, 247
Steinbruner, John, 336, 341
Sterling, Claire, 343
Stevenson, Adlai, 163
Stockholm, 28, 30, 105–10
Stoertz, Howard, 47, 60
Stoessel, Walter, 291
Strategic Air Command (SAC), 10, 14, 147, 198
Strategic Arms Limitations Talks. *See* SALT
Strategic balance (U.S.-Soviet), 144–45, 170, 177, 182, 203–04, 262, 327, 331–32, 342, 388. *See also* Strategic parity
Strategic Defense Initiative (SDI), 355–58, 362, 373
Strategic intelligence, 43, 328–34

Strategic Intelligence for American World Policy (Kent), 43
Strategic Nuclear Delivery Vehicle (SNDV) Freeze, 190, 205
Strategic parity, 203–04, 207, 231, 263, 283, 327, 332, 334, 385
Strategic stability, 244, 263, 264, 332, 334, 355–56
Strategic Surrender: The Politics of Victory and Defeat (Kekskemeti), 13
Strudelhof, 249
Submarine-launched (or sea-launched) ballistic missiles (SLBMs), 209, 211, 233, 331; in SALT, 255, 261–62, 262
Sukhodrev, Viktor, 217
Summit meetings (U.S.-Soviet), Geneva (*1985*), 356; Glassboro (*1967*), 207, 217, 266; Moscow (*1972*), 89, 245, 253, 269, 282, 285, 288, 325; Reykjavik (*1986*), 352, 356; Vienna (*1979*), 336; Washington (*1973*), 282, 283, 290, 325
Surprise Attack Conference (*1958*), 55, 147
Sutterlin, James, 292
Sverdlovsk (Yekaterinburg), 47, 75, 78, 81, 82, 84, 86, 94
Sweden, 105–10; intelligence service, 106–09; interest in nuclear weapons program, 106, 202
Symington, Stuart, 64
Syria, 280, 295

Taiwan Straits crisis, 46, 81
"Talent," 47, 64
Tallin, 91
Taraki, Nur Mohammed, 285
Tashkent, 148, 149, 344
Taylor, Charles, 74
Taylor, Maxwell, 67, 133, 135, 137, 162, 171
Tbilisi, 29, 346
"Team B," 328–34
Tehran, 285, 297
Terror Network, The (Sterling), 343
Terrorism, 312, 343, 387
Thailand, 295, 296–97
Third World, as Cold War arena, 131–38, 214–15, 280, 295–98, 312, 322, 343, 350, 387, 391–92
Tolubeyev, Nikita, 308
Thompson, Llewellyn ("Tommy"), 77, 84, 98, 123, 132, 165, 171, 172, 179, 193, 198, 199, 205, 207, 212
"Thompson Committee" (nonproliferation), 193, 196, 214
Thor IRBM, 74, 152

Time magazine, 36, 64, 394
Timerbaev, Roland, 250
Tito, Josip Broz, 7, 25, 221, 389
TNF (Theater Nuclear Forces, NATO), 345–46, 355
Toon, Malcolm ("Mac"), 123, 340
Trettner, Heinz, 200–01
"Triangular diplomacy," 279
Trivers, Howard, 147
Troyanovsky, Oleg, 182
Truman, Harry S, 15, 24, 391
Truman administration, 13, 57, 122, 381
Truman Doctrine, 3
Tsarapkin, Semën, 148, 160, 161
Tsvetkov, Boris, 305
Tu-16 Badger, Soviet medium bomber, 107, 191
Tu-95D Bear, Soviet naval reconnaissance aircraft, 282
Tucker, Robert C., 17
Turkey, 3, 169, 173, 175, 176, 224, 311
Twining, Nathan, 123, 199
Tyuratam, 47

U-2, U.S. reconnaissance aircraft, 47, 64, 92, 113, 366; shot down in Soviet Union (1960), 86, 89, 123, 366; shot down in Cuba (1962), 168, 173
Ukraine, 17, 101, 103, 373; author's visits, 28, 92–93
Ulyanovsk (Simbirsk), 360
United Kingdom (Great Britain), diplomacy, 24, 34, 123, 148, 151, 152, 166, 192, 201, 224–26, 230, 394; intelligence, 53, 54, 105, 107, 110, 148, 201, 265. *See also* SIS
United Nations (UN), 4, 139, 140, 149, 160–63, 191, 323, 369; Charter, 180; Security Council, 172
United States, policy, 129–31, 144–45, 153–54; relations with the Soviet Union, 1, 24–25, 73–89, 144–45; 153–54, 180–81, 183–84, 189–90, 243–44, 275, 277, 279–82, 283–86, 287–88, 325–27, 338, 340–48, 353–55, 362, 375–77, 383–85, 391–95; strategy and military policy, 66–70, 151–52, 198–201; U.S. Air Force, 108, 123, 182, 203, 299; U.S. Army, 151; U.S. Army Special Warfare Center, 137; U.S. Army Strategic Intelligence School, 62; U.S. Commander in Chief, Pacific, 296; U.S. Information Agency (USIA), 76, 136, 155, 289, 298, 339–40; U.S. Intelligence Board (USIB), 44, 45; U.S. and NATO, xiii, 207, 209, 213, 215, 227, 239; U.S. Navy, 350; U.S. Strike Command (STRICOM), 198, 199

US Policy Toward the Soviet Union: A Long-Term Western Perspective, 1987–2000 (Atlantic Council), 354
Ural region, 82, 84, 94
Uranium mine and mill (Ukraine), 92–93
Urosev, Radovan, 307, 308
Usachev, Igor, 146, 148, 149, 161, 164
U Thant, 173
USSR. *See* Soviet Union

"V" bombers (U.K.), 151
Vance, Cyrus, 303, 304, 306, 314, 322, 327, 333
Vandenberg Air Force Base, 74
Varentsov, Sergei, 113
Vasilieva, Vera A. (Vera Garthoff), 5
Velikhov, Evgeny, 356
Verification (of arms control and disarmament), 55, 142, 148, 150, 157, 161, 190, 196, 206, 218, 258
Vernadsky, George, 6
Vershinin, Konstantin, 81
Vest, George, 303, 322, 336
Vidin, 315
Vienna, 118, 126, 201, 205, 306, 316, 336; MBFR meetings 289; SALT I meetings, 245, 249, 257, 270, 272
Vietnam War, xiv, 132, 138, 181, 188–89, 191, 202, 207, 243, 244, 270, 277, 279, 295, 296, 309, 327, 379, 391, 398–99
Vishnevsky, Sergei, 347
Vladivostok, SALT accord, 335
Vlasov Army, 12, 13, 102
Voice of America (VOA), 16, 311, 319
Volgograd (Stalingrad), 346
Volkogonov, Dmitry, 361
von Karman, Theodore, 9
von Neuman, John, 15
Vorontsov, Yuly, 216, 218–19, 245, 250, 268, 271, 272, 280, 281, 371
Voroshilov General Staff Academy, 30, 114, 363, 366
"Voroshilov Papers," 363–64
VPK (Military-Industrial-Commission, USSR), 250.

Walder, Francis, 252
"Walk-ins," 105–110
"War at Sea," 201
War games, 198–201, 335–36
Wall Street, 26
Warnke, Paul, 206, 208, 215, 218, 335
Warrenton, NPG meeting, 225
"Wars of national liberation," 132–38, 189

Warsaw, 37, 84–85, 148, 371
Warsaw Pact, 48, 115, 120, 149–51, 199, 217, 223, 228, 234, 237, 240, 289, 368, 395; Western estimates of, 46, 120, 169, 236, 237
Washington NATO meeting (1969), 237, 238
Watergate, 286, 288, 291, 379
Watson, Thomas J., Jr., 344
Wattenberg, Ben, 328
Weiler, Lawrence, 251
Weinberger, Caspar, 362
Weinrod, Bruce, 358
Weiss, Seymour ("Sey"), 153, 193, 203, 204, 271
Wennerström, Stig, 105–10
West Berlin. See Berlin
West Germany. See Germany
Western Europe, 4, 5, 7, 39, 288, 299–301
Wheeler, Earle ("Bus"), 206, 211
White, Sir Dick, 110
White (Russian) emigration, 5, 40, 370
White House, 124, 197, 211, 212, 254, 258, 268, 273, 274, 276, 280, 287, 289, 290, 302, 303
Whitman, John, 60, 335
Wiesner, Jerome, 155, 159
Wilson, Charles, 67
Wilson, Woodrow, 394
WIN (Freedom and Independence Movement), Poland, 101–02
"Window of vulnerability," 328, 329
Winks, Robin, 40n
"Winter War," 3
Wisner, Frank, 52
Wizards of Armageddon (Kaplan), 20
Wohlstetter, Albert, 10, 16, 106
Wolfe, Thomas, 29
Woodrow Wilson School of International Affairs, Princeton, 2
Woolsey, R. James, 249, 354
World Communism, 7, 44, 45, 67, 132, 137–38, 189, 342, 389, 392
World War I, 249, 367

World War II, 1, 2, 138, 379
World War III, 332, 377
World Youth Festival (Sixth), Moscow (1959), 29–36
"Worst case" analysis, 21, 384
"Wringer" (U.S. Air Force interview project), 12
Wynne, Greville, 110
Wyman, Willard G., 70
Wyczynski, Stefan Cardinal 85

"X" (George Kennan), 6

Yale University, xii, 1, 2, 4, 5, 6, 7, 8, 9, 10, 11, 22, 40n, 42n, 102, 103, 133, 164, 373; Divinity School, 102; Institute for International Studies, 4; Russian Chorus, 5, 35
Yalta, 74
Yarborough, William Y., 137
Yarmolinsky, Adam, 158
Yazov, Dmitry, 179
Yekaterinburg (Sverdlovsk), 81
Yeltsin administration, 338
Yeltsin, Boris N., 362, 370
Yemelyanov, Vasily, 75, 90–98
Youth, Russian, 30–36
Yueh, Meng, 309
Yugoslavia, 7, 25, 72, 105, 123, 147, 221, 236, 285, 307, 308, 315, 318, 389
Yurchenko, Vitaly, 118

Zaire, 296. See also Congo
Zarubin, Georgy, 27
Zawadski, Aleksandr, 84
Zhëlty Vody, 92–93
Zhilin, Pavel, 202
Zhivkov, Todor, 304–05, 312, 316, 317, 320, 322, 323
Zhukov, Georgy, 29–30, 106
Zhurkin, Vitaly, 343, 359
Zorin, Valerian, 140
Zumwalt, Elmo ("Bud"), 178, 328